NIJINSKY
RICHARD BUCKLE

Simon and Schuster   New York

To Cecil Beaton,
enlivening neighbour, encouraging friend

CONTENTS

ILLUSTRATIONS

Illustrations

vii

Illustrations

viii

LINE DRAWINGS

Line Drawings

ACKNOWLEDGMENTS

The author wishes to express his gratitude to Mme Romola Nijinsky for having kindly granted permission for extensive quotes from her books entitled *Nijinsky* and *The Last Days of Nijinsky*, published by Victor Gollancz Ltd, and from her book entitled *The Diary of Vaslav Nijinsky*, published by Jonathan Cape Ltd.

He is also grateful to Mr Vitale Fokine for permission to quote extracts from his father's memoirs, for the information which Mr Fokine gave him about the details discovered by the researchers working on the Russian edition of the book, and also for Mr Fokine's own opinions.

He would like to thank the following publishers for allowing him to use copyright material: Constable and Co. Ltd (*The Diaghilev Ballet 1909–1929* by Grigoriev); Chatto and Windus Ltd (*Memoirs*, Vol. II by Benois); Putnam and Co. Ltd (*Reminiscences of the Russian Ballet* by Benois).

ILLUSTRATIONS

The largest single group of illustrations – including a number never before reproduced – are from the collection of Mr Roger Pryor Dodge, on loan to the Library and Museum of Performing Arts, Lincoln Center. I am deeply grateful for Mr Dodge's generous permission to reproduce them and to Miss Genevieve Oswald for making them available. But these photographs had to be copied, and it was Miss Martha Swope, most distinguished of American ballet photographers, who undertook the laborious task of re-photographing each print. For this labour of love no thanks are adequate. I could not go to America to see to all this, and my friends Mr Joseph Martinson and Miss Denisa Beach gave time and took trouble to make all the arrangements. Mr Martinson died in the winter of 1970, so my thanks to him must find their way, if they can, beyond the grave: those to Miss Beach I proffer here.

Sources for all the illustrations are acknowledged on pp. vi - x   I should like to express particular gratitude to Mr Robert Tobin, whose Bakst painting of Nijinsky in 'Les Orientales' is reproduced not only in the book but also on the jacket.

NOTE ON SPELLING AND DATES

An attempt has been made at consistency in spelling Russian names. Russian spelling is phonetic, however, and to be really consistent one would write 'Benua' for 'Benois' and 'Burman' for 'Bourman', which would seem freakish.

Dates are given New Style, that is, according to the Western (Gregorian) Calendar.

PRINCIPAL CHARACTERS

ASTRUC, GABRIEL. French-Jewish music publisher, later founder of the Comité International de Patronage Artistique; impresario who made possible the triumph of the Russian Ballet in the west.

BAKST, LEON (born Rosenberg). Painter and stage designer, close friend of Diaghilev and designer of several of his most celebrated ballets.

BENOIS, ALEXANDRE. St Petersburg painter, art historian and stage designer. Originally Diaghilev's mentor, he later designed a number of ballets for him, notably 'Petrushka'.

BOLM, ADOLF. Principal character dancer of the Diaghilev Ballet from 1909 till 1917.

BOURMAN, ANATOLE. Classmate of Nijinsky; member of Diaghilev's company from 1911. Later married to Klementovitch. Wrote with Dorothy Lyman a life of Nijinsky.

CECCHETTI, ENRICO (MAESTRO). Milanese dancer and ballet master, established in Petersburg on and off from 1890 to 1909, later ballet master of Diaghilev's company and teacher of Nijinsky.

CHALIAPINE, FEODOR. Russian singer, foremost bass of his day. First presented in the west by Diaghilev in 'Boris'.

COCTEAU, JEAN. French writer, author of the libretto of 'Le Dieu bleu'.

DEBUSSY, CLAUDE. French composer, whose 'L'Après-midi' was used by Nijinsky and from whom Diaghilev commissioned 'Jeux'.

DIAGHILEV, SERGEI PAVLOVITCH. Russian nobleman, who brought Russian painting, music, opera and ballet for the first time to western Europe. The lover of Nijinsky.

DUFF, LADY JULIET. Daughter of Lady Ripon; one of the Russian Ballet's warmest English supporters.

DUNCAN, ISADORA. American pioneer of a free form of dance to music of great composers.

FOKINE, MICHEL. St Petersburg dancer and innovating choreographer of most of Nijinsky's roles from 'Le Pavillon d'Armide' (1907) to 'Daphnis et Chloë' (1912). With the Diaghilev Ballet from 1909 to 1914 with a gap in 1913.

GREFFUHLE, COMTESSE. Celebrated beauty and queen of Paris society: President of Les Concerts de Paris and the earliest patron of Diaghilev in the west.

GRIGORIEV, SERGEI. Member of the Diaghilev Ballet and its *régisseur* from 1909 to 1929. Husband of Lubov Tchernicheva.

GUNSBOURG, BARON DMITRI DE. Russian-Jewish financier and art patron. A backer of the Diaghilev Ballet.

HAHN, REYNALDO. French composer, commissioned to write 'Le Dieu bleu' for Diaghilev.

KARSAVINA, TAMARA. St Petersburg ballerina, member of the Diaghilev Ballet from 1909 to 1914 and again later. Nijinsky's partner in most works.

KCHESSINSKAYA, MATILDA. St Petersburg ballerina, mistress of Nicholas II when Tsarevitch, then of various Grand Dukes. Friend and enemy of Diaghilev, she appeared briefly with his company in the west in 1911 and 1912.

LVOV, PRINCE PAVEL DMITRIEVITCH. St Petersburg dilettante, patron of sportsmen and artists. Nijinsky's first male admirer. Introduced him to Diaghilev.

MARKUS, EMILIA. Hungary's most famous actress. Mother of Romola de Pulszky.

MASSINE (born MIASSINE), LEONIDE. Moscow dancer, successor of Nijinsky in Diaghilev's affections and as choreographer.

MORRELL, LADY OTTOLINE. Bloomsbury hostess and friend of Diaghilev and Nijinsky.

NIJINSKA, BRONISLAVA FOMINICHNA. Third child and only daughter of Thomas and Eleonora Nijinsky. Member of Diaghilev's company. Later married to Kotchetovsky.

NIJINSKAYA, ELEONORA NICOLAIEVNA. Polish-born, *née* Bereda. Dancer at the Warsaw Opera until her marriage to Thomas Nijinsky. Mother of Stanislav, Vaslav and Bronislava.

NIJINSKY, THOMAS. Polish-born dancer and choreographer. Husband of Eleonora Bereda and father of Stanislav, Vaslav and Bronislava Nijinsky. Toured Russia with his own ballet troupe.

NIJINSKY, VASLAV FOMITCH. Second son of Thomas and Eleonora Nijinsky

PAVLOVA, ANNA. St Petersburg ballerina, only for two brief periods a member of the Diaghilev Ballet.

PULSZKY, ROMOLA DE. Hungarian born, an enthusiast for the arts. Later wife of Nijinsky.

RAMBERT, MARIE (born MIRIAM RAMBERG). Russo-Polish dancer, briefly a member of the Russian Ballet and friend of Nijinsky.

RIPON, THE MARCHIONESS OF. The first English supporter of the Russian Ballet.

SERT, MISIA. Born Godebska, married in turn Thadée Natanson, Alfred Edwards and José-Maria Sert. Close friend and patron of Diaghilev from 1908.

Principal Characters

STRAVINSKY, IGOR. Russian composer launched by Diaghilev, who commissioned from him 'L'Oiseau de feu', 'Petrushka', 'Le Sacre', etc.

VLADIMIR ALEXANDROVITCH, GRAND DUKE OF RUSSIA. Brother of Alexander III and eldest uncle of Nicholas II. The only member of the Imperial Family to support Diaghilev's enterprises in the west.

INTRODUCTION

This book is very much the result of teamwork. When I began it I thought that the most I should be able to do would be to collate the many memoirs and articles by the collaborators of Diaghilev and Nijinsky which had appeared since Romola Nijinsky's life of her husband in 1933. The job of sifting truth from falsehood and putting the evidence in order alone seemed to justify another biography. I could not guess to what a marvellous extent I should have the co-operation of so many people who had lived or worked with Nijinsky.

Some of my conversations with Nijinsky's friends, relations, colleagues or successors took place near home, some in distant lands. My talks with Dame Marie Rambert took place in Kew Gardens, in Holland Park and in her own home on Campden Hill. Those with Mme Karsavina were held in her pretty house in Hampstead. Mr Massine gave me his recollections over dinner on two successive evenings at the Falcon Hotel in Stratford-upon-Avon. I was shown the setting of Nijinsky's early studies in Petersburg by Mme Natalia Dudinskaya, who now rules the school where he worked. I discussed him with M. Pierre Vladimirov in the offices of the School of American Ballet in New York and with Mme Ludmilla Schollar in William Christensen's Ballet School in San Francisco. When I met Mme Bronislava Nijinska for the first time, in her little house perched on a beetling crag at Pacific Palisades near Los Angeles, I felt I had really come to the ends of the earth as well as to the ultimate repository of truth about Nijinsky. Mme Bronislava's second husband had died ten days before, her hearing was poor and her English non-existent – besides which she had long been writing a book of her own about her brother. Nevertheless, she gave up two afternoons to answer my questions and to tell me things I did not know. Her

Introduction

daughter, Irina Nijinska-Raetz, to whom my friend Tamara Toumanova had introduced me a day or two before – thus making the interviews possible – acted as interpreter.

It was the dauntless Mme Irina who, two years later, while her mother was staging a ballet in Florence for the Maggio Musicale, read the whole 200,000 words of my book aloud – very loud – to Mme Bronislava, translating it as she went along into Russian. This took place mostly at night in a hotel bedroom, with people banging on the wall. I then met Mmes Bronislava and Irina in Paris, and in another hotel bedroom, with David Dougill taking notes, received their comments and corrections. It was Mme Irina who sensibly suggested that as technical descriptions of dancing could not be fuller in a book of this nature they should be omitted altogether; and I took her advice as far as I was able and cut them down to the minimum.

Mme Romola Nijinsky had already read my book with devoted diligence during a week spent at the Cavendish Hotel, Jermyn Street, when, on the afternoon the horse Nijinsky won the Two Thousand Guineas, she arrived at my flat in Covent Garden bursting with excitement about the race (which she had watched on colour television at Television House, near the Waldorf Hotel, where her husband had spent his first nights in England), to give me her detailed comments on the typescript. All her suggestions and corrections I accepted. Some months later, during the summer of 1970, I had further talks with Mme Romola Nijinsky, Mme Bronislava Nijinska and Mme Irina Nijinska-Raetz at the Cavendish Hotel: these led to extensive rewriting. Mme Romola Nijinsky later read through the final draft of the book again and approved it.

Through Mr Robert Craft, Mr Stravinsky answered a series of question-naires and checked many points. He also read certain chapters and offered suggestions. Mr Grigoriev answered many detailed questionnaires, his answers being transcribed by his wife Mme Tchernicheva. To my great regret both Mr Stravinsky and Mr Grigoriev died while the book was in preparation.

To these helpful friends, Nijinsky's colleagues, his partner, the com-poser of his 'Sacre du printemps', the chief guardian of classical tradition at his old school, his sister, niece and wife, I am more grateful than I can say.

Other members of the Diaghilev Ballet who gave their time to help me or answered letters were Mme Doubrovska, Mme Sokolova, Mme Lopokhova, the late Hilda Bewicke (Mrs Arfa), Miss Maria Chabelska, Mr Stanislas Idzikovsky, Mr Dolin and that wonderful *chef d'orchestre*, the late Ernest Ansermet.

If I had known twenty years ago that I was going to write Nijinsky's life how much more evidence I could have gathered from illustrious people who have died in that period! What questions I should have asked Alexandre Benois and Jean Cocteau! But I did enjoy the friendship of Lady Juliet Duff, and I have drawn on my memories of conversations with her, as well as on an essay she wrote on Diaghilev which was unpublished at the time of her death.

I never met Mme Valentine Hugo (*née* Gross), who died in 1968, but through the courtesy of M. Jean Hugo, whose first wife she was, a mass of notes and sketches were made available to me. Apart from being the most assiduous of artists in recording Nijinsky in all his roles, she planned to write a life of him. This never materialized, and I hope she would approve of this book which has been made with her posthumous help.

I owe an immense debt of gratitude to my old friend Mr Erich Alport, who invited me to go with him to Russia before I even knew I was to write the book, thus enabling me, as it turned out, to describe aspects of Leningrad at first hand. To the insistence, enthusiasm and generosity of Mr Lincoln Kirstein I owe a trip to the United States, which included my visit to California and the discovery of the Astruc papers in the Museum and Library of Performing Arts at Lincoln Center, New York.

Gabriel Astruc, the most enlightened and daring of musical impresarios, made possible the early triumphs of the Russian Ballet in Paris – and paid for this dearly. The survival of his correspondence with Diaghilev at Lincoln Center, of which I should have been unaware without Mr Kirstein's prompting, clarified a number of important points, helped towards exact dating, and proved the most valuable single group of documents for the study of the Russian Ballet's history. Mlle Lucienne Astruc, daughter of the impresario, has been a friend since the days of the Diaghilev Exhibition, and she has given me many precious documents which will one day find their way to our London Museum of Theatre Arts.

A number of dancers have helped me give some account of the choreography of certain ballets. Mme Karsavina described, mimed and danced for me passages of 'Le Pavillon d'Armide', and Mme Schollar and Mr Wilzak helped me with the same ballet. Miss Amanda Knott of Ballet Rambert corrected my description of 'L'Après-midi d'un faune', as did Mr Vassili Trunoff of Festival Ballet my account, made from memory only, with the aid of a gramophone record, of 'Schéhérazade'.

M. Jean Hugo gave me helpful information about Paris society in the early years of the Diaghilev Ballet. Mme Jean Hugo took much trouble to find out who the person was whose collection of Gauguin paintings excited Nijinsky. M. Philippe Jullian was kind enough to help identify a number of people listed as being present at the first famous *répétition générale* in 1909. I thank these friends in France most sincerely. Mme Natalia Dudinskaya

3

supplied me with a list of Nijinsky's roles at the Mariinsky, as well as the old photograph of Theatre Street, and I am so grateful for her help.

At the suggestion of Mme Bronislava Nijinska I got in touch with the distinguished ballet historian Mme Vera Krasovskaya, who read my chapter about Nijinsky's early years and provided facts from Leningrad sources to which I should not otherwise have had access. Besides making many useful comments, invaluable in that they expressed a Russian point of view, she went to great trouble to find out the truth about certain specific events – such as Nijinsky's pre-graduation appearance in 'Don Giovanni' – so that, thanks to her, valuable information can be published for the first time. My debt to her is considerable, and so is my gratitude.

Not only must I express my warm gratitude to Miss Genevieve Oswald, Curator of the Dance Collection of the New York Public Library at the Museum and Library of Performing Arts, and her staff, but also the Libraries and staff of the Bibliothèque Nationale, the Bibliothèque de l'Arsenal and the Bibliothèque de l'Opéra, Paris, and of the British Museum Reading Room, the BM Newspaper Library, Colindale and the Royal Opera House, Covent Garden.

The research in America was begun by me and concluded by Mr Brian Blackwood, who also did all the research in Paris. Mr David Dougill did all the London research. These two colleagues expedited work on the book and were of incalculable service to the cause.

Mr Blackwood was first called in, however, in his capacity as a musician. He is himself preparing a book on the musical side of the Diaghilev Ballet, and was able during 1969 and 1970 to give me part of his time to supply the deficiencies of my technical knowledge of music. Once I had decided that it was desirable to give wherever possible some sort of choreographic account of the ballets Nijinsky danced or invented, it seemed a pity not to supply also some parallel notes on the music. We therefore together set about working out our descriptions. It was very hard to decide how far to go, because this is not a musical text-book any more than it is a book on ballet technique. Mr Blackwood, if this were his own book, could and no doubt would go into far more detail, and I must take the blame if the reader finds that we have stopped short in 'describing' a score, just as I must be held responsible for any descriptive phrases which to a musician may seem fanciful and imprecise. Mr Blackwood played over for me, at the Music Library of the Senate House, London University, the piano scores of certain almost forgotten ballets, such as 'Le Pavillon d'Armide' and 'Le Dieu bleu', which have never been recorded.

In the case of 'Le Sacre du printemps' – far the most important score dealt with, and the hardest to describe – Mr Blackwood prepared the first

4

analysis, I injected a few of my own thoughts, then cut the piece by half. Mr Stravinsky and Mr Craft read the draft, made certain comments and approved at least one specific phrase. But I was far from satisfied, and in the absence of Mr Blackwood, with my neighbour in the country, the composer Thomas Eastwood, I played over a record of the ballet again, two evenings running, and together we concocted a fuller description. So, some of the phrases are Mr Blackwood's, some Mr Eastwood's and some mine. This draft was then sent back for comment to Mr Stravinsky and Mr Craft.

It was my colleague Mr Desmond Shawe-Taylor who played me a record of Liszt's 14th Rhapsody one Sunday afternoon in Dorset, and with him and Mr John Bryson, a collaborator on my Diaghilev and Shakespeare Exhibitions, I discussed what kind of a ballet Diaghilev would have made of it, if he had got it on.

So many friends made helpful suggestions or provided small pieces of information: the late Antonio Gandarillas; Mr Alexander Tcherepnine; Mr Philip Dyer, who as a child was patted on the head by Diaghilev, who was my assistant on the Diaghilev Exhibition and who is now Wardrobe Master to our incipient Museum of Theatre Arts; my colleague Mr Felix Aprahamian; Mme Nadia Lacoste, Directrice du Centre de Presse, Principauté de Monaco; Baroness Budberg; Mr Miklos de Szakats, former husband of Nijinsky's younger daughter; Lady Diana Cooper; Baron Tassilo von Watzdorf; Mr Ronald Crichton; Mr Nigel Gosling; Mr H.S. Ede; Mr Harold Rosenthal; Mr Raymond Mander and Mr Joe Mitchenson; Mr Richard Davies; Mr John Peter; Mr Stuart Nicol of Royal Mail Lines, Ltd.; Mr Duncan Grant; M. Boris Kochno.

Much of this book was written at a remote cottage in Wiltshire, and at times, when writing it, I would see no one but the postman for several days at a stretch. If it were not that several kind neighbours cheered me up and entertained me in the evenings I might have fallen into a melancholy and broken off the work; so I take pleasure in thanking for their continued hospitality Mr and Mrs John Arundell (she being the great-grand-daughter of Lady Ripon and grand-daughter of Lady Juliet Duff) and their children; Mr and Mrs Julian Bream; Mr and Mrs Thomas Eastwood; Mrs Edmund Fane; and Mr Cecil Beaton, who spurred on my work with his enthusiasm and inspired me with his industry.

Mr David Dougill patiently typed and retyped many versions of every chapter, copying endless insertions and corrections in quintuplicate. As our task drew to a close, and after we had overstepped several deadlines, he prepared the whole of the first draft of the penultimate chapter, incorporating details and press notices of the Ballet's North American tours which have not been published before. He also worked with me on the Notes, and I really do not believe I should have had the courage to complete these without him. (I had so many sources of information that I had forgotten what some of them were.) Finally, Mr Dougill crowned his labours by making the Index single-handed.

In January and February 1970, which was the period of what would have been our final spurt, Mr Blackwood, Mr Dougill and I, working in adjacent rooms in my flat in Covent Garden, had the pleasure and honour of being joined, in a fourth room, by Mrs Margaret Power, who came, out of friendship to me and devotion to Nijinsky's memory, to type, insert and correct and indeed to criticize and improve. A *doyenne* of balletomanes in this country, she became, at the end of the last war, a good friend to the Nijinskys in Vienna. She later helped to care for Nijinsky in England, and after his death continued as a friend to his widow. In more than one sense she was a blessing to our work.

I say 'semi-final spurt' because I had intended to end the book with Nijinsky's illness. At the request of Mr Anthony Godwin of Weidenfeld & Nicolson, I added one more chapter bringing the story up to Nijinsky's death: this was written during the summer of 1970.

At the time of Nijinsky's second funeral in Paris in summer, 1953, I was collecting material for the Diaghilev Exhibition, which was to be held at the 1954 Edinburgh Festival to commemorate the twenty-fifth anniversary of Diaghilev's death. I had been asked to do this simply because I was a critic of ballet known to be interested in Nijinsky and the Diaghilev period, and nothing much was expected of me except to assemble a number of designs and portraits and hang them on a wall: but as I became more and more engrossed in the detective work and correspondence necessary for this collection – and I was helped by many old friends and collaborators of Diaghilev, such as Lady Juliet Duff and Alexandre Benois – I began to devise techniques of display which were considered novel at the time, with the result that I found myself landed with a second career – that of an exhibition designer. The sales in 1968 and 1969 of the Diaghilev wardrobe, which I catalogued for Sotheby's, led directly to the foundation of a Museum of Theatre Arts in London, with sections devoted to drama, opera and ballet, which I hope will soon find a home in the neighbourhood of Covent Garden. Our Museum, for which we have collected some of Nijinsky's own costumes, portraits of him, action studies by Valentine Gross, and the costumes of his great ballet 'Le Sacre du printemps' – still fresh because worn so little during all those years – should prove the most lasting result of a chain of events which can be traced back to my first sight of the photograph of Nijinsky in 'Le Spectre de la rose' on the jacket of his wife's biography, at Liverpool Street Station, half a lifetime ago.

CHAPTER ONE

1898-1908

August 1898–December 1908

On 20 August 1898, Eleonora Nicolaievna Nijinskaya, a pretty middle-aged Polish woman, took her nine-year-old younger son to the Imperial School of Ballet in Petersburg, hoping that he might be accepted as a pupil. Her elder son was simple-minded and she had a seven-year-old daughter. Since her husband had left her, life was not easy; but if the State took over the maintenance of her boy, it would be easier. It was not only a question of bread, however: in her mind were thoughts of art and glory. She had been a fine dancer herself, but had left the stage to look after her family. Her husband Thomas, also a Pole, was a superb dancer, but he had never appeared in the Imperial Theatres of Moscow or Petersburg. He might have done if he had wanted to, even though not a graduate of the Imperial Schools, but he enjoyed a wandering life and made more money on the road.[1] Very little of this found its way to Eleonora.

Poles were slightly underprivileged subjects of the Russian Empire. The last Emperor but one, the liberal-minded Alexander II, who had emancipated the serfs in 1861, had been assassinated twenty years later by a Pole. The present Emperor was extremely conservative.

If the boy Vaslav became a pupil of the Imperial School he would have his foot on the lowest rung of the ladder of the Civil Service: he would be the equivalent of a junior officer cadet. After seven or eight years, if he graduated to the company of the Mariinsky Theatre, he would climb from *corps de ballet* to *coryphé*, from *coryphé* to second *soliste*, from second *soliste* to first *soliste*, from first *soliste* to *premier danseur*. As a leading dancer Vaslav could attain fame and fortune. In Russia the whole structure of society was a graded pyramid culminating in the Tsar. If you were not a member of the

Civil Service you were in limbo and outer darkness – you were nothing. Ninety per cent of the Tsar's subjects were nothing.

Teatralnaya Ulitsa (Theatre Street), to which mother and son had come, was built by the Italian architect, Rossi; it is one of the most beautiful streets in the world and certainly the most regular. Two identical blocks of buildings nearly two hundred yards long confront each other to form the street, which terminates at its northern end in the splendid pile of the Alexandrinsky Theatre (where drama is performed) and at the other in an open space on the quay of the Fontanka, one of the curving rivers and canals which bring an element of unruly romanticism to the regulated vistas of classical Petersburg, much as the Water of Leith does to the New Town of Edinburgh or, less obviously, the old Indian trail of Broadway to the ordered canyons of Manhattan. The arcading of the ground floors of these 'terraces' is repeated above by taller arches which frame not only the big windows of the *piano nobile*, but the semi-circular windows of the second floor, linked by decorative plaster panels in relief; these upper arches being separated by pairs of engaged Doric columns supporting the double cornice. The monotony is imperceptibly broken by projecting bays four arches away from either end of the blocks, their first-floor windows having triangular pediments. Like most of the late eighteenth- and early nineteenth-century buildings in Petersburg, Rossi's blocks are painted a warm pinkish ochre, and against this consoling colour the white columns and decorations stand out. But this is not a street of ostentation, a parade, a *boulevard* or *corso*. Because the Alexandrinsky Theatre presents its *back* to it, blocking its end rather awkwardly, the visitor is aware of a monastic university atmosphere, as in the quadrangle of an Oxford college, or in Jefferson's serene enclosure at Charlottesville. This is a place of training and research. The left-hand building housed the Ministry of Education: the right-hand, students of the theatre and ballet schools.

The mother and son paused at the arched entry of the Ballet School, and, no doubt, as I did when I followed in their historic footsteps a few years ago, inquired the way of a uniformed porter, to be directed diagonally half-left across a courtyard to a corner door. Inside it, even then, was there a crone-like *concierge*, and were there plants and plaques on the wall at the foot of the marble stairs? Herds of fearful, expectant children, fathers and mothers were pouring in – between a hundred and a hundred and fifty boys[2] with one or both parents. From the crowded office at the top of the stairs they would be directed to the rehearsal room, where usually only the senior girls had their classes.

It was (and is) a cheerful big room, because through the tall windows which ran down both sides there were glimpses of trees. The floor had a

8

ramp corresponding to that of the Mariinsky stage so that students could get used to dancing on a slight slope before they graduated to the Imperial company. The wall at the 'deep end' was covered with mirrors. As in all ballet class-rooms a *barre*, on which dancers must support themselves with one hand to perform their preliminary exercises, ran round the other three sides. There was a gallery all round the top, and there were portraits of the Emperor and of old ballerinas and celebrated teachers on the walls.[3]

The boys lined up to be inspected by the staff of teachers, doctors and ballet-masters, the chief of all being the eighty-three-year-old Swede, Christian Johannsen, who had been in his youth the pupil of the Danish choreographer, August Bournonville, who had been the pupil of the Franco-Italian Auguste Vestris, who had been taught by his father, Gaetano Vestris, who had studied under the Swiss-French Jean-Georges Noverre, who had given dancing-lessons during her youth in Vienna to Queen Marie Antoinette and collaborated later in Paris on the production of 'Iphigénie en Tauride' with Gluck.

Because of Thomas's fame the name of Nijinsky was not unknown to the examiners, but there was no question of admitting pupils on any consideraton other than merit. Vaslav was backward at his lessons and a real mother's boy. Luckily, the teacher of the senior boys' class, Nicolas Legat, noticed him.[4] 'The first impression he produced on the examining commission was an unfavourable one, for he appeared awkward in manner and delicate in health. But at the doctor's examination I was struck by the formation of his thigh muscles. . . . I told Nijinsky to move a few paces away and jump. His leap was phenomenal. "That youngster can be made into a fine dancer," I said, and passed him without further ado.'

Happy mother and son! The gates of life were flung open. Although of fifteen boys chosen about ten were due to be eliminated at the end of the first two years' training, Eleonora had to have faith that her boy would prevail. Of the six boys eventually left in the 1898 class, five were destined to come to a tragic end – Iliodor Lukiano poisoned by his own hand at twenty-one, George Rosaï dead of pneumonia at twenty-one, Grigori Babitch killed by a jealous husband at twenty-three, Mikhail Feodorov dead of tuberculosis at twenty-six,[5] Nijinsky insane at thirty-one. Only Anatole Bourman would survive to write a bad book about his great schoolfellow for the bafflement of future biographers.

Eleonora was the daughter of a Warsaw cabinet-maker.*[6] She followed her elder sister into the ballet school of the Warsaw theatre and became a member of the company. There was no tradition of dancing either in her family or

---

* It is not true that he was of gentle birth or that he shot himself.

in that of her husband.* Thomas Nijinsky's father had fought as a patriot and guerrilla in the Polish insurrection of 1863 and lost his small property in consequence.[7] Thomas was handsome in the extreme. An outstanding dancer in both classical and character roles, he was also a gifted choreographer and had his own troupe of dancers. After their marriage, Thomas and Eleonora toured the length and breadth of Russia, and their three children, Stanislav, Vaslav and Bronislava, born within six years, toured with them. Vaslav was born in Kiev on 12 March, New Style (28 February, Old Style) 1888,[8] but not baptized until two years, four months later, in Warsaw in the Catholic faith, his mother post-dating his birth for reasons connected with military service. Not many children are christened four hundred miles from where they were born. Bronislava was baptized at the same time. There can have been few such travelled children in the whole of that immense land which divided the West from the East and stretched from the dark Arctic wastes to the sun-drenched vineyards of the Caspian Sea. We can imagine them, like a family of Picasso's acrobats of the 'blue period', alone in a cold and empty landscape, but, in fact, life was more boisterous and colourful than that. The children watched their parents in Protean disguises from the wings of theatres and even sometimes appeared with them. Although their life was spent moving from one small-town cheap hotel to another, they saw, heard and smelt the landscape and the people of Russia. Such was the background of Vaslav and Bronislava, who were destined to produce to the music of Stravinsky two of the elemental Russian epics of our time, 'Le Sacre du printemps' and 'Les Noces'.

Perhaps Stanislav would have grown up to be a dancer and choreographer too, but one day in Warsaw, when he was six, he fell out of a window, struck his head on the pavement and became mentally retarded. Eleonora had an idea that this insanity might have been latent, because, shortly before he was born, the family had been attacked by bandits in a mountain village in the Caucasus and the shock to her had been so great that she had lost the power of speech for three days.[9] There was no tradition of madness on either side of the family. Thomas, however, was subject to fits of uncontrollable passion, during which he appeared to be out of his mind. These rages Vaslav inherited.[10]

From his father Vaslav also inherited his high cheekbones and slanting eyes, which, in spite of the Nijinskys' Polish nationality, would seem to be indications of Tartar blood. From Thomas too came the extraordinary jump. Not only Vaslav and Bronislava, but also their daughters, were to have both the jump and the Tartar face. From his mother Vaslav inherited his gentle affectionate nature. Eleonora was 'a genius of a mother'.[11]

* The statement that Thomas came of a line of dancers is false.

Thomas was too attractive to be faithful to his wife. When his mistress Rumiantseva joined the troupe and Thomas started another family, Eleonora renounced the stage, took her children off and settled in Petersburg (but she and Thomas were never divorced).[12] It was also easier for her to have medical attention for Stanislav in the western capital. The boy was briefly apprenticed to a watchmaker, but could not concentrate on the work. His mother reconciled herself to the fact that he would never be able to earn a living. He got worse and was eventually confined in a State asylum. Eleonora, Vaslav and Bronislava used to visit him every Sunday.

Thomas Nijinsky came back to Petersburg to see his wife and children at least once, when Vaslav was six or seven. Father and son went bathing on the Neva, and Thomas threw Vaslav into the water thinking that this would teach him to swim. Vaslav sank to the bottom, but managed to save himself by catching hold of a rope.[13]

The Nijinsky family moved into a flat in Mokhovaya Street, which ran north-south between the long Serguevskaya Street (parallel with and not far from the Neva) and the Simeonovsky Bridge over the Fontanka. They were little more than five minutes' walk from the delightful Summer Garden, planted by Peter the Great, in which the opening scene of Tchaikovsky's 'Queen of Spades' takes place. It was an aristocratic neighbourhood, but in Petersburg many princely façades conceal a hinterland of subsidiary courtyards and tenements. The Stieglitz Museum was nearby, and on wet days Eleonora took her children there or to the Alexander III Museum, or to see the Imperial treasures of the Hermitage, which adjoined Rastrelli's red Winter Palace.[14]

In the 1890s Russia consisted of a small nineteenth-century intelligentsia in a seventeenth-century population. The Greek-Orthodox religion was Byzantine, and so were the despotism of the Tsar and the ignorance of the people. But for a century thoughts of liberty had been budding, and these were not unconnected with a slow revolution in the world of art. It is significant that Pushkin, the father of Russian culture, whose poems and plays not only inspired the writers who came after him, but so many musicians who made them into operas and ballets, should have been exiled to the Caucasus for expressing his liberal ideas.

Between the accession in 1825 of Nicholas I, the oppressor of Pushkin, and the abdication in 1917 of Nicholas II, the opponent of Diaghilev, there took place a renaissance in the arts, which may be said to have reached its height in a series of performances staged not in Russia but in Paris and Western Europe during the last decade of the period, and of which Vaslav Nijinsky was the supreme ornament.

Between the death of Gogol in 1852 and the end of the century there appeared Turgenev's *Fathers and Sons,* Tolstoy's *War and Peace, Anna Karenina* and *The Kreutzer Sonata,* Dostoyevsky's *Crime and Punishment, The Idiot, The Devils* and *The Brothers Karamazov,* and Chekhov's *The Seagull* and *Uncle Vanya.* During the same period Glinka would die; Balakirev would compose his songs and symphonies; Borodin 'Prince Igor'; Mussorgsky 'Boris Godounov' and 'Khovanshchina'; Rimsky-Korsakov nearly all his operas and symphonic poems and Tchaikovsky his complete works. In the 'eighties and 'nineties there was a reaction against the dominant school of painters known as Peredvijniki or Peripatetics,*whose academism had a pervasive moralistic and nationalist tone: the new wave of artists, less ready to suppress their personalities for a cause, inclined towards the doctrine of Art for Art's Sake, and were labelled Decadents. From the former group stood out the illustrious figure of Ilya Repine, a painter of real distinction, excelling in historical scenes, *genre* and portraiture, who turned gradually from academism and story-telling towards more Impressionist ideals. His pupil Valentin Serov, son of the composer of 'Judith' and other operas, formed a link between the Peredvijniki and the Decadents: in his work we can find something of Manet, Sargent and even Whistler. The landscapes of Isaak Levitan appear as a bridge between Constable and the Impressionists; he has been compared to Corot and Boudin. Two younger Moscow landscapists, Alexandre Golovine and Konstantin Korovine, were the first painters to be drawn to work for the theatre. Mikhail Vrubel, who, like the latter, used paint with a freedom approaching frenzy, was a completely original painter of Russian life, an expressionist before the word was invented. In the Western capital Alexandre Benois, who, with the Beardsley-influenced Leon Bakst, would play a leading role in the sphere of theatrical design, was a gentler minor talent, specializing in evocative landscapes and townscapes, particularly of Petersburg and its surrounding country palaces, and of Versailles. His friend Konstantin Somov also had a nostalgia for the past – he might be called the Russian Conder; while Nicolas Roerich's unrealistic images and archeological dreams, coupled with the love of pure colour he had in common with both Somov and Bakst, may be seen as parallel to the symbolism of Gauguin.

At the Imperial Ballet School the school year, which was eight months long, began in September, on the day when the Imperial Theatres re-opened after the four months' summer recess. For the first two years, until it was decided which children should be accepted as permanent members of the Imperial School, they lived at home. Vaslav walked to school and back: it took him twenty minutes.[15]

* Because of their travelling exhibitions.

The new day-boys were only issued with caps: these were like an officer cadet's, with patent leather peaks and the Imperial eagle in silver. They must have looked with envy at their seniors and determined to work hard in order to earn the full uniform. The boarders had three uniforms: a black one for every day, a dark blue for holidays and a grey linen for the summer. The tunics were embroidered on either side of the military collar with silver lyres framed in palms and surmounted by a crown. The two overcoats, one for winter with an astrakhan collar, the other for summer, were also of military cut, double-breasted, ankle-length and with silver buttons. There were boots, shoes and six changes of underwear. When Vaslav had earned this wardrobe he would really see himself as a person of consequence.

For ballet classes the boys wore white shirts and black trousers. Vaslav was not entirely a beginner: he had already learnt from his parents the five positions of classical ballet and a few basic steps.[16] From the start it was clear to his companions that this Pole had stolen a march on them. His happiest hours were during the morning class, for all children enjoy best what they do best, and he was behind the others in the afternoon lessons of French, History and Mathematics. Day-boys brought their lunch with them, but Vaslav did not look forward to lunch-time and recreation time because he was treated as an outcast by the other boys. He was despised for being Polish, silent, bad at expressing himself and apparently slow-witted; and he was laughed at for his Tartar or Mongolian features and nicknamed 'Japonczek' – the little Japanese. Vaslav did not submit to his classmates' bullying in silence. He was always quick to defend himself, had many fights and punched many noses. His marks for behaviour were invariably very low. When there was any trouble Rosaï, Bourman, Babitch and the others always tried to put the blame on Vaslav, and as he never told tales he was often punished. Throughout his eight years at school he never made a friend.[17]

His masters, however, were aware of his potentialities. He was quickly promoted from the class of the good-looking, amusing and popular Sergei Legat to that of his elder brother Nicolas, who had spotted Vaslav's jump at the entrance examination.[18] Legat used to have all the windows in the classroom open until a minute before the lesson began. The boys lined up along the *barre* and their teacher accompanied them on his violin. 'In ten minutes,' wrote Bourman,* 'our blood tingled! We had to work to keep

---

* I must explain my policy with regard to Anatole Bourman's book *The Tragedy of Nijinsky* which came out three years after Romola Nijinsky's successful life of her husband. People who write books usually do it because they need money, so we must not judge Bourman too severely for allowing his collaborator, Miss D. Lyman, to work up his reminiscences into as sensational a tale as possible. It was necessary for her purpose to present Bourman as a much closer friend of Nijinsky's than he was, and to make him the eye-witness of all the crucial events in Nijinsky's life. The dancer's most recent (1957) biographer, Mme Françoise Reiss, accepted Bourman's story as the

warm – and we worked until the heat from our bodies created an aura of steam around us while our breath made us look as though we held white plumes between our teeth. I have often remembered how cold it was, and thought of Legat, unable to exercise as we did, patiently teaching us, now shouting excited orders at us, now counting sharply to emphasize the tempo that he set by plucking the strings of his violin. Always happy and smiling, he made his lessons a joy, and loved us both as a friend and a teacher.'[19]

The Legat brothers were, after Pavel Gerdt, the principal male dancers at the Mariinsky. They were clever caricaturists and had published an album of water-colours of their fellow artists which amazed Petersburg. For classes in mime the boys went to Gerdt. This famous man had been a *premier danseur* for thirty-two years: he was equally renowned for his classical dancing, his partnering and his mime, and had played Prince Désiré in the original 'Sleeping Beauty', or rather 'La Belle au bois dormant', eight years before. Its composer, Tchaikovsky, was dead, but its choreographer, Marius Petipa, still reigned supreme over the ballet of the Mariinsky Theatre, for which he had staged over sixty ballets by himself and others since his arrival in Petersburg from France over half a century ago.

The boys' classrooms and the boarders' dormitories were on the top floor. The girls lived and worked down below, secluded as nuns, under the strict eye of their headmistress, Varvara Ivanovna Lihosherstova. Boys and girls were not allowed to speak to each other even when they joined in lessons of ballroom dancing and were waltzing together.

During the last few years a kind of revolution had been taking place in Russian ballet dancing.[20] The Petersburg school had always prided itself on its style and artistry – the Moscow artists went in more for bravura and dramatic effect: then, during the 'eighties and 'nineties a series of Italian guest-artists at the Mariinsky had dazzled Petersburg with their strength and acrobatic feats. Prominent among these were Enrico Cecchetti, who had been the original Bluebird in 'The Sleeping Beauty', Carlotta Brianza, who had been Aurora, and Pierina Legnani, whose thirty-two *fouettés* – a step with which a female dancer whips herself into spinning like a top, rising and falling on the toes of one foot which remains on the same spot throughout – had taken the town by storm. All the Russian dancers became eager to learn the Italian tricks, and the day when the celebrated Matilda Kchessinskaya, who had been the Tsar's mistress before his marriage, and was the favourite of several Grand Dukes, accomplished this *tour de force*, was the occasion for

truth, and was thus able to enliven her narrative with some lurid anecdotes. I have Mme Bronislava Nijinska's assurance that a number of episodes are pure invention. Yet Bourman could not help telling the truth sometimes. I have had to use my discernment and have been readier in crediting unsensational details of school life, which it would have been hard for Miss Lyman to invent, than any other parts of the book.

patriotic rejoicing. In 1898 the school had engaged Cecchetti to hold a 'parallel class of perfection' for the dancers of the company in addition to – or as an alternative to – Johannsen's class. The marriage of Italian strength and Russian style was to be the special glory of the rising generation of dancers: and of these Nijinsky would be the brightest star.

For two years Vaslav walked to school every morning and home every evening. If he liked he could walk by the Fontanka river almost the whole way. Down Mokhovaya, sharp right, and he was by the Simeonovsky Bridge. He could either follow the curve of the river to the right, passing the Anichkov Bridge by the Anichkov Palace where the Dowager Empress lived, and on to the Chernishev Bridge, which was just at the bottom of Theatre Street; or when he came to the Anichkov Bridge with its bronze horse-tamers, he could turn right up the endless Nevsky Prospekt and then left through the gardens in front of the Alexandrinsky Theatre, past Mikeshin's statue of Catherine the Great. This was a little shorter. But if, pausing at the bottom of Mokhovaya before crossing the road towards the river, he happened to glance left, he would have seen on the corner of Simeonovskaya and the Liteiny Prospekt a building in which was living the man who would guide him to his future triumphs. In the top-floor flat Diaghilev, with his friends Benois, Bakst and Nouvel, all Nijinsky's future collaborators, were planning their magazine *Mir Iskustva*, 'The World of Art'.

Born in the Selistchev Barracks in the province of Novgorod in 1872, Sergei Pavlovitch Diaghilev lost his mother a few days after his birth; but his father, an officer in the Imperial Guard, took as his second wife a kind and cultivated woman, Elena Panaeva, and Diaghilev's childhood in Petersburg and later in Perm was spent in a lively and music-loving circle of step-brothers and cousins. Although by 1898 he had assumed leadership of the group of friends who were going to play so historic a role, the man around whom they had all first collected was Alexandre Nicolaievitch Benois, who was two years older.

Benois was one of those Russians without a drop of Russian blood. On his father's side French and German, on his mother's Venetian, he was to prove the ideal interpreter in paint and words of Peter's west-looking capital, and the chronicler of its treasures. His father and maternal grandfather were both architects and had collaborated on the building of the Mariinsky Theatre. Benois was a gentle, studious, amusing man, devoted to all forms of art and applied art. In 1898 he had been married for four years and had known Diaghilev for eight. He describes his first meeting with the latter:

It was at the beginning of the summer of 1890 that I met Diaghilev; I was twenty and he was eighteen. He had just left school at Perm and was in St Petersburg to matriculate at the University at the same time as his cousin, Dima Filosofov, Valetchka Nouvel and myself. We three had also just finished our studies at the K. May school. Dima had already left for the country; but before going he had asked Nouvel and myself to look after his cousin, who was to be in St Petersburg for a few days on his way to the Filosofovs' country house. We plunged into intimacy at this first meeting, and before the end of the evening were calling each other 'thou'. What chiefly struck Nouvel and me about the newcomer was his air of well-being, his full face, fresh complexion and the big mouth which revealed, when he smiled, teeth of a dazzling whiteness. Dima's cousin was smiling all the time, and as often as not his smile would herald a burst of loud, infectious laughter. In sum, Serge struck us as being a good fellow, though a bit simple and provincial: and if we received him on intimate terms from the very beginning it was only because he was a close relation of the Filosofov family. How amazed we should have been to know that we had just welcomed the one who was to become in so few years captain of our team, the man who would help us to realize all our dreams in the varied fields of art! For we all dreamed of nothing less than striving to bring about a renaissance of art in Russia!

Serge Diaghilev, then, was admitted to our circle, but he only really became one of us by gradual stages. We were all rather sedate young men, real mothers' boys, keen on attending lectures, mad about the theatre: we seemed older than we were. Dima's cousin, on the other hand, was a little childish and showed a certain tendency to violent action: he never stopped hitting us, for instance, and would even challenge us to fight – an offer we should never have dreamt of accepting. . . . Anyway, we knew we stood no chance against 'big Serge', who was so much stronger than we were.

Diaghilev's real nature was that of a fighter. So that as all traces of his youthful naïveté vanished and our friendship grew deeper, a kind of struggle became manifest in our relations. In the early years of our friendship I was Serge's chief mentor; and the avidity with which he pounced on whatever information struck him as valuable delighted me and flattered my pedagogic instinct. Even then, however, his attitude would often change with the greatest ease from that of a peaceable and submissive disciple to one of pugnacity, in which he took pleasure in landing well-directed and demoralizing blows. The pupil would suddenly grow arrogant and his studious apprenticeship turn to cynical exploitation. Quarrels would follow which often seemed final. I sometimes wrote him indignant letters, only to receive vague excuses in reply. But all would end in a touching reconciliation and tears from Serge – for, besides being a fighter, and essentially a man of action, Diaghilev was sentimental, and quarrels with his friends upset him greatly.

It was music first of all that brought us together. Without being professionals or virtuosos, we were all passionate lovers of music; but Serge dreamed of devoting himself entirely to the art. All the time he was studying law along with us, he took singing lessons with Cotogni, the famous baritone of the Italian Opera; while for musical theory, which he wanted to master completely so as to rival Moussorgsky and Tchaikovsky, he went to the very source and studied with Rimsky-Korsakov.

However, our musical tastes were not always the same. The quality our group valued most was what the Germans call *Stimmung*, and besides this, the power of suggestion and dramatic force. The Bach of the Passions, Gluck, Schubert, Wagner and the Russian composers – Borodin in Prince Igor, Rimsky and, above all, Tchaikovsky, were our gods. Tchaikovsky's 'Queen of Spades' had just been performed for the first time at the Opera of St Petersburg, and we were ecstatic about its Hoffmannesque element, notably the scene in the old Countess's bedroom. We liked the composer's famous Romances much less, finding them insipid and sometimes trivial. These Romances, however, were just what Diaghilev liked. What he valued most was broad melody, and in particular whatever gave a singer the chance to display the sensuous qualities of his voice. During the years of his apprenticeship he bore our criticisms and jokes with resignation, but as he learned more about music – and about the history of art in general – he gained in self-confidence and found reasons to justify his predilections. There came a time when not only did he dare to withstand our attacks but went on to refute our arguments fiercely.

His attitude towards the plastic arts was quite different. He had no creative ambitions in the direction of painting, sculpture or architecture, not having tried his hand at any of them, so he contented himself with the role of dilettante; and the opinions of those people he acknowledged as authorities (particularly Bakst, Serov and myself) were accepted as Gospel truth. Yet even over these matters Diaghilev managed to surprise us, for he would leap from indifference to enthusiasm, from total ignorance to unusual expertise. It was in this way that we saw him become in the course of a few months the historian of Russian eighteenth-century art, untiring in his researches in the State archives and museums, as well as in private collections, working with the zest he put into any task he took to heart.

One could certainly call Diaghilev a creative genius, although it is not easy to analyse the nature of his creative gift. He practised neither painting nor sculpture, nor was he a professional writer; for his few critical essays, remarkable as they were as proofs of his taste and judgement, did not amount to much – and anyway Serge hated the business of writing. He even lost faith before long in any vocation he may have felt for music, which was his real speciality. In no branch of art did he become an executant or a creator: and yet one cannot deny that his whole activity was *creative*. It is impossible to believe that the painters, musicians and choreographers who gave birth to the movement known as *Mir Iskustva*, 'The World of Art', from the paper we published, would have worked to such good effect had not Diaghilev placed himself at their head and taken command of them. There was one thing lacking in the artists of that generation who have since become world-famous: they lacked the spirit to fight and impose themselves. This spirit Diaghilev possessed in the highest degree, so that we can say he too had his unique speciality, namely *will-power*. . . . This powerful manipulator of men obliged creative artists to become the obedient executants of their own ideas under his despotic sway.[21]

Benois' meeting, at the house of his brother Albert, with Leon Bakst whose real name was Rosenberg, dates from a few months earlier:

On entering Albert's upstairs studio one day in March 1890 I came upon a young man I did not know. Albert introduced his new acquaintance to me as a gifted artist; I took but little notice of this as it was Albert's usual way of introducing any painter. Mr Rosenberg's exterior was in no way remarkable. The rather regular features were spoilt by his short-sighted eyes, his bright red hair and a thin moustache which straggled over his curved lips. His shy and at the same time ingratiating manner seemed to me, if not off-putting, at least unpleasing. Mr Rosenberg smiled very often and laughed too much. It was clear that he was most happy at having been received in the house of such a famous painter as my brother was at that time. . . .

Our friendly feelings for Levushka Rosenberg were mixed with some pity. He told Valetchka Nouvel and me how hard his life was. He had been left without any means of subsistence after the sudden death of his father, a well-to-do man (a stockbroker, I believe) who had only had time to provide his children with a good elementary education. Levushka had been obliged to find the means to keep not only himself but also his mother, his grandmother, two sisters and a very young brother. Moreover, he did not want to leave the Academy of Arts, which he attended as an external student. His work at the Academy took up much of his time and he lacked the means to buy the materials necessary for his artistic work.[22]

Other members of the group of friends – and these had all been at school with Benois – were the painter Konstantin Somov, Walter Nouvel, whose speciality among the arts was music, and Diaghilev's cousin, Dmitri Filosofov, whose interests were more abstract and metaphysical. Diaghilev and Filosofov were both homosexual. They had been on grand tours of Western Europe together. Diaghilev had made a point of meeting celebrated painters such as Lenbach and Liebermann, of hearing Wagner's operas, of seeing the treasures of Florence and Venice, and of buying pictures and antique furniture. He dreamed of founding a museum: at least for the meanwhile he intended to live in style.

The brotherhood called each other by their diminutive or *petits noms*: Serioja for Sergei, Levushka for Leon, Shoura for Alexandre, Dima for Dmitri, Valetchka for Walter, Kostia for Konstantin.

In 1898–9, with the backing of Sava Mamontov, the Moscow millionaire and patron of the Moscow Arts Theatre, and Princess Tenisheva, a collector of pictures on a large scale, Diaghilev and his friends founded the periodical *Mir Iskustva*. This was something entirely new in Russia. Possibly inspired by *The Yellow Book* and *The Savoy*, it was luxuriously produced with half-tone blocks on art paper and decorations in line in the text, but it differed from the English publications (a link with which was provided by an article commissioned from D.S.McColl on Aubrey Beardsley) in that it published no poetry or fiction. It was a mouthpiece for the group of friends through which they would voice their views on ancient and modern Russian art and architecture, foreign art, music, literature, philosophy and the theatre. Not that their views always coincided. Benois, who was in Paris when the first number was produced, was horrified by the importance Diaghilev gave to the neo-archaistic architect and ikon painter Vaznetzov. As the years went on – and although the first backers withdrew after a year and had to be replaced, publication continued until 1904 – the slightly mystical influence of Filosofov on Diaghilev was gradually replaced by that of the more 'visual' Benois. The music section was run by Alfred Nourok and was serious rather than brilliant – among articles of interest were those by Grieg on Mozart and by Nietzsche on Wagner at Bayreuth. *Mir Iskustva* stirred up many contro-versies and earned the friends the epithet of 'decadent'. Repine, for instance, broke with them completely, but this did not prevent Diaghilev devoting a number to his work some months later. By and large, every Russian critic of note contributed to the periodical and the work of every important Russian painter was reproduced in it. The *Mir Iskustva* group also arranged exhibitions of Russian, Finnish, German and English paintings at various museums in Petersburg between 1899 and 1901.

The editorial office of the *World of Art* was Sergei Diaghilev's apartment on the top floor of a big house at the corner of the Liteiny Prospekt and the Simeonevskaya Street. . . . The place of honour was occupied by three portraits by Lenbach (obtained in 1895), two drawings by Menzel, some water-colours by Hans Herrman and Bartels, a pastel portrait by Puvis de Chavannes and several sketches by Dagnan-Bouveret.
    The Jacobean chairs stood . . . in Serioja's dining-room. The drawing-room, which served our editor as study, contained, besides the Blüthner piano, several heavy, gilded, velvet-covered armchairs, a large velvet ottoman and some small antique Italian cupboards on which stood an excellent copy of Donatello's bust of Niccolo da Uzzano, several casts of Pompeian bronzes and numerous photographs of artists, authors and musicians, all autographed for Diaghilev. Here stood in close proximity Gounod and Zola, Menzel and Massenet. These were the trophies of 1895 when the young Diaghilev had found it necessary to convey his respects to a number of celebrities. . . .
    A handsome, large, black, sixteenth-century table served as the 'editor's desk'. It had been brought by Serioja from Italy, and was said to have aroused the envy of Wilhelm von Bode himself. Serioja sat at the head in a very imposing armchair upholstered in old velvet. In front of him lay writing materials and among them a pot of glue and a large pair of scissors which served as a favourite distraction for him – Diaghilev was passionately fond of cutting out photographs from which reproductions were made in the review. . . . The rooms overlooking the yard were dull and dark and really rather resembled one's idea of a business office. Here were heaps of papers, kept in order by poor Dima Filosofov, who had voluntarily taken upon himself the ungrateful jobs of being simultaneously office manager, chief of

staff, tutor and general secretary who had to receive all visitors. The large packages of reproductions sent from abroad were unpacked in these back rooms, where it was again Filosofov who sorted and numbered them before putting them away in the cupboards. It was here also that our other martyr – the next victim of Serioja's despotism – Levushka Bakst spent whole days in inventing elegant titles for the drawings and retouching the photographs, in an attempt to give them a more artistic character. Sometimes the good-natured, easy-going Levushka would have sudden fits of rebellion and indignation, but more often he willingly – and, oh, how artistically! – spent his time manipulating Indian ink and Paris white. This work also helped him to earn something, for he was still in rather difficult circumstances.

The meetings of the editorial staff invariably took place in the dining-room, but they were entirely unlike those of other papers. The mere fact that they took place during tea-time, to the accompaniment of the hissing samovar, gave them a very homely, unofficial character. Serioja's old nurse, who had taken the place of his mother during the first years of his life and was sincerely and tenderly loved by him, usually poured out tea. It was the custom for each of us to approach her and shake hands; I myself usually kissed her, for I had a real feeling of love for this venerable old woman with her faded and somewhat sorrowful face. His love for her did not prevent Serioja from treating her in the 'traditional rather masterly way'. Without, however, really hurting her feelings, he used to scold and shout at her in fun; this she easily forgave, indeed, she was ready to forgive her favourite far graver pranks than those. How delighted the old woman would be when her former charge would suddenly begin hugging and pulling her about during one of his teasing moods. The nanny never took part in our conversation, and she probably couldn't make out what these noisy young people were up to, who disputed ceaselessly and sometimes laughed so unrestrainedly. What could she, an illiterate peasant woman, understand about painting, music, religion, philosophy or aesthetics? Nevertheless, it was clear that in her own way she really enjoyed being with us. She enjoyed seeing that Serioja had so many friends and she probably felt that he was gradually becoming a person of importance, almost as important as his papa, the General Diaghilev. Tea was always served with *krendeli* and *soushki** and lemon cut in rounds. On the very rare occasions that Diaghilev entertained ladies, sandwiches of minced salt beef – *spécialité de la maison* – would be added to the usual fare, but nothing else was considered necessary. Diaghilev seldom took his meals at home and never invited his friends to lunch or dinner. If he found it necessary to entertain anyone, he invited them to a restaurant, for in St Petersburg's French restaurants one could eat and drink exceedingly well.

Besides the old nanny, there was yet another figure who was a characteristic part of Diaghilev's household, his manservant Vassili Zhuikov. . . . Vassili's appearance was not as picturesque as nanny's. He was small, and had an ordinary but rather clever face, to which a black moustache gave a rather military air not quite proper in a servant. Yet Vassili was what one might call the *perfect* servant; not that he

---

* *Krendeli*: biscuits in a figure-of-eight shape; *soushki*: biscuits, shaped in rings, and made of a different dough, strung on a stick.

was servile towards his master or other people in general; on the contrary, Vassili was very independent in his attitude and even, at times, verged on impertinence. Vassili's 'professional' talent expressed itself in unlimited devotion to his master, a capacity that Diaghilev perceived at once, for he possessed a wonderful gift of detecting all kinds of talent. He immediately understood that Vassili was just the servant he needed, although from the purely decorative point of view he was not quite the thing.[23]

In 1899 a friend of Diaghilev's, the charming and cultivated Prince Sergei Volkonsky, was appointed Director of the Imperial Theatres, and at once set about employing the group of friends. Diaghilev became a junior assistant to the Director. Filosofov was appointed to the Repertory Committee at the Alexandrinsky. Benois was to design a production of Taneev's opera 'Cupid's Revenge' at the Hermitage Theatre; Bakst was given a French play *Le Coeur de la Marquise;* Somov designed programmes. Diaghilev's first task was to edit the year-book of the Imperial Theatres; and in 1900 this usually dull and colourless publication was transformed into a magnificent volume with articles on the work of the late Director Vsevolojsky, on the eighteenth-century designer Gonzago and on the architecture of the Alexandrinsky Theatre. Even the Tsar approved.

The friends, however, had bigger ideas than this. They planned a new production of Delibes' 'Sylvia', with Benois supervising and designing the first act, Korovine the second and Benois' nephew Eugene Lanceray the third. Bakst was to design the costumes except for one which would be by Serov. Preobrajenskaya and the Legat brothers would dance the principal parts.[24]

The Mariinsky Theatre was over a mile from the school, but from the beginning of their eight years of study the ballet students took part in performances of ballet or opera there, swelling a crowd or standing in the background to lend perspective, so that the theatre was part of their lives. They were conveyed to and from it by horse-drawn vehicles known as Noah's Arks. Ballet performances were on Wednesdays and Sundays – the latter being the *chic* night – and rehearsals for them usually on Fridays. Climbing to their dressing-room on the fifth floor, the boys were dressed and made-up, to emerge on the vast stage in its blazing lights to face the blue and silver auditorium filled with the Court and Society. On this stage their friendly teachers, Gerdt, Nicolas and Sergei Legat, were transformed into princes and heroes, and there they beheld them partnering the fabled ballerinas and sharing their acclamations.

In December 1900 Pavel Gerdt had a benefit night, dancing with Kchessinskaya in Petipa's 'Bayadère'. In January 1901 Legnani gave her farewell performance and was, with one exception, the last of the Italian guest-artists to appear in Petersburg. In February there was a scandal, but it is unlikely that any word of it reached the ears of the second-year students.

Volkonsky had got into trouble over the production of 'Sylvia' with his heads of departments, who told him that he should not entrust the supervision of such a large-scale work to a junior colleague. Trying to please everybody, the unfortunate director asked Diaghilev to share the honours of the show with the senior officials, but promised that this would only be a matter of form and that artistically everything would go on just as before. Diaghilev was headstrong and refused. He thought he could force Volkonsky's hand, and threatened to discontinue editing the Annual of the Imperial Theatres. The mild prince suddenly lost his temper and ordered Diaghilev to continue his editorial duties. Diaghilev rushed back to his flat, where the friends were working on their 'Sylvia' sketches, and broke the news. Consternation set in. Korovine, the Moscow artist attached to the Imperial Theatres, became scared of losing his job, and Serov, older and wiser than the others, grew silent, evidently disapproving of Diaghilev's intransigence; but Filosofov and Benois wrote letters of protest to the director. Diaghilev wrote confirming his refusal to edit the Annual.

Volkonsky did all he could to heal the breach, even coming round to Diaghilev's flat with his Moscow colleague Teliakovsky and spending two hours discussing the matter with the friends. But Diaghilev was adamant. One reason for his attitude was that the Grand Duke Sergei Mikhailovitch, Kchessinskaya's lover, was backing him up. Both the Grand Duke and the ballerina hated Volkonsky. That day the Grand Duke took the train to Tsarskoe Selo to put in a word with the Emperor. The following day, however, the Tsar signed the order for Diaghilev's dismissal. Two days later Diaghilev opened the *Government Gazette*, hoping to find Volkonsky had resigned, only to read that he himself had been dismissed 'under Article 3' which only applied to rare cases of disgraceful behaviour. This was a shattering blow. His hopes of guiding the destiny of the Russian theatre vanished into air. The consequences to the world outside Russia would be great.[25]

There was a sequel. In April Kchessinskaya was to dance for the first time the role of La Camargo in Petipa's ballet of that name to the music of Minkus, taken over from the departed Legnani, and, as she was so small, did not want to wear the eighteenth-century hooped skirt which was appropriate to the role. When, against orders, she appeared in a short *tutu*, she was fined a small sum, which was the normal consequence of any breach of regulations. The announcement of her fine, pinned on the call-board, was too much for the powerful lady. She appealed through the Grand Duke to the Tsar. The fine was remitted. Volkonsky resigned in July.[26]

That spring there had been a State visit from the French President, and Kchessinskaya danced 'Le Lac des Cygnes' in a theatre in the park of Tsarskoe Selo. The evening was later described by a girl pupil who took part in it just before her graduation:

The gala performance took place in the Chinese theatre of Tsarskoe Selo, which stood in the Chinese Village, a graceful whim of Catherine the Great. Built in 1778, the theatre was kept in good repair. It stood among ancient pagoda-like fir trees. Inside, it was of rare charm – lacquer panels ornamenting the boxes, red and gold rococo chairs, bronze chandeliers with porcelain flowers – all the precious *chinoiseries* of the eighteenth century. All through the evening there was no applause. The bejewelled audience remained mute, passive as a *tableau vivant* in the light of innumerable candles. The Imperial Family and the Court were present. Every artist afterwards received a present from the Emperor, as was always the case with Imperial performances.[27]

The observant girl was destined in a few years time to be Nijinsky's partner, and like him one of the glories of the age. Tamara Platonovna Karsavina, the daughter of a dancer and of a lady of gentle birth descended from Byzantine Emperors, was to develop many wonderful qualities seldom united in one woman, for besides being beautiful, she was also intelligent and good. She had an ivory pallor and huge dark eyes, and she had a sense of humour. Within the next few weeks she passed her examinations and made her debut at the Mariinsky before it closed for the summer recess in a *pas de deux* danced with Michel Fokine, called 'Le Pêcheur et la perle'.

Fokine was five years older than Karsavina, handsome and intellectual, and with a searching mind, already dissatisfied with the traditional artificialities of the classical ballet and dreaming of new forms. He and Karsavina fell in love. She herself described him thus:

Michel Fokine began his career on the stage of the Mariinsky Theatre in 1898. For some years before his graduation he was fondly watched by the elder members of the profession – a remarkable dancer in the making. Prodigious leap, virile execution, most expressive arms, the head of a young Byron.

The inflammable hearts of the girl pupils as well were all a-flutter. Many a bad mark for behaviour did we catch for sneaking into a forbidden passage that bridged our quarters with the artists' studio, to peep at him practising. And the amount of fond names we bestowed on him! When my master told me Fokine consented to partner me at my début I could hardly believe my luck. Four years of seniority meant a lot in our hierarchy. So, during my first year on the stage, I felt flattered when he used to settle by my side with his tea in the lunch interval. Munching sandwiches, we talked of art – or rather, he talked and I listened, enchanted and a little frightened by his daring views. He would see me home, carrying my bag for me – miles out to a distant part of the town. We thought the walk was too short.

We spoke of art – mostly. . . . On the way, he sometimes took me to a museum to show me his favourite pictures: at that time he studied painting and music. Storms – and how frequent! – interrupted our brief idyll. Impetuous by nature, he had in his youth a strain of fanatical intolerance.[28]

During the autumn and winter of 1901 Carlotta Zambelli, the Milanese star of the Paris Opéra, came to give several performances of 'Coppélia', 'Giselle' and 'Pakhita' at the Mariinsky. There were complaints that at the end of the first ballet she only did eight *fouettés en attitude* and only on *demi-pointe* instead of on the tips of her toes, and she was conscious of an adverse clique among the balletomanes and the 'court' of Kchessinskaya, but she earned praise from the critic Svetlov for her lightness, elevation and elegance. She studied the role of Giselle under Cecchetti, but was surprised to find it was the custom in Russia for each ballerina to insert a brilliant variation of her own choice from a different ballet and with music by a different composer. Petipa, the old expatriate, came to watch her practise, sitting with a rug over his knees, and saying 'Well, show me how they dance in Paris.' Old Johannsen in an interview in the *Petersburg Gazette* compared her unfavourably with Taglioni. But to be compared with Taglioni at all must have been rather flattering, one would think. Zambelli was offered a large salary to return in the following season, but refused; and she was the last of the foreign guest-artists.[29]*

Nijinsky was transferred in about 1902, a year or more after he was accepted as a boarder, to the class of Mikhail Obukhov, who was to watch so proudly over his development, while doing what he could to protect him from the jealousy and cruelty of the other boys. Bourman wrote:

Obukhov was also extremely outspoken, remaining a firm disbeliever in praise during the years we spent with him. I never heard him grow enthusiastic. 'Pretty good!' was the acme of approval from his lips. His marking betrayed the same tendency. Twelve was the maximum to be acquired, but Obukhov never gave more than an eight or a nine, except to Vaslav, who was once honoured by an eleven, though even he failed to achieve a twelve. 'Why should I mark any of you with a twelve?' the master would fume. 'Perhaps there is some school in the world better than this, and some dancer who may deserve the highest mark. Here none are perfect!' Nevertheless, he recognized Nijinsky's genius with the highest grade he ever gave and he perceived Nijinsky's need with far more penetration than his mark indicated.[30]

At the beginning of 1902 Gorsky's version of 'Don Quichotte' was given at the Mariinsky, which was the first sign of the new director, Teliakovsky's, reaction against the reign of Petipa. In this Karsavina had the small part of

---

* Kchessinskaya in her memoirs omits to mention Zambelli's visit, and writes that Legnani, who retired in January 1901, was the last guest-artist from abroad.

a Cupid. Although the designer of this spectacle was Korovine, a contributor to *Mir Iskustva* and a friend of Benois, the latter wrote a harsh review of it in the magazine, which now set about attacking Teliakovsky and all his works.

There had been rumours that the Moscow production of the old ballet 'Don Quichotte' was a masterpiece, and that its producer, the ballet-master Gorsky, had revealed new horizons. This proved to be untrue. Gorsky's new version was vitiated by the abhorrent lack of organization that is typical of amateur performances. His 'novelties' consisted of making the crowds on the stage bustle and move about fitfully and aimlessly. As regards the action, the dramatic possibilities and the dancers themselves were depressed to a uniformly commonplace level. 'Don Quichotte' had never been an adornment to the Imperial Stage; now it had become something unworthy of it and almost disreputable.[31]

In spite of the declared editorial policy of Diaghilev and the presumed acquiescence to it of his collaborators Benois and Bakst, the latter did not refuse employment by the director of the Imperial Theatres. Benois accepted to design 'Die Götterdämmerung' and Bakst did not withdraw his collaboration in two Greek plays *Hippolytus* and *Oedipus* for the Alexandrinsky Theatre, or for a small ballet called 'Die Puppenfee' or 'The Fairy Doll' for a Court performance at the Hermitage.

By inviting them Teliakovsky indicated that he was in sympathy with their outlook, though determined not to be run by their domineering colleague and editor. Diaghilev was most indignant at their 'treachery'; and his branding of them in his mind as traitors – though he remained determined to get the best work out of them he could – may have been the cause of his frequently high-handed treatment of them in later years. Not that he was not ruthless by nature when artistic questions were at stake. In 1901 Diaghilev moved to a flat at 11 Fontanka, next to the house of Countess Panina and opposite that of Count Sheremetev; and the headquarters of *Mir Iskustva* moved with him.[32]

Matilda Kchessinskaya, who, after the Tsar's marriage, had been, as we have seen, the friend of the Grand Duke Sergei Mikhailovitch, had met, shortly after her tenth anniversary gala in 1900, his first cousin once removed, the ten-year-younger Grand Duke Andrei Vladimirovitch. After an Italian journey with him in the autumn of 1901, she found she was pregnant. In January 1902 she danced in Gorsky's 'Don Quichotte' at the Mariinsky and in February she appeared at the little Hermitage Theatre in 'Les Elèves de Monsieur Dupré', trying not to show herself in profile lest it become too obvious to her ex-lover, the Tsar, who was sitting very close to her in the front row, that she was pregnant by one or the other of his cousins.[33]

Nijinsky 1898–1908

The Hermitage Theatre was approached from the picture gallery by a bridge, inside which there was a long ante-room in the Chinese rococo style designed by Quarenghi. Its windows along both sides looked down on the little canal connecting the Neva and the Moika, into which Lisa threw herself in Tchaikovsky's 'Queen of Spades'.* The theatre itself was semi-circular, classical and exquisitely pretty, with pink marbled columns against white walls. Intimate as it was, and used only for performances before the Imperial Family and the Court, the stage was spacious and deep, and at the back of it was a wide sloping road up which elaborate machinery could be dragged or companies of soldiers march from the street below.† Karsavina gives a description of what the audience looked like from the stage on one of these special performances, which took place only two or three times a year and which, like the evenings at the Mariinsky, came to be a regular, if more exceptional, feature of Vaslav's life, making him feel part of the Imperial hierarchy.

It was the night of a fancy-dress ball, when the entire Court wore historical Russian dresses. That of the Empress Alexandra Feodorovna was the genuine saraphan of Tsaritza Miloslavskaya. Being on that night only one of the *corps de ballet*, where comparatively little concentration was required, I was entirely taken up with the splendour of all that I could see in front of me. I strained my eyes trying to distinguish figures in the semi-obscurity of the audience. Those three in front, the Tsar and both Tsaritzas, one could see distinctly. The young Empress, in a heavy tiara, put on over a gauze kerchief entirely concealing her hair, looked like an ikon of rigid beauty; she held her head very stiff, and I could not help feeling it would be difficult for her to bend over her plate at supper. I had a better view of her in the interval while peeping through the hole in the curtain, for which there was great competition; her dress of heavy brocade was sewn over with jewels.[34]

Kchessinskaya's part in 'La Bayadère' contained a dramatic solo in which the heroine, Nikia, disappointed in her faithless lover, is bitten by a snake and dances until she falls dead. It was now taken over by a girl who had graduated from the school four years before and was already attracting considerable attention. Anna Pavlova's life had been a struggle. She was the illegitimate daughter of a Jewish laundress who had been deserted by her lover; and she suffered from poor health. However, her very special qualities of ethereal lightness, her delicately arched instep, her lyrical *port de bras* and the extraordinary passion of her acting, soon made her stand out among her contemporaries. Having known the extreme of poverty, it was under-

---

* She did not do this in Pushkin's story.
† On 4 October 1967, Erich Alport and I were shown this theatre, as yet incompletely restored, by Professor Kraminsky, the learned and inspired renovator of war-scarred Leningrad, and I gazed in amazement down this dark slope into the nether regions.

standable that she should consolidate her position by what means she could. She attached herself first to the stage manager of the Mariinsky, a nephew of the director, Teliakovsky, and later to the critic Valerien Svetlov, whose praises helped to enhance her reputation.[35]

Vaslav was dancing in such ballets as 'Casse-noisette', 'Le Talisman' and 'Koniok-goburnok' or 'The Little Hump-backed Horse', one of the first ballets to have as its subject a Russian fairy story. In 'Pakhita', with fifteen other boys and sixteen girl partners, he was to dance the Polish mazurka.[36] For this they rehearsed in the big classroom on the first floor where the girls' class of perfection was usually held;[37] and it was a matter of some excitement to work with their secluded neighbours. Most of the boys pretended to be in love with one or other of the girls, though it was rare that they were able to exchange a word with her.

Varvara Ivanovna Lihosherstova, directress of the Girls' School, was the inevitable cloud. She always discovered something wrong! Her discipline was as unbending as court etiquette. If one boy spoke too often to his partner, if another laughed, Varvara Ivanovna would dart a piercing glance in his direction, and desserts were lost for a week or visiting privileges were gone in the twinkling of an eye, for she protected her girls with the jealousy of a hen with one chick. She prohibited flirting or joking between boys and girls, and no excuse for transgressions was acceptable, punishment was certain, and there could be no quarter expected.[38]

There were nevertheless times when a puckish sense of mischief showed through Vaslav's shyness and reserve. Someone had pointed out to him Teliakovsky's second-in-command, Krupensky, as the 'evil genius' of the theatre. On an evening when the boys were to impersonate demons in 'Tannhäuser' and Vaslav was completely disguised by a grotesque make-up, whenever he passed Krupensky in the wings he wiggled his forefingers over his ears, making horns, and put out his tongue. After the opera Krupensky had all the boys called on the stage and asked, 'Which was the boy who put out his tongue?' There was a silence; Vaslav was afraid to own up. So the whole class was punished and missed a holiday. Vaslav confessed to his tutor, 'It was I who did it.' The tutor said, 'I know.'[39]

One day the boys were playing at jumping over an iron music-stand and when it was Nijinsky's turn to jump Rosaï screwed it up to an impossible height, so that Vaslav fell, was badly injured and had to be in hospital for several weeks. On another occasion, because of a brawl, Vaslav was actually suspended for a period and sent home.[40]

The teachers gave their pupils very individual supervision and devoted themselves to bringing out their latent talents. Vaslav was not particularly fond of reading, but he took to music and learned the piano – which he played more by ear than sight-reading – the flute, the balalaika and the

27

accordion. His mother did not like him playing the accordion as she thought it common.[41]

A Catholic priest occasionally came to visit Vaslav,[42] but this did not prevent him attending the Orthodox services in the school chapel and being on friendly terms with the school priest, Father Vassili.[43] One day the Catholic priest introduced talk of Russo-Polish politics in the confessional; Vaslav was disgusted and gave up going to confession.[44]

In 1903 Tamara Karsavina was given her first leading role in 'Le Réveil de Flore'.

I set to work with a joyous heart. There was no dramatic plot in this ballet, the part being purely a dancing one requiring a certain amount of technical virtuosity of a higher level than I had hitherto attempted. A year of Johannsen's rebukes had not been spent in vain. I could now master considerable difficulties. Being spring, the smart season was over. That consideration didn't worry me; my spirits were always higher in the spring. . . . Marius Petipa was pleased. '*Très bien, ma belle,*' he said. All went well; that is, till the very rehearsal. I must have overworked myself by that time; my toes were blistered, and my strength began failing me. The approach of the performance brought a sickening fear, a frame of mind due, perhaps, to the fact that my friends on the stage wanted to impress me with the importance of success; some, less well-disposed, said it was much too early for me to have a responsible part. Both encouragement and discouragement were equally pernicious to my mental balance. Once the idea of possible failure had been put into my head, it began working ravages with my self-control. It hypnotized me. . . . By the evening I was in a wretched state; there was a lump in my throat. I came on, feeling I was on my trial. All was dizzy before my eyes; I was unsteady, couldn't get my balance, and my legs shook. At the end applause roared, and bouquets filled the stage. It didn't cheer me up; I had sentenced myself as a failure. One hope lurked in my mind – perhaps the audience had not noticed my slips; they were cheering me so.[45]

Karsavina's stern teacher, old Johannsen, died that year.

Change was in the air. Teliakovsky cut down the subscribers' nights at the Mariinsky when only the hereditary box-owners could sit in the lower part of the theatre, and there was a growing middle-class audience for the ballet. This audience was more liberal-minded than the aristocratic traditionalists and it began to find fault with the repertory of Marius Petipa productions.[46] Teliakovsky had already brought from Moscow the painters Golovine and Korovine, the first easel-painters to design scenery for opera and ballet. He tried to promote the work of Russian composers, who, apart from Tchaikovsky, were the laughing-stock of the aristocracy. Now he planned to replace Petipa with Gorsky from Moscow, who was already teaching in the school. The old ballet master was to celebrate his fiftieth anniversary as choreographer to the Imperial Ballet with a new work, 'The Magic Mirror', with music by Koreshchenko and – a sign of the new order – settings by Golovine, at a gala performance on 9 February 1903.

All seats in the theatre were sold out [wrote Teliakovsky in his diary] for the new ballet, about which people talked for almost two years, the testimonial performance for the famous Petipa. Tales about the forthcoming novel spectacle interested everybody. The Imperial box was filled by members of the Imperial family. At eight o'clock sharp the Dowager Empress Maria Feodorovna and the Tsar with the young Empress arrived. The ministerial box was also filled with invited persons of high society. They came to greet their bard who had served three Emperors, to see another song dedicated to 'grandeur of autocracy', to 'be treated to' a tempting novelty. ('Well, with what will you treat us tonight?' asked the Minister of the Court.)

And suddenly, instead of an ecstatic roar there were whistles, shouts and noise in the audience; in the intermissions there were stormy scenes. The noise did not abate during the entire act. Some people began to shout 'Curtain'. The greatest celebration turned into a loud scandal and this decided the fate of the production. The Imperial box was definitely dissatisfied with the ballet. The Minister also did not like the ballet.

Petipa fell. . . . In hostile circles a new candidate was already being discussed, and the newspaper *Birjevye Vyedomosti* printed the following sensational announcement: 'The ballet company will have to get used to a new ballet master, A. Gorsky. He will stage his own versions of "The Hump-backed Horse" and "Swan Lake". He stages both ballets entirely differently and in a much more original manner.'[47]

Although they had begun to arrange choreography at the Mariinsky, the brothers Legat were surprised to find themselves invited to stage a ballet at the Hermitage Theatre.[48] This was 'The Fairy Doll', which had been planned two years before. Nicolas and Sergei were two pierrots, with Kchessinskaya as a doll; and Bakst designed an attractive toyshop set.

About this Benois wrote:

His enthusiasm and love for our native city, St Petersburg, and personal recollections of his childhood, gave Bakst the happy idea of transferring the action to the St Petersburg Arcade, known to every St Petersburg child because of the toyshops that were concentrated there. . . .

Our friend was in love with a young widow – Lubov Pavlovna Gritzenko, the daughter of the famous Russian patron of art, P.M.Tretiakov – and his feeling was reciprocated. Their meetings usually took place in studios of the Mariinsky Theatre under the curious pretext of Bakst having chosen to paint his beloved in these strange surroundings. The result of these seances was still more curious. Bakst really did paint Lubov Pavlovna, but the 'portrait' proved to be one of the dolls in the toyshop, and this doll was suspended from the ceiling, among all sorts of other toys, drums, hoops, carriages, clowns, etc. The Imperial Family had noticed this detail during the performance at the Hermitage Theatre and indeed it was impossible not to notice it, for 'Lubov Pavlovna', smiling gracefully, was dangling in the very foreground. Later, when the ballet was transferred to the Mariinsky Theatre, those who were initiated into the mystery of the strange doll in the black Paris dress and huge hat, so out of place among the other toys, were tremendously amused at the infatuated artist's invention. Lubov Pavlovna's brother-in-law, our great friend S. S. Botkine, was the one who especially enjoyed the joke. 'Look, look at Luba dangling there!' he would repeat, choking and almost weeping with laughter. Soon after this, we learnt that the lovers would be united. After many complications from both sides, the wedding took place. Lubov Pavlovna had to overcome the indignant resistance of all her purely Muscovite relations at the idea of her marrying a Jew, while Levushka could not make up his mind to change the faith of his fathers, as was demanded by the Russian law of that time of Jews who married Christians.[49]

1904 began with the outbreak of the Russo-Japanese war, which no one took seriously at first, but which was to end after a few months so ignominiously for the Russians, providing appalling proof of the corruption and inefficiency of the State. In January Matilda Kchessinskaya gave her 'Farewell Performance' dancing in 'La Fille mal gardée' and 'Le Lac des Cygnes':[50] but this may only have been due to a policy of *reculer pour mieux sauter*, as she would be returning to the stage on and off for another decade.*

The Tsar and Tsarina had only had daughters, but in August the Empress gave birth to a son and heir and there was great rejoicing and a holiday granted to the ballet school. This was the pretty Tsarevitch to whose christening a wicked fairy brought the gift of haemophilia as a final curse on the doomed Romanov dynasty.

It was a time of scarcity caused by the mobilization of peasant workers, a time of unemployment and a time of strikes. Murmurs of political unrest hardly penetrated the walls of the ballet school. But on Sunday, 8 January 1905, the priest Father Gapon, who was the founder of a workers' union, led a deputation, which was followed by an immense crowd, to present a petition to the Tsar at the Winter Palace. The Tsar was at Tsarskoe Selo, twenty miles away, which was his usual residence. Troops fired on the workers. This was the massacre of Bloody Sunday.

Vaslav was on his way home from school to visit his mother, carrying some books. Coming out of the Alexandrinsky Gardens he got caught up in the crowd pouring up the Nevsky Prospekt and was swept along towards the Winter Palace. There was a charge of mounted Cossacks with lead-weighted knouts, and he was struck on the forehead so that the blood flowed down his face. The hungry subjects of the Tsar were falling and dying around him. He managed to escape. His colleague Babitch's pretty seventeen-year-old sister was among the missing.[51] At dusk, returning by sleigh

* And indeed I saw her in a Russian dance at a Gala at Covent Garden in 1936.

to his home on the Vassilievsky Island, Benois was nearly beaten up by an angry crowd. 'What do you think you are doing? Running people over?'[52]

That night was Preobrajenskaya's Benefit at the Mariinsky. Karsavina, who was not dancing that evening, watched from the stalls the performance of 'Les Caprices du papillon' in which the charming little ballerina excelled. 'Towards the last act, alarming rumours ran in the theatre – riots had broken out in the town; the mob were on their way . . . they had already broken into the Alexandrinsky and stopped the performance. Panic spread. The theatre emptied quickly. On the stage the performance never so much as flickered. . . .'[53]

Next morning Vaslav went out with Bourman, Rosaï and Babitch to search for the body of Babitch's sister, but it was never found.[54]

Valentin Serov, who had painted the Tsar's portrait in 1900, was one of many intellectuals shocked by the massacre. The Grand Duke Vladimir, the Tsar's eldest uncle, who commanded the Petersburg garrison, was also President of the Academy of Fine Arts, of which Serov was a member. The painter wrote him an open letter of protest. This was not published; and Serov resigned.

To avoid mass demonstrations it was decreed that the many dead should be buried before dawn. According to Isadora Duncan, she met the endless funeral cortège as she arrived from Berlin. If her train had not been twelve hours late, she wrote, she would not have had this experience which she felt was a turning-point in her life.

There was no one at the station to meet me. When I descended from the train the temperature was ten degrees below zero. I had never felt such cold. The padded Russian coachmen were hitting their arms with their gloved fists to keep the blood flowing in their veins. I left my maid with the baggage, and, taking a one-horse cab, directed the driver to the Hotel Europa. Here I was in the black dawn of Russia, quite alone, on the way to the hotel, when suddenly I beheld a sight equal in ghastliness to any in the imagination of Edgar Allan Poe. It was a long procession that I saw from a distance. Black and mournful it came. There were men laden and bent under their loads – coffins – one after another. The coachman slowed his horse to a walk, and bent and crossed himself. I looked on in the indistinct dawn, filled with horror. I asked him what this was. Although I knew no Russian, he managed to convey to me that these were the workmen shot down before the Winter Palace the day before . . . because, unarmed, they had come to ask the Tsar for help in their distress – for bread for their wives and children. I told the coachman to stop. The tears ran down my face and were frozen on my cheeks as this sad, endless procession passed me. But why buried at dawn? Because later in the day it might have caused more revolution. The sight of it was not for the city in the daytime. . . . With boundless indignation I watched these poor grief-stricken workmen carrying their martyred dead.[55]

31

Isadora Duncan dancing to Schubert.
Drawing by José Clara.

There is something wrong with this story, though, because Isadora had arrived in Petersburg in December 1904, a week or two before.[56] Of course she may have seen the procession from her window at the Europa Hotel. Isadora, the young American who despised ballet and had evolved a new way of dancing naturally which was wonderfully expressive and appeared deceptively simple, had in the last two or three years subjugated Western Europe, and had arrived to extend her conquests in Russia. What was just as extraordinary as her dancing barefoot in flimsy draperies was that she danced not to 'dance music' but to the compositions of the great masters. Her first appearance was in the Hall of Nobles on 26 December before a surprised and elegant audience.

32

How strange it must have been to those dilettantes of the gorgeous ballet, with its lavish decorations and scenery, to watch a young girl, clothed in a tunic of cobweb, appear and dance before a simple blue curtain to the music of Chopin! Yet even for the first dance there was a storm of applause. My soul that yearned suffered the tragic notes of the Preludes; my soul that aspired and revolted to the thunder of the Polonaises; my soul that wept with righteous anger, thinking of the martyrs of that funeral procession of the dawn; this soul awakened in that wealthy, spoilt, and aristocratic audience a response of stirring applause. How curious!

The next day Isadora received a visit from 'a most charming little lady, wrapped in sables, with diamonds hanging from her ears, and her neck encircled with pearls'. It was Kchessinskaya.

That evening a magnificent carriage, warmed and filled with expensive furs, conducted me to the opera, where I found a first-tier box, containing flowers, bonbons, and three beautiful specimens of the *jeunesse dorée* of Petersburg. I was still wearing my little white tunic and sandals. . . . I am an enemy of the ballet . . . but it was impossible not to applaud the fairy-like figure of Kchessinskaya as she flitted across the stage, more like a lovely bird or butterfly than a human being.

Isadora also went to see Pavlova in 'Giselle' and had supper afterwards at her flat, where she sat between Bakst and Benois. Bakst told her fortune and she had an ardent discussion about dancing with Diaghilev.[57]

Diaghilev was about to celebrate his most spectacular triumph to date, an Exhibition of Russian Historical Portraits. All through the previous summer he had travelled about Russia, visiting country houses and unearthing long-hidden or even forgotten paintings, rummaging in attics and playing on the fears of landowners, persuading them to lend their ancestors on the grounds that in time of revolution they would be safer in the capital.[58] The huge exhibition of three thousand portraits represented the past of Russia. Statesmen, princes, ecclesiastics and court beauties were grouped in the echoing immensity of the Tauride Palace, around full-length portraits, under canopies, of the monarchs they had served – imperious Peter, intelligent Catherine, mad Paul and high falutin' Alexander I. In the centre a columned sculpture hall was decorated by Bakst as a trellised winter garden. 'There was something oppressive,' Benois thought, 'in this multi-coloured assembly of magnates in gold-embroidered coats, those dressed-up ladies, all this Necropolis, this *Vanitas Vanitatum*, which doubled the pleasure of relaxing in the greenery among the white marble busts.'[59]

There were rumours of a general strike, and the Benois family left for Versailles before the official opening of the exhibition by the Emperor.

Later I heard from eye-witnesses and my correspondents about the opening ceremony. It followed the traditional pattern: the Tsar arrived, accompanied by members of his family, and walked slowly past the endless rows of his ancestors.

Diaghilev, the Grand Duke Nicolai Mikhailovitch and Prince Dashkov provided explanations. At the end of this review, which lasted for about two hours, Nicholas II thanked his uncle, Diaghilev and Dashkov, but not by a single word did he reveal his personal attitude to all he had seen, although it was all so closely related to his person; everything in it spoke of the past of the Russian monarchy, of his predecessors on the throne and of their collaborators and associates. It was known that the Tsar was interested in history and it might have been expected that this magnificent spectacle would make some kind of impression on him. Perhaps his attitude was due to an emotional paralysis which rendered him inarticulate; or he might have seen in the faces of his ancestors bitter reproaches and terrible warnings of approaching disaster.[60]

But Diaghilev, who had assembled this apotheosis of the Russian past – and most of the portraits were due for destruction – was sworn to the future. At a banquet given in his honour in the Tauride Palace, which had been built by Patiomkin, the favourite of Catherine the Great, after his conquest of the Caucasus, Diaghilev spoke the following words:

There is no doubt that every tribute is a summing-up, and every summing-up is an ending. Far from me the thought that tonight's banquet is in any sense the end of the aims for which we have lived up to now. I think you will agree with me that thoughts of summing-up and ending come to one's mind more and more in these days. That is the question that struck me the whole time I was working. Don't you feel that this long gallery of portraits of big and small people that I brought to live in the beautiful halls of the Palais Tauride is only a grandiose summing-up of a brilliant, but, alas! dead period of our history? ... I have earned the right to proclaim this loudly, because with the last breath of the summer breezes I ended my long travels across the immensity of Russia. It was just after those acquisitive expeditions that I became convinced that the time to sum up was before us. I saw that not only in the brilliant portraits of those ancestors, so far removed from us, but more vividly from their descendants, who were ending their lives. The end of a period is revealed here, in those gloomy dark palaces, frightening in their dead splendour, and inhabited to-day by charming mediocre people who could no longer stand the strain of bygone parades. Here are ending their lives not only people, but pages of history. . . .

We are witnesses of the greatest moment of summing-up in history, in the name of a new and unknown culture, which will be created by us, and which will also sweep us away. That is why, with fear or misgiving, I raise my glass to the ruined walls of the beautiful palaces, as well as to the new commandments of a new aesthetic. The only wish that I, an incorrigible sensualist, can express, is that the forthcoming struggle should not damage the amenities of life, and that the death should be as beautiful and as illuminating as the resurrection.[61]

Thus spoke Petronius Arbiter – but with a touch of Spartacus.

If artists and intellectuals tended to fall immediately under Isadora's sway, it was understandable that young ballet dancers should be shocked by her lack of virtuosity.[62] She came to watch classes in Theatre Street and gave a demonstration. Taken aback at first, Vaslav later came to admire her greatly. Her most immediate influence, however, was on Michel Fokine.[63] For several years he had been dreaming of new forms and here was a goddess moving to sublime music. It was his moment of release – of explosion. For the pupils' display in April he was asked to arrange a ballet. He went to the Public Library in search of Greek subject matter, and the aged, white-bearded Vladimir Vasilievitch Stassov, the Director, who was a celebrated critic of art and music, was so impressed that a ballet dancer should have these interests that he took particular trouble to produce the relevant documentation. In the theatre library Fokine found the libretto of an old ballet made by Lev Ivanov in 1896, 'Acis and Galatea', with music by Kadletz: but the inspector of the school would not allow him to discard the conventional ballet style.

I did not try to prove that between the classic and the Greek art there could be a bridge. I realized that I had been carried away by my ideas. Sadly I left the Inspector's office. However, I still managed to produce the ballet not exactly as customary. The girls danced on their toes, but the costumes were a hybrid between the ballet styles and the Greek. Here and there was also a hint of a different, non-balletic plastique. The groupings were unusual, asymmetrical; some performers were placed on different levels, on mounds, tree stubs, trees; others on the floor (it was intended to be grass) – thus avoiding the usual horizontal line grouping. The Dance of the Fauns seemed to be entirely new. Here I had my freedom. The fauns resembled beasts. They performed no ballet steps and, at the end of the ballet dance, did some tumbling, which was not in accordance with the classical school but corresponded very well with the mood of an animal dance.

The boys played a subsidiary part in Fokine's production, as the little ballet was only intended to show off the prowess of Fokine's female pupils. One boy, however, he found 'outstanding for elevation and effort'. Fokine asked him, 'What is your name?' 'Nijinsky,' he answered. It was the meeting of a man and a boy who would make each other famous. 'Acis' was the first of many Fokine ballets Nijinsky was to dance in. For the same performance the choreographer arranged a spectacular 'Polka' for Elena Smirnova and George Rosaï.[64]

Fokine and Karsavina had parted company. He had begged and begged her to marry him. But her mother did not want her to throw herself away on a dancer. Michel then implored Tamara to run away with him. She loved him, but she obeyed her mother.[65] She had become ill, and was sent to Italy where she took classes in Milan. Fokine transferred his affection to one of his pupils, Vera Antonova, a dark girl with an oval face, who adored him. They were married in 1905.

At last the spirit of revolt spread to the ballet. The dancers signed a petition demanding autonomy.

The autumn of 1905 [wrote Karsavina] I remember even now as a nightmare. A cruel October wind from the sea, chill, sleet, sinister hush in the town. For several days trams had not been running, the strike gaining rapidly. I chose a roundabout way, avoiding pickets. Though they let one pass unquestioned, my heart sank every time I came across their encampments. My thin shoes let in water; my feet were numb. A glimmer of hope that I might catch a severe cold to free me from an impending ordeal was my only comfort. I was going to Fokine's flat to take part in what seemed a conspiracy to me. . . . The light was cut off that night in the whole town. . . . A resolution of the meeting was being elaborated . . . when I came in. . . . One by one the belated members arrived, bringing some fresh information. The Railways had stopped; to prevent a meeting of workmen on the Vassilievsky Ostrov [island] the bridges had been raised. Fokine picked up a receiver to see if the telephone was still working. No reply from the exchange. . . . Two little dancers, mere boys, came in all flushed and excited; they constituted themselves scouts. Their honest admiration for our actions would not allow them to keep quiet. 'We saw some detectives outside,' they bubbled, interrupting each other, 'must be detectives, both in pea-green overcoats and goloshes.' At all times the obviousness of our secret police, their goloshes in all weathers, were everybody's joke. . . . The next step was to try and prevent the matinée performance at the Mariinsky. 'The Queen of Spades' was being given; a considerable number of dancers appeared in it. My duty was to go round the ladies' dressing-rooms and call the dancers off. The task was distasteful to me, and my eloquence not of the most persuasive. A few left the theatre; the majority refused to strike. Within the next few days the circular of the Minister of the Court was made known to the troupe. Our action was qualified as a breach of discipline; all who wished to remain loyal were to sign a declaration. The great majority signed, leaving us, their chosen delegates, in the lurch.[66]

The abortive strike had tragic consequences. Sergei Legat, Vaslav's former teacher, who had been prevailed on to sign the original petition, felt himself a traitor to the Tsar. His anguish was further heightened by unhappy relations with Marie Petipa, with whom he had been living. After a night of raving he cut his throat.[67]

On 13 October the first Soviet of deputies of the workers of Petersburg was formed. This, together with a strike which had brought Russian railways to a standstill, as well as continued risings among the peasants, compelled the Tsar to give out on 17 October that an elected Council or Duma would be established to serve under a Council of Ministers. Russia was to have its first Parliament, with Count Witte as its first 'Prime Minister'.

The Duma would meet at the Tauride Palace, the site of Diaghilev's exhibition.

Having given Russia a glimpse of its own history, Diaghilev's next move was to take a huge representative exhibition of two centuries of Russian painting and sculpture to Paris in 1906. In the halls of the Salon d'Automne in the Petit Palais he hung ikons, the eighteenth-century portraits and scenes of Levitsky and Borovikovsky, the neo-classical compositions of Brullov and a great number of works by artists of the 'World of Art', Vrubel, Serov, Bakst, Benois, Somov, Anisfeld, Dobujinsky, Roerich, Korovine, Maliavin and Larionov. The ikons were hung by Bakst on gold brocade, which Benois thought made it difficult to look at them, although the effect was striking in a typical Diaghilev way. Sculpture, as at the Tauride Palace, was shown in a winter garden. Benois also thought the exhibition was not truly representative because Diaghilev had excluded the Peredvijiniki and any painters who did not interest him.[68] Diaghilev's committee was headed by the Grand Duke Vladimir.

Another member of the committee was the rich and handsome Comtesse Greffuhle, queen of Paris Society, President of the Société Musicale, which had been founded by the brilliant and imaginative music-publisher Gabriel Astruc that year. When Diaghilev first went to see her, she had thought there was something odd about him and feared he might be nothing but a social climber. But he impressed her with his remarks about her pictures and when he sat down at the piano and played some Russian songs 'the music was so fresh, so altogether wonderful and lovely', that when he explained that he intended organizing a festival of Russian music in the coming year she was unhesitantly enrolled in his support and the foundation of the future Russian seasons was laid.[69]

Nijinsky had now been eight years at the ballet school and was a senior student. He was still as quiet and self-effacing as ever, still slow at book-learning, still happiest in class. Music attracted him far more than literature, but he sometimes lost himself in a book; he and Bronislava read *David Copperfield* together in a Russian translation, and even had a go at *Don Quixote*, attracted by its handsome red and gold binding. His favourite composers were Rimsky-Korsakov and Wagner; and he could play a piano arrangement of the overture of 'Tannhäuser' without a single mistake. His sight-reading was still weak, but if someone struck a chord he could tell without looking what notes it was composed of.[70] Because of his exceptional ability he might have been allowed to pass out of the school after only six years – if only he could have got through the examinations in subjects other than dancing and music. He was always gentle and friendly with younger students and never addressed even the newest of them as 'thou', which was customary among senior boys, but always 'you', treating them as equals.[71]

The staff and pupils of the ballet school were aware that they had a remarkable dancer in their midst. *How* remarkable, they could not yet know. And of course it was not only his technical virtuosity they were proud of, for technique was second nature to them – it was the manner and style and expression he put into his dancing. In Petersburg technique was never an end in itself.[72]

Nobody was prouder of Vaslav than his teacher Obukhov.

One morning [wrote Karsavina] I came up earlier than usual; the boys were just finishing their practice. I glanced casually, and could not believe my eyes; one boy in a leap rose far above the heads of the others and seemed to tarry in the air. 'Who is that?' I asked Michael Obukhov, his master. 'It is Nijinsky; the little devil never comes down with the music.' He then called Nijinsky forward by himself and made him show me some steps. A prodigy was before my eyes. He stopped dancing, and I felt it was all unreal and could not have been; the boy looked quite unconscious of his achievement, prosy and even backward. 'Shut your mouth,' were his master's parting words. 'You fly-swallower.' 'Off with you all now.' Like peas falling out of a bag, the boys rushed off, their patter a hollow repercussion in the vaulted passage. In utter amazement I asked Michael why nobody spoke of this remarkable boy, and he about to finish. 'They will soon,' chuckled Michael. 'Don't you worry.'[73]

Obukhov decided to show his prize pupil to the public. Hitherto Nijinsky had appeared only as an inconspicuous figure in *ensembles* at the Mariinsky. It cannot have been without difficulty that his teacher arranged that a boy who had not graduated should take part in a dance with leading members of the company. This was to be a *pas de huit** inserted into Mozart's opera 'Don Giovanni'. The other dancers were Preobrajenskaya, Trefilova, Vaganova, Egorova, Andrianov, Bolm and Leontiev; and it was Trefilova whom Nijinsky supported.[74] The performance took place on 31 January 1906. It was impossible that the young student should not leap higher and turn more *pirouettes* than the other men. So he stood for the first time to hear the world's applause.[75] On 6 February the *pas de huit* was repeated, but with Pavlova replacing Trefilova.[76] The two great dancers appeared together for the first time.

Fokine's success with 'Acis and Galatea' had one unexpected result. He was invited by Alexander Akimovich Sanine, the producer at the Alexandrinsky Theatre, to arrange a dance of buffoons and jesters in Alexis Tolstoi's

---

* Bourman records the appearance in 'Don Giovanni', but makes it a *pas de quatre* with Kyasht, Legat and Obukhov. He makes Obukhov lead Nijinsky forward to receive the applause. It is possible that he emerged from the wings to do this.

play *The Death of Ivan the Terrible*. He was delighted, but told Sanine that as he was not officially a ballet master, the direction of the Imperial Theatres would probably insist on Nicolas Legat doing the job. Sanine undertook to arrange matters; but sure enough, the dreaded Alexander Dmitrievitch Krupensky, assistant director of the Imperial Theatres and head of the production department, told him that he had no business to choose his collaborators without the approval of the office. To the amazement of everybody, Sanine resigned and sent the story to the newspapers.[77]

Shortly after this, in April 1906, Fokine arranged for a charity performance a ballet called 'La Vigne' to music of Anton Rubinstein, in which Kyasht, Marie Petipa, Karsavina, Fokina, Pavlova and himself impersonated various types of wine. After this he was thrilled to receive the accolade of old Marius Petipa in the form of a visiting-card inscribed with the words

> Cher camarade Fokine
> Enchanté de vos compositions.
> Continuez vous deviendrez
> un bon maître de ballet
> Tout à vous.[78]*

Fokine was next invited by Victor Dandré, a member of the City Council who later became manager and perhaps the husband of Anna Pavlova,† to stage a whole evening's programme at the Mariinsky at a benefit for the Society of the Prevention of Cruelty to Children. For this he chose to make a two-act ballet, 'Eunice', on a subject taken from Sienkievitch's Roman novel *Quo Vadis*, and a ballet to Chopin orchestrated by Glazunov, called 'Chopiniana'. The music for the former work by Shtcherbashev contained some un-Roman waltzes, which rather discouraged the choreographer, and it was unthinkable that he should be allowed to have barefoot dancers on the Imperial stage, but he tried to make the best of a bad job and produce something as classical-Roman and as un-classical-ballet as possible. He contrived dances without point work, *pirouettes, entrechats* or *battements*; and on the dancers' white tights Bronislava Nijinska painted toe-nails and rosy heels and knees.[79] The ageing but handsome Gerdt impersonated Petronius, Kchessinskaya was the slave Eunice, and Pavlova as Acte performed a Dance of the Seven Veils. There was also a dance with wineskins, a spectacular dance with lighted torches, and an Egyptian *pas de trois* in which Vera Fokina, Julia Siedova and Rutkovskaya sacrificed themselves by darkening their bodies and elongating their eyes in order to become in

---

*In the English-language edition of Fokine's book (p. 92) the message is quoted slightly inaccurately.

† There is some doubt whether they actually married. Their relationship was primarily a business one.

clinging draperies the first 'Egyptians' not to wear ballet *tutus* on the Imperial stage.[80] Nijinsky had a small part.

Before the performance, which took place on 23 February 1907, Fokine had run into a little trouble with the *doyen* of the balletomanes, Nicolas Mikhailovitch Besobrasov, whose rank as full State Councillor entitled him to the honorary rank of general. This kind, portly, white-haired old gentleman exercised considerable power in the ballet world, was thought the final arbiter of quality in *pirouettes* and was a specialist in organizing the seating at benefit nights for dancers in such a way as to make the smartest audience pay the maximum amount of money for their seats. He thought Fokine's reforms were going too far too quickly. 'Continue your experiments at first with the *corps de ballet*. It is impossible to bring the ballerina out on stage without her *tutu*.' The young choreographer listened respectfully, then continued to work exactly as before: but after the performance Besobrasov was one of the first to offer his congratulations.[81]

In the Chopin ballet, the Waltz in C Sharp Minor was danced by Pavlova and Obukhov. Fokine wrote:

The choreography differed from all other *pas de deux* in its total absence of spectacular feats. There was not a single *entrechat*, turn in the air, or *pirouette*. There was a slow turn of the ballerina, holding her partner's hand, but this could not be classified as a *pirouette* because the movement was not confined to the turn but was used for a change of position and grouping. When composing, I placed no restrictions on myself; I simply could not conceive of any spectacular stunts to the accompaniment of the poetic, lyrical Waltz of Chopin. I was totally unconcerned whether this romantic duet would bring applause or satisfy the audience or the ballerina, for I did not think of success at all. That is probably why I was rewarded with one of the greatest successes which has fallen to any of my compositions.[82]

Simple as it appeared this dance was extremely hard to execute correctly. Other numbers in the ballet were the majestic Polonaise in Polish costumes, a nocturne in which Chopin, impersonated by the mime Alexis Bulgakov, was haunted by ghostly monks and consoled by the vision of his beloved, a mazurka in which Siedova as the young bride of an old bridegroom elopes with her true love, and a tarantella led by Vera Fokina in which Michel used steps they had observed together during their honeymoon in Capri.[83]

Some years before, when he was still on good terms with Teliakovsky, Benois had conceived the idea for a ballet based on a story of Théophile Gautier, to be called 'Le Pavillon d'Armide'. He suggested to his nephew by marriage, Nicolas Tcherepnine, a pupil of Rimsky's, that he should write the music, and together they went to see the director about it. 'Are there any waltzes? It is most important to have waltzes!' Teliakovsky had said. And although waltzes were provided and Benois was even paid a fee for his libretto, it was shortly after this that he and the director quarrelled and the project was dropped.[84] Now, early in 1907, Fokine heard a suite from the ballet, which Tcherepnine had arranged, played at a concert and went backstage to seek out the composer. Tcherepnine was pleased that the choreographer liked his music; and shortly afterwards, with costumes borrowed from the Mariinsky wardrobe, the suite was arranged as a one-act ballet and given on 28 April 1907, under the title of 'Le Gobelins animé' – 'The Gobelins tapestry which came to life' – at a school performance. This production was, more or less, the central *divertissement* of the future ballet in three scenes,* and the great hit was the dance of jesters led by George Rosaï.[85] Surprisingly, the formidable Krupensky saw the ballet, liked it and arranged that the whole work as planned by Benois and Tcherepnine – though slightly abbreviated – should be staged at the Mariinsky in the autumn.

At his graduation performance, which took place the night after, 29 April 1907 at the Mariinsky Theatre, Nijinsky performed in a variety of numbers, dancing, according to the critic of the *Petersburg Gazette*, 'the whole evening'.[86] Koslyaninov, the critic of *Theatre and Music*, records him as dancing the variation called 'Lightning' from Petipa's 'Magic Mirror' and also a dance from 'Pakhita',[87] which was probably the famous *pas de trois*. The critics were extremely enthusiastic.[88] Mme Schollar recalls appearing with Nijinsky in an effective *pas de deux* called 'The Prince Gardener' arranged by Klavdia Kulichevska, one of her teachers. Her costume was sewn with spangles, so that in supporting her *pirouettes* Vaslav's hands were cut between thumb and forefinger and her dress was covered in blood – which was considered a bad omen.[89] Mme Bronislava Nijinska remembers her brother dancing in the *divertissement* of 'Le Pavillon d'Armide' with Smirnova, Schollar and Elisaveta Gerdt (daughter of Pavel), who was not to graduate till the following year.[90] He may have danced all these numbers and more, but the only printed record is of the two dances mentioned in *Theatre and Music*.

The great Kchessinskaya came to congratulate Nijinsky and said she wished to have him as her partner. This meant that although he would officially be only an ill-paid member of the *corps de ballet* he would never dance in the *corps*, but start as a soloist: it was as much as to say his fortune was made.[91]

Then came the other dreaded exams; and Nijinsky failed in history. Authority connived. He was to have another test three days later, set by his own teacher, who gave him warning of the questions. This time he passed.[92] His schooldays were over – not that a dancer's schooling is ever done.

Meanwhile, Diaghilev was back in Paris, and his five Russian concerts

* A fuller description will be found in Chapter II.

took place at the Opéra between 16–30 May. Works by every Russian composer of note from Glinka to Scriabine were performed, Rimsky, Rachmaninov and Glazunov conducting their own. Nikisch and Blumenfeld also conducted; and the singers included Litvinne, Chaliapine, Cherkasskaya, Zbroueva, Petrenko and Smirnov. It was an amazing programme. Even so, as Diaghilev recalled in later years, the first concert ended in a scandal.

The last but one number of the programme was the Prince Galitzky scene from 'Prince Igor', Act I, in which Chaliapine was making his Paris *début*. This was so extraordinarily successful that the applause went on and on and there seemed no limit to the number of times the excited public would recall Chaliapine. Nikisch, who was conducting, made ready to begin Glinka's 'Kamarinskaya', which was the last item on the programme. Several times Nikisch raised his arms ready to start, but the public, by now quite out of hand, refused to be silenced. Then, mortally offended, Nikisch threw down his baton, walked out of the orchestra pit, and left the public stranded. People began to drift out. Upstairs in the gallery the din continued when, in a sudden hush, we heard a deep bass voice thundering out from the remote heights of the house, in Russian, the words 'Ka-ma-rinska-ya! Get stuffed!' Grand Duke Vladimir, who was sitting beside me in the box, got up and said to the Grand Duchess, 'Well, I think it's time we went home.'[93]

Benois and his family had been for over two years living mostly in Paris and Versailles. Besides painting, Benois had written a book, *The Russian School of Painting*, catalogued the Alexander III Museum of Russian pictures in the Mikhailovsky Palace, and contributed articles to various journals. Now Tcherepnine, in Paris for the concerts, told him that their ballet 'Le Pavillon d'Armide' was to be performed; and of course Benois was to design it.[94]

Immediately on his admission to the Imperial Ballet, Nijinsky had been sent on holiday: but his summer was not entirely idle. In June came the awaited summons of Kchessinskaya: Vaslav was to be her partner at performances during the army manœuvres at Krasnoe Selo. These shows, presented in a wooden theatre seating only eight hundred, for the army officers and their families, had an informal picnic atmosphere despite the frequent attendance of Grand Dukes and the Emperor himself. It had been during the Krasnoe Selo 'season', in fact, that Kchessinskaya's romance with Nicholas II, then Tsarevitch, had flowered thirteen years before.[95]

If Vaslav was to dance with Kchessinskaya it could be safely assumed that there would be no more money worries. The family decided to rent a cottage near the Lake of Duderhof, which was in the neighbourhood of Krasnoe Selo, and the Nijinskys settled down to enjoy the summer. One day, unexpected and uninvited, Vaslav's old classmate, Bourman, who had also just graduated, arrived to stay. Knowing that Kchessinskaya was attracted to Nijinsky, he hoped to profit by the connection.[96] Eleonora strongly disapproved of him. Bourman's uncle was some kind of baron, but his father had been disowned by the family because of drink and gambling and he played the piano in a second-rate restaurant. Anatole took after his father. He did not, as he claims in his book, stay the whole summer – he stayed a week:[97] but while discounting most of the sensational stories he propagated, we may take his word for the pleasant way the household passed their time in the country. 'We laughed all day, we ran over the grass with wings on our heels. We read scores of books, and talked and talked, while Mother Nijinsky cooked marvellous Polish dinners for us. . . . When Mother Nijinsky stood in the sunshine shouting "Tola! Bronia! Vatzo!" we ran like children, racing and tumbling in to destroy every vestige of a perfect repast, while she smiled benignly at us. . . .'[98] Bronislava, on the other hand, disliked Bourman for his lying and boasting of success with women, thought him dirty and kept out of his way as much as possible.[99] It was at this time that Vaslav read Dostoyevsky's *The Idiot*,[100] and perhaps identified himself in a vague way with Prince Myshkin, the Christ-like simpleton, the meek, instinctively understanding, all-forgiving, ridiculous, long-suffering lover, friend and philanthropist, whom children turned to, who foretold in Russia the humbling of princes, and thought mankind could be redeemed by beauty.

Bourman's Dostoyevskian characteristic was that he shared the writer's passion for cards. One day he told Vaslav that he must have five hundred roubles for a gambling debt or he would kill himself. Nijinsky said he could not produce such a sum. Bourman asked him to borrow it. Nijinsky said he could not borrow money to pay such a thing as a gambling debt. 'Then, can't you pawn something?' urged his shameless friend.[101]

The weeks of entertaining the troops at Krasnoe Selo passed gaily, with excursions into the surrounding country and parties at the restaurant opposite the rustic theatre, at which Nijinsky and Bourman were the guests of Kchessinskaya and her attendant Grand Dukes. For dancing a solo before the Emperor, Nijinsky along with all the other dancers was awarded the coveted gold watch with Imperial cypher (which was believed to exempt the owner from arrest in Petersburg); and by the end of the summer he had saved over two thousand roubles.[102]

Thomas Nijinsky, whom his wife and children had not seen for years, heard of his son's growing reputation as a dancer and wrote to ask Vaslav to visit him at Nijni-Novgorod.* Eleonora, who had not forgiven her husband his desertion, was reluctant to let Vaslav go. Her son, however, was suddenly anxious to see his father and he persuaded her.

* Not at Kazan, as stated by Mme Romola Nijinsky. According to his sister, Vaslav never travelled on the Volga, though he longed to.

In Nijni-Novgorod the handsome Thomas, now nearing forty, was waiting. Father and son made friends and danced for each other. On his return home Vaslav would tell his family that Thomas was a greater dancer than himself: his father had shown him steps which he found it impossible to execute. Thomas gave him some cuff-links and promised to come and see him dance in Petersburg: but in fact they never met again.[103]

The Nijinskys had moved more than once since Vaslav had walked to school from the flat in Mokhovaya. Now, on their return from the country, Eleonora celebrated her new affluence by taking a much larger apartment in Ulitsa Bolshoi Konyusheunya, the street of the Big Stables, which was a commercial thoroughfare turning off the north side of Nevsky Prospekt, near the Moika Canal and the Hermitage. The flat was over a shop which sold up-to-date Swedish furniture, and it was to be Vaslav's last home in Petersburg.[104]

Whereas the senior boy pupils in the school went to Obukhov for their lessons, the men in the company went to Nicolas Legat. But Cecchetti, who had left the Imperial School in 1902 to pass a few years as ballet master in Poland and Italy, had recently returned. He was shortly to open his own school in Petersburg, but for the time being Pavlova claimed his services and he gave her lessons at her flat in Torgovaya Street near the Mariinsky. Vaslav was anxious to study with the Italian *maestro* rather than with Legat, and Pavlova allowed him to share her private class.[105]

There was another reason not to go to Legat. He was now regarded in the Nijinsky family if not as an enemy, at least as a rival. Legat was jealous of his right to be Kchessinskaya's partner, which Vaslav was beginning to usurp. He was also jealous of a flirtation Vaslav was carrying on with a dancer called Antonina Tchumakova. Legat had formerly had an affair with her elder sister Olga; now he was in love with Antonina, and Nijinsky was a rival twenty years younger.[106]*

Another friend of Nijinsky's was Inna Niesloukhovska, who had graduated at the same time as himself. She was a well-educated girl with pretty eyes, the daughter of the *régisseur* at the Alexandrinsky Theatre, whose house was an intellectual centre. One day, when Vaslav was present at a party there, Inna spoke out in admiration of Isadora, saying that hers was the true art of dancing. Nijinsky was so shocked that he dropped the girl from that moment.† To Bronia he said 'How can I have anything to do with someone

* Antonina subsequently became Legat's (first) wife; and their daughter was the mother of Tatiana Legat of the Kirov Ballet, who is married to that wonderful dancer Yuri Soloviev.

† Niesloukhovska went to Paris with Diaghilev's company in his first 1909 season. She later married a Comte de Chevigné, secretary of the French Embassy in Petersburg and a relation of the Comtesse de Chevigné who would be one of Diaghilev's chief supporters (and who was immortalized as the Duchesse de Guermantes by Proust).

who understands nothing about my work?' Bronia used to tell him when she thought a girl was attracted to him, and she noticed that this would prompt him to take the initiative and pay court to her.[107]

Even at this stage of his career Nijinsky was well known in Petersburg; and one result was that the young prodigy was in demand to give dancing lessons to the children of well-to-do people. A naïve millionaire miller called Sinyagin wrote to ask if he would give ballroom-dancing classes to his boy and girl. He taught them quadrilles, galops, waltzes, polkas and mazurkas. Nijinsky demanded a hundred roubles an hour – and got it. Bourman went along as accompanist.

The family was typical of the Russian merchant class. We were met [by] our host and hostess bowing crudely. . . . The children were a boy of eight and a girl of nine. . . .* During the lesson, given in a spacious hall, the whole family and all the servants congregated. Madame Sinyagin, whose face was beautiful, even if she was fat and had short podgy fingers covered with diamonds, the aunts and cousins, the cook, the grooms, the dish-washers, the laundresses and the coachmen – they were all there to watch the Sinyagin hopefuls at their dancing. . . . After the lesson we would be ushered into a huge dining-room and placed in seats of honour while everything expensive was heaped upon us. . . .[108]

Other houses in which Nijinsky gave lessons were more aristocratic. He began to see how the rich lived. Nijinsky never gave lessons in classical ballet to amateurs.[109]

The Mariinsky season began in September. Although Vaslav was still only a member of the *corps de ballet*, paid sixty-five roubles a month, because of the patronage of Kchessinskaya and because his reputation was already so great the management wanted to make the best use of him they could, and he was given solo roles. On 1 October he danced a *pas de deux* from 'Pakhita' with Lydia Kyasht; on the 7th a *pas de deux* in 'La Fille mal gardée' with Elena Smirnova; and in October a *pas de deux* in 'Giselle' – probably the first act 'peasant' dance, of which the music is by Burgmüller, not Adam – with Karsavina.[110] The rehearsal for this was the occasion of a painful scene, which the ballerina never forgot:

The first time we danced before the whole company was at a theatre rehearsal; I was aware of the intense interest of all the artists; I felt a scrutiny, not unkind, round us both, and was more nervous than at a performance. We finished; the company clapped. From a group in the first wing, a sanctum reserved only for primas, an infuriated figure rushed up to me. 'Enough of your brazen impudence. Where do you think you are, to dance quite naked? . . .' I couldn't realize what had happened. It appeared that the strap of my bodice had slipped off and my shoulder

---

* Bourman says they were fat and clumsy but Mme Bronislava Nijinska ,who confirms his story in general, says Nijinsky would not have accepted them as pupils if they were.

had become uncovered, which I was not conscious of during my dance. I stood in the middle of the stage dumb-founded, helpless against volleys of coarse words hurled at me from the same cruel mouth. The *régisseur* came on and led off the Puritan. By this time a dense crowd of sympathizers had surrounded me; my chronic want of handkerchiefs necessitated the use of my tarlatan skirt to wipe away the tears. Preobrajenskaya stroked my head, repeating, 'Sneeze on the viper, sweetheart. Forget her, and think only of those beautiful *pirouettes* of yours.' The scandal spread rapidly, and an ovation met me at the next performance.[111]

The viper was Pavlova, whose jealousy of Karsavina was to follow her throughout her career.[112]

On 10 November Nijinsky danced again in 'La Fille mal gardée' and – for the first time at the Mariinsky with Kchessinskaya – in the number called 'The Prince Gardener', which he had done on his graduation night with Schollar, and which the latter now taught the *prima ballerina*.[113] On 27 December, Nijinsky danced with Siedova a *pas de deux* in 'Le Roi Candaule', in which he had to black his face and appear as a mulatto, crowned with feathers.[114]

Back from Paris, Benois was introduced to Krupensky in his office in the Square of the Alexandrinsky Theatre, at the end of Theatre Street. His first impression of the Assistant Director was favourable. 'He was a young, pleasant and rather portly man with a dark Assyrian beard.' It was soon clear that the ambitious Krupensky regarded 'Le Pavillon d'Armide' as his own particular show-piece which was going to bring him credit. A scene-painting studio in Alexeyevskaya Street was assigned to Benois and he was lent the assistants of the theatre's principal scenic artist, Oreste Allegri.[115]

The collaborators who were to make history were drawing together. Back from his holiday, Fokine came to the studio and Benois met him for the first time.

What appealed to me at once was his gaiety [Benois recorded]. There was absolutely no affectation or pose about him, no pretence of being a genius; on the contrary, he possessed the simplicity and a certain youthful charm that I consider to be the undoubted sign of real talent. One could see that he was captivated by the problem entrusted to him. We agreed with each other at once. He told me about the way he had produced Armide's dances for the performance in the Theatre School and all his ideas fell in with mine. It became clear that I could trust and depend on him.[116]

Now in September 1907, Fokine took Benois to watch a rehearsal in the ballet school. The painter was overcome by the new experience.

I must confess that when I was taken into the rehearsal hall of the Theatre School I was almost dumbfounded. I had often been present at stage rehearsals and was acquainted with many dancers, and this should have been a guarantee against any surprise. But the sight that now presented itself to my eyes was something entirely unexpected. The daylight, streaming through the tall windows on either side of the hall, seemed to make the sea of tarlatan dresses even more ethereal, transparent, foamy. These young women, maidens and little girls, made no use whatsoever of cosmetics, and their youthful bodies and faces were radiant with health and vigour. It made an unusual picture, infinitely more attractive than those which Degas loved to paint. The atmosphere in Degas' ballet pictures is always somewhat gloomy; the dancers, caught unawares during their exercises, which are often far from graceful, seem to be tormented martyrs. Here, on the contrary, everything seemed gay and carefree and, in spite of the masses of people, one breathed freely. The male and female dancers, who sat along the walls in groups or walked about the hall waiting for the rehearsal to begin, did not in the least look like martyrs or 'victims of their profession'.

Fokine led me in and presented me to the company. My bow was answered by a mass curtsey performed by all the rules of court etiquette. Only after this ritual did I proceed to greet the artists I knew, of whom Gerdt, Kchessinskaya and Solianikov were engaged in the principal parts. . . . Some of them I was seeing for the first time at so close a range and they looked charming in the delightful and becoming costumes, invented during the period of 1830, that were compulsory for rehearsals. Kchessinskaya, who did not conform to rules, was the only dancer to appear in a *tutu* – much shorter than the regulation ones.

The boys of the school stood in a separate group and they, too, wore their working dress and ballet shoes. When I passed them they bowed so deeply that I was embarrassed. A youth . . . was standing with them. I would not have noticed him had not Fokine presented him to me as the artist for whom he had especially composed the part of Armide's slave, so as to give him a chance to display his remarkable talent. Fokine counted on amazing the public by the unusual height of his *sauts* and *vols*, which the youth performed without any visible effort. I must confess that I was rather surprised when I saw this wonder face to face. He was a short, rather thick-set little fellow with the most ordinary, colourless face. He was more like a shop assistant than a fairy-tale hero. But this was – Nijinsky! Little did I expect then, as I shook his hand, that in two years' time he was to gain world renown and end his short but entirely fantastic career crowned with the halo of genius.

Soon silence was ordered. Tcherepnine sat down next to the pianist, the artists took their places and the rehearsal began. The rehearsal was that of the second scene – the coming to life of the Gobelins.

It is impossible to describe the excitement which took possession of me. The performance I had invented and dreamed of was unfolding itself to the music which had, so to say, been made to order for it, had been composed in accordance with my wishes and been actually sanctioned by me. What happiness it was to see my ideas realized *precisely* as I had wished, clothed in the stylish pomposity with which I had endeavoured to express my infatuation for eighteenth-century art, but instinct, at the same time, with the 'Hoffmannish' atmosphere of mystery that had delighted me since my youth. On this memorable day I experienced that very

47

rare feeling – not unmixed, somehow, with pain – that occurs only when something long wished for has at last been accomplished. . . . The faces of the dancers, too, seemed to be shining with happiness. The whole company, with very few exceptions, worshipped Fokine, feeling that in him they had a leader who would bring them, by a new path, to unparalleled triumphs.

But there was trouble in store. For reasons unknown Krupensky turned against the ballet and began to raise difficulties. He started to treat Benois arrogantly, and the painter 'saw red'. Diaghilev came to watch a rehearsal at the Mariinsky and after half an hour was politely but firmly asked to leave by a police officer. Benois thought that after this humiliating incident he must have sworn revenge on the Imperial Theatres. 'Certainly he could not have invented a better way than to create his own, world-famous theatre.'

Next Kchessinskaya, perhaps hoping to please the directorate and put a stop to the production, gave up her role. There was an hour of despondency. Benois and Fokine were discussing the crisis in the directors' box when Pavlova rushed in, flushed with excitement, and, sitting on the edge of the box with her back to the theatre, offered to dance Armida. Then Gerdt tried to get out of his role, saying he was too old, and had to be persuaded. Krupensky refused to allow the expense of real ostrich feathers for the fans carried by Nubian attendants. At the dress rehearsal the dancers could not recognize each other in unfamiliar costumes and everything was chaos; Fokine lost his temper. Clearly another dress rehearsal was necessary, but the direction said the first night could not be cancelled at forty-eight hours' notice, and the programmes had already been printed. Benois resorted to desperate measures. He went to the telephone and rang up Bakst's brother, Isaiah Rosenberg, who contributed a column to the *Petersburg Gazette*, and told him how badly he and Fokine had been treated. Rosenberg made Benois write the article himself. It appeared next day and was a bombshell. The directorate gave in and 'Le Pavillon d'Armide' was postponed by a week.

The first performance of Benois' ballet took place on 25 November 1907, following the whole of 'Le Lac des Cygnes' and ending at one in the morning. It was a great success. After Pavlova, Gerdt, Nijinsky and the other soloists had made their bows, Benois, Tcherepnine and Fokine were called on the stage. For the painter it was the first time he had enjoyed this 'vainglorious pleasure'; and Pavlova, with her arms full of flowers, kissed him.[117]

That winter Nijinsky began to dance more small roles at the Mariinsky. He appeared in the *grand pas hongrois* in 'Raimonda', the *pas d'action* in 'La Bayadère', the *pas de trois* in 'Pakhita', and a *pas de deux* in 'The Little Hump-backed Horse.'[118]

On 21 March 1908, at a charity performance for the Administration of Imperial Theatres, Fokine proved his versatility by arranging an Egyptian ballet, 'Une Nuit d'Egypte', to music of Arensky, and a second version of 'Chopiniana'. In the former, although he was not allowed new scenery and had to make do with a set from 'Aida', he carried further his reform of ballet costume and insistence on correct period style. The principal roles were taken by Pavlova and Gerdt, while Nijinsky had the honour of being paired with the ballerina Preobrajenskaya in a dance for two slaves. The Chopin ballet drew its inspiration from the C Sharp Minor Waltz in the earlier version, and this number was retained while the other pieces for the new solos and *ensembles* were orchestrated by Maurice Keller. Gone were the ballroom, Chopin and the monks. In their place were a poet and a *corps* of sylphs. With extreme economy Fokine had adapted the longest skirts he could find from old ballets to recreate the image of Taglioni, as Bakst had done with the costume he had designed for Pavlova in the original 'Chopiniana'. At last Fokine had completely banished the *tutu*. The white-clad sylphs, all with hair parted in the middle, were led by Pavlova, Preobrajenskaya and Karsavina. Nijinsky in his black velvet tunic was the poet: this was a testing role, in which virtuosity counted for less than the ability to sustain a mood, which he did throughout the ballet with great success.[119]* Rather oddly, Chopin's 'Polonaise Militaire' was played as an overture.

Between its first performance at the Mariinsky Theatre in 1874 and Mussorgsky's death in alcoholic poverty in 1881, at the age of forty-two, his opera 'Boris Godounov' had been performed fifteen times.[120] It was then dropped from the repertory. In the early years of the twentieth century Rimsky-Korsakov rearranged the work, reorchestrating certain passages and eliminating many of the 'barbaric' elements. 'Boris' was revived for Chaliapine. In Petersburg, however, it was seldom given more than once a year, and Chaliapine's scenes were the only ones greeted with applause. It was the most unpopular opera in the repertory. The Court and Society stayed away from performances of 'Boris', which were only supported by a small group of liberal intellectuals known as *koutchkisti*.

Diaghilev loved Mussorgsky's 'Boris Godounov'. He remembered as a child hearing his aunt Panaeva, great grand-daughter of the poet Panaev and a delightful singer, saying to her servants 'I'm going to sing today, so don't forget to send for Mussorgsky.' The composer was her regular accompanist, although naturally it was never his own music he was asked to play. The words 'Don't forget to send for Mussorgsky' haunted Diaghilev all his life. He decided to take a production of 'Boris Godounov' to Paris in the summer of 1908.

*Fuller descriptions of 'Une Nuit d'Egypte' (revised as 'Cléopâtre') and the second 'Chopin-iana' (as 'Les Sylphides') will be found in Chapter II.

First there arose the question of the score. Towards the end of his life Diaghilev wrote:

Certain incidents attendant on the first staging of 'Boris' in 1874 are well known; such as that the scenes in Pimen's cell and the revolutionary scene with the Innocent were banned, and that the direction of the Imperial Theatres insisted on Mussorgsky's adding the Polish scenes to the opera. In the autograph score of Mussorgsky, which has never been recopied and of course never published [in 1927] – the score used in the earliest productions of the opera, before the editing of Rimsky-Korsakov – the scene in Pimen's cell is not included: but I found it among Rimsky-Korsakov's papers. Much has been said about Mussorgsky's inspired idea of ending the opera not with the death of Boris, but with the scene of revolution and the Innocent's song, as was published in the first edition of Rimsky's version. But in Mussorgsky's manuscript the opera ends with the death of Boris, and on the last page the composer wrote 'End of the opera.'

When I came to put on 'Boris' in Paris Rimsky-Korsakov restored certain numbers which had been suppressed from the start, including the famous peal of bells, which was to cause a sensation in Paris. I was terrified of the opera's length and worried about the running order. My friends and I had endless discussions with Rimsky-Korsakov about transposing certain scenes. Among other questions we considered whether we could place the coronation after Pimen's cell, so as to separate the two crowd scenes and end [the act] with the coronation – which was chronologically possible* and theatrically a great improvement. The first year in Paris I gave neither the inn scene nor the scene in Marina's bedroom, so afraid was I of dragging out the opera – which, anyway, most people said the French would never understand! On top of his other alterations I persuaded Rimsky-Korsakov to revise the coronation scene, which struck me as too short, and to complete and elaborate some of the carillons. He threw himself excitedly into this work; and the last word I had from him just before his death was a telegram to Paris from Russia asking me 'How do my new bits sound?'[121]

Feeling that the old Russia before Peter the Great and the Moscow oriental style of architecture were not in his line, Benois refused to undertake the décor. He contented himself with designing the more European Polish scene. The Moscow painters Korovine and Golovine also refused to design the opera, probably through fear of offending their patron Teliakovsky, who would have nothing to do with Diaghilev: but Golovine agreed to contribute certain general ideas for other artists to elaborate.[122]

Bilibine, an expert on Russian history and ikons, was called in to design and advise on the costumes. Following his indications, Diaghilev and Benois went hunting in the Tartar and Jewish shops of the Petersburg markets for silk, brocade, old head-dresses and traditional costumes.[123] Furthermore, Diaghilev sent Bilibine to search the northern provinces, where he travelled

* Benois did not agree with this. (*Memoirs* II, p. 252.)

from village to village, 'buying up from the peasants a mass of beautiful old hand-woven sarafans, which had been hoarded in chests for centuries'.[124] These treasures from the past were displayed on the stage of the little Hermitage Court Theatre (where Benois painted his Polish scene) for the inspection of the Grand Duke Vladimir, whose patronage Diaghilev had secured for the enterprise, as for his concerts in the previous year.[125]

Vladimir, second of the five sons of Alexander II, and uncle of the Tsar, was a big, loud-voiced, convivial man, but nevertheless the one committed patron of art among the twenty-seven Grand Dukes. Ranking after the four-year-old Tsarevitch and the Tsar's only surviving brother Michael Alexandrovitch, he was the fourth man in the Empire. He was sixty. His cousin, Grand Duke Alexander Mikhailovitch, who married the Tsar's sister Xenia, describes him thus:

Grand Duke Vladimir collected ancient ikons, he visited Paris twice a year, and he adored to give elaborate parties at his splendid palace in Tsarskoe Selo. A kind-hearted man, he fell victim to his eccentricities. A stranger meeting Grand Duke Vladimir Alexandrovitch was certain to be taken aback by the roughness and by the shouting voice of this Grand Seigneur of Russia. He treated the younger grand dukes with a maximum of contempt. None of us could have engaged him in conversation unless prepared to discuss subjects of art or the finesses of French cooking. . . .[126]

The Grand Duke had little in common with his devious, reticent nephew, Tsar Nicholas II: conversely, we may assume that much of the latter's secretiveness and lack of frankness may have been assumed after his premature accession as a defence against the big, overbearing, booming uncles. The Grand Duke's wife, Marie Pavlovna, born a duchess of Mecklenburg, was a vivacious, intelligent and brilliant woman, who flung herself into the job of being a leader of society as much as the Empress backed out of hers. Her Court was far more the centre of social and artistic life than that of the cold, proud and shy Tsarina, whom both she and her husband disliked. The Grand Duke Vladimir complained that when he was in the company of the Empress Alexandra Feodorovna he was driven to the desperate expedient of making a genealogical mistake in quoting the Almanach de Gotha in order to arouse his niece to break her silence.[127]

Grand Duke Vladimir was the father of Grand Duke André, Kchessinskaya's friend who was later to marry her. Since first seeing Tamara Karsavina dance, when she was still a pupil in the school, he had prophesied a great future for her and his fatherly interest had continued through the years. He had once caused a flutter in the ballet school by asking Varvara Ivanovna to send him the young Karsavina's photograph. The head-mistress, while obliged to obey, was afraid of making her pupil conceited by singling her out, and after anxious consultations with the staff it had been decided to have a photograph taken of every girl in the school.[128]

When the Dowager Empress heard that Diaghilev was taking 'Boris' to Paris she said, 'Couldn't you find anything more boring to give them?'[129]

The Imperial Theatres gave us every possible help on this occasion [wrote Diaghilev. Such was the advantage of having Grand Duke Vladimir behind him]. The chorus was lent by the Bolshoi Theatre, Moscow, our singers were the best available: namely, Chaliapine, Smirnov, Yougina, Zbroueva and Petrenko. A team of stage mechanics came from Moscow under the leadership of K.F.Valz, the supreme technical wizard of his time. Our conductor was F.M.Blumenfeld.

We had come to an agreement with the Paris Opera that they should place their theatre at our disposal for the performance of 'Boris' on condition that afterwards the whole production with its sets and dresses should become their property. The intention was to add the opera to the Paris repertoire and sing it in French. (As the Opera directors subsequently sold the production to the Metropolitan in New York, this never happened; and after my Paris season 'Boris' was given in the United States before being seen again in Europe.)

So we set off for Paris, where a curious and expectant public awaited us. But we ran into incredible difficulties with the hidebound bureaucracy of the Opéra officials. We were told on arrival that it was out of the question to mount an opera as complicated as 'Boris' in the short time allowed for; that the Theatre's own repertory was more than filling the available rehearsal time, and that there was no possibility of rehearsing the singers on stage or of setting up such elaborate scenery. Whatever I asked for I received the same answer. 'Unheard-of! Impossible!'

When at last we began to rehearse with the orchestra – and we were only allowed two or three rehearsals – the stage-hands set up such a din on the stage that I had to have a twenty-franc gold piece ready in my hand to tip them when Chaliapine or another principal came on to sing. This was the only way to make them stop their hammering and go off for a drink. Three days before we were due to open they told us that we could only hang our sets on the day of the first performance – and there were seven sets.[130]

Benois remembered this emergency rather differently and recorded Diaghilev's immediate reaction, which Diaghilev did not.

On the day of the semi-official rehearsal, forty-eight hours before the *répétition générale*, Petroman sprang a surprise on us and announced that a mistake had occurred for which we were to blame – that the décor had not the necessary dimensions, did not reach the floor, and that there was much repair work to be done which would take three or four days. Here Diaghilev showed his real self and saved the situation. He declared, quite calmly, that he would not put off the show and was ready to produce the opera without décor. Petroman was so terrified of a scandal that the impossible was done. . . .

But even after this, we were still not sure that the dress rehearsal could take place . . . some of the chorus singing had not been sufficiently rehearsed and the only try-out with extras had taken place at midnight and turned into an uncontrollable orgy. This made another unforgettable impression: the huge stage of the Opéra, illuminated by only one candle, and crowding on to it a mass of two hundred filthy, stinking people from the street, with false beards awry, and hastily pulled-on boyar fur coats and caps. No wonder that, surprised at their own appearance, these hungry casual 'actors' decided to have some fun, and began to sing and dance, impervious to all calls to order. A catastrophe seemed inevitable and even our fearless Diaghilev took fright.

Then another theatrical miracle took place. Diaghilev decided to arrange a supper at Larue and hold a council of war to decide whether to give the performance the next day or not. The whole team was summoned, the minor 'props' as well as the artists and the make-up man, a stammerer whom Chaliapine trusted above everybody else. Diaghilev must have been scared to have recourse to such a democratic method![131]

In Diaghilev's words: 'I called a meeting of my collaborators. . . . Everyone was there, including our Russian technicians. The most vociferous speaker was Valz, backed up by his stage mechanics and by the wig-maker Feodor Grigorievitch Zaika, who always reminded me of Hoffmann's Drosselmeyer. They worked themselves into a frenzy, declaring that postponement would mean the ruin of our enterprise. I decided to take the risk and let the show go on.'

On the night before 'Boris' opened everyone went to bed late. In the early hours Diaghilev heard a knock at his door in the Hôtel Mirabeau.

'Who is it?'

'Can I come in? It is I, Chaliapine.'

'What's the matter, Feodor Ivanovitch?'

'Is there a settee in your room? I can't bear to be alone.'

'So that giant,' wrote Diaghilev, 'spent the night in my room, sleeping fitfully, curled up on a tiny sofa.'[132]

Benois wrote:

The coronation, the polonaise, the revolution were rehearsed three times in the afternoon under Diaghilev's supervision. The chief artists rehearsed their parts with the piano, the painter gave the last touch to banners and ikons, and thirty seamstresses sewed, mended and ironed, I dashed up and down like a madman (there were no lifts or telephones), Diaghilev was reading the proofs of the magnificent programme.[133]

The polonaise was to be danced by dancers of the Opéra ballet, but led by two artists from Petersburg. These were Alexandra Vassilieva, a lady no longer young, who was the companion of the balletomane Besobrasov, and Mikhail Alexandrov, a handsome, vain fellow who believed himself to be an illegitimate son of Alexander II,[134]* and who, as we shall shortly see, was perhaps to play a decisive role in Nijinsky's life.

At last Diaghilev and his friends were able to see the sets, which had been painted in Russia, hung up, put together and lit for the first time. Huge crowds of noblemen, archers, peasants and priests in costumes of such colour and splendour as Paris had never seen, moved before them. The production was ready a few minutes before the performance began.

I hardly had time to change before the curtain went up [wrote Diaghilev]. By the end of the first scene the public were beginning to enjoy themselves. Pimen's cell, with unseen choirs of monks singing in the wings, caused a sensation, and during the coronation scene we realized that 'Boris' was going to be a triumph. I hardly saw this scene as I was superintending the entry of processions of supers. During the second interval when the stage-hands, thunderstruck by our success, saw me in my tail-coat and white gloves moving on some hedges and placing benches for the Polish garden scene, they ran to help me. I had been refused any water for the fountain – all available water apparently being reserved exclusively for the firemen – but this did not diminish the success of the Polish scene. French ladies, infatuated with Smirnov, were soon to be heard trilling *O povtori, povtori, Marina!* sounding their guttural r's. The impression made by Chaliapine in the scene of Boris's madness was really overwhelming, and the audience went wild. In the scene of revolution, which I presented in deep snow, the episode of the Innocent, the passing of the imposter Dmitri standing upright in his sleigh and the grand ensembles of the chorus, who brandished torches as they sang, impressed the public most favourably. The only setback in the whole performance was the length of the last intermission, caused by the insistence of Valz on hanging some huge and enormously heavy chandeliers in the set representing the Great Hall of the Kremlin. At this point the audience grew restless and began to stamp. But the scene of Boris's death, when the ascetic monks came on with tall candles and when Boris spoke his last words to his children, was a knockout. The future of Russian opera in the west was assured.

That night, after the opera, Chaliapine strode beside me along the *grands boulevards*, saying over and over again, 'We've done something tonight. I don't know what, but we've really done something!'[135]

Years later Benois still recalled the excitement of that night.

I remember so vividly returning to our hotels at dawn, arm in arm with Diaghilev, reluctant to part, and on reaching the Place Vendôme looking up with a challenge at that other conqueror standing on the column!† Even when we reached our rooms we began calling out to each other across the yards, I from my Hôtel de l'Orient to Diaghilev's Hôtel Mirabeau. The sun was already high in the sky when

* According to Kchessinskaya, a son of Prince Dolgoroukov, the brother of Alexander II's second (morganatic) wife Princess Yurievskaya. Mme B. Nijinska also thought this might be correct.
† Napoleon I.

Diaghilev's cousin, Paffka, also rather tipsy, came to my room, and, hearing that we could communicate with Diaghilev through the window, he too started calling out. Finally people were peering out of their windows, indignant at being disturbed, and the porter knocked at our door. I had great trouble in dragging Paffka away from the window and putting him to sleep on a sofa in my room.[136]

Diaghilev wrote:

To show how dubious our whole undertaking had been considered in Russia I must admit that even the Grand Duke Vladimir Alexandrovitch, who was so fond of me, had not dared to come to Paris for our first performance. It was only when he was bombarded with telegrams announcing the triumph of 'Boris' that he and the Grand Duchess made up their minds to take the Nord-Express as it were straight to the theatre. The Grand Duke was genuinely happy and proud that this project which he had been almost the only one to encourage, which he had thrown himself into heart and soul, and which he had helped me to bring off, should have met with so outstanding a success. He was amazed at the high standard of our performance; and at a party he gave at his hotel, the Continental, for the whole company and stage staff he told them in the course of a little speech 'It isn't thanks to me or Diaghilev that "Boris" is such a success – it's all *your* doing. We only planned it: you made it come true.' The chorus misunderstood these words and thought the Grand Duke was dissatisfied with me.

Before he went back to Petersburg the Grand Duke asked me, 'Is it true that you are down 20,000 roubles? Tell me the truth and I'll ask the Emperor to make it up.' I told him it was not true. He smiled and said, 'Perhaps you'd rather notify me in writing?' I insisted that there was not a word of truth in the story. Getting up and coming over to me, he raised his arm, made the sign of the cross and said 'May this blessing preserve you from all evil intrigues!' Then he embraced me.[137]

One result of the Russian opera's success in Paris was that Diaghilev met a woman who was to become one of his dearest friends. Misia, born Godebska, half Polish, half Belgian, was a vivacious, attractive woman in her early twenties, who had been the friend of Mallarmé, Lautrec, Renoir, Bonnard and Vuillard (the last four of whom had painted her) and who was at this time married to the rich proprietor of *Le Matin*, Alfred Edwards, though soon to exchange him for José-Maria Sert.

Misia declared that 'Boris Godounov' was her second love: Debussy's 'Pelléas' had been her first.

For the first night I had invited a few friends into the big box between the pillars. But in the middle of the first act I was so moved by the music that I made my way to the gallery and remained sitting there on a step till the end. . . . The stage streamed with gold. Chaliapine's voice rose powerful and magnificent above Mussorgsky's overwhelming music. . . . I left the theatre stirred to the point of realizing that something had been changed in my life. The music was with me always. . . . I made incessant propaganda for this work and dragged to it all the people I loved. . . . Not satisfied with attending every performance, I ordered that all the unsold seats should be brought to me, so that no place remained unsold and Diaghilev had the encouraging illusion of financial success.

Some of this may be exaggerated, but Misia was to prove indeed a staunch supporter of Diaghilev.

It was shortly after the first night [she wrote] that, dining one evening at Prunier's with Sert, I saw Diaghilev.* Sert knew him, and introduced him to me. The fervour of my enthusiasm for 'Boris' very soon opened the doors of his heart for me. We remained until five in the morning, and found it intolerable to have to part. The next day he came to see me, and our friendship ended only with his death.[138]

The Serts were destined to prove their friendship in a practical way, for they more than once came to the rescue of Diaghilev's ballet company in times of stress.

According to Bourman, there was a man in the ballet employed as a pimp by rich members of Petersburg society, introducing them to girl dancers who would subsequently appear at the theatre wearing expensive jewels.[139] Although Bourman gives him a different name, there is evidence that he was Alexandrov, who had led the polonaise in 'Boris'.[140] He and an accomplice invited Nijinsky and Bourman to meet a friend at dinner. Why they invited Bourman is not clear, unless they thought Nijinsky would be too shy to come without him. The dinner was at Mdvyed, one of the best restaurants, overlooked from above by a gallery off which opened the private rooms. The host was Prince Pavel Dmitrievitch Lvov.†

This prince was the artistic member of an old family which would contribute a president to the third (reactionary) Duma of 1912. He was thirty, tall, good-looking, with big blue eyes and a monocle. He had seen Nijinsky dance and was fascinated by him; but learning from the two pimps that the young dancer was sexually naïve – had not 'learnt the score' – he hit upon an ingenious ruse (if we are to believe Bourman) to try him out. He said that his cousin – a beautiful princess, of whom he produced a miniature – was in love with Nijinsky and wanted to buy him a ring. Any young man would have been intrigued by such a romantic situation. The dinner led to a visit

---

* According to Benois, who is almost always accurate, it was after the first night of 'Boris' that 'we' – by which I take it he means Diaghilev, possibly Chaliapine, Diaghilev's cousin Pavel Koribut-Kubitovitch and himself – 'celebrated our success quite intimately with Misia Edwards and Mme Bénardaky in the Café de la Paix'. (*Memoirs* II, p. 252.) Yet it would seem that Misia Sert had heard 'Boris' before meeting Diaghilev (M. Sert: *Two or Three Muses*, pp. 111, 112).

† Bourman, who calls Alexandrov 'Vasilev', and gives his accomplice the name of 'Guttmann', when there is reason to believe he was a friend of Kchessinskaya's called Baron Gotch, calls Lvov 'Prince Michail-Dmitri'.

to Fabergé; this led to more dinners, visits to night-clubs – such as The Aquarium, where the American Negro Claude Hopkins demonstrated tap-dancing for the first time in Petersburg – more presents and more parties during which 'Vaslav and the Prince would retire to discuss the merits of the unknown princess.'[141]

Such is Bourman's lurid account. The fact remains that Lvov, a great patron of sportsmen, was a good friend to the whole Nijinsky family, whom he helped financially. Eleonora liked him; and when Bronia had a poisoned foot he took her to a doctor and perhaps saved her career.[142]

Affairs between men were accepted as quite natural in Petersburg society[143] – which was not the case in Paris in those days, and even less in London. It seems safe to state, from his sister's evidence, and in the light of after events, that physically Nijinsky preferred women, even if emotionally, lacking a father, he needed the protective love of an older man.

Nijinsky had never before had such smart clothes, eaten or drunk so well, or been at home in such luxurious houses. To judge from photographs taken at this time, the Prince's admiration brought out in him an inherent vein of feminine provocation. Just as, when dancing, he had the instinctive know-ledge of the pattern his limbs were forming without the need to correct his poses in a mirror as other dancers did,[144] so was he conscious that his high cheek-bones and mysterious faun-like look, half voluptuous, half mocking, which it was easy to assume, could make up for the lack of high spirits and brilliant conversation. He kept trying out different ways of doing his hair: a fringe, a slanting parting, a straight parting slightly right of centre, with the fine hair brushed up at the sides.[145]

Was Pavel Dmitrievitch disappointed in Nijinsky offstage? Did he find after the first weeks of their friendship that the dancer was not quite his type? Nijinsky was small in a part where size is usually admired.[146] It was, incidentally, at the house of Lvov that he had what was probably his first sexual experience with a woman. She was a *cocotte* and Vaslav was frightened and put off.*

The relationship lasted a few months but the Prince, apparently, did not fall in love. At least, he was not jealous enough to wish to keep Nijinsky to himself, for he introduced him to the immensely rich Pole, Count Tishkievitch. Nijinsky, however, apparently loved Lvov. In his *Diary* of 1918, which, admittedly, we have to 'interpret', he wrote 'One day I met a Russian prince who introduced me to a Polish count. . . . This count bought me a piano: I did not love him. I loved the prince and not the count.'[147] According to Mme Bronislava Nijinska it was Lvov, not Tishkievitch, who

---

* So he told his wife. His sister does not believe the experiment, which she knew about, took place under Lvov's roof.

bought Nijinsky the piano. She remembers the Count as a married man with four children who had known her parents years before in Vilna, who bored her with his lectures on morals and did not approve of girls using scent.[148] Her memories, presumably accurate, cast doubt on the exactitude of her brother's *Diary* or, perhaps, on that of its editor.

Then came the meeting which was to be as fruitful for the future of ballet throughout the world as another famous encounter – that of the Emperor and Empress with Rasputin three years before – would prove disastrous to the House of Romanov.

Diaghilev – who at that time was having an affair with a young man called Alexis Mavrine, employed as his secretary – had of course seen Nijinsky on stage before and since his graduation: Nijinsky knew of Diaghilev's reputation as a champion of Russian art. According to Bourman their very first meeting was during an interval at the Mariinsky. Nijinsky was walking up and down with Prince Lvov in the big hall with mirrors, where to this day Soviet citizens circulate on the long carpets which run beside the walls, leaving empty the polished parquet in the middle; and Lvov introduced him to Diaghilev. The two men must have presented an exceptional contrast. The elder with his big head and imposing manner, with the celebrated white streak in his dark hair which had earned him the nickname 'Chinchilla', and the unnecessary monocle, seemed taller than he was. The younger, five foot four inches in height, in spite of his slanting eyes and the long muscular neck which rose from narrow, sloping shoulders, was essentially private-looking and appeared smaller beside him. Later that evening Diaghilev is said to have joined Lvov and Nijinsky at a party *chez* Cubat. Bourman's account of the conversation at this party, of Diaghilev's boasting of the glorious productions he would show to Europe and Nijinsky's tirade on the superiority of the Petersburg to the Moscow school of ballet, is inherently improbable – we know, for instance, that Nijinsky did not express himself in long speeches: yet one detail recorded by Bourman makes it seem likely that a meeting or meetings of this nature did occur in a restaurant (perhaps he telescoped two parties together). Bourman remembers Diaghilev taking offence at being described as an *entrepreneur*, with the result that he bore Bourman a grudge and did not sign him up until his third season in Western Europe. This does not seem to be the kind of detail which is invented.[149]

In Nijinsky's own words:

Lvov* introduced me to Diaghilev, who asked me to come to the Europa Hotel where he lived. I disliked him for his too self-assured voice, but went to seek my

* In the published version of *The Diary of Vaslav Nijinsky* the translator or the editor has misread 'Lvov' as 'Ivor'.

luck. I found my luck. At once I allowed him to make love to me. I trembled like a leaf. I hated him, but pretended, because I knew that my mother and I would die of hunger otherwise. . . .[150]

Now let us interpret. We realize that as the *Diary* was written during the critical period when Nijinsky's mind was breaking down, it might *all* be a fantasy, without a word of truth in it: but we know from corroborative evidence of many of the incidents which he records that this is not the case. We do not look for logic in the *Diary*, and we notice that within a few lines the writer can utterly reverse his point of view. For instance, a 'letter' of accusation to Diaghilev beginning 'I cannot name you because I have no name for you' ends touchingly 'I am a tender being and want to write you a cradle song . . . a lullaby . . . sleep peacefully, sleep, sleep peacefully.' (The editor, Mme Nijinsky, here appends a footnote: 'The lullaby is written in verse and its translation is not possible.'[151]) Rightly or wrongly, in 1918, the sick Nijinsky felt betrayed by Diaghilev, who, besides, had transferred his love to Massine. Most of the passages relating to Diaghilev sound the bitter recriminatory note of a lovers' quarrel and remind us of certain terrible pages in that famous letter – of which only the more Christian part was published under the name of *De Profundis* – written in Reading Gaol. I'm good: you're bad. I'm right: you're wrong. The self-pity, also reminiscent of a lovers' quarrel, which makes Nijinsky introduce several times in his *Diary* the dying-of-hunger theme, here leads him, as it were, to put the blame on Diaghilev for the privations of his childhood. In 1908, of course, there was no conceivable danger of his not being able to support his mother in comfort. So I interpret: 'I was depressed when I found that my friendship with Prince Lvov, whom I was fond of and found attractive, could not be permanent. At least this new life brought me smart clothes and a piano. When I was introduced to Diaghilev I was becoming used to the idea of being passed around, and imagined that this was the way of the world and such was to be my fate. Diaghilev was exactly twice my age. His voice and overbearing manner rather put me off, but I knew he might be helpful in my career. Our first attempt at making love in the hotel room was not very successful.'

Perhaps we should here add, on Nijinsky's behalf and in fairness to Diaghilev, even though it means anticipating a later phase of our story, 'I could not foresee that the sexual aspect of our relationship would sink into unimportance beside the fact that Diaghilev's tuition and encouragement would make me the greatest performer of the age, the most wonderful dancer who ever lived. How could I guess in that hotel bedroom that I should come to depend on Diaghilev as much as any one man ever depended on another?'

Nijinsky 1898–1908

Such, in November or December 1908, was the first encounter of two men whose friendship was to become the most notorious since that of Oscar Wilde* and Alfred Douglas in the previous decade. Their union could produce no children, but it would give birth to masterpieces – and change the history of the dance, of music and of painting throughout the world.

---

* Diaghilev had met Wilde in Paris in 1898. The exiled poet wrote about him to Smithers, his last publisher—and Beardsley's—: 'Have you a copy of Aubrey's drawing of Mlle de Maupin? There is a young Russian here, who is a great amateur of Aubrey's art, who would love to have one. He is a great collector, and rich. So you might send him a copy and name a price, and also deal with him for drawings by Aubrey. His name is Serge de Diaghilew, Hôtel St James, Rue St Honoré, Paris.' (*The Letters of Oscar Wilde*, p. 734.)

CHAPTER TWO

1909

What decided Diaghilev to bring the Russian Ballet to the West?

It could be argued that the existence of the superb Mariinsky company, headed by the celebrated Kchessinskaya, with young artists of genius such as Pavlova, Karsavina and the twenty-one-year-old Nijinsky, made a Paris season inevitable; or that the new ideas of Fokine were bound to find a new public outside Russia; or that Bakst and Benois, the most imaginative stage-designers to have appeared for a century, were inevitably destined for international fame. Yet what ballet company, apart from small groups of character dancers, had ever gone abroad before? In fact two: the Milanese had presented Manzotti's 'Excelsior' in Paris and London in the 1880's,* and during the summer of 1908 Pavlova and Bolm had led a small troupe on a tour of Sweden, Denmark and Germany. Furthermore, what proof was there that Paris, which had seen the flowering of ballet in the Romantic period and its decadence in the age of Degas, could still be persuaded to take an interest in this *démodé* art? Kchessinskaya had made some guest appearances at the Opéra in 1907 and 1908 without sensational acclaim. Then it must be remembered that Bakst and Benois had so far given in Russia only a hint of the marvels they were now on the brink of creating.

Romola Nijinsky wrote that Nijinsky persuaded Diaghilev 'in the early winter of 1909' to present the ballet in Western Europe.[1] Dandré relates how he and Pavlova, at a luncheon in Petersburg in the winter of 1908, 'tried to take advantage of this opportunity [the formation of a committee for the presentation of opera in Paris] to show the ballet as well' and that '[Diaghilev] was terrified at our suggestion.'[2] Fokine had received, during his 1908 summer holiday in Switzerland, which he partly spent giving lessons to the

* Enrico Cecchetti was *premier danseur*.

61

rich amateur Ida Rubinstein, a letter from Benois revealing that he 'had the idea of persuading Sergei Pavlovitch Diaghilev to take the ballet company to Paris' and to present 'Le Pavillon d'Armide' and other Fokine ballets.[3] Astruc, of the Société Musicale, the promoter of the Parisian concerts, whose interests now extended to Russian opera and ballet, describes how it was he who begged Diaghilev, during the season of 'Boris Godounov', to bring the Russian Ballet in the following year.[4]

Nijinsky, Pavlova, Benois and Astruc may all have been quite correct in recalling these conversations and individually quite justified in believing that he or she had been the deciding factor in the history of the Russian Ballet. But Diaghilev had a way of testing people's reactions, of pretending to be opposed to a course he really favoured, of planting the seed of an idea in a colleague's mind, so that the colleague found himself initiating proposals and persuading Diaghilev to embark on a course of action to which he was already in his heart committed.* Certainly it had been Benois who first persuaded him to take seriously the art of ballet, but once Diaghilev had observed the reforms of Fokine taking place on the Mariinsky stage, once he had seen in 'Le Pavillon d'Armide' that a new unity and expressiveness were possible, and once he had realized that in Pavlova and Nijinsky there were ready at hand two artists of genius to interpret the new ballets, he decided that new kinds of triumph could be enjoyed in the West which – with Teliakovsky in command of the Imperial Theatres – would be impossible in Russia. Two of the essential elements were Pavlova and Nijinsky and it was a feat of diplomacy to make both dancers think that they had talked him into exporting the ballet. The third essential was Fokine, and since he had already worked with Benois and got along well with him, it was for Benois to bring him in. The fourth element, Astruc, was indispensable at the Paris end.

The idea of taking Russian ballet to the West had in fact been for some years at the back of Diaghilev's mind. In Moscow in 1906 he had told the French music critic Robert Brussel that in three years he would bring the Russian Ballet to Paris.[5] After the first production of 'Le Pavillon d'Armide' at the Mariinsky in November 1907 Diaghilev told Benois 'This must be shown to Europe.'[6] Suddenly, after the success of 'Boris' these vague thoughts and plans crystallized: the moment had come.

Gabriel Astruc, who had put on the Russian concerts, describes how over dinner *chez* Paillard in summer 1908 he persuaded Diaghilev that Paris must be shown the glories of the Russian dance. This is how Astruc remembered the conversation. He mentioned how he had admired the dancing in

---

* An example of this is Diaghilev's reaction to Benois' proposal to present 'Giselle' in Paris. (See p. 122.) I here draw my own conclusions: but Mme Sokolova, when she read this passage, exclaimed 'Just like the old man!'

the Polish scene of 'Boris', for which Alexandra Vassilieva had come from Petersburg to teach the Opéra dancers – and lead them in – a polonaise.

'You seem so fond of dancing,' said Diaghilev, 'you ought to come to St Petersburg to see our Imperial Ballet. You, in France, do not honour dancing any longer, and the art is incomplete as you show it today. You possess fine ballerinas but you have no idea what a male dancer can be. Our male dancers are stars in Russia. Nothing can give you an idea of how fine our Vaslav is* – I believe that nothing like him has been seen since Vestris.'

'Does he dance alone?'

'Yes – but sometimes with a partner who is almost his equal, la Pavlova. She is the greatest ballerina in the world, excelling both in classicism and character. Like a Taglioni she doesn't dance, but floats; of her, also, one might say that she could walk over a cornfield without bending an ear.'

'But you must have great producers and *maîtres de ballet* to use all those fine talents.'

'We have. There is the old Cecchetti, master of us all, who carries the torch of classicism. Then there is a true genius, Michel Fokine, a descendant of the greatest *maîtres de ballet* of all time.'

'Nijinsky, Fokine and Pavlova must come to Paris – next year.'

'But Paris will never come to see whole evenings of dancing.'[7]

Diaghilev knew perfectly well that he could hold Paris enthralled with whole evenings of Russian ballet – Russian ballet as *he* would present it – but he wanted Astruc to enjoy the illusion of persuading him.

This conversation took place on 2 June 1908, and Astruc preserved in his files the scribbled notes he made at the dinner table. On a double sheet of writing-paper headed 'Paillard, 2 Chaussée d'Antin, Paris' we can see the birth of the Ballets Russes.[8]

First Astruc wrote the names of ballets Diaghilev proposed to give: 'Le Pavillon d'Armide de Chérepnine avec La Pawlowa – dec et livret Benoist [*sic*]. 2 actes. Sylvia – Léo Delibes. 3 tableaux.' But 'Sylvia' is crossed out. Then 'Giselle . . . 2 actes.' It was evidently intended that the evenings of ballet should alternate with opera, as indeed they did in the first Russian season, for next is written 'Mozart et Salieri de Rimsky Korsakoff – Anselmi & Chaliapine'. And the theatre Astruc proposed for this season was not the Opéra but 'Théâtre Sarah Bernhardt. Mai 1909.'

Next Astruc made a list, partly no doubt dictated by Diaghilev, of possible patrons for the season: 'S.A. la Princesse Murat – Mse de Ganay – Csse de Chevigné – Csse Ed de Pourtalès – Csse de Hohenfelsen – Psse de Polignac – Grand Duc Cyrille – Csse Jean de Castellane – Bnne? de Rothschild.'

---

* I have quoted Astruc's text of this conversation exactly; but Diaghilev had no personal acquaintance with Nijinsky at the time.

Opposite, Astruc totted up costs – 265,000 francs including 50,000 for himself as impresario. Sixteen performances, estimated to take 20,000 francs each, totalled 320,000 francs. At the top of the first page where there was a little space left alongside the letter-heading he then wrote the names of proposed ballerinas: 'Pawlowa II. Préobrajenskaia. Gelzer. Trefilowa. Sedowa. Kiakcht.' Finally, in the shallow space above the engraved word 'Paillard' he wrote: 'Nijinsky, Koslow, Mordkine, Andrianow, Bolm, Fokin.'

On 4 June[9] Astruc broached the subject of a season of ballet and opera with the Grand Duchess Vladimir (Marie Pavlovna) at a party of Princesse Edmond de Polignac's. She approved of the idea. Diaghilev and Astruc had further talks, and although the nature of the repertory and the composition of the company remained fluid until almost a month before the Russians came to Paris in the following May, a contract was signed.

In the contract it was stated that Diaghilev accepted entire financial responsibility for the Russian Season, while Astruc undertook the administration, the publicity and the sale of tickets, for which he was to receive only $2\frac{1}{2}$ per cent of the takings, Diaghilev having induced him to accept half his usual fee.[10] Astruc was Diaghilev's sponsor with the Parisian press, a guarantee of good relations. In France the distinction between editorial matter and advertising is not as sharp as in English-speaking countries, and a sum was set aside for the purpose of commissioning articles from distinguished critics. In fact, Astruc would exert himself in a number of ways not specified in the contract, such as dealing with the decorators and upholsterers who were to renovate the shabby old Châtelet Theatre – for it was at the enormous Châtelet, the home of popular spectacle, and not at the Sarah Bernhardt opposite, that the Russian season was to be held.

Diaghilev made himself responsible not only for financing the season and for presenting the artists of the Imperial Theatres in their own décors and costumes, but for establishing a committee of patrons made up of the leaders of Parisian society and headed by the Grand Duke and Grand Duchess Vladimir.

Returning to Petersburg from his annual holiday in Venice, Diaghilev set about planning his repertory for Paris and engaging dancers. Throughout Petersburg the double windows were screwed into position for the winter; the ice grew thicker on the Neva; the carriages, droshkies and a few cars sped through the snowy streets beneath endless façades of palaces; the gold spire of the yellow and white Admiralty and the gold dome of the adjacent St Isaac's could be seen for miles, while across the river the even higher gold needle of the church within the dread Petropavlovsky Fortress – whose gun daily proclaimed noon – pierced the frozen sky.

Diaghilev's latest flat in Zamiatin Pereúlok, off the English Quay, between the Horse Guards Barracks and the Neva, five minutes' walk south-west of the Admiralty, was to be the centre of this winter season of planning which the planners, who were to take part in the conquest of Europe by the Russian Ballet in the following spring, would remember with such pride and pleasure for the rest of their lives. It was a ground-floor flat, of a pattern common in Petersburg. The principal rooms faced the street, and the servants' quarters, kitchen and bathroom looked on to an inner courtyard. The drawing-room had paper with grey and beige stripes; there were the pictures by Lenbach, Repine and others, and a grand piano. Next door was the slightly smaller dining-room with an oval table covered by a cloth: the Jacobean chairs had not survived from the old flat on the Fontanka. It was here that meetings of the artistic committee were held. In Diaghilev's simple bedroom a light burned before an ikon. Diaghilev's old nurse was now dead and he was looked after only by Vassili Zuikov.[11]

The former colleagues of the 'World of Art' days assembled to plan the first joint season of opera and ballet. Bakst, dapper and scented, in *pince-nez*, with upturned reddish moustache, always busy with a sketch pad; Benois, bearded, also spectacled, enthusiastic, gentle and persuasive, with a slight stoop and twinkling eyes; little cynical Walter Nouvel, with a tendency to pour cold water on the more flamboyant schemes. The group was sometimes augmented by Valerien Svetlov, the critic, with his quiff of white hair;[12] by Prince Argutinsky-Dolgoroukov, a diplomat and collector of paintings and Russian porcelain;[13] by Besobrasov, the bluff old balletomane, who could drink an infinite number of cups of tea;[14] by the quiet Valentin Serov, after Repine the most distinguished living Russian painter, the only man whose word Diaghilev obeyed;[15] by the tall, lanky Tcherepnine; and by the genial Dr Sergei Botkine, who had a beautiful house near the Tauride Palace full of Peter the Great furniture;[16] and was married to the sister-in-law of Bakst.*

Then Benois introduced Fokine to the group's session: he was the one man they could not do without. The young choreographer felt the charm and power of Diaghilev's personality. He was delighted to hear that it was intended to include his 'Pavillon d'Armide' and 'Chopiniana' in the Paris repertory. Diaghilev asked him to think over some Russian themes. They needed a third ballet. Benois suggested Fokine's 'Egyptian Nights', and Diaghilev was interested, but thought Arensky's music too feeble to be given in Paris.[17]

The company, to be composed of artists borrowed from the Imperial

---

* He was not the Dr Botkine (whose name was Eugene) who attended the Tsar and died with him in Ekaterinburg. Grigoriev confuses the two men.

Theatres during their vacation, would need a *régisseur*, a manager. After two unsuccessful attempts had been made to employ officials of the Mariinsky, Fokine suggested his friend Grigoriev, who had helped him stage several ballets in the last few years; and the big, devoted and imperturbable Sergei Leonidovitch Grigoriev, who, like Atlas, was to support the whole administration of the Ballets Russes on his shoulders for twenty years, was drawn into the enterprise.

I went to see Diaghilev in a great state of excitement. Eight years had gone by since I had first seen him and heard his name. . . . I rang the bell of his flat with a certain trepidation. . . . A man with a little beard asked me to come in and said that Diaghilev would like me to wait for him. I was rather glad of the delay, which gave me the chance to calm down. . . . Diaghilev came in, and after shaking hands, asked me to sit down. Our interview was very brief. He said that Fokine had recommended me as a *régisseur*; that if I agreed he would pay me so much; and that my first duty would be to sign contracts with the artists. I agreed to the terms and he handed me the contracts. . . . He gave me a curious smile; his mouth alone smiled, the rest of his face remaining entirely serious. . . . On leaving him I felt happy: our meeting, his offer to me, and the coming visit to Paris, had completely changed my life. For the moment everything seemed interesting, eventful and full of meaning.[18]

A week later Grigoriev accompanied Fokine to a meeting of the artistic committee.

They were sitting in the dining-room . . . on the table to Diaghilev's right stood a samovar, and his valet Vassili poured out tea. There were biscuits and jam on the table, and several plates of Russian sweets. In front of every member of the company lay a sheet of paper and a pencil. Diaghilev had a large exercise book in front of him. He presided over the meeting. Fokine and I were introduced to everybody. . . . The only person I knew was Benois.

Grigoriev describes Bakst, Besobrasov, Svetlov and Nouvel. 'There was one more person, a young man, modest and attractive. His name was Mavrine: he was Diaghilev's secretary. . . .'[19]

Everyone who attended these meetings smoked except Diaghilev, Benois, Fokine and Grigoriev.[20]

Diaghilev said he wished to change the name of 'Chopiniana' to 'Les Sylphides'. Fokine argued, but gave in. At the Mariinsky, the ballet was preceded by the 'Polonaise Militaire', a survival from the days before it had become an abstract *ballet blanc*, which was clearly out of keeping. Diaghilev wished to replace this by a prelude, and everyone agreed. The Chopin pieces were also to be reorchestrated.* Benois was to design the scenery and costumes (the latter being imitated from old lithographs of Taglioni).

Another week passed and the committee assembled again. This time

---

* By Stravinsky, Grigoriev adds: but Diaghilev did not meet the composer until 6 February 1909.

Diaghilev announced startling decisions about 'Egyptian Nights', which was to be called 'Cléopâtre'. Arensky's overture was to be replaced by Taneev's from the opera 'Oresteia'. Cleopatra's entrance was to be made to music from Rimsky's 'Mlada'. The Bacchanale would be danced to 'Autumn' from Glazunov's 'Seasons'. The orgy-*divertissement* was to end with the dance of the Persian girls from 'Khovanshchina'.

He paused here for a moment, looking at our astonished faces, then smiled and continued: 'Then the end of the ballet is banal. It must be changed. The youth poisoned by Cleopatra, instead of coming to life again, must be killed for good, and his bride must sob over his lifeless body as the curtain falls. And since we have no music for such a dramatic scene, I will ask our dear Nikolai Nikolayevitch [Tcherepnine] to write this music for us.' Tcherepnine was astounded . . . we all sat silent, till at last Fokine spoke. 'Well,' he said, 'with so many changes – it will be an entirely new ballet!' 'That does not matter', said Diaghilev, 'what I want to know is whether you like the idea.' We all said yes, and he continued, 'As for you Lyovushka [Bakst], you will have to paint us a lovely *décor*.' Lyovushka instantly began tracing the plan of the scene as he visualized it and describing it in his curious guttural accent. 'There will be a huge temple on the banks of the Nile. Columns; a sultry day; the scent of the East and a great many lovely women with beautiful bodies. . . .' Diaghilev shook his head, as if at an incorrigible child; and we all laughed. . . . Diaghilev asked us all to go into the next room, where he sat at the piano with Nouvel next to him and asked us to listen to the altered score. I did not know that Diaghilev could play the piano and watched him doing so. He played very well, biting his tongue the whole time, especially when he came to difficult bits. He would frequently stop and explain to Fokine the passages in the score that had been altered. Fokine sat holding the score and marking them. When the playing was over, everyone started talking and going into the details of the ballet. Nouvel laughed in his peculiar way, remarking that what we had just heard was just a mediocre *salade russe*. Diaghilev replied that this was unavoidable; he required a third ballet; and this was the only music available. He dismissed Nouvel's criticism almost without considering it.[21]

Nouvel, of course, was right: 'Cléopâtre' was a hotch-potch, yet it would be the cause of several of the big sensations of the Paris season. It is curious to reflect that the fastidious Diaghilev presented three ballets in his 1909 season with music which was in some way unsatisfactory. 'Cléopâtre' was this astonishing *mélange* by six different composers; Tcherepnine's score for 'Le Pavillon d'Armide' was old-fashioned and derivative; and while Chopin's mazurkas, valses and preludes used in 'Les Sylphides' are music of a high order they lose their special quality when orchestrated. Even at this stage, about four months before the Paris opening, Diaghilev was predominantly interested in the operas he was going to present, and regarded the ballet merely as an additional *bonne bouche*.

Before the principal dancers could be signed up it was necessary to decide what roles there were for whom. It was inconceivable that Matilda Kchessinskaya should be left out of the expedition, as she was not only the principal ballerina of the Mariinsky, but also one of the most influential women in Russia: yet she was a dancer in the traditional style, too set in her mould to adapt herself to Fokine's new plasticity of movement, and the choreographer objected to her participation. At length, Diaghilev persuaded him to accept her in 'Le Pavillon d'Armide', which was after all a *pastiche* (however imaginatively worked out) and not a revolutionary work; but he refused to have her in 'Les Sylphides'. Anna Pavlova would be ideal for the latter; and could also dance the dramatic role of the abandoned bride, Ta-hor, in 'Cléopâtre'. Who was to be Cleopatra?

Fokine said he had a private pupil, Ida Rubinstein. 'She is tall, beautiful and plastic in her movements; and I consider her most suitable for the part.' Bakst, who knew Ida Rubinstein well, shared Fokine's opinion; and the rest of the committee were inclined to agree, except His Excellency General Besobrasov. Being a very strict balletomane, he considered that no one except professionals should be admitted into the company. . . . He was not convinced and went on grumbling for some time.[22]

Fokine himself would be the hero, Vicomte de Beaugency, in 'Le Pavillon d'Armide' and Amoun in 'Cléopâtre'. Nijinsky would again have the small dance of Armida's Favourite Slave in the former ballet and be given a similar role in the latter. Diaghilev also wanted him for the poet in 'Les Sylphides'. Adolf Bolm was to lead the dance of Polovtsian warriors in the opera 'Prince Igor'; and Pavel Gerdt (soloist to His Imperial Majesty) was to be the old Marquis-magician in 'Le Pavillon'.

We have seen that Bakst and Botkine had married two sisters, the daughters of Prince Tretiakov: a third sister was the wife of Alexander Siloti, who sponsored a series of concerts which bore his name and which he conducted himself. At the Siloti Concert on 6 February 1909, Diaghilev heard an orchestral piece by a young composer, whose 'Feu d'artifice' (Fireworks) and 'Chant Funèbre' had been played respectively at the Conservatoire in the previous year and at the Rimsky memorial concert on 31 January, on both of which occasions Diaghilev may have been present. The new piece was the Fantastic Scherzo by Igor Stravinsky. Unlike the bibulous and unpleasant Glazunov, whose comment was 'No talent, only dissonance', Diaghilev was thrilled with the new music, foresaw future collaborations over ballets and hastened to introduce himself to the composer. Stravinsky was a small man with a big nose, who had been a devoted pupil of Rimsky's. He and Diaghilev at once became friends; and the first of many commissions Diaghilev gave Stravinsky was the orchestration of Chopin's Valse Brillante for 'Les Sylphides'.

Stravinsky went with Diaghilev to visit Benois on Vassilievsky Island; and he was amused by the sight of Diaghilev making an entrance at the Leiner Restaurant on Nevsky Prospekt (where Tchaikovsky drank the glass of water which was supposed to have given him cholera), 'bowing to people right and left like Baron de Charlus'.* After a concert they would dine 'in a little sawdust delicatessen, on marinated fish, caviar, Black Sea oysters and the most delicious mushrooms in the world'.[23]

Diaghilev left for Moscow to recruit more dancers. He engaged the ballerina Vera Karalli, the fiery character dancer little Sophie Feodorova, her good-looking sister Olga – who will be seen to play a small part in the *private* history of the Russian Ballet – the handsome Mikhail Mordkine and others. He then travelled to Paris to make final arrangements for the season of opera and ballet. While he was away, on 22 February 1909, the Grand Duke Vladimir Alexandrovitch died.

The Paris season had been entirely dependent on the subsidy of 100,000 roubles which the Grand Duke had been promised from the Imperial purse. Kchessinskaya's influence had also been counted on, but in recent conversations with Diaghilev she had been shocked to learn that Armida was to be her only role. Now she decided not to appear with his company in Paris. 'I could not intercede on behalf of a project in which I was no longer taking part. I therefore asked that my requests for a subsidy should not be followed up. All Diaghilev's efforts to obtain that subsidy by other means failed.'[24] Gerdt also left the sinking ship.

When Diaghilev assembled the committee again he had to tell them that he had received a letter from the Imperial Secretariat cancelling the subsidy. After reading out the letter he banged the table and cried 'I am most indignant that the Emperor should act in such a way!'[25] He told his friends that he would try to find a way out of the difficulty and asked them to come back in a few days' time.

Diaghilev immediately returned to Paris and told Astruc that unless backing could be raised at his end the Russian season could not take place. He told him that he had a private subsidy of 50,000 francs in Russia,[26] but it is likely that he was anticipating this and lying optimistically. In the event, whatever money he did raise in Russia went to pay for the scenery and costumes. Undaunted, the French impresario applied to several financiers for help and secured the promise of 50,000 francs, only to be drawn on if the average receipts of the season fell below 25,000 francs a performance. The backers were later called upon to sign a form of *abonnement* promising

* But of course Proust had not yet invented Charlus. He did so in the course of that year.

either 'a full share' of 10,000 francs, which is what Basil Zaharoff subscribed, or 'a half-share' of 5,000 which is the sum subscribed by Henri de Rothschild, Nicolai de Bénardaky and Max Lyon. In return they were entitled to one stall at *répétitions générales*, one at first performances, admission to the theatre (presumably to stand) at all twenty performances, admission to the *foyer de la danse*, and 25 per cent of the profits, if any.[27]

Diaghilev never discussed his financial difficulties with Nijinsky (or in later years with Massine);[28] nor did he take Grigoriev into his confidence at this time. Even Benois was bothered as little as possible with talk about money; and probably the only friend to know the whole financial story was Nouvel. Even he did not know all that went on in Diaghilev's mind. Back in Petersburg Diaghilev told his committee that Comtesse Greffulhe and Mme Edwards had come to his support, not mentioning that the underwriting had all been done by Astruc's Jewish friends.[29] At this meeting, according to Grigoriev,

Diaghilev arrived looking very spry and animated. . . . In view of the reduced budget, we should only be able to give one opera in its entirety, namely 'Ivan the Terrible', and only one act of each of the two others, 'Russlan and Liudmila' and 'Prince Igor'. Each of these acts would be given on separate nights, and each followed by two ballets. . . . But since we had only three ballets decided on so far, we were still one short. What he had in mind to complete three programmes was a *grand divertissement*. We all welcomed this decision except Nouvel, who said that since we could not show the operas as intended, and since the ballet would not really impress Paris sufficiently, it would be better to give up the whole season. Diaghilev got very angry with him at this and said he had signed too many contracts in Petersburg, Moscow and Paris itself. If Nouvel was not satisfied, perhaps he would raise enough backing for us to carry out the scheme as originally planned. This argument silenced Nouvel. Besides, no one took his objection seriously. We all thought Diaghilev was getting out of his difficulties brilliantly and rejoiced on his behalf.[30]

Diaghilev's enemies had not finished with him. On 18 March the Grand Duke André Vladimirovitch wrote to his cousin the Emperor:

Dear Nicky,

As was to be expected, your telegram wrought havoc in the whole Diaghilev business, and now in his attempt to save his beastly affair he is resorting to every subterfuge, from the vilest flatteries to absolute falsehoods. According to information given me, Boris, who will be in attendance on you tomorrow, has been got at on behalf of Diaghilev, and sympathizes with his grievances. He therefore means to ask you not to restore your patronage, for that the latter no longer desires, but to allow him to continue to use the Hermitage for rehearsals, and to borrow the décor and costumes used in the Mariinsky theatre for the season in Paris. We very much hope you will not take the bait, which, let me warn you, will be cast very cleverly, nor grant permission for either the use of the Hermitage or the settings. It would only be conniving at a most unsavoury business which sullies the memory of dear Father.[31]

Permission to use the scenery and costumes of the Imperial Theatres for Diaghilev's operas was withdrawn. (The ballets and the danced and sung act of 'Prince Igor' were all having new décors.) Diaghilev's immediate reaction was to cable Astruc on 12 March asking him to find out whether the Opéra would sell back to him last year's production of 'Boris Godounov'.[32] The answer being 'No', two days later we find him telegraphing, 'If sale absolutely impossible try hiring.'[33] Not until the third week of March did he resign himself to the fact that 'Boris' could not be included in the repertory. His operas would all have to have new sets and costumes. The season was due to open in two months' time.

Through the Grand Duke Vladimir's intercession the little Hermitage Theatre, where Benois had painted his Polish scene for 'Boris', had been placed at the disposal of Diaghilev for rehearsals of the ballet. Benois adored working there.

I had grown to look upon the Hermitage Theatre, which formed part of the great Winter Palace, as something of 'my own'. . . . It was entered from the famous Picture Gallery, by crossing the Venetian Bridge over the Winter Canal. As I was almost an *habitué* of the gallery, and was at that time compiling a guide-book of the pictures, I visited it daily. Crossing over, *de plein pied*, from the gallery where I worked as an historian of art, to the delightful rooms where I became a theatrical painter, had a peculiar charm for me. I delighted in the theatre itself – a *chef d'oeuvre* of Quarenghi; admiring its ideal proportions, I tried to imagine what it looked like in the days when the great Empress was enthroned there, surrounded by her magnates and friends.[34]

Karsavina remembered in later years how tea and chocolate would be served to the dancers, when they rehearsed there, by court flunkeys.[35]

A fortnight after the Tsar received his cousin's letter, on 2 April, Benois arrived through the snow, full of anticipation, to attend a rehearsal at the Hermitage Theatre.

The artists were already in their dressing-rooms; the dressers, their arms full of foaming tulle skirts, were hurrying along the labyrinths of corridors. . . . But here I was suddenly accosted by Diaghilev's secretary, Mavrine, who imparted to me the astounding news that we were to collect all our belongings and leave the premises immediately. . . . Fortunately, half an hour later Mavrine had comforting news for us: our indefatigable leader had rushed all over the town to find some suitable rehearsing hall and had already something in view. Shortly after this came a telephone message inviting us all to a certain Catherine Hall on the Yekaterinsky Canal. I shall never forget that romantic exodus. Mavrine and I headed the

71

procession in one cab, all our artists, dressers with their baskets and stage hands followed behind in others. The long procession stretched across the whole town. The day was dismal and dull but luckily dry. The atmosphere of adventure – almost of a picnic – seemed to soften our slight feeling of shame at having been 'turned out', and when we reached the little-known Catherine Hall we liked it so much that our spirits rose immediately. It was the newly decorated building of a German Club with an impressive entrance and monumental staircase overlooked by an excellent full-length portrait of Catherine II. This seemed to us a good omen. We had just been turned out of *her* Hermitage and here she was meeting us in the new place with her famous gracious smile, full of intelligence and benevolence.[36]

Grigoriev recorded:

On 2 April at four o'clock in the afternoon there took place the first, and what may justly be called historic, rehearsal of the Diaghilev Ballet.* The entire committee were present. After I had introduced every member of the company† to Diaghilev, he addressed them in the following words, 'It gives me great pleasure to make your acquaintance. I trust that we are going to work together in harmony. I am delighted to be showing Paris the Russian Ballet for the first time. Ballet, to my mind, is one of the most lovely arts and it exists nowhere else in Europe. It will depend on you all to make it a success, and I greatly hope that you will do so.' The speech was applauded; and Diaghilev was surrounded by the members of the company, eager to ask questions.[37]

The first ballet to be rehearsed was the Polovtsian Dances from 'Prince Igor'. Fokine, realizing nothing was known about the remote Polovtsi tribe, had been reluctant to undertake this choreography, but Diaghilev had told him 'You will do it perfectly, Mikhail Mikhailovitch.' 'On other occasions,' wrote Fokine, 'I began to compose after I absorbed historical, ethnographical, musical and literary material. This time I came to the rehearsals with Borodin's music under my arm. This comprised my total armament.'[38]

Fokine worked at great speed and had almost plotted out the mass groupings of the Polovtsian girls and boys, the dance of the captive women and the charges of the Polovtsian warriors at the first rehearsal. At the end the company crowded round and applauded him.[39] Confident in their heroic employer, Diaghilev, who survived every disaster and inspired their utmost confidence, proud to be involved in the creation of Fokine's novel works of art, conscious that with artists like Benois and Bakst they would be presented to the best possible advantage to the most critical public in the world, the whole company was full of hope and joy.

---

* The companies assembled by Diaghilev could not accurately be described as 'Diaghilev Ballet' until 1911.

† But Pavlova and Rubinstein did not rehearse with the company at the Catherine Hall. Grigoriev confirmed this.

Meanwhile Diaghilev had been arranging through Astruc that the Paris firm of Fontanes should redecorate the proscenium arch and the six different levels of the Châtelet, and that the firm of Belsacq should re-upholster most of the seats.[40] Astruc was clamouring for photographs of the singers and dancers to be used for publicity.[41]

Calm and confident as he appeared in the presence of his company, Diaghilev was inwardly full of doubts as to how much of his enterprise was feasible or whether it was possible at all. He failed to secure the patronage of the Grand Duke Boris and felt at times that he had so many enemies that the success of the season would be jeopardized if Astruc even mentioned his name in the publicity.[42] He veered between optimism and pessimism. Whereas on 31 March he had telegraphed to Astruc in reply to a query about the size of the company 'A hundred walkers-on. Eighty singers. Seventy dancers. Thirty soloists,'[43] by 6 April, within a few hours of agreeing to the estimate of Fontanes and promising to send him an advance of 5,000 francs the next day, he had come to the conclusion that it would not be possible to give opera at all in Paris. He cabled, 'No opera this year. Bringing brilliant ballet company, eighty strong, best soloists, 15 performances. Repertory can be enlarged if you think necessary to take series of bookings. We shall be able to give three ballets per programme. Have we the right to mount Adam's Giselle? Start big publicity. . . .'[44] Not knowing of the weight of Diaghilev's troubles in Russia, Astruc must have thought he was drunk. His refusal to dispense with opera decided Diaghilev to go to Paris as soon as possible to discuss the matter with Astruc and if possible Chaliapine. The very day after his announcement that there would be no opera, he telegraphed to ask whether it would be possible for Geraldine Farrar to sing Marguerite in Boito's 'Mefistofele'.[45] This opera, though not Russian, would provide a role for Chaliapine: it was in fact not given during the Saison Russe.

Back in Petersburg again, Diaghilev had the pleasure of watching the new ballets of Fokine take shape at the Catherine Hall. The windowless auditorium was like that of an ordinary theatre, with rows of theatre seats, but was unusual in being on the first floor.[46] During rehearsals, Diaghilev would order meals to be served for the dancers: these were laid on a long table which was carried in and placed to the left of the orchestra stalls. He himself joined the company at these collations. It was then that Nijinsky was first observed by his fellow artists to be on friendly terms with the great man.[47]

Benois wrote:

I think that the happy atmosphere in which we prepared for our first Paris season had much to do with its subsequent success. It gave the whole company fresh vitality. From ballet-master and *premiers danseurs* to the last dancer in the *corps de ballet*, everyone seemed to unfold and become utterly devoted to the art. . . . The ballet-master's spirit must indeed have been delighted and refreshed by the *happiness* of his contact with the company. Those of us who sat watching the work from the stalls were equally happy; here, we felt something was maturing that would amaze the world.[48]

Happy or not, Diaghilev faced a new problem every day. He was dissatisfied with the publicity Astruc had secured him in the French press, suspected a hostile campaign and grew abusive in his telegrams. On 23 April he authorized Astruc to spend another 3,000 francs. There was trouble in Russia over the authors' rights in some of the operas to be performed and he pulled strings to have the question reviewed in the Duma and then brought before the Imperial Council. As late as 27 April he arranged to add two acts of Serov's opera 'Judith' to the repertory, the orgy scene and the final hymn, with Litvinne, Chaliapine, Smirnov and Zbroueva. This necessitated other changes of programme. On the 28th he was able to announce that besides Tcherepnine there would be an additional *chef d'orchestre* in the person of Emile Cooper. A second telegram on the same day gave instructions for alterations in the publicity circular. A third gave the insurance of 'Judith' at 15,000 francs. The next day he cabled about the hire of a scene-painting studio; in a second cable he refused to allow Litvinne to take part in a concert arranged by a rival management; in a third he dealt with Astruc's apprehensions that 'a certain person' should be consulted over the poster, which Diaghilev was resolved to settle without interference from anyone, in consultation with Astruc alone.[49]

The Mariinsky season ended on 1 May. Karsavina had an engagement to fulfil in Germany and was to travel to Paris from there.[50] Pavlova too was on tour and would follow in a week or two. On 2 May, under the command of 'General' Besobrasov, Nijinsky and the rest of the Russian invaders set off for the French capital. Vaslav, who had travelled all over Russia in his youth, had never been outside it before.[51]

Following a day later, Diaghilev was met at the Gare du Nord by Gabriel Astruc, to whom he announced that he had arrived without a *sou* in his pockets, that all the Russian money had been spent on scenery and costumes, and that he relied entirely upon Astruc to pay the company.

Astruc replied that he could not undertake the responsibility of paying out money he had received in subscriptions and advance bookings, because if the theatre caught fire or there was a strike or if Chaliapine was ill he would be obliged to reimburse it within twenty-four hours.

'In that case,' said Diaghilev, 'there can be no Russian season.'[52] But, of course, a compromise had to be reached.

To the Russians Paris was synonymous with Paradise: none of the Mariinsky dancers had ever been there before. Karsavina, who came from Prague a day or two after the others had arrived from Petersburg, described her emotions at the thought of the French capital. 'Paris to me was a city of eternal pleasure, dissipation and sin. So exaggerated had been my ideas of its extreme elegance that in my heart of hearts I expected the streets to be like ballroom floors and to be peopled exclusively with smart ladies, walking along with a frou-frou of silk petticoats. . . . Above all, I dreaded that I should be too provincial for Paris.'[53] She was staying at the Hôtel Normandie in the rue de l'Echelle, off the Avenue de l'Opéra.[54] Diaghilev and Nijinsky were at the Hôtel de Hollande nearby.[55] Grigoriev and most of the dancers lodged just across the river from the theatre, in various small hotels in the Quartier Latin. Grigoriev too described the feelings Paris aroused in him:

At Petersburg the weather had been cold and damp; the spring had been late; and we were quite surprised to find the sun warm in Paris and the trees in leaf. I took a room in a small hotel in the Boulevard Saint-Michel; and when I came out into the street and looked about, a wonderful feeling of happiness came over me, which was always to remain connected in my memory with this first visit of mine to Paris. I stopped for a few minutes at the corner of the street, gazing across a neighbouring garden. I could scarcely believe that my dream of seeing Paris had come true.[56]

Eleonora Nijinsky had come to Paris to see her children dance – for Bronia too was in the company – and mother and daughter stayed on the Left Bank.[57]

Since 1900 Benois, when he was in Paris, had always stayed at a quiet *maison meublée* in the rue Cambon (now occupied by Chanel's *maison de couture*) and he used to eat at Weber's in the rue Royale: now he became so entranced by the creative fever of the Russian encampment and so delighted with the company of the dancers that he could not tear himself away from them or stir far from the theatre. The restaurant Zimmer was actually part of the theatre building; either there or in humbler restaurants of the neighbourhood, the Bouillon Duval or Bouillon Boulant, he would join a group of dancers, along with Svetlov or Besobrasov or Alexis Mavrine. Three months before, at the Metropole Hotel in Moscow, Diaghilev had pointed out to Benois the good-looking younger sister of Sophie Feodorova as 'the *only* woman he could ever fall in love with'. Now Benois observed to his amusement during these lunches in the shadow of the Châtelet Theatre, where a 'melodrama with shipwreck' called 'Les Aventures de Gavroche' had just been running,[58] that Mavrine, Diaghilev's boy-friend, had fallen in love with the same lady – which gave him food for thought about the theory of elective affinities.[59]

The Russians had just over a fortnight to prepare their season. The

Moscow dancers who arrived two days after the Leningrad troupe had to be taught Fokine's ballets, scenery had to be painted and hung and the productions had to be fitted on to the Châtelet stage. The theatre itself had to be redecorated and the front five rows of stalls removed to allow for the large orchestra. Finally, the legend of the Russians had to be spread round the town. Diaghilev's special method of publicity was to bring his fashionable friends – those who could be counted on to talk in drawing-rooms – to rehearsals; this was particularly liable to enrage Fokine, and there were explosions.[60]

The Châtelet [wrote Karsavina] was well-nigh shaken to its foundations. . . . The stage-hands, gruff as they only can be in Paris, the administration pedantic and stagnant, regarded us as lunatics. . . . At the back of the stage a party of workmen hammered and sawed, making a new trap-door for Armida's canopied couch. In the auditorium a larger gang out-hammered them. 'I don't like the pit, I will have boxes instead,' decided Diaghilev. Hemmed between the rival gangs, we rehearsed. At times the din drowned the feeble tinkle of the piano. Fokine, in a white frenzy, would call out in the dark: 'Sergei Pavlovitch, for mercy's sake, I cannot work with that blasted noise.' A voice from the dark promised that all would be quiet, and entreated us to carry on. We carried on till a new interruption.[61]

When the opera singers gained possession of the stage the dancers were banished to a stifling studio under the roof.[62]

As the fatal day drew nearer, it seemed more than ever improbable that everything would be ready in time. Fokine grew thinner and thinner. There was no longer time to go out for meals. 'Our troupe remained at the theatre all day long,' recalled Karsavina. 'Diaghilev gave orders – roast fowls, pâtés, salads speedily arrived from a restaurant. Empty packing-cases made quite good tables. Picnic feeling, excellent food, young appetite – in themselves a joy. . . .'[63]

So much time was needed for rehearsals that no daily classes were held – an extremely unusual omission in the routine of a ballet company.[64] The dancers would do their warming-up by themselves, holding on to any chair-back or piece of scenery which was the right height to support them while they did their *pliés* and *battements*. Nijinsky never failed to go through a complete class by himself, and from time to time Karsavina would walk over to him to practise supported *pirouettes*.[65] Behind the backcloth there strayed a flock of sheep, needed for the last scene of 'Le Pavillon d'Armide.'[66]

Serov had made a delicate drawing in charcoal and white chalk on blue-grey paper of Pavlova in 'Les Sylphides', and although the ballerina was only to appear a fortnight after the opening of the Saison Russe this was enormously enlarged to become the Russians' first poster. Pavlova, wearing the long tulle Taglioni dress designed by Benois, and crowned with white roses, was shown in profile, head held back on the swan-like neck, with arms raised before her as if pressing back the air, drifting forward on the very front of her pointed toes. This was the first sign of the Russian ballet to burgeon on the walls of Paris.*

The Paris season was in full swing. Today we cannot but see it through the eyes of Proust. Some of the people on whom he based his principal characters were Diaghilev's warmest supporters. The great novel, however, which had been conceived during the same winter as the Ballets Russes, would only be begun in the coming summer.[67] Mme de Chevigné, with her birdlike nose and peasant speech, was to become the Duchesse de Guermantes. The old Duc de Gramont (whose third wife, Maria Ruspoli, had a son on 30 April) would contribute to the Duc de Guermantes, as Guiche, the son of his second marriage to Marguerite de Rothschild and husband of Mme Greffulhe's daughter, would to Saint-Loup.[68] Mme Greffulhe, so rich, vain and resplendent, would be the Princesse de Guermantes, and her cousin Robert de Montesquiou, that hysterical peacock, the Baron de Charlus.[69] One of the guarantors of Diaghilev's season was the Russian expatriate Nicolai de Bénardaky, who would contribute something to the character of Swann, just as would his wife, who had a *salon*, to that of Odette: and their daughter Marie, Proust's childish love, would live for ever as Gilberte.[70]

Paris was full of noble Russians, but many of these held aloof from Diaghilev, knowing of the Tsar's disapproval. The King of England arrived from Naples in a grey-green suit and brown boots. The Etienne de Beaumonts had a dinner-party. Isadora began rehearsals with the Colonne Orchestra at the Gaieté-Lyrique. The sister of her lover the American millionaire Paris Singer, Princesse Edmond de Polignac, sent out invitations to a pink and white ball on 8 June. Sarah Bernhardt was playing at her theatre, just opposite the Châtelet, and Réjane at hers; Lucien Guitry was at the Renaissance.[71]

Sales of tickets for the Saison Russe were so good that on 10 May Astruc announced extra performances.[72] While Astruc sold tickets and Diaghilev went his rounds and the world of society gave its *réceptions*, its *bals très restreints*, its *matinées de comédie*, its *soirées musicales,* its *quatre-à-sept*, innocent of coming immortality in Proust's pages, Fokine worked with the dancers.

* Very few copies of this poster exist. There is one in the Paris Opéra Museum; I saw one in Legat's studio in Hammersmith in 1939; there is one in the Edinburgh College of Art, given by Lady Juliet Duff to commemorate our Diaghilev Exhibition, which was held there in 1954. I saw one very battered copy in the Theatre Museum in Leningrad, at the corner of Alexandrinsky Square and Theatre Street; and I have a copy, given me by Lucienne Astruc, the daughter of Gabriel Astruc, which is at present on loan to the Royal Ballet School in Richmond Park and is destined for our new Museum of Theatre Arts.

Robert Brussel, the music critic, in an article in *Figaro*, described the preparations at the Châtelet and the meeting of Petersburg and Moscow dancers a few days before.

The whole company had assembled at the theatre today – the ladies from Moscow, who work in short tunics of red or green Liberty silk and those from Petersburg, who are already in *tutus*. They have not met for years, some of them since they were children or at the dancing school together, so there is kissing, gossip, reminiscing, secret confidences, laughter and exclamations mixed up with *pirouettes*. The men, who hold themselves so well, kiss the hands of the ballerinas.

The thin, highly-strung young man who looks like a fencing master in his cotton tunic is Michel Fokine, ballet-master and reformer of the Russian Ballet. This dark, slender girl with almond eyes and an ivory complexion, who evokes dreams of the gorgeous east, is Vera Karalli from Moscow. This blonde, so smart and supple in her movements, is Alexandra Baldina. That one in walking dress but with red boots, who is trying out a *Czardas* for 'Le Festin' with Michel Mordkine, is Sophie Feodorova. This elusive, thoughtful beauty who seems wafted by infinite grace is Tamara Karsavina. . . . Among the men there is the extraordinary Nijinsky, a kind of modern Vestris, but whose dazzling technique is allied to a plastic feeling and a distinction of gesture which are certainly unequalled anywhere.

Fokine claps his hands, the talking stops, the dancers take up their positions. They are going to rehearse Tcherepnine's 'Pavillon d'Armide'. Alexandre Benois, author of the libretto and designer of the sets, has something to say. The pianist Pomeranzev sight-reads an unfamiliar score, and plunges into a giddy dance with incredible skill.

They rehearse the *pas de trois* with la Karsavina, la Baldina and Nijinsky. Nijinsky dances his solo and displays his incredible elevation. The graceful Karsavina brings to the following variation a suggestion of gentle reserve. Then the imperious Karalli performs the dance of Armida. Last the stage fills with men; and in the Buffoons' dance prodigies are performed, while the exuberant Rosaï displays his fantastic steps.

All the dances are rehearsed once more, the slightest error of taste – there are no errors of technique – being the subject of severe reprimands and long digressions. Fokine's sharp eye misses nothing. Watchful, stimulating, he restrains exaggerations, demonstrates, mimes, shows everyone his steps, darts from pianist to dancer and from dancer to pianist. . . .[73]

Brussel, a charming little man in his thirties, fell in love with Karsavina and could not keep away from rehearsals at the Châtelet.[74] Fokine resented having to work in front of all Diaghilev's Paris friends, some of whom, such as the poet Anna de Noailles, Proust's 'princess from the East', Jean Cocteau, Proust's Octave, and Misia Edwards, Proust's Princess Yourbeletieff, were non-stop talkers. Diaghilev asked Grigoriev to keep an eye on these and other visitors and to see they did not interrupt the dancers' work. This he

1 Theatre Street, Petersburg. In the background the rear of the Alexandrinsky Theatre. The entrance to the Ballet School is half-way down on the right.

2 Alexandre Benois. Painting by Leon Bakst, 1898.

3 Leon Bakst.
Painting by B. Kustodiev, 1910.

4 Anna Pavlova at home, *c.* 1905.

5 Sergei Diaghilev and his nurse. Painting by Leon Bakst, 1905.

6 Nijinsky in school uniform, *c.* 1900.

7 Mikhail Obukhov.

8 Tamara Karsavina and Michel Fokine
in 'The Fisherman and the Pearl'.

9 Nijinsky in an unidentified role at the
Mariinsky Theatre.
10 Nijinsky in 'Eunice'.

11 Nijinsky in 'King Candaule'. Probably
one of the publicity photographs sent by
Diaghilev to Astruc early in 1909. It
remained in Astruc's hands and was
inherited by his daughter, who gave it to me.

12 Nijinsky in 'La Source'. Perhaps the first photograph
of Nijinsky to be published in the West.

13 Nijinsky in
'Le Pavillon d'Armide',
first version.

14 Caricature of Nijinsky's teacher,
Enrico Cecchetti, by Nicolas Legat.

found by no means easy. Young Cocteau wanted to talk to Nijinsky, who fascinated him, Robert Brussel to Karsavina. It was on Brussel that Fokine's wrath fell. There may have been an element of jealousy in this, because although Fokine was now married to Vera, anyone who had loved Karsavina once must love her for ever. Fokine flew into a rage and ordered Brussel out of the theatre. Brussel, highly offended, complained to Diaghilev, but the latter made light of the affair, giving the soft answer that turneth away wrath. 'Evidently the people in charge of the rehearsal,' he said, 'did not realize that M.Brussel had special permission to distract the dancers.'[75]*

Another music critic, M.D.Calvocoressi, who had written a book on Mussorgsky, attached himself to the company, and ran errands for the girls.[76]

On 16 May the Moscow orchestra, who were to play for the Saison Russe under their conductor Emile Cooper, arrived in Paris.[77] The *répétition générale* would be on the 19th, so time for orchestral rehearsals was short.

The two newspapers Proust read every morning were *Le Figaro* and *Le Gaulois* – the latter being the local paper of the Faubourg and even more right-wing than the former.[78] On 18 May in *Le Figaro*'s column called 'Courrier des Théâtres' he would have read the announcement:

Au Théâtre du Châtelet à 8 h. ½ très précises, soirée de gala pour la répétition générale du premier spectacle de la 'Saison russe'. . . . La toilette de soirée sera rigoureusement exigée à toutes les places du théâtre. . . . On n'entrera plus dans la salle après le lever du rideau.

The composition of the audience by Astruc and Diaghilev was in itself a work of art. Apart from the necessary drama, art and music critics, they had assembled the editors of all the principal papers and journals. Careful for the future Diaghilev had made sure of the presence of several impresarios and directors of Opera Houses. There were Broussan of the Opéra, Albert Carré of the Opéra Comique, Camille Blanc and Raoul Guinsbourg from Monte Carlo, Gatti-Casazza and Dippel from the Metropolitan, New York, Henry Russell from Boston.

Politics and the foreign service were well-represented. In the centre box Pichon, the Foreign Minister, and Nelidov, the Russian Ambassador, sat together with their wives. Also present were MM Barthou, Minister of Works (who would be assassinated with King Alexander of Yugoslavia) with his wife; Doumergue, Minister of Education; Caillaux, Finance Minister, with his wife (who was to kill Calmette, the editor of *Figaro*, in 1914); Dujardin-Beaumetz, Under-Secretary of State for the Fine Arts, who

---

* The French word *'distraire'* has the double meaning of 'to divert the attention of' and 'to amuse'.

established the Conservatoire in the rue de Madrid; and d'Estournelles de Constant who had played a part in the Franco-Russian trade pact of 1903.

In the boxes were Mme Greffuhle, who had given a dinner for the company at the Hôtel Crillon a few nights before, Mme de Chevigné and her daughter Mme Bischoffsheim, Mme Madeleine Lemaire, who had a *salon*, painted roses and was to be partly Proust's Mme Verdurin and partly Mme de Villeparisis, Princesse Alexandre de Chimay, Proust's dear friend and sister of Anna de Noailles, and the blue-stocking Mme Bulteau, the latter's great friend, who also had a literary *salon*.

Couture was represented by Mmes Caron and Paquin and M Doeillet; literature by Jean Richepin, Georges Cain, Leon and Lucien Daudet, Daniel Lesueur (the lady novelist) and Octave Mirbeau; painting and caricature by Paul Helleu, Jacques-Emile Blanche, Sem, and Jean-Louis Forain, whose work Diaghilev had reproduced in *Mir Iskustva* years before; sculpture by Rodin; music by Lalo, Fauré, Saint-Saëns, Ravel and Edouard Colonne; opera by Litvinne, Farrar, Bréval, Cavalieri, Chaliapine, de Reszke and Henri Simon; the theatre by the playwrights Francis de Croisset, Caillavet, Coolus and Henri de Rothschild ('André Pascal') – also a backer, by Clarétie, director of the Comédie Française, by Cecile Sorel, Yvette Guilbert, Jane Marnac, Louise Balthy and Rachel Boyer.

The distinction between actresses and *demi-mondaines* was not in 1909 always clear: but it is interesting to note that Louise de Mornand, whom Proust loved, was present, as also was Madeleine Carlier, one of the only three women in Cocteau's life and whom he made the heroine of 'Le Grand Ecart'.

There were four celebrated but very different dancers present – the revolutionary Isadora Duncan, Carlotta Zambelli, the current star of the Opéra, who had danced 'Coppelia' in Petersburg eight years before, Rosita Mauri, the former ballerina of the Opéra, and Mariquita, who had played at the Funambules at the time of Deburau (1845) and was at this time Ballet Mistress of the Opéra Comique.[79]

There were, however, many more dancers in the house and many more actresses than those named above, for Astruc had had the admirable idea of placing only good-looking young women in the front row of the dress-circle, and to this end distributed tickets among the *danseuses* of the Opéra and the actresses of the Comédie Française. Not a tail-coat, not a bald head to break the lustrous semicircle: only beauty, diamonds and bare shoulders. Blondes alternated with brunettes. This dazzling vision, like a basket of hot-house flowers, made such an impression on *le tout Paris* that in all theatres built after that time the dress-circle was called not *le balcon* but *la corbeille*.[80]

The new red cloth with which Diaghilev had covered the walls of the auditorium, the passages and even some of the floors, thus transforming the shabby old theatre into a bright new box, heightened the expectation of the audience.

Meanwhile, backstage, Nijinsky was in the process of becoming Armida's Favourite Slave, the inhabitant of another planet whose laws he instinctively understood and obeyed. Benois had noticed how he gave little proof at rehearsals of what he would be in performance. 'Nijinsky performed everything with unfailing precision, but there was something mechanical and automatic in his execution. At the final rehearsals he seemed to awaken from a sort of lethargy; he began to think and feel.'[81]

Nijinsky had arrived at the Châtelet between half-past six and seven. He changed into practice clothes and went through a class by himself at the back of the stage. Then he washed and put on his make-up, which took him half an hour. Order ruled in the dressing-room, where costumes were hung just so, and the sticks of make-up were lined up on the dressing-table with military precision. Finally, Vassili helped Nijinsky into his costume; he put on his white turban; and Maria Stepanovna, the wardrobe mistress, came to see if anything needed stitching.[82] Benois described how

the final metamorphosis took place when he put on his costume, about which he was always very particular, demanding that it should be an exact copy of the sketch made by the artist. At these moments the usually apathetic Vaslav became nervous and capricious. . . . He gradually began to change into another being, the one he saw in the mirror. He became reincarnated and actually *entered into* his new existence as an exceptionally attractive and poetical personality. The fact that Nijinsky's metamorphosis was predominantly subconscious is in my opinion the very proof of his genius. Only a genius – that is to say, a phenomenon that has no adequate natural explanation – could incarnate the choreographic essence of the rococo period as did Nijinsky in 'Le Pavillon d'Armide' – especially in the Paris version of my ballet.[83]

To *le tout Paris*, seething with expectancy on the other side of the red curtains, Nijinsky gave no thought.

The programme was to open with Benois' ballet, conducted not by Emile Cooper but by its composer Tcherepnine. There were several changes in 'Le Pavillon d'Armide' since the Petersburg production. A quarter of an hour had been cut, and some numbers had been rearranged to form a new *pas de trois* for Karsavina, Baldina and Nijinsky. Benois considered that he had greatly improved the sets and costumes, which, since the withdrawal of Imperial support, had all been made anew for the Paris season. 'In the St Petersburg version I had been worried by the proximity of lilac, pink and yellow, and by the somewhat motley details of the décor for the second scene. These defects I now corrected.' The perspective of topiary in Armida's garden leading to a baroque *tempietto* at the top of a splendid staircase had in Petersburg been seen at an angle: it was now presented full-on, and this enabled Valz, the wizard–stage-manager from Moscow, to contrive two gigantic water pyramids on either side.[84] The *tempietto* was replaced by a distant palace 'bosom'd high in tufted trees'.[85]

Pavlova would not arrive in Paris for a fortnight, owing to her European tour, and Armida was to be danced on this night and on the night following by Karalli, whom Benois thought 'a good technician and a very beautiful woman, but a pale performer lacking personality'.[86] Mordkine, likewise from Moscow, took Gerdt's part as René de Beaugency. 'He was far too strong and vigorous a dancer for the part and lacked the poetical tenderness which should be a fundamental quality of my hero. But in Paris my ballet gained from the change in the part of the Marquis, which was taken by Bulgakov, in the place of Solianikov. In the latter part of the role, where the ancient Marquis is transformed into the magnificent wizard Hidraot, Bulgakov's interpretation was particularly successful.'[87] The imperfect casting of the hero and heroine made no difference to the success of the ballet, for, as we shall see, the greatest triumphs were not scored by them.

Benois had conceived his ballet as a glorification of 'that most French of epochs, the eighteenth century': he, the descendant of French, Germans and Venetians, and bearing a French name, took pride in showing Parisians that he understood the *style noble* of Versailles better than they did.

Those who were used to the sickly sweetness invariably used in Paris theatres to characterize the Rococo epoch (as for instance the production of 'Manon' at the Opéra Comique) found our colours too vivid and the grace of our dancers too pretentious. But to those who really understood Versailles, the Sèvres china, the tapestries, the gilt apartments of the palaces and the architectural parks, our 'Pavillon d'Armide' was a revelation. Among our most enthusiastic friends were Robert de Montesquiou and Henri de Régnier* himself.[88]

To be exact, 'Le Pavillon' mixed the baroque and rococo styles, Louis XIV and Louis XV, seventeenth and eighteenth centuries – but so, in the course of time, had Versailles itself.

The Russian element in the production consisted in the free way the scenery was painted, Russian designers and scene-painters having caught an element of vigour from the Impressionists before their counterparts at the Opéra and the Opéra Comique. This vigour corresponded to the suppressed passion contained in the Russian dancers' use of the classical vocabulary. Classical dancing at the Paris Opéra in 1909 consisted of a little Italian virtuosity tricked out with a lot of French *coquetterie*. Then, of course, there

---

* The Parnassian poet, son-in-law of Hérédia, had published his poems about Versailles, 'La Cité des eaux', seven years before.

were Russian elements in the music of 'Le Pavillon', and a real Russian character dance for the Buffoons.

Yet a further enrichment of this classical ballet was its romanticism. This was the original, paradoxical and typically Benois element. The story which had given the painter the idea for his ballet had been Théophile Gautier's *Omphale*, and though this was set in a rococo pavilion and dealt with an animated Beauvais tapestry,* it was romantic and Hoffmannesque: it was a mysterious and rather erotic ghost story. One other element removed Benois' work from the conventional ballet of the period and related it to literature, or rather to the drama: there was no dancing, except the Dance of the Hours, in the first scene and none at all in the last. A mime-play combining mystery and humour in the manner of 'The Magic Flute' encased the choreography.

Tcherepnine mounts his rostrum.[89] There is a ghostly roll on the kettle-drums and the clarinet and strings begin a mysterious introduction. Dark chords played *pianissimo* bring up the curtain on the dimly lit interior of a baroque pavilion. 'Tall windows with an ornate *oeil-de-boeuf* over each of them alternate with columns of polished marble, while the plaster modelling above the central niche represents allegorical figures resting on clouds and supporting a sumptuous canopy adorned with feathers which overhangs the magic Gobelins.'[90] In front of the latter stands a giant ormolu clock, with the figures of Time and Love, impersonated by motionless dancers. To the right, a bed in a curtained alcove and a dressing-table. Lanterns are seen through the windows and lackeys open up the pavilion, preceding the entrance of the sinister old Marquis and his benighted guest, Vicomte René, who is accompanied by his valet, carrying luggage. With old-fashioned and exaggerated courtesy the host, who is dressed in the fashion of the last years of Louis XIV, welcomes young René, whose clothes proclaim the date of the action to be nearer the end of the century. René removes his caped overcoat and shakes the rain off it. The servants bring candelabra, the valet (played by Grigoriev) unpacks. The Marquis takes one of the candlesticks and shows René the tapestry. Without using the old conventional sign language (Fokine's anathema) he mimes that the lady represented in the Gobelins, who sits sadly holding a scarf, surrounded by her attendants, is his daughter dead long since, for love of whom three men took their lives. René is struck by her beauty. The host bows his way out and René disappears into the alcove to go to bed. Moonlight floods the room. At first, fascinated by the tapestry, René remains wakeful, but he sleeps at last. The figure of Time (or Saturn) on the clock reverses his hour-glass, and in a brief mime-scene is overcome by Love (Cupid). Midnight strikes, the twelve hours (girls dressed as boys)

* For reasons of his own Benois changed Beauvais to Gobelins.

step down from the clock and dance a mechanical *andantino* punctuated by chords on harp and celesta. A chromatic theme is heard. This awakens René, who gets up, looks at the tapestry, then returns to bed. The theme sounds again. René is afraid. He considers running away but is reluctant to make a fool of himself. The Gobelins rolls up into its frame, and a living image of the Marquis's daughter, in fact the sorceress Armida, in the same pose with the scarf, surrounded by her courtiers, is seen behind it. Armida places her scarf round the neck of an imaginary Rinaldo, then starts on realizing that her lover is not there. Pitifully she asks the women on her left where he is gone. They reply with sad hopeless gestures. She asks the men on her right the same question and receives the same negative answer. To a sobbing tune, whose rising and falling represents alternate hope and despair, Armida comes down from her frame, seems to see Rinaldo, then shakes her head in disappointment. She tells her ladies to play their harps, and the lament ends with her falling mournfully on one knee.

Meanwhile René, clutching his dressing-gown about him, has crept stealthily around behind Armida. Now comes the big moment. As she sinks on her knee he stretches out his arms to raise her from the ground. She starts, recognizes in him her long-lost Rinaldo and greets him with rapture. René's night clothes are whisked down a trap, and he is revealed in periwig and heroic 'Roman' costume of the Louis XIV period, his whole form suddenly imbued by the baroque style, so that he stands gesturing towards Armida like a splendid statue. At the same time, to a mounting frenzy in the orchestra the walls of the pavilion disappear and we are out-of-doors in brilliant sunlight. Framed by a natural arch of boskage – the only romantic-rococo-pastoral element in the décor, suggestive of Fragonard or Hubert Robert – rears up the splendid symmetry of Armida's garden. It is an essay in curves and obelisks. The dancing-area is defined by a semicircle of dark topiary, while Armida's palace, rising from undulant woods in the distance, is circular behind its portico, and recalls in its fantasy the Piedmontese palaces of Juvara – particularly as it is backed by Alps. The palace is topped by an obelisk or spire, like Sacharov's Admiralty in Petersburg; the topiary looms into obelisks like Tiepolo's idea of pyramids; and the two tall fountains on either side of the stage (fed from the nearby Seine), whose splashing mingles with the music, rise in a similar pointed form. It is Versailles with a difference.

At the top of the steps at the back stands a magnificent figure, the old Marquis transformed into a potent magician, King Hidraot. He wears a long frogged golden mantle and a towering mitred headdress surmounted by blue ostrich feathers. He waves his tall staff in indication that it is he who has effected this magic transformation and comes slowly down the steps.

Armida leads Rinaldo across the stage. More courtiers appear and form circular groups. It is Fokine's and Benois' intention that the predominantly pink- and green-clad court – best seen from high up in the theatre – should suggest the pattern of an Aubusson carpet. A further piled-up group of dancers comes up out of the ground. This includes Nubians with tall feather fans. Armida herself wears a Nattier-blue mantle sewn with jewels and trimmed with gold tassels, opening over a plain white muslin skirt. Her white and gold turban is bound with pearls. The Court marches in procession and the enchantress conducts her lover to a dais on the left, from which they will watch the *divertissement*.

The dances which follow include a Brahmsian Valse Noble for eight men and eight women, a grotesque Oriental Bacchanale for eight women (including Fokina, Bronislava Nijinska, Schollar and Tchernicheva), with interjections on the xylophone, and a comic dance in which six limping and hideous monsters discover some beautiful masks, with ringlets made of wood shavings, and with whose aid they delude some young attractive witches to take part in a rather formal Sabbath and go off quite happy. These numbers are varied by processions crossing the stage, one of which stately regroupings is accompanied by solemn Handelian measures for strings, with trumpet calls.

The most spectacular number, however, is the *pas de trois* danced by two of Armida's Confidantes, Karsavina and Baldina, and her Favourite Slave, Nijinsky. His white, yellow and silver costume trimmed with festoons of silk, lace ruffles and ermine tails is a simplified form of the courtly male dancing costume of the eighteenth century, such as Boquet designed, with a *tonnelet* or wired skirt – an exaggerated development of the kilt worn under the stylized Roman armour of dancers in the time of Louis XIV – and knee-breeches. On his head he wears a white silk turban with an ostrich feather: round his neck, high up under the chin, a jewelled band. The two ladies wear yellow and gold. 'It is a marvellous moment [to quote Geoffrey Whitworth] when Nijinsky makes his first and curiously modest entrance into that wonderful scene of pink and green and blue . . .'.[91] The opening section of the *pas de trois* when all three dance together is performed to a lilting tune on the plaintive cor anglais; and the Parisians are suddenly aware as the dancers rise, fall, beat and spin that they have never seen dancing of this calibre before. There is a growing murmur of admiration. At the end of this number the dancers leave the stage, Nijinsky being the last to exit, before reappearing for his solo. Tonight, excited by the warmth of the public's reaction, instead of walking he chooses to leap off. He soars up and up as if he were flying into the tree-tops, and no one sees him beginning to come down. No living Parisian has ever beheld such a leap. The gasps of incredulity turn to a thunder of applause.[92] Vestris has returned to France.

85

The tune for Nijinsky's solo is banal, a typical male variation, scored for full orchestra, *allegro risoluto*. He begins by rising on half point and leaping sideways across the stage. These high jumps alternate with *pirouettes*. Then he performs a simpler but peculiarly elegant movement (which is later to be much copied) of inclining forward and stroking his left leg with his right hand, while his left arm is extended behind him. These stylized *révérences*, repeated twice in different directions, alternate with *cabrioles*. As Nijinsky dances he hears an unfamiliar disturbance in the audience, and is afraid. The noise grows louder. At the end of his dance the cheering breaks out.[93]

The role of the Favourite Slave is a dancing one, inserted by Fokine into his ballet to show off Nijinsky's virtuosity: it is not developed dramatically and plays no part in the story of the subjected René, yet by the projection of some intensity of feeling Nijinsky transforms the whole scene. To quote Geoffrey Whitworth again:

The vivid radiant boy is also the hierophant of mysteries, and in the glamour of his presence 'Armide' comes to seem not merely a matchless display of lovely form in lovely motion, but also a type of the supreme functioning of a state of being most strange and utterly alien from our own. The court of Armide, one believes, is part of a definite and settled polity, with its own laws, its own customs and its own business from day to day. . . . The secret of this effect . . . partly lies in . . . the conviction of *aloofness* which Nijinsky brings to his rendering. . . .[94]

There follows a solo for Baldina, which begins stately and accelerates towards the end, her music being punctuated by brief pauses which allow her to hold striking attitudes.[95]

Karsavina's dance is a gay little *allegro* with celesta and bells (like the Sugar Plum Fairy's solo in 'Casse-noisette') and the combination of her nimble foot-work, her poetic *port de bras*, her lustrous exotic beauty and a magic smile which lights up her whole face, makes an instantaneous impression on the susceptible public of *le tout Paris*. Pirouettes – arms held open, one up, one down, with the head tilted back towards the upheld arm; then the arms and *épaulement* are reversed; and finally the arms come together *en couronne*, tellingly tilted – the whole miniature turned into a masterpiece by the marriage of expression and *épaulement*, which casts a spell. She finishes with a *diagonale* of tripping steps, looking down mischievously with raised eyebrows at her hands held at waist level in front of her, finger-tips almost touching; and comes to rest in an eighteenth-century pose.* Once more Tcherepnine has to wait for the applause to subside before he can begin the coda.[96]

---

* Mme Karsavina's demonstration of this dance, seated as she was in a chair, was one of the most expressive pieces of abstract dance the author ever saw.

Nijinsky leaps on to a swinging tune on clarinets and strings. The two girls take over at a slower pace, then all three join together for the brilliant conclusion of the *pas de trois*, accompanied by the full orchestra *fortissimo*.

The audience has been spellbound by the spectacle and astonished by the revelation of what classical dancing can be. Before the end of the scene they have still one more surprise in store – their first sight of Russian character dancing. The dance of Buffoons, with which the *divertissement* ends, is a high-speed eccentric number to a jerky comic tune, whose rhythm is marked by the tambourine and triangle; and, according to Fokine, it is the most difficult dance, technically, he ever invented. This is led by Nijinsky's old class-mate Rosaï, who performs the cobbler's step, spins in a crouched position, leaps high in the air while he does *entrechats* with his knees, then lands on one knee. The other six boys execute a movement which seems equally improbable, crashing to the floor with crossed legs *à la Turque*, then instantaneously rebounding to catch each other by the feet as they turn in the air.[97] Coming as a climax to what has gone before this excites the public to frenzy and Rosaï enjoys an acclamation as great as Nijinsky's.*

Karalli comes down from her throne to dance a graceful *allegretto* with flute and harp accompaniment and chiming bells. This is her *pas d'écharpe*, her duet with the magic golden scarf. In the ensuing *pas de deux* to a noble tune she completes her spell by looping the scarf round René. After a waltz of the whole Court Armida and Rinaldo have long trains hung on their shoulders, and with these borne behind them by little pages they walk in solemn procession, as if celebrating their union, to a stately tune with harp *glissandi*.

There has been 'a lot of beautiful walking'[98] throughout this scene; now, as the lights dim and the scene changes back to the interior of the pavilion, Karalli and Mordkine mount the staircase at the back, which is now concealed by the walls of the pavilion and step, together with a few courtiers, into the frame of the Gobelins. The group formed within the frame is the same as that at the beginning, except that Armida's gold scarf enfolds her lover. As the light grows even dimmer, the true 'Gobelins' descends to hide them. In this painted composition, of course, there is no Rinaldo.

The stage, with its curtained alcove in which René is supposed to be sleeping, but in which Mordkine is in fact changing back into his travelling clothes, is now almost empty for three minutes, while Tcherepnine's Sunrise and Pastoral, which amounts to an interlude, is played. First, horn calls and chords on flute and oboe create, as it were, a perspective of

* Fokine claimed it was greater. But of course the more obvious virtuosity of character dancing is often more loudly applauded than the artistry of classical dancing. (This was Mme Bronislava Nijinska's comment.)

landscape as in Delibes's 'Sylvia', suggesting that the pavilion is *au fond des bois*. There are sudden arpeggios on the harp, which get quicker and louder until, with a clash of cymbals and bells, the sun rises. The shepherd's pipe is heard, and the texture of the music thickens as the shepherd himself with his shepherdess drive their flock past outside the windows; the piece closes with a *diminuendo* as they disappear into the distance. Tcherepnine's well-orchestrated number looks backward to the Pastoral Symphony and the last act of 'Tristan', and forward to 'Daphnis et Chloë' (whose composer is in the audience).

Now the drama is to be concluded. The bustle of the servants coming to speed René on his way, represented by violins *tremolando*, is rendered sinister by the perversion on bass clarinet and cello of a tune heard earlier, which represents the old Marquis. The latter greets René, who is still under the influence of what he believes to be a dream. Then the Marquis points out the golden scarf hanging on the clock. Aghast, René realizes he is now in fact the slave of the witch Armida. He strikes his brow; and to crashing chromatics, with dominant brass, he falls dead at the old man's feet.

Jean Cocteau.
Drawing by Leon Bakst.

When the curtain came down on 'Le Pavillon d'Armide' there was a storm of applause, and the acclamations continued for some minutes. Mordkine led forward Karalli, and Nijinsky led forward Karsavina and Baldina. Men never took a call without their partners. When the house lights went up, the gentlemen in the stalls, as was usual, rose to their feet, snapped open their silk hats, put them on, lifted their opera-glasses to quiz the ladies in the boxes and raised their hats to those whose eyes they caught.[99] The caricaturist Sem moved down to the front row of the dress-circle to talk to one of the sixty-three beauties assembled there, but Astruc had given orders that no member of the male sex should mar the unity of his diamond horseshoe, and Sem was politely requested to move on by a *garde municipal*.[100] Not every member of this audience, as Jean-Louis Vaudoyer remembered in later years, was carried away by the Russians,[101] and we can imagine that certain dancers of the Opéra on the one hand, and Isadora Duncan on the other, had their reservations. But to the majority it had been revealed that ballet was a serious art, as it had been in the days of Taglioni, and that a male dancer could be a supreme artist. Robert de Montesquiou extolled the perfection of the Russians in his loud falsetto voice, waving his gold-topped cane,[102] the sceptre with which he ruled Paris society. Jean Cocteau moved from box to box, preaching the gospel according to Diaghilev. Mme de Chevigné, wearing her diamond dog-collar, held court.*

If we did not know that Diaghilev's repertory for this season was less the result of careful planning than of making do with existing works and embellishing them, we should salute the placing of the Polovtsian act of the opera 'Prince Igor' after 'Le Pavillon' as a master-stroke of programme-building: no two works could be more different or more calculated to display the range of the Russians. The public was transported on a magic carpet from the splendours of a fairy-tale Versailles to the remote solitudes of the Asiatic steppes.

To give an effect of immensity and desolation Nicolas Roerich has abolished wings and painted his scene on a curved canvas. Although Gordon Craig deals in verticals rather than horizontals, there is something Craigish about the simplicity and power of Roerich's scene. It is nearly all sky – a mottled golden sky barred with pink clouds. Against this are silhouetted some low rolling grey-green hills, parted by a broad meandering river, and

---

* Cocteau, still comparatively unknown in Paris society, had not yet been introduced to Mme de Chevigné, though they lived in the same house. He was longing to meet this bluff lady, who although she had no money and had never opened a book, was somehow a dominant figure in the Faubourg; a few months after the Russian season he lay in wait for her on the staircase of their house. As she came downstairs he snatched up her poodle and began caressing it effusively. Mme de Chevigné was equal to the occasion: she barked out 'Take care or your powder will come off all over him!' But they became friends later. (Told to me by Jean Hugo.)

half-hidden by the russet beehive tents of the Polovtsi. As an evocation of the desolate heart of a vast continent it is superb.

From the moment the curtain rises the audience are seized by a sense of the utter strangeness of this unknown land between Persia, Tartary and China, sparsely populated by warring tribes. The oriental colour of Borodin's music is evident from the languorous opening song of the girls attendant on Khontchakovna, the Khan's daughter. There are dancing girls as well as singing girls, and, led by Sophie Feodorova, these perform a contrasting *presto* number, the only dance which will occur until Fokine's choreographic frenzies are let loose at the end of the act. Khontchakovna, sung by Petrenko, delivers her love-starved *cavatina* 'Now the daylight dies'. Some Russian prisoners are led by, returning from labour. Khontchakovna orders her women to give them a drink, and they sing their thanks. There is a patrol of Polovtsian soldiers. Night falls. Now appears Vladimir, Prince Igor's son, a tenor role sung by Smirnov. He and the Polovtsian princess are in love. His aria 'Daylight is fading' is followed by their passionate duet. They part, and Prince Igor comes on to lament his captivity – this is the baritone Charonov. The wheedling Ovlour offers to help him escape, but he refuses. Now follows the entry of the great Khan Khontchak himself in the person of the bass Zaparojetz, and a heroic dialogue ensues in which the Tartar chieftain offers to grant any wish which will make his prisoner's captivity more tolerable, while the Russian declares that he lacks nothing but liberty. This too the Khan is willing to grant Igor if the latter will swear to make war against him no more. Igor cannot promise this and his honourable frankness spurs the Khan to summon his tribesmen, their children and captive slaves to provide for Igor the danced diversion which in Fokine's arrangement will reverberate through Europe and America for many years to come. A barbaric crowd invades the stage. 'Ferocious of aspect, their faces smeared with soot and mud, their coats green and mottled red and ochre, their trousers striped in bright hues, one is reminded of a lair of wild beasts rather than a camp of human beings.'[103]

First the oriental slave girls undulate with their crimson and purple veils to the languid, voluptuous tune on the oboe and cor anglais, which is taken up by the violins and has woodwind and harp accompaniment. After a quicker dance of wild tribesmen, pounding timpani bring on the Khan's warriors, led by Bolm, who charge and leap, brandishing their bows, to the sound of chorus and full orchestra. Starting on a breathless off-beat their music climbs the scale until the top note screams out on strings and woodwind playing in their highest register. The slave girls hover and at the end of their number the warriors fling them over their shoulders. There is a jaunty dance of boys, who have wooden cups attached above their knees and wooden clappers on their hands, which they strike together as they leap and run on the spot and kick up their legs behind them: this builds up to a second entry of the warriors, again matched by the chorus. From now on boys, girls, slaves and warriors, with their appropriate melodies, alternate in swift succession. The singers, praising the Khan, provide a sustaining bourdon to the rapid rhythms of the dancers, and the scene ends with an overpowering climax of movement and sound. At the head of his warriors Bolm charges at the audience, spins in the air and crashes to the ground on one knee, firing his bow.

In the following interval the audience launched a counter-invasion. 'I realized,' Karsavina recalled, 'something unusual was happening to me and around me: something to which I could give no name, so unexpected, so enormous as to frighten almost. My senses were all blurred that night. The familiar barriers between the stage and the audience were broken. The side doors with their ingenious locks and stern notices – of no avail. . . . The stage was so crowded with spectators that there was hardly room to move.'[104] Karsavina and Nijinsky had had a full hour – the duration of the second act of 'Prince Igor' – to change their costumes for the final *divertissement*. 'To perform our usual rite of practising our steps and lifts before going on, Nijinsky and I had to dodge. Hundreds of eyes followed us about. . . . "He is a prodigy" and awed whispers "C'est elle!" '[105] In the middle of the hubbub Reynaldo Hahn ran into Lucien Daudet, and lisped, with calculated absurdity, 'C'est joli, ces danses du Poitou.'[106]

'Le Festin' is only a *divertissement,* but the Russian music – although by various composers – and the fact that it is made up of character or national dances – with the exception of one *pas de deux* – give it a certain unity. Since it is pretending to be a ballet (and for all the Paris public knows it may be the traditional finale of every performance in Petersburg or Moscow) Fokine will not allow his dancers to take calls after the individual numbers. The setting of 'Le Festin' is Korovine's first act of 'Russlan', designed for the Mariinsky and painted afresh for Paris – a medieval Russian banqueting hall. The costumes are by Bakst, Benois, Bilibine and Korovine. First the company process on stage to Rimsky's march from the last act of 'Coq d'or'. Then follows the Georgian Lesghinka from 'Russlan' adapted by Fokine from Petipa, danced by Fokina and ten men. Next comes the *pas de deux* for Karsavina and Nijinsky, which Kchessinskaya would have danced if she had come to Paris and which is curiously entitled 'L'Oiseau de feu',*

---

* I do not believe that this was, as Fokine thought, because Diaghilev had announced a ballet called 'L'Oiseau de feu' which was not ready. I do not think he had announced it, nor did he commission it successively from Liadov and Stravinsky until the end of 1909.

and which was really Petipa's Blue Bird number from the last act of 'La Belle au bois dormant'.

The fantastic costumes of Bakst obligingly turn Karsavina into the bird (whereas it is really the man who is the Blue Bird in Petipa's *divertissement*) with flaming ostrich feathers on headdress and skirt, and Nijinsky into a turbaned prince with a mustard, lime-green and gold tunic sewn with pearls and topaz. The dazzling choreography creates an immediate impression, which Michael, the company's courier, is to describe afterwards in his own vivid way: 'But when those two came on, Good Lord! I have never seen such a public. You would have thought their seats were on fire.'[107] So Karsavina balances and spins and flutters in *pas de bourrée* and Nijinsky swings through the wonderful *diagonale* of *cabrioles* and *brisés volés*. Difficult indeed to obey the orders of the ruthless Fokine and not to acknowledge the ovation which follows this dance.

A Czardas by Gorsky arranged to music of Glazunov is danced by the fiery Sophie Feodorova with Mordkine. Olga Feodorova and Kremnev lead a Hopak of Mussorgsky from 'The Fair at Sorochinsk', and a Glinka Mazurka from 'A Life for the Tsar' is danced by four couples. Rosaï scores for the second time in the evening with a solo Trepak to the music of the Buffoons' Dance from 'Casse-noisette'. Karalli and Mordkine lead the celebrated Grand Pas Classique Hongrois, in which Nijinsky dances a subordinate role, from Glazunov's 'Raimonda', invented by Petipa. The Finale is danced to the march from Tchaikovsky's Second Symphony; and the programme is over.

But the evening was not over. Karsavina wrote:

All was happy confusion; crowds again, somebody exquisitely dressed staunched the blood trickling down my arm with a cobwebby handkerchief – I had cut myself against Nijinsky's jewelled tunic; Diaghilev picking his way through groups of people, calling 'Where is she? – I must embrace her.' From that day he always called us his children. Somebody was asking Nijinsky if it was difficult to stay in the air as he did while jumping; he did not understand at first, and then very obligingly: 'No! No! not difficult. You have to just go up and then pause a little up there.'[108]

Nijinsky took off his costume, removed his make-up; and went out to supper and fame.

Next morning dawned hot and beautiful, and *Le Figaro* exclaimed about the size and brilliance of the audience at the Châtelet and the transformation of the theatre, comparing the occasion to a *fête* at Versailles in the days of the Empire:[109] but criticism was postponed until after the official première on the 19th, which was only marred by Rosaï hurting his leg in the Buffoons' Dance and having to be replaced in the Trepak. Thursday the 20th was Ascension Day and there was no performance. Karsavina describes how a gruff and cynical old man called Oneguine, a political exile to whom she had been sent an introduction and who had taken her under his wing, brought her the newspapers.

He sat with me as I had my coffee, himself refusing to share the meal. I wore the wrap of double usage, that of opera cloak and dressing-gown, and, as usual, darned stockings. Both items memorable through Oneguine's sneers. I learned amazing things about myself this morning, and that I was 'La Karsavina'. There was quite an extemporaneous feeling of wonder in me as at suddenly perceiving my double. . . .[110]

Brussel's article in *Le Figaro* was mostly about the music: but he found room to refer to 'Mme Karsavina, whose subtle technique and marvellous sense of music are combined with expressive grace and poetic feeling and whose success in "L'Oiseau de feu" stopped the show. . . .' He went on to praise Nijinsky's extraordinary suppleness and dizzy technique.[111] Other writers called Nijinsky 'Vestris', 'God of the dance', 'prodigy'.[112] One critic, coached by Diaghilev perhaps, became so technical as to describe how Nijinsky could execute *entrechat-dix* and *triples tours en l'air*.[113] In *Commedia* Henri Gauthier-Villars (the husband of Colette) wrote:

The blond and queenly Baldina, Mlle Karsavina of the irresistible charm, the magic of the Feodorovas – I would celebrate them all if I did not feel bound above all to proclaim my admiration for the dancer Nijinsky, wonder of wonders, breaker of the record in *entrechats*. . . . Yesterday when he took off so slowly and elegantly, describing a trajectory of $4\frac{1}{2}$ metres and landing noiselessly in the wings an incredulous *Ah*! burst from the ladies. It was truly *le Bond des Soupirs*.[114]*

Once the *répétition générale* and the première were over, although there were two other ballets to be rehearsed, it was possible for the company to look around them and enjoy Paris. Nijinsky did a full class every morning alone by himself, rehearsed and had a late lunch. Then he would either go with Diaghilev to the Louvre, drive in the Bois with Bakst or Nouvel, have a massage or sleep. After the performance Diaghilev usually entertained his committee of friends at Larue or Viel – Benois, Bakst, Roerich, Nouvel, Besobrasov, Svetlov, Argutinsky – and Nijinsky began to appear at these gatherings, listening in silence while the older men discussed the season and planned new projects.[115]

Meanwhile, two elopements took place which changed the history of the Russian Ballet. Karalli ran off with the tenor Sobinov and Mavrine ran off with Olga Feodorova. Whether Karalli's disappearance had something to do with Karsavina's success we can only surmise. There is reason to believe she was jealous of her[116] – and, after all, one can have an affair with a tenor without breaking one's contract. Karsavina became the company's star and

---

* Pun on *Le Pont des Soupirs* – the Bridge of Sighs.

on 25 May, six days before Pavlova arrived, she danced the role of Armida opposite Bolm, who had been much scolded by Fokine for his clumsiness in partnering during rehearsal. She was replaced in the *pas de trois* by Fokine's sister-in-law, Alexandra Feodorova: but in the role of Armida she was allowed to retain her old solo from the *pas de trois*, because it suited her and she considered it the most effective choreography in the ballet; and Feodorova danced something else. Mavrine had more reason to take himself off, as it was clearly awkward to continue as Diaghilev's official friend while enjoying a passionate romance with the one woman who had ever attracted Diaghilev. The latter was already more interested in Vaslav than Alexis, but his pride was hurt at his favourite's treachery. He later forgave him, and was to employ Olga Feodorova again.

Paris, that magic season between spring and summer, the triumph of Russian art and the adulation in which the dancers basked – everything went to the head: so that even if one did not fall in love and elope one felt unusually light-headed and bought, perhaps, an expensive hat. Valz, the *chef machiniste* and miracle worker from Moscow, who was an elderly lady-killer with dyed moustache and high heels, gave an extravagant dinner for twenty, including all his favourite *danseuses*, at Le Doyen in the Champs-Elysées.[117] It is a curious fact that in this sort of highly charged atmosphere, in which love flourishes, a man's passion can just as well be directed towards one person as another. Where all seems delightful and desirable there is an element of chance in whom we fall for. Although Diaghilev was more than ever attracted to the withdrawn and serious-minded Nijinsky, he was also a bit in love with Karsavina, his new star, whose intelligence appealed to him as well as her beauty.[118] One sunny morning she was practising alone on the dark and empty stage, when Diaghilev appeared and said 'We are all living in the witchery of Armida's groves. The very air round the Russian season is intoxicated.'[119]

Dr Botkine drove Karsavina to Versailles. It was in the Bosquet d'Apollon that the ballerina learnt a lesson. 'The sun, merciless in the clipped walks of the formal avenues, here only dappled the marble of the fountain through the thick foliage.' Karsavina, virtuous herself in spite of all her adorers, had been worried about Diaghilev's homosexuality, a side of life she had only recently become aware of. Botkine said, 'It is a cruel misjudgement to give an ugly name to what is, after all, but a freak of nature.' From his wide experience of human beings, he gave her examples of homosexuals who had lived good lives. 'Botkine made me see that it was the quality of love that makes it beautiful, no matter who the object. The quality of Diaghilev's affections was single-hearted, true and deep, bury them as he would beneath his blasé mask.'[120]

Apart from such functions as an official party given for the company by Briand at the Quai d'Orsay, and at which they performed Russian dances, Ida Rubinstein, Karsavina and Nijinsky were the only dancers who went out in society. Montesquiou became Ida's devoted knight and carried her off to his Pavillon at Neuilly. Karsavina's life was overcrowded with admiration. When she was not being driven to Fontainebleau by Robert Brussel in a hired car filled with all the cushions from his flat, another beau was escorting her to a party at Misia Sert's house on the Quai Voltaire, from which Proust, shy, polite and green as a ghost, would drive her home. Nor was Karsavina excluded by Diaghilev from gatherings predominantly male. At one of these she observed Nijinsky enthralled by Emmanuel Bibesco's collection of paintings by Gauguin. 'Look at that strength!' he said.[121] Vaslav at once felt an affinity with the painter of Polynesian mysteries, and Gauguin's influence was to mould his thought when he became a choreographer in later years.

Because the success of the Russians was partly due to the new miracle of male dancing, there was something scandalous about it. Since the Romantic period it had been the woman, the Muse, the diva, the ballerina who had been worshipped: to admire a man for his grace and beauty was unheard-of and in some circles unthinkable.[122] The scandal of Count Eulenberg's disgrace at the Kaiser's court in the previous year was fresh in people's minds, and it was only nine years since Oscar Wilde had come to an appropriately bad end in Paris. In 1838 Théophile Gautier, deploring the nasty muscular male dancers of his period, intruders in the fairy paradise of the ballet he loved, had disliked them for their excessive masculinity.[123] What would he have thought of the more epicene apparition of Nijinsky in the ballet inspired by his short story? As a matter of fact, if there was a homosexual conspiracy in the air to seduce the public by male charms – and Diaghilev had become overnight a leading figure of the Paris homosexual set, and it rather went to his head[124] – a conspiracy to exalt the male dancer – or rather, Nijinsky, with whom Diaghilev was now in love – at the expense of the ballerina, Gautier cannot be wholly cleared of collusion. In his story *Omphale*, which gave Benois the idea for 'Armida', the Beauvais tapestry represents a long-since-dead Marquis and Marquise in the guise of Hercules and Omphale. Now, Hercules was condemned by the oracle to three years hard labour, and he chose to be the servant of Omphale. In order to please his lovely mistress – or, as some think, himself – he performed his duty in female attire. It made a change, no doubt, from that lion-skin and club. In the tapestry imagined by Gautier the Marquis-Hercules is decked in silk *panniers*, his neck festooned with ribbons, rosettes and ropes of pearls. He is spinning flax, his little finger 'cocked with peculiar grace'. When the Marquise steps out of the tapestry at night to teach the facts of life to the youth who has been accommodated in the pavilion, he asks her, 'But what will your husband say?' and she replies, laughing, 'Nothing. . . . He's the most understanding of husbands!' From this and from the Marquis's decision to be depicted *en travesti*, with pearls, we are meant by Gautier to understand that his inclinations are distinctly *rococo*. Then, surely when a role was inserted in the existing ballet scenario of 'Armida' simply to show off Nijinsky, must it not have been a memory, conscious or unconscious, of Gautier's girlish and domesticated Hercules that prompted Benois to call the new character 'Armida's Favourite *Slave*'? And was not the costume Benois then designed for Nijinsky related to that of the Marquis which Gautier painted only in words? One final proof of a mysterious conspiracy, into which even such heterosexual gentlemen as Gautier and Benois were drawn in spite of themselves! Which old master does Benois draw most like? Tiepolo. Among the frescoes adorning the Villa Valmarana near Vicenza, which Benois had certainly seen, are two depicting the story of Rinaldo and Armida. Although Tiepolo's Rinaldo is meltingly feminine, it is Armida who wears the necklace. Benois took Armida's pearls and gave them to Nijinsky, adding a few diamonds for good measure. We know it is the same necklace because it is worn as high as it will go, right under the chin. (It started a fashion: Cartier copied it.) Nijinsky's very first entry on the stage of the Châtelet, because of his equivocal personality, because of his allure, because he combined the strength of a man with the grace of a woman, because of his frilled and skirted costume, and because of his jewelled choker, had sped this most homosexual of centuries on its vertiginous course.

After all the trials he had gone through, Diaghilev had reason to be delighted with the success of the Russian season. In spite of the Russian Court's intrigues against him, in spite of the enmity of the Tsar and the Grand Dukes, in spite of the opposition of Kchessinskaya, in spite of the withdrawal of subsidies and the struggle to raise funds, he had proved what Petersburg had refused to believe possible – that the new ballet as conceived by Benois, Bakst, Fokine and himself, was the art-form of the moment and a wonder of the world. He had scored off the Emperor of all the Russias. So he was the greatest man in the world! And it was in this glorious light – or something like it – that Nijinsky would now regard him. Can admiration grow into love and can love live without physical desire?

Eleonora Nijinsky came every night to the theatre. Karsavina was touched to see Vaslav go dutifully up to kiss his mother and say 'Dobra noc', and amused that the mother, who had come to Paris to chaperone her daughter,*

---

* This was Mme Karsavina's phrase: but Mme Bronislava Nijinska commented 'She never was a chaperone because she believed a good girl will always know how to behave. It was Vaslav and Diaghilev who "chaperoned" me!'

would go quietly off with Bronia, while her son went off with Diaghilev.[125]

Chaliapine, who made his first appearance of the season in Rimsky's 'Pskovitianka', renamed by Diaghilev 'Ivan le Terrible', on 25 May, had naturally been counted on by Astruc as the chief attraction of the Saison Russe – and he was paid almost as much as the rest of the company put together – but though his success was great that of the ballet as a whole was to prove greater. 'Ivan' was, of course, the only full-length opera in Diaghilev's season, and there was no dancing in it. Here it is necessary to correct certain errors propagated by previous writers. It may seem impertinent for one who was not present in Paris in 1909 to question facts stated in print by those who were, but the entire French press cannot have conspired to lie. Chaliapine did not, as we have seen, sing in 'Prince Igor', as Grigoriev describes him doing, at the opening of the season: he did not sing in it at all that season. Pavlova and Fokine did not dance in 'Armide' at the première as he states. Pavlova had not arrived and Karalli danced with Mordkine not only at the *répétition générale*, described above, but also at the première.[126] It is interesting that Benois thought Pavlova could have arrived before, but waited to see how the ballet was received in Paris.[127] If this is so, she made a mistake which affected the history of ballet – one might say, of the whole world of art – because Karsavina was acclaimed in the press and became the toast of Paris a fortnight before Pavlova (who was already a *prima ballerina* in Russia – which Karsavina was not) ever showed her face at all. From so redolent a book as *Theatre Street* one does not expect exactitude over boring dates and numbers, but Mme Karsavina is wrong in saying 'Pavlova made but a fleeting appearance and left us after a couple of performances',[128] because once Pavlova had arrived she stayed till the end of the season and danced six times, performing in 'Armide' as well as 'Les Sylphides' and 'Cléopâtre'. Had Mme Karsavina remembered the small fact that Pavlova's delayed arrival enabled herself, Karsavina, to conquer Paris – and Diaghilev's good opinion – she might have found it easier to explain certain unpleasant incidents in later years. But Pavlova had always been and always would be jealous of her – which was absurd, as they were such different artists and Pavlova was an ethereal divinity. Indeed, it seems possible that had Pavlova appeared at the beginning of the season to gather the first fruits of acclamation she might never have been impelled to part with Diaghilev and form her own company.*

On 2 June was given the *répétition générale* of the second mixed programme of opera and ballet, and on 4 June this programme comprising the first act of 'Russlan and Liudmila', 'Les Sylphides' and 'Cléopâtre' received its first

---

* Possible, but not probable. As Dame Marie Rambert has pointed out, Pavlova had to be her own master, and knew it.

public performance in Paris. It was Benois who had urged Diaghilev to include in the Paris repertory the second version of Fokine's 'Chopiniana', renamed by Diaghilev; and the latter, constitutionally unable to leave any score alone, had ordered new orchestrations of the Chopin piano pieces from Liadov, Glazunov, Taneev, Sokolov and Stravinsky. Benois had designed a romantic setting of a ruined Gothic church in a moonlit glade which called up memories of Sir Walter Scott, just as his drifting white dresses were reminders of those designed by Ciceri for Taglioni in 'La Sylphide' and for Grisi in Gautier's 'Giselle'. The painter was not quite happy about the costume he had created for Nijinsky.

It seemed to me to be a trifle comic when I saw it on the stage. It consisted of a black velvet jacket, a collar *à l'enfant*, a light tie, long curls and white legs. And yet, his slightly caricatured appearance made the artist more like a figure from some old beaded *réticule* or painted lampshade. It was just such funny improbable troubadours who formed the dreams of our own grandmothers, the creators of the embroidered *réticules* and painted lampshades.[129]

Yet as so often happened with Nijinsky, a marvellous and inexplicable instinct made him bend the costume to the service of the role he was to dance. He understood the costume in relation to the choreography and his part in it, he became one with it and he ended by making it seem inevitable.

For the dress rehearsal of this programme 'the house was packed . . . and people were sitting on the steps of the balcony and in the aisles of the stalls. Everyone was bursting with curiosity. When the curtain went up . . . the whole house gasped with admiration and surprise . . . the dancers were like blue pearls. . . .'[130]

Like the middle act of 'Armide', Fokine's 'Les Sylphides' was a series of dances – yet how different! While the first portrayed the formal splendours of Versailles where classical ballet was born, the second evoked the tormented dreams of the 1830s. In the former technical virtuosity was essential: in the latter it was utterly out of place. 'Les Sylphides', which, as we have seen, was first given in its final form at the Mariinsky in Petersburg in the previous year, was totally unlike anything seen on the ballet stage before. Dance melted into dance, group into group, and although traditional *pas* were used all formality was taken out of the *port de bras*, all virtuoso steps were omitted. The object was not to display technique but to create a mood. All the same, it was extremely hard to dance and the sustained poses called for considerable strength and experience.

Never before had principal dancers been so merged with the *corps de ballet*; never before had a dancer turned her back on the audience; never before had a male solo contained no double turns in the air or failed to end with a *préparation* and a series of *pirouettes*. An example of how instinctively

Fokine breathed the air of a new age (inaugurated by Isadora) is that without his even planning it, each solo that he arranged ended differently. In the first Valse Karsavina finished with a *pirouette* and stopped on her toes with her back to the audience; in the first Mazurka Pavlova ran off the stage; in the second Mazurka Nijinsky, after a jump, fell on one knee, stretching out his right hand as towards a vision; in the Prelude Baldina froze on her toes facing the audience, hand to lips, as if catching the sound of a distant nightingale – or, as Fokine put it, 'imploring the orchestra to play still more softly'.[131]

It is too easy to write poetically about 'Les Sylphides'. The male dancer is a poet, or he is Chopin, which comes to the same thing. But the three principal girl dancers and the *corps de ballet* of sixteen are anything but dancers although all they do is dance. They are fairies or figments of the poet's imagination; they have been compared to water, trees, clouds, mist, festoons of flowers. In his 'Ode to Melancholy' Keats has an epithet which is apposite: 'cloudy trophies' – 'And be among his cloudy trophies hung'. Indeed, if melancholy is the dominant mood of 'Les Sylphides', though there are bursts of joy in it, we might do worse than take as a motto for the ballet another line from the same poem, 'Joy, whose hand is ever at his lips, bidding adieu.' Yearning, hope, disappointment, regret.

The short Prelude (Op. 28, no. 7) which is the most contemplative of the Chopin pieces used, is played before the curtain rises. As the sweet Nocturne (Op. 32, no. 2) begins the first group is revealed, with Pavlova and Karsavina leaning their heads on Nijinsky's shoulders, the *corps* and Baldina reclining at their feet. Some of the *corps* are lined up on either side of the central group, leaning inwards. Others are at the sides. Almost immediately they begin to move, running forward. Throughout the ballet the patterns and motions of the *corps* are as important as the dancing of any one principal; and the fact that they will often regroup themselves in silence between numbers gives the work a gentle continuity, removes it from the old-fashioned *divertissement* and discourages applause.* During the opening Nocturne, while Nijinsky lifts Pavlova and supports her in *arabesque* or stands poised, suspended on his toes, his arms looped like a garland above his head, or kneels yearning, and while Baldina runs through the arch formed by Pavlova's and Nijinsky's arms, hopping and curtseying, the *corps* dip and kneel, their backs to the audience, with undulating arms, tiptoe, rotate, scoop the air with their arms, form into parallel lines and finally into a semicircle.

* According to Dame Marie Rambert (who was with the company in 1913 during the absence of Fokine) Nijinsky acknowledged applause after his solo in 'Les Sylphides'. (Mary Clarke: *Dancers of Mercury*, p. 64.)

Karsavina's is the first solo, the Valse (Op. 70, no. 1), and to receive her the *corps*, who at the end of the Nocturne were like festoons, move into two lines at right angles to the audience. This is an ecstatic solo which Fokine thinks Karsavina executes with 'rare romanticism'.[132] To a tripping rhythm, she leaps on, runs backwards *sur les pointes*, flutters her arm, drifts, hand to mouth, as if calling up the 'horns of elfland', then makes a spreading open gesture of both hands as if parting the curtains of the air. She turns *en attitude*, arms *en couronne*, makes a sweeping gesture towards her foot, circles the stage and ends with back turned, arms drifting, looking over her right shoulder.

In silence the *corps* form three sides of a square to prepare for the first Mazurka (Op.33, no.2). This is a kind of *perpetuum mobile* and Pavlova, with sylphlike indecision, makes three diagonal entries, as the *corps* do *port de bras* in different directions before forming a semicircle, alternate girls standing and kneeling, with an arch in the middle through which the ballerina will be satisfied to make her fourth entry and begin to dance. With swirling arms she hops in *relevé*, like 'a maenad at the centre of a calm night',[133] pausing to hold an *arabesque* before running off – apparently to continue dancing to another air in another place. In silence the *corps* with their arms speed her on her way, then form a solid group in the centre.

As the curved melody of the slower Mazurka (Op.67, no.3) begins, Nijinsky 'seems to cast himself loose upon the music's tide'. He diagonals forward with slow *jetés* and sweeping gestures, crosses the front of the stage with *cabrioles* and turns, backs with *entrechats*. 'He is the sport and plaything of the flood of melody; dancing not to it, but with it or by it – almost, indeed, *on* it.'[134] At last he kneels with rapt gaze, his right arm yearning forward, while with the back of his left hand he brushes aside a lock of hair. He rises and runs off. The *corps* turn their backs, forming an espalier on three sides of a square. Then they move into three groups, each made up of four kneeling girls with one standing in the centre.

Now the *andantino* of the Prelude is repeated as Baldina swoops without jumping and twirls with drifting arms. She makes the sweeping hand-to-toe gesture and poses *en arabesque penchée,* with hands crossed on her chest. She stalks forward and poses on tiptoe, hand to lips, hearing voices. The *corps* form a semicircle, the girls in pairs, leaning confidentially together.

The next Valse (Op.64, no.2) is the *pas de deux* danced by Pavlova and Nijinsky, and to the first long note the ballerina, who has been lifted off-stage, appears to descend – with pointed toe visible through her long diaphanous skirt – from the trees. This choreography fits the shape of the music very closely. She trips, he yearns. He lifts her through the air, supports her *en arabesque*, turns her *en attitude*, kneels and receives her hand on his shoulder. Dancing quicker, he jumps and turns inside out as she trips after him. He lifts her *en arabesque* first to one side, then to the other. By now, the *corps*, who were in two lines, facing each other in pairs, are reclining, hand to chin. Pavlova runs backwards, half drawn by Nijinsky's magnetism as he barely touches her wrists. They dance to and fro and as he runs off he pauses, suspended, on one foot, before he follows her with right arm raised in appeal and longing.

To the final Valse Brillante, orchestrated by Stravinsky, the *corps* canter in circles. Two lines advance and retire, then turn diagonally. To a stirring, swinging tune Nijinsky jumps on between the groups, and draws Pavlova off. The *corps* dance round with drifting arms. A sinuous questioning melody leads to a reprise of the opening music. Everyone stops, then to a faster tempo they charge round and the ballet ends with a re-forming of the opening group. Nijinsky stands at the back with the two ballerinas leaning their heads on his shoulders. A line of dancers run forward to recline in the foreground as the curtain falls.

'Les Sylphides' was the first abstract ballet. 'Cléopâtre', which followed, was as much of a contrast to it as 'Prince Igor' had been to 'Armide'. There had been publicity about a mysterious society woman of striking beauty who would appear in the title role – this was, of course, Ida Rubinstein; and the public had reason to be curious. Rubinstein was to be carried on in a sarcophagus, wrapped up like a mummy. This idea had come to Benois while he listened to Rimsky's music for 'Mlada'. 'I suddenly visualized the Queen's journey through the sands of the desert in this closed coffin, and it logically followed that she should be swathed like a mummy to prevent the least grain of sand penetrating through the covering to blemish her divine body.'[135] Benois found Rubinstein lying like a corpse in her coffin in the wings of the Châtelet, and said, 'Well, Ida Lvovna, how are you feeling?' 'All right, thank you,' she replied, 'but I can't move.'[136]

'Cléopâtre', with its melodramatic theme and its six different composers, sounds rather absurd to us today, but it was nothing of the kind in 1909. In it Fokine was able to realize more than ever before his ideals of a dance-drama divorced from the conventions of the old ballet. 'Cléopâtre' was not a ballet: nobody in it wore point shoes or stood in one of the five positions or executed classical *port de bras*. The novelty of this cannot be overstated. Benois, however, was perfectly aware of the absurdities.

Egyptian young gentlemen never paid court to the temple slaves and never shot arrows with love-letters to the feet of the queen. The daughters of Pharaoh would not dream of indulging in love-affairs on the threshold of a temple and never poisoned their temporary favourites before the eyes of the people who had come to worship them. Lastly, if Cleopatra did keep Greek dancers it would not have

Leon Bakst.
Caricature by Jean Cocteau.

been in front of the gods that she would have allowed them to dance the mad bacchanale. . . .

Yet 'Cléopâtre' brought the fullest houses. . . . Its success surpassed that of Chaliapine.[137] The power of the miscellaneous music, the décor of Bakst, the choreographic invention of Fokine and the extraordinary talents of the performers made the drama convincing.

Bakst's setting, with its huge columns and pink gods framing a glimpse of the Nile in the purple dusk, was a grand conception and the impression it made on Paris was so powerful that it launched a new age of exoticism.

Following a file of girls bearing pitchers, Pavlova as Ta-hor comes to meet her lover Amoun.[138] This is Fokine, who bounds on with a bow, a splendid, heroic figure. They express their love in a dance and are blessed by the High Priest. A messenger announces the approach of Cleopatra. To a triumphant burst of music a glittering procession winds on to the stage. The rear is brought up by a painted sarcophagus, borne by bearded men. Beside it walk Karsavina and Nijinsky, Cleopatra's slaves. They give the impression of 'two tender and carefree creatures, who, growing up on the steps of the terrible queen's throne, are absolutely devoted to her'.[139] The sarcophagus is opened to reveal a mummy-case, and from this is lifted the swathed body of Cleopatra. Twelve veils of different colours are ceremoniously unwound from her body and the queen with a sweeping gesture throws off the last. The imperious beauty of Ida Rubinstein is revealed to Paris, her pallid features framed by a turquoise-blue stylized wig, bound with gold and jewels. Nijinsky darts forward crouching, and she supports herself with one hand on his head as she moves slowly to a couch. Her court gathers around her and tall fans begin to wave.

Meanwhile Amoun has fallen under Cleopatra's spell and Ta-hor is watching him anxiously. He approaches the queen's couch and Nijinsky snarls at him, baring his teeth like a dog. Cleopatra gives no sign of having seen him and Ta-hor drags him away; then Cleopatra's eyes follow the lovers. The ritual dances begin, led by Ta-hor. Suddenly an arrow lands at Cleopatra's feet. Consternation of the court! – but the queen gazes impassively ahead of her. Amoun is dragged on bearing the tell-tale bow, and as Cleopatra rises to face him and he gazes passionately at her, Karsavina as the slave girl 'reads' the message attached to the arrow, in which Amoun declares his love. Ta-hor's pleading is met by Cleopatra with godlike indifference. The queen tells Amoun that he may spend one night of love with her if he drinks poison in the morning. He agrees. Again, as Ta-hor battling with her beloved, Pavlova shows her wonderful dramatic gift. When her pleading proves vain she creeps forth broken-hearted into the desert.

Placing an arm round Amoun's neck Cleopatra draws him towards her couch. They are showered with flowers and their embraces are now hidden, now revealed by the waving draperies of Cleopatra's maidens. It is left to others to express in dance the ecstasies which are being enjoyed on the couch. First, to the Turkish dance from Glinka's 'Russlan', Karsavina and Nijinsky perform a bounding number with a golden veil. As he lifts her from side to side the veil describes a loop or arch in the air. Karsavina runs backwards on her toes, dragging the scarf, then flings it over her head as she turns.[140] Then comes Glazunov's 'Autumn' from 'The Seasons', to which Fokine has arranged a Bacchanale embodying all his feeling for classical Greece. In this wild dance girls are pursued by satyrs. Fokina sweeps across the stage like a whirlwind, while Sophie Feodorova freezes into sensual poses.[141] As the pace quickens, all revolve like a maelstrom, and the girls throw themselves on the floor in attitudes of suggestive abandon, while the satyrs hang over them lasciviously. Many people are shocked by this.[142]

Benois, who had suggested to Diaghilev the use of Glazunov's Bacchanale, considered this to be one of Fokine's finest arrangements, on a par with the 'Polovtsian Dances' and the Buffoons' Dance in 'Armide'. He called it 'a wonderful vision of the radiant beauty of the ancient world'.[143] It aroused such enthusiasm in the audience that Tcherepnine, who was conducting, was held up for several minutes. The dancers, in despair of the show being able to continue, thought they had better acknowledge the applause though the drama was not yet over – something quite contrary to Fokine's principles. From the couch, screened by veils, he witnessed the argument going on in the wings. In his own words,

To my horror I saw that the bacchantes of ancient Greece had joined hands with the bearded fauns and, forming a line, were coming out to take a bow. I rapidly disengaged myself from Cleopatra's embraces and pounced like a tiger, running towards the wings to meet these dancers who were destroying the unity of the scene in defiance of my orders. I did not know myself what I was going to do. I did not have time to consider. After a few steps of my 'Egyptian' run, however, the applause ended very abruptly. A tomblike stillness followed. My Greeks, embarrassed, backed into the wings. After holding my threatening position during the pause which followed, I pretended I saw the approaching figure of my weeping fiancée, and then, turning round, I again threw myself into the arms of Cleopatra.[144]

The High Priest brings the poisoned cup. Cleopatra bears it to the centre of the stage, driving Amoun before her. He searches her eyes for a sign of mercy, but she is adamant. He drains the cup; the poison does its work. The Queen raises him by his chin to observe impassively the agony in his eyes, then lets him fall lifeless to the ground. She stands for a moment enjoying her sadistic pleasure, then, motioning to her attendants, leaves the temple, leaning on her slaves. The High Priest throws a black cloth over Amoun's body as he passes. Dawn begins to rise. Ta-hor steals in, in search of her lover, a tiny figure in the huge empty temple. She uncovers his body, kisses his lips, caresses his arms; then, realizing that he is dead beyond recall, she beats her breast and flings herself across him.

'Cléopâtre' was such a draw that Astruc and Diaghilev began to give it after the long opera 'Ivan the Terrible', as if Chaliapine alone could not be counted on to fill the house. There were other changes of programme. Extra performances were announced. Serov's opera 'Judith', as planned, was added to the repertory on 6 June; it was sung by Chaliapine and Litvinne; and 'Le Pavillon d'Armide' completed the programme. Curiously enough, although Glinka's 'Russlan' is music of a superior order to 'Judith', all performances of it were cancelled after the première and 'Judith' was substituted.[145] This may have been because there was no role for Chaliapine in 'Russlan'.

It was Diaghilev's hope to bring a company the following year to appear at the Opéra, so with this in mind he contrived that on 19 June, the day after his season closed at the Châtelet, the Russians should take part in a special Gala performance in aid of the Société des Artistes Français at Garnier's gorgeous theatre, which had seen the success of 'Boris Godounov' in the previous year. There was a rehearsal during the afternoon, to which Pavlova came in street clothes, looking wonderfully smart. As she sketched the movements of her Mazurka, holding up the skirt of her dress, Fokine said to Karsavina, 'I don't know if it's the sunshine, or the success of our season or her summer frock, but I don't think I've ever seen her looking so elegant before.'[146] Besides 'Les Sylphides' the company danced 'Le Festin' and Chaliapine sang two acts of 'Boris' with the Russian chorus. The performance was naturally a great success, and Diaghilev, pleased that his dancers (who were not yet really his, but the Tsar's) should have appeared for the first time on the famous stage, began negotiations with Messager and Broussan for a Russian season in 1910. At a party afterwards Diaghilev thanked the company in a speech, and a Minister bestowed the Palmes Académiques on Pavlova, Karsavina, Fokine, Nijinsky and Grigoriev.[147*]

There were two reasons, however, why Diaghilev's happiness should not be complete. One was financial and the other was that Nijinsky was ill. Already on the night of the Opéra gala he had been suffering from a bad throat. He was not fit to dance at a private party given on the following day.

This *'soirée artistique inoubliable'* as *Commedia* called it, was at the house of M. and Mme Ephrussi in the avenue du Bois. In the gardens, with their great clumps of trees lit by electricity, the Russians performed character dances from 'Le Festin'; Smirnov sang the tenor aria from the last act of 'Tosca', Rimsky's 'La nuit de mai' and some popular Russian songs; and 'Les Sylphides' found its perfect setting.[148] Diaghilev had arranged that Nijinsky should be paid 1,000 francs for the evening and Karsavina 500. As we have seen, Nijinsky did not appear and Astruc, who never stopped letting fall to Karsavina that she had in Mme Ephrussi 'a fervent admirer', told the ballerina secretly that the hostess wanted her to have 1,000 too, which was an enormous sum for her in those days. Mme Ephrussi's admiration for Karsavina was boundless and the ballerina found her dressing-table festooned with white roses.[149]

Diaghilev called in his friend Dr Botkine to look at Nijinsky, and typhoid fever, probably due to drinking tap water, was diagnosed. The hotel management were afraid of infection, so Diaghilev took a small furnished flat, and set about nursing the invalid. It was in this flat that Diaghilev proposed they should live together and Nijinsky agreed.[150]

Svetlov looked in at the Châtelet to see the company moving out.

---

* Grigoriev omits the name of Karsavina. She always wore the ribbon when she wanted a sleeping-car on the Petersburg train.

The huge, deep stage was dark, gloomy and deserted. A few workmen in blue blouses were packing up scenery. At the rear of the stage the *régisseur* [Grigoriev] was paying the artists their final salaries. The critic Calvocoressi, who had contributed so passionately towards the Russians' success, had been so helpful to the dancers* and even contrived with a heroic effort to express himself in Russian by the end of the six weeks' season, was pacing up and down the stage, the prey of a puzzled sorrow. He was obviously depressed. From all around women's voices were calling 'Monsieur Calvo' or just 'Calvo'. . . .[151]

Basking in the dazzling sunshine of Parisian acclaim and in love with Nijinsky, Diaghilev had been for a month under a spell and everything had seemed possible: money trouble was the last thing that could be allowed to spoil his happiness. But already on 15 June Astruc had sounded a warning note. He wrote to Diaghilev that takings to date were 405,000 francs, which made it possible to expect 500,000 or 510,000 by the end of the season in a few days' time: but expenses would total 600,000. While disclaiming all financial responsibility, Astruc felt a moral one as Diaghilev's sponsor in Paris, and asked how the bills were going to be paid.[152]

Pressure from creditors had nearly prevented the Opéra Gala from taking place. Once again Astruc's credit had saved the situation.[153] Enjoying their ovations, not one of the company – not even Nijinsky or Grigoriev – knew about the deficit Diaghilev had to face on the morrow.†

On 20 June, Diaghilev gave Astruc a complete list of outstanding debts and the truth was known at last: the sum to be found was 86,000 francs. One of the guarantors, who was under no obligation to hand over any money since the average receipts per performance had exceeded 25,000 francs, generously paid up 10,000 francs: but Diaghilev's creditors were beginning to appeal to Astruc. The latter acted quickly and took possession of Diaghilev's only tangible asset, the sets and costumes of the Russian season. On these he secured a loan of 20,000 francs from the Société de Monaco, on the understanding that the décors passed to the Casino if not redeemed in a certain period. At the same time he carried out a *saisie foraine*, an official seizure of Diaghilev's possessions at the Hôtel de Hollande. Belsacq the upholsterer had already taken this step on his own behalf. Diaghilev owed his hotel several thousand francs. Astruc then set about making Diaghilev bankrupt at the Tribunal de Commerce de la Seine.[154] Finally, Diaghilev signed a bill undertaking to reimburse Astruc 15,000 francs on 7 October.[155]

Pavlova stayed on in Paris to make another guest appearance in a Gala at the Opéra – a Gala which Kchessinskaya came from Russia to dance in.[156]

---

* He had even taken Nijinsky to buy a bathing costume. (Calvocoressi, p 210.)

† And Grigoriev had not heard about it in 1953 when he published his book, for he wrote 'The result of our first Paris season was highly satisfactory, both artistically and financially.' (p.35.)

Karsavina had signed a contract to dance in music-hall at the London Coliseum. Her agent, Marinelli, had asked her to try to bring Nijinsky too, but Nijinsky told her he had already been offered 'thousands' and refused.[157] Karsavina herself had received many offers, including some from Australia and the United States: she chose England because of her love for Dickens,[158] and thus became the first of the Russian stars to shine in London, a year before Pavlova, Mordkine, Kyasht, Bolm and Preobrajenskaya, and two years before Fokine and Nijinsky. Rosaï and Armida's other buffoons were also given a London contract.[159] Benois, though he could ill afford it, had brought his wife from Russia to share the excitements of the season: they now returned home. 'Roaming through the parks of Peterhof and Oranienbaum,' he wrote, 'it seemed to me that I could hear in the rustle of the pine-trees the melodies of the "Camp" or the "Enchantment of Armide", and my stories of how the Polovtsian maidens, headed by Sophie Feodorova, dashed like a hurricane about the stage and of the wild leaps of Bolm, so impressed my children that they would try to reproduce it all – and not without success.'[160]

Diaghilev and Nijinsky left for Carlsbad, and since it is always agreeable to have a third person, an old friend, on a honeymoon, Diaghilev took Bakst along too. Perhaps he thought he might be bored alone with his new lover. Their hotel, the Villa Schüffler, stood on a hill amid pine-forests next to the Russian church. Vaslav did not take the cure: he did no work, but was regularly massaged. They went on drives through the woods and Vaslav was reminded of a spa called Narzan in the Caucasus, which he had seen on his youthful travels.[161]

After two weeks isolated from the world the friends were parted temporarily. Diaghilev had business in Paris, so Bakst escorted Vaslav to Venice, where, after a few days, Diaghilev would join them. Vaslav loved the train journey through the Tyrol and the Alps and he was glued to the window of their compartment, feasting on the mountain scenery throughout the day.[162]

One result of the season's success was that Diaghilev felt confident that it was only a beginning. So without a penny to his name, but feeling like Lorenzo the Magnificent, he had commissioned 'Daphnis et Chloë' from Ravel and a work called 'Masques et Bergamasques' from Debussy. He also set going discussions between Cocteau and Reynaldo Hahn, which would result in work being started on 'Le Dieu bleu' the following year. At Calvocoressi's suggestion he asked Gabriel Fauré for a ballet, but the latter was working on his opera 'Pénélope' and the project came to nothing.[163] Now Diaghilev went to Paris to talk to Debussy. In a letter to Louis Laloy, dated 30 July 1909, Debussy excused himself for having stolen a march on Laloy, who was hoping to write a scenario for Diaghilev, and written that of a ballet to be called 'Masques et Bergamasques' himself. He summarized the sequence of events thus:

1. You brought Diaghilev to see me. We talked things over without exactly getting anywhere. 2. I met Diaghilev *chez* Durand [the music publisher] and he discussed with me a possible collaboration with P.J.Toulet . . . (a further complication). At the same time he told me that as he was leaving for Venice in three days to meet the choreographer he would like to take a scenario to show him. 3. As we were only talking about a *divertissement* lasting at the most fifty minutes I saw no point in turning the world upside down or bothering you, so I wrote the scenario, providing no more plot than was necessary to link up the danced passages. Diaghilev liked it and at once said that Nijinsky and Karsavina must dance it. You see how easy the whole thing was. . . . So things are going ahead. We are dealing with a Russian who speaks our language and who will understand exactly what I want. Naturally I shan't expect Nijinsky's legs to deal in symbols, nor Karsavina's smile to expound the philosophy of Kant. I intend to enjoy myself writing this ballet, which is the right state of mind for a *divertissement*. . . . [164]

Three days later Debussy wrote to Laloy: 'Kipling says the Russian is a charming person until he puts on his shirt. . . . Our Russian friend thinks the best way to get what he wants from people is to lie to them. He may not be as sharp as he thinks; and this is certainly not a game *I* play with my friends. However, nothing has changed between you and me, whatever chicanery Diaghilev has been up to. . . .'[165] Debussy did not like Diaghilev, but it seems clear that he was using him as a scapegoat for his own behaviour towards Laloy, so the chicanery was not all on one side.

'Masques et Bergamasques' never saw the light of day: but the interesting fact to emerge from this correspondence is that as early as the first Saison Russe Diaghilev was intending Nijinsky to be a choreographer,* for of course it was Nijinsky not Fokine who was awaiting Diaghilev in Venice.

Before leaving for Venice Diaghilev took care to get Astruc to return all the Ballet's musical scores.[166] And on 6 August we find him writing to Astruc from the Hôtel de Hollande asking for the return of Serov's original sketch for the Pavlova poster, which belonged to Dr Botkine.[167]

With what pleasure Diaghilev must have looked forward, as he travelled south, to showing Vaslav the beauties of his favourite city! They stayed at the Grand Hôtel des Bains de Mer on the Lido.† Diaghilev and Bakst took Vaslav to the Accademia, the Scuola di San Rocco and the churches. Vaslav swam in the lagoon, and Bakst made an enormous oil sketch of him, sunburnt and naked except for some scarlet bathing pants and a handkerchief knotted on his head, standing with head tilted to observe his outstretched left hand,

---

* Mme Bronislava Nijinska does not believe this.
† Where Diaghilev was to die twenty years later.

a golden faun against a peacock sea. Diaghilev never bathed, partly because he was afraid of the sea and partly because he thought only the young and slender should expose their bodies in public. In the evening they would sit outside the gilded café of Florian under the arcades of the immense Piazza San Marco, observing people and pigeons. There were parties at the palace of the flamboyant Marchesa Casati, who led panthers on a chain, and Vaslav met D'Annunzio, who asked him to dance, and Isadora, who suggested having a baby by him, both of which offers he turned down. At night the friends returned by gondola across the lagoon.[168]

The Mariinsky season began on 1 September and Vaslav had to start practising again at least a week before. Diaghilev and he were in Paris on 19 August.[169] Because of the debts Diaghilev left in his wake, which soon became common knowledge in the Russian capital, it was not such a triumphant return to Petersburg as it might have been. While Nijinsky, whom Diaghilev never bothered about his money troubles, began classes and rehearsals and told his mother about his stay in Germany and Italy, Diaghilev had to try to pay for the past season while planning the next one at the Paris Opéra.

Diaghilev had sensibly but perhaps rather dishonestly concealed from Astruc his negotiations with the Opéra, and Astruc's financial anxiety turned to vengeful fury when he discovered what was afoot. If Diaghilev dealt directly with the Opéra Astruc could be dispensed with: and this transaction after all he had done to ensure the triumph of the Russians in Paris, seemed to him the blackest treachery. What made it doubly serious was that Astruc was planning a season of Italian opera with Caruso and the Metropolitan Opera Company of New York at the Châtelet at the very same time next year; and so as not to clash with the *jours d'abonnement* at the Opéra both Astruc and Diaghilev would expect to give their performances on Tuesdays, Thursdays and Saturdays. They were in direct rivalry and Astruc exerted himself to blacken Diaghilev's name with the Russian establishment in the hope that he would never be allowed to bring artists of the Imperial Theatres to Paris again.

His first step was to try to detach Chaliapine from Diaghilev.

Astruc in Paris to Chaliapine in Moscow, 9.10.09

My dear friend,

I have just received your telegram, and I must admit I am shocked to the core.

It is not only the disappointment I feel as a friend at getting so terse a telegram, when you know how anxiously and even passionately I have been waiting for your answer to a question put to you very clearly five months ago and repeated at regular intervals by letter and telegram. You must have known, my dear Fedia, what importance I placed on this matter, and I should have thought that friendship, apart from practical considerations, would have told you that you should let me know before definitely signing with someone else. . . .

The question is: who have you signed with?

I must tell you, my dear Fedia, that if you have signed with M. Serge de Diaghilev without telling me you may have made a big mistake. . . . Let me remind you that if the Russian season was able to take place in Paris this *was entirely due to me*, because it was I alone who got Diaghilev the credit in Russia without which the season could not have happened. . . .

[Astruc then tells the story of the financial side of the Russian season.]

To show his gratitude to me Diaghilev's sole gesture was to plan a new season in competition with me. He will profit by all the work I put in during the last year to stage performances in Paris and London in an unprofessional way.

Under the circumstances I should warn you that I intend to take the most drastic steps to put an end to this scandal. As you know I possess certain weapons: but there are even more lethal ones which I shall resort to when the moment comes. War has been forced on me and I declare war today.

You have been warned. Make up your mind. . . . I should have thought that Boito, Toscanini and Gatti-Casazza, who all played a part in the beginnings of your career and with whom you have so many happy memories in common, would somewhat have influenced your decision. But it appears that all this goes for nothing. I am not trying to influence you, but one thing I will say. Your decision has made both them and myself very sad indeed.

Yours ever,

GABRIEL.[170]

Astruc next began systematically to attack Diaghilev through the Russian court. He wrote to Count Friederickx, Minister of the Imperial Court, asking if he might submit a report on the Russian season to the Tsar;[171] and received a reply in the affirmative from General Mossolov,* Head of the Chancellery.[172] In the second week in November he told his story to the Grand Duke Nicolas Mikhailovitch, who was in Paris for a few days.[173] On 18 November, he paid a morning visit to the Grand Duke André Vladimirovitch, Kchessinskaya's lover, at his Paris hotel.[174]

The report to the Tsar,[175] which took nearly eleven pages of foolscap, covered the financial aspect of the story as unfolded above (and indeed is the source for much of it). Astruc takes to himself the credit for making the Russian season financially possible (which he certainly had), and for its success with the press and public; he also points out that he secured a reduction of 50 per cent for Diaghilev with the Société des Auteurs et Compositeurs dramatiques de Paris, thus saving Diaghilev 25,000 francs, and that he himself agreed to take a minimal percentage of $2\frac{1}{2}$ per cent. He

* Author of interesting memoirs. See Bibliography.

accuses Diaghilev of fulfilling none of his undertakings. He points out that in all the documents he signed Diaghilev inscribed himself 'Attaché à la Chancellerie Personelle de Sa Majesté l'Empereur de Russie'. He inserts a little scandal.

One morning when he [Astruc] was on the point of handing over a sum of 10,000 francs to Diaghilev's 'accredited representative' M. Astruc received a letter marked 'urgent and personal' which read as follows: 'Dear friend. Please do not on any account pay money to *any single one* of my secretaries *without a card from me for each payment.* Yours ever, Serge de Diaghilev.' M.Astruc, alarmed at this sudden indication of mistrust, asked for an explanation but failed to receive one. However, he heard a few days later that the confidential associate and *very intimate friend* who acted as accountant and who was trusted with delivery of monies had left Paris suddenly on the very evening the famous letter was sent – a fact which could lead to all kinds of suppositions.

This reference, of course, is to the elopement of Mavrine, Diaghilev's former secretary and lover, with Olga Feodorova.

It is curious – but perhaps typical of the cut-throat world of theatre* – that Astruc, who was to collaborate so closely and so successfully with Diaghilev for several years to come, should have been responsible in the course of this winter of 1909–10 for damaging Diaghilev's reputation at the Imperial Court once and for all. It was conceivable that although the Emperor distrusted him and although none of the Grand Dukes felt the same friendship for him as the late Grand Duke Vladimir had done, and although since her husband's death the Grand Duchess Marie Pavlovna had been influenced against him, Diaghilev might still, as a result of the glory his Paris season had brought to Russia, have received subsidies from the Imperial purse. Astruc made this improbable, if not impossible: so that at the end of his life, jotting down fragmentary reminiscences of the beginnings of his enterprise for the benefit of Kochno and Lifar, Diaghilev was able to state that never at any time had he received a single rouble for the mounting of his ballet seasons from the Emperor.

To facilitate his plotting with associates in St Petersburg, and knowing that letters were often opened and censored in Russia, Astruc invented a code for referring to the persons most closely concerned.[176] It is significant that there is no code-name for Nijinsky: he was already considered to be so inseparable from Diaghilev that any attempt to use him as a pawn in the war-game was not even considered. Some of the code-names are less meaningful than others.

---

* This was the comment of Mr Jerome Robbins when I told him the story.

Emperor	Pierre
Grand Duchess Vladimir	Jacqueline
André	Joseph
Boris	Gabriel
Serge	Emile
Directors of the Opéra	Eléments
Diaghilev	Chemineau
Astruc	Chrysale
Kchessinskaya	Mélanie
Chaliapine	Ivan
Calvocoressi	Valet
Bankruptcy	Eugénie
Russian opera	Printemps
Russian ballet	Hiver
Direction of Imperial Theatres	Maxime
Friederickx	Babylas
Artistes	Oiseaux
Material	Fenêtre
Engagement	Fonction
Gunsbourg	Tapir
Pavlova	Amour
Karsavina	Raison
Mefistofele	Diablotin
Barber of Seville	Sévillane

'Chemineau', of course, is the French word for a tramp. Such was the role assigned in this code to Diaghilev, in contrast to Astruc's 'Chrysale': Chrysale was the honest man, the *bon bourgeois*, in Molière's *Les Femmes Savantes*.

On 8 December one Jules Martin wrote from St Petersburg about the Diaghilev 'dossier' which was to be shown to Babylas (Count Friederickx). He said he had seen Mélanie (Kchessinskaya) and had long talks with Emile (Grand Duke Serge) and Joseph (Grand Duke André); that he would shortly be seeing Jacqueline (Grand Duchess Vladimir) and would tell her the whole story of Chemineau's (Diaghilev's) behaviour. The latter had failed to raise any money in St Petersburg and was in difficulties because in addition to the 10,000 francs he would have to pay out to the Paris Opéra he was expected to advance a large sum towards the expenses of a projected London season. Martin had heard (erroneously) that Diaghilev's principal guarantor in Paris was the Marquise de Ganay – the Comtesse de Chevigné too, though to a lesser extent. Martin would be seeing Maxime (the direction of the Imperial Theatres) on the following day; Pierre and Babylas (the Tsar and Count Friederickx) would be back (from Livadia in the Crimea) in a fortnight.[177]

However, in the middle of December Diaghilev went to Paris and through the good offices of the Comtesse de Béarn, Mme de Ganay, Mme de Chevigné and Misia Edwards he and Astruc were brought together to discuss their differences. Sert and Robert Brussel were present at these meetings, and in a letter to Brussel dated 23 December Astruc summed up his conclusions.

Astruc in Paris to Brussel in Paris, 23.12.09

Dear friend,

Following the talks which have taken place during the last few days between M.Serge de Diaghilev, M.Sert, yourself and me, and which were due to the kind intervention of a mutual friend* anxious to reconcile two former collaborators divided by a serious disagreement, I now put forward a detailed specification of the conditions which I think will make it possible to arrange matters.

The awkward situation which our friends have been considering is as follows:

1. I am organizing next May and June at the Châtelet Theatre a season of Italian opera in which the company, the chorus and the corps de ballet of the Metropolitan Opera, New York, will appear in their own sets and costumes. This was announced in the Paris press some time ago.

2. M.Serge de Diaghilev, for his part, is giving at the same time at the Théâtre de l'Opéra a season of Russian opera and ballet similar to that which he gave last year with my help at the Châtelet.

The days chosen by me for our performances at the Châtelet, in agreement with the direction of the New York Theatre, are the Tuesdays, Thursdays and Saturdays between 19 May and 25 June. These days were planned to avoid clashing with the subscription days at the Opéra, which would have been definitely detrimental to my season.

The days chosen by M.de Diaghilev are necessarily the same Tuesdays, Thursdays and Saturdays because they are the only days when the Opéra does not perform and can therefore let the theatre.

After reviewing at length the various ways of finding grounds for agreement, it was agreed:

1. That M.de Diaghilev could not get out of his agreement with the Opéra and postpone his season till 1911.

2. That M.de Diaghilev could not put back his season by three weeks because of contracts signed with London for periods preceding and following his Paris season.

The only solution of our problems was that suggested by M.de Diaghilev, namely that I should agree to upset my plans and change my performances at the Châtelet from Tuesdays, Thursdays and Saturdays to Mondays, Wednesdays and Fridays.

* In the feminine.

In spite of the serious damage this change of days might do me, with the danger of entirely losing the season-ticket-holders [*abonnés*] of the Opéra and of having to subtract the takings of that theatre (22,000 francs a night in May) from my potential receipts, I am disposed to agree to the proposed change.

My conditions would be as follows:

1. M.de Diaghilev would undertake to assure me the collaboration of Chaliapine between 19 May and 25 June for three performances of Boîto's *Mefistofele* and three of *The Barber of Seville* (in the roles of Mefistofele and Basilio).

2. The administration, *abonnements*, sale of tickets, publicity etc. of the Russian season to be entrusted to me by M.de Diaghilev on the same terms as stated in my contract with the Metropolitan Opera Company, that is that I should receive 5 per cent of the gross takings of every performance, payable nightly in the same way as the Assistance Public and the Droit des Pauvres, plus 25 per cent of the total profits, if any, this sum to be paid within a week of the final performance.

3. Immediate payment today of the sum of 24,711 francs, plus costs and interest, which M.de Diaghilev still owes me from the last Russian season.

4. Messrs G.Astruc & Co. to nominate the Paris representatives of the Russian season, and these persons to be paid by M.de Diaghilev.

5. Financial guarantees to be established which would ensure the carrying out of the above conditions. . . .

Yours very affectionately,

GABRIEL ASTRUC

P.S. For your information, after our first discussion I telegraphed to New York: 'Hope to obtain Chaliapine three Mefistofele three Barbers.' I received the following reply: 'Chaliapine affair must be decided within ten days. Later decision would make change of plans impossible. Gatti-Casazza.'[178]

So Diaghilev and Astruc were friends again: their collaboration was necessary for the Russian Ballet to fulfil its destiny. A new associate, Dmitri de Gunsbourg, paid up Diaghilev's debt to Astruc.

Still, the fate of both seasons, the Russian and the American, seemed to depend on Chaliapine. On 5 January 1910 Astruc despatched Robert Brussel to Russia to talk to the great man and to ensure his co-operation. Brussel welcomed the opportunity of seeing his beloved Karsavina again, though aware that his editor on *Le Figaro*, Gaston Calmette, would grow impatient if he stayed away too long. The course of negotiations can be followed in an exchange of telegrams between Brussel, in Petersburg and Moscow, and Astruc, in Paris, as well as some addressed to Baron Elter, the chancellor of Grand Duchess Marie Pavlovna, in Petersburg, and to Chaliapine in Moscow.[179]

Robert Brussel in Petersburg to Gabriel Astruc in Paris, 8.1.1910

Arrived safely. Yvan [Chaliapine] in Moscow. Chemineau [Diaghilev] insists we leave Monday evening. Yvan adamant against 'Diablotin' ['Mefistofele']. Reasons the work, the décor and the cast. Verdi's 'Don Carlos' perhaps less impossible. Could be magnificent. Consult Louis engagement. Mélanie [Kchessinskaya] uncertain. Arrange presentation Jacqueline [Grand Duchess Vladimir]. Have seen copy instructions admittedly late. Fault Valet [Calvocoressi]. Send 500. Telegraph. Robert.

Robert Brussel in Petersburg to Gabriel Astruc in Paris, 9.1.1910

Chemineau ill. Hope leave Monday evening. National Moscow. Have seen Amour [Pavlova] Raison [Karsavina]. Long talk Mélanie who wavers. Seen Joseph [Grand Duke André]. Shall dine. Monday shall know date audience Jacqueline. Has Chevigné written? Shall see Minister Commerce, possibly Emile [Grand Duke Serge]. Situation complicated. Your reputation stands high. Sorry huge expenses. If you disapprove can make private arrangement elsewhere. If stay extended implore Barthou explain Calmette am useful here 'Figaro'. Worried Sarraut and Nice urgent. Cannot write, kept busy every minute. Ill, cold 22 degrees. Say you approve. Affectionately Robert.

Gabriel Astruc in Paris to Baron Alexandre Elter in Petersburg, 10.1.1910

Mme Litvinne advises me telegraph you to expedite solution present difficult problems. Should like respectfully to assure Her Imperial Highness that I shall do everything to ensure complete agreement hoping Russian season will enjoy same triumph as last year. Unfortunately am not alone in directing Italian season. It is Chaliapine who is holding everything up. If he agrees sing Mefistofele everything all right. Hope with Litvinne singing Marguerite the Italian production would bring together two glories of Russian theatre. Gabriel Astruc.

Félia Litvinne in Paris to Baron Alexandre Elter in Petersburg, 10.1.1910

Love and every good wish for New Year. Have advised Astruc telegraph you. Deeply grateful if agreement possible. Félia.

Gabriel Astruc in Paris to Robert Brussel in Petersburg, 10.1.1910

Have sent very important telegram Elter care of Grand Duchess about Chaliapine. See him tomorrow morning 25 Moika. Gabriel.

Gabriel Astruc in Paris to Robert Brussel in Petersburg, 10.1.1910

Primo, warn Chemineau deal cancelled if lawyer doesn't pay 20,000 today unconditionally. Secondo, New York cables important plans held up awaiting Yvan's reply. They insist decision essential within three days. Go Moscow alone if Chemineau ill. Spend what you must but be reasonable. Don't worry about Calmette and Nice. Thanks. Best wishes. 500 telegraphed. Astruc.

Robert Brussel in Petersburg to Gabriel Astruc in Paris, 11.1.1910

Telegram received last night. Saw Diaghilev this morning. He had just received Chaise-Martin's letter saying you accept call off legal actions... two months. Have myself a telegram from Diaghilev to Chaise-Martin in Paris saying 'Letter received. Agree in principle Astruc to administrate coming Russian season. Pay him if your conditions are accepted, if not advance 500 unconditionally, signed Diaghilev.' Chaliapine expects me Thursday. Shall leave Wednesday evening for Moscow, back in Petersburg Friday morning. Continue to cable Hôtel France. Elter is away. Saw Joseph at two. He is warning Jacqueline to expect me. My cheque not arrived. Thanks. Love. Robert.

Robert Brussel in Petersburg to Gabriel Astruc in Paris, 12.1.1910

Tapir [Baron Dmitri de Gunsbourg] is getting Valet [Calvocoressi] to write to Chemineau to prevent agreement insisting that you are trying to take over Russian season in order to make it fail. I have parried the blow. Can I go up to 10,000 with Yvan. Telegraph urgent. Robert.

Gabriel Astruc in Paris to Robert Brussel in Petersburg, 12.1.1910

Tapir's behaviour in keeping with his past record. Reassure Chemineau who will be sure to understand it is in my interest to make both affairs succeed. You can go as far as 20,000 with Yvan for three 'Mefistofele'. Gabriel.

Gabriel Astruc in Paris to Fyodor Chaliapine in Moscow, 13.1.1910

Robert Brussel will speak for me. Please think things over once and for all. The situation is serious. Consider above all this is a matter of friendship. Gabriel.

Robert Brussel in Moscow to Gabriel Astruc in Paris, 13.1.1910

Chaliapine definitely not on artistic grounds. You know the real reason. Diaghilev and myself in despair. Cable instructions Petersburg. Love. Robert.

Gabriel Astruc in Paris to Robert Brussel in Petersburg, 14.1.1910

Terribly sorry. Nevertheless return immediately bring in cash the 5,000 for Diaghilev's second payment and letter for Chaise-Martin confirming authorization to pay first 5,000. Ask Diaghilev to prepare contract coming season. Gabriel.

Robert Brussel in Petersburg to Gabriel Astruc in Paris, 15.1.1910

Arriving Monday Nordexpress. Chaise-Martin's letter sent off. Worried about my mother and *Figaro*. Cable at once. Robert.

Robert Brussel in Petersburg to Gabriel Astruc in Paris, 15.1.1910

Arrive today 4 Gare du Nord. Robert.

On his return to Paris Brussel sent Diaghilev a letter drafted by Astruc summarizing the situation. Once Diaghilev's debt to Astruc was settled they could go ahead. Astruc was only too delighted to show that his skill and resources were so great that he could make a success of both the Italian and Russian seasons, though they ran simultaneously. It was essential for Diaghilev to announce his repertory so that publicity could be started and tickets sold at once.

In fact there was to be no opera in the Russian season at the Paris Opéra.

The first Diaghilev season of ballet alone was largely due to the non-co-operation of Chaliapine: without him it was too risky to transport a large company of singers and several elaborate productions. But, as in the previous year, the exact composition of the ballet repertory would be arrived at only after much trial and error.

CHAPTER THREE

1910

The period of January–March 1910 was no less critical in the story of Diaghilev and his influence on the arts than the same period a year before, when the decision to take the new Russian ballet to the west had been made. We have evidence of the problems facing Diaghilev during these three months. He had to pay the debts of the past season and raise a subsidy for the next one. He was torn between ballet and opera. His desire to make Nijinsky preeminent was very strong – and ballet had been the chief success of the 1909 season: but ballet had been a late-comer in his life and he could not rid himself of the accepted notion that opera was a higher art. Anyway, would the Paris Opéra accept a Russian Season of ballet alone? And was it feasible to take opera to Paris without Chaliapine? If ballet alone was acceptable by Paris, what new works could be taken to augment the previous repertory? Kchessinskaya was a stumbling block. If she consented to go to Paris she would have to be shown in one of her roles from the old repertory. This would probably ensure financial support from the Imperial purse, but Fokine neither wanted Kchessinskaya in his ballets nor did he want anyone else's ballets – Petipa's, for instance – in the repertory.[1] The problem of new ballets and their casting was acute. If Kchessinskaya was important from the point of view of money and prestige, Pavlova, Nijinsky and Karsavina were essential artistically.

Benois, who had first interested Diaghilev in the ballet, and who thought he had been the chief instrument in persuading him to take Russian ballet to Paris, had struck up a friendship with Fokine, and insisted that 'there could be no talk of opera.'[2] We may imagine that Nouvel took the opposite point of view.

Since the first discussions of a new ballet repertory a year before, everyone

118

had thought it desirable to produce a Russian folk ballet, a fairy story – only more magical and less childish than 'The Little Hump-backed Horse'. For months Fokine had been revolving this in his mind. He read through Afanasiev's collections of folk tales and began to combine some of them into a scenario.[3] Benois wrote:

By joint effort we started to search for the most suitable story, but soon came to the conclusion that no single story existed that was entirely adequate and that one would have to be created by merging several together. The music was to be composed by Tcherepnine, the dances to be arranged by Fokine; the fundamental elements of the subject were inspired by the young poet Patiomkin. The working out of these elements was undertaken by a sort of conference in which Tcherepnine, Fokine, the painters Steletzky, Golovine and I took part. Our excellent writer Remizov, who was not only a great crank but a great lover of all things Russian, was carried away with our idea. During the two meetings I had with him, his very tone seemed to give life to our collective work.[4]

Remizov [Prince Peter Lieven recalled]

was a little, odd, extremely ugly man, resembling an overgrown sparrow and forever muffled in warm clothes. . . . He bewildered the friends with various tales, incomprehensible strange-sounding improvisations at which he was a master. 'There are also Bellyboshkies,' he would say, 'Evil sort of creatures, some with tails and some without.' What Bellyboshkies were nobody could make out, but this nonsensical word sounded so attractive that the Dance of the Bellyboshkies in the train of the wicked sorcerer was produced.[5]

Fokine, who was certainly the prime instigator of the scenario, and who was ultimately given all the credit for it, does not name these other collaborators in his description of how 'The Firebird' came about.

We met very often, during the evening hours, at the home of Alexandre Benois for tea. During some of these tea-drinking sessions, I narrated the story of the Firebird. Every time some artist visitor appeared who was not familiar with the new ballet, I had to repeat the libretto . . . and I would describe the ballet and be carried away by my own fantasy. With each description I added new details. . . .[6]

The recollections of Stravinsky, the 'new boy' on the committee, are different: 'Fokine is usually credited as the librettist of "The Firebird", but I remember that all of us, and especially Bakst, who was Diaghilev's principal adviser, contributed ideas to the plan of the scenario.'[7] Perhaps Grigoriev has a small claim to co-authorship, even if he only borrowed the books of Afanasiev for Fokine, for he wrote many years later: 'I obtained several collections of Russian fairy tales; and between us we evolved a story by piecing together the more interesting parts of several versions. This took us about a fortnight.'[8] Eventually, Benois describes, Tcherepnine, 'who was prone to inexplicable changes of mood, and whose attitude was in those days cooling towards ballet in general', lost interest.[9] It was just as well.

Already, during his holiday in Venice, Diaghilev had written to his old professor, the composer Liadov: 'I want a ballet and a *Russian* one; there has never been such a ballet before. It is imperative that I present one in May 1910 in the Paris Opéra and at Drury Lane in London. We all consider you now as our leading composer with the freshest and most interesting talent.'[10] At one of the early meetings of the 'committee' at Diaghilev's flat in autumn 1909, Diaghilev received Fokine's scenario and announced that he was asking Liadov to compose the score. Liadov was a slow worker. When, a few weeks later, Golovine met him in the street and asked him how he was getting on, he replied 'Fine. I've bought the music paper.'[11]* Diaghilev must have anticipated something of the kind, because, with his usual fore-thought – which some might call duplicity – he had discussed the new fairy-tale ballet with the young Stravinsky. Liadov relinquished the commission. When in December Diaghilev rang up Stravinsky to tell him he was to compose 'The Firebird' Stravinsky admitted to Diaghilev's surprise that he had already begun it.[12] 'The Introduction,' Stravinsky remembers, 'up to the bassoon-and-clarinet figure at bar seven was composed in the country, as were notations for other parts.' He would finish the composition in March, and the orchestration a month later: the complete work (apart from a few retouchings) being posted to Paris in mid-April.[13]

Stravinsky was not attracted by the subject of the ballet.

Like all story ballets it demanded descriptive music of a kind I did not want to write. I had not yet proved myself as a composer, and I had not earned the right to criticize the aesthetics of my collaborators, but I did criticize them, and arrogantly, though perhaps my age [twenty-seven] was more arrogant than I was. Above all, I could not abide the assumption that my music would be imitation Rimsky-Korsakov, especially as by that time I was in such revolt against poor Rimsky. However, if I say I was less than eager to fulfil the commission, I know that, in truth, my reservations about the subject were also an advance defence for my not being sure I could. But Diaghilev, the diplomat, arranged everything. He came to call on me one day, with Fokine, Nijinsky, Bakst and Benois. When the five of them had proclaimed their belief in my talent, I began to believe, too, and accepted.[14]

For a composer who had started work on the ballet a month before receiving the commission he was being remarkably coy.

* He was overdoing the self-disparagement: he had in fact made a few sketches. (Alexander Tcherepnine conversation.)

All this time it was assumed that the birdlike Pavlova would dance the Firebird.[15] If Diaghilev had known sooner that Pavlova would not dance it he would certainly have created a new work for Nijinsky instead.

Stravinsky had reason to fear being lumped together with Rimsky-Korsakov 'for Russian export', and it is interesting that at the very beginning of Diaghilev's 'export drive' of Russian colour and folklore, one so young should have sensed the danger. (It is almost as if he foresaw with a shudder the excesses of *l'âme slave*, the White Russians in exile, the nightclub 'Schéhérazade' in Paris, staffed by ex-officers of the Imperial Guard, the Russian Tea-room in New York.) Whether because Diaghilev thought the Rimsky numbers in 'Cléopâtre' and 'Le Festin' had been particularly effective in Paris, or because Rimsky's harmony made him appear the most advanced of the Five – the Russian Debussy – or out of piety for his old teacher, lately dead, or because he genuinely admired his music, he hoped to present not only Rimsky's opera 'Sadko' but also the symphonic poem 'Schéhérazade,' in the form of a ballet, in Paris.

It was because the friends were intending to mount 'Sadko', or part of it, that Fokine agreed to a slight change in the libretto of 'The Firebird'. In the opera the hero charms the inhabitants of the Kingdom of the Sea with a magic *gusli*, a kind of zither or psaltery. Fokine had intended that Prince Ivan, the hero of his ballet, should use the same method of subjection on Kastchei's unholy court. Benois persuaded him to substitute a feather from the Firebird's breast.[16] A more important change was made in Fokine's libretto. The choreographer wrote: 'Yielding to the wish of Igor Stravinsky, I agreed to substitute a coronation for the gay processional dances with which I had wanted to end the ballet.'[17]

'The Firebird' has always been quoted as the earliest example of close collaboration between a composer and a choreographer. Many years before Fokine's own memoirs were published (1961), he was telling Lincoln Kirstein – and Arnold Haskell[18] was spreading the story – how the music and choreography had been worked out together.

Stravinsky brought him a beautiful cantilena on the entrance of the Tsarevitch into the garden. . . . But Fokine disapproved. 'No, no,' he said. 'You bring him in like a tenor. Break the phrase where he merely shows his head, on his first intrusion. Then make the curious swish of the garden's magic horse return, and then, when he shows his hand again, bring in the full swing of the melody.'[19]

Fokine's later description emphasizes his theory of those days (which used so to annoy Stravinsky) that music should be a mere accompaniment to the dance, but it probably gives an exaggerated picture of his own influence on the score.

Stravinsky played, and I interpreted the role of the Tsarevitch, the piano substituting for the wall. . . . Stravinsky, watching, accompanied me with patches of the Tsarevitch melodies, playing mysterious tremolos as background to depict the garden of the sinister immortal Kastchei. Later on I played the role of the Tsarevna and hesitantly took the golden apple. . . . Then I became Kastchei, his evil entourage – and so on. All this found most colourful interpretation in the sounds that came from the piano, flowing freely from the fingers of Stravinsky. . . .[20]

Flowing freely! Are we meant to think that Stravinsky improvised an accompaniment, then went away and wrote it down? Not very likely. Stravinsky says

I like exact requirements. . . . To speak of my own collaboration with Fokine means nothing more than to say that we studied the libretto together, episode by episode, until I knew the exact measures required of the music. In spite of his wearying homiletics, repeated at each meeting, on the role of music as *accompaniment* to dance, Fokine taught me much, and I have worked with choreographers in the same way ever since.[21]

It was naturally Benois, with his love for Gautier and the whole Romantic period, who suggested taking 'Giselle' to Paris. It was in Paris in 1841 that this famous ballet on a theme by Gautier, danced by Carlotta Grisi and Jules Perrot, had first seen the light of day. Giselle was Pavlova's great role. Benois pointed out to the committee that, as the Russian school of ballet grew out of the French, in taking 'Giselle' to Paris they would be paying a compliment to France. (Of course, he was longing to design the ballet.) General Besobrasov and Svetlov were both in favour.

But Diaghilev made a face and said 'Shura is quite right, of course. But "Giselle" is too well known in Paris,* and would not be likely to interest the public. I'm quite prepared to consider it, though.' At the next meeting he asked Benois 'What about "Giselle", Shura? Do you still insist on "Giselle"?' 'I do indeed,' said Benois. 'I feel sure that it would give our repertoire variety and show our dancers at their most brilliant. Besides, I should like to paint you a décor for it!' Diaghilev gave a sly smile, and wrote 'Giselle' in large ornate characters in his exercise book.†

Grigoriev thought the question had already been decided in his mind.[22] Probably Diaghilev guessed that if Benois, Fokine's new friend, could be got to insist on 'Giselle' there would be less opposition from the opinionated Fokine, to whom the old ballet with its set dances and conventional mime was a thing of the past. 'Giselle' had in fact been one of the first ballets Diaghilev thought of bringing to Paris, as the notes made by Astruc *chez* Paillard in summer 1908 bear witness.

* It had not in fact been danced there since 1868.
† The word 'Carnaval' appears for the first time on p. 83 of Diaghilev's black book, along with 'Giselle' in fairly ornate capitals, but 'Giselle' had appeared seven times on previous pages.

Calvocoressi was asked by Diaghilev to find out the position with regard to the copyright of Adam's score for 'Giselle'.

We had a lot of trouble . . . and we did not know in whom the copyright was vested. Eventually we discovered the assignee, a music publisher who lived in a side street in Versailles. We went to see him. I believe he had quite forgotten the very existence of 'Giselle'. He gave us the required permission with glee and prepared for the novel experience of pocketing the performing fees that were falling to him from the skies.[23]

The planning, designing and tentative casting of the new repertory went on over Christmas 1909 and well into the New Year: and this strategy was of course dependent on whether or not there was to be opera as well as ballet, on whether terms could be agreed with Paris, on the reconciliation with Astruc, on the payment of debts and other considerations. Contracts with the dancers would only be signed in March,[24] and rehearsals only begin in April.[25] Meanwhile, Nijinsky, Karsavina, Fokine, Grigoriev and the rest had resumed their duties at the Mariinsky. Nijinsky danced nearly every Wednesday and Sunday, his roles being the poet in 'Chopiniana', the Slave in 'Une Nuit d'Egypte', the Slave in 'Le Pavillon d'Armide', Blue Bird in 'La Belle au bois dormant', the Act III *pas de deux* in 'La Fille mal gardée', Vayn, God of the Wind, in a *grand pas d'action* in 'The Talisman' and a number of *pas de deux* and *pas de trois* in ballets of the old repertory.[26] He was also present, this year, at many of the meetings of the 'committee', but he lived with his mother and did not move in with Diaghilev.[27]

Just as with 'The Firebird', the collaborators retained in later years different memories as to the authorship of 'Schéhérazade'. There can be no doubt that the general idea was Benois'. Rimsky's symphonic poem had only hints of a programme based on episodes from the 'Arabian Nights'. Ever since his first experience of the music many years before, Benois, ignorant of Rimsky's name for the turbulent fourth movement – 'Festival at Baghdad: the Sea' – had heard in it 'the voluptuaries of the harem and their cruel punishment'.[28] From the beginning it was agreed that Bakst should do the décor and costumes,[29] but before he or anyone else was consulted Diaghilev had a pianist play over the piano score several times to excite Benois' imagination.[30]

Benois had been hurt during the first Paris season at being given no credit as part-author of 'Cléopâtre'. After all, the ideas for the entry of Cleopatra and for her disrobing had been his. Now, as the scenario of 'Schéhérazade' came to him he wrote down his ideas on the score itself. 'I did this solely to help my memory. One evening, however, as Argutinsky and I were returning home from one of these creative evenings I said to him half-jokingly: "This time my notes are in black and white, which will guarantee that this work will be considered *mine*." '[31] He was not considering the money point of view,[32] although if he had – and he may not have been aware of this – he would have found that as author of the libretto of a ballet he would be entitled, in France at least, to royalties on every performance. The Société des Auteurs were very active in exerting the rights of those they represented. But Benois was too optimistic.

By the time Fokine was called in the friends had discussed the story between them and the choreographer got the impression that Bakst was the author.[33] Bakst wanted the unfaithful wives to be sewn in sacks and thrown into the sea. Nobody else was in favour of this ending. As Fokine pointed out, 'To hide the dancers in bags at this most tragic moment would mean to give up a very effective scene. The bags would be heavy and cumbersome to look at. Besides, to throw them when they contained artists would be dangerous. . . . A mass slaughter of lovers and faithless wives in front of the spectators presented a much more enthralling problem for me.' This was agreed on.[34] Ida Rubinstein would be the Sultana Zobeïda; Bulgakov, who had been an impressive Marquis in 'Le Pavillon', would mime the Shah; and Nijinsky would be the Negro slave who was the Sultana's lover. Nouvel said to Diaghilev, 'How odd it is that Nijinsky should always be the *slave* in your ballets – in "Le Pavillon d'Armide", in "Cléopâtre" and now again in "Schéhérazade"! I hope one day you'll emancipate him.'[35]

All this planning of new works was absorbing and delightful for the friends, but for Diaghilev the months of January, February and March were a time of increasing doubt, struggle and despair. He must continually have been on the point of throwing up the whole idea of another Russian season abroad, and we may imagine that only his love for Nijinsky and the shining hope of giving him greater roles to dance and act than ever before, in ballets yet to be composed by Debussy, Ravel and Stravinsky, kept him going. Karsavina, whom Diaghilev had not warned of his projected season at the Opéra, had returned from London with another Coliseum contract for the spring, which presumably would prevent her from appearing with the Russians in Paris. This was a fearful blow, not only because Diaghilev needed her talent and glamour in the company, but because she was one of the artists whom he was obliged by his arrangement with the Opéra to present. 'The anguish was great on both sides,' wrote Karsavina, who would willingly have given up the financial benefits of her London engagement, but was bound by her signature. She began to dread the sound of the telephone, 'as it was not easy to resist Diaghilev's pressure'.[36] By the middle of January, as we have seen, Brussel had finally failed to secure the co-operation of Chaliapine, so the whole enterprise might very well founder. About 1

February Pavlova told Diaghilev that she could not come to Paris as she was to appear in music-hall at the Palace Theatre, London.[37] So Diaghilev had lost in her his Firebird and his Giselle. Her decision was undoubtedly arrived at for financial reasons and because she felt she could shine more brilliantly in an old-fashioned repertoire of her own choosing away from Nijinsky and Karsavina, but her dislike of Stravinsky's music may have helped to turn the scale. (Diaghilev had taken Stravinsky to a party at her flat, but she was incapable of understanding the new music.)[38] So Karsavina would have to dance the Firebird: but whether she could take part in the season at all depended on an arrangement with Oswald Stoll of the London Coliseum. Without at first breaking this news to Astruc, Diaghilev racked his brains for ways to please him and at the same time make some money. Knowing what a draw 'Cléopâtre' had been, he cabled on 2 February offering Astruc three performances of it at the Châtelet during the Metropolitan season of Italian Opera for 50,000 francs. On 8 February Astruc agreed to pay 45,000 francs for three performances of 'Les Sylphides', 'Cléopâtre' and 'Le Festin', provided that Kchessinskaya, Pavlova, Karsavina, Rubinstein, Nijinsky and Fokine all appeared and provided these works were exclusive to him and not performed at the Opéra. These were impossible conditions. Diaghilev naturally could not eliminate half his repertoire for the Opéra season, and of course he could not produce Pavlova and had come to no firm arrangement with Kchessinskaya, so Astruc called off the deal. On 10 February Diaghilev, who had clearly gone straight to see Kchessinskaya after Pavlova's defection, cabled to Astruc, 'All well here. Giselle replaced by short version of La Belle au bois dormant.' On 11 February Diaghilev bravely cabled, 'Everything else is going all right.'[39] But on top of all his other troubles Rimsky's widow and son were placing every possible difficulty in the way of his presenting 'Schéhérazade' as a ballet.[40]

Dr Sergei Botkine, devoted as ever to Tamara Karsavina, used to send his assistant or a nurse to see her daily, to keep an eye on her health and sometimes give her an injection. Karsavina now had a sledge of her own, with a horse and a fat coachman. One cold evening the doctor had tea with her and he told her, 'I am so happy, I have just found a cure for ulcers of the stomach. My whole being is singing with joy.' She dropped him in her sledge at the house where he was dining, on her way to the theatre. Next morning she heard he was dead.[41] Botkine's death was not only a personal loss to Diaghilev, Benois and the friends – and Prince Argutinsky, who had not spoken to the doctor since a row over an antique which they had both coveted and which Botkine had bought, was inconsolable[42] – it was a blow to the prospects of their enterprise. For Botkine, apart from being married to a rich Tretiakov, knew many influential people in the capital and had always been helpful in raising funds and pulling strings.[43] In fact, far from everything going all right with Diaghilev, everything was going wrong. *Les quatre cents coups.*

On 11 February Schidlovsky, one of Astruc's contacts in Petersburg, wrote to him about the possibility of getting him a Russian decoration (Brussel had just received one), and mentioned that Diaghilev was totally failing to raise money in Petersburg, that Kchessinskaya had refused to appear, that the Grand Duchess Marie Pavlovna (Vladimir) had withdrawn her patronage because of all the scandals surrounding Diaghilev's name, and that the Paris season could not possibly take place.[44] What were Astruc's thoughts, after reading this letter, when he cabled to ask Diaghilev to name the dates of his *générale* and *première* at the Opéra?[45] On 16 February Diaghilev gave him two dates without knowing who or what he was going to be able to show. (The suggested dates, 22 and 24 May, were not adhered to.)[46]

Meanwhile, 'The Firebird' was being written.

We have seen how in January Brussel had reason to believe Dmitri Gunsbourg wished to prevent a reconciliation between Diaghilev and Astruc. A dilettante and a lover of ballet, it seems that Gunsbourg saw himself at the head of a ballet-company, another Diaghilev but one with money. Perhaps he thought that if he could prevent Astruc from showing a Diaghilev-led company in Paris, there would be more chance that Astruc might present a Gunsbourg company. Did Diaghilev trust him? The question is academic, because we know that Diaghilev, who admired clever rogues, was quite capable of working with and turning to his advantage people he did not trust or like.[47] His marvellous diplomacy – which could be called insincerity in a good cause – was to sustain a ballet company for twenty years and make possible the creation of many masterpieces. Now he charmed and flattered Gunsbourg, making him think of himself as the joint-Caesar of the enterprise, in order to get his money. He was capable almost of persuading Gunsbourg that the new ballets were his – Gunsbourg's – inspiration; and even if Gunsbourg was too intelligent to be deceived or to deceive himself, he may still have derived a certain pleasure from being treated by Diaghilev in society if not as 'the onlie begetter' at least as someone whose intelligence, taste, name, cosmopolitan Jewish connections, business experience and money were essential to the enterprise of taking Russian art to Western Europe. It must have been Gunsbourg who enabled Diaghilev to pay Astruc 5,000 francs on 14 February and to honour a bill for 17,432 francs on 10 March,[48] for while continually postponing a visit to Paris for discussions with Astruc, after six weeks of shilly-shallying, Diaghilev cabled to Astruc on 10 April that Nouvel and Gunsbourg, his powers-of-attorney (*fonds de pouvoir*), would be leaving on the morrow.[49] However, Gunsbourg had not left on 23 April, when he cabled Astruc he would be 'leaving Tuesday'.[50]

All this time Diaghilev was negotiating with London and New York,[51] juggling with prospective seasons, tours and combinations which might make his projects more feasible financially. He had also arranged that the Russian Ballet (opera having been finally renounced in mid-March) would dance in Berlin on the way to Paris and in Brussels after Paris. But with no opera on the programme, Diaghilev realized he needed two more new productions besides 'The Firebird', 'Schéhérazade' and 'Giselle'. The last ballet had not been abandoned on the withdrawal of Pavlova. They counted on Karsavina to dance it with Nijinsky instead, and Benois had designed two charming *pastiche* Romantic sets, which had already been painted. There had been some hesitation in entrusting the great role to Karsavina in spite of her successes in Paris.[52] She had had little occasion hitherto to reveal her genius for mime. Fokine spoke against her,[53] which seems incredible as she was his supreme interpreter. Either he wanted her to appear only in *his* ballets, or, more likely, his marriage to Vera had brought out in him a tendency to decry his former love. Getting to know Tamara Karsavina better, Benois was enchanted with her character: 'Tatochka now really became one of us; she was the most reliable of our chief artists and one whose entire being was suited to our work. . . . Tamara Platonovna was not only a beautiful woman and a first-class, highly individual artist, but had as well a most attractive personality, was open to varied interests and infinitely more cultured than most of her comrades. . . .' What a relief for the friends to find that 'unlike Pavlova, with whom one could not talk except in a half-coquettish ballet fashion, Karsavina was capable of sustaining a serious conversation'![54]

Karsavina was delighted to find herself admitted to the flat in Zamiatin Pereulok off the English Quay, where the new Russian Ballet had been born.

In Diaghilev's small flat beat the pulse of his formidable enterprise. Strategic moves and counter-moves of his ingenuity, planning, budgeting, music in one corner, discussion in another. A Chancery and a small Parnassus in the restricted space of two rooms. The lines of each production were discussed there first. Around the table sat wise men; the Artistic Committee drinking weak tea and hatching daring ideas. . . . Benois topped the Areopagus. . . . He overflowed with benignity, and his erudition was unique. His mastery of blending fantastic with real was the more wonderful because he effected his magic by the simplest means. . . . Quite different assets were those of Bakst. He was exotic, fantastic – reaching from one pole to another. The spice and sombreness of the East, the serene aloofness of classical antiquity were his. Roerich – all mystery; a prophet with impeded speech, he could do infinitely more than ever he promised. . . . While they sat in one room, in the next Stravinsky and Fokine worked over a score and appealed to Diaghilev in every collision over the tempi. . . . He brought quick, unhesitating decision to every doubt. He had a sense of the theatre to an uncanny degree. Engrossed as he was in his part, he kept a vigilant eye on his collaborators. 'Gentlemen, you are wandering off your point,' came now and then from his corner. Diversions constantly occurred. Tradesmen burst in; alarming news arrived; unless Anisfeld has more canvas at once, he won't be able to finish painting the scenery.[55]

There was evidently a limit to the funds Gunsbourg was willing to put at Diaghilev's disposal, for the latter, having failed to raise money in Russia for the forthcoming season, set out at Easter for Paris.[56] To Benois he sent off such despairing cables describing his set-backs and disappointments that the friends began to fear he might commit suicide.[57] It seemed that the season was doomed.

On 5 March a ball was to be given by the magazine *Satyricon* in the Pavlov Hall. Two young men, Mikhail Kornfeld, later the editor of the magazine, and Pavel Patiomkin, the celebrated poet who died young, came to Fokine and asked him to stage a ballet to be given at the ball. He suggested Schumann's Carnaval as eminently appropriate and also as something he had long wanted to arrange. The young men were enthusiastic. Let Fokine describe how his delightful ballet came into existence.

We sat down with the German biography [of Schumann] and [Kornfeld] quickly translated to me the past pertinent to Carnaval which had a connection with Schumann's personal life. . . . From this and from the titles indicated on the music, such as 'Harlequin', 'Columbine', 'Pantalon', 'Pierrot' and 'Papillon' I was able immediately to visualize and construct the picture of the ballet: the series of separate characters linked one to the other – the proverbially hapless Pierrot, the comical Pantalon, the Harlequin always emerging victorious from his escapades; and the light plot around the love between Columbine and Harlequin. The luckless Pierrot and Pantalon were literally improvised during rehearsal. The ballet was staged in three rehearsals, the last of which took place . . . minutes before the opening of the ball. The staff of the *Satyricon* magazine were finishing the decoration of the hall, banging with their hammers, shouting to one another, arguing and climbing ladders to hang cloths and garlands. During all this commotion and racket I created the Finale. . . .[58]

Apart from the actor Meyerhold, all those taking part in 'Carnaval' were members of the Imperial Ballet. But as it was against the rules for them to appear elsewhere than at the Mariinsky during the ballet and opera season, they danced anonymously and all were masked. Everyone knew who they were, including members of the Directorate of the Imperial Theatres who were present, but because of the polite fiction of the masks, discipline could be said to be unbreached.[59]*

* For that matter, Meyerhold, who had been working since September 1908 as a producer at the Alexandrinsky Theatre (following his successive breaks with Stanislavsky in Moscow and

'Carnaval' [wrote Fokine] I composed in the following way: the ballet started and developed on the stage, and continued amidst the audience.... During the number which Schumann called Promenade the dancers left the stage, and the Finale was done amidst the spectators. At the very end the dancers ran back on the stage. Just before the end Harlequin and Columbine tied up Pierrot and Pantalon with the long sleeves of the former. When the two of them finally managed to disentangle themselves and run towards the stage, the curtain fell right in front of their noses, leaving them alone on the proscenium.

In the final dance everything was built on runs. Florestan pursued Estrella, Eusebius chased Chiarina, Papillon ran away from Pierrot and Pantalon; everyone ran in and out of the audience, the dancers mingling with the spectators. This was novel and entertaining, but not too easy because the dancers, wearing masks, had difficulty in locating and identifying each other.[60]

The enforced anonymity of the dancers meant that their names could not be mentioned in the press: this has led to a confusion over the exact casting which I have had some difficulty in clearing up. In the English-language edition of his autobiography Fokine gave the name of Leontiev as having danced Harlequin; Mme Karsavina says Fokine danced it; Mme Bronislava Nijinska says her brother did.

I wrote to Mr Vitale Fokine, the choreographer's son, about this. He told me that when preparing the fuller Russian edition of his father's book for the press, his researchers in Leningrad had found that Leontiev had indeed danced Harlequin, and that Nijinsky had taken the role of Florestan. (In the English edition of Fokine's book, Florestan is given to Vassili Kiselev.) Karsavina was Columbine; Vera Fokina was Chiarina; Ludmilla Schollar was Estrella; Alexander Chiriaiev was Eusebius; Bronislava Nijinska was Papillon; Alfred Bekefi was Pantalon; and Vsevolod Meyerhold, the actor and director (already famous for his experiments), was Pierrot. The ballet was accompanied by the piano suite as Schumann wrote it.*

Time being scarce, Fokine, apart from showing the dancers their moves and timing, left certain details for them to fill in themselves. When Bronislava

Komisarjevskaya in Petersburg), was asked by Teliakovsky, shortly after this, to adopt a pseudonym for his private theatrical activities.

* In Beaumont's *Michael Fokine* and in his *Complete Book* he gives the role of Florestan to I. Kchessinsky. In the English-language edition of Fokine's memoirs Florestan is Vassili Kiselev. In his *The Diaghilev Ballet*, Grigoriev gives the roles of Columbine and Harlequin, at the first performance of 'Carnaval' by the Diaghilev Ballet (in Berlin, 20 May 1910) to Karsavina and Nijinsky. But Karsavina was at the London Coliseum and Mme Lopokhova, who in fact danced the Berlin and Paris premières, confirms that her Harlequin was Leontiev. Arnold Haskell in his *Diaghileff* does not make this mistake: on the other hand he states that it was Diaghilev who had Schumann's music orchestrated by the four composers – overlooking the fact that Rimsky would have to have made his contribution posthumously. In his *Complete Book* Beaumont also states wrongly that the first performance of the ballet in Western Europe was in Paris. Nijinsky did not take over the role of Harlequin until 1911.

was practising her Butterfly dance, it was Vaslav who invented and taught her the rapidly changing positions of the arms, now together in front, now behind the back, and the fluttering hands which, with the non-stop movement, seem to us today the essential characteristics of this role in Fokine's famous and much-loved ballet. We can imagine the brother, putting on his coquettish face, flitting about the room and then correcting his sister. Bronia stayed up half the night perfecting in front of a looking-glass the gestures he had shown her.[61] So what was possibly Nijinsky's first effective essay in choreography was embedded in a work of Fokine's, just as Leonardo's angel is said to smile from the corner of Verocchio's 'Madonna' in the National Gallery. Vaslav's mind had perhaps already been directed by Diaghilev since the last summer into thoughts of doing choreography.

It was Grigoriev who told Diaghilev about 'Carnaval'.

Diaghilev looked up from his exercise book and said that he did not particularly care for Schumann, and that though he had not seen Fokine's ballet, he had heard that it was arranged for only a small number of dancers and would therefore be unsuitable for a large stage. However, Benois arrived at this point, and, on hearing my suggestion, supported me. . . .[62]

By chance Schumann's suite had already been orchestrated by Rimsky-Korsakov, Liadov, Glazunov and Tcherepnine: this was done as far back as 1902 for a concert in memory of Anton Rubinstein. With a short *divertissement* called 'Les Orientales', for which Diaghilev himself[63] chose music by Glazunov, Sinding and Arensky, and commissioned an orchestration of Grieg from Stravinsky (for which he was paid seventy-five roubles), the repertory was now complete.

Somehow, with the aid of Astruc, Diaghilev contrived to make the season in Paris possible. The financial responsibility was all to be his: he simply hired the Opéra for a number of days.[64] It was hoped to pay for the season out of box-office receipts. Astruc, who was now naturally as anxious as anyone to make this season a success, even though in competition with his opera season at the Châtelet, would have his percentage, but he also helped by raising money on the prospective takings. In all these negotiations, no doubt, Misia, Mme Greffuhle, Mme de Chevigné, Mme de Béarn, Mme Ephrussi and others played their part.

Soon after Diaghilev's return from Paris it was time for Karsavina to depart for London. She had promised to try to get leave from the Coliseum in order to join the Russians in Paris as soon as possible, on the condition that she returned to the Coliseum later in the summer.[65] The young Lydia Lopokhova would dance Columbine in Berlin and on the opening night in Paris; and 'Giselle' and 'The Firebird' would be postponed till Karsavina's arrival.

Diaghilev did not argue with us. He merely went on thinking.[62] On the eve of my departure for London [wrote Karsavina] a more than usually pressing 'come to talk things over' brought me again to Diaghilev's flat. I think he wanted to re-exercise the almost hypnotic power he had over me before I could escape from his influence. There the air was tense, all nerves worn down, as usual nothing ready and time short. He took me to his room, the only uninvaded spot. . . . Diaghilev reminded me of my promise. We both had outlived the strife, if there was one; mutual anxiety had brought us closer. Diaghilev spoke affectionately; we cried a little. I looked round. The image lamp was lit; Diaghilev looked weary, a mere human. The room was bare of adornment, I had expected it to be fastidious. I could not realize then that the glamour of his personality spent itself in creation of fancy. His gentle words had a touch of resignation. He knew that on his way one obstacle hardly removed another will arise.[66]

On 7 May, King Edward of England died, and all hopes of a London season in 1910 fell through. This was a bitter blow.[67]

The final problem was to find the money to pay for the artists' tickets to Berlin and Paris. More string-pulling, more persuasion. The Finance Minister, Count Kokovtsov,* advised the Tsar to grant Diaghilev 10,000 roubles, the equivalent of £1,000. The Tsar signed the report. The friends heard of this at three in the afternoon, a day or two before the company was due to depart. Diaghilev rushed round to a banker friend and on the security of the Tsar's order borrowed £1,000 for a few days. The tickets were bought. But the Tsar was not a man of honour. Under pressure perhaps from the Grand Duke Sergei Mikhailovitch, who is said to have persuaded him that Diaghilev's ballets were decadent, he withdrew the small subsidy. The banker had to be repaid. Prince Argutinsky and another loyal friend Ratkov-Rognev signed a bill for the sum needed. This was later paid back to them out of receipts in Paris. The Tsar, however, circulated his embassies with the command to refuse all support to Diaghilev's enterprise.[68]

The mild affectionate Benois was subject to occasional fits of temper, sulks – even passion. He had at least one serious quarrel with Diaghilev every year. For Diaghilev, his 'pupil', had now assumed command – by right of having taken all the dirty work on himself in order to allow his painters, composers, choreographer and dancers to get on happily with their jobs – and he was apt to adopt a high-handed manner. On the day before the company's departure Benois called at the passport office to collect his passport for Germany and France and found Diaghilev had not made the necessary arrangements for him, so that he would be held up for two days and deprived of the fun of travelling with the company. Is it possible that in the last anxious weeks Diaghilev had found his old friend increasingly

* He became Prime Minister on the assassination of Stolypin in the following year.

fractious and had hoped to pass a few days without him? Benois returned home, and in an onrush of rage, banged his right fist against a window-pane and severed an artery. He might have lost the use of his hand, but after an operation and a month in Petersburg with his arm in plaster he recovered, and left with his family for Lugano – thus missing Berlin and the Paris opening.[69]

In the middle of May the Russians arrived in Berlin. They were to appear in the Theater des Westens in Charlottenburg, a quiet western suburb grown up around the palace and formal gardens created by the Prussian kings. The dancers from Moscow arrived a few days later. Karalli had not been re-engaged, but Sophie Feodorova returned to dance not only her roles in 'Prince Igor' and 'Le Festin', but one of the three Odalisques in 'Schéhérazade' – which she had already rehearsed in Petersburg. Moscow's most celebrated ballerina, Ekaterina Gelzer, came as a guest artist to dance in 'Le Festin' and 'Les Orientales'. Plump, pretty and excitable, she had a strong classical technique, but very little else.[70] Alexander Volinine, who accompanied her, was the son of a rich Moscow merchant[71] – an unusual parentage for a dancer in 1910: he was quiet, amiable and a good partner.[72]

Of the new ballets only 'Carnaval' was to be shown in Berlin, and, in the absence of Karsavina in London, the role of Columbine would be interpreted by the irrepressibly gay Lydia Lopokhova, whose ingenious virtuosity was 'tempered by the imperceptible awkwardness of youth'.[73] Leontiev would be her Harlequin. It had rightly been considered essential to show the Schumann ballet to the Germans. It was given on the opening night of the season on 20 May and proved enormously popular.

The setting Bakst designed for 'Carnaval' is so familiar to us today that it is easy to forget how startling it must have seemed in its simplicity to the theatre-goers of 1910. The dark blue curtains have a poetic ambiguity, for they suggest both a tent in which a party is being given and the booth in which the characters of the Commedia dell'Arte entertain their audience. Along the top of the curtains runs a dado of stylized poppies in red, black and gold, which, together with two red and black striped sofas with curly arms, the stage's only other adornment, place the date of the action in the Viennese Biedermeyer period, that is, 1840. For the 'programme' of Schumann's composition, closely followed by Fokine, contains references to his love-life and embodies not only the (gallicized) characters of the Italian comedy, Harlequin, Columbine, Pierrot and Pantalon, but also autobiographical allusions: Florestan, who chases Estrella, representing the headstrong, impulsive side of Schumann's character, and Eusebius, who is shyly and reverently in love with Chiarina, the solitary, dreamy and romantic side. Estrella is Ernestine von Fricken, with whom the composer was in love;

and Chiarina the fifteen-year-old Clara Wieck, the pianist whom he later married.

The girls all wear flounced crinolines with bonnets or frilled caps. Some are white and yellow; Chiarina has a white jacket and a royal blue skirt with tassels; Papillon's white dress is shorter, more childish than the others, with little painted wings, and she has bunches of ribbons attached to her wrists; Columbine's big white skirt has cherries painted round one of its innumerable scalloped frills, and she has black silk ballet shoes. The men, mostly top-hatted, wear brown or bottle-green frock-coats with high collars, nipped-in waists and full-skirts in the D'Orsay style, worn over buff or striped peg-top trousers. Pantalon is excessively dapper in ginger, with dyed moustaches and green gloves; and Eusebius, with his long black poetic hair, has a carnation-pink velvet jacket, shorter than the others, and striped black trousers. Pierrot is traditional, in baggy white trousers and smock with a limp black ruff, green pom-pom buttons and long trailing sleeves that hide his hands. The lozenge pattern on Harlequin's tight trousers is apple green, vermilion and white to match Columbine's cherries; he has a floppy white silk shirt, a black bow, black skull cap and (painted) black domino mask.

The charm of Fokine's ballet is that there is just enough story to give interest to the dancing but no more than the music itself contains – nothing had to be twisted or added. Diaghilev, the arch-cutter, cut only the brief number called Réplique. The work is delicate, pretty, but also faintly satirical, with a touch of sadness and a hint of cruelty to add spice to the comedy. Harlequin mocks the world and makes love only in jest; and it seems to be through his eyes that we are intended to see the absurd yearning of Eusebius, the Angst of Pierrot and the senile philandering of Pantalon.

After the preliminary stately chords there is a flight of girls, crossing the stage pursued by their lovers – a tripping of feet, an urgency of overtaking, male impatience, feminine provocation. Are they on their way to a party, these dancers to the *valse brillante* of Schumann's Préambule, or merely leaving the ballroom for the secret shadows of the garden? We see for the first time Florestan chasing Estrella, and after the heartfelt sighs of Eusebius for Chiarina the pace quickens from *animato* to *vivo* to *presto*.

Pierrot tiptoes through the curtain, down-sloping eyebrows over tired eyes, to mourn his loveless life. His arms are extended upwards with dangling sleeves, but every glimmer of hope is at once extinguished by his realization of the impossibility of communicating with another human being. To the bounding waltz expressive of his carefree character Harlequin capers on and feigns friendship for Pierrot. He dances round him, points at him derisively, pulls his sleeves, but finally pushes him over and runs off. For the next few numbers Pierrot lies dejectedly by the proscenium arch. There follows a Valse Noble for six couples. Then comes Eusebius to dream of love on a sofa. His languid tune, orchestrated, has seven notes on the clarinet to two on the string accompaniment, which seems to want to trip him up. Chiarina appears to him and gives him a rose, and he dotes on her. How vivid a contrast is Florestan's exuberant onrush to a passionate waltz, his whirlwind flirtation with Estrella. His tune is interrupted in mid-career as he makes his high-pacing exit-run after her! During this dance Pierrot has also been yearning after Estrella and at the end of it he lopes off. To the air called Coquette, Eusebius and Chiarina go through their romantic paces, she throwing him flowers. Then Papillon flits on – *prestissimo* semi-quavers on the flute and piccolo alternating with violins – fluttering hands and tittupping feet. Pierrot stalks her, but she cannot for a second come to rest, and just as he thinks he has caught her in his conical white hat she vanishes through the curtains. To Lettres Dansantes, another fast waltz, we watch the palpitations of Pierrot – his expectation of finding in his hat a butterfly all of his own, his disappointment, as the tune ends in mid-phrase, on finding the hat empty. Chiarina has an *apassionato* solo with a strong rhythmic melody scored for strings. To the tune called Chopin she and her two friends, tip-toeing like three Graces with arms raised and gloved hands meeting, in and out and round and round, impede Florestan's pursuit of the expectant Estrella and 'share with each other the virgin's secret armoury of cruelty'.* Then, having celebrated, as it were, to this solemn and valedictory nocturne, scored for clarinet, harp and strings, the mysteries of girlhood, they back away from each other, still on tip-toe, drawn by fate in three different directions; and we see the extremities of Chiarina's hand disappearing through a parting of the curtains at the back. There follows a short rapid entry for Estrella.

When Columbine and Harlequin enter, linked together, to Reconnaissance, his high-hopping knees-up steps follow the *animato* melody, scored for flute and clarinet, while her rapid *pas de bourrée* echo the staccato semi-quaver string accompaniment. They circle the stage and kiss. Pantalon bustles on in a great fuss and hurry to Schumann's *perpetuum mobile*, afraid to be late for his assignation with Columbine. He looks at his watch, sits on a sofa and re-reads her letter. She steals up behind him and puts her hand over his eyes while Harlequin snatches the note. When Columbine introduces Harlequin to the old man, the latter holds out his hand, but the former flourishes the love-letter, then tears it into little pieces, and scatters them in the air as he executes *entrechats*, wagging his head grotesquely. To the dipping Valse

---

* I could not resist borrowing this sentence of Adrian Stokes's, although it was applied to a later production of 'Carnaval'. (*Tonight the Ballet*, p. 41.)

Allemande, Columbine circles round the offended Pantalon and tries to include him in her dance with Harlequin, but at the end they push him playfully off. Harlequin's triumphant solo, to the tune called Paganini, is made up of *cabrioles, entrechats, pirouettes* and rapid hand-claps above the head. At the end he executes a *grande pirouette à la seconde*, spinning gradually more slowly as he sinks into a sitting position, cross-legged on the floor. In Aveu the lovers, on opposite sides of the stage, argue about who should cross over to whom, then to this sigh-heaving amorous tune Harlequin, kneeling, lays a symbolic heart at Columbine's feet. When the other couples gradually come on and fill the stage to the ambling Promenade, they discover Columbine on the sofa, with Harlequin stretched out on the floor, whispering to her. Congratulations are offered to the engaged couple, and all the men kiss Columbine's hand. General rejoicings. Papillon flits on, pursued by Pierrot. The young dancers march against a group of old 'Philistines' (musical reactionaries in Schumann's mind) who carry umbrellas. Pantalon and Pierrot are spun round in an involuntary embrace and knotted together by the latter's sleeves, but mollified in time to hold hands with Columbine and Harlequin in the final group.

Fokine's 'Carnaval' contained some wonderful ideas and was to provide Nijinsky, a year later, with one of his most effective roles. The virginal *pas de trois* of Chiarina and her two friends, the entry of Columbine and Harlequin and the end of the latter's solo, had the simplicity of genius. Perhaps only in the rather pointless attack on the Philistines can we see signs of the ballet's rapid composition and the transfer of the final number from ballroom to stage.

Vera Fokina with her mannered romantic languor and Bronislava Nijinska with her speed and strength were ideally suited to the roles of Chiarina and Papillon. Maestro Cecchetti was so experienced a mime that he could make even the small role of Pantalon into a masterpiece. That people found Bolm's Pierrot profoundly moving gave an extra dimension to the comedy. As Columbine, Lopokhova was irresistible.

The company arrived in Paris at the beginning of June and Lopokhova was so excited by the beauty of the Gare du Nord that she fainted.

The Paris Opéra had less elaborate machinery than the Châtelet; the stage staff were as unco-operative as in the days of 'Boris'; it was with the greatest difficulty that the Russians could get the stage to rehearse on; and 'Schéhérazade', of which nobody had yet seen the scenery hung, had still to be finished – and its dress rehearsal went badly.[74] However, it was a satisfaction for the company – as well as an honour – to appear in this great gilded palace, even if it seemed a little shabby and in need of redecoration.[75]

The endless wide passages backstage and the large, comfortable dressing-rooms, furnished by their permanent French occupants, each with its private amenities, were superior to anything the dancers were used to in Russia.[76]

Could the Russians, without opera or Chaliapine, without Pavlova – and opening without Karsavina – recapture the Parisian public? If Paris proved fickle and stayed away from the Opéra, or was stolen away by the Metropolitan Opera season at the Châtelet, there would probably never again be a

José-Maria Sert, Jean Cocteau, Misia Edwards (Sert) and Diaghilev in a box. Caricature by Jean Cocteau.

Saison Russe. Fokine, Nijinsky and the other dancers would return to shelter beneath the wings of the Imperial eagle. Bakst and Benois did not live solely by designing for the stage: they had their reputations and livelihoods as art historian and painter to keep them going. But Diaghilev? What would his future be if the season was a failure? He had none in Russia. He would be ruined and there would be many who would rejoice. Outwardly, as ever, he wore an air of supreme self-confidence: inwardly he must have been devoured by anxiety and doubt.

Yet he need not have worried. The Opéra would be sold out. Nijinsky would reveal his versatility in 'Schéhérazade' and 'Giselle'. Little Lydia Lopokhova would be acclaimed. Karsavina would triumph in 'L'Oiseau de feu'. 'Schéhérazade' would astound the public and change the appearance of women and drawing-rooms throughout Europe and America. In 'L'Oiseau de feu', his first very-own commissioned 'Diaghilev ballet', the heroic Sergei Pavlovitch would proclaim to the world the genius of our century's greatest composer. What glories after what trials!

The opening programme on 4 June was made up of 'Carnaval', 'Schéhérazade', 'Le Festin' and the Polovtsian Dances from 'Prince Igor'.

Six months before his death two summers earlier, Rimsky-Korsakov had written of Isadora Duncan: 'What I dislike about her is that she connects her art with musical compositions dear to me. . . . How vexed I should be if I learned that Miss Duncan danced and mimed to my "Schéhérazade". . . .'[77] Diaghilev had had trouble persuading Rimsky's widow to allow him to present the symphonic poem as a dance-drama – it was certainly not a ballet; and we may be almost certain that if the composer could have seen Fokine's production he would have been displeased. When we consider, looking ahead, what shocks Debussy and Stravinsky would sustain when they saw dancing to the accompaniment of scores actually commissioned for ballet, it seems inconceivable that Rimsky could have been pleased with what happened to his 'Schéhérazade' – any more than Chopin or Schumann with the ballets made to their orchestrated piano compositions. When Fokine, taking his cue from Isadora, had arranged dances to Chopin, he was – for a ballet-master – breaking fresh ground. But 'Les Sylphides' had no story: there was one danced number for each waltz or mazurka. By imposing, with the help of Benois and Bakst, a passionate drama on an elaborate symphonic composition complete in itself, Fokine and his collaborators were going much further – and probably in the wrong direction. In view of the numerous compositions, including symphonies, concertos, quartets and parts of operas, which have been 'used' as the basis of story ballets in recent years, it may be of interest to consider the problems facing the librettists and choreographer of this work which was the first of its kind.

Rimsky wrote in his autobiography:

The programme I had been guided by in composing 'Schéhérazade' consisted of separate, unconnected episodes and pictures from 'The Arabian Nights', scattered through all four movements of my suite: the sea and Sinbad's ship, the fantastic narrative of Prince Kalender, the Prince and the Princess, the Baghdad festival and the ship dashing against the rock with the bronze rider on it. The unifying thread consisted of the brief introductions to Movements I, II and IV and the intermezzo in Movement III, written for violin solo and delineating Schéhérazade herself as telling her wondrous tales to the stern Sultan. The final conclusion of Movement IV serves the same artistic purpose. In vain do people seek in my suite leading motives linked consistently with ever the same poetic ideas and conceptions. . . . The unison phrase, as though depicting Schéhérazade's stern spouse, at the beginning of the suite appears as a datum in the Kalender's Narrative, where there cannot, however, be any mention of Sultan Shahriar.[78]

Benois, Diaghilev and Fokine, having seized upon the 'unifying thread', a tendrilly *arabesque* for solo violin with slight harp accompaniment, as a theme for Schéhérazade – or rather for Zobeïda, as the Sultana was called in their ballet – could not but use the *pesante* opening theme – which Rimsky calls 'the unison phrase' – for the Sultan, Shah or King.

So the first movement is to be an overture, and the third is to be omitted. The ballet opens with the sinuous blandishment of Zobeïda. The King of India, Shah Shahriar, is sulking because his brother Zeman, the King of Persia (down here on a visit), has told him his wives are all unfaithful. The Shah sits cross-legged on a divan being coaxed by his queen while Persia sits on his left glowering over his *tchibouk* and keeping a suspicious eye on the whispering harem. The fat old Chief Eunuch is in attendance. A dance of three seated Odalisques, who undulate their arms to the *andantino* in 3/8 time, fails to divert the Shah from his gloomy thoughts. At the end of the dance he rises (to brusque chords in the basses), waves aside the beguiling Zobeïda and announces his intention to go hunting. Echoing trumpet fanfares confirm his decision. As the preparations are made he converses with his brother. Zobeïda's begging him to stay will not be her own little *cadenza* on the violin but *roulades* on the clarinet. The fanfares and the marches are varied and prolonged considerably before the Shah's expedition can be lost sight of, so he has to be armed, and huntsmen and soldiers have to be brought on and eventually marched off. A bassoon solo will accompany the Eunuch, whom the ladies of the harem implore to unlock the doors to admit their Negro lovers, and their pleading will be represented by warbling in the higher woodwind. But there is no theme for the Golden Negro, Zobeïda's lover; and a reappearance of the Shah's theme in the background during the movement's final *accelerando* must be explained away in his absence as an imminent threat or a guilty thought at the back of the Queen's or the Eunuch's mind.

The last movement, which Rimsky called 'Festival at Baghdad: the Sea', can be relabelled 'Orgy: Slaughter'. In the ballet it follows the preceding movement without a break. The firm statement of the Shah's theme at the very beginning needs some accounting for when he is away out hunting, as indeed its reappearance twice before the orgy has reached its climax. Perhaps it is a forecast of the Shah's return; certainly it helps to dramatize the tense wariness of the slaves as they enter the Shah's private realm. Zobeïda's solo violin accompanies the embraces she exchanges with her Negro. The surging, terrifying music of the storm and ship-wreck will lend itself admirably to the wrath of Shahriar when he returns to find his wives enter-taining their paramours, but Fokine will have a problem because hints of the Storm, represented by a suppressed statement of the Shah's theme and distant fanfares, occur during the Festival, so he will have to bring on, as it were, outriders of the Shah's revenge, before the janissaries really set to with their scimitars to slaughter the wives and slaves. The Shah's tune, blasted out by trombones and tuba during the massacre, returns at the end to be played softly on cellos and basses, this final gentle treatment representing, no doubt, in Rimsky's mind not only calm after the storm but also the happy ending of 'The 1,001 Nights', when sentence of death is remitted: but the mildness of its restatement can easily be accepted in the dance-drama as due to the breaking of Shahriar's heart. Zobeïda's final violin cadenza is her pleading for her life. At the end of it she kills herself. As the curtain falls in silence the Shah weeps.

Designing the setting for 'Schéhérazade', Bakst had given himself up to a vision of the barbaric and voluptuous Orient which was his spiritual home, and in doing so created what was to become the most famous décor of the age. This harem had a kind of architecture – one vaguely related to the mosques and pavilions of Shah Abbas at Isfahan, with their blue and green tiled walls and painted coffered ceilings: but it was rather formless and depended on a debauch of colour to create its Monticellian impression. Anyway, the architecture of the backcloth, with its three blue doors leading to the slave quarters, was lost in purple twilight. The dominant feature of the set was an immense looped curtain framing the top and left side of the stage, apple green striped with sky blue, spotted with pink roses, and with larger circular patterns in black and gold; from this hung golden lamps. Green and blue was the overall colour-scheme but this amazing peacock green-and-blueness (an unheard-of combination in 1910, which inspired Cartier to set emeralds and sapphires together for the first time in history) was challenged by the coral-red carpet painted with blue and rose-pink rugs, and piled with incredible cushions and bolsters. Behind the Shah's raised divan to the left, where the great curtain fell to the ground, was a curious platform supported on the shoulders of highly improbable quasi-Indian caryatids and approached by a steep staircase, the sole purpose of which was to display a feat of daring and endurance by the dancer Orlov, who was one of the Negroes. At the end of the drama he was killed by one of the Shah's guards on the platform and then 'had to hang head downwards, spreadeagled on the steps with open arms, and hold this painful but effective pose till the curtain fell'.[79] To describe Bakst's invention is to belittle it, for this was no mere composition of architecture, furnishing and light, but an Aurora Borealis, a fantastic musical chord, a new and intoxicating smell.

Bakst was probably an even greater designer of costumes than of sets: his invention of pattern and his imaginative juxtaposition of colours has never been surpassed. In the blues and crimsons of his turbaned kings, in the scarlet Eunuch, the orange-vermilion and chrome-yellow high-capped janissaries, in the rose-pink and green Odalisques and the diaphanously clad, speckled and bejewelled ladies of the harem, and in the braceleted Negroes with their strange encrusted *brassières* linked to their bunched metallic *lamé* trousers by ropes of pearls, he showed more even than in 'Cléopâtre' the fantastic profusion of his genius. When the splendours of 'Schéhérazade' were contrasted with the quaint simplicity of 'Carnaval', who could doubt that he was the greatest designer in the world?

Yet Rimsky's music and the setting and costumes of Bakst were only there to give occasion for the drama devised by Fokine and the performances of Rubinstein as Zobeïda, Bulgakov as Shah Shahriar and Nijinsky as the Golden Slave.

Grigoriev wrote of the choreography for the *ensemble* dances in the Orgy:

By means of intricate evolutions for the various groups of dancers woven in with a number of individual moves, Fokine contrived to endow this dance with such rich variety that its climax was tremendous. The strongest choreographic moment came when, having combined all the different groups into one, he used a pause in the music suddenly to halt them, and then, while accelerating the pace still more, as it were to unravel this human tangle. The effect was overwhelming. The audience roared its applause. . . .[80]

Here is what Fokine thought of Ida Rubinstein's Zobeïda:

My creation of the role . . . and her performance were remarkable for giving powerful impressions accomplished by the most economical means. Everything was expressed with one single pose, with one movement, one turn of the head. Nevertheless, everything was outlined and drawn clearly. Every single line was carefully thought out and felt. She is displeased by the departure of her husband, and expresses her displeasure with a single movement, turning away her head when he comes to kiss her farewell. She stands in front of a door through which her lover is momentarily due to emerge. She waits for him with her entire body. Then (and to me the most dramatic scene) she sits utterly still while slaughter takes place around her. Death approaches her, but not the horror nor the fear of it. She majestically awaits her fate in a pose without motion. What powerful expression without movement! I consider this one of the most successful accomplishments among my ideas of the new ballet.[81]

The tall, ivory-pale Bulgakov, with his black beard, Benois thought 'a king from head to foot'.[82]

Now, a few opinions of Nijinsky's Golden Slave.

Fokine: The lack of masculinity which was peculiar to this remarkable dancer and which made him unfit for certain roles (such as that of the leading Warrior in the Polovtsian Dances) suited very well the role of the Negro Slave. He resembled a primitive savage, not by the colour of his body make-up, but by his movements. Now he was a half-human, half-feline animal, softly leaping great distances, now a stallion, with distended nostrils, full of energy, overflowing with an abundance of power, his feet impatiently pawing the ground.[83]

Geoffrey Whitworth: From the moment of his entrance the drama takes on to itself a new and terrible meaning. The dark youth flickers here and there among the mazy crowd of slaves, hungry for the faithless wife of the sultan. . . . He finds her soon, and his lecherous hands play over and over her body with a purpose too subtle, it seems, to take and hold her once and for all. And presently he leaves her, threading his way in and out of the passionate dancers, to lie at last on a soft cushion, like a flame of lust that smoulders and sinks but never dies. Now he has joined the orgy again. See him leap in the air, no man but a devil. . . .[84]

Benois: . . . Half-cat, half-snake, fiendishly agile, feminine and yet wholly terrifying.[85]

Vaudoyer: He was undulating and brilliant as a reptile.[86]

Bronislava Nijinska: From his first bound on to the stage the whole characterization of the Negro Slave was present. He was first a snake, then a panther.[87]

Estrade Guerra: I remember well how he fell forwards, pivoted on his head, then fell back on the other side, his arms and legs completely slack. . . . It was like seeing a hare wounded by the huntsman's shot and rising before the final fall.[88]

Francis de Miomandre: The transport of his movements, the encircling giddiness, the dominance of his passion reached such heights that when the executioner's sword pierced him in the final tumult we no longer really knew whether he had succumbed to the avenging steel or to the unbearable violence of his joy in those three fierce somersaults.[89]

Cocteau: He beat on the boards like a fish at the bottom of a boat.[90]

Savage, devil, stallion, cat, snake, hare, panther, fish!

The extraordinary first night at the Opéra which had begun with Lopokhova in 'Carnaval', continued with Nijinsky and Rubinstein in 'Schéhérazade', ended with 'Le Festin' and Fokine in 'Prince Igor'. Gelzer was rather vulgar in a Russian boyar dance,[91] with Volinine, but she had to be shown in something.

Marcel Proust was present to see the first performance of 'Schéhérazade', with Jean-Louis Vaudoyer and Reynaldo Hahn. Writing a few days later to comment on Reynaldo's article in *Le Journal*, Marcel protested: 'I don't see how you could possibly see Nijinsky miming, because there were always two hundred people dancing in front of him'; and he added, 'I never saw anything so beautiful.'[92]

Karsavina, having cajoled the Coliseum management into giving her leave, joined the company two days later, and was delighted with her well-furnished dressing-room, which had 'Mlle Legrand' painted over the door.[93]

It is curious that the ballet which Karsavina had been dancing twice nightly at the London Coliseum with Koslov and Baldina was the second act of 'Giselle' in the Moscow version[94] (though Karsavina in her role followed the Petersburg version), which was billed as 'Gisella, or La Sylphide': and now she had to rehearse the Petersburg version of the whole ballet with Nijinsky and perform it in the city of its origin. It had not been given in Paris since it was danced by Adela Grantsova in 1868.

The old Romantic ballet, conceived by Théophile Gautier and Vernoy de Saint-Georges as a vehicle to show off the wide range of Carlotta Grisi's gifts, had a strong role for the man as well, and we know Jules Perrot had been as vivid a mime as he was agile as a dancer. The artist impersonating the village girl, carefree and loving at the beginning, has when she finds her young suitor is a count in disguise and engaged to a princess, to go mad and die with the bravura of a Bellini or Donizetti heroine. When she reappears in Act II, disembodied, as one of the sylphlike Wilis, the dreaded '*dames des bois*', she must not only possess a technique strong enough to dance her lover almost to death, but also the ability to convey a tender love which outlasts the grave. Count Albrecht must be both prince and peasant, Hamlet to her Ophelia; he has to perform in the second act an exhausting series of *entrechats, cabrioles, pirouettes* and *tours en l'air* ending in crashing (but not noisy) falls to the ground, while giving an impression of remorse and heartbreak. This must all be done with period style.

It is typical of Nijinsky's seriousness that he was chiefly worried about the conventional mime. To dance an old ballet of this kind as part of the traditional repertory of the Mariinsky was one thing; to make something living out of it in a repertory otherwise consisting wholly of Fokine ballets was another matter. Fokine had abolished the old sign language. True, there was a little of it in 'Carnaval', with Harlequin laying his heart at Columbine's feet, but that was quite in keeping with Commedia dell' Arte characters. In 'Cléopâtre' Amoun did not declare his love for the queen by pointing first at himself, then placing both hands on his heart, then pointing at Cleopatra: he looked at her with passionate admiration.[95] In 'Schéhérazade', when the Shah was battling with himself whether to kill Zobeïda along with all the other wives, his vengeful brother did not embark on a long spiel such as:

15 Nijinsky in street clothes, Paris 1909.

16 Décor for 'Le Pavillon d'Armide', Act II, second version.
17 Vera Karalli and Mikhail Mordkine in 'Le Pavillon d'Armide', Act II, second versio
Photograph by Bert.

18 Nijinsky in 'Le Pavillon d'Armide', second version.
Photograph by L. Roosen.

19 Nijinsky in 'L'Oiseau de feu'
(Bluebird *pas de deux*) in 'Le Festin'.
Photograph by L. Roosen.

20 *and* 21 *(opposite)* Nijinsky in
a character dance in 'Le Festin'.
Photographs by Bert.

22 and 23 Nijinsky in 'Les Sylphides'.

24 Tamara Karsavina and Nijinsky
in 'Les Sylphides'.

25 Nijinsky in 'Le Pavillon d'Armide'.
Drawing by John S. Sargent, 1911.

26 Nijinsky in practice clothes. Drawing by Maxime Dethomas.
27 Nijinsky on the Lido. Painting by Leon Bakst.

Listen (hand extended to the Shah). Just think (tapping his forehead) that your queen (pointing at Zobeïda, then sketching a crown over his own head) was making love (cuddling his own body with both arms) to a Negro (making a fierce grimace and passing his hand like a shade down in front of his face to convey darkness). No, the King of Persia, hand on sword-hilt, paced very slowly across the front of the stage and with one foot turned the Negro's body over, so that he lay face upwards.[96] Karsavina could understand very well the charm of the old sign-language – the convention of a past age and a reminder of 'Giselle' 's origins.[97] But Nijinsky was so carried away on Fokine's new wave that he could not see his way satisfactorily to reconciling old fashions with heartfelt emotions.* One day at rehearsal Diaghilev complained to Nijinsky during Karsavina's mad scene that he was standing still doing nothing. Vaslav replied, 'I am acting with my eyes.'[98] He filled a notebook with his reflections on the ballet, and with his analysis of what Albrecht's reactions would be at different moments. And how was he to make the transition from mime to set dances as natural as in Fokine's dance-dramas? The choreographer himself shared Nijinsky's dissatisfaction: he had only been persuaded by Diaghilev to rehearse 'Giselle' when threatened with the engagement of a second *maître de ballet*.[99] After Chopin, Borodin, Schumann and Rimsky, the genuine ballet music written to order by Adolphe Adam in 1841 seemed terribly insipid.

Karsavina had been taught the role of Giselle by her old professor Mme Sokolova: Pavlova, who had made a speciality of the role in Petersburg, could have been extremely helpful to her, but was not.† Karsavina had not had the experience of dancing in the ballet at the Mariinsky, where Pavlova kept it for herself; but she had at least grown used to dancing the steps of the second act in London. She wrote:

So intent were Nijinsky and I on making masterpieces of our own respective parts in 'Giselle' that our eagerness to impose on one another our individuality led to tempestuous scenes. 'Giselle' on our stage was a holy ballet, not a step to be altered. . . . I loved every bit of it. I was sadly taken aback when I found that I danced, mimed, went off my head and died of a broken heart without any response from Nijinsky. He stood pensive and bit his nails. 'Now you have to come across towards me,' I suggested. 'I know myself what to do,' he said moodily. After ineffectual efforts to go through the dialogue by myself, I wept. Nijinsky looked sheepish and unmoved. Diaghilev led me off to the wings, proffered a handkerchief and told me to be indulgent: 'You don't know what volumes he has written on that part, what treatises on its interpretation.'[100]

Volumes! an exaggeration of course. And it is clear that *thinking* a role out

---

* The public, on the whole, and particularly in London, would prove to share his confusion.
† When I asked Mme Karsavina if Pavlova had helped, she exclaimed, 'Not her!'

was not a successful method with Nijinsky, though of course he forced himself to try: he had to *feel* it, and this feeling might only come to him suddenly and at the eleventh hour.[101] The straightforward princely role, romantic or heroic, was not really in his line. Whereas most male dancers spent their lives being just that and nothing more – cavaliers always at hand to lift the ballerina and take a secondary place – he had begun to specialize in roles that were more fantastic. There was also something awkward to him in the normal man–woman relationship in ballet. In 'Schéhérazade', though an embodiment of lust, he had been in a way more feminine than Ida Rubinstein.

'From now on,' wrote Karsavina, 'Diaghilev acted as a buffer between us. We were both inflammable, and the learning of "Giselle" was not without tears and many. Eventually understanding came; and we got well attuned together. "Giselle", according to notices, was a great personal success for the interpreters – nothing more.'[102]

Perhaps Diaghilev's instinct had been right in doubting whether Parisians would be interested in an interpretation of their old ballet by the Russians. Benois' nostalgic sets – the first an autumn landscape with a distant hill-top castle, beetling on its crag, the second a dark blue moonlit forest – were wonderful evocations of Gautier's dreams – Benois seemed destined to collaborate with *le bon Théo* across the years. When eventually the painter saw his ballet, he thought Karsavina 'almost outshone Pavlova'.[103] Svetlov, comparing her to the dramatic Pavlova, thought that she

took the part in another key. In her interpretation there enters no deep tragedy. On the contrary, it is the lyrical song of a woman's grief, sad and poetic. The pathos is tender, restrained. In the mad scene it is an almost timid complaint. In the act of the Wilis, in all her dances there is something soothing, almost a quiet satisfaction, a submission to fate and a hope for a happier future.[104]

In the photograph of Nijinsky as Count Albrecht his eyes shine and even his wig seems alive.

Now Karsavina and Fokine, Lopokhova and Leontiev alternated in the parts of Columbine and Harlequin in 'Carnaval'. Of Karsavina Svetlov wrote: 'The fine irony and tender smiles of Schumann's Carnaval are blended in her dancing into plastic visions set in an atmosphere of melody.'[105]

Benois was in Lugano with his family, but of course he was longing to share in the excitements of the Paris season, and, in response to 'insistent letters' from Diaghilev, he made the twelve-hour journey. On his arrival his friends Misia, Sert, Vaudoyer and the painter Dethomas made much of him; but a shock was in store.

How great was my amazement when, having taken my seat in the stalls of the

Paris Opéra, I unfolded my programme and read under the title 'Schéhérazade' the words 'Ballet de L. Bakst'. I was so amazed I could hardly believe my eyes, but at the first sounds from the orchestra and the raising of the curtain I forgot everything and gave myself up entirely to intense enjoyment of the performance. My enthusiasm was so great that when I went on the stage to embrace Bakst and Diaghilev after the performance I was quite unconscious of having been hurt by them. It was only after I had re-read the programme in my hotel that I became conscious of the real meaning of the words printed under the title, and my heart was filled with bitterness and indignation. This disappointment of mine had nothing to do with practical considerations; they did not enter my head. In spite of my age – forty years – I had only a very vague idea of the existence of 'royalties'. . . . Next day I was finally flabbergasted by Serioja's answer to my question as to how this could have happened: 'Que veux-tu? Bakst had to be given something. You have "Le Pavillon d'Armide" and he will have "Schéhérazade".'[106]

Never greedy of credit for himself, Diaghilev had made the mistake of overlooking the feelings of his friend, who was already getting a complex about being elbowed out of the new Russian Ballet, of which he was a founder-father. Diaghilev considered that as all the friends pooled their ideas, they might as well pool the spoils. If Bakst – whose décor for 'Schéhérazade', far more than Benois' story, was the epoch-making thing about it – could receive not only credit but also royalties on the work, it would go far to reconciling him to nominal or tardy payment for his many designs.[107] Back in Lugano, Benois wrote to Diaghilev telling him that he was 'breaking with him for good'.[108]

Diaghilev was too busy to be bothered. Like the Pope in Firbank's *Cardinal Pirelli* he probably thought, 'Why can't they all behave?' We have evidence that he not only thought but spoke bitterly against Benois, and ruled him out of his life – until he needed him again.[109] Benois, however, paid generous tribute to Bakst's triumphant décor in an article for the Russian magazine *Rech*.[110]

If 'Giselle' had too subtle a flavour for the pampered palate of *le tout Paris*, it was not wasted on Marcel Proust. From Cabourg in July he was to reproach Reynaldo by letter for calling it 'the celebrated and insipid "Giselle" ';[111] and when he began to write *A l'Ombre des jeunes filles en fleur* that summer with the first descriptions of Balbec's (Cabourg's) hotel, casino and *plage*, he gave the name Gisèle to one of the girls in Albertine's 'little band'.[112]

When Diaghilev and Nijinsky and their friends were supping after the ballet *chez* Larue, Proust would sometimes be sitting in a corner drinking chocolate and writing letters. It was here that Cocteau jumped on the back of the *banquette* and climbed over the table (as Bertrand de Fénelon had done in 1902, to be commemorated for his gallantry as Saint-Loup) to put Marcel's fur coat over his shoulders. Proust made a rhyme about the incident.

> *Afin de me couvrir de fourrure et de moire,*
> *Sans de ses larges yeux renverser l'encre noire,*
> *Tel un sylphe au plafond, tel sur la neige un ski,*
> *Jean sauta sur la table auprès de Nijinski.*
> *C'était dans le salon purpurin de Larue. . . .*[113]*

Proust found Nijinsky uninteresting off-stage, but he took to Bakst and thought his liking was reciprocated. 'It is true he is charming to everybody, but I thought I detected a *nuance*.'[114] After one of these evenings Diaghilev played a practical joke on Cocteau, who had dropped him home at the Hôtel Mirabeau, by telling the cab-driver to drive on to the Hôtel des Réservoirs at Versailles.

It became clear during rehearsals of 'The Firebird' that Karsavina was going to score a tremendous success. Diaghilev would have preferred Nijinsky to have enjoyed this, and he determined to put matters right in the following year. The ballet which Cocteau and Reynaldo Hahn were devising must have an oriental theme, since this had become all the rage; it must have décor and costumes by Bakst even more striking than those of 'Schéhérazade', and Nijinsky must have a role, like that of Karsavina as the Firebird, which set him apart from and above the other characters, a supernatural being and *deus ex machina*, who, moreover, would not have to support and take second place to any ballerina. In fact, in no new ballet by Fokine or himself would Nijinsky ever 'support' – in the sense of acting as a *porteur* – a ballerina again. (In 'Le Spectre de la rose' he would support Karsavina in an *arabesque*, but lift her very little. In 'Petrushka' it would be the Moor who supported the Ballerina. In Greek ballets, because of the nature of their movement, the question would not arise.)

Cocteau asked Karsavina to tell him the story of 'The Firebird'; and he incorporated several of its elements in the libretto of 'Le Dieu bleu'.[115]

Benois thought the story of 'The Firebird' was weak and that the friends had

only succeeded in creating another fairy-tale for children [like 'Koniok Gorbunok'] – not a fairy-tale for grown-ups. The worst of it is, that the hero, Ivan Tsarevitch and the Beautiful Tsarevna are always remote from the audience. One does not believe in them, and therefore it is impossible to suffer with them. The Evil Being, incarnated in Kastchei, is more alive and convincing. . . . But Kastchei appears too late and perishes too quickly. . . .

---

* Literally, 'To cover me with fur and shot silk, without spilling any of the black ink of his eyes, like a sylph on the ceiling or a ski on the snow, Jean leapt on the table near Nijinsky. It was in the crimsony hall of Larue. . . .'

Benois thought that Diaghilev's stipulation that the ballet should last no more than an hour had restricted Fokine and Stravinsky, accelerated the action and made the drama superficial.[116] While admitting that there is a disunity and oddity about the story, I find it hard to imagine the ballet longer or to see what could be gained by drawing the characters more profoundly: as a pageant, a tapestry, the ballet has always satisfied me. The disunity, of course, consists in the Firebird's having her chief dance, one of the longest and hardest solos ever invented, at the very start, when we have hardly caught a glimpse of Ivan and before the action really begins. The oddity is that there are no dances in the processional finale. On the stage these difficulties disappear. It seems wonderful that after the magic introduction we should at once be startled by the flashing apparitions of the bird of fire, who will return later only to lull the powers of evil to sleep; and the wedding procession and solemn immobility of Ivan and his Tsarevna at the very end are grand and moving.

Nor did Benois think Golovine's setting helpful to the drama, beautiful as it was. Diaghilev had wanted Vrubel to design the ballet, but Vrubel was dying or going mad,[117] and Golovine was chosen instead. 'Unfortunately,' wrote Benois, 'Golovine, a wonderful colourist and a lover of ancient Russian art, remained true to himself. . . .' He meant that Golovine's fine design was just a typical 'Golovine' and unhelpful dramatically. 'A group of poisonous toadstools, not unlike Hindu pagodas, symbolized Kastchei's residence; beneath were layers and outlines of different colours, suggesting overgrowths and thickets that were soft, green, damp and close. . . .' There were also the figures of knights, petrified by the evil Kastchei when they had attempted to rescue the captive princesses. 'It seemed like a huge chequered carpet, blazing with colour but devoid of any depth. No one could *penetrate* into such a forest – indeed, it seemed scarcely to be a forest at all.'[118] Benois may have been right, but the design of Golovine, who was a kind of archaic *pointilliste*, seems marvellous to us today – a semi-representational mosaic made up entirely of green, gold and silver beetles.

Golovine's costumes partook of an equal richness and their glitter merged with the set.

Kastchei's servants and followers were elaborately attired, but they were neither frightening nor repulsive. . . . The result was that Fokine's choreographic ideas, performed by the artists in working clothes at rehearsals, seemed to be extremely fantastic and eerie, but on the stage everything was submerged in uniform, sumptuous luxury: the Kikimoras looked like page-boys, the Bellyboshkies like Turkish janissaries. Even Kastchei himself (in spite of the performer's terrifying gestures and make-up) was hardly frightening. . . . Ivan Tsarevitch would never, as the tale demanded, have spat from sheer disgust in the face of such a Kastchei.[119]

Diaghilev found Golovine's costumes for the Firebird, the Prince and the Princess unsatisfactory, and Bakst made new designs for these.[120]

Thrilled as he was to find himself in Paris, Stravinsky had reservations about the score he had provided and the way Fokine was going to interpret it on stage. The conductor was Gabriel Pierné; and the composer stood in the darkened Opéra throughout eight orchestral rehearsals. One day Pierné put him in his place in front of all the musicians. He had written at one point in the score (no.90) '*non crescendo*', and Pierné said, 'Young man, if you do not want a *crescendo*, then do not write anything.'[121]

At last came the great day, 25 June, when a ballet of Stravinsky's would be given for the first time in the theatre and when his music would be heard for the first time in Western Europe. The composer was always to remember the rival glitter of the stage and of the audience.[122]

The introduction, played before the rise of the curtain, sets the scene. It is the ancient terror of the woods at night, the home of malevolent powers. It is Grendel's Mere in *Beowulf*:

> In a doubtful land
> Dwell they, wolf-shapes,   windy nesses,
> Fearsome fen-paths,   where the force from the mountains
> Under misty nesses   netherwards floweth,
> A flood under the fields.   'Tis not far from hence
> As miles are marked   that the mere standeth,
> Above which hang   rimy bowers;
> A wood fast-rooted   the water o'er-shadows.
> There will, every night,   a wonder be seen,
> Fire in the flood.   There is none found so wise
> Of the sons of men,   who has sounded those depths.

Lost in this horrible solitude the palace of evil sleeps, but we hear the tread of some of Kastchei's loathsome sentinels. When the curtain rises the Firebird's incandescent music is heard and we see her, apparently luminous, dart across the darkened stage. Karsavina does not wear a ballet *tutu*, but transparent Oriental pantaloons of bluish-green, drifting draperies, gold-braided tresses, flaming ostrich and pheasant feathers in her jewelled headdress. A fragment of the folk tune which represents Ivan steals in as we see his head appear over the wall and realize he is stalking her. Fokine has a medieval Russian prince's costume adorned with gold and jewels, and a cap with upturned brim. The Firebird sports in the garden, picking at the tree of golden apples. Her music is inhuman fireworks. Ivan puts down his bow, deciding to capture her alive. He clasps her in his arms. Karsavina's great dark eyes gaze in terror at him over her shoulder. She flutters, palpitates. Her dance of supplication is a *pas d'action*. He holds her by the waist as her arms are now clasped fearfully across her chest, now spread out as beating wings, now wrapped tightly round her head. Although she dances on point and her movements are extremely hard technically, with many *jetés*, there are none of the conventional coloratura steps of classical ballet – no *entrechats*, no *battements*, no *préparations*, no turn-out. Her pleading sounds very Schéhérazade-like. Ivan feels pity – he is a Christian prince – and this is ultimately to be his salvation: for the Firebird gives him a magic feather. He releases her and she darts exultantly away.

Ivan is alone and looks up as we imagine the bird flashing across in the treetops over his head. The prince's simple downright man-of-honour theme is contrasted with the lurking menace of Kastchei's sinister chromatics played by three bassoons. Down the slope from the castle come, barefoot, twelve princesses in their white embroidered nightgowns, the moonlight falling on their long hair. A thirteenth princess, the beautiful Tsarevna, interpreted by Vera Fokina, is more gorgeously nightgowned than the others. To a sparkling scherzo they dance and play catch with the golden apples. With formal bows and salutes Ivan introduces himself and is greeted with dignity by the Tsarevna. All join in a slow, stately round dance or Khorovod. A brief dialogue of two flutes in canon leads into an old folk-song (from Novgorod), 'In the Garden', played *cantabile* by oboe, then clarinet and bassoon; this is followed by another folk-tune, slightly faster, on the strings, and the dance ends with the prince and princess face to face, and we see that they love each other. Offstage trumpets herald the dawn. The princesses scamper off fearfully, the beautiful Tsarevna looking behind her, longingly. Prince Ivan, in manly desperation, decides to assault the castle single-handed.

As he batters at the castle gate, an unearthly *carillon* breaks forth, beginning with harps and celesta over chromatic waverings by the violas *sul ponticello*. Woodwind, brass and piano join in the movement which is worked up to a *fortissimo* climax, and the trombones play the main theme of the Infernal Dance in canon. No such incredible sounds have ever been heard in the Opéra before. On to the stage crawl, hop or leap the Kikimoras and Bellyboshkies of Kastchei's monstrous court. Ivan struggles but is made prisoner. Six sinister bars played on all the bass instruments of the orchestra (bassoons, contra-bassoons, horns, trombones, tuba, bass) lead to a sharp *staccato* chord as, whiskered, cadaverous, bent double, with bones showing through his golden skin, his shoulders rising into horned humps, with long talons on his skeleton hands, Kastchei enters. There follows a musical dialogue between hero and villain. Kastchei rages, the princesses plead with him in vain, and with loud chromatic scales, up and down, alternating with *pianissimo tremolando* in the strings, the ogre begins the spell which will turn

Ivan to stone. Tingling *glissandos* on harp and horn combine with wild upward flourishes in the woodwind, ending on a crash. Before the formula is repeated a third time Ivan waves his magic feather and with a whirr of wings the Firebird appears. She forces the monsters into a non-stop dance. Quietly at first, cor anglais and violins begin a nervous spinning tune. Wind and then full orchestra take over until Kastchei's retinue, half crazed, begin their Infernal Dance. A low *dies irae* alternates with jagged brass phrases. Snatches of oriental melody are heard from the violins. Xylophone and woodwind join in the *danse macabre*. A flute plays more gently but the respite is short-lived. Ruthlessly the *dies irae* returns. Brass fanfares lead to a diabolical finale for full orchestra with unison strings playing the princess's tune. The dance reaches a height of frenzy. A quiet *staccato* figure for strings works up to a full orchestral *fortissimo*. As the wind shrieks up and down, to a final sharp chord Kastchei's followers sink exhausted to the ground.

Now begins the Firebird's Lullaby – a melody of poignant beauty played by the bassoon with occasional sighs from the oboe. Muted strings quietly sustain, then play a high counter-melody. As the bassoon begins again violins play the Firebird's *motif* in descending chords. The oboe plays, fading into nothingness. As Karsavina circles the stage in *pas de bourrée* with outstretched arms, the whole crowd is lulled to sleep. Kastchei awakens, but Ivan has found the casket containing his soul, which is a huge egg. The ogre sways in terror from side to side as Ivan tosses the egg and finally flings it to the ground. The stage is plunged in darkness.

The music of the conclusion is another folk-song turned into a hymn of thanksgiving which becomes the wedding procession of Prince Ivan and the Tsarevna. The princesses and their knights, no longer petrified, file slowly on; line after line of boyars crowd onto the stage. Ivan and his bride, crowned and sceptred, turn about to display their long encrusted trains, and advance solemnly to take their place like idols in the middle of the crowd; the Firebird flashes by to give her blessing; and with a triumphant swinging rhythm like bells the ballet reaches its happy ending.

With what a glow of glory must Fokine, dancer, choreographer and pioneer, have stood there with his wife beside him and a proud company behind, facing a Paris which rose to acclaim his ballet and Stravinsky's score! And Karsavina, what a triumph for her in the first big role Fokine had moulded on her!

Seated in Diaghilev's box, Stravinsky met all the celebrities, hostesses and balletomanes of Paris. On this and on subsequent nights he was introduced to Proust, Jean Giraudoux, Paul Morand, St John Perse, Paul Claudel and Sarah Bernhardt. 'I was called to the stage to bow at the conclusion, and was recalled several times. I was still on stage when the final curtain had come down, and I saw coming toward me Diaghilev and a dark man with a double forehead whom he introduced as Claude Debussy. The great composer spoke kindly about the music, ending his words with an invitation to dine with him.'[123]

The East was in fashion, just as it had been in the early days of Victor Hugo nearly a century before; and the *divertissement* that followed 'The Firebird' – and which was the last new offering of the season – had the same title as Hugo's second book of poems, *Les Orientales*. Gelzer and Volinine appeared in this, and Nijinsky had two numbers. One was 'Kobold', danced to Grieg's piano piece of that name, orchestrated by Stravinsky.* For this Nijinsky wore greenish-blue all-over tights with patches of *paillettes* – even his face was covered. He was a capering goblin. All that remains of this are three photographs in the Museum and Library of Performing Arts in New York. Of the other number, a more static dance made up mostly of poses in the Siamese style – Fokine had seen a troupe of Siamese dancers in Petersburg a few years before – there are numerous mementoes. For Nijinsky was photographed in it by Druet and Baron de Meyer, and drawn or painted in it by Jacques-Emile Blanche, Jean Cocteau, Georges Barbier and others.

Karsavina took her Firebird costume and Nijinsky took his gold and bejewelled Siamese costume and helmet to the studio of Jacques-Emile Blanche at Passy to be photographed: for the painter intended to save the dancers some hours of posing by working partly from Druet's photographs. It was a sunny Sunday morning and 'the operator', as Mme Blanche called him, arrived at one o'clock.[124]

The garden of Blanche with its chestnuts, catalpa and English lawns had inspired, one stormy evening, Debussy's 'Jardin sous la pluie', which was one of an album of piano pieces dedicated to the sociable painter.[125] Nijinsky posed out on the lawn as well as in the studio, and the poses he took – crouched, half serpent, half tiger on the floor or standing, finger-tips to tilted chin – together with a jump he performed for one of the earliest ever action photographs, legs crossed in the air and hands joined over the head, are indications of the nature of his Danse Siamoise. Karsavina posed, as he did, in front of their host's fine Coromandel screen. Some of the surviving photographs show her roaring with laughter, which was very un-Firebirdlike behaviour. This was the fault of Cocteau, who had arrived to watch the session, and who kept striking poses and making funny speeches from the gallery which ran round above the studio.[126] He also sketched Nijinsky in his Siamese role.

---

* Grigoriev attributed the choreography of this number to Nijinsky, but Mme Bronislava Nijinska says it was by Fokine.

Nijinsky 1910

The painting Blanche made of Karsavina *sur les pointes*, with imperious outstretched arms, never got beyond the stage of a sketch, although a vivid one: it is in the collection of Serge Lifar. The big painting of Nijinsky was bought by Princesse Edmond de Polignac and after her death hung for years at Donnington Priory near Newbury, the house of her niece Mrs Reginald Fellowes, who lent it to me for the Diaghilev Exhibition in 1954–5. But Blanche was not the only artist to work from Druet's photographs. A few years later a secret admirer of Nijinsky commissioned a painting of him from Bakst, and the latter copied the crouching pose from Druet's photograph, interpreting somewhat freely the costume he had himself designed (he left the trousers plain *bleu-de-roi*, unadorned by *paillettes*) and subtly varying the face so that it is even more alive than the photograph. This was never exhibited or reproduced – in fact it was hidden from the world – until discovered in Washington in 1969 by Baron Tassilo von Watzdorf of Sotheby's. When it was put up for sale in July of the same year it fetched £11,400, a record price for any work of Bakst. Such were the far-reaching consequences of that jolly photographic session in Passy, which ended in a late but delicious luncheon.

Nijinsky and Karsavina returned to pose for Blanche on other Sundays

Tamara Karsavina.
Drawing by Gir.

and in subsequent seasons, and occasionally Karsavina brought her friends to witness the sitting. Being at that time very *gourmande*, she described to the assembled company how impressed she had been in the restaurant at the Savoy Hotel by the trolleys laden with varied sweets which were wheeled up for her choice. On her next visit to Passy Blanche had procured a trolley and there was a lavish spread of delicacies to choose from.[127] Blanche painted Ida Rubinstein too, in her Zobeïda costume, reclining on cushions and showing her noble Semitic profile against the black and gold lacquered screen.

Rubinstein also posed for Serov in a building in the Boulevard des Invalides which had once been a monastery:[128] he painted her seated naked on cushions, turning her bony back, head twisted over the right shoulder. She now had not only Montesquiou but also D'Annunzio as *cavalieri serventi*. She liked to attract attention; the admiration of distinguished men flattered her.[129] She bought a black tiger cub and told Diaghilev she wanted not only to mime, but also to dance. This was clearly out of the question. People believed that she drank champagne out of Madonna lilies, but this was probably part of a deliberate publicity campaign.[130]

Stravinsky, poor as he was – Diaghilev paid him 1,500 roubles (£100) for 'The Firebird' – was so elated by the success of his ballet and so confident in a golden future with Diaghilev that he sped back to Russia to fetch his wife and children.[131] The last performance of 'The Firebird' was on 24 June, and he was determined that she should hear the music. Already, when he had been finishing his orchestration two months before, the idea had come to him for a new ballet. 'I had dreamed a scene of pagan ritual in which a chosen sacrificial virgin danced herself to death. This vision was not accompanied by concrete musical ideas, however. . . .'[132] Before leaving Petersburg for Paris, he had talked to Roerich, the mystic interpreter of ancient Russia, about the scenario and they had agreed to collaborate. Now, at Ustilug, his family house, two and a half days' journey south of Petersburg, he began a letter to Roerich which was to be finished in France ten days later.

Stravinsky to Roerich, 19.6.1910

Dear Nicolai Konstantinovitch,

. . . My 'Firebird' was a great success in Paris, but the music proved to be so difficult that it cannot be performed anywhere else this year. It required nine rehearsals, which shows you how unthinkable it would be to attempt to play it with other orchestras. Because of this we had hoped to double the number of performances here, but that was impractical for various reasons, and there will be only two supplementary performances, the 22nd and 24th (next Tuesday and Thursday), after the three alternate subscription performances. I expect to arrive in time only for the Thursday performance, as I said.

Naturally the success of 'The Firebird' has encouraged Diaghilev for future projects, and sooner or later we will have to tell him about the 'Great Sacrifice'. In fact, he has already asked me to compose a new ballet. I said I was writing one which, for the moment, I did not wish to talk about, and this touched off an explosion, as I might have guessed. 'What? You keep secrets from me, I who do my utmost for you all? Fokine, you, everyone has secrets from me.' Etc., etc. I had to tell him, of course, but I begged him not to repeat it. As soon as I said that I was working with you both Diaghilev and Bakst were delighted, Bakst saying he thought our idea was a noble one. They were greatly relieved, obviously, to hear that my secret did not concern Benois: Diaghilev would have been greatly offended if Benois had been involved.

. . .

Later. I have had to complete this letter in La Baule, having found no time in Paris, where we spent only three days. Again the 'Firebird' had an immense success, and I was greatly pleased, but I must say that some of Golovine's work, and some of the lighting, was not very fortunate. I had thought, from the very first, when I saw Golovine's costumes and his beautiful sets, that he had failed to create anything satisfactory for the spooky Kastchei dance, and this opinion was also shared by André Rimsky-Korsakov and Kolya Richter, who came for the final performance. Music and costumes are at odds in this scene, and the dancers look like dressed-up actors. Diaghilev took charge of the lighting himself, but with imperfect results and at times serious mis-synchronizations. In addition to these failures of the company, the Management and Direction of the Grand Opera did everything in their power to hinder and handicap us. To begin with they did not want to rent the house to a company of Russians, and it was only because of the Comtesse Greffuhle and the help of a few others that we succeeded. I do not know the exact reasons for it, but the quarrel between Diaghilev and Fokine began because of difficulties in producing the 'Firebird'. I prefer to stay out of this imbroglio myself, and I regret Diaghilev tattled the remark to me that Fokine's participation in our 'Great Sacrifice' would only be a question of money. (Note that Diaghilev never for a moment considered whether *we* wished to work with Fokine!) If the Fokine feud is not settled soon Diaghilev thinks we should work with a certain Gorsky, of whom I know nothing. Now it may be that this Gorsky is a great genius, but Diaghilev is bluffing, and is really very upset by Fokine.

As you see, I am living in La Baule, by the Atlantic Ocean. It is a small city, crowded now with children of all ages. I often thought about you during the journey from Ustilug to Paris. How right your advice to go *via* Warsaw and Berlin. Please excuse my last conversation on the telephone.

Now this: I cannot find the paper on which I wrote the libretto of the 'Great Sacrifice'. For God's sake send it to me, registered, and with it the small page of manuscript which I forgot about, as I went away, and left with you. I am using your St Petersburg address as you did not give me one in Hapsal. Awaiting your answer, I shake your hand and kiss you three times.

With love, yours

IGOR STRAVINSKY[133]

Thanks to Astruc's good management and to the popularity of the new ballets, the season had been a much greater success financially than that of 1909.[134] It was arranged that some extra performances should be given at the Opéra. But the Brussels engagement had to be fulfilled first, though it was only two performances; and Karsavina had to get back to do a bit more 'Giselle' at the Coliseum, where the Koslov troupe had been giving an Oriental ballet, 'Salammbo', in her absence. Gelzer was rehearsed in Karsavina's Valse in 'Les Sylphides' and Fokine persuaded Diaghilev with some difficulty to allow Lopokhova, who had already made a success of 'Carnaval', to replace Karsavina in 'The Firebird'.[135] With her fine *élévation* she brought it off, but she was quite different from Karsavina, a humming-bird as opposed to a phoenix.[136]

To guard against any future rivalry with London music-halls, Diaghilev now offered Karsavina a two-year contract to dance for him from 1 May to the end of August, during the closure of the Mariinsky.[137] She hesitated to renounce all holidays, all private life. He raged at her for 'prostituting her art' by appearing in a music-hall. He was possessively jealous, saying, 'I hate your family. It takes you away from me. Why could you not have married Fokine? You would both have belonged to me.'[138] In the same breath he began to complain that Fokine's choreography was old-fashioned and a thing of the past. There had been disagreements between them during the staging of 'The Firebird'. He did not like Fokine, who was so sure of himself and had formulated his new creed without the aid of Diaghilev and the friends. With his greed for novelty (which was to become more and more noticeable as he grew older), Diaghilev had already begun to see the limitations of Fokine's folkloric approach and passion for local colour and period style. He was thinking of replacing him by someone with newer ideas or someone he could help to mould. There was Gorsky in Moscow; and there was Nijinsky. Karsavina was astounded. It was a year and a month since Paris had been captured by the novelty of the Polovtsian Dances and 'Cléopâtre', and here was Diaghilev brushing Fokine aside. At the same time she had the feeling that Diaghilev was trying her out. Would she be faithful and follow him in his artistic adventures or would she fall short like Pavlova? 'What are you going to do with Fokine's ballets, Sergei Pavlovitch?' 'Oh, I don't know. I may sell it all, lock, stock and barrel.' She was shattered, but assured him of her adherence.[139]

Bombarded in London by a barrage of Diaghilev's telegrams, the long-suffering Karsavina managed to extract a little more leave from Oswald Stoll and was able to dance at one of the two performances in Brussels. These were attended by the Belgian Royal Family and received with enthusiasm. Diaghilev welcomed Karsavina like 'a fond father' and 'his joy was touching'.

At luncheon with Nijinsky and the ballerina on the day of her performance Diaghilev asked her not to mind if Gelzer danced her Valse in 'Les Sylphides'; he explained that Gelzer had helped him out in Karsavina's absence and he felt he could not now take the part away from her this season. Karsavina, who, a year and a half before, had been almost too shy of Diaghilev to open her mouth in his presence, 'raged and stormed for form's sake, meaning all the while to meet his wishes'. That evening, while she was making up, she saw him in her looking-glass. He never knocked on doors. She was no longer angry but thought her dignity required her to look daggers.[140] He said, 'You have slapped one cheek. Here is the other.' Then he added sadly, 'Tata, I am desperately in love.' 'Who with?' 'She doesn't care for me any more than for the Emperor of China.'[141]

After the final Paris performances, the 'Diaghilev Ballet' once more ceased to exist: but its triumphant creator, who was not only negotiating for another Paris season, but planning seasons in London and New York, told Grigoriev as he bade him goodbye that in the following year they would work longer together. As Grigoriev and the other members of the Mariinsky had devoted their whole four months' leave to working for Diaghilev, the *régisseur* found it hard to understand what he could possibly mean.[142] But Diaghilev was dreaming of forming his own company, independent of the Tsar. The trouble was that in return for their schooling, training and the money spent for eight years on their board, lodging and clothes, members of the Imperial Ballet were obliged to dance for a minimum of five years after they left school. This was only fair. Older dancers, if they did not mind renouncing their pensions, were at liberty to leave. Not so Nijinsky and his contemporaries.

Lydia Lopokhova, however, had taken the plunge and cut herself off from the homeland – the first of a long line to do so. She had signed a contract to dance in the United States and would never return to Russia, though she was to rejoin Diaghilev during the war.[143] Meanwhile, Ida Rubinstein, who was tired of miming and was ambitious to dance, speak and if possible sing, was leaving Diaghilev – she had never, of course, had any connection with the Imperial Theatres – to finance with her own money and that of Walter Guinness, her English lover, immense spectacles of her own. From that moment she became ridiculous.

Summer 1910. The friends scattered: when they reunited their 'holidays' would have borne fruit. After a stay with his family at La Baule by the sea in Brittany – from which he declined Diaghilev's summons to Paris, saying he could not afford the fare,[144] and where he composed the setting for two songs of Verlaine – Stravinsky moved to Switzerland.[145] After visiting Benois for a few days, to make up the quarrel, at Montagnola near Lugano,

Diaghilev and Nijinsky went to Venice.[146] Bakst and Serov made the longed-for pilgrimage to Greece and Crete.[147] Vaslav was thinking more and more about how to evolve a new kind of choreography: from these thoughts of his and from Bakst's passion for the remains of Hellas would be born 'L'Après-midi d'un faune'. From Stravinsky's stay in Switzerland, where he decided to interrupt work on the preliminary sketches for 'Le Sacre du printemps', begun at La Baule, to compose a *konzertstück*, would come 'Petrushka'.

In September the Stravinskys moved from their pension at Vevey to a clinic at Lausanne, where their second son was to be born on 23 September, and the composer rented an attic studio across the street to work in. Here he began his would-be piano concerto, the starting point for which seems to have been a fascination for the discord produced by superimposing the chords of C major and F sharp major, and which developed into a kind of argument or battle between the piano and the orchestra. When Diaghilev and Nijinsky arrived towards the end of the month, after six weeks in Venice, to hear how the music of 'Le Sacre' was getting on, Stravinsky played them his new and almost finished composition, which he had by now decided was 'Petrushka's cry'.[148]*

Both Stravinsky and Diaghilev had known in Petersburg the Butter Week fairs which preceded Lent, when temporary wooden theatres, switchbacks and *carrousels* appeared in the Square of the Winter Palace. They also remembered the Russian equivalent of the English Punch-and-Judy show, in which the adventures of Petrushka would be acted out by puppets. Petrushka was in fact the Russian Punch: he beat his wife, killed people and was finally hauled off to Hell by the Devil. While one man, hidden, worked the puppets, the organ-grinder provided music and dialogue. He would continually warn Petrushka 'Look out! You'll get into hot water', and Petrushka would merely give a shrieking laugh 'He, he, he!' When speaking Petrushka's lines the organ-grinder put into his mouth 'a little contrivance which gave a nasal tone to his voice', and it was the strange sounds thus produced that Diaghilev heard in the new composition.†

When Stravinsky played them a few bars of another piece for piano and orchestra which he was planning as a companion to the first, a Russian dance, Diaghilev at once had the idea – or perhaps it occurred to him overnight – of using the two as the basis for a ballet about the Russian

---

* According to Lifar it was Diaghilev who associated the music with Petrushka. Mr. Stravinsky denied this. He remembered the idea coming to him by the lake at Clarens.

† I have taken the brief description of the Petrushka play from Prince Peter Lieven; but the Prince is wrong in stating that Petrushka's shrieks inspired Stravinsky's composition, for, as we have seen, the music was written before the idea of connecting it with Petrushka occurred to anybody.

carnival. All agreed that Benois, with his nostalgia for the architecture and traditions of old Petersburg, would be the man to work out a libretto and design the scene; and Diaghilev wrote to him in Petersburg a day or two later.[149] Although, at Montagnola, Benois had been reconciled with Diaghilev, he had still insisted that his collaboration with the ballet was over. Little did he guess that his greatest work was still to come! Now he had to be coaxed. Diaghilev begged him to forget old grudges and create the new masterpiece with Stravinsky. Indeed, the idea was irresistible to him.

Benois reflected:

Petrushka, the Russian Guignol or Punch, no less than Harlequin, had been my friend since my earliest childhood. Whenever I heard the loud, nasal cries of the travelling showman: 'Here's Petrushka! Come, good people and see the show!' I would get into a kind of frenzy to see the enchanting performance. . . . As to Petrushka in person, I immediately had the feeling that it was a duty I owed to my old friend to immortalize him on the real stage. I was still more tempted by the idea of depicting the Butter Week Fair . . . the dear *balagani* [fairground booths] which were the delight of my childhood, and had been the delight of my father before me. The fact that the *balagani* had for some ten years ceased to exist made the idea of building a kind of memorial to them still more tempting. . . .[150]

So Benois set to happily and began to work out the possibilities of the libretto; Stravinsky moved to Clarens, where in another bohemian attic he completed the Russian Dance;[151] and Diaghilev went to Paris for discussions with Astruc and to London to work out something for the following year with Sir Joseph Beecham.[152] Diaghilev was in London on 10 October, as we know from the date of a cable he sent to Astruc.[153] He had probably left Vaslav at the Hôtel Scribe, but they were together again on the 27th as is proved by the post-mark on the following lettercard. After a convivial lunch spent plotting 'Le Dieu bleu', the collaborators were suddenly seized with fear that if the secret of their new work leaked out something might happen to prevent its realization. So they wrote to Astruc from the Restaurant Le Grand Vatel, 275, rue St-Honoré: 'In the name of all you hold dear not a word to *anyone* about the ballet we are planning, and especially about the possibility of including it in the Coronation celebrations, Yours ever, Reynaldo Hahn, Serge Diaghilev, Leon Bakst, Jean Cocteau, Nijinsky.'[154] Nijinsky was going to be two months late for the Mariinsky season and would be in trouble for it.[155] Was he deliberately trying to provoke Teliakovsky to dismiss him?

Whereas Fokine had presented Stravinsky with a complete libretto of 'The Firebird' (only slightly modified later) and the music had then been composed to fit it, Benois wrote *his* libretto around music that had already been composed. This applies absolutely with regard to the second scene, in which

Petrushka's loneliness and claustrophobic panic in his dark cell were cleverly adapted to Stravinsky's *staccato* and violent 'piano concerto'. It applies partly, but not entirely, to the rest of the ballet: more music was composed and more story was worked out before Stravinsky and Benois met, but there was an increasing degree of give-and-take.[156]

When Diaghilev arrived back in Petersburg in November he told Benois more about the music and discussions began.[157] Bakst was in Paris being 'unfaithful' and planning 'Le Martyre de St Sébastien' with Ida Rubinstein, D'Annunzio and Debussy; and Fokine was not called in till a later stage: but a nucleus of the friends, of which band Nijinsky was now a silent but accepted member, pushed forward with their cosy discussions.

We met daily in Diaghilev's flat in Zamiatin Lane, where at the traditional evening tea with *boubliki* . . . 'Petrushka' took shape and fitted ultimately into four fairly short acts, without any intervals. The first and last acts were to take place at the Carnival Fair; the two middle ones were to show the interior of the Conjuror's theatre. The puppets that had come to life in the first act, under the magic spell of the Conjuror, were to continue living a real life in their own quarters, where a romance was to begin between them. . . .

For Benois had already imagined the pretty, brainless Ballerina, whom ugly Petrushka was to love, and the resplendent Blackamoor whom the lady would prefer. Benois remembered that 'in the street performances of Petrushka there was invariably a separate *intermezzo*, inserted between the acts: two Blackamoors, dressed in velvet and gold, would appear and would start unmercifully hitting each other's wooden heads with sticks'. Benois endowed Petrushka with a soul: he was no longer the knockabout bullying Punch but the pathetic Pierrot, capable of imagination, love and sorrow, a Hamlet among puppets.

If Petrushka were to be taken as the personification of the spiritual and suffering side of humanity – or shall we call it the poetical principle? – his lady Columbine would be the incarnation of the eternal feminine; then the gorgeous Blackamoor would serve as the embodiment of everything senselessly attractive, powerfully masculine and undeservedly triumphant.[158]

In October the Stravinskys had moved to Beaulieu, near Nice. Here more music was written. In December Stravinsky paid a short visit to his mother in Petersburg – finding the city, after his travels, 'sadly small and provincial'[159] – and Benois was at last able to hear the parts which had been composed. The latter wrote: 'Igor played them to me in my little dark blue drawing-room; the piano was my old, fearfully hard Gentsch. . . . What I now heard surpassed my expectations. . . .'[160] They conferred about the

159

plot and when Stravinsky returned to Beaulieu* the collaboration continued by letter. Before and after his trip to Petersburg Stravinsky finished the first scene – of which the Russian Dance had been the starting point – and composed both the third, the Moor's cell, and most of the fourth. The ballet would be completed when the friends met in Rome in the spring. Only then was Fokine called in.[161]

As Nijinsky heard parts of Stravinsky's score – and particularly the second scene, which was to be to all intents and purposes a long solo for himself – several times before it was ever played to Fokine, it is probable that Petrushka's typical spasmodic sideways jerks of the hands and perhaps his pattering run were his own invention.†

Shortly after his return to Beaulieu Stravinsky fell ill with nicotine poisoning which bent him double and he was weak for months. He continued work on the score, nevertheless. Needing the music of a certain popular Russian song for one of the two street-dancers he wrote asking André Rimsky-Korsakov to find him a copy. This was sent, but his friend derisively put some comic words of his own to the song, and asked Igor how he could use such trash. The tune for the other street dancer had a different source. Stravinsky heard it played daily on a barrel-organ outside his window in Beaulieu, was struck by its appropriateness for his purpose and wrote it in. It did not occur to him that the composer might be living, and Maurice Delage, who was with him at the time, thought the tune must be very old. It was not until several months after the première of 'Petrushka' in 1911 that Stravinsky learned that the tune, 'Elle avait une jamb' en bois', was by a Mr Emile Spencer, who was alive and living in France. From then on Mr Spencer and his heirs have received a proportion of the royalties on 'Petrushka'.[162]

In snow-girt Petersburg Benois set about designing his sets and costumes for the new ballet, the period of which was not to be that of his own childhood in the 1870s, when he had first seen the travelling puppet-shows and the pre-Lent fairs, but a period forty years earlier, in the days of the Emperor Nicholas I, his father's patron. His latest flat was near to the palace of Count Bobrinsky and the room he had taken to work in was directly over the lodgings used by the Count's coachmen. 'Unceasing revels and dancing went on there all day long to the sounds of the balalaika and the laughter of gay ladies. At any other time this would have greatly disturbed me, but in the

---

* Benois mistakenly wrote 'to Switzerland'. (*Reminiscences*, p. 328.)

† I put this idea to both Mme Bronislava Nijinska and Mr Stravinsky. Each agreed separately that it was very probable. But it is interesting to note that – for a day or two at least – the ugly Petrushka was not considered a suitable role for the glamorous Nijinsky. In Diaghilev's Black Note-Book (p.141) Leontiev is cast as Petrushka. And Nijinsky is even considered for the Magician.

present case all the noise, shouts and stamping only helped to inspire me. It was almost a gift of providence.'[163]

Winter brought Astruc the usual blizzard of telegrams from Diaghilev. There was a dancer called Dombrovska in Paris – would Astruc engage her?[164] Had Astruc heard from Chaliapine (who denied hotly that he intended to sing in a Russian opera season in Paris in the spring)?[165] If Paradossi would negotiate as instructed without delay Diaghilev knew how to quash all possibility of rivalry from the Argentine opera (probably with regard to Chaliapine).[166] If Reynaldo Hahn did not accept the terms agreed upon by Saturday Diaghilev would give up the idea of staging 'Le Dieu bleu'.[167] Then, on Christmas Eve,* in reply to some doubts of Astruc about a rival attraction, there was despatched the haughty statement – which by this time was also literally true – 'Am above all competition. Diaghilev.'[168]

* New Style, Western Calendar. The Russian Christmas would be thirteen days later.

CHAPTER FOUR

1911

Nijinsky wanted to create choreography and Diaghilev wanted him to. What form was it to take? Just as Fokine had rebelled against the academic dance, throwing out *tutus*, turn-out and virtuosity for its own sake, so were the two friends feeling for different reasons dissatisfied with the results of Fokine's revolution. Their dissatisfaction took different forms and no doubt expressed itself in different ways, if indeed it found an exact definition.[1] Diaghilev foresaw a dead-end to the ballet of local colour and the evocation of past periods or distant lands, and he had a prejudice against stories and drama in ballet.[2] Fokine, brilliantly abetted by Benois and Bakst, had conjured up Versailles and the Romantic era; he had made an Egyptian, a 'Polovtsian', a Persian and a Russian ballet with the help of Bakst, Roerich and Golovine. When Ravel's 'Daphnis' was ready he would no doubt make a Greek ballet, and with Reynaldo Hahn's 'Dieu bleu' he would make an Indian ballet. What had these fairy-tales to say to the people of a world which was beginning to realize it was 'modern'? Better than to *evoke* past eras would surely be to re-interpret them or even to speak for your own. Diaghilev felt a stirring of the new spirit which was moving artists throughout Europe to seek new forms with which to greet a new age.

To Nijinsky, as a dancer, these thoughts probably came in a different shape. There was certainly something to *interpret* in such roles as the Golden Negro in 'Schéhérazade', but this character was just an outstanding figure in a general orgy who had to make love, lie on cushions, cower, somersault and die. Was this dancing? The stilted old ballets had form, if they had nothing else. In gaining expressiveness Fokine had thrown much overboard. The present writer believes that Nijinsky's feelings were similar to those of

Cézanne several decades before, when he said that he wanted to make of Impressionism something as solid as the art of the old masters.

But how? Every young artist of talent in this century has been afraid of making or writing something that has been made or written before. The young of this age, more than of any previous one, were and are afraid of the obvious, the *déjà-vu*. In the old days everyone began by copying his master: now this seemed out of the question. To be entirely oneself, totally original, owing nothing to anybody, that was the thing – and a very inhibiting thing too for a young man. What form was the breakaway to take? No wonder if a man has to hesitate for years before allowing himself to put pen to paper. Then the trouble with being twenty-three is that one has nothing to 'say'.

And how was Diaghilev, who had never danced or learnt the secret springs of movement or what the body was capable of or what felt right or wrong or what rhythms the body could accept and what reject or the value of sometimes being heavy and sometimes light – how was he to help Nijinsky devise a new system of movement? He could conduct him to picture galleries, show him sculpture, play him music and hope that some magic process would take place: that was all.

Isadora described how, in the early years of the century, when she first came to Paris and began to evolve her art, she would stand in the dark for hours, with her hands on her solar plexus, plumbing the forgotten sources of natural movement.[3] Like Isadora ten years earlier and like Martha Graham a quarter of a century later, Nijinsky had to put aside all he had learnt and been in order to discover how to tell the truth in his own way.

The great moment of release had happened in Paris during the previous summer. We cannot call it a moment of revelation, because in his first essay in choreography Nijinsky was only beginning to realize some of the things he could do. But release it was. To make a 'ballet' like a moving frieze, to animate Greek and Egyptian reliefs and Greek vase paintings seen in the Louvre, this was the idea that dissolved his inhibitions; for he would then owe nothing to the classical academic dance and would be doing something neither Isadora nor Fokine had done before. He would find by instinct and experiment a valid way of movement for figures seen only in profile, a way of making his dancers pass from one static group to the next. Did he realize he was taking the first step towards abstraction? He was doing what Picasso had done when he painted his first cubist pictures three years before.

In later years Michel Larionov told the story, repeated from Diaghilev no doubt, and turned into a joke, that Bakst and Nijinsky had agreed to meet in the antique sculpture department of the Louvre; that the painter waited in vain in the Greek section and went away without making contact with the dancer, who was lost in admiration of Egyptian reliefs on the floor below.[4]

Nijinsky 1911

Dancer: interpreter: creator. Nijinsky, who had danced the choreography of Petipa as no man ever before, had interpreted the new dance-drama of Fokine like an actor of genius, and who had only to continue dancing and interpreting for the rest of his active life to enjoy fame and fortune and the canonization of posterity, chose instead the hardest, most uncertain road, turned the sharp corner and began to scale the steep and rocky mountain-track of invention.

One of the first events of the new year, 1911, was the arrival in Petersburg of Emile Jaques-Dalcroze, the deviser of eurythmics, who gave a demonstration with the aid of his pupils during January. This was no doubt the occasion when Diaghilev and Nijinsky, who were later to visit Dalcroze at his headquarters in Germany, became interested in his system.

Bakst had arrived back in Petersburg at the end of December 1910[5] and a few days later, probably at the very beginning of 1911, at their flat in the Street of the Big Stables, Vaslav and Bronislava showed him and Diaghilev what had been worked out in the way of a moving Greek frieze.[6] Fokine had made ballets without brilliant steps, but in Nijinsky's creation there was not only nothing but walking – there was one jump – but this was all done with the torso full on to the audience and the head, arms and legs in profile, and a new heavy way of walking had been invented. The human figure was dehumanized: the dancers were elements of composition. And what story was this choreography in profile to tell, what mood were its patterns to convey, and to what music should it be danced? It was probably Diaghilev, after several possible scores had been rejected, who proposed the use of Debussy's 'Prélude à l'Après-midi d'un faune', inspired by Mallarmé's poem and composed nearly twenty years before. Nijinsky's movement was so little related to the tone-poem, chosen perhaps *after* the style of choreography had been invented,[7] that the score was reduced to background music. A new step had been taken in the history of the relationship between music and dancing. Suddenly it was possible to imagine a dance in opposition to music – or without it.

Diaghilev had asked for something new and he had been given it with a vengeance. Did he get a shock? Was he afraid? If so it was probably the remoteness of music from movement that most filled him with misgivings. If in January 1911 the dance had not yet been tailored in length to fit the Debussy piece and even to coincide marvellously with it in a few crucial places, this operation was soon to be performed, and a remarkably successful marriage would take place.[8] Diaghilev, however, professed himself delighted. Bronia, who had complete confidence in the work her brother had invented, guessed that the right wing of Diaghilev's committee, the balletomanes, might try to influence him and persuade him to modify Nijinsky's stark new movements – as Besobrasov had formerly begged Fokine not to make such radical costume reforms or to suppress the ballerina's virtuoso solo in

'Eunice', and later to soften down 'Prince Igor'. She said, 'You won't let them make you change anything, will you?' Holding up his hand to show an infinitesimal space between thumb and forefinger, Nijinsky replied 'Not by *that* much.'[9]

Diaghilev may have been nervous about the new work and the balleto-manes may have got at him; Debussy may have been raising objections to the use of his music, and anyway, with Fokine's and Tcherepnine's 'Narcisse' on the stocks, there was already one new ballet on a Greek subject to be presented; but the chief reason that 'L'Après-midi d'un faune' was postponed was Diaghilev's and Nijinsky's fear that Fokine would walk out without completing the ballets necessary for their next season.[10]

Diaghilev in Petersburg to Astruc in Paris, 10.2.11

... Debussy replaced by Spectre de la Rose: Théophile Gautier music Weber Nijinsky Karsavina only. Gautier's anniversary.[11]

'Le Spectre de la rose', which was to become so famous, was born from the rose Chiarina threw to Eusebius in 'Carnaval'. While writing some (rather adverse) notes on the latter ballet for *La Revue de Paris*, Jean-Louis Vaudoyer had on a sudden impulse placed two lines from Gautier's poem 'Le Spectre de la rose' at the head of his text.

> *Je suis le spectre d'une rose*
> *Que tu portais hier au bal.**

The article appeared in print in July 1910,[12] when the Paris season of the ballet was over, and it was then that it suddenly occurred to Vaudoyer to associate the poem with 'L'Invitation à la Valse' by Weber, a composer whom Gautier had much admired. This piano piece had been orchestrated by Berlioz. Vaudoyer wrote to Bakst suggesting that a short ballet might be made of it.[13] Probably Bakst only received the letter on his return from Greece, but on arrival in Petersburg he told the friends about it. Fokine created the *pas de deux* very quickly and spontaneously in two or three rehearsals, working not on the usual stage of The Crooked Mirror on the Catherine Canal, but on a smaller stage in the theatre's restaurant.[14] Bakst saw the rehearsals and understood what would be necessary as a set.[15]

Now that Diaghilev had resolved to form his own company to perform all the year round it would no longer be sufficient for him to borrow the dancers of the Imperial Theatres of Petersburg and Moscow during their four months' summer leave. Karsavina presented the least problem, for she had now been appointed a prima ballerina of the Mariinsky and could arrange her infrequent performances to fit in with Diaghilev's bookings,

---

* Most writers misquoting these lines, make Gautier write '*Je suis le spectre de la rose.*'

and she was devoted enough not only to renounce her lucrative music-hall career in London but to resign herself to continual journeys to and fro.[16]

Bolm, who had graduated in 1904, having served well over the necessary five years with the Imperial Ballet, was at liberty to hand in his notice: being an intelligent man he realized that the new ballets of Fokine offered more interesting opportunities than the Mariinsky repertory; and he gave up the assurance of a pension in order to see the world and seek more laurels such as he had won in 'Prince Igor'. The Muscovite Sophie Feodorova also threw in her lot with Diaghilev. Naturally, Diaghilev had to offer more money than the Imperial Theatres.[17] But Grigoriev, who was helping Diaghilev to enlist a troupe and arrange the contracts, considered that the forming of a *corps de ballet* was harder than to secure a few principal dancers.[18] General Besobrasov was dispatched to Warsaw to enlist recruits;[19] and Diaghilev cabled Astruc about a touring troupe headed by the brothers Molodsov, believed to be in Paris, and of whom Fokine expressed doubts.[20] Perhaps Diaghilev realized that whatever novelties Nijinsky might produce, he was a slow worker and could not be relied on for four new ballets a year. So Fokine was to be re-engaged, but in the capacity of choreographer only, since Diaghilev wanted no competition for Nijinsky as *premier danseur*. Fokine fought strenuously for his right to perform, and finally only consented to abandon the Mariinsky in return for a very large salary and for being billed as Choreographic Director.[21] Benois was to be called Artistic Director.[22]

And what about Nijinsky? Of his five years' obligatory service there were still two to run. It was unthinkable that he should not dance with the new Diaghilev Ballet, which centred on him, all the year round, but how was this to be arranged? Fate played into Diaghilev's hands over this matter, but it is not unlikely that Fate was given a gentle push.

At the end of January Nijinsky was to dance for the first time at the Mariinsky in 'Giselle' with Karsavina, and he decided to wear the costumes Benois had designed for his appearance in Paris. The first-act costume was an early-Renaissance tunic of felt ending in a skirt over the thighs, which Diaghilev had ordered to be shortened by two inches. It was very much the costume that Perrot wore in the original production, but ballet fashions had changed in Russia since the Romantic period and it had become customary to wear trunks over the tights in mediaeval or Renaissance-style ballets. Benois had not included these in his sketch and would probably have agreed with Diaghilev that they spoiled the line. The omission of trunks had the effect of making Nijinsky appear, by Russian standards of the time, distressingly nude. (There was no question, as some writers have inferred, of Nijinsky leaving off his athletic support or jock-strap, an article which male dancers in classical ballet would feel very uncomfortable without.)[23] An official in charge of the production protested to Nijinsky before the curtain went up, but the dancer refused to make any addition to the costume he had worn in Paris.[24]

Teliakovsky was away at the time, but the Dowager Empress was present and so, inevitably, were a number of enemies. During the interval, while Karsavina was sent for by the Empress and congratulated on her success (in music-hall) in London,[25] two friends of Kchessinskaya's did some telephoning and made mischief.[26] Motives are always mixed, and ill-wishers often find that by getting their way they achieve the opposite results to those they had intended: so it is of little importance whether Kchessinskaya, out of jealousy, seized the opportunity to get a rival for popularity out of the way, or whether Krupensky sought revenge on the lover of his enemy Diaghilev, or whether a Grand Duke gave orders, hoping to discredit the Diaghilev enterprise. The next day Nijinsky was told to apologize or resign. He refused to apologize and was dismissed. Almost immediately, it seems, the management of the Imperial Theatres realized their loss – perhaps Teliakovsky on his return disapproved of Krupensky's action – and gave Nijinsky an opportunity to rejoin the company. This he declined to take.[27]

On 26 January, *Petersburgskaya Gazeta* announced Nijinsky's dismissal. The next day they published a long interview with him. He told the journalist that he had asked permission to dance Albrecht in the costume Benois had designed for Paris. This was accorded, but when he was dressed in his first-act costume he was told that it was too revealing. Nevertheless, Krupensky, Golovine and other officials did not prevent him from going on with the performance. Next morning he was summoned by the Direction and told that he was dismissed from the Imperial Theatres because of his first-act costume.

I don't want to discuss the matter [said Nijinsky]. I can only state that if the direction of the Imperial Theatres wanted to retain me in its employment it had two alternative courses of action: either to insist on my changing into the costume which was the property of the theatre, or to give my part to another dancer – either Legat or Andrianov. They were both on stage and both had danced the role more than once. I do not know why I have to answer for other people's behaviour. During my long course of study at the Theatre School and during my three short seasons at the Theatre I have given all my energy to uphold – first in Russia, then abroad – the high standard of my training and the glory of our art. As a reward I was dismissed with twenty-four hours' notice. Personally, I should not dismiss even a servant who had done something much more serious in such a way. . . .

Before the year was out Kchessinskaya would be dancing with Nijinsky in

London. The Diaghilev enterprise was in no wise discredited. Most important of all, Diaghilev got his heart's desire. Nijinsky was free to conquer the world in his own time.

It would be reasonable to guess that Diaghilev did not finally decide to form his own company until after Nijinsky's dismissal: but this was not the case. He had begun to sign contracts with other dancers as early as 1 December 1910.[28]

Jubilant as he was, Diaghilev determined to wring every drop of indignation out of Nijinsky's predicament and to use it as publicity for his own enterprise. Late on the Thursday afternoon, when it was certain that Nijinsky was well-and-truly dismissed, he cabled to Astruc:

Diaghilev in Petersburg to Astruc in Paris, 10.2.11

After triumphant début presence all Petersburg Vestris was dismissed within twenty-four hours. Reason costume Carpaccio designed Bakst. Monstrous intrigue. Press indignant this morning. Interview director announcing willing take back Vestris who refuses. Appalling scandal. Use publicity. Acknowledge receipt. Serge.[29]

Astruc was naturally incredulous and doubted whether Diaghilev could be telling the exact truth, particularly as he had attributed Nijinsky's costume – the work of Benois – to Bakst. These attributions, such as the authorship of 'Schéhérazade', were becoming a habit. (The only conceivable reason for this was that Bakst's name had greater publicity value in Paris.) He therefore cabled to Gunsbourg. The same evening Gunsbourg replied:

Gunsbourg in Petersburg to Astruc in Paris, 12.2.11

Costume revealing* but responsibility of direction. No difficulty bookings abroad nevertheless foresee possible trouble London Gala.[30]

He was referring to the relationship of the Dowager Empress to Queen Alexandra. The direction of the Imperial Theatres had put about the rumour that the Empress Marie Feodorovna had professed herself shocked by Nijinsky's appearance and asked for his dismissal. She later denied saying anything of the kind.[31]

On Friday Diaghilev cabled again.

Diaghilev in Petersburg to Astruc in Paris, 13.2.11

Try to obtain and send me at once letters or interviews with Duncan and Zambelli about Nijinsky and his grotesque dismissal. Reply.[32]

And again the next day:

---

* 'Costume décolleté' was Gunsbourg's rather odd description in French.

Diaghilev in Petersburg to Astruc in Paris, 14.2.11

Incriminating costume same as Paris Giselle style Carpaccio. Worried direction invent Dowager demanded dismissal. Let's stir something up.[33]*

An hour later:

Diaghilev in Petersburg to Astruc in Paris, 14.2.11

Whole family present applauded. Mother seeing for first time declared she had never seen anything like it. Next day direction gave out mother shocked insisted dismissal. Acknowledge receipt. Send me press interviews.[34]

Before leaving his office that Saturday Astruc wrote back.

Astruc in Paris to Diaghilev in Petersburg, 14.2.11 (Registered)

My dear friend,
    I enclose all the articles that appeared this morning about the Nijinsky affair.
    I must admit that your telegram worried me quite a lot. I cannot see why you want us to take this Carpaccio-Bakst line when the real reason is Giselle-Benois? You must have your reasons, but I can't give the French press information which differs from what Nijinsky and Benois told the Russian press in great detail in the columns of *Novoye Vremya* and the *St Petersburg Journal*.
    Anyway, you will see that I got going in a big way within half an hour of receiving your telegram. Paris seethed. Every columnist and balletomane in Paris arrived at the Pavillon de Hanovre. So we have [a list of articles follows]. . . .
    I am very anxious for detailed information about your programmes. . . . Let me know also how you stand over your tours and whether you reckon to be in a position to keep all your promises.[35]

Benois was working on his designs for the numerous costumes in 'Petrushka', while in distant Beaulieu Stravinsky pushed on with the score; Tcherepnine was finishing 'Narcisse', for which Bakst had designed a pastoral scene and some striking costumes; Anisfeld, who had painted so many admirable décors by other designers, had now been given the submarine act of 'Sadko', with its ballet of sea-monsters, all for himself.
    Ravel had still not completed 'Daphnis', but Reynaldo Hahn had made progress with 'Le Dieu bleu' and Diaghilev now invited him to Petersburg and set out to fête him. On 28 March Diaghilev gave a great dinner for Hahn *chez* Cubat, which was attended by Glazunov, Liadov, Tcherepnine, Davidov, Serov, Bakst, Golovine, Roerich, Karsavina, Nijinsky, Mikhail and Vera Fokine, Schollar, Bolm, Baron Benckendorff, Gunsbourg and other notabilities. (Kchessinskaya, who had celebrated her twentieth anniversary on the stage with a gala at the Mariinsky three nights before, supported by Gerdt and Nicolas Legat and in the presence of the Emperor and both

* *'Moussons.'* The French brevity cannot be achieved in translation.

Empresses, was not present.)[36] After dinner Reynaldo Hahn and Baron Medem of the Conservatoire played 'Le Dieu bleu' *à quatre mains* to universal applause. This, incidentally, was the nearest Diaghilev ever got to presenting one of his ballets in Petersburg. It was also probably the last time Diaghilev and Nijinsky were ever at Cubat's together. The evening ended with Reynaldo at the piano singing his own songs, and with Glazunov playing some of the latter's piano pieces. A small apotheosis for Diaghilev the conqueror, who had not only shown Russian art to Europe, but was now commissioning French composers to work for his new company. Surrounded by his friends and triumphant before Nijinsky, whom he had only known for just over two years, how he must have enjoyed the dinner! He who had been dismissed 'without right to appeal' from the Imperial Theatres, who had even been ordered out of a rehearsal of Benois's 'Le Pavillon', who had been thwarted by the intrigues of Teliakovsky, Krupensky and Kchessinskaya and ostracized by the Imperial family, and whose lover had in his turn been dismissed from the Mariinsky, was now in fact, and would soon be acknowledged as, the Tsar of artistic Europe. Diaghilev hastened to cable Astruc a report of the banquet, in order to make publicity out of the occasion.[37]

He could not foresee that 'Le Dieu bleu' would *not* be presented in 1911, and that when it was shown in 1912 it would be a failure; nor that his dear friend Valentin Serov, whose enthusiasm for Persian miniatures had just inspired him to paint a fine front-cloth for 'Schéhérazade',* would be dead within the year; nor that within a month Nijinsky would have left Russia for good; nor that within three years he and Nijinsky would have parted company!

Diaghilev had signed contracts to present his Ballet at Monte Carlo, following the annual winter season of opera, and in Rome during the World Exhibition of Art. The Paris season would come next in June; and he was negotiating for a Coronation season in London and a visit to America.

Five weeks before his Monte Carlo season opened and two months before his Paris season, which was to be at the Châtelet as in 1909, Diaghilev's proposed repertory was as follows: 'L'Oiseau de feu', 'Schéhérazade', 'Narcisse', 'Petrushka', 'Sadko', 'Le Dieu bleu', 'Le Spectre de la rose', and a ballet to Liszt's 14th Rhapsody.[38] We shall see how the last, which never came to anything, was still under discussion three weeks before the Paris première.

Another novelty was contemplated. As it was Liszt's centenary as well as Gautier's, Diaghilev planned to play his 'Orpheus' as a symphonic

* Sold at Sotheby's on 17 July 1968.

entr'acte, while the audience looked at a big decorative curtain by Bakst.[39] This was never realized, but a similar project was. An interlude, 'The Battle of Kerjenez' from Rimsky's opera 'Grad Kitej' was to be played, and Roerich was to paint for its visual accompaniment a 'striking red and green curtain, representing a battle between Slavs and Mongols'.[40]*

A company had been assembled; a repertory had been sketched out. Tcherepnine was to conduct in Monte Carlo. Diaghilev still had to find two conductors for the Paris season. He negotiated with Cooper in Moscow and, through Astruc, with Pierné in Paris.[41] In the end it was a newcomer to the ballet, Pierre Monteux, who would conduct 'Petrushka'.

On 13 March Bakst arrived in Paris to paint the décors of 'Le Dieu bleu' and 'Le Spectre de la rose'.[42] On the 15th Diaghilev cabled to Astruc that he would be in Paris on Sunday. Could they lunch together and would Astruc book two stalls for the Colonne Concert that afternoon?[43] On Saturday, 18 March, Diaghilev and Nijinsky set off together in the wide luxurious train and that night Nijinsky crossed the Russian–German frontier for the last time.

They spent only the Sunday and Monday in Paris, but during that time Astruc aroused Diaghilev's interest in a new composition by the French composer Paul Dukas entitled 'La Péri', which he thought would make a good ballet.[44] Perhaps Diaghilev's jealousy that Debussy should have composed 'Le Martyre de St Sébastien' for Ida Rubinstein before writing anything for him – and Diaghilev had given Fokine permission to arrange dances for her production – prompted him to snatch at this work by another eminent French composer. Astruc was to conduct negotiations, and it was hoped to give the ballet in Paris.

Arriving at Nice on the morning of Tuesday, 21 March, Vaslav saw a Mediterranean coastline which was very different from Venice. He and Diaghilev took the train along the coast, tunnelling through the red rocks and passing the as yet unsophisticated fishing-villages and the promontories of Cap d'Antibes and Cap Ferrat on which the villas and gardens were still few and far between. They did not at once go on to Monte Carlo, but got out at Beaulieu to see the Stravinskys and hear the latest parts of 'Petrushka'.[45] Here they remained at the Hôtel Bristol for two or three days, during which time Diaghilev went backwards and forwards between Beaulieu and Monte Carlo, twenty minutes away. He met Raoul Guinsbourg, the Director of the Opera, rented a disused theatre, the Palais du Soleil, for classes and rehearsals, booked rooms for Vaslav and himself – not at the smart Hôtel de Paris, opposite the Casino, where he was always to stay in

* This was later bought back for Russia, and, according to Prince Peter Lieven, was hung in the Kasansky railway station in Moscow.

post-war years, but at the Riviera Palace at Beausoleil, high up on the steep mountain slope above Monte Carlo, which was in France, not Monaco, and only approachable by funicular or by a very zig-zag road.[46]

Then the company arrived from Petersburg, Moscow, Warsaw and Paris; and we can imagine the delight with which these northerners, some of whom had never set eyes on any sea before, beheld the Mediterranean and saw the oleanders and bougainvillea in flower, and cascades of pink or red geraniums tumbling from the rocks. But they had hard work ahead of them, for their season was due to open in a fortnight's time.

Maestro Cecchetti had to drill into shape a mixed bag of dancers, few of whom had yet worked together, and of whom only the St Petersburgers had experienced the iron rigours of his class. 'These wonderful lessons,' wrote Grigoriev, 'which began from the day of our arrival, were not only of enormous assistance to everyone, but at once imposed a new style and attitude on the dancers not drawn from the Imperial Theatres and were a boon to Fokine by welding the company into a whole.'[47] Fokine had to rehearse the heterogeneous troupe, most of whom were unfamiliar with his ballets, in 'Les Sylphides', 'Armide', 'Prince Igor', 'Schéhérazade', 'Cléopâtre' and 'Carnaval', as well as 'Giselle', which works, together with two of the new ballets, made up the repertory for Monte Carlo.

Fokine was not as happy as he should have been. Although his position as 'Choreographic Director' of the new company ought to ensure him all the scope that had been denied him at the Mariinsky – and on top of this he was to stage the dances for Rubinstein's 'St Sébastien' – he had all too short a time to do what was necessary. He had counted on mounting 'Daphnis' this season, in which he hoped to embody all his dreams of classical Greece, but Ravel had still not finished the score; Diaghilev had obliged him to undertake another Greek ballet to the hastily-composed score of Tcherepnine, and Bakst was diverting to 'Narcisse' some of the ideas he had had for 'Daphnis'.[48] Fokine would start rehearsing 'Narcisse' after the opening of the season on 9 April.[49] 'Le Spectre' at least had been worked out in Petersburg. 'Petrushka', to whose 'non-danceability'[50] he was not completely reconciled, would have to be rehearsed in Rome. And when could he possibly find time to arrange 'Le Dieu bleu' and the other works which Diaghilev was hoping to present in Paris?

'Diaghilev watched all our proceedings closely,' wrote Grigoriev.[51] He was outwardly as confident and imperturbable as ever: what was going on in his mind? Now that he had his own company he must keep them employed. He knew that, in spite of Nijinsky and a few superb principal dancers – and Karsavina and Preobrajenskaya arrived from Petersburg at the end of March[52] – it was not yet so strong a team as he had captained in the last two years. They must be perfected. And they must be paid. At least Dmitri Gunsbourg was by his side in case of emergencies and there were advances to be had from managements who had booked him in Rome and London. His chief interest – apart from watching the interpretations of Nijinsky and Karsavina – was the creation of new works of art; and if he was to be able to continue commissioning scores from Debussy, Stravinsky, Ravel and others life would be worth while.

Most of the telegrams to Astruc over the next two months were about 'La Péri'. The whole trouble with this ballet was that Paul Dukas had a mistress, Trouhanova, who was a dancer – a plump and amateurish one; and Dukas wanted her to dance his music. Even this Diaghilev might agree to on certain conditions. On the day after his arrival in the south we find him telegraphing from Beaulieu. Fokine agrees in principle to 'La Péri', particularly if Dukas will conduct: Stravinsky agrees to play the piano part in 'Petrushka' (23 March 1911). The Dukas question must be settled forthwith – six thousand francs for four performances: the moral effect of this is all-important and the dancers are delighted (25 March 1911). Then from Beausoleil: Trouhanova's conditions are acceptable so long as after the Paris season Diaghilev has the right to give 'La Péri' in every country throughout the world. Nijinsky agrees to dance only if Dukas conducts. If this does not work 'La Péri' must be replaced by the 14th Rhapsody of Liszt (3 April 1911).[53]

Playing over this rhapsody today, which was written first for piano, then for piano and orchestra, then as an orchestral composition (sometimes called 'Hungarian Fantasia'), it is amusing to conjecture what sort of 'Diaghilev ballet' it would have turned out to be. While its brevity (ten minutes) and the nature of the music indicate that it would probably be a dance for only two people, its veering moods – funereal, tender, patriotic, capricious, gipsyish, emphatic, vertiginous, trippingly gentle and dazzling at the end – make clear that it must have been a passionate *pas d'action* with Hungarian colouring, which Karsavina and Nijinsky would have danced in red boots.

For Nijinsky life was regular, agreeable and not as hectic as for other members of the company. He was anyway happiest in the routine of class and rehearsal. He knew the whole repertory, he had learnt 'Le Spectre' in Petersburg and had merely to perfect it with Karsavina. He would only have the one role of Narcisse to learn after the Monte Carlo season opened. So he began working again in private with Bronia on his Greek ballet, the existence of which was a secret from Fokine and the company.[54]

Though Bakst was kept busy on Ida Rubinstein's massive production in Paris and would only appear in time for 'Le Spectre de la rose', a group of the friends had gathered to assist at the *accouchement* of Diaghilev's own company. Svetlov had brought the contingent from Russia[55] and Besobrasov that from Poland.[56] Paffka Koribut-Kubitovitch, Diaghilev's kind and gentle cousin, was there to do odd jobs.[57] Stravinsky, when he could tear himself away from the composition of 'Petrushka', arrived from Beaulieu to watch the preparations.[58] Benois had come to supervise details of production.[59] Gunsbourg, gay and immaculate, kept a vague hold on the purse strings.[60] The Botkine girls, Bakst's nieces, were there to enjoy the fun.[61] Chaliapine, whose season of opera at Monte Carlo preceded the ballet season, lingered on to relax in the sunshine and to drink with his compatriots at the Café de Paris.[62] The Aga Khan, who had a villa at Monte Carlo and very much admired Karsavina, but who, in view of her implacable virtue, had to console himself instead with the blonde and more accommodating Kovalevska, was sometimes drawn into the conferences, as Diaghilev hoped he would be helpful financially.[63] The Grimaldis, the princely family of Monaco, naturally viewed the Diaghilev enterprise with a paternal eye from their neighbouring rock.[64]

The Théâtre de Monte Carlo had been built in a great hurry by Charles Garnier in 1878. It stands on terraces overhanging the sea. Approaching it from the town, past gardens planted with palms and giant magnolias, one sees a cream-coloured rococo façade surmounted by two tiled and pinnacled domes: between the latter is a clock flanked by green bronze seated youths. To one's left, as one faces the theatre, is the Café de Paris, with its *terrasse*: to the right the Hôtel de Paris. The Casino, which is joined to the theatre, extends to the left. Mounting the steps to the triple doors, one enters a rich brownish foyer with marbled columns, serving as an antechamber both to the Casino on the left and the theatre straight ahead. The auditorium, though small, is ornate and golden, with carved oak *fauteuils* upholstered in red plush. As it is rectangular, there are no boxes round the sides, the walls being adorned with huge mirrors.* There is a canopied central box for the Prince. Over the proscenium is the painting of an angel conducting a rather oddly-composed orchestra out of doors in a breeze; and the justifiably boastful inscription 'INCEPTUM IULIO 1878–19 IANUARIO EXACTUM'. Four art-nouveau ladies with gilded drapery and palm-leaves support the square dome and there are more beautiful athletes seated round the cornice.

Walking down steps, between the theatre and the Hôtel de Paris, one passes on the left the Prince's private entrance to his box and on the right a fine bust of Berlioz by Roussel, rising from a bed of pink and white begonias, and arrives at the broad terrace overlooking the sea. On the base of the Berlioz bust are reliefs depicting Faust, Mephistopheles and Marguerite.

* Now covered by curtains.

'La Damnation de Faust' had its first performance as an opera* at the Théâtre de Monte Carlo on 18 May 1893. And this was the theatre where Diaghilev's Ballet was to have its début on 9 April 1911, to be followed by the première of Weber's 'Le Spectre de la rose', which Berlioz orchestrated, ten days later.

Meanwhile, in Paris, Astruc was anxious to have a good poster designed for the Châtelet season and he appealed to Bakst; but the painter was either too busy to make a special sketch or thought his own designs were too detailed or in too many colours to be practical for a poster. He sent another suggestion.

Bakst to Astruc, 29.3.1911
Weber,
    rue Royale,
    Paris

My dear friend,
    I thought about the poster you need and I have had a good idea. You must get Cocteau to do it. He draws very well and will do you a stunning Nijinsky, for he has often sketched him. I think Diaghilev will agree. What do you think?
                    See you soon
                    LEON BAKST[65]

Bakst wrote from *chez* Weber because it was a restaurant and café he frequented, not far from his studio in the Boulevard Malesherbes: that its name was that of the composer of 'L'Invitation à la valse' was a mere coincidence! Astruc without delay asked Diaghilev's opinion of Cocteau's potentialities as time was short for the colour printing, and Diaghilev telegraphed on 31 March 'Let us use the Russian poster' – presumably meaning the Serov of Pavlova.[66] The logical Astruc, however, who had resisted the attribution of Benois' 'Giselle' costume to Bakst, thought it would be cheating to use a picture of Pavlova to advertise a company in which she no longer danced, so he asked Cocteau to try out some sketches. One of Cocteau's first ideas was to adapt a drawing he had made of Nijinsky in 'Les Orientales' in the studio of Blanche at Passy. He made a bold line drawing of Nijinsky standing on one bent leg, the other crossed over it (as in Druet's reclining photograph) and painted the name NIJINSKI in large capital letters on the right. Not satisfied with the profile, he stuck a scrap of paper over the face and drew it again.[67] Astruc probably advised him that it would be better if the dancer were portrayed in one of the new productions. At this point, doubtless, Cocteau went to Bakst or to the dressmaker to study Bakst's design for the Rose costume. Having made notes of this, he adapted his drawing of Nijinsky in 'Les Orientales', flinging the right arm backwards over the shoulder, and

---

* It had been composed as an oratorio, and was so performed at the Opéra Comique on 6 December 1846.

bending the legs back into a classical *arabesque*, but retaining the downward tilt of the head and the backwards extended left arm almost unchanged.[68] It seems clear that the final result of the now famous poster was arrived at without Cocteau going to Monte Carlo and without his ever having seen Nijinsky dance in 'Le Spectre de la rose'. Whether the poster, together with a companion one of Karsavina in the same ballet, was used to advertise the Châtelet season of 1911 is not clear – they were reproduced in the programme: for the few known surviving copies are posters for the season at the Champs-Elysées in 1913.[69]

On 5 April Diaghilev spent the day with Astruc in Paris, travelling there and back on the night train. Apart from settling a number of problems with Astruc, he was obliged to use persuasion on Bakst to quit his labours for Rubinstein in order to spend two days at Monte Carlo setting up 'Le Spectre de la rose'; and he was probably shown Cocteau's sketches for the poster. He had so much on his mind on this busy day that he left behind in Astruc's office a parcel of photographs by Bert which were needed in Monte Carlo.[70] On Thursday, 6 April Diaghilev had his dress rehearsal in Monte Carlo. The programme, to be repeated at the première on Sunday, was made up of 'Giselle' and 'Schéhérazade'. Only ten of the company had been with him at the Châtelet two years before, namely Nijinsky, Karsavina, Bolm, Schollar, Rosaï, Vassilieva, Nijinska, Grigoriev, Alexandrov and Semenov. A few old hands, such as Kremnev and Orlov, would be joining him later. (Alexandra Vassilieva, Besobrasov's friend, and Mikhail Alexandrov had in fact been with him in 1908, and had led the French Opéra dancers in the polonaise in the Polish scene in 'Boris'.) Cecchetti had been with Diaghilev in 1910, but not in 1909.

It was a good programme, the two ballets being well contrasted, and the two stars being able to display their versatility. For Karsavina was dancing not only Giselle but, for the first time, Zobeïda. Diaghilev had expected Ida Rubinstein to travel from Paris for the first two public performances on Sunday and Monday, 9 and 10 April, but she had cried off on the very day of the dress-rehearsal.[71] (She would turn up on the 24th, thus saving Diaghilev from breaking his contract, which stipulated that he must present certain artists, including Rubinstein, in Monte Carlo.) There was barely time to have a costume fixed up for Karsavina.[72]

Schollar was Myrthe, Queen of the Wilis; Bolm was Hilarion, the rival lover of Giselle, called on the programme 'Le Garde forestier'; and Giselle's mother was mimed by no less a person than Cecchetti himself. In 'Schéhérazade' Bolm played the Shah and Grigoriev enacted his embittered brother.

Between the *répétition générale* on the Thursday and the première on Sunday there occurred an accident which cast a gloom over the birth of the new company. A rehearsal of 'Le Pavillon d'Armide' was in progress and the trap-door through which the group of Nubian pages made their appearance with their fans during the transformation scene was open. The theatre's resident stage-manager, Muoratori, an ex-singer, came on stage from the wings, brushed aside Cecchetti, who tried to restrain him, and fell headlong down the trap into the basement many feet below. The shock was so violent that the rings came off his fingers, and he was killed instantly. Diaghilev was profoundly depressed by this useless sacrifice, which he took as a sinister omen.[73]

This was the only cloud to mar the happy spring season, which no one doubted would be the first of many. Diaghilev was worried about 'La Péri' and about Fokine's rehearsal time and he resented the 'treachery' and absence of Bakst, but he only occasionally vented his ill-temper by telegram on Astruc. It was an interlude of hope and construction. After the day's work Vaslav and Diaghilev often supped with Karsavina and Chaliapine at the Café de Paris, whose tables were crowded with their friends.[74] April was the Grand-Ducal season, and one night four Grand Dukes, Serge, Boris, André and George, were seen dining together at the Hôtel de Paris;[75] and of course Kchessinskaya was there too, holding court.[76] Perhaps it was the omnipresence of these potential enemies at the Hôtel de Paris that had made Diaghilev decide to settle further up the hill. Another visitor who was to become a dear friend to Diaghilev, Nijinsky and Karsavina, and who would help to support the company materially in years to come, was Lady Juliet Duff, who arrived with her husband in time to see the first performance of 'Le Spectre de la rose'.[77] And a photograph survives, taken by General Besobrasov after a gay lunch-party at the Riviera Palace Hotel on Sunday, 16 April,[78] of Koribut-Kubitovitch, Nijinsky, Stravinsky, Benois and Diaghilev peering between the immense hats of Karsavina and the Botkine sisters.[79] Vaslav's hair is cut in a fringe once more, as it had been before he graduated; and he is wearing not his mysterious, sultry faun face, but his mischievous little-boy Puck face.

Three days after this luncheon at Beausoleil there took place the first performance of 'Le Spectre de la rose'.

The ballet is set in the romantic 1830s, the furniture imagined by Bakst being the *bois clair* of Biedermeyer rather than that of Charles x. A girl in white returns from her first ball, dreaming of love. She sinks into an armchair, takes the rose from her bosom, smells it, and as her eyes close in sleep, lets it fall to the ground. Then the Spirit of the Rose leaps in at the window, capers round the room, raises the sleeping girl to her feet and dances with her. At last he returns her to her chair and disappears out of the window. The girl wakes, then, finding her rose on the floor, presses it to her heart.

There were several unusual things about this little ballet, which has since become so famous that it is hard for us to imagine how new and original it seemed in 1911. First, Bakst's set, with its wallpaper, curtained bed, open french windows, draped table and urn of flowers, sofa, dressing-table, harp, birdcage and embroidery frame, was more like the set for a Musset play than for a Russian ballet. Second, this *pas de deux*, which was mainly a solo for the man, was about the longest dance ever invented. Third, there was what Nijinsky did with his role as Spirit of the Rose.

To the opening passage on cellos and woodwind, Karsavina walked on – she did not dance. As the first gust of waltz music broke forth Nijinsky flew through the right-hand window, like a leaf blown by the breeze. The rapid swinging rhythm kept him leaping and twirling incessantly round the room. As a gentler rocking waltz unfolded he raised the still-sleeping Karsavina from her chair and drew her across the floor. The whole of her dance with him to a variety of waltz tunes was made up of *pas de bourrée*, that is, tripping steps on the tips of her toes, and performed with apparently closed eyes. At length Nijinsky led her back to her chair, extending one leg in *arabesque* behind him as he bent to kiss her. His first hectic waltz was now repeated. Round and round, to and fro, he bounded with whirling, drifting arms, until as the tune drew to an end he fell reclining at Karsavina's feet, right arm extended back over his shoulder towards her in passionate acclaim. One more phrase and he crossed the stage diagonally at a run and soared out of the left-hand window, appearing to fly up and up into the night. To a quiet slow passage for solo cello, Karsavina then enacted the girl's awakening and finding of the fallen rose.

When Bronislava Nijinska had seen Fokine arranging 'Le Spectre' in Petersburg, she had been depressed by the banality of Fokine's classical *enchaînements*: but in the course of rehearsals her brother completely transformed his role.[80] He instinctively sensed that for a *man* to be dressed in rose petals and to carry on in this giddy non-stop way, waltzing by himself, as he did at the beginning and end of the ballet, was absurd. That a sexless inhuman being should appear and dance thus was a different matter. He abolished the classical correctness of the *port de bras*, curling his arms round his face and holding them, when extended, with broken wrists and curled-up fingers, so that they became art-nouveau tendrils. Bakst had had dyed and sewn to the pinkish-purple leotard the limp silk petals of pinks, reds and purples which merged into each other like the colours of Tiffany glass, abolishing contours and camouflaging sex: but Nijinsky himself devised his make-up. 'His face was like that of a celestial insect, his eyebrows suggesting some beautiful beetle which one might expect to find closest to the heart of a rose, and his mouth was like rose-petals.'[81] As ever, when costumed and made up, he became possessed. As he danced the endless dance, hardly coming to rest for a moment, weaving evanescent garlands in the air, his lips were parted in ecstasy and he seemed to emit a perfumed gaze. This shows in photographs.

The dress-rehearsal was not without its nerve-racking moments. When Nijinsky's costume arrived at the eleventh hour it was found to have been badly interpreted by the dressmaker. Benois later recalled that

important corrections had to be made there and then. There was no other course but to pin the silk rose petals direct to the flesh-coloured *tricot*. Naturally this could not be done without pin-pricks and scratches, which caused poor Vaslav to squirm and cry out in pain. Diaghilev, in evening dress and top hat, looking very pompous and solemn as he always looked on first nights, stood by, giving directions with growing anxiety, while the role of costumier was being improvised by our stage-manager [the scene-painter] O.P.Allegri, as the professional costumier seemed no good at all. Kneeling on the floor with his mouth full of pins, Allegri cleverly performed the complicated and responsible operation of correcting the costume on a living body. . . .[82]

Bakst arrived for the first performance to find that his birdcage, which was to hang in one of the open windows, had been removed because Nijinsky said it would inhibit his jump. He wandered round the set, trying to find a place for it. Diaghilev exclaimed, 'Levushka, for God's sake, chuck the canary, the public is growing impatient. Oh, don't be ridiculous; canaries don't stand on the chest-of-drawers.' 'You don't understand, Serioja; we must give the atmosphere.' Bakst protracted the interval alarmingly, Karsavina was to remember, but he finally had the birdcage hoisted high up under a cornice.[83]

'Le Spectre' had been turned out with such ease and was such a slight affair that Diaghilev and his friends, who tended to count on more elaborate or exotic spectacles to excite the public, were somewhat taken aback by its exceptional success. It would gradually dawn on them that this was the most popular ballet in the repertory. In the Rose, Nijinsky, weaving his variations on a theme of Fokine, had created what was to be his most famous role.

Ida Rubinstein tore herself away from Paris to arrive on 23 April for two performances of 'Schéhérazade' and two of 'Cléopâtre', in which latter ballet Preobrajenskaya interpreted Pavlova's old role of Ta-hor.[84] It had been hoped that Rubinstein would be the chief Nymph in Nijinsky's Greek ballet,[85] but these appearances as Zobeïda would be her last for Diaghilev. From now on, a series of annual spectacles, all designed by Bakst, of which the first was 'Le Martyre de St Sébastien', presented a month later, turned her into a rival for Diaghilev – a rich but not a serious one. She stayed five days at Monte Carlo, during which time Fokine invented for her the dance she would perform as St Sebastian.[86]

Somewhat *à contre coeur* Fokine began to rehearse 'Narcisse'. Benois disapproved of the subject, which Bakst had insisted on and which naturally appealed to the paederastic side of Diaghilev (as it had to that of Caravaggio three centuries before), because he considered it totally unsuitable for ballet.[87] The characters of Echo and Narcissus he thought were 'the most static in Greek mythology', Echo being 'imprisoned in her cave' and Narcissus 'immobilized in the contemplation of his own beauty'. For this and for other reasons the ballet was one of Diaghilev's semi-failures – in spite of an attractive score, a good set and the performances of Karsavina and Nijinsky.

Tcherepnine had written a woodland introduction, reminiscent of Delibes' 'Sylvia', and there was singing by a backstage chorus *à bouche fermée* before the curtain rose. This droning would be used throughout as the symbol of Echo. Bakst had painted against a blue sky with dancing clouds a green landscape of weeping willows, with a stream in the foreground and at the back an arch of rocks through which a meadow could be seen and across which the nymph Echo would sometimes move on a higher plane. (She was not, in fact, 'imprisoned in her cave' throughout nor even confined to her bridge, but descended to the same level as the other dancers.) There was a statue of Pomona on the right.

Little green furry creatures with horns, long pointed ears and tails, woodspirits, caper about the stage. (The idea of these shy monsters who only appeared when there were no humans about was charming, as Benois pointed out,[88] but there is always the risk of monsters appearing ridiculous on the stage as we have seen in 'Firebird' and shall see again in 'Le Dieu bleu'.) The creatures are banished by the arrival of a party of Beotian peasants who celebrate the rites of Pomona, splash the water of the pool and lie about in the shade. The bold stripes, spots and checks of their simple smocks in colours of honey, lemon, orange, rust and garnet, are among Bakst's happiest inventions. There follows a dance for Bronislava Nijinska as a Bacchante in coral-pink, with a royal-blue shawl attached to her wrists, carrying an amphora and cup. She is borne on at speed by two satyrs, leaning backwards and kicking her legs high in the air; and her dance, made up of jumps and spins, is extremely strenuous. Other Bacchantes in periwinkle-blue join her and at the climax of their dance they all fall to the ground. The distant voice of Narcissus is heard, repeated by Echo, and Nijinsky leaps on, followed by two amorous Nymphs. Clad in a white *chlamys* and wig of long fair hair, he enters gaily to a curving *moderato* in 4 time, with trills, and all the girls on stage follow his movements adoringly. Karsavina, as the melancholy Echo, appears on the bridge with flowing black hair, in purple silk draperies stencilled with silver; she descends and prostrates herself adoringly at Nijinsky's feet. He, who loves to be admired, raises her and gazes into her eyes. Their dance together is an elegiac poem, accompanied by the *bouche fermée* singing. The jealous nymphs, to music reminiscent of the Gypsies in Messager's 'Les Deux Pigeons', explain that Echo is incapable of making an original statement but can only repeat those of others. Narcissus tries her out, and for every few steps he dances Echo repeats the final phrase. He mocks her by improvising faster, more difficult steps and gestures, till, tired of this too-easy game, he runs off with his companions into the woods. Echo, left alone, prays to Pomona that Narcissus may suffer from unrequited love, then leaves the stage. Narcissus returns to drink from the pool and is fascinated by his own reflection. He tries to charm the subaqueous stranger by the beauty of his poses. Echo returns and is ready to love him all over again, but he has no

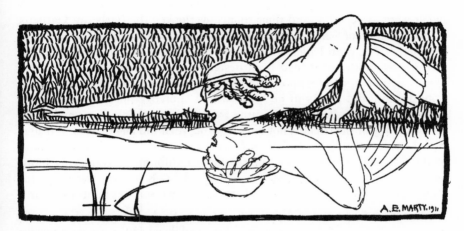

Nijinsky in 'Narcisse'. Drawing by André-E. Marty.

eyes for anything but his image in the pool. (Fokine had had trouble introducing some variety into what Benois thought an 'interminable choreographic soliloquy'. And 'even Karsavina's beauty and her genuinely classical poses did not prevent the melancholy mood demanded of Echo from becoming tedious. Both dancers seemed to be the victims of a strange fancy and one felt sorry for them'[89].) Karsavina goes off. Nijinsky sinks into the pool – that is, down a gaping trap-door; and a huge artificial narcissus rises from the ground to take his place, while the sylvan creatures steal out of their holes to observe the new phenomenon, and Karsavina passes sadly across the bridge to merge with the rocky landscape, as the mournful ululations of the chorus are resumed.

The ballet had so many good elements, but the episodes were 'strung together' and did not achieve unity.[90] There was evidently just too much plaintive posing; and the goblins and the artificial flower did not come off. For once the Diaghilev touch had not worked. But he had given Karsavina one helpful bit of advice, the suggestive power of which she never forgot. 'Don't trip lightly as a graceful nymph; I see rather a monumental figure, a tragic mask, Niobe.' 'In my vision,' she wrote, 'the heavy metric structure of the tragic name became the mournful tread of sleepless Echo.'[91]

Diaghilev was in Rome on Friday the 5th, ahead of Vaslav and the company.[92] The latter had the pleasure of travelling round the coast of Piedmont and Tuscany. Diaghilev and Nijinsky stayed at the big modern Hôtel Excelsior at the bottom of the busy Via Veneto.[93] Benois and Stravinsky put up at a smaller quieter hotel, the Albergo Italia near the Quattro Fontane,[94] which was between Diaghilev's hotel and the Teatro Costanzi, where the Ballet were to perform; and their rooms overlooked the Barberini Gardens, to the murmur of whose fountains the last pages of 'Petrushka' would be completed. The great ballet, which could be regarded as a culmination of the *Mir Iskustva* movement, had been designed in Petersburg, the city whose life it celebrated, and composed mostly by the Lake of Geneva and on the Côte d'Azur, and it was to be finished and choreographed in Rome, then perfected in Paris. Benois' wife came from Lugano to join him; and to increase the joy of the friends, not only Nourok, their old ally of 'The World of Art' days, but also Serov and his wife were in Rome – Serov being in charge of the Russian section of the International Exhibition.[95] Karsavina found her brother and sister-in-law in Rome: Lev Karsavin was studying philosophy.[96] Finally Maestro Cecchetti on his own soil was in his element.[97]

These were indeed wonderful days for us [wrote Benois]. Seen from a distance they seem as radiant as the happy days of my childhood and as the most poetical years of my youth. It was wonderful to be working in an atmosphere of complete friendship and harmony on a task of whose significance we were all fully conscious. It was wonderful to bring our work to conclusion in such unfamiliar and beautiful surroundings. . . . We roamed about the town, visiting the churches, the museums and the World Exhibition of Art, at which Serov had scored a notable triumph, and where we welcomed the King and Queen of Italy when they came to the opening of the Russian section. . . . Our excursions to Tivoli and Albano I shall never forget. I already knew those places well, but I was in a state of spiritual ecstasy and everything seemed fresh. . . .[98]

There were, of course, the usual draw-backs. In spite of the friendly attitude of Conte di San Martino, director of the World Exhibition, the management and stage staff of the Teatro Costanzi were hostile. Impossible to gain possession of the stage for rehearsals. (It was the Paris Opéra all over again.) 'Even access to the theatre was difficult. The doorkeeper would be outside the entrance; as one approached the stage-door his gesticulation, usually vivacious, took on a highly dramatic tenor. In the corridors there would be more "hushers" and all around walked on tip-toes – Toscanini was rehearsing.'[99]

Fokine had arrived ahead of the company for talks with Diaghilev about the repertory for Paris, and these put him in a bad temper.[100] It was a month to the opening night in Paris, and Diaghilev expected him to produce not only 'Petrushka', but 'Sadko', 'La Péri' and 'Le Dieu bleu', as well as rehearsing 'Firebird' with a company who were mostly unfamiliar with it. It was a battle of wills between two extremely obstinate men, which Diaghilev – being the more persistent of the two – would probably have won had not his demands been, in fact, impossible. When Grigoriev came to discuss the rehearsals for the Roman season with Fokine the latter sulked and refused to speak. When Diaghilev suggested that Fokine should work on 'Petrushka' and 'Sadko' simultaneously, Grigoriev wrote,

he was still more annoyed and merely said that he would see me about it. I did my best to calm him down, seeing that he was in no fit state to tackle the arrangement of a ballet like 'Petrushka', of which not only was the music difficult, but parts of the scenario, and particularly the middle scenes, had not yet been properly worked out. Yet when he began composing, as he shortly did, he turned out to be full of ideas; and the rehearsals went quickly ahead. Only when he reached the third scene, where the Moor is left by himself for a time, did his invention fail him. He could not think what to make him do, and lost his temper, throwing the music on the floor and leaving the rehearsal. Next day, however, he appeared looking happier, and said that he had thought of some 'business' for the accursed Moor: he would give him a coconut to play with – which would carry him at least through the first part of the scene.[101]

Some extra music had to be written in.

Rehearsals took place in a buffet in the theatre's basement, the floor of which was covered in worn, dirty crimson carpeting; and on this the dancers had to dance and even lie. The weather was stifling and ventilation non-existent. Stravinsky, at the piano, asked the ladies' permission to remove his coat.[102] Diaghilev, looking worn out, but immaculately dressed, perched on a hard chair and watched the great ballet take shape. Benois sketched them both, and in the margin of his drawing of the composer, the designer wrote of their choreographer: 'Fokine can make *nothing* of the rhythms of the Coachmen's dance!' and added, 'Appalling heat!'

The Ballet opened on 15 May with 'Le Pavillon d'Armide', 'Les Sylphides' and 'Prince Igor' and was warmly received. Diaghilev lost no time in cabling to Astruc about the elegance of the audience and the sixteen curtain calls. The King of Italy, the Queen and the Queen Mother attended the second performance, which was greeted with 'infinite ovations'.[103]

With his Roman triumph and with the progress made on 'Petrushka', Diaghilev's spirits improved.[104] Karsavina was staying at a hotel opposite the Queen Mother's palace, near the Borghese Gardens.[105] She wrote:

Diaghilev often came round in the morning to fetch me on his way to the Teatro Costanzi. 'Maestro, you say? The old man will wait; it is a sin to be indoors on such a morning', and he would take Nijinsky and myself for some enchanting drive, pointing out here and there an arch, a view, a monument. He would hand us over to the Maestro with a request not to scold his children for being a bit late. Maestro, with unusual blandness, would excuse his unpunctual pupils; he knew he could make up for time lost. . . . For the sake of discipline, though, Maestro would go through a show of disapproval; twirling his cane, thus giving time for escape, he would sling it at my feet; a well-timed skip cleared the missile. . . . He was in a frenzy of teaching, and an equal frenzy of learning possessed both Nijinsky and myself.

If, on the other hand, they arrived early for their lesson, the old teacher would still have got there before them, and they would find him 'cracking jokes with the stage hands, making the wise black poodle of the doorkeeper perform his tricks. The dog loved money and knew the use of it. Given a soldo he sedately walked across the road to the pastrycook's, put his coin on the counter and came with a cream bun to eat at his leisure.'[106]

Time was getting on and the Battle of the Paris Repertory was engaged. Diaghilev wanted to give Paris as varied and novel programmes as possible, even though there were only to be two of them, with four performances of each: but by now he realized that in announcing 'Le Dieu bleu', 'La Péri' and a revival of 'L'Oiseau de feu', he had promised more than he could fulfil.[107] Torn between a Fokine who refused to be hurried and an Astruc who demanded that he should present the scheduled ballets, he was to find his diplomatic skill tested to the utmost. While fighting to get as much work out of Fokine as he could, he decided to put all the blame on to Astruc and Bakst for the non-appearance of any ballets he failed to present. On 22 May he wrote as follows:

Diaghilev in Rome to Astruc in Paris, 22.5.11 (typed)

My dear Astruc,

This is the situation: we have a fortnight till the Paris opening, and there are still two ballets we have not even touched for reasons which have nothing to do with me or my company.

First Péri. I have still not received Trouhanova's contract signed. Indeed, you tell me there are still things you cannot agree on with her. You realize that I cannot start working on something which may not come off. Then, Mlle Trouhanova, having given her word to come to Monte Carlo, never managed to do so during the entire two months* we were there. Now, having finished her recitals, she still gives no sign of life. Obviously we can't plan a work without the co-operation of its chief interpreter.

I have certainly received the piano score (in which there are some obvious mistakes), but it is of no use to me for the reasons given above and above all for the following reason, which I must now put to you most seriously.

You have followed my work for five years and you know the principles on which it is based. I am not a professional impresario, and my speciality is to make painters, musicians, poets and dancers work together.

Of all my collaborators the most indispensable has always been Leon Bakst, my childhood friend,† who has taken part in all my enterprises. He owes his Paris reputation entirely to the Russian seasons which, as you well know, have cost me such superhuman efforts.

This year I gave him four productions to do. One, Narcisse, we all worked out together. As for the second, le Spectre de la Rose, Bakst watched the rehearsals in Petersburg and saw it arranged choreographically. So he had only to adapt his décor to a ready-made work.

As for 'Dieu bleu' and above all 'Péri' we have had nothing but vague suggestions, possible treatments – nothing more, not even a pencil sketch. I believe there has to be a temple in the set of 'Dieu bleu', but I do not know how or where it is situated. I don't even know if it is the interior of a temple or the square outside it, and I don't know where the pool and the grill stipulated in the libretto are meant to be. In short I know nothing about the construction or the very idea of the décor. And it is under these conditions that Fokine, Benois and myself are supposed to devise a production?

As far as Péri is concerned the situation has become absolutely ridiculous, for we are in total ignorance of whether the action takes place in a palace, on a mountain-top or in the clouds – and this is two weeks before the first night. Bakst claims that we lack confidence in his work, but I must say that I have never seen so astounding a betrayal of every artistic and aesthetic principle as he has shown in his dealings with us. When Bakst took on the production of S. Sebastien he swore to me that it would in no way interfere with our work, which he held much dearer. Now I declare that we have been completely sacrificed to the work of Rubinstein and d'Annunzio. We are the victims of our too great trust in him. Certainly Kchessinska never played us such a dirty trick as you have done over this negotiation, which, as you will remember, I was so helpful about. Kchessinska never obliged us to abandon anything we had undertaken. Now, thanks to you and Bakst, at the last moment we are forced to give up the production of two ballets planned for a season beginning in a fortnight's time, and I warn you that you must take the consequences.

I need not remind you that by giving up the *répétition générale* of Dieu bleu we lose almost a hundred thousand francs. But what hurts me most is not to be

---

* i.e., just under six weeks.

† When they first met in 1890 Diaghilev and Bakst were eighteen and twenty-four respectively.

able to give Paris the whole splendid repertory we planned – and you know that that is the one thing I really care about.

I leave you to judge who is to blame for what has happened. It was not for nothing that I put myself out to go to Paris to beg Bakst to come to Monte Carlo just for two days. Now I am in the most embarrassing position with regard to Dukas and above all Reynaldo Hahn, who took the trouble to come to Petersburg; and I must ask you to make your excuses for what has happened and to explain to them the reasons for this delay. I have suffered too much from the financial and moral worries that you and Bakst have brought upon me.

Yours,
[signed] SERGE DE DIAGHILEV

P.S. [in manuscript] Copies of this letter have been sent to Bakst and Reynaldo Hahn.[108]

The letter was no doubt carefully timed to arrive on Astruc's and Bakst's breakfast tables simultaneously with the press notices of Ida Rubinstein's 'St Sébastien'. Thus are traitors punished.

Bakst telegraphed at once.

Bakst in Paris to Diaghilev in Rome, 24.5.11

. . . Protest vehemently against responsibilities you try to place on my shoulders. Two sketches and plantations [explanations?] Péri dispatched last month Monte Carlo remained undelivered returned Paris. Nevertheless began painting backcloth. Costumes sent to Muelle. Costume Nijinsky Péri used cover programme Brunhoff. I telegraphed and wrote accepting Fokine Benois production Dieu Bleu. No reply. In despair adopted Fokine method of staging eve of departure Petersburg. Sketch Dieu Bleu finished costumes designed.

BAKST[109]

Astruc seems to have protested furiously against any change in the programme announced. On the night of the 25th Diaghilev, Benois, Fokine and Grigoriev sat up till the early hours discussing possibilities; and next day Diaghilev telegraphed to Astruc.

Diaghilev in Rome to Astruc in Paris, 26.5.11

After discussion entire night decided definitely renounce revival Firebird in favour following programmes. First Carnaval with Nijinsky Harlequin Narcisse Rose Sadko. Second Scheherazade Peri Kerjenetz Rose Petrushka. Stage director Allegri arriving Paris Sunday with music. . . . Begin rehearsals Monday.[110]

Diaghilev had entirely abandoned the possibility of putting on the extremely complicated 'Dieu bleu' and he probably thought it would be better to give up 'La Péri' too, but in the letter Allegri took to Astruc that weekend he tried a different tactic.

My dear Astruc.

Your telegrams full of words like disastrous, immoral and deplorable are getting on my nerves. You seem to be willing disaster on our season. . . . It is obvious that if Bakst and Trouhanova had come to Monte Carlo for a few days Péri would have been arranged already.

Now the unanimous revolt against this intruding ballet has reached its climax. Karsavina refuses to come to Paris to dance alongside Trouhanova. Fokine declared yesterday that to put on Péri with Trouhanova would be the most idiotic thing he had ever let himself in for and something he could never forgive himself. Benois disclaims all responsibility for this inartistic business. The artists are disgusted. I don't speak of Besobrasov and de Gunsburg.

The only thing which makes them entertain the project at all is that I am determined to get Péri on.

Yesterday, after hearing the music Fokine declared that he would need at least twelve rehearsals to arrange it, not counting orchestral ones! !

He doesn't feel ready to start work on it because the libretto is quite inadequate and he has no idea how to produce it.

Under the circumstances I realize that the revival of Firebird, our most complicated ballet and one we have not danced for a year, is a physical impossibility if we do Péri. I had to decide between the two and to give up the work put in on the revival of Firebird.

I made that decision against the wishes of all my colleagues as a result of all the abusive words in your interminable telegrams.

And now I hear from you that the cancelling of Firebird is deplorable too.

Well, I am quite lost and I simply don't know what to do.

I shall have to show your telegram to all these people and the scenes will start all over again and will be worse than ever, since even you don't back me up in a decision come to simply because you say I have given my word and can't go back on it. It's really too much.

There is one thing I must ask you to do. See your friend Bakst and let me know by telegram what you both agree which scheme is likely to be less damaging to my reputation and financial prospects.

I am no longer in control of a season, which will be my sixth in Paris, and since I have obligations towards my company and my backers, I am obliged to submit totally to the decisions of my friends Bakst and Astruc.

If there is a possibility of postponing Péri until another season, the London one, for example, or the American one, I shall resume work on the revival of Firebird.

But I must know by Monday at the latest.

Therefore please cable as soon as you have made up your mind.

Yours ever

SERGE DE DIAGHILEV[111]

In fact there was no necessity to give 'Firebird', and, whatever had been announced, the second programme was quite long enough without 'La Péri'. Admittedly, it was a bit awkward that Trouhanova had already been photographed for the programme, wearing her Bakst costume, and that Bakst's designs for her and Nijinsky were also reproduced. The scenery had even been painted. (It would come in useful six years later, in São Paulo in Brazil, of all places, when the Bakst setting of 'Cléopâtre' was burnt in a railway tunnel!)[112] There would be a few complaints in the press about the changes,[113] but the success of the new productions put these quite out of mind. On the 31st Diaghilev cabled that Tcherepnine would conduct the first and Monteux the second programme; that he needed twenty men, twenty women and eight children as walkers-on (these being for the crowd in 'Petrushka'); that an extra rehearsal room would be needed besides the stage of the Châtelet as there would often be three rehearsals a day; that the company would arrive in Paris on Friday morning and begin rehearsals at the Châtelet at once.[114]

Les Ballets Russes de Serge de Diaghilev arrived for their first Paris season off the night train from Rome on the morning of Friday the 2nd of June and began a busy weekend's work. Their opening night was on the Tuesday.

So it was the Châtelet that saw Nijinsky's first performance of Harlequin in 'Carnaval', Fokine's and Leontiev's role, but one Nijinsky was to make inimitably his own. As was increasingly the case, Nijinsky brought to a would-be straightforward role something extra and unexpected which transformed the ballet magically. We have seen how he created an atmosphere even in the classical *enchaînement* of 'Le Pavillon d'Armide', making Armide's Slave appear like the inhabitant of another world. In how many of his roles would he portray a character not quite human! His airborne, knee-lifting, head-wagging, finger-pointing, hand-clapping Harlequin appeared feline – 'an unforgettable figure,' wrote Geoffrey Whitworth,

not at all the blustering, magnificent Harlequin of Italian comedy, but a sly fellow, slickly insinuating, naughtily intimate. He is always whispering subtle secrets to Columbine, and is saved from viciousness only by his unerring sense of fun. Certainly he is the most uncanny and least human of all Nijinsky's creations. For this Harlequin is the very soul of mischief – half Puck – but Puck with a sting and with a body like a wire of tempered steel.[115]

His head [wrote Valentine Gross, a young painter who attended every performance to make drawings in the dark] seemed even smaller in the black skull cap; while the painted black domino mask hid everything but the lower part of his face and the eyes, which were prolonged, slanting up to the temples, and had such a shine and mystery like the eyes of a cat. I have never seen anything to equal the liveliness of his interpretation or the precision of his muscular control – such as at the moment when, with insect rapidity, he tore the letter into innumerable pieces like white butterflies, while wagging his head from left to right so quickly that one could hardly see it. . . . The famous *entrechat-dix* executed as he shot up into the air were done so coolly, with such elegance and wit.[116]

It seems incredible to us today that Nijinsky, after dancing his first Harlequin, should have gone on to perform in 'Narcisse' and 'Le Spectre de la rose'. Here is Jean Cocteau's description of him in the latter ballet.

In his costume of curling petals, behind which perhaps the Girl perceives the image of her recent dancing-partner, he comes through the blue cretonne curtains out of the warm June night. He conveys – which one would have thought impossible – the impression of some melancholy, imperious scent. Exulting in his rosy ecstasy he seems to impregnate the muslin curtains and take possession of the dreaming girl. It is the most extraordinary achievement. By magic he makes the Girl dream she is dancing and conjures up all the delights of the ball. After he has bid a last farewell to his beloved victim he evaporates through the window in a jump so poignant, so contrary to all the laws of flight and balance, following so high and curved a trajectory, that I shall never again smell a rose without this ineffacable phantom appearing before me.[117]

The enchanted evening ended with the submarine act of Rimsky's 'Sadko', which was the kind of exotic spectacle with exotic music that Paris had come to expect from the Russians. Anisfeld's green sea-monsters performed Fokine's ingenious undulations to the marvellous water-music; and the roles of Sadko and the Sea King were sung by Issatchenko and Zaporojetz. This first programme was repeated four times, but at subsequent performances Leontiev took over the role of Harlequin.[118]

In one night the French had seen Nijinsky in two of his greatest roles: but critics like to find something to complain about, and to the charge of blasphemy at dancing to an orchestrated version of Schumann's 'Carnaval', repeated from the year before, at least one critic added that of dancing to Berlioz's orchestration of Weber. He thought it was lazy of Diaghilev not to order new music for 'Le Spectre de la rose'![119]

After the run-through of 'Le Spectre' before its first Paris performance Karsavina had made a new friend who was to become in time her almost official admirer.[120]

Two young men, both tall and both in check trousers, had been to congratulate me after the morning rehearsal; one of them was the author – I only learned afterwards which was which. So I addressed my heartfelt thanks for giving me such opportunity as the part offered to the wrong young man, and for a long time I disapproved of the right one on account of a flicker of a *sourire moqueur*, which on closer knowledge proved to be the most enchanting touch of persiflage in an earnest and refined mind.[121]

This of course was Jean-Louis Vaudoyer.

Diaghilev imagined as the Girl in 'Le Spectre de la rose'. Caricature by Jean Cocteau.

When the orchestra began to rehearse the score of 'Petrushka' they burst out laughing. Monteux had some trouble persuading them that Stravinsky's music was not a joke.[122] (It took even Fokine many years to appreciate it.) Benois' scenery and costumes arrived from Petersburg: but time for finishing the ballet was short. Fokine only had one two-hour rehearsal with the crowd, including a number of French walkers-on, before the orchestral and dress rehearsals.[123] Diaghilev always remembered one incident which took place during the final rehearsals of the crowd. When Cecchetti as the Magician mimed the playing of his flute solo before animating the puppets, a young girl in the crowd was literally 'charmed' by the hypnotic music and strayed unconsciously forward into the clear space in the middle of the stage. Fokine kept this in.[124]

190

The excitement of staging his ballet was too much for Benois, who was not well, and he made one of his scenes.

'Petrushka' opened the wound that had hardly healed after the 'Schéhérazade' incident [he wrote]. The décor of Petrushka's room was badly crushed during the journey, and considerable damage was done to the Conjuror's portrait, which occupied the centre of one of the walls. According to my plan, this portrait was to play an important part in the drama: the Conjuror had hung it there so that it should constantly remind Petrushka that he was in his master's power, and must therefore be humble and submissive. But it is just this portrait of his master that arouses Petrushka's indignation when he finds himself in solitary confinement: he shakes his fists at him and pours on him maledictions and curses. It was indispensable to have the portrait repaired as quickly as possible, but I, unfortunately, had developed an abscess on my elbow and was obliged to sit at home. When Bakst kindly offered to repair the portrait, I gratefully agreed, having no doubt that he would do it perfectly.

How great was my surprise at the dress-rehearsal two days later when I saw instead of 'my' portrait of the Conjuror a totally different one, showing him in profile, with his eyes looking sideways! Had I been in good health, I would of course have tried to arrange it all in a friendly way; Bakst had probably no evil intentions at all and had only exhibited too much zeal. But I had come to the theatre with a temperature and unbearable pain in my arm, the atmosphere of the rehearsal was tense – in short, I considered the alteration of my portrait an unpardonable outrage against me as an artist, and my whole plan for the ballet. Last year's insult came immediately to my memory. My fury expressed itself in a loud shout across the theatre, filled with a highly select audience: 'I shall not allow it! Take it down immediately! I can't bear it!' After which I flung my portfolio full of drawings on the floor and rushed out into the street and home. . . .

My state of fury continued for two whole days. It was in vain that Serov immediately offered to give the portrait its original form and executed it with touching diligence; it was in vain that Nouvel kept coming to explain that it had been a misunderstanding and that both Serioja and Bakst were very sorry about what had occurred. I would not listen, nor give in. Nor would the pain in my arm stop until the doctor operated on it.

I sent in my resignation to Serioja, giving up my post of Artistic Director, and announced my refusal to go to London. . . .[125]

The second programme of the Paris season was given on Tuesday, 13 June, a week after the first. It began with 'Schéhérazade', Karsavina replacing Rubinstein. Beautiful, passionate and moving as Karsavina was, the sadistic ballet had owed something of its effectiveness to the cold, inhuman quality of the angular mime, and without Rubinstein it would never be the same again. Once again Karsavina and Nijinsky were to dance in three ballets. The orchestral interlude from 'Grad Kitej', with Roerich battlescape, was played while they changed into their 'Spectre' costumes. 'Petrushka' followed.

Benois' ideas for staging 'Petrushka' must have owed something, though he did not acknowledge the debt in his books, to certain of Meyerhold's productions.* (He and Meyerhold were always criticizing each other.) On 9 October 1910 the latter had presented at the Interlude House, a cabaret-restaurant, a programme including Arthur Schnitzler's 'Veil of Pierrette', renamed by Meyerhold 'Columbine's scarf', with music by Dohnanyi and décor by Sapunov. Like 'Petrushka' this aimed at producing an eerie Hoffmannesque atmosphere; the lovelorn Pierrot who has a suicide pact with Columbine, which she does not fulfil, is a parallel to the tormented Petrushka; the master of ceremonies, a huge-headed Kapellmeister who from his high stool controls the destiny of the characters, and who at the end, when Columbine falls genuinely dead beside Pierrot, flees in terror through the auditorium, as if acknowledging his guilt, presages Benois' flute-playing Magician and his final exit haunted by Petrushka's ghost.[126]

When the curtain rises on Benois' décor for 'Petrushka' the French audience see before them a picture of the Russian winter – that terrible foe who defeated their ancestors in 1812. But Benois has created a scene of colour and gaiety amid the snow. It is Shrove Tuesday, the day before the Lenten fast begins; the period is the 1830s; and Nicholas I, the younger brother of Napoleon's ally and enemy, Alexander, is on the throne. Over the booths and flags of the fair rises the attenuated golden spire of the Admiralty, beyond which, out of sight, lies the frozen Neva and the islands, where Pushkin has yet to fight his fatal duel. On either side are the *balagani* or temporary wooden theatres, with their painted signs, the left-hand one having a yellow balcony from which the old man or father of the fair will dangle his long false beard, and red and grey striped curtains below. Just to right of centre, half-hiding a distant merry-go-round and overhung by a helter-skelter, is the curtained booth of the Russian Punch-and-Judy or rather Petrushka show, with a sign showing a devil pitchforking Petrushka into hell. This is, as it were, the stage within a stage, where the microcosmic drama of the Magician's puppets will take place while the careless crowd orbits around them. But Benois the Master-magician and Puppet-master has, with typical Hoffmannesque (or Pirandellian) humour –

* But in the ephemeral world of the theatre it is only natural to enrich this year's productions with good ideas from last year's. In Meyerhold's 'Columbine's scarf', the 'flapping white sleeve' of Pierrot, though traditional, appears to be a reminiscence of Fokine's 'Carnaval', first staged in February of the same year, 1910, and in which Meyerhold himself played Pierrot. But was Fokine's ballet itself partly inspired by Meyerhold's production of 'Balagan' – 'The Fairground Booth' – by Alexander Blok at Vera Komisarjevskaya's Theatre in Petersburg on 30 December 1906? For this the stage was 'hung at the sides and rear with blue drapes' and Pierrot 'sighs and flaps his arms'. (Meyerhold: *O Teatre*, p. 198, quoted by Edward Braun: *Meyerhold on Theatre*, p. 71.) 'Balagan' was one of the discarded titles for 'Petrushka' (other names considered for it were 'Maslanetsa' – 'Butter-week', and 'Mardi-Gras' – 'Shrove Tuesday'). Its action was heralded by a big drum: no doubt, Stravinsky or Benois or Diaghilev remembered this when they decided to link the three scenes of 'Petrushka' and cover up the scene-changes by a roll of kettle-drums.

and his humour equals poetry – framed the fairground in the arch of a greater theatre, with people looking out of the windows of its painted boxes. Is it by accident that this outer theatre is blue like our sky and that the reveal of a narrow strip of ceiling, painted in false perspective just above the gold-fringed pelmet of its proscenium, is decorated with a yellow sun? Box within box: world beyond world. The artist is teasing us, suggesting that the 'real' people in the crowded fair are as much puppets as the painted sawdust figures behind the curtain of the booth, or even that we, so safe beyond the footlights, are really puppets too. He seems to be asking, with Omar Khayyam, 'Which is the Potter, pray, and which the pot?'

The stage is filled with a circulating crowd and Benois would later describe what pains had been taken to make them 'live'.

I used to watch carefully during the rehearsals to see that every walker-on fulfilled the part that had been given him. The mixture of various characteristic elements gave the illusion of life. The people of good society showed elegant manners, the military men looked like real soldiers and officers of the time of Nicholas I, street-hawkers seemed really to be offering their goods, the peasant men and women looked like real *moujiks* and *babas*. I allowed nobody to improvise or overact.[127]

There are aristocratic couples arm-in-arm, followed by a cockaded footman carrying an extra coat; grooms and coachmen tipple; cadets salute their officers. 'One admires a samovar, others listen to the senseless chatter of an old man, a youth plays a harmonica, the boys reach for pretzels, girls crack sunflower seeds with their teeth.'[128] The sails of the windmill-like big wheel revolve and children ride on the *carrousel*.

'This merry-go-round,' wrote Benois, 'was a genuine *manège de chevaux de bois* of the time of Napoleon III which we had contrived to acquire at some fair.'[129]*

The stridency and bustle of the fair are represented in Stravinsky's music by a shrill figure on the flute and by an impatient rhythmical stamping which will frequently interrupt the various borrowed tunes that give the score a kaleidoscopic and Shakespearian diversity, and will at the same time serve to bring on a fresh incursion of boisterous revellers. The steady animal panting of the accordion seems to convey the surrounding enormity of winter.

The imminence of Lent and Easter as well as a kind of popular religious element are suggested at the very beginning by the introduction of a tune we recognize at once as Russian, even if we do not know that it used to be sung at Easter by bands of peasants walking from village to village in the department of Smolensk. A street musician enters with a barrel-organ, whose music –

---

* It is now at the bottom of the River Plate, having been dropped by a crane when the Ballet's luggage was unloading at Buenos Aires. (Benois: *Reminiscences*, p. 335 footnote.)

the whining tune Stravinsky wrote to ask André Rimsky-Korsakov for – is represented by clarinets. He is here to accompany a street dancer, Schollar, who spreads her little square of carpet and begins to perform to the tune of 'Elle avait une jamb' en bois', to the second verse of which her accompanist adds a cornet *obbligato*. A rival dancer, Nijinska, now appears, her manager turning the handle of a musical-box while she executes *ronds de jambe* and strikes a triangle. For a moment the two dancers' tunes overlap as they vie for attention. The stamping rhythms of the crowd and the strains of the Easter song overwhelm them. Two drummers, the Magician's assistants, clear a space for the puppets' performance, and the Magician, Cecchetti, puts his head through the curtains of the booth. After a moment of silence and suspense, he comes out closing the curtains behind him. He wears an astrological cloak and somewhat papal headdress, which hints at his moral tyranny over the puppets whom he is able to endue with life. His sinister aspect is represented by eerie chromatic slides and he proceeds to charm the crowd with a Weber-like flute solo, whose un-Russian nature with its elaborate ornamentations are calculated to seem utterly mysterious and exotic to the unsophisticated merry-makers. Suddenly he draws back the curtains of the booth to reveal the three puppets held up under the arms by metal supports. He touches them each in turn with the magic flute. As the pulsing clockwork rhythm breaks forth their legs are galvanized into life and perform an animated heel-toe dance. To the left is the splendid figure of the black-faced turbaned Moor, Orlov, his emerald-green velvet tunic decorated with gold frogging. In the centre the Ballerina, Karsavina, rosy-cheeked with doll's eyelashes, in a fur-edged crimson tam-o'-shanter, neat crimson bodice, pink skirt and lace-trimmed pantaloons. On the right, Nijinsky's Petrushka has chalky features like painted wood, a scarlet and white bonnet, a white belted smock with a floppy Pierrot collar, checkered red and green trousers, helpless black-mittened hands and turned-in awkward black-booted feet. The puppets get down from their stands and take the centre of the stage. From the crude pantomime that follows we gather that Petrushka loves the Ballerina but that she is repelled by his convulsive spasms of movement and prefers the gorgeous, brainless Moor.

Kettledrums maintain suspense during the change to Scene II. This is Petrushka's cell or the box in which he is flung by the old Magician between performances. The black walls of this gloomy room, which we see at an angle, are relieved only by a dado of white clouds round the top and a few stars. The door is guarded by painted devils, so perhaps this is an Arctic hell; and there is a portrait of the Magician – the eye of Big Brother is upon you – on the right-hand wall. The music for this scene is Stravinsky's original Konzertstück for piano and orchestra. Petrushka's dual nature, half-puppet, half-human, is represented by the bitonality of a figure on the woodwind, which is also associated with a gesture of his (fingerless) gloved hands jerked sideways and upwards stiffly into the unpitying air. The trepidations of the creature's heart are illustrated by scampering runs on the piano. 'Several instruments in the orchestra try to console him upon his miserable destiny' and the 'impotent rage' with which he cuts them short, cursing the Magician his master, is a harsh fanfare. He tries to dance, but his knees turn in and his arms shield his awkward body in shame. 'There is a moment' (according to Fokine) 'when Petrushka, being sorry for himself, examines his own pitifully unsightly figure. He picks up his pants to knee level, but when he pulls to the right, both knees move to the right; then in order to see himself from the other side, he pulls himself by the pants to the left.'[130] The Ballerina comes to call on him, entering to a somewhat liturgical tune. Petrushka's transports of passion and hope scare her away. He dances his frustration, darting round his prison, to a piano cadenza, and as his wild fanfare sounds again his flaying arms break a hole in the paper wall of his cell, he falls headlong through and, half in, half out, hangs limp.

The Moor's apartment, in which Scene III takes place, is also shown at an angle, but its decoration affords an extreme contrast to that of Petrushka's. The walls are painted like a garish jungle, with green coconut palms against a scarlet sky and white rabbits scampering on the grass beneath. There is a cushioned divan. The eastern music represents a wild beast sullenly pacing his cage and in the rising arpeggios on piano and strings we can hear the thrashing of the tiger's tail. The Moor, all of whose movements are bold, crude, decisive and turned out, in contrast to Petrushka's, stamps around, knees bent and wide apart, arms held up as if in childish astonishment. This scene is interrupted by an episode, inserted at Fokine's request, in which the Moor, hearing the milk inside a coconut, attacks it with his scimitar. Failing to make an impression on the nut, he kneels down and worships it. A roll of drums heralds the entrance of the Ballerina, who, cornet to lips, dances a stiff little *vivandière* dance to the delight of the Moor. She then performs a waltz, repeats it with variations and breaks into another waltz, played on the harp, whose tune is borrowed from Josef Lanner. The Moor now joins the Ballerina in dancing to the previous tune, his own astraddle stamping, as he grasps her by the waist, forming an awkward counterpoint to her tripping in three-time. Suddenly Petrushka's cry is heard and the lovesick creature bursts in to threaten the Moor with his ineffectual gestures to dissonant fanfares. The Ballerina stages a provocative faint; the Moor drives Petrushka out with his scimitar, then seats himself on the divan with the Ballerina on his knee. From the way he opens his mouth wide and gnashes his teeth it seems that he thinks she is edible.

In Scene IV we return to the fair where, as the evening has worn on, the revelry has become more uproarious. The complex music of this scene is a miracle of ingenious orchestration. Out of the initial twangling, piping, tingling and tooting, there emerges the dance of the Wet-nurses in their ornate traditional dress, with their gliding, dipping steps and arms akimbo or folded over their breasts. Their music is based on two folk tunes, 'I was at a feast' and 'Oh my room, my little room'. Next there appears a bear and his keeper. The crowd surround them, half afraid, half teasing, as the keeper plays his pipe, represented by the clarinet, and the bear's lumbering is conveyed by the tuba. A pulsing monotonous breathing of accordions again suggests the all-enveloping cold. A swaggering drunk merchant, Kussov, appears escorting two Gypsy girls with tambourines, and he throws money to the crowd. Then comes the stamping of the booted coachmen, Rosaï and Orlik, who break into a squatting, kicking dance with a marked rhythm to another folk tune, 'I was going up a hill.' A party of merrymakers bursts in wearing over their heads the masks, at the end of long wobbling necks, of the Goat, the Crane and a Devil. With a return of the Easter tune from Scene I, the crowd stamp and beat their arms across their chests to keep warm. They

George Rosaï as a Coachman
in 'Petrushka'.
Drawing by Valentine Gross.

have not noticed that the curtains of the booth are agitated by the Moor's pursuit of Petrushka. The latter's shriek is heard and he shoots from the booth, running on tip-toe, hands clasped between his legs, with the armed Moor in hot pursuit. The Ballerina has her hands over her ears in terror as Petrushka is struck down. The crowd gathers round to watch his brief death scene, hear his last pathetic piping cry, watch his final gesture of appeal. A watchman goes to fetch the Magician, who appears, top-hatted this time, from a refreshment stall. There are a few threatening gestures from the crowd. The Magician lifts the limp puppet which has by now replaced Nijinsky (who has run off to the right under cover of the crowd) and shakes it to show it is nothing but wood and sawdust. The crowd disperses and the pumping accordions again emphasize the bleakness of the winter night. The Magician, left alone, passes slowly across to the left of the stage, dragging the puppet. Suddenly Petrushka's squeaking fanfare is heard and Nijinsky as the puppet's ghost appears menacing over the booth where he learned sorrow, with 'frantic, waving arms'.[131] Has his soul survived? The terrified Magician slinks off, the ghost of Petrushka falls forward and hangs with swinging arms over the top of the booth, and the music ends with a curious question-mark on the plucked strings.

Although he was not speaking to Diaghilev, Benois went to two performances of his ballet before leaving Paris, and 'derived considerable pleasure from them'.[132] 'Petrushka', as we know, was to become one of the most famous of the Russian ballets. But Stravinsky has always thought that Fokine had arranged the ballet all wrong,[133] and that Benois had designed the wrong sort of costumes for the Magician and the Moor;[134] while at the time Fokine did not really appreciate the music.[135] Benois, on the other hand, would look back on the first production of his ballet as perfect.[136] He was to design five subsequent productions, in Leningrad, Copenhagen, Paris, Milan and London, each being a variation of the original.

Fokine wrote at length about 'Petrushka' in later years. Here are his comments on the performances of Karsavina and Nijinsky.

The Ballerina must be an attractive, stupid doll. When Tamara Karsavina performed this role exactly and well – as no one has since her – just as I staged it for her, she caused a great deal of favourable comment. I was grateful to her for her efforts, but still could not understand what could be considered difficult in this role. She performed all the required gestures, attached doll-like eyelashes to her eyelids,* and rouged her cheeks to look like two red apples. There was nothing further to create, no personality. It only remained for her not to alter or forget a single movement. Yet I saw many dolls in 'Petrushka' later, and none of them ever approached this first interpretation. I posed this question to myself: 'Why don't

* In fact, I think she *painted* crude black rays radiating from her eyes.

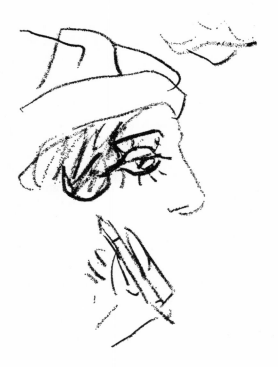

*Tamara Karsavina making up
for 'Petrushka'.
Drawing by Valentine Gross.*

they perform the way Karsavina did? It seemed so easy.' But – they simply couldn't.[137]

Of Nijinsky he wrote: 'I sincerely admired his every movement . . . he played his role wonderfully well. . . . Never again did I see such a splendid Petrushka.'[138]

Benois wrote:

I was particularly enchanted with Nijinsky at the first performance of 'Petrushka'. He had not been successful in the part during rehearsals and it seemed as if he did not completely understand what was needed. He even asked me to explain his role to him, which was very unusual for Nijinsky. But in the end he amazed us as he had in 'Pavillon', 'Sylphides', 'Schéhérazade' and 'Giselle'. This time also the metamorphosis took place when he put on his costume and covered his face with make-up – and it was even more amazing. I was surprised at the courage Vaslav showed, after all his *jeune premier* successes, in appearing as a horrible half-doll, half-human grotesque. The great difficulty of Petrushka's part is to express his pitiful oppression and his hopeless efforts to achieve personal dignity *without ceasing to be a puppet*. Both music and libretto are spasmodically interrupted by outbursts of illusive joy and frenzied despair. The artist is not given a single *pas* or a *fioriture* to enable him to be attractive to the public, and one must remember that Nijinsky was then quite a young man and the temptation to 'be attractive to the public' must have appealed to him far more strongly than to an older artist.[139]

Robert Brussel praised the new ballet in *Le Figaro*, admired Stravinsky's 'extraordinarily fascinating, varied and inventive orchestration', adored Karsavina and thought Nijinsky's puppet was the height of 'naïvety and desolating melancholy'.[140] The public were enthusiastic. In fact, thanks largely to 'Le Spectre' and 'Petrushka', Diaghilev's third short season of ballet in Paris was almost more successful than its predecessors.

Nijinsky's first night in London (and indeed his first five weeks' stay in England) was spent at the Waldorf Hotel in the crescent of the Aldwych. On subsequent visits he and Diaghilev would always put up at the smarter Savoy, a few minutes' walk away from the Waldorf, between the Strand and the river, but if Diaghilev had tried to book rooms there in June 1911 and failed it was no doubt because London was crammed with Imperial and foreign dignitaries and their suites. Anyway the Waldorf, with its convex back overlooking the roofs of Drury Lane, was as near as you could possibly get to Covent Garden. It had only been open for three years, having been built as part of the Kingsway–Aldwych slum clearance scheme; it is the centre of a pompous stone block with the twin Strand and Aldwych Theatres at either end. Although designed in a mixture of traditional styles of architecture, with French *mansard* pavilion roofs at either end and a colonnade in the middle, it was one of the first steel-framed buildings erected in London and had a spacious Palm Court.[141]*

The Aldwych was the theatre at which the Russians would have appeared in 1910 if King Edward had not died, and where Vaslav's 'Sacre du printemps' would be rehearsed in 1912. Like many London theatres, including the Gaiety across the street, where George Grossmith's *Peggy* was running, and like the Adelphi along the Strand, which was showing *The Quaker Girl*, it was controlled by George Edwardes, a connection of Benois'. Martin Harvey was playing Sidney Carton in *The Only Way* at the neighbouring Lyceum; the Savoy had a festival of Dickens adaptations; and Shaw's *Fanny's First Play* was on at the Little, in John Street, Adelphi.

A more surprising feature of the London theatre and a proof of the extent to which Karsavina's pioneer appearance at the Coliseum in 1909 had changed the whole scene, was that there was a Russian ballerina at every one of the big music-halls except the Coliseum, where the Danish Adeline Genée – for years the unchallenged queen of the dance in London – held the fort. Pavlova was dancing at the Palace; Gelzer and Tikhomirov were

---

* In which Ernest Ansermet, three months before his death, received me to talk about Diaghilev and Nijinsky.

at the Alhambra; a 'Mme Sobinoff, Russia's premier singer and dancer', was at the Hippodrome; and Karsavina's old class-mate, Lydia Kyasht, was appearing with Phyllis Bedells and Fred Farren in a short version of Delibes' 'Sylvia' at the Empire. On her first visit to London in 1910 Kyasht had won the heart of Juliet Duff's uncle Hugh, the sporting Earl of Lonsdale, who had set her up in a comfortable house in St John's Wood.[142]

Karsavina by now was an experienced 'Londoner'; she took a flat with Elsa Will near Baker Street.[143] Gunsbourg was at the Carlton in the Haymarket,[144] in the same block as Tree's His Majesty's Theatre. The rest of the company stayed in small hotels in Bloomsbury. The plain brick eighteenth-century squares and terraces of WC1 amazed the Russians, who were used to the painted plaster of Petersburg, and had taken for granted the grey stone of Paris and the marble of Rome.

We were surprised [wrote Grigoriev] by the extreme simplicity of the architecture; London houses seemed to us almost excessively plain. We found rooms in the neighbourhood of the British Museum ... but here again the gardens of the squares were all locked up, and only the residents had keys to them. . . . Something we had certainly never encountered before were the curious two-wheeled vehicles, with the driver seated behind his passengers, known as hansom cabs. . . . What amazed us above all, however, was the Theatre Royal [the Opera House] in Covent Garden itself. It stood in the midst of a vegetable market and was closely hemmed in by greengrocers' warehouses and vast mountains of cabbages, potatoes, carrots and all manner of fruit. . . . On the other hand, the interior was excellent. . . . The stage, to be sure, had one drawback from our standpoint: it was flat instead of raked; and since our dancers were used to a sloping floor, they found this flatness somewhat disconcerting.[145]

Diaghilev, Nijinsky and Karsavina were welcomed as old friends by Lady Ripon and her daughter Lady Juliet Duff. Lady Ripon had seen the ballet in Russia and it was she who had been responsible for arranging that Diaghilev's company should be included in the programme of the Coronation Gala, which would otherwise have been entirely opera.[146] Juliet Duff, as we have seen, had been at Monte Carlo in the spring. Gwladys Ripon was a daughter of the Sidney Herbert (created Lord Herbert of Lea) who, as Secretary for War, had helped Florence Nightingale establish her hospital at Scutari; and as his mother Lady Pembroke had been a Woronzov, Gwladys was a quarter Russian and probably distantly related to Diaghilev. She had married the fourth Earl of Lonsdale, but as he was constitutionally incapable of having relations with women of his own class, it was taken for granted that the only child, Juliet, was by one of Gwladys Lonsdale's innumerable lovers. Some thought the father was the Grand Duke Michael, who lived with his morganatic wife, Countess Torby, in exile at Ken Wood:

but Lady Juliet's true father was almost certainly Lord Annaly.[147] Three years after Lord Lonsdale's death (in a brothel) in 1882, the earldom went to his brother, later famous as a patron of sport, and his widow married Lord de Grey, heir of the rich Marquis of Ripon. It was during her incarnation as Lady de Grey that the exiled Oscar Wilde, in gratitude for her friendship during his troubles, dedicated to her the printed edition of his play *A Woman of No Importance*. On the death of her father-in-law in 1909 Gwladys became Lady Ripon. She was one of the few members of Edwardian society with a real interest in the arts. Queen Alexandra, so beautiful, brainless, deaf, deserted and bored, relied greatly on her for distraction; and the Queen's friendship on at least one occasion saved her from social ostracism after a scandal.[148] Lady Randolph Churchill described her as 'a luxurious woman with perfect manners, a kind disposition and a moderate sense of duty'.[149] In 1911 she had abandoned her vast house in Carlton House Terrace for her big suburban villa Coombe, with what Reynaldo Hahn called its '*jardin de curé*',[150] near Kingston in Surrey, an hour's drive from London. Juliet, who had married Robin Duff of the Life Guards in 1904 and had a daughter and a son, lived in Upper Brook Street between Grosvenor Square and Hyde Park, but was much with her mother.

How would the straitlaced, puritanical, conservative and philistine English react to the Russian Ballet – as opposed to single stars in music-hall acts? How would the exotic Fokine repertory be received in the world of Kipling and Elgar (W.S.Gilbert had died in the previous month), a world which had been shocked by young Epstein's carved nudes on the British Medical Association building in the Strand three summers before? Diaghilev was experienced enough to realize that the enthusiastic Lady Ripon and her daughter were hardly typical members of the audience. He knew that Karsavina, Pavlova, Kyasht and Preobrajenska had been acclaimed in the music-halls, but they had danced fragments of the old classical repertory and could not therefore, in that context, have seemed very different from Adeline Genée who had been the darling of music-hall audiences for years. Playing for safety, Diaghilev had included neither of the Stravinsky ballets in his London repertory. 'Firebird' he had anyway had no time to rehearse. He could have brought 'Petrushka', but didn't. He would first try the Londoners out on the barbarous Russian music of 'Prince Igor', 'Cléopâtre', and 'Schéhérazade'. With 'Le Pavillon d'Armide', 'Les Sylphides', 'Carnaval' and 'Le Spectre de la rose' he had reason to feel fairly safe. 'Narcisse' and 'Sadko' had also been left behind.

During this first London season the ballet would alternate with Italian opera, and of its sixteen performances six would be shared with the opera company – for instance 'Pagliacci' would precede 'Carnaval', 'Le Spectre' and 'Prince Igor' (24 June), 'Les Sylphides' and 'Armide' (30 June), or 'Les Sylphides', 'Le Spectre' and 'Prince Igor' (3 July); 'Il Segreto di Susanna' would be sandwiched between 'Cléopâtre' and 'Carnaval' (11 July) or between 'Les Sylphides' and 'Cléopâtre' (17 July) or followed by 'Schéhérazade', 'Le Spectre' and 'Prince Igor' (26 July). 'Les Sylphides' would be given ten times, 'Prince Igor' eight, 'Armide' seven, both 'Carnaval' and 'Schéhérazade' six times, 'Le Spectre' five and 'Cléopâtre' four.[151]

The dress-rehearsal was to be held on the afternoon of Tuesday, 20 June, and a small group of Diaghilev's friends had assembled to watch it. But the wardrobe staff had been detained by the Immigration Officer at Folkestone and Diaghilev received a telegram asking if he could guarantee that they would leave the country after his engagement. The director of Covent Garden telegraphed his guarantee, but there was no one to sort out complicated costumes, headdresses, boots, jewellery and accessories and the small audience dispersed, leaving the Russians to rehearse in plain clothes.[152] The Immigration Officer was no doubt on the look-out for Russian terrorists and revolutionaries. (The fifth congress of Social Democrats, attended by Lenin, had been held in London four years before.)

The Diaghilev Ballet opened at Covent Garden on Wednesday, 21 June with 'Le Pavillon d'Armide', 'Carnaval' and 'Prince Igor'. Karsavina, Nijinsky and Bolm of course danced in 'Le Pavillon'. Elsa Will was the first Columbine the English saw in 'Carnaval', with Nijinsky as Harlequin and with Fokina, Schollar, Nijinska, Bolm and Cecchetti in their old roles of Chiarina, Estrella, Papillon, Pierrot and Pantalon, with Semenov as Florestan and Ivan Kussov, who had just joined the company in Paris as *premier danseur de caractère* (and had been the drunk merchant in 'Petrushka'), as Eusebius. In 'Prince Igor', as at the first performance two years before, Bolm, Feodorova and Rosaï led respectively the Warriors, Girls and Boys, and a newcomer, Anna Gachevska was the principal Captive Slave. Petrenko and Zaporojetz were singing Khontchakovna and Khan Khontchak as in Paris, and Issatchenko took Smirnov's part of Vladimir, the role of Igor being reduced to a *persona muta*. The company had, according to Diaghilev, 'an immense success, though during the "Prince Igor" dances, half the public went home. At least a hundred old ladies, covered with diamonds as though they were ikons, went out past me with a look of disgust on their faces. The business manager came running up, crying "You've spoilt your magnificent opening by this barbarian horror at the end – it isn't dancing – it's just savages prancing about." '[153]* The next

* Writing in 1926, Diaghilev forgot that his company had given two performances *before* the Coronation Gala. He wrote 'The next evening [after the Gala] came our real opening. . . .' Grigoriev

day, somewhat stealing the Russians' thunder, King George V was crowned; and there was no performance at Covent Garden.

Diaghilev in London to Astruc in Paris, 23.6.11

Announce unparalleled triumph . . . audience indescribably smart. London has discovered Nijinsky and given a warm welcome to Karsavina, Will, Fokine, Tcherepnine.[154]

But the Russians really were a revelation to the British public. On Thursday, 22 June, the Diaghilev Ballet had its first notice in *The Times*.

It has been obvious for some years that Russians are the ideal dancers of the world . . . the quality in which they all seem to excel is accuracy of rhythm, as if they were creating the rhythm, not timing their movements according to it. . . . As for Mme Karsavina . . . no words can do justice to her actual dancing; yet her face is so expressive that one forgets all about her feet. M.Nijinsky may possibly not realize the Pheidian ideal quite as perfectly as M.Mordkine, but his technique is even more assured and his leaps are not only of extraordinary height, but his descents from his native element are timed so perfectly that every jump is a separate ecstasy. . . .

The Schumann 'Carnaval' was an unqualified joy from the beginning to end, with never a moment when one felt that the music had been treated with anything but complete sympathy. . . . M.Nijinsky dances with incredible virtuosity during the number called 'Paganini', and at the wonderful point where the dominant seventh on E Flat emerges by the deft use of the pedal, the dancer represents the effect to absolute perfection by suddenly sitting down. . . . The stage-management of the whole was among the most purely artistic things the stage has ever seen.[155]

On Saturday, 24 June, two days after the Coronation, the Russians gave their second performance, and 'Le Spectre' was danced for the first time in England. One critic described the ballet as 'a dream of perfect beauty and all too quickly over'.[156] In 'Carnaval', instead of wearing patterned trousers buttoning above the ankle, which Fokine and Leontiev had usually worn and which Diaghilev had made him put on for fear of shocking the English, Nijinsky reverted to his usual lozengy tights, and *The Times* noticed his dress was 'less conventional and more effective than before'. 'Prince Igor' was given without the singing.[157]

That morning *The Times* had devoted a long and serious article to the 'new and enchanting pleasure' which the novel art form provided. It is interesting that in his very first paragraph the writer envisaged a time when British artists might even 'arrive at some imitation of it on our own stage'. The thoughtful critic went on:

made the same mistake. (p. 67). I have transferred Diaghilev's story of the disconcerted dowagers to the *real* 'real opening' night, from Saturday to Wednesday.

Nijinsky 1911

What then are the essential characters which differentiate the art of the Russian Ballet from that which we have hitherto known in England? That they dance better – the simplest explanation – is one of the most misleading, for the elusive differentia does not lie in technique. Certainly their technique is exquisite; all of them can do the most wonderful things with no appearance of effort, and they can do many sorts of wonderful things. But technique is no more the source of the highest pleasure in dancing than it is in painting, in music, or any other of the arts. It is a channel of communication; it is the means by which the artistic idea comes from the mind of the creator to the senses of the spectator. The Russians, in fact, have so long since brought their technique of dancing, their command of their limbs and bodies, their instinct for balance, for energy without exertion, to the highest point that they have been able to develop the art for which that technique exists – namely, the conveyance of choreographic ideas. Russian ballet-dancing never for one moment escapes from its subjection to ideas – and, moreover, to artistic ideas, ideas that is, conceived at a high pitch of emotional intelligence. . . .

Our English ballets have had so little concern with the imagination that even the most pitiful little crumbs of imaginative food, the evolution of recent English choreographic impressionists and mysterious orientals from Montmartre, have caused something of a flutter among us. And now that we have suddenly set before us the abundant fare supplied by the inventive genius of a Benois and a Fokine, inheritors of a great tradition that has been gradually developing, all unknown to us, beyond the Baltic, and the interpretative genius of a Nijinsky, a Karsavina, an Elsa Will, is it to be wondered at that we fall to so greedily? For here we are introduced to a whole range of ideas such as we have never met before.[158]

The critic had a real admiration for Pavlova but he realized the shortcomings of her presentations.

How much of the work of a ballet-master suffers from being given piece-meal may be seen by comparing the effect of the detached 'turns' of Pavlova and her company at the Palace Theatre before an irrelevant purely 'decorative' back-cloth, with the effect of 'Carnaval' in its entirety at Covent Garden. 'Carnaval' is an exquisitely delicate artistic whole, from the first coy scamperings and hidings of Chiarina and Estrella to the good-natured *grand rond* in chase of the Philistines; and not a detail of it could be spared; least of all the black dado with the giant golden tulips and the two little roguish Pierrots of sofas, crouching against the wainscot, which make one alert from the beginning for the airy mockery of the whole intention. It is the sum of all these details which leaves us in the end with a quite new and brilliant vision of Schumann's work, purged of all possible suspicion of any Germanic seriousness of purpose.

He understood how the Russian art was a collaboration between choreographer and dancers.

In all ballet-dancing there is a dim attempt to represent the spiritual and the fantastic by means of the material: the tip-toeing and the lifting-up of the women is a suggestion of the ethereal; but the perfect ease and grace of the Russians enable them to carry this to a far higher point, so that in their suggestion of things flying, things swimming, things poised, or blown by the wind, the sense of the material passes altogether away. The dancers are able in their turn to create the art of the ballet-master for him by offering him new possibilities, such as Karsavina's instinctive plant-like correlations of balanced extremities, and the contrary movements of head and limbs with which Nijinsky is able to create the grotesque abstract, half-mathematical sensations.

Praising the Russians for their restraint he even noticed such details as 'the excellently-judged waving of the feather-fans . . . in the Armida Palace dances'. He admired in 'Prince Igor' 'the women that crouch, unconscious of themselves, or rise and stretch lazy limbs, and in the end fling themselves prone when their dance is over; the savage-joyful panther-leaping of the men; the stamping feet and quick nerve-racking beat of the drum; and, more threatening than all, the gambolling of the boys, like kittens unwittingly preparing themselves for the future chase'. He wrote charmingly of 'Carnaval'.

A Coquette dancing with two roses at the Carnival shows the graces of the early Victorian period at their daintiest, but all the time you guess that she is making fun of them and of the absurd people who believe in her. . . . No need to shed tears for young ladies who languish forlorn on the tips of their toes, or for poor gentlemen who die of love for such elfin creatures. Remember that this is an aristocratic tradition, with something of Boucher and Beaumarchais clinging to it, arch, mischievous, *gouailleur*. It is immensely serious as Art, but never for a moment serious as Life.[159]

The next day the critic of the *Sunday Times* wrote of 'the peerless Nijinsky':

It would savour of hyperbole to say of his dancing that the half of it had not been told, but the foreword of him had certainly not been extravagant. He has great charm of personality: the grossness of contour and sensuality of lineament which so often mark the male dancer are conspicuous by their absence; and his every movement is instinct with spontaneity and grace. He seems to be positively lighter than air, for his leaps have no sense of effort and you are inclined to doubt if he really touches the stage between them. His precision is faultless and his technique generally as polished as it is resourceful.[160]

It is interesting to note the effect of the Diaghilev Ballet on at least one English dancer. The seventeen-year-old Phyllis Bedells, who was appearing in 'Sylvia' at the Empire in the company led by Kyasht, had seen Karsavina dance before, but the Diaghilev company was a great new experience, as she was to record many years later.

When the Diaghilev Ballet made its first appearance at Covent Garden with the full company it was maddening not to be able to see them as there were no matinée performances.* All London was raving about their success, and eventually I had to go to the Empire directors and say that as part of my education I must be given the opportunity to see them. Very reluctantly it was agreed that I take one night off which, unless one was ill, was an almost unheard-of thing. I booked a seat in the circle – just one. I could not afford to pay for another seat on my small salary. My father took me to the theatre and collected me when the performance ended. For the first time in my life I heard Grand Opera sung. The ballet programme followed the performance of *I Pagliacci*, with Emmy Destinn, Sammarco, and Robert Martin. Then the curtain rose on *Carnaval*. . . . And afterwards there were the *Prince Igor* dances. As long as I live I shall not forget that night. I could hardly keep still in my seat. Because people who were sitting in neighbouring seats would keep chatting away in a blasé manner I worked myself into a state of fury. It seemed impossible to believe that anyone could behave like that while the magic of those artists filled me with such delight. Several times, young as I was, I asked them to be quiet. . . . I cannot write about Nijinsky. It is useless. Then he was at the very height of his powers. I was breathless as I sat there in my seat and watched his dancing.[161]

The impression made by the Russian Ballet on one non-professional member of their new audience can be judged by the reaction of the Duchess of Rutland, whose youngest daughter, Diana Manners, was coming out that season. She was a gifted artist and one of the 'Souls', that group of high-minded intellectuals – Wyndhams, Horners, Elchos, Grenfells and Asquiths, A. J. Balfour and Lord Curzon – who reacted against the philistinism of Edwardian society. She had always loathed the idea of ballet, which she considered quite unconnected with art and a mere diversion for the kind of man she most particularly disliked. Her conversion was as sudden as St Paul's. Her very first sight of Karsavina in 1909 had been a revelation, now the Diaghilev Ballet turned her into a passionate devotee of the new art.[162]

For the Coronation Gala on Monday, 26 June, the Opera House was decorated with 'over a hundred thousand roses, and the boxes', according to Diaghilev, 'contained almost as many maharajahs'.[163] Among the flowers were plaques emblazoned with the names of countries over which the King Emperor ruled, with INDIA occupying a central position under the Royal Box. 'The audience began to assemble at seven o'clock, Lady Ripon and her daughter, Lady Juliet Duff, being very early on the scene.' While upstairs, 'the gallery slips were much sought after for their view of the audience.' Queen Mary wore the huge Cullinan diamond and the Star of Africa on her bodice.[164]

---

* But because of the Ballet's success matinées were introduced quite soon after the beginning of the season, as Covent Garden programmes prove.

28 Nijinsky in his dance to Grieg's 'Kobold' (arranged by Stravinsky) in 'Les Orientales'. Photograph by Bert.

29 Nijinsky in 'Schéhérazade'. Photograph by Bert.

Nijinsky in his 'Danse Siamoise' in 'Les Orientales'.
31 (*opposite*) Painting by Jacques-Emile Blanche.
32 Photograph by Druet.
33 Gouache by Leon Bakst (done from Druet's photograph), sold at Sotheby's in July 1969 for £11,400, the highest price ever paid for a work by Bakst.

(*top left*) Nijinsky in his 'Danse Siamoise' in 'Les Orientales'. First project for the poster. Drawing by Jean Cocteau. It seems that Cocteau adapted this sketch to design the poster Plate 38 without ever having seen 'Le Spectre' on stage.

(*top right*) Nijinsky's costume for 'Le Spectre de la rose'. Watercolour by Leon Bakst.

(*bottom left*) Nijinsky in 'Le Spectre de la rose'. First sketch for the poster by Jean Cocteau.

(*bottom right*) Poster of Nijinsky in 'Le Spectre de la rose'. From the gouache by Jean Cocteau.

39 *and* 40 Tamara Karsavina and Nijinsky in 'Le Spectre de la rose'.
Details from on-stage photographs by Bert.

41 Framed by the hats of the Botkine sisters, Pavel Koribut-Kubitovitch, Tamara Karsavina, Nijinsky, Igor Stravinsky, Alexandre Benois, Sergei Diaghilev, with Alexandra Vassilieva seated in the foreground, at Beausoleil. Photograph by Nicolas Besobrasov.

42 Nijinsky in 'Narcisse'. Photograph by Balogh. One of the only three photographs I know of Nijinsky in 'Narcisse', this has only been reproduced before in a Sotheby's catalogue.

43 Alexander Orlov, Enrico Cecchetti, Tamara Karsavina, Nijinsky and (with backs turned) Bronislava Nijinska and George Rosaï in 'Petrushka', Act I. Photograph by Bert. The spire of the Admiralty was no doubt an afterthought arising from the necessity to move the 'big wheel' further to the right, as it does not occur in Benois's original design (now in Russia), reproduced by Svetlov.

44 Tamara Karsavina and Nijinsky in 'Petrushka', Act II. Photograph by Bert.

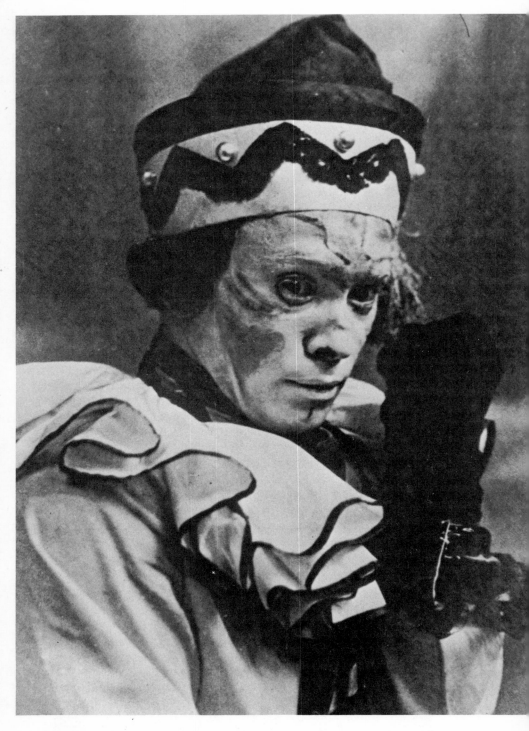

45 Nijinsky in 'Petrushka' (close-up). Photograph by Elliot and Fry, in Dodge Collection. Copied Martha Swope.

46 Nijinsky. Drawing by Oskar Kokoschka.

47 Nijinsky in street clothes. Photograph by Elliott and Fry.

48 Maurice Ravel, Nijinsky and Bronislava Nijinska on the balcony of Ravel's flat. Photograph by Igor Stravinsky.

49 Tamara Karsavina and Nijinsky in 'Carnaval'. Watercolour drawing by
Ludwig Kainer. Kainer made a lithograph based on it, one of a series published in
Leipzig in 1913.

50 Nijinsky in 'Le Dieu bleu'. Photograph by Bert.

Although Destinn and Kirkby Lunn sang the duet from 'Aida', Melba the second-act aria from Gounod's 'Roméo et Juliette', Tetrazzini, Béval, Malatesta and John McCormack part of Act III of 'Il Barbiere', 'applause was restrained.'[165] But what can you expect from a lot of Maharajahs? The critic of the *Daily Mail* was not kept down.

The regal spectacle ended with one of the most enchanting creations ever seen on any stage [this was the second *tableau*, the Gobelins *divertissement*, of 'Le Pavillon d'Armide']. . . . Both the King and Queen freely used opera glasses and the interest of the whole assembly was excited. The pauses after the various dances, meant for applause, were at first silent. As the marvellous ballet progressed there was more and more admiration for the delicious Mme Karsavina, M.Nijinsky, who seems the incarnation of youthful joy, the astonishing company of buffoons and the others.[166]

Diaghilev's spirits, however, must have been considerably dampened by the mouselike response of the princely audience. His memory of the evening was gloomy: 'Our reception was icy, and neither Karsavina's variations, nor even those of Nijinsky . . . received the slightest applause. It was only after the dance of the buffoons that the strangest of sounds came to us: the public was gently clapping its kid-gloved hands.'[167]

If Diaghilev and Nijinsky were not used to such 'effortless superiority' as the English showed on this occasion, the public's response on other nights was very different; and the box-office returns coupled with the determination of Sir Joseph Beecham to have nothing but the best, regardless of expense, soon made it clear to them that they could plan for longer seasons in London even than in Paris. It was arranged that they should pay a return visit in October.

The newspapers were soon recording that the success of the Ballet had exceeded all expectation. 'There has been nothing like the vogue of the Russian ballet for a generation. So attractive are their performances that many people are postponing their departure from town in order to see them out, and we are getting "tiara" nights to the end of the season, even though we are in the very stew of the dog days.'[168]

On 27 June 'Les Sylphides' was given, with Karsavina and Nijinsky in their inevitable roles, Bronislava Nijinska in Pavlova's Mazurka and Will in the Prelude. Richard Capell, the *Daily Mail* music critic, wrote that although a music-lover naturally looked askance at this 'free handling of the masterpieces of the immortal dead . . . the imponderable Karsavina floats once more across the stage and he is conquered utterly'.[169] Karsavina alternated with Will as Columbine in 'Carnaval'. On 11 July 'Cléopâtre' was given, with Seraphine Astafieva as Cleopatra, Sophie Feodorova in Pavlova's role as Ta-hor and Will in Karsavina's as the Slave, Nijinsky's partner. On 20 July London saw for the first time 'Schéhérazade' with Karsavina, Nijinsky, and Bolm as the Shah. On the last night of the season, 31 July, odd as it may seem, 'Cléopâtre' and 'Schéhérazade', sandwiching 'Les Sylphides', were on the same bill. Elsa Will had perhaps been called away and Schollar replaced her in the Prelude, while Karsavina resumed her original small role in 'Cléopâtre' and played Zobeïda in the Rimsky work.

Before the end of the season Nijinsky's name was on everybody's lips, but another Russian had had what was to prove an even more pervasive influence – Leon Bakst. His décors banished for ever from the dress shops and furnishers the favourite Edwardian colours of white, cream, grey and pale mauve. The windows of Harvey Nichols blossomed in purple and red.[170] To be fair it must be admitted that Bakst had been preceded by more than one imaginative theatre designer in England in recent years. Gordon Craig, the starting-point of whose art had been the melodramatic compositions (usually four-poster beds) of James Pryde,[171] with their exaggerated verticals, had designed several productions in the past decade (and would be holding an exhibition at the Leicester Gallery in September). Charles Ricketts, on whom, as on Bakst, Beardsley had been an influence, had made imaginative designs for plays by Yeats and Shaw; and it was he who had devised the production of *Fanny's First Play*, which was running at the Little Theatre, between the Strand and the Thames, and enjoying a big success there. But the stage work of these two artists had been on a small scale, on minute budgets, and for the delectation of a happy few. Ricketts, who, like Diaghilev, had known Oscar Wilde (only he had known him better), and, like Bakst, had just made the pilgrimage to Greece, was a painter, illustrator, printer, connoisseur and collector who would become one of the most fervent admirers of the Russian Ballet.[172] At the end of the first London season Lady Ripon gave Diaghilev a black pearl stud. Its temporary disappearance in subsequent years would always be a sign of bad times.[173] Vaslav, Bronia and Karsavina also received presents.

Stravinsky, who had not been in London with the company, was working with Roerich on 'Le Sacre du printemps' in Russia.

In July 1911 [he wrote], after the first performances of 'Petrushka', I travelled to the Princess Tenichev's country estate near Smolensk, to meet with Nicolas Roerich and plan the scenario of 'Le Sacre du printemps'; Roerich knew the Princess well, and he was eager for me to see her collections of Russian ethnic art. I journeyed from Ustilug to Brest-Litovsk, where, however, I discovered that I would have to wait two days for the next train to Smolensk. I therefore bribed the conductor of a freight train to let me ride in a cattle-car, though I was all alone in it with a bull! The bull was leashed by a single not-very-reassuring rope, and as he glowered and slavered I began to barricade myself behind my one small suitcase. I must have looked an odd sight in Smolensk as I stepped from that *corrida* carrying my expensive (or, at least, not tramp-like) bag and brushing my clothes and hat, but I must also have looked relieved. The Princess Tenichev gave me a guest house attended by servants in handsome white uniforms with red belts and black boots. I set to work with Roerich, and in a few days the plan of action and the titles of the dances were composed. Roerich also sketched his famous Polovtsian-type backdrops while we were there, and designed costumes after real costumes in the Princess's collection. . . .

I became conscious of thematic ideas for 'Le Sacre' immediately after returning to Ustilug, the themes being those of Les Augures printanières, the first dance I was to compose. Returning to Switzerland in the fall, I moved with my family to a *pension* in Clarens and continued to work. Almost the entire 'Sacre du printemps' was written in a tiny room of this house, in an eight-feet-by-eight closet, rather, whose only furniture was a small upright piano which I kept muted (I always work at a muted piano), a table, and two chairs. I composed from the Augures printan-ières to the end of the first part and then wrote the Prelude afterwards. My idea was that the Prelude should represent the awakening of nature, the scratching, gnawing, wiggling of birds and beasts. The dances of the second part were com-posed in the order in which they now appear, and composed very quickly, too, until the Danse sacrale, which I could play, but did not, at first, know how to write.[174]

By the beginning of the following year the titanic composition would be complete except for a few details.

Diaghilev, who did not dare to risk frightening off the English with Stravinsky's music, had a hunch that they would take to classical ballet. (In fact, he was to anticipate this appetite by thirty years.) He would show London not only 'Giselle' but Petipa's 'Le Lac des Cygnes'. Because Karsavina was committed to the Mariinsky for certain performances she would begin the second London season in October, return to Petersburg for several weeks and be back for the end of the season in December: so her role of Giselle must be taken over in mid-season by Pavlova. 'Le Lac' would be danced by Matilda Kchessinskaya. All three ballerinas would be supported by Nijinsky.

Diaghilev had urgent business in Petersburg: he wanted to show his company in Russia. The only available theatre was the Narodny Dom or People's Palace, a big modern building which was neither attractive nor fashionable: but there was nothing else to be had. On 29 September he telegraphed to Astruc offering him the running of the season of twelve or fifteen performances between 29 December and 1 February,[175] but Astruc could not see his way to take on the job. Nevertheless Diaghilev looked forward to showing Russia the new art to which, with the aid of himself as *accoucheur*, she had given birth.

Grigoriev wondered how Diaghilev would get the scenery and dresses for such a big production as 'Le Lac' – even though it was reduced to two acts: but Diaghilev arranged to buy the whole Moscow production of the ballet, which had been designed as early as 1901 by Golovine and Korovine.[176] Benois was to write, with a touch of jealousy, 'Serioja had decided to include this rather sentimental old-fashioned ballet in our repertoire chiefly to give M.F.Kchessinskaya an opportunity to shine; also because he had a genuine admiration for the sets and "Carpaccio" costumes . . . for the Moscow production.'[177]

Diaghilev left Petersburg on 7 October and was in London by the 10th.[178] There was some trouble over engaging Monteux to conduct the London season, also over securing Zambelli of the Paris Opéra as a possible replacement for Karsavina, if Pavlova let him down.[179] He was in Paris in the week beginning 14 October,[180] but was back – at the Savoy Hotel – with Nijinsky in time for the opening of his second London season at Covent Garden on 16 October.[181] There were a few changes in the company. Elsa Will had departed. Maria Piltz, who was tall and handsome, had been engaged in Warsaw. Vaslav's old school-friend Anatole Bourman had arrived from Russia.* And Max Frohman, whose sister had been with the company since the spring in Paris, came from Moscow. He was extremely good-looking with an oval face and classical features, and it was not long before Diaghilev 'had his eye on him'.[182]

During the first London season it had been noticed that the poor stage lighting had prevented the colours from making their full impact. 'Great shadows lay across the front of the stage,' wrote one observer, 'amid which the pure reds and greens and blues fought bravely to be articulate . . . while two appalling muddy proscenium wings stood like ogres devouring the colour values.'[183] For the second season a number of improvements were made at Covent Garden. The sides and top of the proscenium were framed with black cloth, the footlights were lowered and the stalls raised to improve sight-lines, and projecting lights were installed in the gallery which, by the use of exchangeable lenses, could be either floodlights or spotlights.[184] A hydraulic curtain was installed, and a new oak stage laid specially for the Ballet.[185]

On the first night Nijinsky and Karsavina danced 'Giselle' and 'Schéhérazade'. London had seen Karsavina in a version of the second act of 'Giselle' with the Koslov troupe at the Coliseum, but never Nijinsky's Albrecht, and the touching old ballet was now seen complete again in England for the first time in living memory.[186]

* Bourman's story that he ran into Bronislava Nijinska at the Alexandrinsky Theatre and that she persuaded Diaghilev to engage him is, according to Mme Nijinska, an invention.

Diaghilev had miscalculated. London did not take readily to the classic. 'In the first act,' wrote *The Times*, 'M.Nijinsky's solo dance was the most conspicuous feature, and was the most warmly applauded. In the early part of the act the audience hardly seemed to know what to look for . . .'[187] Richard Capell of the *Daily Mail* considered 'Were the dancing anything less than perfect "Giselle" would, truth to tell, be a thought tedious. . . . The Russians have for the first time done something incongruous. The dances in every other spectacle they have presented here have been part of a harmonious whole. In "Giselle" we see that even this wonderful troupe of dancers cannot always steer clear of that incongruity which rightly rendered the old ballet a laughing-stock.' He deemed Karsavina 'truly pathetic', admired Nijinsky's flying leaps and *entrechats*, the 'deep-dyed villain' of Bolm's rejected lover, and saw in Cecchetti, who played Giselle's mother, 'an actor of singular and sinister power', but thought the classic style involved motions 'which are acrobatic rather than purely graceful', while the music of Adam 'in an opera or in the concert-room would be wearisomely trivial'.[188] The critic of the *Sunday Times* thought Karsavina 'was delightfully gay and natural in the early scenes' and 'gave a poignant suggestion of a mind distraught in her mad dance'; and Nijinsky 'acted in the final scene with a rare tenderness of feeling'.[189] But, as the *Observer* put it, 'it is difficult to see how these fine dancers were attracted by their parts.' 'Giselle' 'is not a work of art, and can never become one'.[190] 'Schéhérazade' followed. Capell rebuked the audience for talking during the 'overture', though doubtless discussing the 'provocative' perspective of Serov's 'Persian miniature' curtain; but found in Fokine's drama 'not a gesture or motion . . . incongruous in the dramatic scheme. The splendid and cruel spectacle made an overwhelming effect. There is one moment – when a procession of scarlet-and-gold clad youths prance through the harem bearing high-piled dishes of fruit – which seems to sum up all the luscious poetry and pageantry of the Orient.'[191] 'In its wonderful expression of pent-up passion let loose in flood,' wrote the *Sunday Times*'s music critic, 'and in the unity of all its constituents . . . "Schéhérazade" is *sui generis*; its impression bites deeper into you each time you see it.'[192]

On the second night, 17 October, the hard-worked Karsavina and Nijinsky danced all three ballets, 'Le Pavillon', 'Carnaval' and 'Schéhérazade' – but so did both Bolm, playing René, Pierrot and the Shah, and Maestro Cecchetti, miming King Hydraot, Pantalon and the Chief Eunuch. Piltz made her début as one of Armida's confidantes, along with Nijinska, Schollar and Vassilievska, and danced Chiarina.

After appearing in five programmes Karsavina had to leave for Petersburg and on Saturday, 28 October Pavlova danced once more with the Diaghilev

Ballet. She did 'Giselle' with Nijinsky, but in 'Cléopâtre' played not her old part of the despairing, abandoned mistress, Ta-hor, which was taken by Sophie Feodorova, but that of Nijinsky's fellow Slave, the dancer with the scarf. The critic of *The Times* thought Pavlova's roles in 'Giselle' and 'Cléopâtre' 'gave her no proper scope' and was disappointed not to see her as Ta-hor. However, he qualified this with some discerning praise: 'The main thing about Pavlova is that, when she dances, the whole of her dances. . . . She dances with her feet, her fingers, her neck (how much expression there is in the various inclinings of her head), her smile, her eyes, her dress. . . . She is all dance and all drama at the same time. After the wildest caper she and Nijinsky are instantly poised in perfect balance ready to stand stock still or start off again in any direction.' He went on to wonder how two such expansive people as this Giselle and 'her old mother, Cecchetti' could live in such a very little cottage; and to decide that 'the Wilis ought to be either vampirical or else plaintive and pathetic'.[193] The critic of the *Daily Mail* thought Pavlova 'danced with consummate expressiveness' and that 'her acting in the scene of Giselle's death at the close of Act I was truly poignant.' At the same time the latter critic gave us a hint of how Nijinsky appeared as Loys-Albrecht: 'A young faun from some Slav Arcadia straying here among mortals, was her fantastic cavalier.'[194]

Pavlova continued to perform in these ballets, as well as 'Le Pavillon', 'Les Sylphides' and 'L'Oiseau d'or' (which was the Blue Bird *pas de deux*, called in 1909 'L'Oiseau de feu'); and she danced for the first time Columbine in 'Carnaval' on 6 November and danced it for the last time on the following day. (These two performances might be described as collectors' items!) Her last-ever appearance with the Diaghilev Ballet – or with Nijinsky – was on 11 November, when she danced 'Le Pavillon', 'Les Sylphides' and 'L'Oiseau d'or'.

'L'Oiseau d'or' – or 'The Golden Bird' as Lord Northcliffe's newspaper rendered it – was given in Korovine's setting of an old wooden Moscow palace which had been designed for the opera 'Russlan' and used for 'Le Festin'. In the critic's description of Nijinsky's costume of a 'Muscovite Prince in russet green and barbaric jewels' and Pavlova's 'lemon-coloured tutu and orange corsage, and an audacious crest of scarlet and yellow ostrich feathers, and so many jewels that the dancing was over before one had fully seen them',[195] it is possible to recognize the clothes Bakst designed for Nijinsky and Karsavina in the same dance in 1909.

Gordon Craig, who lived in Italy and was about to mount his production of *Hamlet* at the Moscow Arts Theatre, was temporarily in London and had taken a house at 7 Smith Square, Westminster. Here he set up his large model stage and invited actors and theatre managers to see demonstrations of his system of moving screens. Diaghilev and Nijinsky came with Count Harry Kessler, the German patron of the theatre, but Diaghilev continued talking while the demonstration was in progress, so Craig switched on the lights and refused to go on with the show.[196] This cannot, though, have been the only reason why Craig persisted in animosity towards the Russian Ballet until he saw Balanchine's 'Apollon Musagète' in Paris in 1928.

Lady Ripon took Vaslav down to John Sargent's studio in Tite Street, Chelsea, and the artist made a charcoal head of him in the turban and jewelled choker of 'Le Pavillon d'Armide', exaggerating the length of his neck and recording the curious impression he gave in this ballet (which we have seen Geoffrey Whitworth and others trying to describe) of his being a mysterious but sexless creature from another planet. The head is tilted arrogantly back, the eyes are half closed and the lips parted in Olympian mockery and provocation.

Kchessinskaya had arrived! She was not unaccompanied. She brought her son Vova, a Dr Milk 'for Vova fell ill on journeys', her faithful henchman Baron Gotch,* who used to do female impersonations, her ladysmaid, her dresser, and the Grand Duke André Vladimirovitch. They stayed at the Savoy Hotel. She had left the keys of her luggage behind in Petersburg, but 'when they found out who I was the Customs officers very politely, and as a special favour, believed me about the contents of the luggage and allowed us to take them away.' Her jewels had travelled separately.

My diamonds and other precious stones were so valuable that they raised delicate problems. On the advice of Agathon Fabergé, the famous jeweller's son, who was also one of my great friends, I had entrusted the dispatch of my jewels to his firm, the London branch looking after them until my arrival. Two catalogues were made, and each piece of jewellery was numbered: I had only to know the numbers of the jewels I needed every evening, without giving further details. At the appointed hour an official of the firm, who was also a detective, brought them to me in my dressing-room and prevented any unauthorized person from entering; when the performance was over he took the jewels away again. I also had a number of pieces which I wore every day, and these the hotel management had asked me to place in their safe at night. One night there was a big dinner-party at the hotel, and I asked Fabergé to send me my diadem, which was very valuable. The official brought it, but must have told the management of the Savoy, who informed me that as an added security measure plain-clothes police would dine at a neighbouring table; so I was not to be surprised at their presence. Two young Englishmen in tails did in fact follow me like my shadow the whole evening, but so skilfully and discreetly that nobody except the initiated could tell them from the Savoy's elegant clientèle.[197]

---

* Who, according to Mlle Françoise Reiss, who had it from Kchessinskaya, with Alexandrov introduced Nijinsky to Lvov (p. 51).

On Tuesday, 14 November, Kchessinskaya, 'Dancer of Honour to the Emperor of Russia', made her London début with Nijinsky in the *Grand pas de deux* from 'La Belle au bois dormant', called for the occasion 'Aurore et le Prince'. Diaghilev himself had chosen for her 'a very beautiful blue costume' and discussed the question of the jewels she was to wear. 'I had an undeniable success at the first performance,' the ballerina considered, 'but in spite of Diaghilev's claims it was not as great as I had hoped. It was more a *succès d'estime*, due to a famous artist, the prima ballerina of the Imperial Ballet.'[198] The *Daily Mail* described her skirt as mauve and silver, so no doubt the costume was a kind of heliotrope blue: perhaps the bodice was too covered in diamonds to be seen. Nijinsky wore a Russian costume in black and orange trimmed with ermine, which must have flattered her colour-scheme.[199]

At the end of the same programme Kchessinskaya danced Columbine in 'Carnaval', which we can imagine was one of the few roles in Fokine ballets which would suit her very well, for a high-spirited bubbling gaiety was her most attractive characteristic. Diaghilev's circle of friends, however, tended not to admire the famous ballerina and used to make fun of her. Bakst was in Lady Juliet Duff's box and so was the Grand Duke André; and the designer looked as if he was missing Karsavina. Kchessinskaya was, after all, forty. Lady Juliet prompted him to say something nice about her to the Grand Duke: but all Bakst could manage was the remark 'Montheigneur, tha robe a l'air bien fraîche' ('Her dreth lookth very new, Thir.')[200]

That night and on three subsequent occasions the role of Zobeïda in 'Schéhérazade' was taken, in Karsavina's absence, by a mystery lady called Roshanara. She had been doing oriental solos with Pavlova's troupe at the Palace Theatre,* and the *Daily Mail* judged her 'an accomplished actress, though she fails to express the intensity and pathos of Mme Karsavina'.[201] At these last three performances Kchessinskaya danced 'Le Pavillon d'Armide'. *The Times* compared three Armidas. 'Even with Mme Karsavina it was still a little dull. Mme Pavlova displayed her talent by making this somewhat lifeless affair a thing of real beauty and interest. Mme Kchessinska . . . displays a technical skill which is remarkable, but she has not the personal magnetism of her predecessor. She never makes one forget that she is a *prima ballerina*.'[202]

---

* In a programme for Pavlova's provincial tour of 1910 (Walford Hyden: *Pavlova*, p. 43) Roshanara is listed as a member of the Imperial Ballet. But the *Sketch* of 7 July 1911 states that she was born in Calcutta and 'picked up her dancing more or less by intuition, for she never received any lessons in the art.' She had danced in Indian palaces but never on the public stage until Oscar Ashe and Lily Brayton brought her to England to perform the oriental dances in 'Kismet' at the Garrick Theatre. Such a background would appeal to Diaghilev in his search for a successor to Rubinstein.

Since the beginning of their second London season the company had been looking forward happily to showing themselves and being acclaimed in Petersburg after Christmas, but there was a gap in their bookings at the end of the year; so Diaghilev crossed the hated Channel and on 17 November met Astruc in Paris to see what could be arranged.[203] Negotiations were set afoot with Amsterdam, Vienna and Budapest, and three performances were arranged for the Paris Opéra at the end of December. There was also the question of a special gala performance on New Year's Eve in aid of French aviation, and a Berlin season was booked for January.

Rehearsals now began for the first production of 'Le Lac des Cygnes' ever to be seen outside Russia except for one staged at Prague in the composer's lifetime.* This would be given on 30 November. Diaghilev had reduced the four-act ballet to two acts, retaining what he thought were the best passages of Petipa's and Ivanov's choreography. In his version the story could be summarized as follows.[204] Act I: the lake by night. The Prince comes hunting with his companions. They encounter the group of girls bewitched by the Evil Genius, who become swans by day; and the Prince falls in love with their leader, the Swan Queen. When the Evil Genius, a gaunt monster, appears among the trees, the Prince tries to shoot him with his cross-bow, but is powerless against his magic. The dancing of the girls is interrupted by the dawn, and they become swans again and swim away. Act II, Scene 1: the castle ballroom. The Prince's mother is giving a party to celebrate her son's betrothal to a neighbouring Princess. After a waltz by eight couples, the Master of Ceremonies ushers in a sinister stranger who is the Evil Genius in disguise; and he is leading the Swan Queen. The Prince, greeting them, is startled to find himself gazing into the eyes of his beloved. But she is led away and he resumes his seat. Neither the Spanish dance, nor the Czardas or Mazurka, which follow, can draw the Prince out of his deep reverie. The Swan Queen reappears and fascinates the Prince anew with her solo. She goes off and the Prince in turn flings himself into an exultant dance, at the climax of which she reappears. When their *pas de deux* ends in an embrace, the court is scandalized, the Queen embarrassed, the fiancée indignant. The Evil Genius snatches the Swan Queen away and carries her off on his shoulder. The Prince, deaf to his mother's pleading, follows them through the crowd. Act II, Scene 2: the lake again. The Evil Genius drags on the Swan Queen, pursued by the Prince. But it is dawn once more, the beloved has vanished and a swan with a crown is seen gliding across the lake. The Prince falls dead.

The chief differences between the version of 'Le Lac des Cygnes' prepared

---

* And a condensed version which Schollar and George Kyasht (brother of Lydia Kyasht) had danced at the Hippodrome, London, in the previous year.

by Diaghilev and that of Petersburg, which was written down by Sergueev and reproduced by him in England in the 1930s, were the omission of the first act and of all the swans' dances, with their elaborate and beautiful groups in the fourth; and the creation of a fiancée for the Prince instead of the Prospective Brides who, in the Sergueev version, are brought to court to compete for the Prince's favour, only to be snubbed for their pains.

Korovine's lake scene was a somewhat wishy-washy landscape, pinkish-mauve, with fir-trees in the foreground and bare hills beyond the lake. For the Prince's companions Golovine had created subtly elegant 'Carpaccio' costumes in velvet and suède, some with short capes. The court scene by Golovine was a medieval Russian palace, mostly golden, with a wide flat arch through which was seen an apse adorned with coats-of-arms. The costumes for the courtiers who stood around to watch the *divertissement* (mostly walkers-on), gowns and tunics in heavy brocade or high-waisted velvet dresses with long dagged sleeves in garnet or russet colours, were magnificent.*

'I firmly decided,' wrote Kchessinskaya, 'to insert my classical solo to music by Kadletz into the ballroom scene . . . counting thus on scoring a true success. Diaghilev agreed with me . . .'[205] Diaghilev had little option. Having bought the Moscow production of the ballet, with over a hundred costumes, simply to show off the famous lady in three performances, he could not risk her walking out on him. To play the violin solo which accompanied the *pas de deux* in the lake scene and for the inserted Kadletz piece Kchessinskaya engaged Mischa Elman, who was in London for some concerts at the Queen's Hall.† He was a pupil of Auer, who used to play the *adage* at the Mariinsky. The *adage* was rehearsed with Nijinsky in front of the company at Covent Garden, but the Kadletz solo, which Elman was 'very anxious' about, was prepared *in camera* at the Savoy Hotel with no other audience but the Grand Duke André.[206] In which suite overlooking the river, one wonders, did this rare event take place!

It is clear from press notices that, contrary to Diaghilev's hopes, the English were not bowled over by the old classical ballets: to present them at this moment when the public had rapturously accepted the new art-form of Fokine was bad timing. In the first act of 'Giselle', we have seen, they 'had hardly known what to look for'. After the passionate acting of 'Schéhérazade' the old sign language in which the Swan Queen told her story to the Prince seemed almost a betrayal. England was not yet 'ready' for

---

* Though they were made in 1901 they are mostly in good condition today.

† The story told by Haskell and repeated in her memoirs by Mme Kchessinskaya, that Elman dashed across London to play for her during the interval of his concert at the Albert Hall is apocryphal.

the long Tchaikovsky ballets, which would become so alarmingly popular in the middle of the century – and would not even be 'ready' when Diaghilev nearly ruined his whole enterprise by putting on 'The Sleeping Beauty' for a run in 1921. At the end of his life he would write 'Tchaikovsky will never be understood in the west. . . . I presented him too soon and in the wrong way.'[207] Could he but have known!

There are very few descriptions of Nijinsky in 'Le Lac des Cygnes' – which, anyway, not many people in England can ever have seen, since it was given only three times in 1911 and twice in 1912. Two accounts survive. A.E.Johnson, author of one of the only three pre-war books to be published in England on the Russian Ballet (Ellen Terry's essay and Geoffrey Whitworth's book on Nijinsky were the others), wrote as follows:

The ballet presents Nijinsky in the kind of role more definitely associated with Adolf Bolm, and it is interesting to note the emphasis which it lays upon the essential difference between the two artists. Bolm is an actor who can dance when occasion demands; Nijinsky, a dancer who seems almost ill at ease when constrained to limit his movements to the actor's pedestrian paces. One would prefer to see the part of the Prince taken by Bolm, and an excuse found (as in 'Le Pavillon d'Armide') for Nijinsky's appearance, in his true function as dancer, in the court scene.[208]

This is an interesting observation. We saw in the previous chapter how hard Nijinsky found it to think himself into the role of Albrecht in 'Giselle'. Princes, cavaliers, manly straightforward lovers – these were the stock heroes of the old ballets, and he was not at home in such conventional roles, in which all that was needed, besides firm support for the ballerina, were a proud bearing and good manners. To become a ghost, a puppet, a half-animal creature, a faun, a character from the Commedia dell' Arte or even a Greek boy in love with himself was much easier for him. He needed a mask.

One guesses that Nijinsky would have felt easier about the role of the Prince if he could have introduced an eerie, haunted element into his character (like Ernest Thesiger, say, in Barrie's play *Mary Rose*, produced in 1920 and conceivably partly inspired by 'Swan Lake'), but that it would be hard to reconcile this with a bounding solo in the ballroom scene is borne out by a description written nearly thirty years later:

The Prince, attended by his friend, entered the glade. Nijinsky wore doublet and hose; on his head was a cap decorated with a long feather. The costume was entirely black except for the hose, which were relieved with vertical pink stripes. Nijinsky's slanting eyes and pale make-up, made paler still in contrast with his dark clothes, gave him a mystic air, the appearance of a man haunted by a vision which he yearns to see again. As he walked near the lake, peering up at the tree-tops or gazing towards the placid water, he made you aware of the presence of mist by the contraction and dilation of his nostrils, and by an almost imperceptible groping movement of his hands, as though he were brushing the mist aside.

In the second scene, I remember his sitting at a table watching the dancers dancing in his honour. But his eyes stared beyond the dancers as though he saw some haunting vision, that cherished form of the phantom Swan Princess, visible to him alone.[209]

The music for Nijinsky's solo was taken by Diaghilev from 'Casse-noisette'.[210] It was the Sugar Plum Fairy's tinkling tune with the celesta; and it is hard to imagine the dance which could have been arranged to this essentially feminine music.* Nothing, indeed, could be more out of keeping with the fey character of the lovesick Prince which it seems Nijinsky was trying to create.

Kchessinskaya was satisfied. 'It was a real feast. Although it was the first time he had accompanied dancing, Mischa Elman did it as a great master, and if the adagio from the swans' scene delighted the public, it was in my classical solo that I secured the resounding triumph I had dreamed of.'[211] This, of course, was followed in the coda by her famous thirty-two *fouettés*. Elman played for her again on 5 December, but not at the last performance of the ballet on the 7th.

Whenever Kchessinskaya danced the stage was covered with enormous bouquets. According to her,

Nijinsky did not like anybody but himself to receive ovations when he was dancing. His pride was hurt, and he indulged in a scene of jealousy with Diaghilev, threatening never again to dance with me; it was even said that in his fury he tore his costume. But Diaghilev was as skilled in avoiding scandal and smoothing down even the gravest incidents as he was in exciting them, and in the end everything was quickly arranged to everybody's satisfaction.[212]

Although we have evidence that Nijinsky did get rather spoilt as the years went on, his was not a jealous nature and it seems improbable that any young man's jealousy of a famous and favoured ballerina twice his age could have been very violent. More likely Diaghilev, to enhance Kchessinskaya's confidence in the genuineness of her success, invented the story to please her. After all, what could be more flattering than that this triumphant young god should envy her?

And what was the first reaction of the press to this ballet which has now become as regular a feature of British theatrical life as used to be *Peter Pan*,

---

* I asked three choreographers at dinner one night if they could imagine a man's dance to this music: Ashton, Taras and Nureyev all replied that they couldn't. Yet the *Sunday Times* (3 December 1911) spoke of Nijinsky's 'characteristic display of his graceful leaps and bounds' to the Sugar Plum Fairy tune.

Charley's Aunt or the Savoy operas? The famous Ivanov lake scene with the swans' dances bored them. 'Some of the early dances are exceedingly dull and . . . full of padding', thought the critic of *The Times*, while in the music 'there is nothing that quite touches the tiny masterpieces in the "Casse-noisette" ballet until we come to the second scene.'[213] 'The music is of little account. . . . It would be unkind to bring this dancing into comparison with Mme Pavlova's magic "Swan" dance' (*Daily Mail*).[214] Kchessinskaya 'did some extraordinary feats of precisely calculated design with *finesse* and a mathematical exactness which suggested a pair of magic compasses controlled by a fantastic philosopher with a taste for humour as well as a sense of beauty' (*The Times*).[215] The national dances were 'fascinating' (*Daily Mail*).[216] 'Nijinsky . . . as usual, combined skilful and delicate mimicry with astonishingly beautiful dancing. In the second scene he made a radiant figure in cream, gold and orange, with peacock plumes waving in his hair' (*The Times*).[217]

Kchessinskaya, with infinite means at her disposal, was always extremely hospitable to her fellow dancers. One Sunday she, the Grand Duke and Diaghilev organized an outing for Nijinsky and the leading dancers to Windsor Castle. An extra coach was attached to the train at Paddington and there were buses to meet them at Windsor station: but when they arrived at the Castle they found, as so many Sunday visitors have done and still do today, that it was shut. It was, of course, raining, but they drove through the Park and observed the Guardsmen at the windows of Combermere Barracks.

She gave a supper for the dancers, with *blinis* and caviare, at the Savoy, and at this Reynaldo Hahn was present; and before she returned to Russia with her suite she had the whole company to luncheon.[218]

Karsavina had returned from Petersburg in time to dance on 29 November with Nijinsky in 'Les Sylphides'. This was the only evening that season that she and Kchessinskaya appeared on the same programme, and she was able to watch her friend dance her part of Columbine in 'Carnaval'.

On 7 December, Karsavina, Nijinsky and Diaghilev, who was just back from Paris,[219] had lunch with Lady Juliet Duff in Upper Brook Street and signed her birthday-book. Diaghilev, after his signature, wrote 'L'ami des dieux' – 'The friend of the gods'. Nijinsky, more modestly and flatteringly, wrote 'Le Spectre *a* la rose'.[220]

The London season ended on Saturday, 9 December, with Karsavina and Nijinsky dancing 'Carnaval', 'Les Sylphides', 'Le Spectre de la rose' and 'Schéhérazade' – some evening! The applause was so great after the *pas de deux* – the C Sharp minor Valse – in 'Les Sylphides' that Karsavina and Nijinsky repeated it. This was the first encore that had been given during the

Ballet's two London seasons.[221] And who led the tumult of applause which produced it? No less an aesthete than the designer of *Fanny's First Play*. Charles Ricketts was to describe the raptures of that evening in a letter to a friend a few nights later: 'I am bitter and melancholy . . . the Russians have left us! . . . On that last night they danced as they dance only in Paradise – Karsavina destroyed utterly all the diamonds which the Tsar had given to the rival lady! (I forget her name), and Nijinsky never once touched the ground, but laughed at our sorrows and passions in mid-air. It was I who got the encore for Chopin's ironical and immortal valse.'[222]

The devoted Richard Capell of the *Daily Mail* reflected that 'the one sad aspect of the Russian season' which had 'revealed to us a new art – ballet-dancing resuscitated and transformed from a decrepit bore into an unimagined joy' was that 'at least a hundred thousand spectators too few have been granted a glimpse of this new beauty.' Of 'Schéhérazade' he wrote, 'There is compensation for some of the depressing conditions of modern life in the reflection that our epoch is alone, in the history of art, capable of producing just such a stage spectacle.'[223] Was he subconsciously echoing Oscar Wilde, who said that yellow satin was a consolation for all the miseries of life?

After the three first ballets there had been 'thunderous applause'[224] but on this electric evening the drama of 'Schéhérazade' almost overwhelmed the spectators. Of the final slaughter Ricketts wrote 'They put such beauty into their deaths that we became amorous of death and a Jew behind me cried out, "Oh! My God." The audience was cowed and applauded silently, one faded round of sound, whereupon that pimple of a French conductor struck up "God save the King", which of course suggests to the Britisher coats, hats, and trains to the suburbs.' Poor Monteux had probably realized that after the prolonged evening his orchestra were impatient to get away. Ricketts was not to be thwarted. 'I was white with rage and, the moment he ceased, I yelled "Karsavina" twice at the top of my voice; there was a pause, then came the roar from the gallery, like the boom of a distant gun, and the house applauded for twenty minutes.'[225] Richard Capell, who should have been on his way to Fleet Street to write his article, stayed to join in the applause and to time it. 'The audience from the front row of the stalls to the dark mass of enthusiasts standing at the back of the gallery applauded, cheered, and waved handkerchiefs for fully twenty minutes. The dancers received many tributes. Among them was a sheaf of flowers and a gold trinket in the form of a ballet-shoe with an inscription for Mme Karsavina, and a huge laurel wreath tied with the British colours for M.Nijinsky, which had been subscribed to by frequenters of the Covent Garden Gallery.'[226]

*Nijinsky in the wings after 'Le Spectre de la rose'. Caricature by Jean Cocteau.
From left to right: Bakst, an unknown, Diaghilev, Misia Edwards, Vassili,
Sert, Nijinsky.*

The next day, leaving Nijinsky behind with his mother and sister, Diaghilev was in Paris for two hours and signed his contract with the Opéra at the Crillon Hotel.[227] While in Paris he cabled to London to find out Pavlova's whereabouts.[228] He then caught the night train for Berlin, where he clinched the deal for his season in January.[229] By the 15th he was in Petersburg, cabling to Astruc to stop Karsavina, who was in Paris at the Hôtel Wagram, leaving for Russia on the following day.[230] He had to find a replacement for Schollar, who presumably wanted to go home for Christmas, and he engaged Nadine Baranovitch.[231] Because Karsavina was a doubtful starter he engaged Elsa Will, who had danced with him earlier in the year, to take the role of Columbine.[232]

Diaghilev left Russia in time to be back in Paris for the first performance at the Opéra on 24 December. This and the subsequent three were highly successful, and at one of them Karsavina and Nijinsky actually repeated the whole of 'Le Spectre de la rose',[233] and Karsavina made a speech. 'Diaghilev sent me before the curtain and I delivered my maiden speech to the effect that we would like to please our public by encoring, and that we entertained a hope that a charity collection about to begin would be generously supported.' This was no doubt the occasion which inspired Cocteau to make his caricature of Vaslav being fanned like a boxer in the corner of the ring by Vassili's towel, watched by a benign but anxious Diaghilev. Lady Ripon came over to Paris for the New Year and so did Lady Juliet Duff – the latter thus establishing a kind of record in having seen Vaslav dance 'Le Spectre' in three cities in the first nine months of its existence. The first year of Diaghilev's own company had been a glorious one. Lady Ripon had a party at the Ritz for her friends on New Year's Day, 1912, and Cocteau did a drawing for her of Nijinsky as the Rose, inscribing it: 'À madame la marquise de Ripon, un *dessinateur accidental*, respectueux et charmé'; and Vaslav signed it too.[234] Lady Ripon and her daughter were the first society ladies to follow Vaslav around.

CHAPTER FIVE

1912

January – August 1912

1912, which dawned for the Russians in Paris, was to be the year of the French composers, of Reynaldo Hahn, Debussy and Ravel; the year of Nijinsky's first choreography and the consequent departure of Fokine; the year of Thomas Nijinsky's death and Bronislava's marriage.

Stravinsky had driven himself to finish the composition – but not the orchestration – of 'Le Sacre' because he hoped that Diaghilev would produce it in the spring, but this was not to be.

At the end of January [he wrote], I went to Berlin, where the Ballet then was, to discuss the performance with him. I found him very upset about Nijinsky's health, but though he would talk about Nijinsky by the hour, all he ever said about 'Le Sacre' was that he could not mount it in 1912. Aware of my disappointment, he tried to console me by inviting me to accompany the Ballet to Budapest, London, and Venice, its next stops [presumably Vienna, Budapest and London]. I did journey with him to these cities, all three new to me then, and all three beloved ever since. The real reason I so easily accepted the postponement of 'Le Sacre', however, was that I had already begun to think about 'Les Noces'. At this Berlin meeting Diaghilev encouraged me to use a huge orchestra for 'Le Sacre', promising that the size of our Ballet orchestra would be greatly increased in the following season. I am not sure my orchestra would have been so large otherwise.[1]

Nijinsky was prone to influenza,[2] but one of the factors which was affecting his health was probably overwork. As well as 'Cléopâtre', 'Les Sylphides' and 'Carnaval' which Berlin had seen two years before, the company were dancing 'Schéhérazade', 'Prince Igor' and 'Le Spectre' – which were extremely popular – 'Le Pavillon', 'Giselle' and 'Le Lac des Cygnes'. In the last work Karsavina was appearing for the first time, and Diaghilev was surprised and delighted by her virtuosity.[3]* She and Nijinsky danced in

---

* Grigoriev does not mention that Karsavina danced 'Le Lac des Cygnes' for Diaghilev.

every ballet in the repertory except the Polovtsian dances from 'Prince Igor'.

'Le Dieu bleu' was to be staged at last, and in Berlin Fokine began to build up this complicated work, in which he incorporated bits of Siamese dancing remembered from the troupe which had visited Petersburg a few years back.

Diaghilev had signed with his German impresario to give fifty-three performances in Berlin during 1912,[4] which would be divided into two seasons, one at the beginning and one at the end of the year. His January stay in Berlin was to be followed by the eagerly awaited season at the Narodny Dom in Petersburg, which was due to begin – rather later than had been planned – on 24 February and to continue into March.[5] Early in January Diaghilev was cabling from the Hôtel Kaiserhof to Kchessinskaya in Petersburg about the possibility of once more obtaining the services of Piltz.[6] He was also in communication with two exotic dance recitalists, Napierkovska and Mata Hari (later notorious – and shot – as a spy), whom he wished to create the roles of the Goddess and the Girl in 'Le Dieu bleu', and who would be new to the Russian capital. It was a desperate attempt to repeat the sensation caused by Ida Rubinstein in his earlier exotic ballets. He settled with Mata Hari for seven performances at 3,000 francs plus her journey, but failed to secure Napierkovska's services for six weeks for 6,000 francs.[7] To strengthen his company he also signed a contract with Carlotta Zambelli of the Paris Opéra. She was to be paid 20,000 francs for seven performances, plus her journey, and to dance 'Giselle', 'Le Spectre', 'L'Oiseau de feu' and one other work to be agreed, presumably on the nights Karsavina was on duty at the Mariinsky.[8]

Meanwhile plans were afoot for the Russian Ballet to appear in August at the new resort of Deauville in Normandy, which its sponsor Cornuché was determined to turn into the most elegant and expensive millionaires' playground, with a summer season to rival the winter and spring seasons of Monte Carlo. The South American Ciacchi,[9] whom Astruc with his passion for codes always referred to as Chimène – giving him for a reason now unfathomable the name of the heroine of Corneille's *Le Cid* – was hoping to whisk the Russians off over the ocean as soon as they had finished their stay in Deauville.[10] In the event this trip would be postponed by a year.

Then on 20 January the blow fell. Narodny Dom was burnt to the ground.[11]* All Diaghilev's efforts to find another theatre for his Russian

---

* Not only does Grigoriev state that Diaghilev announced the burning of Narodny Dom to him on his arrival in Paris from London just before Christmas, nearly a month before it happened, but he describes the effect of this on Diaghilev's spirits – 'I had quite a shock, he appeared so dejected . . .' (p. 70).

season were in vain. He not only had to get out of his contracts with Zambelli and Mata Hari,[12] he had to find engagements for the company to fill in until their Monte Carlo season opened in April. Some frantic cabling took place. The German impresario went into action. By a miracle it proved possible to obtain at short notice three days in Dresden, eight performances spread over three weeks in Vienna and a week in Budapest. The situation was thus saved.

But Karsavina was due back in Russia, where she had been counting on fulfilling her obligations and taking part simultaneously in Diaghilev's season at Narodny Dom. She relates:

Quite casually Diaghilev said, 'You are not of course going to leave us, Tata; they have made stipulations for your appearance.' – 'My leave will be over, Sergei Pavlovich.'–'Nonsense, it is carnival now, nobody in the Mariinsky but moustache-less youth, send a telegram asking for prolongation of leave.' Though it was only a matter of matinée performances for schools, my reiterated demands were refused. Through side channels Diaghilev addressed high circles in Petersburg. It was of no avail; Teliakovsky remained adamant. There was nothing for me but to go. Luckily for my shattered fortitude, Svetlov took my side. He followed us pretty often, a faithful friend. No fortitude unsupported could have stood against what I had to stand the last ten days in Berlin, miserable days spent chiefly in tears in the telephone cabin. Diaghilev called me up at short intervals; every evening he got hold of me 'to talk things over'. I realized that he risked forfeiting his contract should I fail him. His arguments exhausted, he bowed to the inevitable, and it was heart-breaking to see his dejected face. On the last night he sat in my dressing-room. My eyelids were swollen with continuous crying, and looked like two little red sausages. Diaghilev sucked the knob of his stick, a sign of depression, and then very wearily, on the off-chance, he said, 'Let us look up the ABC'. He then calculated that starting on the night after the Dresden performance and travelling by the North Express I could arrive at Petersburg early in the morning on the day of my matinée. It seemed a Heaven-sent solution.[13]

It was during their stay in Berlin[14] that Vaslav and Bronia heard from their mother that their father had died while on tour at Kharkov in the Ukraine. They could not be expected to grieve very deeply for the loss of one who was almost a stranger to them, but at least one member of the company was taken aback by Vaslav's lack of demonstrativeness. Bolm crossed the classroom to offer his condolences, and was shocked by the smile with which Nijinsky thanked him.[15] Diaghilev ordered the Bach music for the Mass they had sung for the repose of their father's soul.[16]

Two other deaths that winter which touched the company more closely were those of Serov, over which Diaghilev wept for days,[17] and Rosaï, Nijinsky's classmate, who was carried off by pneumonia.

In almost every town they visited Nijinsky, Karsavina and Bolm found there were artists anxious to draw, paint or sculpt them. Ludwig Kainer made some vivid sketches in Berlin which he subsequently worked up into a series of lithographs.[18] In Dresden, where they performed in the pretty baroque Royal Theatre and went to see Raphael's Sistine Madonna,[19] they were sketched, then modelled by the celebrated Professor Paul Scheurich of the Meissen porcelain factory, and a set of characters from 'Carnaval', brilliant in their modern kind of rococo exaggeration and coloured in a very free variation on Bakst's original designs, were eventually put on the market.[20]

While in Dresden Diaghilev and Nijinsky paid one or two visits to Dalcroze's School of Eurythmics in the suburb of Hellerau.[21] They never ceased to explore opportunities of extending the language of the dance or of studying the possibilities of varying its relationship with music. And it was in Dresden that Grigoriev heard either from Bronislava or Vassilievska – the other girl who worked with Nijinsky – about the secret rehearsals which had been taking place of 'L'Après-midi d'un faune'.

The reason [he wrote] for the secrecy in which this activity had been shrouded was that, owing to Diaghilev's exclusive interest in Nijinsky, he and Fokine had been getting on less and less well, and that before allowing anyone to know about it Diaghilev wished to make sure that the experiment would succeed. I must confess that I was somewhat disquieted by this discovery, foreseeing what might happen when Fokine learnt of it. But I did not let this perturb me for long, since my leave from the Mariinsky would in any case expire in the autumn, when my service with Diaghilev's company would come to an end.[22]*

The train Diaghilev had discovered for Karsavina may have seemed a 'Heaven-sent solution', but, as she found out, he had not taken the elements into account.

I danced at Dresden, rushed off the stage immediately after the performance, threw a shawl over my ringlet wig, a coat over my Egyptian dress and arrived at the station just in time to catch the last train. I washed off my nut-brown complexion of an Egyptian maiden as best I could in my compartment. The express sped on till, on the second day, when a large snowdrift caused a delay, the train was six hours late. From the station I hurried to the theatre. My understudy had been got ready, but there still remained ten minutes of interval. When, in the costume of Sugar Plum Fairy, I came on the stage, the overture had finished and the curtain was going up. Teliakovsky thought it sporting of me.[23]

By persuasive cables Diaghilev was able to lure Kchessinskaya from

* Grigoriev either was not told or had forgotten when he wrote his book that 'L'Après-midi' had been more or less completed a year before this: and he was wrong in connecting it with Dalcroze, of whose principles it is the complete antithesis.

Petersburg and Kyasht from London to divide Karsavina's roles in Vienna and Budapest.[24]

The Vienna season opened at the Hofoper on Monday, 19 February, and continued for two and a half weeks. The Russian Ballet was well received.[25] Not only was Igor Stravinsky there with Diaghilev to witness the company subjugate yet another capital, but Benois, reconciled once more, was summoned to discuss the project of a new Debussy ballet, 'Les Fêtes', which was to be prepared for Paris. Benois suggested that this should be designed in the sumptuous style of Veronese's decorations for Venetian palaces. The fact that, while 'Les Fêtes' came to nothing, another project discussed by Diaghilev in Vienna with Count Harry Kessler and Strauss's librettist Hugo von Hofmannsthal, would see the light in 1914 as 'La Légende de Joseph' with a 'Veronese' décor by José-Maria Sert and 'Veronese' costumes by Bakst, is another instance of Diaghilev's high-handed treatment of his old friend.[26] The Strauss ballet was to be arranged by Nijinsky.*

Nijinsky became ill on 5 March at the end of the company's stay in Vienna; however, he travelled on with them to Budapest. Discussions with 'Chimène' kept Diaghilev an extra night or two in the Austrian capital.[27] In Budapest Grigoriev ran into trouble.

The theatre in which we were to perform, though it possessed a very large auditorium, had only a very small and inconvenient stage. The stage-manager in charge of our scenery declared that it could never be used in so small a space and that we could not give our performances. But all the tickets for the latter had meanwhile been sold; and the management would not hear of cancellation. I therefore made a thorough examination of the stage, and decided that with some adjustment the scenery could be used after all and the performances take place. But no sooner was this settled than Diaghilev's secretary, a Pole named Trubecki,† rushed in to say that Nijinsky was ill and could not dance – an even more serious blow. Nijinsky had never been known to be ill, and to replace him was practically impossible.‡ But while Trubecki, on my instructions, was informing Diaghilev by telephone... Nijinsky, in fact, felt much better the next morning, and by working all day on the scenery with the *régisseur* of the theatre I managed to adapt it satisfactorily to the small stage, and overcome the many technical difficulties involved, so that we were ready for the performance in the evening...

This *régisseur* was a plump middle-aged man with a limp. He wore a shapeless dressing-gown of indefinite hue and had obviously not shaved for days; but he

* Strauss had rejected Hofmannsthal's first idea for a ballet on Orestes and the Furies (*Hofmannsthal-Strauss Correspondence*, p. 121.)

† This is the man whom Romola Nijinsky and Grigoriev call Drobetsky, but I am following his own spelling of his name in telegrams to Astruc.

‡ As we have seen, Nijinsky had been ill in Paris in 1909 and in Berlin a few weeks before.

possessed a will of iron. Within an hour of the performance he was still sitting on a high stool in the middle of the stage, being shaved by a barber, while giving last-minute orders to the stage-hands; and every now and then he would get down off the stool and stump about with soap-smeared cheeks: a sight to be seen. After the performance, now properly dressed, he limped up to me and placed a large envelope in my hands, informing me in French that it was a small mark of gratitude from the management of the theatre for the trouble I had taken to make the performance possible. When I politely but firmly declined this tribute, he was quite taken aback. It would have been interesting to discover what remuneration the management considered appropriate to my achievement.[28]

In Vienna Kchessinskaya had already danced her familiar roles in 'Le Lac des Cygnes' and 'Carnaval'. In Budapest she added to these the Girl in 'Le Spectre de la rose'.[29]

It appears, however, that Nijinsky did miss the opening performance.[30] Even so, the artistry of the Russians overwhelmed the audience of smart, rich, intelligent and critical Hungarians. One of these, a girl of twenty-one, wrote later:

On leaving the theatre, I learned that the brightest star of the company had not been able to appear this evening because of a slight indisposition. I determined to attend all their performances. The next evening found me again at the theatre. The programme was composed of 'Cléopâtre', Schumann's 'Carnaval', and 'Prince Igor'. Once again the audience was a brilliant one. Seeing 'Cléopâtre' a second time, I was better able to appreciate the perfection of Astafieva, Feodorova and Bolm's dancing. The scenery used for Schumann's 'Carnaval' was a heavy velvet curtain of royal blue, painted with beautiful garlands of roses. The costumes were of the lovely Biedermeier period. The audience instantly grasped its light-hearted gaiety. Pierrot, Papillon and Pantalon flirted and swept across the stage, like so many little whirlwinds. Suddenly a slim, lithe, cat-like Harlequin took the stage. Although his face was hidden by a painted mask, the expression and beauty of his body made us all realize that we were in the presence of genius. An electric shock passed through the entire audience. Intoxicated, entranced, gasping for breath, we followed this superhuman being, the very spirit of Harlequin incarnate; mischievous, lovable. The power, the featherweight lightness, the steel-like strength, the suppleness of his movements, the incredible gift of rising and remaining in the air and descending in twice as slow a time as it took to rise – contrary to all laws of gravitation – the execution of the most difficult *pirouettes* and *tours en l'air* with an amazing nonchalance and apparently no effort whatever, proved that this extraordinary phenomenon was the very soul of the dance. With complete abandon the audience rose to its feet as one man, shouted, wept, showered the stage with flowers, gloves, fans, programmes, *pêle-mêle* in their wild enthusiasm. This magnificent vision was Nijinsky.[31]

Within a year and a half the enthusiastic writer of these lines, who had gone on the second night believing that the famous Nijinsky was a ballerina,[32] would be Nijinsky's wife. She at once set about getting to know some members of the company and was introduced to Bolm. 'Bolm', she thought, 'was not only a powerful dancer, but very sociable, extremely cultured, well-read and musical. He was the son of the concert master of the Imperial orchestra. We entertained him, showed him Budapest, and through him I made the acquaintance of many members of the company with whom he seemed to be very popular. I could find no opportunity to meet Nijinsky, nor was I certain whether or not I wished to know him. His genius swept me off my feet, but at the same time I had an uncanny feeling of apprehension. Bolm spoke of him in the highest terms, almost as a priest might speak of divinity.'[33]

The Russian Ballet's first season in Budapest was only a week long, at the beginning of March. If we are to believe Anatole Bourman, there was a scandal because Nijinsky took a call one night after 'Le Spectre de la rose' on his own, without Kchessinskaya, who had gone back to her dressing-room.[34] That he should have done so seems not improbable, besides being symptomatic of the changed status of the male dancer, Nijinsky's genius backed by Diaghilev's force of will having thrust him into extraordinary pre-eminence above the heads of all the ballerinas. Kchessinskaya probably did make a scene and threaten to leave at once for Russia. The absurd frequency with which Bourman, telling his story, turns out to have been on the spot whenever anything of importance happened to Nijinsky – his first meetings with Lvov and Diaghilev, his dismissal, a supposed attempt on his life – need not lead us to assume that he invented *everything* in his book. He took small incidents and, with the aid of his journalistic collaborator, blew them up into sensational dramas. Kchessinskaya does not mention the occurrence, merely recalling that Diaghilev let her miss the last performance of the season so that she could be home in Russia for her name day, 15 March (new style).[35] The Ballet travelled to Monte Carlo without her: but they had three weeks' rehearsal time before they opened and she would be back for the first night.

Diaghilev and Nijinsky returned to the Riviera Palace Hotel at Beausoleil,[36] with its uninterrupted view of the sea. Eleonora stayed down below with Bronia. Puccini had arrived to rehearse 'The Girl of the Golden West',[37] the Aga Khan was at the Hôtel de Paris,[38] and there were a number of distinguished English visitors. Lord Curzon was at the Grand Duke Michael's Villa Kazbeck,[39] Lord and Lady Dunsany at the Jerseys' Villa Capo di Monte,[40] the Joseph Chamberlain family were at the Villa Victoria[41] and Lady Ripon and Lady Juliet Duff, who had been absent from felicity for three whole months, joined their devoted friends at the Riviera Palace.[42]

Although Karsavina was still in Russia and the role of Thamar, in the

229

work planned to Balakirev's symphonic poem of that name, was to be for her, Fokine began rehearsing the Caucasian dances which made up most of the ballet.[43] These involved most of the company and the trouble began when Nijinsky wanted some of the girls to rehearse 'L'Après-midi d'un faune'.[44] Much has been written about the many rehearsals needed to produce this short piece, but Bronislava Nijinska, on whom it had been worked out, is our evidence that it existed complete and finished a year before the other dancers began to learn it, and it was not Nijinsky's uncertainty or stupidity, as has so often been alleged, that entailed such unusually protracted work, but the total inability of the dancers to adjust their bodies to the new form of movement and their minds to the new relationship of dance to music.[45] Admittedly, Nijinsky was far better at demonstrating what they had to do than at analysing it in words.[46] Bronia herself was not to portray the principal Nymph, because Nijinsky wanted a taller woman with a distinctive profile;[47] and Lydia Nelidova was fetched from Moscow to dance the role. She was also to take that of the Goddess, which might have been Mata Hari's, in Fokine's 'Le Dieu bleu'. She had a big nose and was in fact quite plain – apart from being rather stupid and entirely out of sympathy with Nijinsky's experiments,[48] but she fulfilled his qualifications. The other six nymphs were to be Bronia, Tcherepanova, Khokhlova, Maicherska, Klementovicz and Kopyshinska. There was by now no more attempt to conceal from Fokine that Nijinsky's first choreography was taking shape, but rehearsals were still held *in camera*.[49] Fokine could not conceive of the company containing another choreographer besides himself. Even the staging of old ballets like 'Giselle' and 'Le Lac des Cygnes' had seemed to him to mar the unity of his new repertory. We can imagine the long discussions with Vera that must have taken place.

Soon after the arrival of Matilda Kchessinskaya, who was staying with the Grand Duke André at their villa behind Cannes, her small son fell ill, and her time was taken up nursing him.[50] This meant that she could not stay the night in Monte Carlo after a performance, but was obliged to motor home along the coast, a journey of at least an hour and a half. She did not, however, let Diaghilev down, and her boy gradually got better.

With all these worries, and in the absence of Karsavina, it was a comfort for Diaghilev and Nijinsky to have Lady Ripon and her daughter at the same hotel. They were of course present when the Ballet opened at the Théâtre du Casino on Monday, 8 April. The programme consisted of 'Carnaval', 'Le Spectre de la rose', 'Prince Igor' and 'Schéhérazade'.

While it is understandable that Fokine should resent his authority as sole choreographer and ballet-master of the company being challenged, it is easy to see how Nijinsky would have warmed to a little encouragement from his old master, whose chief interpreter, along with Karsavina, he had been from the start. But this was not to be. The touchy Fokine had brought off one revolution in the nature of dancing: he could not see that in the twentieth century life and art were speeding up. To the liberal in office further reforms seemed mere anarchy. So although in all docility Nijinsky would learn and rehearse his roles in Fokine's ballets, a spirit of resentful rivalry was at the back of both their minds. This, Diaghilev, with his infinite diplomatic skill, could have contrived to dispel: but there was a part of Diaghilev's character which was glad when his collaborators did not get on together. We have seen how he played Bakst and Benois off against each other (and this year the company's Artistic Director was Bakst).[51] He liked to be the only essential link between two colleagues. Divide and rule.[52]

What made Fokine's bad feeling even worse was the realization that his 'Daphnis', which he had hoped would embody all his dreams of classical Greece, was taking second place to Nijinsky's Greek ballet 'L'Après-midi d'un faune'. 'Daphnis' meant a lot to him, not least because he considered himself its originator, having planned a scenario on the subject as early as 1904,[53] but Ravel had taken so long over the composition* that 'Narcisse', also on a Greek subject, had been thrust into last season's repertory in its place. Fokine maintained, not quite exactly, that Bakst had used his 'Daphnis' décor for 'Narcisse',[54] thus stealing the thunder of the postponed and more important work. It was at least true that there were statues of gods or nymphs as well as flocks of sheep in each.

Because of Fokine's work on 'Le Dieu bleu' and 'Thamar', and because of the rehearsal time and space needed for Nijinsky's ballet, 'Daphnis' was to be prepared last and given only in the final programme shortly before the end of the Paris season. After long and bitter discussions with Diaghilev, Fokine decided to resign as soon as it had been produced.[55]

Now that Fokine had decided to leave the company in June [wrote Grigoriev], he grew more and more restless and nervy, till it became almost impossible to work with him. He suspected everyone who stood close to Diaghilev of being his enemy, including myself. I was obliged by my work to be constantly referring matters to Diaghilev; and my doing so never failed to arouse Fokine's wrath. He even began accusing me of treachery; and a particularly painful incident led to a final quarrel between us. Diaghilev insisted on Nijinsky having a great many rehearsals for 'L'Après-midi'; and however hard I tried to do so, it proved impossible to avoid refusing Fokine the services of the same dancers at the same time. He flew into a rage with me; and the quarrel that ensued was the end of our friendship, a close friendship of many years. I was so much upset that I asked

---

* The part of 'Daphnis et Chloë' now known as the First Suite was played at the Colonne Concert on 2 April.

Diaghilev to relieve me of my duties; and though he, of course, refused, he agreed to provide me with an assistant, in the person of N.Semenov, the *régisseur* from Moscow; and this relieved me of some of my responsibilities.[56]

Meanwhile, on 16 April, Diaghilev was led to believe that an article about the forthcoming Russian Season in Paris had appeared in *Le Figaro*, announcing that among other ballets *Fokine* would be creating 'L'Après-midi d'un faune'.* After all Diaghilev's passionate drive to promote Nijinsky's first ballet and ensure him the maximum of publicity, this was too much. A storm broke out.

Diaghilev in Beausoleil to Astruc in Paris, 17.4.12

After seeing article front page *Figaro* announcing that Fokine was staging L'Après-midi faune Nijinsky refuses point blank to take part our Paris season. Have never seen him so determined or unreasonable. Have written Bakst about replacing him. Situation more than dangerous in view of the plans of certain people who were just waiting for this. There is no word too bad for your lack of attention. Diaghilev.[57]

Diaghilev could certainly be extremely rude when he wanted, as well as hysterical. The 'certain people' may have been Fokine or Oscar Hammerstein in New York,[58] who had long been plotting to lure Nijinsky away, or even Gunsbourg or another impresario. But although Nijinsky may well have made a terrible scene, Diaghilev must have known that he could calm him down in time, and the telegram was probably as much inspired by Diaghilev's petulance as Nijinsky's rage. Astruc was used to these insults. He adopted appeasing tactics and telephoned Bakst, a fellow-sufferer from Diaghilev's abuse, to help mollify the tyrant.[59]

Bakst in Paris to Diaghilev in Beausoleil, 19.4.12

All our Paris friends talk of nothing but the eagerly awaited L'Après-midi d'un faune. Décor going well. Bakst.[60]

Meanwhile 'Petrushka' made its appearance in the repertory, and on 18 April Bronislava Nijinska danced Karsavina's role of the Ballerina. This was to be followed on 2 May, now that Karsavina was back from Russia for the season's last three performances only,[61] by 'L'Oiseau de feu'. Diaghilev planned to make a trip to Paris on 27 March in order to see one of a series of Trouhanova recitals at the Châtelet, which opened on the 22nd, but he postponed it.[62] Like Rubinstein, she had stolen a march on Diaghilev and got in before him with French composers. Rubinstein had staged Debussy's 'St Sébastien' in the previous year: now Trouhanova was dancing – or rather posturing – to Ravel's 'Valses nobles et sentimentales' (called 'Adelaide ou le langage des

---

* Untraceable. It appears to have been imaginary.

fleurs'), to d'Indy's 'Istar', to Dukas' 'La Péri', which Diaghilev had failed to put on in 1911, and to Florent Schmitt's 'La Tragédie de Salomé', which he would stage for Karsavina in the following year. Calvocoressi, writing in *Comoedia Illustré*, politely described the rotund Trouhanova as giving first place to the music.[63] Her movements were evidently not too distracting.

Eleonora Nijinsky had enjoyed her stay by the Mediterranean, hobnobbing with the Cecchettis, whom she had known since the Maestro had been ballet master in Warsaw, and with Diaghilev's new secretary, the Pole Trubecki, the husband of Sophie Pflanz. One day Vaslav took her on a spending spree to Nice, from which she returned with a number of silk dresses and some unfashionable feathered hats, about which her son was tactful enough to make no comment. Nevertheless, remembering her own youthful tribulations, she disapproved of Vaslav's life of perpetual touring, thinking he would be better off safely ensconced at the Mariinsky.[64]

The company left Monte Carlo for Paris on 6 May,[65*] and Besobrasov in a white suit waved them off. They were never to see him again, for he died of diabetes at Monte Carlo soon after.[66] He was the third of Diaghilev's committee of friends who had planned the first season of ballet in 1909 to cross the frontier, Botkine and Serov having preceded him.

But Svetlov was still helping Diaghilev to run the company, and a handsome volume of his essays was to be published that year simultaneously in Petersburg and Paris (the French translation being by Calvocoressi). Its cover by Lanceray and decorations by Bakst seem to make it a bridge between *Mir Iskustva* and 1912, its other splendid illustrations, many in colour, bearing witness to what a force the ballet had already become in the field of visual arts in the West. Besides designs for décors and costumes by Bakst, Benois, Roerich, Golovine, Korovine and portraits of these designers and of Diaghilev and Fokine by Serov, Koustodiev, or by each other, and photographs of the principal dancers, there were impressions of 'L'Oiseau de feu' and 'Schéhérazade' by R. Lelong, and drawings of Nijinsky by Dethomas and Paul Iribe. The book was called *Le Ballet contemporain*.

For the third time the Russians opened at the Châtelet (it was their fifth season of ballet, if you count the few performances at the Opéra in the winter of 1911, but Diaghilev announced it as the *'septième saison russe'*).[67]

It is an extraordinary thing, looking at Astruc's full-page announcement in *Comoedia Illustré* of the season's sixteen performances, divided into four programmes with one new work in each, to realize that the only ballet in the repertory which could be called classical was 'Le Spectre de la rose'. So far had Fokine's reforms changed the aspect of Russian Ballet since 1909 that all the ballets given were works of local colour rather than virtuosity – Greek,

---

* Grigoriev says 5 May.

Nijinsky and Gabriel Astruc.
Caricature by Sem.

Russian or Oriental. The only female dancer – with two tiny exceptions – who was called upon to stand *sur les pointes* throughout the Paris season was Karsavina in 'Le Spectre', 'L'Oiseau du feu' and 'Petrushka'. The two exceptions were Nijinska and Schollar as the two street dancers in the last ballet.

On the opening night on 13 May were given 'L'Oiseau de feu', 'Le Spectre de la rose', 'Prince Igor' and – at last – 'Le Dieu bleu'.

How little of what we think of as Cocteau's typical qualities – modernity of spirit and transfiguration of the everyday – can we find in his libretto for 'Le Dieu bleu'! Did he himself realize as he watched it that it already belonged to a period of the Russian Ballet which was past? (Within exactly five years 'Parade', his collaboration with Satie and Picasso, would be given at the same theatre.) And what a mistake it had been to commission Reynaldo Hahn, that most witty and poetical composer of songs which embodied the very spirit of the boulevards and drawing-rooms of Paris, to write an oriental drama, which would turn out at the best to be reminiscent of Massenet and Delibes! Fokine's invention and the performance of his principal dancers were bound to be hampered by the pseudo-Hindu-Siamese idiom. Bakst alone, at the height of his powers, had insouciantly produced an extraordinary décor and a crowd of costumes which exceeded the bounds even of his own high-stepping fantasy.

The sacred place in a cleft between two vast cliffs must have been chosen for the god's shrine because of its spring, which forms a pool in the centre.

The steep cliff to the left is in shadow and, between it and the sun-baked orange mountain which fills the centre and right of the stage, the sky descends in a burning azure V, at the base of which can be spied a distant horned pagoda. The orange rock is carved with great heads which emerge from foliage, and springing out from it to the right in exaggerated perspective are two poles from which monstrous snakes hang in trailing loops. Exoticism, mystery and horror can go no further.

As for the costumes, predominantly white, but with varied appliqué patches – triangles, lozenges, zig-zags or peacocks' eyes – of slate blue, purple, magenta, yellow and green, there has never been such an elaboration of gold and pearl embroidery, such luxuriously twined or dizzily towering turbans, hung with such yards of pleated gauze or festooned with such swags of beads!

Entry of the Priests and Temple Attendants – a chromatic oriental music with odd scales. A Young Man (Max Frohman the beautiful) is to become a priest. Over his gorgeous costume* he wears the initiate's simple white robe. Ritual dances of musicians, the bearers of offerings and the Bayadères of the sacred lotus succeed each other; then as the Young Man stands in rapt contemplation before the shrine, there breaks out the dance of the Yogis, who are spinning dervishes with long ropes attached to their hats and shoulders which appear to form discs in the air as they rotate.[68] Here the rites are interrupted. A Girl (Karsavina) in winged headdress and spreading,

---

* As an example of the elaboration of the costumes of this ballet may be appended my description of Frohman's costume in the catalogue for the sale of part of the Diaghilev Ballet wardrobe by Sotheby's on 17 July 1968. The costume now belongs to our Museum of Theatre Arts.

'The basic garment is a skirted tunic with elbow-length sleeves. The upper part of this is chrome yellow silk with an embroidered collar of mother-of-pearl shells and a large peacock's-eye-shaped brooch on the chest of magenta and silver enamel surrounded by white beads and with a ruby at the centre. The sleeves are flesh-coloured moiré silk with bands of silver braid and shell embroidery; the skirt split at the sides appears as a curved apron of flesh-coloured moiré silk bordered with silver braid and shells with a panel of magenta silk down the front with a rectangle of shell embroidery.

'The coat, worn over this, ends at the waist and has long slashed hanging oversleeves and a knee-length "collar" which hangs in a low loop in the front to reveal the magenta silk panel of the skirt in its opening. The jacket oversleeves are magenta silk repp embroidered with a stylized flower pattern in shells; the jacket terminating in a magenta silk belt with bands of silver braid; the sleeves end in elaborate cuffs of oyster silk and flesh-pink moiré silk with silver braid, silver embroidery and mother-of-pearl raspberries. The "collar" is of chrome-yellow silk edged with silver braid and a fringe of white beads, appliqué with a band of purple velvet encrusted with rings of pearls enclosing mother-of-pearl raspberries on a backing of silver lace.

'Ankle-length trousers in purple satin with cuffs of white silk embroidered with shells, dotted with gold sequins and appliqué with lozenges of chrome-yellow satin bound with gold braid, also hand-stencilled with smaller scarlet lozenges. Indian cap (similar to a Doge's cap) covered in flesh-pink moiré silk with bands of shells and embroidered with a pine pattern and arabesques of gold lace with pearls. In the front a silver crest holds a tassel of human hair and there are tassels of silver thread falling over each ear.

'The costume is marked with Frohman's name and the trousers with that of Bolm as well.'

stiffened skirts, breaks through the guards and flings herself at the feet of the neophyte. She is his mistress and she pleads with him not to leave her and the world behind. *Tremolando* strings. The young man rebuffs her gently. Dance of supplication to naïve Adam-like music. Indifferent to the wrath of the priests, the Girl dances the story of their past happiness and as the Young Man watches her his mind is troubled and he begins to doubt his vocation. To a very conventional waltz tune the Girl's movements become faster and more seductive. Scandal! The Young Man is seized and hustled away, while the High Priest (Feodorov) condemns the Girl to a terrible death. The crowd moves off in procession, leaving the Girl alone. By now it is night. Moonlight music. The Milky Way appears shining aloft. (This is a real Cocteau touch.) The Girl looks for a way out, and on opening a door, releases a stampede of monsters and fiends. (Reminiscence of 'L'Oiseau de feu'.) They circle round her to a trampling music. The Girl flings herself in supplication before the sacred lotus. Change of lighting, the monsters cower, the pool lights up. The Goddess (Nelidova) rises, seated, clad all in gold with a conical gold Siamese helmet, from the pool. She is only the herald of the Blue God's appearance. In a hieratic posture Nijinsky now looms out of the water. His flesh is blue and he wears a glittering crown.* The Goddess indicates to him the plight of the Girl. He proceeds to charm the monsters. In Cocteau's words:

His gestures are alternatively gentle and frantic. He leaps from one to the other with supple and terrible bounds. He glides amid their grovelling mass. Now he fascinates them with cabbalistic poses, now scares them with imperious threats. They try to drag him down, but he escapes them. He crouches as they jump, and flutters in the air when they crouch. At his command the tendrils of jungle plants entwine them and bind them, and the scent of blossom overpowers them.[69]

He shows the Goddess, smiling, what he has done; and she picks him a lotus stem to use as a flute. There follows the dance of Divine Enchantment. The flute solo reduces even the God himself to a state of heavenly intoxication. At the end of it he squats triumphant amid the becalmed and docile monsters.

Lights! Lights! Hubbub. Entry of apprehensive priests. At the sight of the miracle they fall flat on their faces. The Goddess orders the priests to release

---

* Nijinsky's costume was sold by Sotheby's on 13 June 1967, and is now on display at the Royal Opera House, being destined for the future Museum of Theatre Arts. Though equally elaborate, it took less words to describe than Frohman's:

'Short-sleeved skirted Oriental costume in yellow watered silk, appliqué with a printed cotton in violet, blue and white, also with white satin; with bands of green velvet studded with green stones; embroidered in green, blue, yellow, black and gold; pink and white stones round the hem of the skirt. Yellow woollen pantaloons with an embroidered white border. Headdress of gold gauze on a wire base, with pearls and an embroidered rose.'

I pointed out to Mme Karsavina that the jewelled buckle over the navel was missing. 'And how it used to scratch me!' she said.

the Girl. Terrified, they obey. 'A feeling of Buddhist blisss pervades the scene.'[70] The lovers are re-united. The Young Man tears off his white robe, The Girl describes her ordeal and dances for joy. The Goddess conjures up a vast golden staircase which stretches into the celestial blue, and as she stands in the heart of the lotus, blessing the young couple, the Blue God ascends to heaven.

'Le Dieu bleu' did not receive the acclaim reserved for Diaghilev's outstanding successes, but Brussel could find no fault with it in *Le Figaro*. The composer, a lover of Mozart, 'tended to write increasingly simply'. The designer's work was 'the zenith of decorative art'. Fokine's staging was as fine as that of 'L'Oiseau de feu', and the way he had arranged the God taming the monsters ' – a thing which had so often been unsuccessfully attempted in the past – was a triumph of originality, invention and plastic beauty'. He praised Nijinska's possessed Bayadère; acclaimed Nelidova's personality (noting her Paris début); sang Karsavina's infinite variety, observing that her art was the expression of a refined soul; and thought Nijinsky had never appeared more marvellous than in this role, which was worthy of his talent.[71]

The second novelty of the season, performed on 20 May, was 'Thamar'. This gave an opportunity for playing a masterpiece of Russian music, drew from Bakst an extraordinary décor and provided Karsavina with one of her most powerful roles. The scene was the interior of a raftered tower, with crimson and purple bricks rising in giddy perspective. On piles of cushions, surrounded by her attendants, the nymphomaniac queen of Georgia awaited the passing travellers whom she would love and kill. As the music's oriental languors changed to pulsing Caucasian dances – in one of which the whirling men, who danced on the toes of their boots, flung their daggers into the floor – the drama merged with dance. The stranger prince, Bolm, arrived, was loved, spurred on to dance, stabbed and flung down a trap-door into the river below. The queen slumbered until the next horseman came in sight. The vampire beauty of Karsavina, with her white face and eyebrows drawn – at Diaghilev's suggestion – in one unbroken line,[72] has been recorded in a painting by Glyn Philpot.

Diaghilev spared no trouble or expense to create a favourable climate of opinion for Nijinsky's first ballet. Following the *répétition générale* – which, according to Fokine, was so silently received that after a hurried backstage conference Astruc appeared in front of the curtain to announce that since 'such a new exhibition could not be understood in a single viewing, the ballet would be repeated' – champagne and caviare were served to critics and supporters in the foyer. This had never happened before.[73]

Bakst's setting for 'L'Après-midi' was much less literal and representational a landscape than his designs for 'Narcisse' or 'Daphnis'. It was as if, in

237

creating this mottled, speckled, stripy, deliquescent composition in greys, russets and greens, he had tried to find an equivalent for Debussy's music in terms of Nabi pattern and colour; and more than any other of his works the design resembles one of those overallish decorations of Vuillard in which a rug, a cat, wallpaper and people are treated impartially as elements of dappled colour. Andrew Marvell's lines come to mind –

> Annihilating all that's made
> To a green thought in a green shade.

All the action of the ballet took place in a narrow strip at the front of the stage, the dancers appearing to move in parallel grooves, so the backcloth was set forward 'on the line of the second wings'. The floorcloth was black as far back as the Faun's rostrum on the left, after that green. The lighting was planned to give an effect of flatness to the dancers.[74]

The characters in Bakst's costumes were not, however, camouflaged: they had to stand out to give the effect of their frieze. The nymphs wore long pleated tunics of white muslin stencilled in blue or rust-red with stripes, wavy lines, leaves or checkered borders. Their feet were bare and white with rouged toes, and on their heads they wore tight-fitting wigs of golden rope which fell in long strands. They wore very little make-up.[75] Bakst painted their eyes 'whitish-pink . . . like those of a pigeon'.[76] Nijinsky wore cream-coloured all-over tights painted round the shoulders, elbows, sides, buttocks and knees with dark brown splotches, like the skin of a calf. He had a small tail and a wisp of green vine leaves round his middle. He wore a woven cap of golden hair like the nymphs, but with two gold horns lying flat on either side so that they formed a kind of circlet.

His facial make-up utterly changed the apparent structure of his face. He under-lined the obliquity of his eyes, and this brought out and gave a slumberous expression. His mouth, chiselled by nature, he made heavier. Here also was an infinite languor and a bestial line. His face, with its high cheekbones, lent itself admirably to the transformation. His ears he elongated with flesh-coloured wax and made them pointed like a horse's. He did not imitate; he merely brought out the impression of a clever animal who might almost be human.[77]

Only Nijinsky and Nelidova as the tall nymph wore gilded sandals.

The première of 'L'Après-midi d'un faune' was on Wednesday, 29 May.

Whether Debussy's eddies of sound represent a breeze through birch trees – but there were probably no birch trees in ancient Greece – or sunlight coming through leaves and dappling water, or the light in Monet's poplars, or the youthful euphoria of Renoir's 'Déjeuner des Canotiers', it is beyond question that they are in some sense about the languid ecstasy of a summer afternoon. But it is not an afternoon on the suburban Seine or in Normandy or in the birch forests of Russia, nor even in a wood near Athens, for as the music goes on we hear an exotic strain; and it seems that this must come from Cyprus, or from Crete with its dark pleasures, or from Daphne, the grove of love near Antioch, or from Thessaly, through which the train of Bacchus had to pass, bringing the dangerous gift of wine from Asia.

And in these glades Debussy has placed Mallarmé's Faun, whose pipe, represented by the flute, from the beginning helps to paint the sylvan scene; the following surges of sound conveying the pulse of desire and summer joy in the breast of this pagan creature, just as certain musical scurries suggest little encounters and furtive disappearances among the trees.

Nijinsky had never read Mallarmé's poem,[78] but his animated frieze adapted itself very comfortably to Debussy's score, finding apt cues for entries, confrontations, sudden incursions and panicky exits.

The ballet opens with a breathy warble on the flute and the curtain rises slowly to reveal the Faun seated on top of his bank, supporting himself on his left arm, right knee raised, head tilted back and pipe to lips; as the phrase is partly echoed by the horns against a background of harp *glissandi*, then repeated on the flute, the Faun goes through the action, in his angular, stylized way, of squeezing first one then another bunch of grapes over his face. On the third repeat of the flute phrase, three nymphs walk slowly on the left. They are followed by two more. In the course of a long tendrilly *arabesque* on two flutes with harp then string accompaniment a sixth nymph (Nijinska) walks rapidly to the centre of the stage, and takes up a pose. She then walks backwards and joins in behind the fourth and fifth nymphs as the seventh nymph (Nelidova) comes on. The first six nymphs remain motionless until the tall nymph has crossed the stage at a rapid mechanical walk, one arm across her breast, and undone a clasp on her shoulder to let fall her outer veils revealing a short golden undergarment. Then they move.

The Faun has not stirred during the entry of the first six nymphs. When the tall nymph came on he followed her with his eyes. Now a warbling clarinet sets his head moving and a *spiccato* cello brings him to his feet. Forming interesting patterns as they kneel or stand with elbows turned out from their sides and hands either pointing at their waists or above their heads, the nymphs move in and out as they bathe the tall nymph in the imaginary stream to a wistful tune on the oboe. Violins pick up the oboe phrase. A *crescendo* brings the Faun down his slope on to the same level as the others. The tempo quickens. The fourth and fifth nymphs bear off one veil to the right; and the first, second and third nymphs bear off the other veil to the left. The music subsides into a clarinet solo '*doux et expressif*'. The sixth nymph is stage centre with her back to the Faun. She turns her head and on seeing him raises her hands in surprise to shoulder level, fingers splayed, and scurries off right. The Faun and the seventh nymph are left motionless as the woodwind sing a new theme of quiet exultation. A sudden *crescendo* to the languorous triplet theme. The violins take the new tune over rippling harps. In sharp bursts the Faun courts the nymph with a jump and changes of direction. His jump is to cross the imaginary stream flowing from the waterfall painted on the backcloth.[79] They link arms, elbows locking, but the tall nymph escapes the Faun, walking off on flat feet to the left. The music surges to *fortissimo* then down again as singly and in pairs the other nymphs return to fetch the remaining veil. A solo violin plays, accompanied by sustained horns and warbles on the flute and clarinet. The Faun tilts back his head and bares his teeth in stylized laughter; then picks up the veil and contemplates it ecstatically in profile. Over an *arpeggio* harp accompaniment the flute plays its original tune. An oboe clucks away. To a downward rush of *staccato* chords in the woodwind three nymphs glide on to mock the Faun. The oboe takes up the tune, and they scuttle off, hands raised. As the cor anglais trills and flutes flutter the sixth nymph (Nijinska) walks on from the right, confronts the Faun with a defiant stare, then goes off abashed. Again the flutes repeat their tune supported by shimmering strings and the quiet ring of *cymbales antiques* (the playing of which has already been mimed by the nymphs brushing their hands together). The Faun, alone again, nods his head over the veil, and slowly bears it up to his ledge. A solo cello joins the flute over a slower harp figure. Wisps of familiar melodies float by. The Faun holds up the veil, nuzzles in it, then stretching it out on the ground, lowers himself on it, head tucked under, and finally, as muted horns and harp harmonies over a quiet flute chord conclude the choreographic poem, consummates his union with it, taut on the ground, by a convulsive jerk. We are to imagine that this is his first sexual experience.[80]

The audience sat through the new work in silence, but at the end there was a tremendous clamour made up of a mixture of cat-calls and applause. It was impossible to tell whether shouts of praise or abuse predominated.[81] In the past some ballets given by the company had been more coolly received than others – and we have seen that there had been a flight of dowagers during the first performance of 'Prince Igor' in London[82] – but none had ever been booed. Diaghilev was 'visibly put out'.[83] He went on stage. Nijinsky was convinced his work had been a failure. Then through the curtain they could hear that a body of supporters had got together to shout '*Bis!*'[84] (One suspects that this may have been the devoted Valentine Gross and her friends.) Partly to establish a victory, but also perhaps to make Nijinsky happy and to convince him that he had won more approval than disfavour, Diaghilev gave orders for the twelve-minute-long ballet to be repeated.[85]

Paris was of course familiar with the music of 'L'Après-midi d'un faune', and it was to be expected that some critics and members of the public would resent an attempt at dancing to the famous score. Diaghilev had been accused in the past of sacrilege to Chopin, Schumann and Rimsky-Korsakov: none of these had been *French*. That Nijinsky should have imposed so new a kind of dancing on the music – which some people might claim with justification was not dancing at all – while establishing at the same time a freer relationship between dance and music than had ever existed before, might well have made him and Diaghilev apprehensive of a hostile reaction. Even so, they were taken by surprise. There was something for everyone to dislike in the new work – musicians could allege blasphemy, balletomanes deformity, and respectable people immorality – that is, if it did not happen to strike them that they were watching a spectacle of transcendent beauty – a kind of masterpiece. How much the adverse reaction of a section of the public was due to musical or choreographic objections and how much to the Faun's final movement of stylized orgasm, it is impossible to know: but it is clear that anyone who had not enjoyed the ballet as it unfolded would like it even less when he had seen it through to the end.

Historians disagree about the exact nature of Nijinsky's final erotic movement, which was anyway slightly modified after the first performance. Grigoriev makes clear that it was shown at the last rehearsals exactly as given at the première and that Diaghilev, warned that it was shocking, refused to have it changed.[86] Prince Peter Lieven's suggestion, based on information from Prince Argutinsky, that the movement was an accident on the first night caused by the breaking of one of a bunch of glass grapes* attached to Nijinsky's tights is certainly nonsense, since what the dancer wore across his private parts was a spray of leaves, not grapes, and they were not made of glass; but the story may have originated in some misleading improvisation of Diaghilev's.[87] In the choreography as handed down to us by Dame Marie Rambert, the Faun, lowering his body on to the veil, slides his arms down by his sides, then makes the last barely perceptible thrust with his pelvis. From the final photograph by Baron de Meyer in the excessively rare book *Le Prélude à l'Après-midi d'un faune*, published by Paul Iribe in 1914, it seems clear to me that on the first night Nijinsky slid his hands *under* his body in such a way as to suggest masturbation. An unpublished water-colour of Valentine Gross shows an even later stage of the movement and confirms this theory. Nijinsky's ultimate gesture could have been slightly out of keeping with the non-representational choreography of the ballet and the subsequent change was probably an improvement.

The press was in the main favourable and *Commedia*, the daily paper which

* His actual phrase in the English translation of L. Zarine is 'vine clusters', which I take to mean grapes.

covered all the theatrical events of Paris and the provinces, not only carried on its front page a three-column article by the editor, Gaston de Pawlowski, a keen supporter of the Ballets Russes, with photographs of the dancers, and profuse quotes from Mallarmé's poem with three of Manet's (rather weak) illustrations to it in line, but on page 2 another photograph of the full-stage scene, showing Bakst's décor and the eight dancers, and two more articles by Louis Vuillemin and Louis Schneider. All these were unanimous in praise.[88]

There was, however, one thundering exception to the dawn chorus of approval. Calmette, the powerful editor of *Le Figaro*, professed to be shocked. Instead of printing Brussel's article he denounced the ballet himself on the front page.

Calmette in *Le Figaro*, 30 May 1912:

UN FAUX PAS*

Our readers will not find in its usual place on the theatre page an account by my esteemed colleague Robert Brussel of the first performance of 'L'Après-midi d'un faune', a choreographic scene by Nijinsky, arranged and danced by that amazing artist.

I am not printing that account. This is not the place to assess the value of Debussy's music . . . [etc., etc.]

I am, however, certain that any of our readers who were present yesterday at the Châtelet will join with me in protesting against the extraordinary exhibition which they had the audacity to serve up to us in the guise of a serious work, decked out with all the refinements of art and imagination.

Anyone who mentions the words 'art' and 'imagination' in the same breath as this production must be laughing at us. This is neither a pretty pastoral nor a work of profound meaning. We are shown a lecherous faun, whose movements are filthy and bestial in their eroticism, and whose gestures are as crude as they are indecent. That is all. And the over-explicit miming of this mis-shapen beast, loathsome when seen full on, but even more loathsome in profile,† was greeted with the booing it deserved.

Decent people‡ will never accept such animal realism.

M. Nijinsky, ill-suited to such a role, and little accustomed to such a reception, took his revenge a quarter of an hour later with an exquisite rendering of 'Le Spectre de la rose' so delightfully conceived by M. J.-L. Vaudoyer.

That is the sort of show to give the public, with its charm, good taste, *esprit français*. . . [etc., etc.][89]

Diaghilev rallied his forces for the counter-attack. On the same day he was

---

* Literally, of course, 'a wrong step'.

† Calmette seems to be trying to imply, in the manner of vulgar columnists with whom we are familiar in this country and who titillate while they denounce in the name of morality, that Nijinsky gave some ithyphallic exhibition.

‡ 'Le vrai public' – a meaningless phrase.

able to have delivered to Calmette his reply with two enclosures, which the editor of *Le Figaro*, out of fairness or perhaps nothing loth to stir up controversy, published on the following day.

Calmette in *Le Figaro,* 31 May 1912:

I had not expected to return to the subject of the Châtelet affair, but among the hundreds of letters which my readers have been so flattering as to write to me, and which have given me so much pleasure, there has come one from M. de Diaghilev, the director of the Russian Ballet Season, which I print in the interest of impartiality.

Paris, 30 May 1912

Sir,

I cannot in a few lines defend a ballet which is the fruit of several years work and of much serious research.

It seems simple in view of the article by M. J.-E. Blanche published by you on Tuesday to submit to the public the opinion of the greatest artist of our day, M. Auguste Rodin, together with that of another master, M. Odilon Redon, who was so close a friend of Stéphane Mallarmé.

First of all, here is the letter I have received from M. Odilon Redon:

Sir,

Joy is often coupled with sorrow. I could not help regretting, amid the delights of this evening's performance by your company, that my illustrious friend Stéphane Mallarmé was not with us. More than anyone, he would have appreciated this wonderful evocation of his thought. . . . I recall how Mallarmé was always bringing dance and music into his conversations. How happy he would have been to recognize, in that living frieze we have just been watching, his faun's very dream, and to see the creatures of his imagination wafted by Debussy's music and brought to life by Nijinsky's choreography and the passionate colour of Bakst. . . .

ODILON REDON

Here now is an important passage from the article published by M. Auguste Rodin [in *Le Matin*]:

Nijinsky has never been so remarkable as in his latest role. No more jumps – nothing but half-conscious animal gestures and poses. He lies down, leans on his elbow, walks with bent knees, draws himself up, advancing and retreating, sometimes slowly, sometimes with jerky angular movements. His eyes flicker, he stretches his arms, he opens his hands out flat, the fingers together, and as he turns away his head he continues to express his desire with a deliberate awkwardness that seems natural. Form and meaning are indissolubly wedded in his body, which is totally expressive of the mind within. . . . His beauty is that of antique frescoes and sculpture: he is the ideal model, whom one longs to draw and sculpt. When the curtain rises to reveal him reclining on the ground, one knee raised, the pipe at his lips, you would think him a statue; and nothing could be more striking than the impulse with which, at the climax, he lies face down on the secreted veil, kissing it and hugging it to him with passionate abandon. . . .

243

I wish that such a noble endeavour should be understood as a whole; and that, apart from its gala performance, the Théâtre du Châtelet would arrange others to which all our artists might come for inspiration and to communicate in beauty.

AUGUSTE RODIN

I call attention to these authoritative opinions and to our obstinate experiments, of which 'L'Après-midi d'un faune' is the culmination, in the belief that our works are worthy even of the respect of our enemies.

I have the honour to be, Sir, etc.,

SERGE DE DIAGHILEV

I do not want to argue with M. Serge de Diaghilev [Calmette goes on]: he is the impresario of the business and is bound to find the programme chosen by himself very good. This programme contains beautiful works, I admit, and we have only instanced one 'faux pas'. About this 'faux pas' there can be no argument. . . .

After concluding that Redon's opinion could only be his own, since Mallarmé had gone where 'the dead rest in the bosom of the earth', Calmette turned the attack on Rodin, whom he accused of living at the tax-payers' expense in the old Hôtel Biron (which had been given to him as a studio for life) and exhibiting indecent drawings in the former chapel of the Sacré Coeur attached to it, surrounded by swooning lady-admirers and self-satisfied snobs. 'There is the real scandal,' he concluded, 'and it is for the government to put a stop to it!'[90]

The controversy was turning political; and the suspicious Parisians, who love to find fantastic explanations for everything that goes on, leapt to the conclusion that Calmette's real object of attack was the Franco-Russian Alliance. Nijinsky always remembered the excitement of the few days following the première of his first ballet.

Diaghilev's friends, and the balletomanes, as well as the personal admirers of the Russian Ballet, came to the Crillon at once. They had all discussed what would be the right thing to do by the time Nijinsky, who had taken a well-deserved rest, awoke from his late sleep and came in to Sergei Pavlovitch's rooms. All sides of the question were considered. Followers and newspapermen called up, came to the hotel, and tried to talk to Diaghilev or to see Nijinsky, to know what they thought of the Calmette attack. Members of the Russian Embassy came in and explained that they were convinced that Calmette had made his attack, merely using 'Faune' as a pretext, because in reality he wished to attack the policy of the French Foreign Office, Poincaré, and the Russian Ambassador, Isvolsky, who were trying to strengthen the Franco-Russian alliance and friendship. The *Figaro*, and the political group which the paper was representing, pursued a different attitude in politics, and, in attacking the Russian Ballet, the strongest propaganda for Russia in France, they attacked the *rapprochement* with this country itself.

News came that the prefect of police of the city of Paris had been requested to stop the next performance of 'Faune' as an obscene spectacle. The news went through Paris like a hurricane, and threw the whole city into a great state of excitement. . . .

In an incredible agitation, rumours were repeated and grew. The *Gaulois* appeared with an article stating that an apology was due to the public. The anti-Faunists seemed to gain ground. What was to be done in this purely artistic matter which now rocked the whole public? . . . Nothing was definite by evening,* except that they learned that Calmette had obtained from the police an injunction to prevent the further performance of 'Faune'. Inquiries were immediately made, and Diaghilev was informed that the last gesture of Nijinsky, the Faun lying on the veil, was the one to which the police objected. Sergei Pavlovitch and the others devised a subterfuge. They requested Nijinsky to change this last movement, but he refused, saying that he could not see any offence to the public morals in his conception. Nevertheless, for one or two performances the end of the ballet was slightly modified, but without any appreciable difference.

A world-wide controversy exploded. A storm of protest was hurled at Calmette. The admirers of Rodin were up in arms. M.Pierre Mortier, editor of *Gil Blas*, sprang to the defence of Rodin, pointed out that the 'Faune' was the *leitmotiv* of his art, and declared that instead of expelling Rodin, as Calmette had suggested, the State should maintain him in the Hôtel Biron for life, and convert it into a Rodin Museum, providing he could leave his work to France; which was in fact done later.

A campaign to support Rodin was started, in which the names of the most eminent figures of France in the artistic, literary and political world were enlisted. . . . Then the rest of the Paris public tried to get in to a performance of 'Faune,' to judge for themselves what this question was that had stirred the intellectual world to its depths. It was a real *tour de force*, however, to get in, as all the tickets for the Russian season had been sold weeks before, and every conceivable influence and political pull was called into play to obtain places at the Châtelet.

Then *Figaro* published a huge Forain caricature[91] showing Rodin, in his studio at the courtyard of the Hôtel Biron. A model enters with a dress over her arm:

'Oh, Master, where can I put my clothes when I pose?'

Rodin: 'Just there, in the chapel.'

This was carefully designed to arouse the clerical animosity of the Faubourg, and a fresh list of adherents swarmed to Rodin's side. The new petition was signed by Isvolsky, the Russian Ambassador; the Senators Dubost, d'Estournelles de Constant, Gaston Menier; MM Edmond Haraucourt and Pierre de Nolhac, and Mmes Alphonse Daudet and Lucie Félix-Faure. Forain, the cartoonist, was attacked by the critic Louis Vauxcelles for his lack of aesthetic self-respect in demeaning himself to draw the caricature in the first place. A Government commission was asked to report, which was favoured both by the President of the Republic and the Prime Minister.

Le Figaro, *Le Gaulois*, *La Liberté*, the anti-Faunist papers, were silenced.

The police appeared and witnessed the performance, but they inclined before the public opinion and 'Faune' was not forbidden.[92]

* The second performance of 'L'Après-midi d'un faune' was on 31 May; the third and fourth were on 1 and 3 June.

Fokine had been shocked to the core when he had seen, at one of its final rehearsals, the erotic ending of Nijinsky's ballet. His comments on the choreography are interesting. First, he accused Nijinsky of plagiarism. He claimed that the latter had taken three things from his own production of the Venusberg scene in 'Tannhäuser', which Nijinsky had performed so excellently. These were: the Faun's walk 'with the palm of the fore hand extended flat and turned to the audience', the pointing out elbows, when the Faun held the veil, and the slow descent upon the veil at the end. In 'Tannhäuser', though, the dancer had lain down not on a scarf but on a woman.[93] Why the movement should be perfectly permissible with a human partner and 'pornographic filth'[94] – as Fokine called it – when performed on a scarf it is hard to see.

Fokine thought that the style of movement devised by Nijinsky was a dead-end, and in this he was probably correct. But he did praise the young choreographer for having the courage to stand still at moments when the music *seemed* to demand agitated movement,* and concluded that 'In general, Nijinsky's archaic, angular choreography suits Debussy's music.'[95] This was quite a concession. My opinion is that although 'suits' is hardly the *mot juste*, implying as it does a quality of matching or paralleling, whereas the angular movement is in sharp contrast to the fluid music, the ballet's magic lies precisely in this contrast, which Nijinsky's instinct, plus a little bit of luck, had marvellously led him to discover.

The first performance of Fokine's 'Daphnis' was to be on 5 June, a week after that of 'L'Après-midi', and the season's fourth programme, of which it was a part, would be given, like the other three, four times. The season would finish on 10 June. A few days before the première of Nijinsky's ballet, Fokine had already completed the choreography of his new work, all but the final dance of rejoicing. Once 'L'Après-midi' had been got over, there was still a week before 'Daphnis', of which three days were '*relâche*', that is, without performances.† There was plenty of time – or should have been – yet mysteries, scandals and an atmosphere of disaster preceded the first performance of this ballet whose score was destined to be one of the most famous symphonic compositions by a French composer in this century, and which would contain, besides, the last role created by Fokine for Nijinsky. By Fokine's own account, there was so little time left that Diaghilev not only tried to cancel the Ravel ballet altogether, but wrote to Vera asking her to persuade Michel that it was impossible to get it on.

My Vera tried to 'influence me' but was not able to do it. Instead I exploded. 'Are you on Diaghilev's side?' I shouted. 'You want me to drop the work which

* Such as at the confrontation of the Faun and the principal nymph, no doubt.
† 30 May, 2 and 4 June.

was my first dream of the new ballet, so that I may never see on the stage what I have created, so that I should watch my ballets staged by another choreographer?'

She replied: 'But you have only three days left, and there still are more than twenty pages of music to choreograph. Besides, the rest needs rehearsing. Wouldn't it be better not to present the ballet rather than show it in an unfinished condition?'

No doubt it was my ballet that was dear to Vera and not the interests of Diaghilev. But at that moment I looked upon her as a Diaghilev advocate. The more she tried to persuade me to agree to a postponement, the more firm was my determination to present the ballet as scheduled. I thought: *Twenty pages of the finale and in a very unusual tempo – 5/4 time nearly continuously. Yes, Vera has a point there!*

I had no idea how I would find a way out of this predicament, but I knew that somehow I would.

'Leave me alone,' I said to my weeping wife, and, almost in tears myself, sat down in front of Ravel's score.

To postpone was impossible. There was no time to sit and wait for an inspiration. There was no time either to console my wife, whom I had offended unjustly.

Soon it would be time to go to the rehearsal and to show the steps as fast as the dancers could learn.[96]

If Fokine was being exact, the conversation with his wife took place on 2 or 3 June.[97] If so, what had been happening during the last few days, apart from newspaper controversy, which should surely not have prevented the company working? And even if, for some reason, Fokine had only three days to complete the choreography of 'Daphnis', twenty pages of the score only represented a few minutes of time. For the man who had arranged 'Prince Igor' almost at one go, who had evolved certain groupings of 'Les Sylphides' just before the curtain went up, and who had sketched out 'Le Spectre de la rose' in a couple of rehearsals, this was child's play.

We can only suppose the trouble arose for one of the following reasons, or a combination of several of them. That Diaghilev, who for months had had doubts about the score for 'Daphnis' – though it was one of the greatest he ever commissioned – genuinely wished not to present it. That he wanted to save it for Nijinsky to arrange at a later date. That he was so elated by the interest 'L'Après-midi' had aroused that he hoped to substitute extra performances of that work. That he did not want to diminish the repercussions of Nijinsky's ballet by following up too soon with another work on a Greek subject which might give critics a chance to say 'Now, *that's* more like ancient Hellas!' That he did not want Nijinsky to have the fatigue of working on a new role so soon after 'L'Après-midi'. Or that he genuinely disliked Fokine's choreography or thought it was in too rough a state ever to be finished in time.

Whatever objections Diaghilev had, one would have thought the ambition to enrich the splendour of his Paris season by adding yet another new work – and one by a distinguished French composer – must have overcome them. It is hard to believe that his wish to cancel 'Daphnis' arose, as Fokine thought, from sheer malevolence. It would have been extremely awkward to announce a change of programme.

But Fokine's glorious talent was equal to the occasion.

When I arrived at the rehearsal I used a unique method of staging the end: I sent one bacchante across the stage, then another, then two at a time, then three together, then an entire group with interwoven arms reminiscent of Greek bas-reliefs. They rushed across the stage again, singly and in groups. I gave each a short but different combination of steps. Each dancer was required to learn only her own brief passage.

Having thus led everyone upstage from one wing to the other, I then had the remaining mass emerge from the downstage wing. The entire ensemble lurched together in a whirlpool of a general dance, and – the biggest part of the most difficult finale was ready! It only remained to stage a small passage for Daphnis and Chloë, a solo for Darkon, and the general end. It was clear that I would make it. I glanced at Diaghilev.

'Yes, you have managed it very quickly and well,' he said, obviously disappointed.[98]

Karsavina recalled:

There were many stumbling-blocks in the music of 'Daphnis and Chloë'. In sonority suave, noble and clear as a crystal spring, it had some nasty pitfalls for the interpreter. There was a dance in it for me in which the bars followed a capricious cadence of ever-changing rhythm. Fokine was too maddened, working against time, to give me much attention; on the morning of the performance the last act was not yet brought to an end. Ravel and I at the back of the stage went through – 1 2 3 – 1 2 3 4 5 – 1 2, till finally I could dismiss mathematics and follow the pattern of the music.[99]

The première, however, had been postponed till the 8th. This meant that, since there was a performance on the 7th, there could not be the regular evening *générale*, and that as the 9th was a *relâche* and the season ended on the 10th, 'Daphnis' could only be given twice. Ravel was annoyed.[100]

The worst of the nightmare was to come. Diaghilev decreed that 'Daphnis' should be given not as the middle ballet, which was traditional for a *création*, but first, before 'Schéhérazade' and 'Thamar'. He also arranged that the performance should start half an hour earlier than usual.[101]* Fokine felt sure that he intended the new work to be performed to an empty house.

That was too much. I decided to stop at nothing. In the auditorium, after the last

* This is difficult to believe. I have no way of checking whether Fokine's story is true.

rehearsal, I had a violent argument with Diaghilev. I used words which described his relationship with Nijinsky in plain terms. I shouted that the ballet company was turning from a fine art into a perverted degeneracy . . . and so forth and so forth.

At the end I added that, if the ballet were presented as a curtain raiser, I would come up on the stage and address the spectators and explain the situation. Let Diaghilev have me dragged off stage by force. It would be a beautiful expression of gratitude for my staging an entire repertoire of ballets for him![102]

And so the day of the première of this doomed ballet, commissioned four years before, came at last: and nobody was happy.

When I arrived at the theatre [wrote Fokine] I noticed that the scenery of 'Schéhérazade' was set up. Diaghilev had surrendered. 'Daphnis' would go on second. I was right when I claimed that the audience would pay no attention to the earlier curtain time, as can be substantiated by the following unusual episode.

I was standing on stage dressed in my tails with my opera hat in hand. From nervous tension I kept on toying with the hat, continually opening and closing it. The orchestra was playing the overture to 'Schéhérazade'. It is a long overture, consisting of the entire first part of the orchestral score. Only at its end do the dancers assume their positions on stage. I was talking to someone also dressed in a non-oriental costume. The property men were arranging the pillows and bringing out the oriental water-pipes. Suddenly the curtain went up. By accident someone had given the order. I looked into the auditorium and slowly walked across the stage through the harem to tell a stage-hand to bring down the curtain. I walked slowly, because there was no one in the auditorium. And it was to such an auditorium that Diaghilev had wished me to present the première of my new ballet.[103]*

It seems likely that Diaghilev had made mischief by alleging that Fokine had said something unpleasant about Nijinsky. Anyway, after Fokine's abuse of Diaghilev, any semblance of civilities was out of the question. The company was divided into Fokine and Nijinsky factions, and it did not make matters easier that Fokine had not spoken to his old friend Grigoriev, the *régisseur*, since Monte Carlo.[104] Nijinsky, with his gentle nature, would have longed to part on good terms with the man who had created so many great roles for him, but 'whispering tongues can poison truth . . . and youth is vain; And to be wroth with one we love Doth work like madness in the brain.'

While the performance was on [wrote Fokine], in the wings, and during the intermission behind the closed curtain, an uprising was brewing. Some dancers, followers of Nijinsky, said that I had insulted their director as well as the company; others, taking my side, spoke about the intrigues. I heard the words, 'We will not allow. . . .' As I later learned, I was to be presented with flowers and a gift, since this was the last day of my many years of work with the company. Part of the

---

* So, according to Fokine, there was no one in Paris in 1912 who wanted to see 'Schéhérazade' only two years after its creation. This seems incredible. Where was Valentine Gross?

company was protesting the presentation. It subsequently turned out that Nijinsky had forbidden the dancers to present anything to me.*

There was also another altercation during the intermission. I was surrounded by a group of angry, threatening dancers. Other dancers formed a ring closer around me, ready to come to my defence if necessary. At the critical moment, the overture ended and someone called out 'Curtain!' Both factions ran to the wings to take their places. I went to the first wing to direct the performance.

The curtain rose; the first performance of 'Daphnis and Chloë' began to a house filled to capacity. The ballet was performed perfectly, by the dancers loyal to me and by my enemies, alike. A whole herd of sheep walked across the stage. They were tended by shepherds and shepherdesses. The prayers, the offerings of flowers and wreaths as gifts to the nymphs, apotheotic dances, pastoral peace, harmony – how far off this was from the belligerent atmosphere and the narrowly averted riot just a few seconds before on the very same stage![105]

One reason that Diaghilev may have been averse to 'Daphnis', apart from the fact that Ravel would not allow the smallest cuts and apart from the expense of the chorus, was that it was the first work he had presented, excepting the old classical ballets and 'Le Pavillon d'Armide' – which was anyway a link with the old kind of ballet – that did not preserve the unities of time and place. The action did not take place within the time it took to perform the ballet, nor even within twenty-four hours, and the scene changed from a sacred grove to a pirates' camp and back again. Diaghilev liked a ballet to have as little story as possible,[106] preferring merely to create a mood or an atmosphere, and the story of 'Daphnis et Chloë', with its rival lovers, dance competition, onslaught of pirates, captivity of Chloë, her rescue by the god Pan and restoration to her beloved, must have seemed, in his eyes, too much like the old five-act ballets against which his whole movement in art was a reaction. Then, at least, in the old ballets the hero went hunting for his swan bride or broke through thickets of thorns to revive his sleeping beauty; while the feeble Daphnis lay in a swoon until the raped Chloë was returned to him by supernatural means. The middle scene was all Chloë's with the pirates, and so Karsavina would be sharing the honours unequally with Nijinsky.

One must also bear in mind how much bigger a work Fokine's Greek pastoral was than Nijinsky's, employing not only the whole company and an orchestra of at least eighty but also a chorus; it was in three scenes and lasted nearly an hour. Nijinsky's 'Faune' had eight dancers in one set for twelve minutes.

The setting by Bakst for the sacred grove is a flat green hollow in a rocky landscape striped by the verticals of innumerable cypresses. Among the

* I must again emphasize that I am merely quoting Fokine. Mme Romola Nijinsky put a question-mark against this sentence in the typescript, as if to show her surprise that anyone should believe Nijinsky acting so out of character.

trees to the left rear the statues of three nymphs, archaic in style, but with arms improbably extended before them, the rocks beneath them being strewn with garlands and other votive offerings. On a distant hill looms a little golden shrine against a cloudy sky.*

The music begins gently, building up a sustained chord while the stage remains empty. The flute plays an urgent yearning tune while the offstage chorus warble a wordless rocking song – like a lullaby. A procession of young men and maidens crosses from right to left, bringing offerings to the nymphs. The theme of Daphnis is heard on the horn, sounding rather like one in Messager's 'Deux Pigeons'. The music swells to a *crescendo* as the young people kneel before the shrine, then dies away. There follows a stately Religious Dance on strings, taken up by woodwind. Daphnis (Nijinsky) has a wig of fair bobbed hair, bound by a fillet, and a plain white pleated kilt. His entry, with goats, is followed by that of Chloë (Karsavina) in flowered draperies. They go off together. The religious dance tune swells and ebbs. Daphnis and Chloë come on to Daphnis's tune and prostrate themselves before the nymphs. A passage for solo violin leads to a more vigorous dance in 7/4 time (beginning on the trumpet), in which Daphnis is involved by some of the girls, somewhat to Chloë's resentment; then, with strings playing alone, the girls drag in Chloë. She arouses the attentions of Darkon, the cowherd (Bolm), who tries to kiss her, but Daphnis pushes him away. Parting the lovers the villagers propose a dance contest between Daphnis and Darkon, the prize to be a kiss from Chloë. Fast timpani and grunting bassoons introduce Darkon's grotesque dance, which Fokine has planned in a more archaic and angular manner than the rounded movements of the other dancers. His outlandish performance, punctuated by trombone *glissandi*, is mocked and imitated by the onlookers, who finally burst out laughing (*staccato* woodwind chords). Daphnis now dances, his arms wound round a staff which rests on his shoulders, to warbling flutes in slow 6/8 time, with harp *glissandi* followed by pauses to allow for Nijinsky's leaps. Daphnis is awarded his kiss to a plaintive oboe solo (Chloë's tune), and Darkon is chased away. The 'Two Pigeons' tune accompanies the embrace of the lovers, and the singers are heard again, humming. Now, to a flutter in the clarinets, enters Lyceion (Marguerite Frohman), a fast married lady from the local town, and she dances to a tripping version of the same tune on the flute over harp accompaniment. She drops veils, which Daphnis picks up with rising excitement as the music gets faster. Then to the same clarinet figure she runs off provocatively. A figure on the cor anglais announces the invasion of a band of pirates, who are seen pursuing the girls. Chloë flings herself before

---

* Above the sky is painted a border of tawny rocks and green bushes, which I have never been able to reconcile with any law of probability, perspective or design.

the altar of the nymphs but is carried off by a group of pirates, to the sound of furious *arpeggios* in strings and woodwind. Daphnis finds a sandal she has dropped and curses the nymphs (*fortissimo* crashes by the full orchestra). He faints. Night is falling: the yearning tune from the beginning is heard on flute, muted horn, then clarinet against *tremolo* chords on muted strings. The Nymphs come to life and dance three hieratic solos. Wind machine and general atmospherics in the orchestra. The Nymphs raise Daphnis and lead him to the rock, invoking Pan to horn-calls. The god appears to a slow *crescendo* over a subterranean bourdon on bass and horn, and Daphnis kneels before him as the curtain falls.

The keening wordless chorus accompanies the change of scene, and distant trumpet and horn calls announce the pirates' camp. To anyone who has seen Rubinstein's production of 'Helène de Sparte', which preceded the Russian season at the Châtelet, the orange rocks of the second scene must seem rather familiar (and indeed they are not unlike the rocks of 'Le Dieu bleu'): but this is not a populated landscape with houses and temples, as in 'Helène', but a bleak cove in which the tawny stones shoot up like gigantic teeth against a dull blue sky with dancing clouds, allowing a glimpse of the peacock-blue Aegean and the black and orange pirate ship moored in the secret bay. The Pirates' costumes are smocks, cloaks, blankets and ponchos of coarse material, stencilled with bold, barbaric patterns – spots, checks, stripes and zig-zags – in primary colours. The Pirates dance a wild measure to a marked rhythm in the basses, whirling woodwind scales and *staccato* trumpets; then, after a quieter passage with an oriental tune in the woodwind, the tempo quickens, the chorus pants passionately, there are three successive *crescendi* ending in crashes, and the men fall exhausted. Chloë is led in bound and Bryaxis, the Pirate Chief (Feodorov), orders her to dance. Harp *glissandi*, then sinister chords. Karsavina's solo is a dance of supplication to a pleading tune on the cor anglais, punctuated by attempts to escape, and coloured by heartbroken thoughts of Daphnis represented by his theme.

The music grows faster and Bryaxis roughly seizes Chloë and flings her over his shoulder (loud trumpet fanfare). Suddenly the scene grows dark and the music sinister, with strings *tremolando* and duets in the woodwind. A harp *glissando* heralds flashes of fire, and fantastic satyrs appear and dart among the Pirates, who are seized with panic and fight each other. An animated *staccato* phrase is tossed around among the trumpets and woodwind, faster and louder. After a brief pause, a tam-tam crashes, the earth appears to gape open and the great shadow of Pan is seen; the Pirates flee, and Chloë is left alone with a crown on her head, while the harp and strings play *glissandi* against sustained chords.

In Scene III we are back in the sacred grove. With the stage empty except for the prostrate figure of Daphnis, there is heard Ravel's sublime dawn music. 'The murmur of brooklets formed by the dew which has run down the rocks'[107] is represented by *arabesques* on woodwind, harp and celesta. Birds sing and shepherds pass by with their sheep. As the orchestral texture thickens, the chorus joins in this wordless hymn to the rising sun. Shepherds find Daphnis and shepherdesses restore Chloë to him (Daphnis's tune on flute and strings). He understands from her crown that Pan has saved her. The Old Shepherd (Cecchetti) explains that the god has done this in memory of his love for Syrinx. Daphnis and Chloë mime the courtship of Syrinx by Pan, which is brought to a successful conclusion by a solo on the reed pipe, represented by a tender flute solo. The plighting of the lovers' troth is followed by a frenzied Bacchanale (reminiscences of 'Schéhérazade') with kicking and tambourines. Finally the music switches into a frantic 5/4 time and the ballet ends in protracted frenzy.

To quote Robert Brussel, who had nothing but praise for Ravel's masterpiece, Fokine's choreography and the artists' interpretation in his next morning's article (which Calmette did not suppress): 'The work was received with acclamation. M. Fokine and his interpreters were recalled several times: but M.Maurice Ravel modestly avoided the ovations.'[108]

Fokine thought his ballet was 'a tremendous success'.[109] If there was a lack of clarity in the choreography, as one critic would complain,[110] this could doubtless have been sorted out, given time. This may have been increased by the use of some Beotian costumes from 'Narcisse', not suited to the new stage groupings of 'Daphnis'.[111] When the ballet was revived two years later, this fault would be put right by some new designs of Bakst.[112]

Saying farewell to no one [wrote Fokine], I left the theatre and my latest ballet, certain that I would never work again for the Diaghilev company and probably would never again see my ballet. My wife and I went somewhere to have supper. We sat in silence, unable to eat.

Very late at night we returned home to the Hôtel des Deux Mondes on the Avenue de l'Opéra. At the entrance to the hotel we were met by a group of waiting dancers. In their arms they held flowers and a vase.

'We, Mikhail Mikhailovitch, were not allowed to bid you farewell on the stage and present you this. So we came here.'

I was deeply moved. I looked. Who were these daring people? I noticed a group of my former pupils who were just recently graduated from my class at the Imperial Theatre School, several dancers from Moscow, several from the St Petersburg troupe. None of the Poles. Serge Grigoriev, my former pal and protégé, whose whole life was intertwined with my ballets, was also not among them. Thus, late at night in front of the hotel entrance, farewells were exchanged between me and a small group of dancers brave and loyal to me, dancers from the company to which for many years I had given an entire repertoire, and with whom I had worked in a friendly, enthusiastic and, at times, joyful manner to create the new Russian ballet. And so I left Diaghilev.[113]

Whether this sad parting took place after the first performance of 'Daphnis' or after the second, two nights later, is not clear. It may have been a small consolation to the great choreographer to watch Ida Rubinstein in the dance he arranged for her 'Salomé', which succeeded the Russian Ballet at the Châtelet. The company left for London without him.* After these first two performances of Fokine's ballet, Nijinsky was never to dance Daphnis again.†

The repertory for London was to be more classical than the Paris one. 'Carnaval', 'Les Sylphides', 'Le Spectre de la rose', 'Le Pavillon d'Armide' and eventually 'Le Lac des Cygnes' were to be included; and besides 'Prince Igor' and 'Schéhérazade' there would be the novelties of the two-year-old 'L'Oiseau de feu', the one-year-old 'Narcisse' and the new 'Thamar'. Bolm would be the first Prince Ivan seen in England, and Piltz would take Fokina's parts of the Beautiful Tsarevna and of Chiarina. Karsavina would be seen for the first time as Queen of the Swans. Pierre Vladimirov, one year's class junior to Nijinsky at the Imperial School, had joined the company in Paris and was to alternate with Nijinsky in 'Les Sylphides'. A first-rate classical dancer with a noble presence, he was a dancer of the old school, and there was no other role of Vaslav's he was capable of replacing him in,[114] just as Bolm was only able adequately to alternate with him in 'Schéhérazade'.

After the dramas of Paris, there was nothing really to worry about except whether the English would like 'Thamar' and 'Narcisse' or be shocked by their first hearing of Stravinsky's music in 'L'Oiseau de feu'. In Paris Vaslav felt he was on trial: dancing in London, where his audience was always loyal and appreciative, he found comparatively relaxing.[115]

The season was eagerly awaited by the Russians' English friends and by many others who had to be content with admiring them from afar. Charles Ricketts wrote to the poet Gordon Bottomley:

We both [meaning himself and Charles Shannon] look forward to the Russian dancers, they have been something like a passion during the past seasons; with them the lambent sense of beauty and desire for perfection is so great, that one watches the dancing of Schumann's 'Carnaval', in crinolines and toppers, before a purple curtain, with authentic tears in one's eyes, and with crumpled gloves which are split to ribbons at the end. The Chopin Valse, Opus 64, no. 2, passes into an indescribable twilight world of beauty and tender irony; the rapid portions are played *à la sordina*, to soundless dancing so rapid that it seems disembodied. All that the antique world thought and said about the famous male dancers who were seduced by Empresses, etc., is quite true. Nijinsky outclasses in passion, beauty, and

---

* Grigoriev is evidently mistaken in stating that Fokine left in the middle of the London season.
† I believe no one has commented before on this rather odd fact.

magnetism all that Karsavina can do, and she is a Muse, or several Muses in one, the Muse of Melancholy and of Caprice, capable of expressing tragedy and even voluptuous innocence; the wildness of chastity and the sting of desire; she is the perfect instrument upon which all emotion can be rendered. Nijinsky is a living flame, the son of Hermes, or Logi perhaps. One cannot imagine his mother – probably some ancient ballerina was answerable; but I prefer to believe in some sort of spontaneous nativity, at the most a passing cloud may have attracted some fantastic and capricious god.[116]

When, at Covent Garden, on Wednesday, 12 June, according to the critic of *The Times*, the curtain went up . . .

and disclosed the familiar view of two rococo sofas (red and cream this year instead of red and blue), the sole note of colour against the green of the curtains (green this year instead of purple), a thrill of joy went through the house. The world was once more a world of fantasy, where Pierrot might sob and wave distracted sleeves and Harlequin spin lightning *pirouettes* before the laughing eyes of Columbine, but where neither tears nor laughter were allowed to scratch more than the surface of our emotion. . . .[117]

The faithful and appreciative Richard Capell of the *Daily Mail* let out a paean. 'The Russians are back at Covent Garden. This means that the Londoner of 1912 is offered a series of pantomimic and choreographic spectacles of a complete and luxurious beauty such as was beyond the command of Nero and Sardanapalus. The three great arts of music, of painting and of dance contribute to these incomparable shows – all three in their most daring and sumptuous expression. . . .' He admitted to having seen 'Carnaval', in Paris and London, about thirty times, and to having been as fascinated on the previous night as ever. He complained of the new green curtain which quarrelled with Estrella's and Chiarina's blue skirts. He wrote of Karsavina in 'Thamar', 'lithe in miraculous lilac clothes and of a dreadful pallor – the victim of her own cruel voluptuousness'.[118]

After a postponement, 'L'Oiseau de feu' was first given on Tuesday, 18 June. Even the *Morning Post*, which had been stuffy in the past about the Russians, being, in a Tory way, suspicious and resentful of anything new, seemed amazed. 'One of the most remarkable things of its kind seen in England . . . perfect harmony . . . intensely pleasing . . . complete novelty . . . instrumental colouring as remarkable as that of the costumes. . . .'[119]

The Times thought the music 'extremely vivid and highly coloured, and although not very interesting melodically, [it] is bound together by firm, incisive, sharply defined rhythms. . . . Mme Karsavina surpassed herself in agility, grace and sensuous beauty of movement, although she had already taken part in two other ballets.'[120] The *Daily Express*, which had been incredulous a few days earlier that Thomas Beecham was actually going to conduct in person,[121] reported his saying Stravinsky's music was 'the most difficult he has hitherto wrestled with, not excluding "Elektra."!'[122] In the *Daily Mail* Richard Capell wrote that it was 'an enchantment and a jewel of fantasy'. While acclaiming its score as perhaps its chief attraction – 'a little masterpiece of brilliancy, wit and eccentric grace . . . something new in music', he found Karsavina 'incomparable'. 'When the Bird of Fire is captured by the bold Prince . . . there is a fluttering of white arms, a quiver of feathery crest and violated plumage, a bird's beating heart, a wild, would-be escape, with a woman's frightened refusal of caresses.'[123]

That evening brought a newcomer to the audience, a twenty-one-year-old red-head, trained as a research chemist, but with a passion for toy theatres and the theatre. He had already been converted to Russian Ballet by the visions of Karsavina, Pavlova and Mordkine in music-hall, and had in consequence decided to open a small bookshop at 75 Charing Cross Road. His first sight of the Diaghilev Ballet changed his life. His name was Cyril Beaumont.*

He wrote:

'Thamar' was a fine dramatic conception and the opening notes of Balakirev's score set the mood for the ballet. The air seemed suddenly heavy and the darkened theatre charged with foreboding. A half-wistful, half-tragic melody rose above a throbbing undercurrent of sound, a suggestion of a swiftly moving river coursing and churning over a rocky mountainside. Then the curtain rose slowly to reveal Bakst's setting – a great room with walls coloured mauve and purple, and slanting ceiling painted green. The lighting was subdued, save for the dull glow of a dying fire. The scene was dominated by a huge divan set against the far wall, and upon the divan reposed Karsavina in the role of Thamar, Queen of Georgia. Stretched at full length, she occasionally stirred uneasily in her sleep. A waiting-woman sat near her couch, other retainers stood in the shadows, their attitudes strained and watchful.

I can still recall the mood established by that scene. It was just as though some terrible menace had been halted, leaving behind a perceptible tenseness which suggested that the threat was about to be renewed. There was only that silent group of watchers; all was still save for the restless stirring of the sleeping woman. But the curiosity aroused was intense. What was about to happen?

Karsavina was a splendid Thamar, a dangerous, feline creature, as she stretched languorously on her couch, her pale brooding features made sinister by the dark eyebrows which crossed her forehead in a single line.[124]

Of Nijinsky in 'Les Sylphides' Beaumont wrote years later:

Until that evening I had regarded Mordkine, a splendidly virile dancer with a figure that would have delighted Pheidias, as the supreme male dancer. Henceforth,

---

* Mr Beaumont's description of 'Le Lac des Cygnes' was introduced into the last chapter.

Nijinsky was and still remains my ideal, and nothing I have seen during twenty-eight years of ballet-going has changed my opinion. . . . His *pas seul* in 'Les Sylphides' was outstanding. . . . In essence its especial quality was its suggestion of melody. When you watch a great violinist playing, it is not the violin alone that is a sounding-board for the precious tunes called forth by the bow gliding over the taut strings, the violinist's very body seems to respond to his music. Nijinsky's dancing in this ballet was imbued with the same quality. He danced not only with his limbs, but with his whole body, and the sequence of movements composing the dance flowed one into the other, now swift, now slow, now retarded. now increasing in speed, with a suggestion of spontaneity that had all the quality of melody. So I recall memories such as the billowing of his white silk sleeve as he curved and extended his arm; then that lovely movement when, on extending his leg in a *développé*, his hand swept gracefully from thigh to shin in a movement so graceful and so delicate as to suggest a caress; and then again the end of a *pirouette*, when he came smoothly and with increasing slowness to rest, like a spun wheel which had exhausted its momentum. I always think of Karsavina and Nijinsky as the perfect partners. . . . But these two were not mortals. It was the poet's shade visiting, in company with the spirit of his dead mistress, the moonlit grove which had once inspired his imperishable odes.[125]

But the new enthusiast, who as a historian of ballet was destined to add more books to its literature than any man ever before, did not lose his critical faculties. Admiring as he passionately did the music of Stravinsky for 'L'Oiseau de feu', the atmosphere of magic and the encounter of Karsavina and Bolm, he still thought that 'from the moment the gates closed upon the princesses, the ballet became stagy. The demons and Kastchei (even though played by Cecchetti), the dance with which the Bird of Fire forced the demons and their leader to dance until they fall exhausted, were all too obvious. It was good theatre, but the ballet was no longer a choreographic poem.'[126]

Nijinsky had met briefly in Paris Lady Ottoline Morrell, who was to become a warm and perceptive friend. With her passionate idealism, love of people, interest in their problems and longing to serve, she was the hostess, confidante and would-be 'mother' to most of the best writers and painters of her time, notably the Bloomsbury set. Many of these – even Lytton Strachey, who most depended on her affection – had an unfortunate habit of mocking her behind her back. She was tall and wore fantastic clothes, in which we have many records of her by Augustus John and Henry Lamb, so she was an outstanding figure and made a strange contrast to the short, stocky Nijinsky, so inconspicuous in his conventional street-clothes. But she had an eye to observe him and a heart to comprehend, and she has left one of the most understanding descriptions of him that we possess. 'Lytton and most of my friends,' she wrote, 'were such enthusiastic admirers of him, that I, from contrariness, had rather pooh-poohed him, but when I saw him dance I was completely converted, for I saw that anyone who so completely lost himself and embodied an idea was not just a good ballet dancer – he seemed no longer to be Nijinsky, but became the idea which he was representing.'[127]

Lady Ottoline was a Duke's daughter, but she felt rather shy as she drove down at Lady Ripon's invitation to meet Diaghilev and Nijinsky for luncheon at Coombe. She and Lady Ripon were both devoted to the arts, but the latter still had a foot firmly planted in the palatial, sporting, pleasure-loving world from which Lady Ottoline had broken free. Gwladys Ripon's was the 'smart artistic set', while the liberal Ottoline Morrell's friends were comparatively Bohemian. It was the difference between the brilliant and amusing Maurice Baring, with whom Lady Ottoline shared the car to Coombe, and D.H.Lawrence.

Lady Ottoline was placed next to Nijinsky at luncheon, and they got on well together from the start. 'He was very quiet and rather ugly,' she wrote, 'but one at once recognized that the flame of genius burned within him.' She invited him to Bedford Square.[128]

Lady Juliet Duff and Nijinsky were often put next to each other at meals and they managed to communicate although, as she recalled, her few words of Russian

always provoked shouts of laughter, which was one way of making the evening go off well. He literally knew only two words of English: one the name of a London thoroughfare, which he called 'Piccadill' and the other was 'Littler', by which he meant neither Prince nor yet Emile Littler (the theatrical impresario, not yet famous), but Little Tich, an eccentric dancer, celebrated in London and Paris. . . . He wore boots with exaggeratedly long feet, and one of his turns was to bang his forehead on the floor from an upright position. 'Littler' Nijinsky would say inquiringly each time he arrived in London, and if his idol were performing, seats would immediately be booked and he and Diaghilev would sit gazing spellbound; and one got just as much pleasure from watching their faces as from the antics of 'Littler' himself.[129]

There would be a chance for Vaslav to see Little Tich (and Pavlova) at a Command Performance at the Palace Theatre on 1 July, for it was an opera night at Covent Garden.

Duncan Grant, arriving at Lady Ottoline's full of expectation at meeting Nijinsky and hoping to see him leap over the tennis net, found him seated beside his hostess in her drawing-room and heard her asking, as he entered the room, '*Aimez-vous Platon?*' ('Do you like Plato?').[130]

Nijinsky and Bakst came one afternoon, Lady Ottoline recalled, 'when Duncan Grant and some others were playing tennis in Bedford Square garden – they were so entranced by the tall trees against the houses and the figures flitting about playing tennis that they exclaimed with delight: "*Quel décor!*" '131

For years I was puzzled by the house in the background of Bakst's design for Nijinsky's ballet 'Jeux', which was to be put on in the following year.132 It was not like a French country house, nor even, with its rows of small windows, like the Riviera Palace Hotel at Beausoleil: it had a prison-like plainness, in spite of the 'dreaming garden trees' which half concealed it. Suddenly, on reading Lady Ottoline's lines above for the third or fourth time, I realized that the architecture which had puzzled me was a version of that of a Bloomsbury square, a reminiscence of that summer afternoon in London. And perhaps even the subject of the ballet was suggested by the tennis-party.*

He was very nervous and highly-strung [wrote Lady Ottoline], and his guardian and jailer, Diaghilev, did not allow him to go out into society as it tired and upset him, and I was one of the few people that he was allowed to come and see, as at my house he could be quiet and only meet other artists. 'He is like a jockey,' I laughingly told Lytton, but really I grew very fond of the little figure with long, muscular neck and pale Kalmuk face, and the hands so expressive and nervous. He always seemed lost in the world outside, as if he looked on as a visitor from another world, although his powers of observation were intensely rapid. For on entering a room he would see all the pictures hanging in it before he had been there but a few minutes. It was not easy to talk to him as he didn't speak English and his French was very vague, but we managed to understand each other, and he was glad, I think, of real understanding and appreciation of his serious work. I was lamenting one day that I was not able to create anything myself and he quickly answered 'Oh, but you do create, Madame, for you help us young artists to create.'

There were at this time fantastic fables about him: that he was very debauched, that he had girdles of emeralds and diamonds given him by an Indian prince; but on the contrary, I found that he disliked any possessions or anything that hampered him or diverted him from his art. He was incessantly thinking out new ballets, new steps; also he was absorbed by the ideas of the old Russian myths and religions which he wanted to express in his ballets as he did in 'Le Sacre du printemps'. Such ballets as 'Le Spectre de la rose' did not interest him; he said it was *trop joli*

---

* In his interview with Emile Deflin for *Gil Blas*, 20 May 1913 (quoted on p. 290) Nijinsky is made to say that 'Jeux' originated from his watching tennis at Deauville in the previous summer. The Deauville season, of course, followed immediately after the London one. Perhaps, in giving to the press a French as opposed to an English origin for his ballet he was merely being diplomatic in the way that visitors to London were formerly supposed to express admiration for our police. In his *Diary*, Nijinsky wrote 'The story of this ballet is about three young men making love to each other. . . . "Jeux" is the life of which Diaghilev dreamed. He wanted to have two boys as lovers. . . . In the ballet, the two girls represent the two boys and the young man is Diaghilev' (pp. 147, 148). I do not take this very seriously. There is also a story that the idea for 'Jeux' came from watching moths round the lamp on an outdoor restaurant table in the Bois de Boulogne. Of course, every work of art has several origins.

and was rather annoyed when people admired it. He gave me a photograph of himself as he was in ordinary life and another to put by its side, as he was in 'Petrushka'.* He said that he made up in this part as an old traditional Russian figure – 'the mythical outcast in whom is concentrated the pathos and suffering of life, one who beats his hands against the walls, but always is cheated and despised and left outside alone.' Perhaps the same myth Dostoyevsky turned into *The Idiot*. Many years later I found in Charlie Chaplin something of the same intense poignancy as there was in Nijinsky.[133]

The worldly Jacques-Emile Blanche, with his flashes of 'impeccable bad taste',[134] was less sympathetic that July than Lady Ottoline to Nijinsky and the creative struggles which were disturbing him.

Chaliapine [he wrote] was one day entertaining Lady Ripon to lunch in the large hall of the Savoy, and I was among the guests. A waiter brought me a note from Diaghilev; I opened it and read: 'Dear friend, we are in the grill-room with Bakst. Vaslav would like to see you; he wants to talk to you about a mad scheme, but you know his fancies – he wants us to collaborate in a "games" libretto and Debussy is to do the score. Come as soon as you leave the table. We have a rehearsal at the theatre at four o'clock.' Vaslav was drawing on the tablecloth when I reached the grill-room. Diaghilev looked as if he were in one of his cross moods, he was biting his fingers; Bakst looked at the drawings on the cloth aghast – but Nijinsky understood only Russian, and it took me some time to find out what was in the wind. The 'cubist' ballet – which became 'Jeux' – was a game of tennis in a garden; but in no circumstances was it to have a romantic décor in the Bakst manner! There should be no *corps de ballet*, no ensembles, no variations, no *pas de deux*, only girls and boys in flannels, and rhythmic movements. A group at a certain stage was to depict a fountain, and the game of tennis (with licentious *motifs*) was to be interrupted by the crashing of an aeroplane. What a childish idea![135]

It is hard, in fact, to imagine a more appealing idea than for three dancers to represent a fountain. As for the aeroplane, it was not until 1926, in 'Roméo et Juliette' that one landed (off-stage) in a Diaghilev ballet!

'I sent the scheme to Debussy,' wrote Blanche, 'who replied: "No, it's idiotic and unmusical; I should not dream of writing a score." Diaghilev pleaded Debussy's cause; Nijinsky was obstinate, and threatened to dance no more in London. Debussy was again wired to; his fee was to be doubled.' When Blanche saw and heard 'Jeux' in the following year he thought it 'a bad score'![136]

Far from Diaghilev leading Nijinsky into virgin forests of experiment, it seems that in 1912, Nijinsky's creative ideas were already leaving Diaghilev behind. The lack of unison and understanding between them made them both nervous. And Diaghilev, Juliet Duff observed, 'was an odd mixture of

---

* These two small signed photographs were sold at Sotheby's on 18 July 1968 for £150 each.

ruthlessness and vulnerability. He could make others cry, but he could cry himself, and I remember a day at my mother's house on Kingston Hill when he had had a disagreement with Nijinsky, who had refused to come, and he sat in the garden with tears dripping down his face and would not be comforted.'[137]

What other society ladies, in the England of 1912, would a man have dared to cry in front of because his boy-friend had been unkind – apart from Lady Ottoline Morrell?

Off the stage [wrote Lady Juliet of Nijinsky], he seemed in those days like a backward child who sometimes surprises and delights one by sudden flashes of perception and wit. One day at luncheon at the Savoy, Diaghilev embarked on a somewhat lengthy anecdote. Nijinsky bore it with ill-concealed impatience and at the end of it looked up and said with firmness and finality '*Histoire longue mais pauvre*'. On another occasion we were discussing the likenesses of people to animals and birds. Nijinsky sat staring at my mother, who had a lovely but aquiline nose, and said '*Vous perroquet.*' My mother, readier than anyone I ever knew to laugh at herself [she was very tall, with a slight stoop], murmured to me 'It's lucky he didn't say "*Vous chameau*".'[138]*

This fine summer it was the rage to have Russian dancers perform at parties. During July Nijinsky danced with Karsavina and Zambelli at a party given by the Aga Khan at the Ritz;[139] Kyasht and Volinine danced for Lord and Lady Londesborough at St Dunstan's;[140] Pavlova was partnered by Novikov at Lady Michelham's at Strawberry Hill;[141] and Nijinsky and Karsavina danced at a party Lady Ripon gave for Queen Alexandra at Coombe.[142]

Pavlova was again at the Palace and Adeline Genée at the Coliseum. Genée had opened her season in May with a new ballet, 'La Camargo', for which she arranged the choreography and in which she impersonated the eighteenth-century dancer. The designer, C. Wilhelm, had taken great pains to collect genuine period furniture for the set: but he failed to find an authentic screen and had to improvise. Soon after his arrival in London Diaghilev had gone one evening with Eric Wolheim, his agent, to see the ballet – and immediately spotted the fake screen. But he was very impressed by Genée's dancing, and he took Karsavina and Nijinsky to the Coliseum for a matinée in July. 'There was not a comfortable seat left in the house, and they climbed up into the gallery where they were shown into three seats at the side from which they had to crane their necks to see the stage. But all their exertions were amply repaid when Genée appeared. Diaghilev was as excited as a child, and superlative praises poured from his lips.' He hoped to get the ballerina to dance in his next London season, but in this he was unsuccessful.[143]

---

* In Stravinsky's version of the story (*Memories*, pp. 36, 37) Nijinsky *does* say '*Vous chameau*'.

'Narcisse' was given on 9 July and received much more favourably than in Paris. *The Times* critic, although he found 'something irritating in the insensibility of Narcissus to the charms of the Nymphs who wreathe themselves around him and literally lay themselves at his feet' and thought the latter part degenerated 'from a ballet into a prolonged tableau', praised the groupings of the Beotian men and girls, the dances of the Bacchantes and 'the unsullied joy of the first dances of Narcissus, a joy which M.Nijinsky portrays perfectly'; these he thought 'as captivating as anything which the Russians have given us'. The new ballet, he noted, was very well received.[144]

The *Morning Post* opined that Nijinsky had 'not before displayed so wide a command of graceful action as distinct from mere physical exercise'.[145] The *Daily Express* found 'Narcisse' 'an immediate and pronounced success', judging that Nijinsky scored 'a triumph'.[146] In the *Daily Mail* Richard Capell wrote of 'a glimpse of the antique world, a Theocritan idyll made visible . . .' and considered that 'M.Nijinsky's role is the most elaborate of those in which he has been seen here and the performance is curious and wonderful. But he seemed less a simple narcissus than an odd orchid. . . .'[147] The critic of the *Sunday Times* said of Nijinsky's performance: 'Every pose, every movement, every gesture was instinct with sexless insensibility and vacuous complacency, and you feel the punishment fits the crime.'[148]

Cyril Beaumont, like everyone else, was struck by Bronislava Nijinska's Bacchante and disliked the artificial flower that rose from the pool at the end. He admired Nijinsky's final pose, when 'crouched by the edge of the pool, he gazed spellbound at his own image, bending down with infinite grace closer and closer to the water, until he disappeared beneath its surface'.[149]

Charles Ricketts wrote his impressions of the ballet to two different friends. To one: 'I confess that the Russian Ballet, with its perfection of dancing and beauty of setting, haunts and enchants me like nothing else. Karsavina as Echo has achieved a new triumph of poetic insight of a touching and lovely order. Her Thamar is also in its way a triumph.'[150] To another:

Karsavina surpassed herself as Echo in 'Narcisse'. She creeps on to the stage, enamoured of Narcisse, and approaches silently, hiding behind trees; she dances in a trance and sinks at Nijinsky's feet at the end of each musical phrase. He leaps like a faun, with such rare clothing on that Duchesses had to be led out of the audience, blinded with emotion, and with their diamond tiaras all awry. On the second performance he wore long knickerbockers, it seems at the request – not of the censor – but of the Russian Embassy.[151]

On 15 July, in the presence of her mother and brother, Bronislava Nijinska was married to the dancer Alexander Kotchetovsky at the Russian Orthodox Church in Buckingham Palace Road. Diaghilev, *in loco parentis*, gave her away and it was he who bought the ring set with sapphires and brilliants, which he declared firmly was 'to wed her to her art' – rather than to Kotchetovsky. (She had to sell it during the Russian Revolution.)[152]

It is interesting that the English should have felt that in Narcissus Nijinsky had a more extended and demanding role than any other they had seen him in. Yet, if they had not so far been allowed to undergo 'Petrushka', news of this masterpiece had filtered across the Channel in the form of an enthusiastic article with effective illustrations in the July number of the maga-

*Nijinsky and Karsavina
in 'Petrushka'.
Drawing by George Banks,
from 'Rhythm'.*

zine *Rhythm*, edited by Middleton Murry and Katherine Mansfield.[153] The gifted young Frenchman, Henry Gaudier, who added to his own name that of his twenty-year-older, eccentric and tormented woman friend, Sophie Brzeska, had contributed some drawings to an earlier number of *Rhythm* – before quarrelling with Murry and Mansfield;[154] and he made sculptures this summer both of Nijinsky alone* and of Karsavina and Bolm in 'L'Oiseau de feu'.† (For the latter he was paid the highest price he ever received in his lifetime, £20.)[155] It is hard to resist the conviction that could

* I have not been able to trace this statue, but Mr Ede, the authority on Gaudier, thinks that it was probably the figure of an imagined dancer to which the sculptor gave the name 'Nijinsky'.
† One casting of this is in the collection of Lord Harewood. I do not know if another exists.

Nijinsky have been brought together with this lonely, fanatical and hungry pair he might have been united with them in an odd, practicable friendship – but perhaps the Savoy Hotel would have come between them.

The young poet Rupert Brooke fell in love with the Russian Ballet that summer. A few months later he was to write of the company: 'They, if anything can, redeem our civilization. I'd give everything to be a ballet-designer.'[156]

It should have been a happy time for Nijinsky. Every night he danced was a triumph. Ahead lay an easy August, with very intermittent performances of 'Les Sylphides', 'Le Festin', 'Carnaval' and 'Le Spectre' at Deauville;* a visit to Bayreuth, where with Diaghilev and Stravinsky he would hear 'Parsifal',[157] and then a Venetian September.[158] But he was battling in his mind to give birth to a new language of the dance and the labour-pains made him irritable.

* Five performances between 6 and 22 August.

CHAPTER SIX

1912-1913

Autumn 1912–September 1913

It has been observed in an earlier chapter that as a boy Nijinsky never had friends.[1] He was by nature a solitary creature and at school circumstances made him an outsider. In 1908, graduating suddenly from boyhood to manhood, he had been, as it were, adopted by Prince Lvov and then by Diaghilev. This kind of relationship with an older man who gave him confidence and a sense of security was obviously ideal for someone of his temperament; and the worst that could be said of it was that the faun might occasionally need to escape briefly from the dominant personality of his tamer, and scamper off into the woods. He might dream from time to time of another kind of relationship, of a flirtation or love affair with a pretty girl. Prettiness, however, was not enough: sympathy was essential, and this included total absorption in the problems of the art of ballet.[2] What girl could feel the holiness of the vocation of a dancer and choreographer enough to give Nijinsky the dedicated understanding he was bound to need and demand? Half measures were worse than nothing.

From the other members of the Russian Ballet he felt utterly removed. They were his colleagues and the raw materials of his art. They worked hard, though nothing like as hard as he did;* and some were even a little intelligent and well educated. Most of the girls were pretty, but most had lovers. Anyway, his closeness to Diaghilev put a distance between him and them. A friendship with one of the men seemed as impossible – however much the rakish Bourman might push himself forward, presuming on schoolday familiarity – as an affair with one of the women.

There was Karsavina, his partner. In a passage of the *Diary* written in

---

* Mr Vladimirov told me that he had seen Nijinsky doing a *barre* after evening performances. He found this beneficial.

1918 there would be something about a secret passion for Karsavina.[3] This I do not take seriously, and if it existed even for a few weeks or days the ballerina was never aware of it – and she had been adored by enough men to be alert to the signs of infatuation.[4] For the truth is that Karsavina was unattainable. Just as he felt the rest of the company, judged not from a snobbish point of view but from that of high seriousness, to be utterly below him, so did Karsavina, an artist as dedicated as himself, seem utterly above. To find in a fellow-dancer such natural distinction, such nobility of manner and mind, was as disconcerting as to find the opposite. Then, she was an intellectual, and even if she did not want to create ballets her grasp of ideas was quicker than his own. Finally there was her lustrous beauty. She was loved not only by princes but by poets. In private life he could not compete. Only the dance could unite them.

His sister Bronia was the nearest to a friend that he had ever had. His mother understood and loved him and so did Diaghilev. Bronia alone understood the workings of his choreographic mind and so was closest to his secret heart. They were very much alike in their thoughts about ballet and their attitude to it, conscious of their duty and of a kind of royal prerogative. It was a little awkward that Bronia, with her more downright masculine intelligence, should be the younger and a woman. It was also awkward that Diaghilev's friendship for Nijinsky had removed the latter from daily contact with his sister. They worked together at class and rehearsal, but Bronia's marriage to Kotchetovsky raised another barrier between them.[5] They were not as close as they had been. If Bronia went away Diaghilev would be his only friend.

Now in the winter of 1912–13 something would happen to alter the situation.

The season at Deauville and the summer holiday over, Diaghilev made a flying trip to Paris to persuade Debussy to prolong the ending of 'Jeux'.[6] Debussy had already complained in a letter to Jacques Durand on 12 September that his score had to make a rather improper situation acceptable. But, as he said, 'in ballet, immorality escapes through the dancers' legs and ends in a *pirouette*.' The action must have been plotted in some detail by Diaghilev and Nijinsky by then; and we can imagine Diaghilev being more interested in the 'literary' aspect of the theme – sporting and amorous – which would give Paris '*un frisson nouveau*' and Nijinsky caring most for the ballet's abstract and sculptural side. Now they had decided that the ballet's story must be cyclical and end where it began, with another ball bouncing on to the stage to break up the children's forbidden games: so Debussy was asked on 31 October to reintroduce at the end the chords of the opening Prelude. This he did with a subtle variation.

The German tour opened at the Stadttheater, Cologne, on 30 October. (And, incidentally, the first month of this tour was the only one during which Grigoriev was separated from the Diaghilev Ballet in its twenty years existence: back in Petersburg he could not make up his mind to resign from the Mariinsky to devote himself to Diaghilev all the year round. He had been continually granted extensions of leave, but the time of reckoning had come. After a period of heart-searching he rejoined the Diaghilev company.[7]) Following their visits to Frankfurt and Munich, the company arrived in Berlin in November. The Berlin season opened on 11 December with the first performance of 'L'Après-midi d'un faune'. Diaghilev, as ever mindful of publicity, cabled Astruc.

Diaghilev in Berlin to Astruc in Paris, 12.12.12

Yesterday triumphant opening at New Royal Opera House. Faune encored. Ten calls. No protests. All Berlin present. Strauss, Hofmannsthal, Reinhardt, Nikisch, the whole Secession group, King of Portugal, ambassadors and court. Wreaths and flowers for Nijinsky. Press enthusiastic. Long article Hofmannsthal in Tageblatt. Emperor, Empress and Princes coming to ballet Sunday. Had long talk with Emperor who was delighted and thanked the company. Huge success.[8]

Gunsbourg was in Paris at the Hôtel Majestic, Avenue Kléber, and active on the company's behalf. On 15 December he telegraphed to London to engage an English girl, Hilda Bewicke, who had presumably been auditioned in London during the summer.[9] She was the first of a number of English dancers who worked for Diaghilev.

Diaghilev was becoming extremely concerned – though he kept it to himself – about the difficulties Stravinsky's score for 'Le Sacre du printemps' would present when Nijinsky got down to composing his choreography. While they were in Berlin in November he had taken the opportunity of re-visiting, with Nijinsky, the Dalcroze Academy at Hellerau, a two hours' journey away. Dalcroze had no intention of training dancers: his pupils were taught to analyse music by a new system of bodily movement. Among them was an intelligent Russo-Polish girl of twenty called Miriam Ramberg, who had previously studied ballet under Slovatsky of the Warsaw Opera. The pupils of Dalcroze despised what they considered the frivolous and pretty-pretty art of ballet, making up satirical rhymes about it and doing comic imitations of ballerinas.[10] Dalcroze himself found that Ramberg, because of her ballet training, tended to give a performance when doing her rhythmical exercises. '*Vous êtes trop extérieure,*' he told her.

None of the Dalcroze students, not even Ramberg, was at all impressed when this heavy imposing Russian gentleman with his small, high-cheek-boned companion appeared in their class: they did not know who they were.

Diaghilev was hoping to engage someone to help Nijinsky with the music of 'Le Sacre', and his eye fell on the diminutive Ramberg, probably because she moved more like a dancer than the others. No doubt he talked to Jaques-Dalcroze about her character and background, and satisfied himself that she was likely to take her work seriously rather than indulge in flirtation and frivolity. Apart from speaking Polish, Russian, German, French and a little English, Ramberg was a very well-educated woman. She had stayed in Moscow and Petersburg with relations and knew the masterpieces of Russian literature.

A few days later Dalcroze told Ramberg of Diaghilev's interest in her. She was packed off to Berlin, where a ticket for the ballet awaited her, and an invitation to have supper afterwards with Diaghilev and Nijinsky. So her first sight of the Russian Ballet was at the Kroll Opera House. She saw in that first programme 'Cléopâtre' with Nelidova, barely noticed Nijinsky in the *pas de deux*, but loved the Bakst décor. She next saw Nijinsky in 'L'Après-midi d'un faune' and was puzzled by the dichotomy between music and movement. 'Carnaval' with Kyasht and Nijinsky ravished her, and she was moved by the Polovtsian Dances from 'Prince Igor'. At supper, being (in her own phrase) 'badly brought-up', when Diaghilev asked her opinion she dared to criticize. 'Why don't the women who escort Cleopatra when she is carried on in her litter walk on the beat of the music?' she asked. 'They just slouch on.' It had not in fact been Fokine's intention that these supers should march in time, but Diaghilev appeared to agree with her. 'Yes, they are just like cooks,' he said. Nijinsky sat silent as she complained that his choreography only coincided in two or three places with the music of 'L'Après-midi'. She could not at that time see the point of the extreme contrast between the impressionistic music and the abstract dancing in this work which she would come later to admire so passionately. In spite of her independent attitude, or perhaps because of it, Diaghilev decided in consultation with Nijinsky that she would be useful, and a few days later she heard that she was engaged.

Ramberg joined the Russian Ballet in Budapest at Christmas 1912, and when the new year of 1913 began, she was with them in Vienna. Her first duty was to give Dalcroze classes to the company, but the dancers, being overworked, tended to drop out of these; and Grigoriev suggested to Diaghilev that she should merely be asked to help individual dancers analyse and learn their roles. This was agreed.

So, as the crucial year of Nijinsky's life began, he had a new colleague.

It is extraordinary that within a few days of meeting Ramberg, who grew to understand him very well and who, if given the chance, might have become his wife, Nijinsky also came into the orbit of another young woman

Nijinsky in class.
Caricature by Jean Cocteau.

who actually did marry him. Romola de Pulszky, who had so admired Nijinsky on the Ballet's previous visit to Budapest, belonged to a distinguished Polish family, which emigrated to Hungary early in the eighteenth century. Her great-grandfather had taken a leading part under Kossuth in the Hungarian revolt against the Austrians in 1848. He represented Kossuth in England, and after the suppression of the rebellion remained in exile there; so that Romola's father was born at Highgate. A great-great-uncle of Romola's was Count Morice Benyovsky, a celebrated traveller and first reigning Prince of Madagascar. Rómola's father Károly, a godson of Garibaldi, was one of several brothers eminent in the world of politics, art and science. He married Emilia Markus, the first actress in Hungary, whom Rostand considered the equal of Bernhardt and Duse as Roxane in 'Cyrano'. The seventh child of a button manufacturer, at thirteen she had sat on the knee of Liszt; at fourteen she had entered the Academy of Dramatic Arts; and at sixteen she had played Juliet. She was known as the 'Blonde Wonder' and was considered by many to be the greatest actress of all time.[11]

269

With Prince Esterhazy, Károly de Pulszky founded the National Gallery of Hungary and became its Director. Romola, the second daughter, was born in his flat there in 1891. From childhood she was interested in art. When her father told her stories they were not about fairies but about the great painters of the Renaissance, and she grew up with the ambition to be the Vasari of her day. But Károly de Pulszky fell victim to a political plot against his brother August, the Minister of Justice, and was accused of buying fake pictures in Italy. He went to Australia; and it was in Brisbane that he shot himself in 1899 at the age of forty-six. Emilia Markus married again, her second husband Oskar Pardany, a Jew, being converted to Christianity for the occasion, with Romola as his godmother. Romola had two English governesses and also studied at the Lycée Fénelon in Paris. With the second governess, Miss Mabel Johnson, she spent over a year in England, mostly at Eastbourne: but they were staying at Southsea in August, 1909, when the Tsar reviewed the British Fleet. Both Romola and her sister Tessa studied acting, Romola with Réjane and Le Bargy. Tessa appeared at the Burgtheater in Vienna, but gave up the stage on marrying the Danish tenor Erik Schmedes. Romola also had ballet lessons from Guerra at the Budapest Opera.[12] She was pretty, with fair hair, very white complexion and bright Sèvres-blue eyes.

Since the Russians' last week-long visit to Budapest Romola had seen them in Paris, and admired them so much that she longed in some way to be associated with them. She saw the new form of Russian ballet as a second Renaissance and wondered if she could be its chronicler. Some of the company had been entertained at her mother's house in February and Romola had made friends with Maestro Cecchetti and with Bolm: but she had met neither Diaghilev nor Nijinsky. Romola had 'a genuine admiration' for Maestro Cecchetti, she wrote years later, 'but I had to use him in order to achieve my purpose – to become permanently attached to the Ballet.'[13] It was not Cecchetti, however, who first introduced Nijinsky to Romola, but a lady journalist.

At rehearsals [wrote Romola], I always hid in some dark corner of the theatre, fearing that if I attracted attention I might be sent away. On this occasion I happened to be sitting in the back of the house with a newspaper-woman. . . . She raved on and on about Nijinsky. Impatiently I interrupted her paeans by saying, 'If you really know this "wonder" so well, then please introduce me to him at once.' We went over to the group of men where Nijinsky was conversing with Diaghilev. It was an exciting moment. One would never have thought that this unassuming young man, with his Tartar face and the appearance of a Japanese student in his badly fitting European clothes, was the same being as the marvellous apparition the whole world had learned to admire. The introduction actually

51 Nijinsky in 'L'Après-midi d'un faune'. Photograph by Bert.

54 Nijinsky, Lydia Nelidova and five of the other six Nymphs in 'L'Après-midi d'un faune'. The missing Nymph is Bronislava Nijinska. Photograph by Baron de Meyer as laid out for *Comoedia Illustré*.
55 Nijinsky in 'Daphnis et Chloë'. Painting by Valentine Gross. I have never seen a photograph of Nijinsky as Daphnis. Probably none was taken.

52 *and* 53 (*opposite*) Nijinsky in 'L'Après-midi d'un faune'. Photographs by Baron de Meyer. The lower photograph and a drawing by Valentine Gross are evidence of Nijinsky's final gesture, which was thought so shocking, and later suppressed.

56–61 Tamara Karsavina, Ludmilla Schollar and Nijinsky in 'Jeux'.
Pastels by Valentine Gross.

62–65 Tamara Karsavina, Ludmilla Schollar and Nijinsky in 'Jeux'.
Photographs by Gerschel.

66–68 Three male dancers in 'Le Sacre du printemps'.

69 Six female dancers in 'Le Sacre du printemps', (*left to right*) Julitska, Ramberg (M
Rambert), Jejerska, Boni, Boniecka, Faithful. Plates 66–69 are four of the only five exis
photographs of Nijinsky's 'Sacre'. The top ones were taken against the same wallpaper
the bottom one, but it has been touched out. The actual costumes, however, have survi
and most are in the collection of the Museum of Theatre Arts, London.

70 *and* 71 Groups from 'Le Sacre du printemps',
Act I (*above*) and Act II (*below*).
Pastels by Valentine Gross.

72 Josefina Kovalevska, Miriam
Ramberg (Marie Rambert),
Ekaterina Oblokova and Sophie
Pflanz on the *Avon*.

73 The first-class dining saloon on
the *Avon*.

occurred. In the ensuing conversation there was a bit of confusion, which was greatly aided by the diversity of languages spoken. Nijinsky misunderstood my identity, and thought I was the *prima ballerina* of the Hungarian Opera, whose name had been brought into conversation at that moment . . . it was probably due to that error on his part that he greeted me with so charming and respectful a bow. For many, many times after that first introduction I was introduced to him, and never was there more than a polite, fleeting acknowledgement and never by any chance did he recognize me.[14]

Compared with the professional dancers who had begun training at ten years old Romola could not dance at all, so if she was to join the company it was a question either of bribing Cecchetti or of bringing social pressure to bear on Diaghilev, who naturally liked to keep on good terms with influential people in every country. When the Ballet left for Vienna, Romola followed them. Through her godfather, who was head of the Imperial Family's Archives, and her brother-in-law Schmedes, she obtained a pass which allowed her access to the Opera House at all times.

The Vienna season was a brilliant one, but it was not without its troubles for Diaghilev. On the one hand Karsavina, who had rejoined the company in Budapest, was there to add her aura to the Ballet's radiance, and scored a triumph in 'Thamar':[15] on the other hand the Opera orchestra pronounced the music of 'Petrushka' to be '*Schweinerei*' and at first refused to play it. When the violinists threw down their bows at a rehearsal Diaghilev went to the orchestra pit and said, 'Gentlemen, in ten years you will be proud to have been the first Austrians to play Stravinsky's music.' When they did play it – only twice – they tried to sabotage it. Thus was Stravinsky, who was present at rehearsals, snubbed in the city of Mozart.[16] Then, Nijinsky was at his most incredible in the Blue-bird *pas de deux* from Tchaikovsky's 'La Belle au bois dormant', which had been called 'L'Oiseau de feu' when included in 'Le Festin' four years before, but which was now billed as 'La Princesse enchantée';[17] on the other hand, 'L'Après-midi d'un faune' was not appreciated in Vienna.[18] Most of the critics were lavish in praise of the Russian Ballet, but Ludwig Karpath, the music critic, had reservations.[19]

Nevertheless, it was Karpath whom Romola knew best and it was him she persuaded to ask Diaghilev for an interview and to take her along. It must have been embarrassing for the kind fat old critic to bother Diaghilev after criticizing his company adversely, but Romola had once done him a service and he could not resist her pressure.

Romola wrote:

I was neither awed nor embarrassed when we went to see Diaghilev. I was determined to obtain my point, and, when my mind was definitely set, nothing and nobody mattered. Diaghilev received us in the middle of the afternoon, in an empty public reception-room at the Hôtel Bristol. As soon as he entered we felt his dominating personality. We expected a cold, a resentful reception. But Diaghilev, who with every gesture and word expressed at the same time the superiority of an emperor and an irresistible charm, confused both Karpath and myself by the warm interest he took in our requests. He made us feel absolutely that nothing interested him more than my intention to be a dancer. . . . Apparently a young society girl had come to the great artistic organizer with a request. In reality, two powerful enemies had crossed swords for the first time. Diaghilev held the thing I most wanted – Nijinsky.* And he sensed at once, with his fine instincts, however subconsciously, the approaching danger. I just as quickly realized that he wished to read my mind. . . .

'I think Bolm is wrong in advising you to go to the Wiesenthals' [Diaghilev told her]. One thought seemed to follow the other, aloud. 'The ideal thing for you would be to become a pupil of the Imperial Dancing School in St Petersburg. But of course it is not feasible, even with the greatest possible pull, for you are not a Russian, and you are long past the required age. . . . I think the best thing for you to do would be to take private lessons from Fokine in St Petersburg.'

With apparent joy I jumped at the idea.

'I would love it.' I misled him deliberately. 'It has always been my dream to go to Russia.'

He then asked my impressions of the different ballets and the artists of his company. My answers must have been correct. He smiled approvingly. During all this time I felt that gradually I was falling under his spell. I tried to fight against his almost hypnotic power. With a desperate effort I began to rave about Bolm as a man, not as an artist, like any little 'flapper' would. And then Diaghilev, with unexpected strategy, turned and asked, 'What about Nijinsky?'

Without hesitation I answered, 'Oh, Nijinsky is a genius. As an artist he is incomparable. But somehow Bolm is more human to me' – and I continued my extravagances about Bolm. By this time he was convinced of my good faith, and then said the fatal words:

'I will speak to Maestro Cecchetti. He has taught all our greatest artists. I am sure he will take you as a special, private pupil. This way you will have not only a marvellous teacher, but also the possibility of travelling with us and closely studying our work.'

I thanked him gratefully, and so our interview ended. I had won my first battle. I could scarcely believe I had succeeded in fooling such an inconceivably clever man as Diaghilev.

The same evening, when I went backstage, Maestro greeted me from afar with enthusiastic gestures and loud shouts of Italian joy. 'Sergei Pavlovitch has decided that you should study with me. I am overjoyed, *bambina*. . . .' He embraced me and kissed me on both cheeks. He always liked to kiss young girls. . . . We finally

---

* As Mme Romola Nijinsky has always insisted to me that in pursuing Nijinsky she had no idea of the possibility of marrying him, the passages in her life of her husband (published in 1933) which imply the opposite must be put down to romantic exaggeration.

settled when and how I would start to study. I was to join them on 4 February in London.[20]

On their way to London the company gave two performances at Prague, two at Leipzig and one in Dresden. Diaghilev made a flying trip to Petersburg.[21] From Dresden on 27 January Nijinsky telegraphed to Astruc asking for a stage plan of the new Théâtre des Champs-Elysées,[22] which was to be opened with a production of Berlioz's 'Benvenuto Cellini' on 31 March. In London rehearsals took place on the stage of the Aldwych Theatre, lent

Tamara Karsavina in 'Carnaval'.
Drawing by August Macke.

by Beecham,[23] and it was here that Nijinsky got down to work on the choreography of 'Le Sacre du printemps'.*

'Petrushka' was shown to the English for the first time on the opening night at Covent Garden. Cyril Beaumont noticed 'the startled expressions on the faces of the audience' and was himself surprised by Stravinsky's music

* Grigoriev writes: 'After finishing our season in Vienna, and visiting one or two German towns on the way, we arrived in London six weeks before we were due to start performing' (p. 89). As the Vienna season ended on 16 January and was followed by performances at Leipzig and Dresden, this is of course inaccurate – and as Nijinsky was still in Dresden on 27 January there would have been less than a week before the London opening on 4 February.

'which then sounded incredibly daring and uncouth': but he was 'soon captivated'. He admired the way that Nijinsky, when he was supported on the iron stand inside the booth, 'succeeded in investing the movements of his legs with a looseness suggesting that foot, leg and thigh were threaded on a string attached to the hip'. There was 'a curiously fitful quality in his movements, his limbs spasmodically leapt or twisted or stamped like the reflex actions of limbs whose muscles have been subjected to an electric current'. Beaumont's description of Nijinsky's make-up is interesting.

His features were made up a kind of putty colour, presumably a suggestion of wood; his nose was built up to have a thicker base; his eyebrows were painted out and replaced by a wavy line set half an inch higher; his lips were compressed together; his eyes seemed devoid of lid and socket, and suggested a pair of boot-buttons or two blobs of black paint; there was a little red on his cheeks. His features were formed into a sad and unhappy mask, an expression which remained constant throughout the ballet.[24]

The Times found the work 'refreshingly new and refreshingly Russian';[25] and Stravinsky, who had taken a curtain-call after the performance, told the *Daily Mail* that 'Petrushka' and 'Firebird' had never been better played in France, Austria, Germany or Hungary than by Thomas Beecham's orchestra.[26]

The young writer Osbert Sitwell had fallen under the spell of the Russian Ballet and thought Stravinsky, Diaghilev, Karsavina, Fokine and Nijinsky all partook of the quality of genius. 'The part of Petrushka,' he wrote, 'showed Nijinsky to be a master of mime, gesture, drama. . . .' Looking back later, he saw Fokine's work as a portent. 'This ballet was, in its scope as a work of art, universal; it presented the European contemporary generation with a prophetic and dramatized version of the fate reserved for it, in the same way that the legend of the Minotaur had once summed up, though after the event and not before it, the fate of several generations of Greek youths and maidens.'[27]

On 11 February – a day on which was announced the death of Captain Scott* in the Antarctic – Cyril Beaumont saw for the first time Nijinsky and Karsavina dance the Blue-bird *pas de deux*, which had been given so many names by Diaghilev, and was now 'L'Oiseau et le prince'; and he was dazzled by the way in which, during the *diagonale* of the coda, 'he seemed not to touch the ground but to glide forward on air, his feet flashing to and fro in the brilliance of his *brisés* and *cabrioles*.'[28]

'L'Après-midi d'un faune' had its first English performance on 11 February, and, although there were a few hisses, was so warmly received by

---

* Whose widow, then Lady Kennet, introduced me to Mme Karsavina in 1947.

the majority that, as in Paris and Berlin, it was repeated. The critic of *The Times* considered the work seriously and at some length, deemed Nijinsky's 'stiff poses, and particularly his last action when he lies down to dream beside the scarf . . . extraordinarily expressive' and paid the budding choreographer a fine compliment in his concluding words: 'We realized again how apparently inexhaustible are the resources of the ballet, for we had been given a new phase of its art which appealed through quite different channels from those with which anything else in the repertory has been concerned.'[29] Richard Capell wrote in the *Daily Mail*:

The miracle of the thing lies with Nijinsky – the fabulous Nijinsky, the peerless dancer, who as the faun does no dancing. The two inspirations of his subtle and unapproached miming in this piece would appear to have been the Greek pottery at the British Museum and a study of the gambols of chamois or goat. He wears a mottled or rather piebald skin – rather like the coat of a young calf; it is admirable. His movements are at once abrupt and stealthy. He leaps once. This one leap is a surprise and an illumination. It is a full evocation of a being half-boy, half-brute, consummate and also uncanny.[30]

On 19 February Queen Alexandra saw 'L'Après-midi', which was again encored.[31] On the 21st the *Daily Mail* reported that

M.Nijinsky, having telegraphed to M.Debussy, the composer, news of the success at Covent Garden of the new ballet 'The Afternoon of a Faun' – which is now being regularly encored – has had the following telegraphed reply: 'Thanks, my dear Nijinsky, for having sent me that telegram, whose words flame like the gold of victorious trumpets! Thanks to your peculiar genius for gesture and rhythm the arabesques of my "Prélude à l'Après-midi d'un faune" have been endowed with a new charm. Congratulate the English on having understood it.'[32]

One suspects that Diaghilev had a hand in this telegraphic exchange.

The Russian Ballet already had one English dancer, Hilda Bewicke. Now some vacancies had to be filled and Tarasov, a young man who had appeared with Diaghilev in a previous season but was now dancing with the Koslov troupe at the Coliseum, arranged to bring some of his colleagues to be auditioned. An English girl, Hilda Munnings, recorded the occasion.[33]

It was arranged that four of us girls, with Zverev and Tarasov, should be given an audition to show our ability, if any, at the awful hour of ten o'clock on a Monday morning. And so I came to the greatest ordeal of my life up-to-date. We changed into practice dress, and stupidly put on brand new ballet shoes. We had to face a committee more terrifying than any first-night audience: they sat with their backs to the towering safety curtain on the stage of the Royal Opera House, Covent Garden. Diaghilev, of course, was there, and Nijinsky, Maestro and Madame Cecchetti and Grigoriev. We had no music, and nothing arranged. We girls lined ourselves up to do some of our dances from 'Schéhérazade'. Just as we started I caught my uncomfortable shoe in something, and down I went with a crash. The stage was slippery and my feet had not got used to the shoes. Before we finished I had gone down three times. At last Diaghilev suggested that Cecchetti should give us some classroom steps to do, and with these I got on better. I cannot remember how the other girls danced, but Zverev jumped and did his *entrechats* and *pirouettes* splendidly, which seemed to save the situation. Still, we hadn't much hope as we crawled out of Covent Garden and down Henrietta Street to the Coliseum. That same evening during our performance we got the news that five of us had been accepted; Anna Broomhead (later Bromova), Doris Faithful, Zverev, Tarasov and myself.

Miriam Ramberg had already begun to work on Stravinsky's score for 'Le Sacre' with Nijinsky. Even she found it extremely difficult to tell where one phrase ended and when another began – so novel, so unexpectedly interrupted and so strangely superimposed were Stravinsky's rhythms. They could never decide when to call a halt to the day's work. There was no question of Ramberg collaborating on the choreography: she respected Nijinsky's vision of a primitive Russia and admired the awkward unclassical poses in which he planned to group his dancers. Her only suggestion, diffidently recalled (apart from purely musical analysis), was made one day when Nijinsky said 'Here I'll form a big circle. What do you think? Say something'; and Ramberg said 'Why not try several little circles for a change?' – and he did.

When he was composing his ballets the idea of virtuosity, of showing off brilliant steps, never entered Nijinsky's head – not even when he was arranging a dance for himself. He first looked for a basic position, then kept to it right through the work. In 'L'Après-midi' it had been that Egyptian combination of a full-on torso with head, hands and legs in profile. In 'Jeux', the ballet about flirting tennis-players which he was planning – almost the first ballet to be made on a contemporary theme – it was the sideways and upwards swing of two arms across the body – a sort of composite sport movement. (In fact, since tennis-players use one hand and not two, this movement was more like golf – but Nijinsky hardly knew the difference between the two games.) In 'Le Sacre' the awkward closed fists half supporting a lolling head, the turned-in bent knees and turned-in feet (reminiscent of Petrushka's) gave the idea of a prehistoric species at the mercy of the weather, the harvest and their own fearful superstitions.[34]

As with 'L'Après-midi d'un faune' Nijinsky had grave difficulty in imparting his intentions to the company, and they resented not only his experiments in movement but his attitude towards them as dancers. When Fokine devised steps, however inventive, they always followed the logic of classical choreography. They had a natural flow. With Nijinsky, the body was no longer one single instrument, but four; and there seemed to be no continuity in his sequences, so that there was no chance of letting yourself go. When composing, Fokine would sometimes take an artist like Karsavina into his confidence and ask 'What do you feel about this?' Dancers could ask him questions and he allowed them a certain freedom of interpretation. Nijinsky was very young[35] – there had never in history been a twenty-four-year-old ballet-master before. Not only his sense of being out on an experimental limb and his curious position with regard to Diaghilev, but also his fanatical dedication to art, made him treat dancers in rehearsal as if they were puppets who had no purpose in life except to interpret his ideas. Human relationships were in abeyance. If Karsavina, when he was thinking something out, asked him the sort of question she would have asked Fokine, he was furious. Then, he preferred to show dancers what to do, rather than explain or analyse a movement. He expected them to copy him.

Considering the unwillingness of the dancers to be the raw material of his experiments, it was a miracle that he and they together really produced such wonderful results. There was the case of Nelidova, who danced the principal Nymph in 'L'Après-midi d'un faune'. She loathed the ballet and it made her long to go back to Moscow. 'Have I come all the way for *this*?' she used to exclaim. But Nijinsky, by persistently eliminating from her technical performance every hint of personal idiosyncrasy, moulded her – in Ramberg's phrase – into a likeness of Pallas Athene.

With all his seriousness, Nijinsky was not unaware of the humour of the situation, as Ramberg discovered. When she asked him if Nelidova wasn't proud to have been turned into a goddess, he replied 'Not at all. She would much rather I invented a little Spanish number for her – ' (mimicking in a funny way, hands on hips) 'with a carnation between her teeth and a rose behind her ear.'

Another instance of his sly observation was provided when Ramberg asked him what sort of man Trubecki was. Now, Trubecki was a muddled and ineffectual Pole, who used to get worked up into an hysterical state when anything went wrong. Diaghilev had engaged him as his private secretary and as treasurer of the company presumably because he was the husband of the dancer Sophie Pflanz. 'You can judge the sort of man he is,' said Nijinsky, 'when I tell you he secretly writes stories with titles like [in Polish] "*Fartoushek*" – "Her little pinafore" – for the *Warsaw Courier*.' (This was, incidentally, the only time Nijinsky spoke a word in Polish to Ramberg: they always spoke Russian together.)

No one in the company except his sister and perhaps Karsavina had ever seen this side of Nijinsky's character before. Ramberg found that when she

Nijinsky in evening dress.
Caricature by Jean Cocteau.

was alone with him they talked quite easily together. She was at his side during the agony of creation, and this led to an ease of intercourse between them. Suddenly, Nijinsky had someone who understood him. But it was an intellectual friendship without warmth.

On the way from London to Monte Carlo the company broke their journey at Lyons, where they gave one performance, dancing 'Les Sylphides', 'Cléopâtre', 'Carnaval' and 'Prince Igor'.[36] By the time the Ballet reached Monte Carlo on 15 March, Ramberg, whose presence they had at first resented, calling her 'Rithmitchka', had settled down and been accepted. She even had an admirer, Vladimir Romanov, whom she did not find attractive, and she rather dreaded the moment when she had to roll on the cushions with him in 'Schéhérazade'. Her intelligence and vivacity were particularly appreciated by the more educated members of the company, such as Hilda Bewicke[37] and Olga Khokhlova. One evening she was doing an imitation of Sarah Bernhardt in a dressing-room, when an old dresser put her head round the door and exclaimed, '*On dirait Mme Sarah!*' Ramberg's friends called her 'Mimi'.

With Fokine gone and since Nijinsky was a slow worker as a choreographer, Diaghilev decided to go to Russia and enlist the services of Boris Romanov and Alexander Gorsky:[38] Nijinsky was left behind in Monte Carlo, and, as in the last two years, stayed at the Riviera Palace Hotel at Beausoleil, coming and going by funicular or car. Vaslav and Ramberg continued to work together on 'Le Sacre' in the classroom under the Casino. They had three clear weeks before the season began on 9 April. They were alone except for a fat German pianist whom Diaghilev had nick-named '*Kolossal*' – not only because of his size but because he was always using this then fashionable expletive.* During their sessions Vassili would frequently come in on some pretext – to close a window to protect Nijinsky from draughts or to put a cardigan over his shoulders – but really, instructed by Diaghilev, to see that he and Ramberg were not flirting. Nevertheless, because of the absence of Diaghilev Mimi Ramberg did see much more of Nijinsky than she would otherwise have done.[39] Eleonora Nijinskaya noticed the growing intimacy of Ramberg with her son and warned him that she thought Mimi was attracted by him. But Vaslav told her there was no danger.[40]

'Jeux' was to be danced by Karsavina, Bronislava Nijinska and Vaslav himself. Because Karsavina had been obliged to return to Petersburg after the London season, Vassilievska deputized for her while Nijinsky was working the ballet out, which he did with a volume of Gauguin reproductions open before him.[41]

After their afternoon's work together it would often happen that Nijinsky and Ramberg met *chez* Pasquier, the café with a *terrasse* where dancers went to drink chocolate and eat cakes, and they would sit talking until it was dark and the time came to go to their respective hotels. One evening Nijinsky pointed to the trees which had artificial green lighting on them, and said 'That is how I like them and how I want the trees to be in "Jeux".' He also told Ramberg some of his ideas for the ballet about Joseph and Potiphar's wife, the score of which Diaghilev had commissioned for an enormous sum from Richard Strauss. In the banquet scene he would suggest the frivolity of this decadent society by making the guests perform a stylized dance with imaginary knives and forks. (This idea was used in 1917 by Massine in 'Les Femmes de bonne humeur', so perhaps it was a legacy of Nijinsky's to his successor, conveyed by Diaghilev.) His plans for 'Joseph' were much more original than the choreography eventually produced by Fokine.

They discussed Fokine's ballets.

M.R. Don't you think 'Petrushka' is Fokine's masterpiece?

N. (*doubtfully*) Ye-e-e-s.

---

* '*Kolossal*' was a period word in Germany then – just as '*épatant*' or 'super' or 'smashing' would be in other countries in subsequent years.

M.R. You don't sound convinced. What is there that you don't like about it?

N. The three puppets are certainly very good.

M.R. And the wet-nurses.

N. Yes. But I can't understand how he can just say to one member of the crowd 'Follow this tune' and leave him to improvise. A choreographer should oversee every tiny detail of choreography and leave nothing to chance.

Nijinsky laughed at Fokine's arrangement of 'Schéhérazade'. When Cecchetti as the Chief Eunuch unlocked the doors and the Negroes bounded on (as we have seen above), each seized a woman and began to caress her passionately on a cushion. They were expected to improvise these embraces and did so *con amore*, as Ramberg had found to her dismay. 'What kind of choreography is that?' asked Nijinsky. 'Choreography should be precise.'[42] He was indeed the very first choreographer to give exact instructions in every detail,[43] and this must have seemed cramping and pedantic to the dancers at the time. It would be normal practice today.

One day at rehearsal Nijinsky, after demonstrating something strenuous, looked round for a chair.[44] Ramberg got up and gave him hers. Later she was mercilessly jeered at by the company for this. She was told she had no sense of a woman's dignity. It was taken for granted that she loved Nijinsky, though this had not yet occurred to her.

Mimi Ramberg was sitting alone *chez* Pasquier one evening when Nijinsky arrived, white with rage and shaking. He said, 'I have just nearly killed a man.' He was referring to his brother-in-law Kotchetovsky. 'Bronia is leaving the cast of "Faune" and she is not to dance in either of my new ballets. That man has prevented her.' To calm him down Ramberg began to walk him along the gardens and recited Edgar Allen Poe's 'Annabel Lee'.

> It was many and many a year ago,
> In a kingdom by the sea,
> That a maiden there lived whom you may know
> By the name of Annabel Lee.
> And this maiden she lived with no other thought
> Than to love and be loved by me.

She translated the poem for him and he became interested. Then she spoke of dance notation and said she had a copy of Feuillet's *Choréographie* at her hotel. He went back to the Hôtel Ravel with her, where most of the company stayed, and sat on her bed to study the book. It was quite normal among young Russians and Poles in those days that a girl should bring a boy back to her room – particularly among students who would not have more than one room of their own: but when he left he was seen by members of the company whose suspicions were merely confirmed that he was having an affair with Ramberg. It was only the next day that Mimi learned the reason – which Nijinsky had neglected to mention – why his sister would not be dancing in his ballets, prevented as he said by her husband Kotchetovsky: she was going to have a baby. Nijinsky could not forgive this when the fate of a work of art was at stake.

'L'Après-midi' was still in the repertory, of course, and a replacement for Bronia as the sixth Nymph had to be rehearsed. This was Bewicke. When, towards the end, she had to come on alone to confront the Faun, then walk off with hands raised, she put on a frightened expression. Nijinsky reprimanded her, asking, 'Why do you make that face?' She replied, 'I thought I was meant to be frightened.' He said, 'Never mind what you thought. Do no more than I tell you. It is all in the choreography.'[45]

Meanwhile Diaghilev and Karsavina were travelling from Petersburg together. 'I had a powerful attraction in my compartment,' she wrote, 'an ornamental bucket of caviare, brought, together with chocolates, flowers and a small ikon, as a farewell gift.' Having Diaghilev temporarily in her power, Tamara decided to profit by the occasion.

T.K. Do you say your morning prayers, Sergei Pavlovitch?

S.D. (*after a slight hesitation*) Yes ... I do. I do kneel down and think of those I love and all who love me.

T.K. Do you ever search your conscience for hurts you may have inflicted?

S.D. (*emphatically*) I do! So often I reproach myself for lack of consideration. I think of how at times I went out in a hurry without saying good-night to Nanny, forgetting to kiss her hand.[46]

On Karsavina's return, rehearsals for 'Jeux' began. Bronia's place was to be taken by Schollar. Nijinsky had been practising in women's ballet shoes as he intended to dance *sur les pointes* in this ballet, as he is shown doing in sketches by Gross of 'Schéhérazade' and 'Petrushka'; but he soon decided this was out of keeping and returned to his ordinary slippers. It was during a rehearsal of 'Jeux' that Ramberg had another sample of Nijinsky's rages. Karsavina asked him a question and he lost his temper and began to rave. She walked out of the room without a word. Nijinsky complained to Diaghilev that Karsavina had the mentality of a *prima ballerina*. Ramberg heard Diaghilev's furious reaction and the abuse he poured on Nijinsky. 'She is not just a ballerina, but a woman of enormous intelligence and distinction, and you are an ill-mannered guttersnipe.' He had seldom been seen in such a fury. Nijinsky was made to apologize and was forgiven.[47]

When Stravinsky arrived from Switzerland, where he and Ravel had been working together on the orchestration of 'Khovanshchina' for Diaghilev's Paris season, and he first saw the work that had been done on 'Le Sacre' there was another tremendous row. Nobody could possibly dance some of Nijinsky's steps to some of Stravinsky's *tempi*, so Nijinsky had slowed the music down. Stravinsky raged and stormed and banged the piano lid.[48] In later years he would write in his book *Chronique de ma vie* that Nijinsky was too ignorant musically to be fit to do choreography: but the *Chronique* was ghosted by Walter Nouvel, and in his old age Stravinsky took back these words. Yet, whatever he thought of the choreography for 'Le Sacre', at the time Stravinsky adored 'L'Après-midi d'un faune'. Perhaps seeing your

Nijinsky making up for 'Carnaval', watched by Igor Stravinsky.
Caricature by Jean Cocteau.

music interpreted in movement is like having your portrait painted. You admire the artist's gift for catching the likeness of your friends, but are appalled by the caricature he does of you. Debussy doubtless preferred Nijinsky's work for 'Le Sacre' to his choreography for 'L'Après-midi' and 'Jeux', which he detested.

Maria Piltz, who was to dance the role of the Chosen Virgin in 'Le Sacre' in place of Bronia, was a tall handsome girl with Slav features. Her dance of sacrifice would be the overwhelming climax of the barbaric rite, but, like the *corps de ballet*, she found Nijinsky's new movements so alien to everything she had ever been called upon to do before that she was slow in realizing his intentions. One afternoon Nijinsky rehearsed with her alone, only Ramberg being present. The latter watched in silent dismay, for Piltz could not see what was needed. Nijinsky showed her the dance. If only *he* could have taken the role, thought Ramberg, if only the Harvest God could have been propitiated with a male sacrifice, this might have been Nijinsky's most wonderful creation. With clenched hand across his face, he threw himself into the air in paroxysms of fear and grief. His movements were stylized and controlled, yet he gave out a tremendous power of tragedy. It was a unique rendering of the solo by its creator, something to be remembered for ever. When Piltz came to dance the role in public, she kept the bones of Nijinsky's performance, but according to Ramberg it was a poor copy, a postcard reproduction of what he had been that afternoon: even so Piltz made a profound impression on the audience. [49]

The little group of dancers who had been auditioned in London, two Russian men and three English girls, arrived to join the company; and Hilda Munnings has given us an account of her first reactions to the Diaghilev Ballet.

My first impression of the company was one of richness and profusion. There seemed to be such an abundance of everything, whether of ballet shoes and costumes or of the hats, shoes and gloves which the dancers wore in private life. We three English girls felt so dowdy in our blouses and skirts. Most of the girls were exceedingly pretty, particularly the Polish ones. Women all had long hair in those days, and most of the company were dark; but Olga Khokhlova had glorious dark auburn hair. I was one of the few blondes in the company.

Every day began with Maestro Cecchetti's class at nine o'clock ... we wore white tutus and pink silk tights, but for the rehearsal which followed immediately we wore *crêpe-de-chine* dresses which took three and a half metres of material to make. They were caught in with one bit of elastic under the breast and another around the thigh, and they fell in pretty draperies just below the knee. Although there was a lot of stuff in them, they were easy to move in and as we all had them made in different colours we must have been a wonderful sight. Rehearsals were conducted by Serge Grigoriev, our *régisseur* or stage-manager. He was about thirty, and to us English girls he seemed tall and terrifying. He had a perpetually worried look and seldom smiled, though, when something amused him, he would let out a short, loud laugh. Not understanding much of what he said, I had the feeling that he was usually complaining. ... When we failed to understand some explanation, he grew impatient and began to shout, covering us with a shower of spit. Being nervous, I never knew whether to wipe it off or leave it. ... I got pushed around a good deal at first, not knowing any of the ballets and speaking no Russian, and the Polish girls used to get annoyed with me and shove me about the stage,

283

saying, 'Pooosh, Meeess.' . . . When Diaghilev came for the first time to one of our rehearsals I was scared stiff. His presence was awe-inspiring and he radiated self-assurance, like royalty. Tall and heavy, with a little moustache and a monocle, he advanced into the room, followed by a group of friends. Everyone who was seated stood up, and silence fell. With Grigoriev following discreetly a yard or two behind, he passed through the crowd of dancers, stopping here and there to exchange a greeting. Any male dancer to whom he spoke would click his heels together and bow.[50]

Hilda observed Nijinsky.

In appearance Nijinsky was himself like a faun – a wild creature who had been trapped by society and was always ill at ease. When addressed, he turned his head furtively, looking as if he might suddenly butt you in the stomach. He moved on the balls of his feet, and his nervous energy found an outlet in fidgeting: when he sat down he twisted his fingers or played with his shoes. He hardly spoke to anyone, and seemed to exist on a different plane. Before dancing he was even more withdrawn, like a bewitched soul. I used to watch him practising his wonderful jumps in the first position, flickering his hands; I had never seen anyone like him before.[51]

Romola de Pulszky had her private lesson with Cecchetti at eleven when the company class was over. Nijinsky and Karsavina came for theirs at twelve. One day Romola sprained her ankle, but the Maestro made her go on working. Vaslav, who had arrived early, took her foot in his hand, felt the ankle and told Cecchetti she should be sent home to rest. He cannot have been unaware of her existence, even if he held aloof.[52] Romola was rather jealous of Mimi's friendship with Nijinsky, but she cultivated her acquaintance in the hopes of hearing useful information about him or obtaining access to him.[53] Ramberg, on her side, found the young Hungarian most attractive and affable.[54] She dressed well, had winning manners and a captivating way of smoking a cigarette. In those days only Nihilists and the most sophisticated people smoked cigarettes, and Romola was certainly no Nihilist. When the company moved to Paris the two women continued to meet; and Mimi would leave her aunt's flat in the old, historic quarter of the Marais to dine with Romola at her Hôtel d'Iéna in the modern fashionable district on the way to Passy. Ramberg was completely innocent of the Hungarian's state of mind. She had no inkling that Romola was in pursuit of Nijinsky: but then she had not analysed her own feelings for Nijinsky either, so completely did her admiration for him as an artist and a creator of genius dominate her thoughts.

The situation was ironical. Romola's friendship with Ramberg enabled her to learn everything she could about Nijinsky's character, his ideals, his method of working, the way his mind functioned, what amused, what shocked and what pleased him. Mimi was flattered and attracted by her sophisticated rival; and there can be little doubt that her confidences went far to helping Romola charm and win Nijinsky away from her when she eventually found herself alone with him.

The Monte Carlo season ended on 6 May. Diaghilev would have taken his company to the Opéra for his spring season in Paris, but Astruc wanted him for the new Théâtre des Champs-Elysées, of which he was manager. How much were the Opéra offering, he had asked Diaghilev; was it 12,000 francs a performance, his usual price? 'Yes,' Diaghilev had replied, 'but you must understand that people are saying that Astruc invented the Russian Ballet. That, my dear friend, must be paid for.' Astruc was obliged to settle for 25,000 a performance. 'This folly,' he wrote, 'which I had not the right *not* to commit, made possible the creation of "Le Sacre", but cost me the life of my management.'[55] In fact he went bankrupt shortly after.

The Théâtre des Champs-Elysées was (and still is) not in the Avenue des Champs-Elysées, but in the Avenue Montaigne, which led off it, near the Place de l'Alma and the Seine. It was large, luxurious and magnificently up-to-date. Its architecture marked the transition between art nouveau and 1920s 'modernistic', and was prophetic of the Metro-Goldwyn style. Both the sculptured reliefs by Bourdelle on the outside and the painted frescoes by Maurice Denis in the auditorium were inspired by Isadora at her most Dionysian.

Together with his own ballet company – Sophie Feodorova and Ludmilla Schollar were the only guest artists[56] – Diaghilev was to present singers of the Imperial Theatres in 'Boris Godounov' and 'Khovanshchina', but as they could not arrive until 18 May the season was to open with ballet, and the first performance on the 15th was to include 'Jeux'. Nijinsky, however, had not finished 'Jeux' when he and Diaghilev arrived in Paris and put up at the Elysée Palace Hotel. Diaghilev was extremely anxious and said the ballet must be completed without delay. A rehearsal was called in the new theatre, but it was one of Nijinsky's bad days. 'He stood in the middle of the practice-room,' wrote Grigoriev, 'his mind an obvious blank. I felt that the situation was desperate and suggested a run-through of what had been composed, in the hope of stimulating his invention. This luckily produced the desired effect.'[57]

One of the first visits Diaghilev and Vaslav paid in Paris was to Ravel, and they took Bronia and Stravinsky with them. Stravinsky photographed Ravel and Nijinsky playing *à quatre mains* and also looking down from the balcony of the flat on to the Avenue Carnot, near the Etoile. Ravel was a passionate admirer of Stravinsky's 'Le Sacre', the première of which he thought would prove 'an event as great as "Pelléas" '.[58] According to Stravinsky he was 'the only musician who immediately understood "Le Sacredu printemps" '.[59]

If 'L'Après-midi d'un faune' was a vase painting or a frieze in low relief, one has the impression from the few photographs that survive and from the seven pastels of Valentine Gross that in 'Jeux' the relief had grown bolder. Although 'Jeux' was partly inspired by the paintings of Gauguin it looks as if the choreographer was also aiming at a compact, enclosed sculptural form, the very opposite of the extended *arabesques, attitudes* and *port de bras* of classical ballet, which, as we know, does not on the whole lend itself to sculpture. Few painters, of course, have been more flat and decorative than Gauguin: yet it seems hardly less paradoxical that the choreographer, admiring the coloured masses of the painter, should aim at imparting to their realization in terms of human bodies in the round some of the monumentality he had for the last few years been observing in the sculptures of Maillol, Renoir and of his friend Rodin, than that his ballet, pretending to be about sport and triangular love-making, should in reality be abstract, concerned neither with sporting movements nor human feelings, an essay in formal relations.

How Nijinsky married his 'stylized gesture' – which was the name for the new kind of dancing – to Debussy's music we shall probably never know. The composer thought it was too literal in some places and totally unrelated in others. Valentine Gross thought that Nijinsky had followed the music admirably, but too closely, and that a certain disparity between the nature of the movement and that of the score came from the ballet having been rehearsed to piano only.[60]

The most sculptural of the groups is that in which Karsavina embraces Schollar.* The latter stands facing us, with right foot slightly advanced, hanging hands curled up – the right just above the left – head leaning over the left shoulder. Karsavina is arrested in a stride on half-point; she leans a little forward from the waist, right arm slanting across the front of Schollar's body to grasp her above the left elbow, left arm placed round her neck so that the curled hand is visible on Schollar's left shoulder. The most striking aspect of this group is the line formed by the underneath of Karsavina's hair, continued by her back and skirt down to her foot. Then there is a kind of interlocking which is highly satisfactory, and the gesture of Karsavina recalls that of the Virgin Mary in the Leonardo painting of St Anne, the Virgin and the infant Christ, in the Louvre.

The group in which the three dancers stand in a row with Nijinsky in the middle is a version of the Three Graces. The composition in which the slightly bending Karsavina addresses Schollar, who sits, knees tucked under

* These few observations on the surviving records of 'Jeux' may be read in conjunction with Plates 56–65.

her, one hand in her lap, the other at her breast, the head sadly inclined, while Nijinsky watches them both, is, of all these groups, the most reminiscent of Gauguin. In the group where Nijinsky appears to threaten the two girls, his pose with upraised right forearm and left hand clenched tightly to the side of his belt, is like one of those little Etruscan bronzes of warriors with spear and shield, except that the dancer's head is bent, ready to butt faunwise, rather than held back in defiance. In the similar pose where Nijinsky, taking the weight on his left leg, has his right fist to his forehead, he recalls the sculptures of Roman athletes.

At the first dress-rehearsal Bakst's set was revealed. The heavy summer trees are seen at dusk with painted stylized patches of electric light. Behind them looms a big white building with rows of little windows, perhaps, as we have remarked, inspired by Bloomsbury. On the green floor-cloth are painted four circular flower-beds. Bronislava Nijinska thought the setting had too much sense of space, and that the choreography asked for something more confined. Rightly or wrongly, it seems that Bakst's intention was to dwarf the dancers and make them appear more childlike. Diaghilev was sitting in the middle of the *corbeille*. On the appearance of Nijinsky in his red wig, rolled-up shirt-sleeves, red tie and knee-length trousers with a red border, held up by red braces, and his white stockings with red tops, Diaghilev exploded. 'No, no, it's quite impossible!' Bakst was to the left of the *corbeille*. 'What's the matter, Serioja? It's a very good costume.' 'I'm sorry, my dear Levushka,' came the answer, firm but gentle. 'It won't do at all. He looks ridiculous.' The argument continued in the most affectionate manner, but Diaghilev was adamant. He redesigned Nijinsky's costume himself,[61] retaining the white shirt and red tie, but giving the dancer white trousers which grew narrower below the knee, and gripped the calf, ending just above the ankle. The girls' white dresses with their tight-fitting bodices and knee-length skirts were made by Paquin. Incidentally, it is clear from Bakst's original design that Nijinsky's costume is for a footballer, and the ball at his feet is a football. It was the size of the white tennis ball which began the action of the ballet by bouncing on to the stage that was to provoke mirth in the Paris audience, and comment from the sporting English. And we have seen that a basic movement planned by the choreographer (and of which we have no picture) was derived from golf. It seems that the Russians were as vague about the distinction between one game and another as Sarah Bernhardt, who stopped her car in the suburbs of Manchester to observe a game of football, exclaiming in rapture, '*J'adore ce cricket – c'est tellement anglais.*'[62]

The music of 'Jeux', barely appreciated in 1913, has latterly been recognized as one of Debussy's finest achievements. The composer himself confessed, 'Before I composed a ballet I didn't know what a choreographer was. Now I know – he is a very strong and mathematical gentleman.'[63] Nevertheless, the overall musical plan is more accommodating than Debussy pretends: thinly veiled by the magical sonorities are all the dance-episodes of the scenario.

After a short, slow, dreamlike introduction, a *scherzando* passage sets the scene. Scraps of melody are tossed around, drums patter, a xylophone is heard. A brief reprise of the introductory bars, and the piece is under way. A tennis ball has fallen on the stage. A young man in tennis clothes holding his racket high in the air leaps across the stage and disappears. Two girls enter, shy and inquisitive. They have something to confide to each other, and are seeking a suitable corner. They begin their dance, first one, then the other, but suddenly stop, put off by the sound of rustling leaves. The young man has been watching them through the branches. They want to run away, but he gently leads them back, and persuades one of them to dance with him. The music surges restlessly, seldom loud, always fluid in rhythm and melody. 'The imaginatively rich structure, ever changing, establishes a very elastic line of thought based on the concept of irreversible tempo' (Boulez).[64] The feeling is that of a light-hearted waltz, *molto rubato*, which speeds up, slows down, almost stops, then rediscovers its momentum. The young man steals a kiss from his partner; the jealousy of the other is immediately aroused which she expresses in a mocking dance in 2/4 time, '*ironique et léger*'. A soft muted horn-call is accompanied by plucked strings. *Staccato* semi-quavers in the woodwind lead back to the waltz tempo. The young man's attention is caught – he tries to teach the steps of the waltz to the second girl. The girl at first mimics him (scale passages in flute and cor anglais) but is eventually won over, after a miming passage in 3/4 time. The waltz is resumed. *Pizzicato* strings accompany the woodwind melody over a timpani *ostinato*. The music surges to a climax. To a rhapsodic passage in the violins the abandoned girl decides to leave. In a winningly persuasive section the other girl retains her, and all three now join in a dance, in the original tempo. The high point of the action has been reached – upper woodwind, strings, xylophone and celesta play descending phrases based on the chromatic scale. The cor anglais plays, in *tempo rubato*; block *legato* chords in the strings lead to a musically reminiscent section. Two harps provide an *arpeggio* background. The tempo quickens. As the melodic scraps of the whole piece are passed in review, the entire orchestra begins to play, working up to a loud climax. Another tennis ball falls on the stage. The dancers flee. Over a murmuring accompaniment in divided strings we hear again the mysterious whole-tone chords of the opening. A chromatic slide, two plucked chords, a final slide, and the ballet is over.

Two days later there appeared in *Le Figaro* Henri Quittard's review of 'Jeux', for which, as he said,

Debussy had not scorned to write the music. . . . Even with such a childish libretto, one would think that this haphazard essay in affectation might provide something graceful or pretty to look at. But the new art, of which M.Nijinsky is the prophet, manages to turn even the insignificant to absurdity. What could be more ungraceful than the meaningless, pretentious contortions, dreamt up by this nimble aesthete. It goes without saying that modern dress does not enhance these poses inspired by Greek vase paintings, with which 'L'Après-midi d'un faune' took us by surprise last year. Furthermore this so-called reformed choreography employs the most old-fashioned and conventional gestures and mime, without any attempt to make them less funny.

It is said that M.Nijinsky's intention was to provide, in this ballet, an apologia in plastic terms for the man of 1913. If this is so, we have nothing to be proud of. But it is annoying that he should almost have succeeded, by some evil spell, in turning those exquisite ballerinas, Mlles Karsavina and Schollar, into stiff and awkward puppets. The public, apart from a few quite lively interruptions, submitted good-humouredly to these mystifications. No doubt people would have been content just to listen to the music. Composer and choreographer take absolutely no notice of each other in this ballet. Just as well for the music.[65]

An article signed 'Swift' in the *Bulletin de la Société Musicale Indépendante*, though it may not have reached a wide public, is funny enough to deserve quotation. 'Summer sports. A number of readers have enquired about the rules of Russian Tennis, which is bound to be the rage of country house-parties this season. They are as follows: the game is played at night on flood-lit flower-beds; there are only three players and the net is dispensed with; the tennis-ball is replaced by a football and the use of the racket is forbidden. Hidden in a pit at the edge of the court, an orchestra accompanies the game. The purpose of this sport is to develop suppleness of the neck, wrists and ankles; and it has the blessing of the Academy of Medicine.'

On 20 May, an interview with Nijinsky, signed Emile Deflin, appeared in *Gil Blas*:

You can't just walk into the Debussian dancer's dressing-room as if it were the Moulin de la Galette. I had to use a bit of cunning in order to get into the Faun's cage. My friend Robert de Tomaz, most Parisian of expatriate Slavs, who reads Tolstoi as easily as Stéphane Mallarmé, the lucky devil, scribbled a few words of Russian on his card and the door gaped wide at this Open Sesame as if passwords had been exchanged – 'Toulon?' 'Kronstadt!'

In the dressing-room there is a faint smell of scent, but it is very simple without a hint of luxury. None of the innumerable photographs of the dancer are to be seen – only a few designs by Bakst and some sketches of Rodin. There are no flowers; the wreaths are all in the wardrobe. Sunk in an old divan whose springs have given way, Nijinsky is sponging himself. His white flannel shirt is open to the waist, his tennis belt, undone, is hanging loose. Huge drops of sweat outline the slanting ridges of his cheek-bones. He has just been dancing 'Jeux'. After we have been introduced Nijinsky, with a slight effort, begins to speak French, but Robert de Tomaz comes to the rescue and from then on their conversation is held in the sonorous tongue of our allies.[66]

It must not be imagined from the following interview that so long a speech was typical of Nijinsky. His words have been edited by the journalist and turned into 'prose'.

'I was rather surprised and sad,' the dancer says, smiling, 'at the public's reaction to "Jeux", but I don't despair. I thought they would understand what I was trying to do and didn't expect them to laugh at my experiments in stylized gesture. You probably know that it was while I was watching tennis at Deauville last year that I was struck by the beauty of certain poses and movements and had the idea of putting them together in a work of art, treating them symphonically, so to speak. . . . M. Debussy's music was a remarkable help in the realization of my aim and, I must say, I went about my work with a good deal of confidence. As I said, the rather unkind reception of the ballet has not discouraged me, because even if most people disapproved there have been one or two whose judgement I value who have liked what I did. I wanted to show my experiment first in France, because it has always struck me that the French public is the most artistic. In England, where I danced for a long season last winter, there is a great understanding of dancing, especially classical dancing. The French, on the other hand, have more flair and I think make better judges of something new. I hope still to interest them in my experiments in stylized gesture. I'm not afraid of hard work; I shall just keep trying to do something really good.'[67]

Debussy did not like Nijinsky's ballet. On 9 June he was to write to Robert Godet:

Among recent pointless goings-on I must include the staging of 'Jeux', which gave Nijinsky's perverse genius a chance of indulging in a peculiar kind of mathematics. This fellow adds up triple crochets with his feet, checks them on his arms, then suddenly, half-paralysed, he stands crossly watching the music slip by. It's awful. It's even Dalcrozian – for I consider Monsieur Dalcroze as one of the greatest enemies of music and you can imagine what havoc his method can create in the mind of a young savage like Nijinsky![68]

Listening to Debussy's wonderful score today, our minds boggle at how Nijinsky could have found movements – if not to match or parallel it – at least which would seem acceptable as something to watch while listening to it. It is clear that he sought a most venturesome solution. What would we not give to see revived his choreography to the music of Debussy in Bakst's décor (which is sentimentalized in the pastels of Valentine Gross) and with its original cast! That Diaghilev should have commissioned such a score (which the composer was unwilling to write) and should have made it possible for Nijinsky to rehearse to it his dangerous experiments enhances our awe of him. That the composer of such a score should have been so derisive of pioneering in another medium and that his derision should be shared by both critics and public fills us with such pity for the heroic Diaghilev and Nijinsky that a phrase of Isadora's, written as the postscript of a despairing letter from Turkestan, where she was wasting her sweetness on an unappreciative provincial public, comes to mind: 'Hell of a life anyway.'[69]

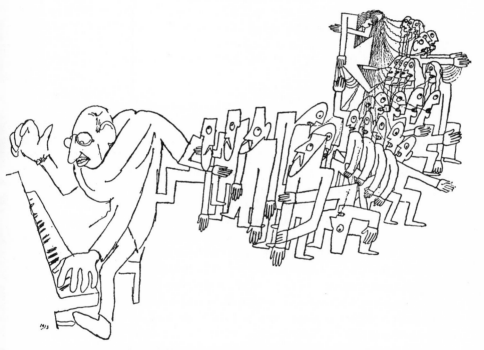

Stravinsky playing 'Le Sacre du printemps'. Caricature by Jean Cocteau.

Now the time was near for 'Le Sacre du printemps'.

How sure of himself and his innovations in choreography was Nijinsky? Did the cool reception of 'Jeux' give him doubts? Confident or doubting, any artist who has battled all night with his angel and won through to his own satisfaction must be relatively unconcerned about the way his work is received: to captivate the public scores only five points out of a hundred. Of course Nijinsky needed the approval of Diaghilev, of Stravinsky, of Bakst – his earlier mentor, even though it was Roerich who had designed the sets and dresses for 'Le Sacre' – and perhaps of Bronia. The question of having to please the public in order to make money – if it had entered his head as a boy – had long since been something to which he gave no thought, so entirely had Diaghilev isolated him from worldly cares. An anecdote recorded by Jacques Rivière gives a key to Nijinsky's state of mind on the eve of battle, as well as illustrating his puckish sense of humour. An acquaintance asked him what 'Le Sacre' was like. 'Oh, you won't like that either,' said the choreographer. Then, making the angular sideways gesture of 'Faune', he said 'There's more of that kind of thing.'[70] People who are not sure of themselves do not joke about their masterpieces.

Let us consider first the ballet of 'Le Sacre du printemps' itself, its music and choreography; second its rating in the eyes of Jacques Rivière, its most intelligent critic, who wrote a long essay about it in *La Nouvelle Revue Française*; third the reaction of the public on the opening night; lastly its handling by the press.

It is impossible to describe in a few words the novelty of Stravinsky's score for 'Le Sacre du printemps', or to judge to what extent its novelties made it the masterpiece it was. A new kind of marvellous monster, it sprang without warning from the forehead of Jove, leaving the doctors a long way behind with their explanations of its conception, birth and magical anatomy. First, it was new in rhythm. Stravinsky overthrew the whole rhythmic system – or rather, invented a new one. Bar after bar there was a different time signature. The composer himself was baffled as to how to write out the final 'Danse Sacrale'. Second, the ballet was new in its orchestration, using both string and woodwind in extreme registers, thus producing new sounds – and, of course, at Diaghilev's specific request it had been scored for an exceptionally large orchestra (there were eight horns). A peculiarity was the accumulation of special instrumental effects – such as the use of harmonics, *col legno*, flutter-tongue on the flute and *campanella in aria* on the French horn.

Nijinsky's stupendous task was to parallel or find an equivalent for this titanic composition in choreographic terms. But he already had in his mind, as we know, new things he wanted to do, and it must have been a question to what extent his new *plastique* – the chief novelty of which was that it had been conceived as much from a painter's, sculptor's and dramatist's point of view as from a ballet-master's – could be wedded to the composer's inventions. He had to imagine his new kinds of pose, of movement, of grouping – devoid of classical virtuosity, but which would certainly be so hard to execute accurately that only ballet dancers would be able to perform them. Then he had, as in 'Faune', only more so, to overcome the reluctant minds and recalcitrant bodies of these dancers, trained to think, count and move so differently. Finally he had to find the key to the unfathomable score. It was an undertaking to baffle the most experienced choreographer, the most professional musician. Nijinsky was neither. He had only his vision and his genius.

In the Introduction a strange nasal solo on the bassoon playing in its highest register – later joined by the horn – evokes the first stirrings of some primeval Russian spring. Irrupting *arpeggios* on other wind instruments suggest sudden spurts of growth, vegetable or animal, in the womb of darkness. The first violins *pizzicato* set the strict pace of the opening dance which is to follow and lead into the Augurs of Spring. In Roerich's green landscape with its lake and birch-trees beneath a cloudy sky boys in embroidered white smocks are jumping up and down in circles to a steady rhythm of heavy string chords supported by the eight horns in block harmony accenting their syncopated beats. (This percussive effect is achieved without drums.) The boys are being taught by an old woman, represented by an *ostinato* figure on the bassoons shadowed by cor anglais and *pizzicato* cellos, certain spells and divinations which must be performed every spring. It is a question of fortune-telling. Squawks from the upper woodwind are like convulsions of nature (as it were vegetable birth-pangs magnified a thousand times) which happen throughout the human ritual. The groups take turns to dance and sit. A simple almost Greek dance-tune on the alto flute is followed by a Russian chorale-like tune on four trumpets. A variation of the dance-tune is carried on incredibly by violins and piccolos only above the whole orchestra, which abandons itself to a Bacchanalian frenzy, and, as the dancers fall to the floor, spills over into the *presto* of the Ritual of Abduction. Two groups of red-clad girls enter in succession to string chords and syncopated drum-beats. Their sight of the boys induces a sexual panic, represented by vociferous brass and twittering woodwind. The groups of challenging men (frenetic horn calls) and trampling, jumping women confront each other from opposite sides of the stage, as the orchestra emits short *staccato* ejaculations interrupted each time by heavy single punches, with drums to the fore, which later become double and take over the music's texture. To these clashes of brass the men grasp the women in a gesture of stylized rape: this is briefly elaborated on by two pairs of dancers before the movement ends.

Spring Rounds are introduced by an expectant trill which, when heard earlier, seemed a kind of spell, and now played on flutes and alto flutes is extended with shattering effect. Against this clarinets are playing a simple, almost primeval melodic sequence. The dance proper begins with a distinctive dragging rhythmic figure, which is repeated over and over again. When the Russian chorale tune reappears in a slightly different form, some continue to follow the basic rhythm while others follow the melody. As the whole orchestra take up the solemn tune and render it threatening, men and girls form up and revolve in separate circles. Two tribes are established for the ritual games. The dance ends tranquilly with a repetition of its opening bars. The Games of the Rival Tribes open with swaggering martial passages on the brass. These alternate throughout the number with more lyrical dipping sections. Short bursts of warfare between the men alternate with pleading from the swinging, clapping women and competitive dances. At the built-up conclusion a barbaric tune on the tubas serves as a ground bass supporting the orchestral frenzy and runs straight into the Procession of the Sage. To crashing chords the Elders of the tribe lead on their Sage or High Priest with his long white beard. The tribe trembles with religious awe. To a quiet interlude the Sage, supported by the Elders, lays himself spreadeagle on the ground. This is the Adoration of the Earth. Auspices are taken. As the music ends with a held spidery chord on the strings, which somehow suggests the presence of the god, the people run to form a square representing the tribal compound.

The Dance of the Earth, which concludes the first scene, is a frenzied celebration of the people, drunk with spring. A single drum in triplet rhythm is joined by another in quadruplet rhythm: this metric contrast gives the number its wild pulse. *Staccato* outbursts of the orchestra with the brass prominent play snatches of figuration and detached off-beat chords. A quieter passage, dominated by horn colour, is like the stirring of a dark whirlpool. The insistent double drum rhythm is taken up and played with various permutations by the whole orchestra. The whirlpool becomes a boiling cauldron as, to syncopated shrieks on the brass and woodwind, the dancers in separate asymmetrical clumps leap and fall convulsively and the scene ends.

The Introduction to the second part paints a melancholy twilit landscape with small creatures and brooks. A sense of desolation is imparted by the strange colour of the muted trumpets and by mysterious muted horn calls, which seem far away. *Arpeggios* on E flat clarinets and strings suggest water falling among the rocks. A Russian tune introduced very gently on alto flute and solo violin implies that this landscape is inhabited.

Roerich's second scene is a dusky hilltop, with sacred stones and three poles hung with votive skins and antlers. In a number called Mystic Circles of Young Girls one of the virgins will be chosen through the hazard of the dance to be sacrificed to the Sun God. When the curtain rises all the girls stand welded into one group, trembling, facing outward. Their toes are pointed in, their knees bent and their right elbows rest on their left fists, while their right fists support their heads, which are bent sideways. The men and Elders stand watching them. To a languid *legato* tune on six solo violas, against the background of *pizzicato* cello, the ring of girls moves round, and at certain counts the whole group rise on tip-toe, dropping their right hands to their sides and jerking their heads to the left. When one circuit has been completed every other girl leaps out of the ring, then back in again. A spurting clarinet trill and a chromatic *tremolo* passage on violins introduces a romantic Russian tune (reminiscent of the 'Firebird' princesses) on the alto flute. The girls walk with a bell-swinging gesture, start and stop again. One of them is chosen. Guitar-like *pizzicato* chords on violas and cellos provide a new colour; a short passage for two solo violas doubled with flutes adds a further sensuousness. The Russian tune is developed and a *sforzando* chord on muted horns starts a *crescendo* and *accelerando*. Eleven double-stopped string chords supported by four-part timpani chords lead into the next number.

This is the Glorification of the Chosen Virgin, who has fallen into a trance. To ecstatic shrieks on the wind the dancers, divided into five groups, male and female, leap and stamp convulsively to chugging or fragmented rhythms. As they approach and surround the Chosen Virgin her emotions are expressed by a hysterical outburst on upper woodwind and brass.

The Evocation of the Ancestors opens with declamatory fanfares alternating with a three-note figure on the drums and basses, distantly echoed by woodwind and drums. To celebrate the Ritual of the Ancestors the Elders enter covered in animal skins and process round the Chosen Virgin. To an oriental tune, against the steady rhythm of bass drums with off-beat timpani and tambourine, the tribe recall their forbears in a slow reflective dance. A new murmuring dancing tune on the alto flute is joined by a counter-tune on muted trumpets, which takes over and assumes a striding, pounding rhythm. There is a return to the oriental tune and the rhythmic texture of the earlier part. A rhapsodic clarinet leads with little warning into the sacrificial dance.

To *staccato* shrieks and percussive chords the final ritual begins as the tribe stamp round the Chosen Virgin, whose dance of exhaustion will be the culmination of the dance drama. Then there breaks out a persistent but halting and convulsive rhythm on the strings, and the Virgin is drawn first to assist then to lead her fellows in the celebration of her own sacrifice. Meanwhile, there are heard blood-curdling ejaculations, which seem to be threats or warnings from the erupting forces of nature. These are played first on loud muted trombones answered by two loud muted trumpets, then by a piccolo, E flat clarinet and D trumpet call, twice. A hysterical trill on the violins, augmented by piccolos ascending in a nightmarish way, leads back to the wild, chaotic rhythms of the opening. These are developed and intensified, becoming ever more complex and unbalanced. The members of the tribe repeat the same jumps again and again, turning in ritual despair to left and to right, while the Virgin is galvanized into leaps of an increasing

Maria Piltz in 'Le Sacre du printemps'. Five drawings by Valentine Gross.

frenzy. At last she falls exhausted. She tries to rise, but in vain. Her last breath, which is also the orgasm of the god, is a gurgle, like the spilling of sap, heard as a little upward run on the flutes. A short silence, then to a final convulsive chord, not on full orchestra, but on cellos, basses, horns, trombones and tuba playing *fortissimo*, she dies. Six men raise her body at arms' length above their heads.

Taking a metaphor from the kitchen, Jacques Rivière wrote that the novelty of both the music and the choreography of 'Le Sacre' consisted in their lack of 'sauce' or 'dressing'. From a musical point of view 'sauce' meant atmosphere, Debussyish impressionism, shimmering orchestration. In dancing it could mean two things: first the veils and lighting of Loie Fuller which merged the dancer in a vague coloured haze (Debussy again) – this the Russians, with their classical geometry, had always eschewed; second, the dazzlement of the dance itself, such as that of Nijinsky in 'Le Spectre', in which virtuosity and physical magic masked the lack of meaning and inner truth. Rivière rightly imagined – and he had not heard the young choreographer criticizing Fokine as Ramberg had – that Nijinsky, the supreme executant of Fokine's choreography, had begun to feel while dancing it a certain *malaise* caused by a growing consciousness of its soft centre, its lack of inner truth. 'And from that moment he had no rest until he

himself had given the final turn to the vice and tightened the screws of the choreographic machine so that it was in perfect working order.' Rivière never doubted for a moment that the twenty-four-year-old Nijinsky had shot far ahead of Fokine and made the greatest of all the Russian ballets.

In Fokine's ballets dancers were disposed in symmetrical groups: this was not the absurd symmetry of the Opéra, but there was a regular distribution of masses ... this equilibrium did not apply only to static poses, it was carried through the movements of the dance no matter how abandoned that dance might be. ... Every pattern was conceived on the principle of response, of give and take; the dancers seized on a gesture and passed it continually backwards and forwards from one to the other like a ball. No group moved except in response to the movement of the opposite group.... After a while Fokine had no other way of being original except to vary the subject and the props. In vain that for the golden apples of 'L'Oiseau de feu' he substituted the daggers of 'Thamar' and the crooks of 'Daphnis et Chloë': it was a losing battle. The only way to rediscover the source of all variety was first to pull the whole thing apart and then start by considering the emotions of the individual.* This is what Nijinsky has done. Taking each group separately ... he studied its cellular formation and recorded its instincts at the

* The French reads: '*Pour retrouver la source de la variété, il eût fallu d'abord redescendre au détail, reprendre contact avec l'individuel.*' I have put in a few extra words to clarify what I believe to be Rivière's meaning.

very moment of their birth; he became the observer and historian of its slightest impulse. The dancing of each group consists of movements hatched in isolation from the other groups, like those spontaneous fires that break out in haystacks. The absolute asymmetry which reigns throughout 'Le Sacre' is the very essence of the work. . . . There is no lack of composition; on the contrary, there is the subtlest composition imaginable in the encounters, the challenges, the frays and the conflicts of these strange battalions. But composition does not take precedence over detail, does not condition it: it makes the best use it can of diverse elements. The impression of unity which we never cease for a moment to enjoy is like the sensation of watching the inhabitants of a given state moving about, passing, accosting and parting from each other, each intent on his own business, taking his neighbours for granted and putting them out of mind. . . .

What advantage did Nijinsky gain by renouncing 'sauce'? To what end has he broken the flow of movement and destroyed choreographic *ensembles*? What kind of beauty is hidden in this spare, restricted dancing? Without insisting further on its marvellous appropriateness to the subject of 'Le Sacre du printemps', it seems to me easy to see in what way it surpasses the work of Fokine. The latter is fundamentally unsuited to the expression of emotion. All one can read in it is a vague, entirely physical and faceless joy. . . . By breaking up movement, by returning to the simplicity of gesture, Nijinsky has restored expressiveness to dancing. All the angularities and awkwardness of this choreography keep the feeling in. The movement encloses it, grasps it, contains it; and by the continual changes of direction it blocks every possible outlet. . . . The body is no longer an escape-route for the soul: on the contrary, it gathers itself together to contain the soul. . . . Fokine's choreography was so inexpressive that to convey to the spectators a change of mood the performers had to resort to facial mimicry, frowns or smiles. That this was added to and superimposed upon their gestures was for that very reason a proof of the ineffectuality of these. It was a reinforcement, something borrowed from another medium to help out the poverty of choreography pure and simple. But in Nijinsky's choreography the face plays no independent role; it is an extension of the body, its flower. Nijinsky makes the body itself speak. It only moves as a whole, as one block, and its speech is expressed in sudden bounds with open arms and legs, or in sideways runs with bent knees and with the head lying on one shoulder. At first sight it seems less skilful, less varied, less intelligent. Yet, with its wholesale displacements, its sudden turns-about, the way it comes to rest only to begin a frantic trembling on the spot, it says a thousand times more than the long-winded, facile, charming chatter of Fokine. The language of Nijinsky is infinitely detailed; it lets nothing get by; it penetrates into corners. No figures of speech, no *pirouettes*, no elliptical allusions. The dancer is no longer wafted by a slight, indifferent inspiration. No longer does he, in his flight, brush lightly against the world around him, he falls on it with the full force of his weight, leaving the imprint of his fall. . . . Since he is no longer obliged to run one gesture into another or to consider their relationship with those which follow, he holds nothing of himself in reserve for the transition.

If we can but stop associating grace with symmetry and *arabesques*, we shall find it everywhere in 'Le Sacre du printemps', in the heads in profile contrasted with bodies full-on, in the elbows hugged into the waist, in the horizontal forearms, in the stiff open hands, in the wavelike vibration which runs through the dancers from head to foot, in the minimal and mysterious parade of brooding girls in the second scene. We shall even find it in the dance of the Chosen Virgin, in her quick, awkward convulsions, in her confusion, in her awful waits, in her constrained, twisted bearing and in the arm raised stiffly skywards above her head as a call for help, in threat and in self-protection. . . .

This is a biological ballet. It is not only the dance of the most primitive men, it is the dance before man. . . . Stravinsky tells us that he wanted to portray the surge of spring. But this is not the usual spring sung by poets, with its breezes, its birdsong, its pale skies and tender greens. Here is nothing but the harsh struggle of growth, the panic terror from the rising of the sap, the fearful regrouping of the cells. Spring seen from inside, with its violence, its spasms and its fissions. We seem to be watching a drama through a microscope. . . .[71]

Not since the reception of 'Tannhäuser' at the old Opéra in the rue Le Peletier in 1861, or even since the first night of Hugo's 'Hernani' at the Comédie Française in 1830, had there been such a battle as took place at the new Théâtre des Champs-Elysées on 29 May 1913. At the première of Hugo's play blocks of free seats had been distributed to art and architectural students and poets: these were the passionate supporters of Hugo, the young Romantics with their long hair and exotic attire; and he described looking through a hole in the curtain: 'From floor to ceiling the theatre was a mass of silk, jewels, flowers and bare shoulders. Amid all this splendour, in the pit and the second balcony, could be seen two broad patches of a darker colour marked by the waving of huge manes of hair.'[72] Much the same situation arose on the first night of 'Le Sacre'. Valentine Gross,* a hundred of whose studies of the Russian Ballet (including fifty of Nijinsky) were on exhibition in the foyer, describes it well:

I look back with delight at the uproar of that evening. At that time in the new theatre there was an ambulatory between the boxes of the *corbeille*† and the big boxes – and in those days there were no *strapontins* [folding seats]. It was here that stood all the painters, poets, journalists, and musicians who were friends of Diaghilev, all the representatives of the new ideas and movements of that marvellous period. This band of Apollo was like a delightful river – calm, for the most part – flowing between the ramparts of the boxes, which were ablaze with diamonds and pearls. I knew already that the music of this ballet outstripped in violence and in dangerous experiment anything that had gone before. I also knew that the choreography had necessitated an incredible amount of work and that Nijinsky had

* Who was to marry Jean Hugo, the great-grandson and heir of the poet.
† A novelty of the Théâtre des Champs-Elysées was that the front of the dress-circle was divided into pew-like boxes. The enclosed boxes of the horse-shoe were some way behind these

shown a terrible determination during the countless and arduous rehearsals – had even, one day at the theatre, lost his temper to such an extent, teaching the ballet to the company, that he had literally nearly hit the ceiling of the rehearsal room – but I was expecting neither so great a work of art, nor such a scandal.

Nothing that has ever been written about the battle of 'Le Sacre du printemps' has given a faint idea of what actually took place. The theatre seemed to be shaken by an earthquake. It seemed to shudder. People shouted insults, howled and whistled, drowning the music. There was slapping and even punching. Words are inadequate to describe such a scene. Calm was briefly restored when the order was suddenly given to put up the house lights. It amused me to see how certain boxes whose occupants had been so noisy and vindictive in the dark quietened down when the lights went on. I must admit that our calm river had become a raging torrent. I saw Maurice Delage, beetroot-red with indignation, little Maurice Ravel truculent as a fighting-cock and Léon-Paul Fargue spitting out crushing remarks at the hissing boxes. I cannot think how it was possible for this ballet, which the public of 1913 found so difficult, to be danced through to the end in such an uproar. The dancers could not hear the music. . . . Diaghilev thundered orders from his box. . . . I missed nothing of the show which was taking place as much offstage as on. Standing between the two middle boxes, I felt quite at ease at the heart of the maelstrom, applauding with my friends. I thought there was something wonderful about the titanic struggle which must have been going on in order to keep these inaudible musicians and these deafened dancers together, in obedience to the laws of their invisible choreographer. The ballet was astoundingly beautiful.[73]

Jean Cocteau thought the public's reaction inevitable:

All the elements of a scandal were present. The smart audience in tails and tulle, diamonds and ospreys was interspersed with the suits and *bandeaux* of the aesthetic crowd. The latter would applaud novelty simply to show their contempt for the people in the boxes. . . . Innumerable shades of snobbery, super-snobbery and inverted snobbery were represented, which would need a chapter to themselves. . . . The audience played the role that was written for it. . . .[74]

Between the two scenes the police were called in to seek out and eject the most violent demonstrators. But it was in vain. No sooner had the curtain risen on the trembling girls of Part II, their tilted heads propped on the back of their hands, than a voice called out '*Un docteur!*', then another: '*Un dentiste!*', followed by another: '*Deux dentistes!*'[75] There was laughter, shouting and whistling; and the battle was renewed. One smart lady in an orchestra box stood up and slapped the face of a man in the box next-door, who was hissing. Her escort rose and cards were exchanged by the two men, who fought a duel next day. Another society woman spat in the face of one of the demonstrators.[76] Comtesse René de Pourtalès* (whose photograph

* Whom Mme Romola Nijinsky calls 'La Princesse de P'.

reveals an expression of fatuous pride) rose to her feet in her box, tiara askew, and cried out, brandishing her fan, 'I am sixty years old and this is the first time anyone has dared to make fun of me!'[77] Florent Schmitt shouted at the boxes '*Taisez-vous, les garces du seizième!*', of which the London equivalent might be 'Shut up, you Kensington bitches!' And a woman called Ravel 'a dirty Jew'.[78] Carl van Vechten described how 'The young man seated behind me in the box stood up during the course of the ballet to enable him to see more clearly. The intense excitement under which he was labouring betrayed itself presently when he began to beat rhythmically on the top of my head with his fists. My emotion was so great that I did not feel the blows for some time.'[79] At one point Diaghilev climbed to the gallery, and his voice was heard by the dancers coming from very far away, calling '*Je vous prie. Laissez s'achever le spectacle!*'[80] Leaning from his box, Astruc shouted, '*Ecoutez d'abord. Vous sifflerez après!*'[81]

I was sitting in the fourth or fifth row on the right [wrote Stravinsky], and the image of Monteux's back is more vivid in my mind today than the picture of the stage. He stood there apparently impervious and as nerveless as a crocodile. It is still almost incredible to me that he actually brought the orchestra through to the end. I left my seat when the heavy noises began – light noise had started from the very beginning – and went backstage behind Nijinsky in the right wing. Nijinsky stood on a chair, just out of view of the audience, shouting numbers to the dancers. I wondered what on earth these numbers had to do with the music for there are no 'thirteens' and 'seventeens' in the metrical scheme of the score.[82]

Bronia was standing beside her brother. Eleonora was in the front row.[83]

Romola had rushed behind the scenes after Part I, to find the dancers on the verge of tears. The passage leading to the dressing-rooms and stage-door of the Théâtre des Champs-Elysées is at the back of the stage, to the left. So great were the crowds of excited Russians in the wings – and there were singers in the theatre as well as dancers, because the programme would finish with 'Prince Igor' – that she could not get through them to return to her seat. Grigoriev and Kremnev tried in vain to break up this throng. There was a similar crowd behind the backcloth, through which Vassili had to force a way for Nijinsky. He was in practice costume, not yet having dressed or made up for 'Le Spectre', which was to follow. 'His face was as white as his *crêpe-de-Chine* dancing shirt. He was beating the rhythm with both fists shouting "Ras, dva, tri" to the artists. The music could not be heard. . . . His face was quivering with emotion. I felt sorry for him. . . .'[84]

'*Dans l'adversité de nos meilleurs amis,*' wrote La Rochefoucauld, '*nous trouvons toujours quelque-chose qui ne nous déplaît pas.*' Some of the warmest admirers of Stravinsky and Nijinsky, like Valentine Gross, had enjoyed the battle. It was an experience, something to talk about. Even Diaghilev – or one side of him – must have been conscious that the scandal was not without its 'news value'. But Diaghilev and Stravinsky could seek consolation with their friends. Nijinsky had to dress, make up and dance 'Le Spectre de la rose' immediately afterwards. And the *corps* had to get ready for 'Prince Igor'. It could hardly, by the way, be called a well-planned programme.

It was the anniversary of 'L'Après-midi d'un faune', chosen deliberately by the superstitious Diaghilev. Reflecting on the reception of his third ballet, Vaslav must have wondered if indifference was the only alternative to scandal.

After the 'performance' [Stravinsky recalled], we were excited, angry, disgusted, and . . . happy. I went with Diaghilev and Nijinsky to a restaurant. So far from weeping and reciting Pushkin in the Bois de Boulogne as the legend is,* Diaghilev's only comment was: 'Exactly what I wanted.' He certainly looked contented. No one could have been quicker to understand the publicity value and he immediately understood the good thing that had happened in that respect. Quite probably he had already thought about the possibility of such a scandal when I first played him the score, months before, in the east corner ground room of the Grand Hotel in Venice. [85]

But, of course, whatever his real feelings were, Diaghilev was trying to cheer Nijinsky up, to make him a little proud of the results of his hard work. 'Le Sacre' was the child of their love, even though initially conceived by Roerich and Stravinsky.

Roerich's décor, being less revolutionary, attracted little notice in comparison with the music and choreography of 'Le Sacre'. If all the arts kept in step together to aid the historian's generalizations the designs of Nijinsky's ballet should have been by Picasso. But in the world of Proust, Reynaldo Hahn, Jacques-Emile Blanche and the Russian Ballet the name of Picasso had not yet been spoken. It would not be for four years that, recruited by Cocteau, the young cubist painter worked for Diaghilev. Roerich was not made much of and returned to Russia, feeling he had not been given his due.[86] (He later became a hermit in the Himalayas, dying in 1947.)

After Calmette's attack on 'L'Après-midi d'un faune' in the previous year and the subsequent controversy which Rodin may be said to have won on Nijinsky's behalf, we could hardly expect a critic on *Le Figaro* would dare to give any new creation of the young choreographer's a good notice. Henri Quittard had scorned 'Jeux': 'Le Sacre' he insultingly brushed aside.

I think we can pass over M. Nijinsky's choreography and the inventions with which this frantic beginner gives proof of his newly discovered genius. If we could for a moment doubt his good faith, we might justifiably be angry. To pull the public's

* Cocteau's much-quoted story.

leg not just once but again in this heavy-handed way would not be in the best of taste. Unfortunately for M.Nijinsky he is evidently dead serious. He will no doubt persevere and if his creations appear daily more ridiculous he will not be able to help it. . . . This new art form, such as it is, already has its admirers. If only their enthusiasm were less noisy! 'Le Sacre du printemps' was rather badly received yesterday and the public was hard put to restrain its mirth. It would therefore have been in better taste if those who thought differently – and there were not many of them – had refrained from applauding the authors on stage in a way everybody found not only impertinent but absurd.[87]*

Quittard denied Nijinsky's admirers the right to express their approval. Bigotry could go no further.

The turncoat Louis Laloy, who had wanted to collaborate with Debussy and Nijinsky in 1909, wrote: 'Some of us would have liked to rescue the score from the stage spectacle, had not M.Stravinsky opposed this suggestion with all his strength, insisting that the choreography was just what he wanted and surpassed his expectations. His loyalty is praiseworthy. The consequence is total disaster.'[88] He was to elaborate on his views in *La Revue française de la musique*. Repeating the great joke which nearly all the critics made about 'Le Massacre du Printemps', Laloy wrote:

Massacre, firstly because we managed to hear so little of it . . . massacre also because it seemed monstrous to more than one theatre-goer that the spring should be celebrated by the epileptic fits of M.Nijinsky and by so sadly discordant a score. . . . The dancing is absurd: to spin out for an hour and a half [*sic*] a choreography of puppets on strings would seem like a bad joke if one had not ample proof of the sincerity and devotion of M.Nijinsky, who is an acrobat of incomparable elevation, but a ballet-master totally devoid of ideas and even common sense. . . . The composer has written a score that we shall not be ready for until 1940.[89]

Georges Pioch in *Gil Blas*:

Not once can the strings be heard. Listen to the Prelude, which is dominated by a wind instrument. We ask each other 'What instrument produces these sounds?' I say 'It's an oboe.' My right-hand neighbour, who is a great composer, insists that it is a muted trumpet. My left-hand neighbour, who is no less of a musical scholar, declares 'I should have thought it was a clarinet.' In the interval we ask the conductor himself, and we are told it was a bassoon that gave us such heart-searchings. . . . I must persist in thinking what a pity it is that M.Nijinsky, who is such a good dancer and jumps better than anyone, should one day have discovered he was a genius – like everyone else in the theatre in these years of plenty. His experiments hitherto have been damaging to the Russian Ballet; and we cannot forget that all the marvellous creations this company have given us were the work of M.Fokine, who was content to be a choreographer. . . .[90]

* Mr Stravinsky denies that he took a call after the first performance of 'Le Sacre'.

Henry Postel du Mas, interviewing Stravinsky, suggested, 'Nijinsky's production has been criticized as being opposed to the music.' 'That is not true. Nijinsky is a remarkable artist, capable of giving new life to the whole art of ballet. Not for a second have we ceased to think along the same lines. You'll see later on what he will do. He is not only a marvellous dancer: he is capable of creation and innovation. He has played a vital part in the collaboration of "Le Sacre du printemps".' But M.du Mas did not agree with the composer. 'Let him give up . . . making out of the "Sacre" the "Massacre du printemps".'[91]

In *Le Monde Musical* Auguste Mangeot wrote, 'As for the choreography, this time, unlike that of "Jeux", it is far from uninteresting. Although grotesque and absurd it is oddly impressive.'[92]

However, Gaston de Pawlowski, editor-in-chief of *Commedia*, himself wrote a long, illustrated, front-page article on the 31st, castigating the manners of the public and affirming the artist's right to experiment. 'Where were those shits* brought up?' – he quotes one of the politer remarks heard on 'the elegant and memorable' evening which was not ' "Le Sacre" but "Le Massacre du Printemps" '. He thought that Nijinsky's 'ugly' movements had gone on too long, and could have been contrasted, with Romantic antithesis, with more 'beautiful' movements; but intelligently saw in them a kind of reflex action – thus showing that he had caught a glimpse of the new truth, the new way of expressing emotion which Nijinsky had hit upon.[93]

There were four performances of 'Le Sacre' in Paris – and Valentine Gross, among others, went to every one. A few cat-calls were heard at the last three performances but the battle was not repeated.[94]

Chaliapine's success in 'Khovanschchina' followed fast upon. Since Diaghilev was not satisfied with all of Rimsky's orchestration, parts of this opera had been reorchestrated by Stravinsky and Ravel. The Moscow painter Feodorovsky had made some splendid designs; Bolm arranged the Persian dances; and Mussorgsky's second opera, heard for the first time in the west, was acclaimed almost as much as 'Boris' had been in 1908.

The third new ballet of the season was 'La Tragédie de Salomé', with music of Florent Schmitt, choreography by Boris Romanov and décor by Sergei Sudeikine. This had been put on specially for Karsavina, who had reason to feel that she had lately been playing second fiddle to Nijinsky. The most striking part of it was the décor by the young Russian designer, much influenced by Aubrey Beardsley, though not in black and white but in sumptuous purple and gold. Karsavina wore an exiguous costume and a rose painted on her right knee. The latter miniature work of art was recreated for each performance by Dmitri Gunsbourg, who fancied himself as a painter.[95]

* *Salauds.*

'La Tragédie de Salomé' was not the story of Herod, Herodias, Salome and the Baptist in choreographic terms. St John's head was present on a pedestal, but Salome was the only character apart from some Negroes and Executioners. The Princess was supposed to be performing her frantic dance of expiation in limbo. After some preliminary caperings by the Negroes, Karsavina appeared at the top of a flight of steps, and as she descended, an endless black and gold train unrolled behind her. Then followed her bizarre solo: that was all.[96] As a youthful experiment by Fokine's pupil, the budding choreographer Romanov, the ballet deserved some credit: but of all Karsavina's roles it was the one which was least successful in showing off her wonderful qualities. Yet she contrived to give an air of aloofness to her performance, a subtle suggestion that she was not so much dancing as reliving the dance in her mind; and this was no small achievement.[97]

It could not be said, however, that 'Salomé' was a success. That made three new ballets which had failed with the public and the press. After all the work which had gone into them, particularly 'Le Sacre', this was a bitter disappointment to Diaghilev. While hoping that the new works would meet with a better reception in London, he concentrated his publicity on the opera.[98]

Since 1909, when she was an art student and sat in the gallery, the devoted Valentine Gross had seen every performance of the Russian Ballet in Paris. Scribbling in the dark, then working up her sketches later, then reworking them and producing finished paintings, pastels and pen-and-ink drawings, she had recorded Nijinsky in all his roles. She was an academic artist, and struggled continually to become less so, but her faithful eye and careful hand have bequeathed us the most extensive documentation of the Russian Ballet. This season, as we have seen, she had exhibited her work in the upstairs foyer of the theatre. She could not know that she was seeing the adored Nijinsky dance for the last time, but she would bear witness to his genius up to the end of her long life. One evening, shortly before the company left for London, she came into the wings immediately after a performance of 'Le Spectre de la rose'. She was amazed to find Nijinsky quite alone, curled up on the floor, panting, like a bird fallen from a nest. His hands were clutched over his heart, which she could hear beating in spite of the distant roar of applause.

He was like a crumpled rose in pain, and there was no one near him. I was so touched that I left him alone and said nothing. Then he saw me and sprang up like a child taken by surprise and came smiling towards me. As he stood beside me in his leotard sewn with damp purplish petals, he seemed a kind of St Sebastian, flayed alive and bleeding from innumerable wounds. In a halting but quite accurate

Nijinsky in 'Le Spectre de la rose'.
Drawing by Valentine Gross.

French he began to tell me how pleased he was with some pastels I had made of
'Jeux' and to thank me for the article I had written to go with them in *Comoedia
Illustré*. I was almost the only person to appreciate his choreography. When I said
goodbye, he took my hand in both of his in such a charming way that for the rest
of the evening I kept glancing down at it in wonder – this hand which had been
covered in dew on contact with the miraculous dancer.[99]

Diaghilev went to London ahead of the Ballet. Nijinsky and Nouvel
travelled separately from the company, and Romola went on the same boat
and train. During the journey from Paris to London she managed to exchange
a few words with Nijinsky, both in the corridor of the train, where she stood
outside the door of the compartment he shared with Nouvel, and on the
boat, where she braved the wind and weather to settle near him on deck. He
still had very little French and she hardly any Russian, but pantomime came
in useful. It seems inevitable – though Romola did not realize it – that
Vaslav had some idea by now that she was running after him. If in the
ensuing weeks he was to give few signs of knowing or noticing her, this may
have been partly catlike diplomacy and partly doubt of his own inclinations

and of her character and charms. Diaghilev in a straw-hat was at Victoria to meet him and shot Romola a surprised glance as Nijinsky raised his cap on saying goodbye to her. She herself was surprised at Vaslav's courage.

Romola stayed at the Stafford Hotel in St James's Place,* but took every chance that offered to lunch or dine at the Savoy Grill, where Diaghilev held court at a table by the open fireplace.[100]

The London season was to be for the first time at the Theatre Royal, Drury Lane. It was again sponsored by Sir Joseph Beecham, with Pierre Monteux conducting the ballet and Emile Cooper the opera. In the enforced absence of Monteux a newcomer, Rhené-Baton, would take over the last evenings of ballet. What made this season historic was that London was hearing Russian opera for the first time. To hear Mussorgsky's epic operas and to experience the Stravinsky–Nijinsky 'Sacre du printemps' – not to mention 'Jeux' and 'L'Après-midi d'un faune', which last ballet Diaghilev had been afraid to show the English in the previous year – to be able to hear Chaliapine one night and to see Karsavina and Nijinsky the next – that was something to keep one in London during July! On their side, Diaghilev and Nijinsky experienced a lessening of tension once the Paris season was over; the Savoy Hotel had become a kind of home to them, and they were always happy to see Lady Ripon, Lady Juliet Duff and Lady Ottoline Morrell again.

Hilda Munnings, who had been given the hideous name of Muningsova, which would surely deceive no-one, recorded some impressions of this fabulous season, during which she appeared for the first time with the Diaghilev Ballet in her home town – and on the stage where she had seen Dan Leno as a child.

Every pay-day – that is, once a fortnight – we would line up in the green-room behind the stage at Drury Lane, and Grigoriev would be sitting there at a table, with piles of golden sovereigns and half-sovereigns, silver crowns, half-crowns, shillings, sixpences and threepenny pieces. In those days, salaries in the Diaghilev ballet were calculated in French francs, and it cannot have been easy for Grigoriev to work out the sums due to different artists. It was quite a sight to see our company, all so elegantly dressed, lining up to receive those piles of gold and silver, and signing the ledger. Even I, with my fifteen gold sovereigns, plus a little silver, would feel as rich as Croesus as I walked out into the sunshine of Russell Street.

Classes were held at the Territorial Drill Hall in Chenies Street, off Tottenham Court Road. They always began at nine o'clock, and woe betide anyone who was late. We would arrive to find Maestro Cecchetti watering the floor and whistling

---

* Mme Romola Nijinsky says in her book, p. 172, 'a very smart but small hotel in Mayfair behind St James's Palace.' St James's is not, of course, in Mayfair. She confirmed during conversations with the author that the hotel was the Stafford.

an unidentifiable tune. He had a funny way of breaking into a whistle as he was talking to you.

Diaghilev allowed several painters and sculptors to watch these classes. Among them were Laura Knight and Una Troubridge, whose head of Nijinsky as the Faun – the only sculpture of him except Rodin's little sketch* ever done from life – I was to find in a junk-shop forty years later. Nijinsky was certainly the main target of these artists, and sometimes when he worked privately with Cecchetti during the lunch hour they were allowed to stay and sketch. There was one girl who was always sitting, watching in silence, and we were surprised to find that she was allowed to join in our classes with Cecchetti. As she was not a regular member of our company this was exceptional. We learned that she was the daughter of a famous Hungarian actress. Diaghilev, who never let pass an opportunity to make up to influential people, had allowed her to study with us, although she was not really a dancer. Her name was Romola de Pulszka. She spoke English and used to come and sit in the *corps de ballet* dressing-room and talk to me.

Nijinsky, I noticed, even though he was always surrounded by people, seemed always to be alone; he was incapable of mixing in any way. If he spoke at all it was to somebody with whom he was dancing, and then he would talk softly and shyly, without looking at the person, and move away as quickly as possible. Before working, Nijinsky used to walk about a lot on the tips of his toes. He would move a few steps to the right, then a few to the left, holding his hands up in a curious characteristic way with the backs touching his cheeks, his head tilted downward. He used to do a lot of jumps in the first position, gradually jumping higher and higher, then lower in a *diminuendo*. This is a very good way to practise jumping, and I have always copied it.[101]

The London season opened with 'Boris Godounov' on 24 June, and Mussorgsky and Chaliapine were alike acclaimed by a new public.

Each scene [wrote the critic of *The Times*] was so absorbing that one was immediately caught in the spirit of the thing; it was intensely real and even the distressingly long pauses between the scenes and the ineptitude of an audience who would insist upon applauding as soon as the curtain fell and before the music was finished did not betray the sense of reality. It is difficult to say how far Mussorgsky, how far the extraordinarily powerful acting of M. Chaliapine and the other principals, the fine singing, and natural action of the crowds, or the beauty of the scenery were responsible for the effect. They were all fused together in the total result.[102]

On the second night 'Jeux', called in England 'Playtime', was shown. Richard Capell, writing in the *Daily Mail*, seemed mystified, but tried to be loyal.

The new 'Playtime' is disconcerting, delicious and discreetly amusing as is M. Debussy's music. . . . The dancing seems inspired by the archaic, but should perhaps be called 'futuristic'. What was the antique stiffness that seemed well in

---

* If this really is of Nijinsky.

place in M.Nijinsky's first ballet doing here? The piece in effect struck one as a parody of 'The Afternoon of a Faun'. While it was in progress the audience were hilarious in a way not kind; but afterwards there was so much applause that it cannot be denied success.[103]

The critic of the *Morning Post*, likewise, was not sure what side he found himself on. Remarking that there was a fuller house for the Russian ballet than for the Russian opera on the previous night – which was understandable as Russian opera was an unknown quantity – he wrote of 'Jeux':

It works out as a highly impressionistic business enacted in front of a weird green and red background with round splotches of white here and there to represent the electric lights. . . . Their [the dancers'] actions are of the quaintest. They suggest that they are suffering from 'tennis wrist' all over. They move with the angularity of clockwork figures. Everything is at an angle. The only thing with a curve in it is the lost ball. . . . All . . . is expressed by angles, obtuse, acute, right angle, and, of course, triangle. The business is conceived in the vein of the Cubists. It is a triumph of angularity. It fits M.Debussy's music very well, and the music is wholly suited to it. . . . The cumulative rhythms – wholly meaningless – are suited with action of similar character. Mlles Karsavina and Schollar and M.Nijinsky turn themselves very successfully into clockwork figures. The absence of the doll-like costume as found in 'Petrushka' spoils a good deal of the effect, for in a country like this, where tennis is understood, the ridiculous character of the whole thing is perfectly clear. The audience first laughed and then applauded.[104]

Diaghilev took pains to make 'Le Sacre' acceptable to the London public. A longer scenario was printed and Edwin Evans spoke from the stage to introduce and explain the ballet.[105] The English received the work with respect, if without enthusiasm.

The first night of 'Le Sacre du printemps' on 11 July was described in *The Times* as follows:

London takes both its pleasures and its pains more quietly than Paris. When 'Le Sacre du Printemps', the latest joint product of MM.Nijinsky and Stravinsky, was produced for the first time in England last night at Drury Lane, the applause was measured, but so were the cries of disapproval. Mr Evans, it is true, was obliged to cut short his preliminary remarks before the curtain, and a certain amount of whistling and half-suppressed laughter was heard during the performance; but that was, perhaps, not very surprising, for Mr Evans forgot that it was for the ballet and not the lecture that people were there, and there are limits to what an English audience can endure when presented with something quite new, especially when it is not certain whether the oddest features of it are purposely or accidentally grotesque. However, M.Nijinsky had not much to complain of in his reception, and both Mlle Piltz, upon whom the heaviest burden fell (amongst those on the stage), and M.Monteux, who achieved a miracle of conducting, were very warmly applauded. . . . The music, at any rate on the harmonic side, though again perfectly consistent, has moved so far ahead even of 'Petrushka' that it parts company with anything coming even from Paris that one has heard before. This at least ought to convince Mr Gordon Craig that even if the Russian ballet belongs, as he has lately been telling us it does, to the theatre of yesterday, the music is not always exactly retrospective. . . . Most of the time one seems to be looking at marionettes rather than children or savages, and many of the movements seem to be the result of some stern and invisible hand moving the puppets by an inexorable decree, the purport of which is known to the owner of the hand, but has only at certain moments been declared to others.[106]

The *Morning Post* was antagonistic. 'These early individuals, clothed in picturesque dresses of many centuries later, indulge in gestures that are supposed to be "of the period". They better suggest a physical culture class. . . . M.Monteux, the conductor, was called on to the stage at the end, also M.Nijinsky, who seemed relieved at the indifferent attitude of the audience.'[107] There was no notice by Richard Capell in the *Daily Mail*: perhaps he had gone on holiday. After the third performance of 'Le Sacre' on the 23rd, which was conducted not by Monteux but by Rhené-Baton, *The Times* concluded that Stravinsky and Nijinsky 'have achieved something that, in spite of its defects, is a step nearer to a real fusion of music and dancing'.[108]

Writing to Astruc from the Savoy Hotel, Bakst described the 'fantastic success' of the season and reported that the Russian opera was as popular as the ballet. 'That's the difference between London and Paris.' He continued, 'Wonderful weather, hectic life. In fact London is a marvellous place, but alas! very expensive.' He was writing to ask for money.[109] But the gallant and audacious Astruc had undertaken in his Théâtre des Champs-Elysées something which could not possibly pay its way, and by the middle of October he would be bankrupt. For the everlasting glory of having presented Nijinsky's 'Sacre du printemps' the price was ruin.[110]

So London saw for the last time Nijinsky dancing with the Diaghilev Ballet, which had made him glorious and in whose productions he and Karsavina had raised the art of ballet to a higher plane than it had ever before attained. And the devoted English admirers, who had watched him so often in 'Les Sylphides', in 'Carnaval', in 'Le Pavillon d'Armide', in 'Le Spectre de la rose', in 'Schéhérazade' – the critics, the artists, the writers, the noble ladies – Richard Capell, Cyril Beaumont, Osbert Sitwell, Rupert Brooke, Lytton Strachey, Duncan Grant, Ottoline Morrell, Violet Rutland, Gwladys Ripon, Juliet Duff – would see him in these works no more.*

Nijinsky's 'Le Sacre du printemps' had been given four performances in Paris, and it had three in London: seven in all. When Diaghilev wanted to revive it seven years later no one could remember the choreography and

---

* But they would see him in a new version of 'Les Sylphides'.

Massine had to start again from scratch. Now that we have the piano score annotated by Stravinsky, with reminders for Nijinsky of the timing of certain movements they had planned together, which came to light in 1967; and with the few hitherto unpublished pastels by Valentine Gross found among her papers after her death; with recollections by Dame Marie Rambert and Mme Sokolova set beside descriptions by one or two historians – with all these added to the tremendous essay of Jacques Rivière we are able to form some idea of what the ballet was like. I am convinced that even Diaghilev and Stravinsky did not entirely appreciate the power of Nijinsky's Blake-like vision or recognize how far ahead of his time he was, and I acclaim 'Le Sacre' not only as a masterpiece, the climax of Nijinsky's career, but also as a seminal work, a turning point in the history of the dance, the ballet of the century. Isadora had asked Nijinsky to have a child by her and he had refused: yet their progeny are legion. Their names are Martha Graham, Doris Humphrey, Merce Cunningham, Antony Tudor, Paul Taylor, Glenn Tetley, Norman Morrice, John Chesworth, Christopher Bruce, Alwin Nikolais, Robert Cohan, Rudi van Dantzig, Geoff Moore.

After this most resplendent of seasons the company had only a fortnight's holiday before sailing to fulfil their engagement in South America. Romola de Pulszky went to enjoy the English sunshine with her old governess in Sussex. Diaghilev, Nouvel and Vaslav travelled to Baden-Baden and stayed at the Hôtel Stéphanie once again. Here they were joined by Benois. A ballet to music of Bach was planned, which was to have 'all the elaborate splendour of Court festivals of the rococo period – the splendour of pageants and fireworks and illuminations'. Benois had already decided on the inclusion of certain pieces, but at Baden-Baden the friends settled down to a systematic perusal of Bach's works, and hired a German pianist to play through the master's innumerable compositions on the modest hotel piano. Nouvel would sometimes replace him, and Diaghilev and Nijinsky joined with the others in discussing which pieces would go well together to make a ballet. In a week the music had been chosen. The selected compositions were from the Englische Suiten, the Klavierwerke, the Praeludien, Fugen und Suiten and the Wohltemperiertes Klavier. (A complete list with indications as to which number is a solo, *pas de deux*, dance for men, women, peasants or the whole company, is in the Musée de l'Opéra, Paris.) Books were next sought to help Vaslav with the choreography and period style. It was understood that on their return from South America, Diaghilev would take him to the Cabinet des Estampes in Paris and the Museo Correr in Venice. In the meanwhile Benois conducted him on a tour of neighbouring rococo palaces and churches. They visited Einsiedeln, Bruchsal and the Archbishop's palace at Würzburg, 'places where eighteenth-century music seemed to have been crystallized in enchanting architectural forms'.[111] So the last great works of art Vaslav set eyes on before crossing the Atlantic into the unknown were Tiepolo's masterpieces, the ceiling over the Archbishop of Würzburg's staircase depicting Olympus, and that of the Kaisersaal with the dizzy Triumph of Apollo.

How incredulously Diaghilev and Nijinsky would have received the information, had they been told, as they listened to the music of Bach and craned their necks to study the rainbow frescoes, that they would never be alone together again! But Diaghilev dreaded the ocean voyage; he was totally uninterested in South America, which presumably had no picture-galleries, museums or Archbishops' palaces; he was doubtless drawn to spend the rest of August and September in Venice, where perhaps adventures with pretty dark-eyed boys awaited him; and he decided to stay in Europe.

When the S.S. *Avon*, 11,073 tons, captain C. E. Down, sailed from South-ampton on 15 August[112] Romola de Pulszky's dismay at finding Nijinsky was not on board with the rest of the company was only to be equalled by her rapture when he boarded the ship at Cherbourg on the following day without Diaghilev.* There were other absentees. Karsavina, dreading a long voyage, was travelling on a faster ship.[113] Bronislava Nijinska was in Petersburg with her mother, expecting a baby in two months. Piltz was pregnant too, and had stayed behind.†[114] If someone wanted to marry Nijinsky – whether Romola de Pulszky or Miriam Ramberg – Vassili was the only person who might be able to stop them, and then only by cutting their throats.

But Ramberg was in a second-class cabin on a lower deck, which she shared with Hilda Muningsova. Romola's second-class cabin was occupied by her maid Anna: for herself she had bought a first-class ticket, and her state-room was within sight of Nijinsky's.[115]

As the *Avon* sails down the west coast of France in summer weather, and 'birds of calm sit brooding on the charmèd wave', the narrative takes on the unreal character of certain kinds of drama, such as the Barrie fantasy where people change their natures in a mystic wood or come into their own on a desert island, or the more prosaic kind in which a group of heterogeneous types are stranded through a wreck, snowstorm or breakdown in a lifeboat, airport waiting-room or isolated mountain hotel.

Life on a luxurious ocean liner was a new kind of holiday for the company

---

* Since Nijinsky boarded the *Avon* at Cherbourg, Grigoriev's assertion, possibly arising from a misunderstanding with his editor, Vera Bowen, that Diaghilev travelled to London to 'say goodbye' to the company, which he had only left a fortnight before, is inherently improbable. Mme Sokolova has no recollection of such a scene.

† Mme Romola Nijinsky writes of her as being on the South American voyage, possibly confus-ing her with Pflanz.

and one which even the sophisticated Romola had never experienced. Only Muningsova – in her previous incarnation as Hilda Munnings – had ever crossed the Atlantic to dance in America before.[116] The voyage would last twenty-one days, but the *Avon* was to call at Vigo, Lisbon and Madeira, and until she left European waters a regular routine of ship-board life would not be established. There were three constant factors, however, in the company's daily life. Olga Khokhlova was sick every day;[117] Ramberg, who hated the heat and sometimes fainted on account of it, intent on self-improvement, did a class alone in her cabin;[118] and Romola de Pulszky made herself charming to anyone who might be useful in bringing her into contact with Nijinsky, systematically patrolling the deck – although she hated walking – in pursuit of her shy quarry.[119]

Putting ourselves in Romola's place and banishing from our minds the knowledge of what came after, we must admit that there was nothing fundamentally wrong in her pursuit of Nijinsky. After all, men have been so struck by the beauty or talent of actresses or dancers that they have followed them round the world in hope of love, sex, friendship or even a crumb of attention. They do not even have to be in love to act in this way, only stage-struck or beglamoured by the personality of a star. Nobody blames them. To deny a woman the right to chase a man of genius one would have to be a really die-hard anti-feminist. That Romola should set her cap at Nijinsky without being in love with him was odd, but it was not wrong. She was twenty-three and determined and it was an adventure. She had the good taste to admire Nijinsky's genius: how could she weigh the consequences to the Russian Ballet if she succeeded in separating him from Diaghilev, or foresee the effect it would have on Vaslav himself? Young people do not look ahead. And of course, she could not *really* believe it possible, strong-willed though she was, that she would be engaged to Nijinsky before setting foot on South American soil. It was a kind of game for her, an impossible test she set herself. If we admire Alexander of Macedon for marching forth to conquer India, we must concede a little admiration for the spirit of Romola de Pulszky (whose grandfather had rebelled against the Habsburgs and whose uncle had subdued Madagascar) which spurred her on to connect herself in some way with the artist she admired above all others.

And what was in Nijinsky's mind at the beginning of this long hot voyage? Certainly he had no idea of getting married and none of leaving Diaghilev. His whole life was the Russian Ballet and he loved his work. He cannot but have worshipped Diaghilev for giving him such glorious roles and the opportunity to create ballets, for having made him the idol of the European world. Even if he did not adore him physically, he must have felt for him the love of a successful pupil for an inspiring master who has opened a door on all the wonders of the world. His every action must have been designed to win Diaghilev's approval. But he was twenty-four; he was at sea; and the sun was shining. He wanted – needed – to make love.

Whether, as he lay alone in his state-room, he dreamed of a male or a female partner seems comparatively beside the point. Perhaps either would have done. (Incidentally, although a relationship of Vaslav with a woman need not – and did not in the event – make it utterly impossible for him to work in Diaghilev's company, an affair with another man would put this out of the question. Diaghilev's jealousy could never rise above that.) I think it is possible that on this voyage, separated from Diaghilev, he could have been seduced by another young man and even fallen in love with him; but it is more likely that his thoughts were of girls.

Girls, however, presented a problem for this reticent, hard-working and secluded young man; and his exalted position placed a barrier between him and the other dancers. He could not possibly, for instance, expose himself to comment, gossip or ridicule by going courting the lovely auburn-haired Khokhlova, or blonde Muningsova, or clever Bewicke in the second class! Then, he was such a well brought-up boy, so sensitive and with such gentlemanly principles that an ephemeral affair must seem sordid and beneath him. Only a beautiful romance would sanctify sexual relations – that or marriage. And even if he was prepared to let down Diaghilev, how could either of these come about? For Nijinsky to make love at all was very difficult.

But Nature, the blind matchmaker, had provided for this exceptional situation. Just as M. de Charlus, in the opening scene of Proust's *Sodome et Gommorrhe,* by paying a call on Mme de Villeparisis, because of her indisposition, at the odd hour of ten in the morning, had the luck to meet the tailor Jupien, one of the rare homosexuals who only liked old men, and who had not yet left for his office; and just as the bee brought the improbable pollen to fertilize the rare orchid of the Duchess, which would otherwise have been condemned to sterility: so did Nature bring into proximity with this rare orchid of a dancer, who could not seek for love among the members of his company and had little time or opportunity to look outside it, a young woman who was attached to the company and yet not of it, one who was a dancer and yet could be excepted from the rules applying to other dancers, an attractive girl of good birth and yet born into an artistic and theatrical family, and one who had inherited from courageous ancestors the spirit to take the initiative when her prospective partner could not. As Proust wrote about the good fortune of M. de Charlus and of the orchid: it was 'an accident so unlikely that one might call it a sort of miracle'. Viewed either as a sport of nature or as a trick of chance, there was something beautiful about it.

Nature was not the sole matchmaker: there were others on board the *Avon* who, once the subject of the play was announced, would be only too willing to fill their appointed roles – Gunsbourg, his middle-aged mistress Ekaterina Oblokova, and a friend of hers in the *corps de ballet*, the chic, pretty Josefina Kovalevska, who had lived with the Aga Khan.[120] If Gunsbourg had already formulated a vague plan to run a ballet company without Diaghilev[121] – and, to give him credit, he had every reason to believe that no enterprise of Diaghilev's would ever attain solvency – it is still extremely unlikely that at the beginning of the voyage he could have imagined it possible to detach Nijinsky from Diaghilev – particularly by means of a woman. For with the naïveté of heterosexuals of that period he probably took it for granted that Nijinsky, because he lived with Diaghilev, was homosexual; and thought that if you were 'like that' you were 'like that' and did not change.

Only a few of the company travelled first class. At meals Nijinsky and the Batons sat at the captain's table; Gunsbourg and Oblokova shared a table with Kovalevska; Romola sat with Trubecki, his wife Pflanz, Bolm and a French-Argentinian dressmaker called Chavez.[122] From the day after the *Avon* left Cherbourg, however, the main body of the company who were travelling second were allowed to come up and visit their colleagues on the upper deck. Romola witnessed the meeting of Nijinsky and the Batons. Rhené-Baton had taken over from Monteux to conduct the last five performances of ballet at Drury Lane, but he had evidently made no contact with Nijinsky except across the footlights. He began to pour out his admiration for the dancer's art, and Mme Baton joined in. But Nijinsky's French was at that time extremely limited, and he shook his head, saying '*Non, non, moi pas comprend, moi parle petit nègre.*' Touched by his simplicity, Baton embraced him and declared that he would be his nurse and look after him during the voyage.[123] On the 17th the *Avon* docked for a few hours at Vigo.[124] The next day Romola went ashore at Lisbon with her friends; Vaslav with the Batons and Chavez.[125] When parties were made up to go ashore at Madeira on the 20th Romola was disappointed not to be included in that of the Batons and Nijinsky. Instead she went with Gunsbourg, Oblokova, Trubecki, Pflanz, Bolm, Kovalevska and Chavez. They nearly got left behind, having missed the last boat back. Romola saw her chances of getting to know Vaslav evaporating. The next ship was in three weeks' time. Oblokova and Kovalevska were in despair at the thought of being stranded without their clothes. Bolm wondered how the company could give 'Prince Igor' or 'Thamar' without him. But a rowing-boat was hired, the *Avon* sent out a launch, and they were saved.[126] They would not sight land again for a week.

Romola found that when she passed Nijinsky, seated with a book in his deck-chair, he never looked up or seemed to recognize her. He was reading Merejkovski's essays on Tolstoy and Dostoevsky.[127] In the afternoons, when most passengers lay with books in the sun or sleeping in their cabins, Nijinsky worked, with Baton at the piano, in a small hall on C deck where a companion-way led to the dining-room. He was working on his Bach ballet. Romola discovered him there and settled down to watch, seated on the steps, but was asked to move on by a steward. The next day she returned and this time it was Baton who asked her to go. Suddenly Nijinsky looked up from his notes and gestured that she might stay.[128] Had he been conscious of her admiration for weeks, and was this the first sign of his returning it? Or did the interest she now showed in his work first arouse his interest in her as a woman? Contact of a kind had been re-established.

Baton played the piano and Nijinsky stood beside him. Sometimes he closed his eyes and gave the impression that he did it to concentrate more on a whole choreographic theme. Or with his fingers he danced a full variation, which he composed while Baton played the piece; or he stopped him suddenly, made him play the same bar several times. All the time, as he stood there, one could feel that he was dancing constantly the steps he invented. And so a whole ballet was created before my wondering eyes. Occasionally he searched with Baton for hours for a suitable chaconne or prelude. He stopped Baton often, saying, '*Crois plus vite*' and Baton laughed, 'How true. I made a mistake. It is supposed to be faster.' . . . Baton told me Nijinsky was composing a new ballet on the music of Bach, to be as pure dancing as his music is pure sound. He wanted to lay down the harmony and fundamental truth of the movement. . . . Always when Baton failed to make himself understood Gunsbourg was summoned as interpreter. Very soon I tried to make myself liked by them. As I had been educated in Paris and I spoke French like a native, I won Mme Baton's heart easily. But I liked them both. They were kind good-hearted people. Among all the Russians we formed the little western European colony. Of course nobody knew that I was admitted to observe these hours of composition. I often wondered why I was. . . .[129]

Vaslav must have thought of Romola when he was alone. If he spoke to the Batons and Gunsbourg about her, would it not be natural that the idea of bringing together the solitary Nijinsky and the pretty Hungarian should take shape in their minds, and would not Gunsbourg discuss it with Oblokova and she with Kovalevska – the two *chic* bejewelled ladies putting their heads together – and would they not enjoy a gossip about the romantic possibilities with Chavez, the dressmaker?

Romola wondered why Vaslav never came on deck (in his usual smart light-coloured suit or navy-blue blazer and white trousers) until about eleven in the morning. Then, waking up earlier than usual one day, she found him practising to starboard, watched by a party of admiring English, with Vassili and Williams the masseur in attendance. She now set about making friends with Williams, who told her that though he could massage the strongest boxer indefinitely, Nijinsky's muscles were so like iron that after an hour's work on them he was exhausted.[130]

Ramberg was trying to avoid the attentions of the handsome Vladimir Romanov, who did not attract her. She had another admirer in a young Polish boy, Loboiko. In Lyons he had proposed that they should take a flat together in Monte Carlo, and when asked why, replied innocently, 'It would be cheaper.' One of Ramberg's friends was a lively little Polish girl, even smaller than herself, Jejerska, who had danced in the same group with her in 'Le Sacre'. They used to laugh together a lot. Jejerska had a lover in Warsaw who was a Russian officer. When asked by Mimi what she would do when she got home, she replied simply, 'I shall go to his house and give myself to him.' Another Polish girl of extreme prettiness was Maicherska. She was the mistress of Feodorov, and when he bit her in an excess of passion, she naïvely explained this away by saying her wash-stand had fallen on her. Ramberg also made friends with Oblokova, Kovalevska and Pflanz, with whom she was photographed on deck. Kovalevska was teased for her simplicity. During the Paris season a group of dancers had gone to her dressing-room and said, 'Have you heard the terrible news? Napoleon is dead.' She put down her hand-mirror, gazed at them in consternation and exclaimed, 'What a misfortune for Paris!' Diaghilev could not prevent the Aga Khan giving Kovalevska money and jewels – indeed, he rather liked his dancers to have grand lovers – but he had steadily refused all pressure to give her roles beyond the limits of her talent. The only concession the Aga Khan ever wrung from him was to allow her to wear a black dress instead of a white in the dance of the Jewesses in 'Cléopâtre'. Now she had been rejected and presumably pensioned off by the oriental religious leader; and she complained tearfully to Ramberg, 'I who have had my clothes from Doucet now have to go shopping at the Magasin du Louvre!'

Mimi saw Nijinsky from time to time and discussed the Merejkovski essays with him. He lent her some volumes of *Mir Iskustva*. She got to know and like the Batons. It was also one of her pleasures to visit Romola in her cabin, because it was so much cooler than her own: they talked while Anna combed Romola's pretty long fair hair. Romola took great pains to look her best. One night she wore a dark blue lace-trimmed dress by Doucet, with a hobble skirt and a big bow, known as a *noeud japonais*, at the back of the waist.[131]

As Nijinsky sat reading in his deck-chair before lunch Romola would make a point of greeting him, yet the voyage was half over before they had any real conversation and it was humiliating for her one moonlight night to find herself being introduced to him yet again by Chavez.

Nijinsky was half leaning against the railing in a 'smoking', holding a small black fan which was ornamented with one gold painted rose. He was rapidly fanning himself. He looked so strange. His eyes were half closed and oh! so slanted. He conversed in a soft melodious voice with Kovalevska in Polish. I was trembling as Chavez said '*Monsieur Nijinsky, permettez-moi de vous présenter Mdlle de Pulszky.*' He did not move; his eyes just closed with an imperceptible *nuance* and he slightly inclined his head. Kovalevska at once began to explain to him who I was.

Did not Romola's instinct tell her that he knew very well who she was, and that he was putting on his mysterious, irresistible faun face for the woman he had longed for and had been expecting God to send him?

I felt that both Chavez and Kovalevska were expecting me to say something. But suddenly every thought deserted me. I felt a chaos of emotion, saw nothing and nobody any more except the dark graceful silhouette of Nijinsky and his fascinating eyes. I suddenly heard myself speaking. '*Je veux vous remercier que vous avez élevé la danse à la hauteur des autres arts.*' Kovalevska translated. He did not move. Suddenly he looked at the small ring I wore. I followed his gaze and, pulling it off my finger, I passed it to him, explaining: 'My father brought it from Egypt; it is a talisman supposed to bring luck. My mother gave it to me as I left with the Russian Ballet.' It was a green-gold serpent whose head was crushed by a scarab. It had a strange design. Nijinsky held it for one moment and then put it on my finger, saying in Polish, 'It will bring you happiness, surely.' We all four of us began to walk around the deck. Suddenly Nijinsky stopped, looked into the phosphorescent waves. They were more luminous tonight than I had ever seen them before. I saw he was fascinated by the motion of the sea. He looked and looked. For a long time we watched in silence. Then I began to talk in French, choosing the easiest words, about dance, music, and Wagner, whose work I idolized. . . . Bayreuth and my childhood days which I had spent with my sister and brother-in-law at the Wahnfried at the rehearsals in the Festspielhaus. I don't know whether he understood a word of what I said, but he seemed to listen attentively. . . . Then Chavez called us. 'Come, come and look at the new constellations, the stars which cannot be seen in the northern hemisphere.' We looked up and saw in all its brilliant splendour the Southern Cross.[132]

Gunsbourg and Bolm were assiduous in organizing amusements. There was a fancy-dress ball. Gunsbourg told Romola that as she had the figure of a boy she should wear a pair of his apple-green silk pyjamas. Was this his idea of the best way to attract Nijinsky? At the last moment she put on a dress by Callot Soeurs, and, making her entrance to cries of disappointment from her friends, saw a look of relief in Nijinsky's eyes. He was the only other person, apart from the officers, not in fancy dress.[133] For him, we may guess, a costume was a magic thing which had to be lived up to and which transformed his spirit as well as his body. There was a party when they crossed the Equator on 28 August,[134] and a ball in the steerage at which

Nijinsky enjoyed watching the flamenco dancing.[135] Company classes were held.[136] Kovalevska taught Romola some of the roles she would have to dance in the *corps de ballet*.[137] Life passed pleasantly for everybody except poor Olga Khokhlova, who continued to be sick, and for those like Ramberg, who could not bear the heat.

After the *Avon* had docked for a day at Pernambuco and was sailing down the coast of Brazil,[138] Vaslav and Romola were several times observed to be seated together on deck in 'animated conversation'.[139] Animation was rare with him and his words were usually few and far between, but if Romola provided most of the sparkle and the talk, his few words of French, helped out by gestures, and his pleased expression made it clear to everyone that they were getting on very well together. The company were amazed – Gunsbourg, Oblokova and Kovalevska perhaps less so than the others. If Gunsbourg planned to form his own company with Nijinsky at its head, it was now up to him to do everything in his power to bind Vaslav and Romola together. The company began to discuss the surprising situation.[140] Bolm did not believe there could be anything in it.[141]

Nijinsky told Ramberg that he was in love with Romola. She did not take him seriously, convinced that he was as totally devoted to Diaghilev as Diaghilev was to him, and assuming that the love affair was no more than a ship-board flirtation. 'But how can you talk to her?' she asked. He replied vaguely 'Oh well. . . . She understands.'[142] In his imagination, as usual three jumps ahead of everyone else's, he no doubt already saw himself happily married with a large family.

On Saturday, 30 August, the *Avon*, having put in briefly at Bahia the day before,[143] was sailing south along the coast of Brazil, due to dock at Rio de Janeiro two days later. Romola was sitting before lunch in the bar with the Batons, Kovalevska and a few others when Gunsbourg approached her, saying he must speak to her privately. She was alarmed, thinking that Grigoriev or Kremnev, who took the classes, might have reported her for not being up to her work, but she went with Gunsbourg on deck. 'There he stopped and with a terrible formal face he said, "Romola Karlovna, as Nijinsky cannot speak to you himself, he has requested me to ask you in marriage." We looked at each other, and then I burst out "No, really, Dmitri Nicolaivitch, it's awful. How can you?" and, blushing, half crying, I ran as fast as I could down to my cabin, where I locked myself up for the rest of the day.'

Romola, unable to believe that her wish had come true, thought her friends had conspired to make fun of her. She remained shut up in her cabin, pretending to have a headache and refusing admittance even to Anna and Kovalevska. In the evening, however, she received a note from

Gunsbourg, saying that he could not keep Nijinsky waiting any longer and requesting her answer to the proposal. She dressed and went on deck. It was after eleven o'clock.

Unexpectedly, from nowhere Nijinsky emerged and said '*Mademoiselle, voulez-vous, vous et moi?*' and pantomimed, indicating on the fourth finger of the left hand, a ring. I nodded and, waving with both hands, said '*Oui, oui, oui.*'

Very gently, taking my hand, without a word he led me up to the upper deck. This was deserted. He pulled two deck-chairs under the captain's bridge, and there we sat in silence, hearing the rhythmically recurring steps of the officers on duty, the sound of the waves, following the line of the smoke which rose from the funnels, a dark ribbon against the clear night sky, which was covered by milliards of stars. I could feel the soothing, unceasing throb of the boat, and my own wildly beating heart. Everything was so peaceful in this tepid tropical night. I knew Nijinsky felt as I did. And as this white boat sailed placidly, with an inward hidden tremor, in the vastness of the infinite ocean towards its destination, so did we towards our fate.[144]

Next morning most of the company were up by six to see the fantastic harbour of Rio with its Sugar Loaf Mountain in the morning light. This was one of the unforgettable moments of Ramberg's life, like her first sight of the sea and sense of infinity on the North German coast, and her glimpse of golden clouds on arrival in Switzerland, which turned out to be the summit of Mont Blanc.[145] Josefina Kovalevska arrived in Romola's room on the heels of the morning coffee.

J.K. Ah, Romola Karlovna, I am so happy, so happy! This is wonderful news. I congratulate you with all my heart. Unbelievable. But somehow I always knew Vaslav Fomitch is not as people say.[146]

Not the most tactful way of putting it, one might think, but indeed the situation was so exceptional that the company would have to draw on every possible reserve of tact in order to react politely to news which must fill them with incredulity and dismay. 'Oh, to see the faces of the others when they hear,' cried Kovalevska. But it was Mme Baton who rushed into Ramberg's cabin with the announcement.

Mme B. Unbelievable news! Nijinsky is engaged to Romola!

And she did not see her friend's face, because Mimi in a sudden flash realized at last, with a sense of loss, that she loved Vaslav, and she bent over and pretended to be getting something out of a suitcase under the bunk in order to hide her tears.

When the bear-like Baton came up on deck to congratulate the happy couple he wrung Romola's hand so warmly that Vaslav was spurred to eloquence.

N. *Peux toucher, pas casser!*[147]

Nijinsky 1912–1913

The *Avon* docked at Rio on the evening of Sunday, the 31st, and was not to sail until 5.45 on the following afternoon;[148] so excursions were planned. People are only granted a few days of perfect happiness in their lives. Just as it is a joy to recall one's own, so is it a pleasure to consider those of others. Vaslav and Romola, on the first day of their engagement, not only had the excitement of going ashore after so long at sea, but that of setting foot on a new continent in a New World and of beholding the bay of Rio de Janeiro and exploring the surrounding mountains. Did anything – flies, the heat, shyness, the presence of Kovalevska, who acted as interpreter – mar their absolute content? After six months' perseverance Romola had got her way; and God had sent Vaslav a girl. The hour of consummation was not far off. Before driving out of the city they went into a jeweller's and Vaslav ordered two wedding rings to be engraved with their names and the date. Then they drove up Sylvestre Mountain, where in a chic hotel in the middle of the tropical forest they had lunch. This was the first time Vaslav and Romola had sat at a table together. In the afternoon they were driven through the mountains, beneath the orchid-laden trees, Romola feeling like a schoolgirl on a Sunday treat, seated between the God of the Dance and the ex-mistress of the Aga Khan. After calling for the rings, they returned to the boat to receive more congratulations. That night Romola sat beside Nijinsky at the captain's table.

After dinner Bolm took her aside. Many of the company must have foreseen disaster, but Bolm was the only one of those not afflicted by match-making madness whose position and whose friendship with Romola gave him the courage or the right to intervene.

A.B. Romola Karlovna, I have heard – I can't believe it – what is this talk about you and Nijinsky? I never imagined – why, you did not seem to be interested in him. What happened?

R.de P. Well, well, I don't always say what I think and feel.

A.B. But, after all, to get married – to a man you don't know – a perfect stranger – a person you can't even talk to.

R.de P. But I know Nijinsky, I've seen him dancing many, many times. I know his genius, his nature, everything.

A.B. You are a child. You know him as an artist, not as a man. He is a kind young man, a charming colleague, but I have to warn you he is utterly heartless.

Bolm tells her the story of Nijinsky's reaction – or lack of reaction – to the death of Thomas Nijinsky, stating that Vaslav must be without normal human feelings.

R.de P. Not necessarily. No, no, I am sure he has a kind heart. Anybody who dances as he does must be so. And I don't care.

A.B. Romola, I have to warn you. I know your parents. I have received the hospitality of your family. It is my duty. Nijinsky's friendship with Diaghilev, you may not understand, is more than merely a friendship, you see. He can't possibly be interested in you, and it will ruin your life.

R.de P. (*Very determinedly*) I thank you. I know you mean well, but I am going to marry him in spite of everything, even if you are right. I'd rather be unhappy serving Nijinsky's genius than be happy without him.

Bolm bows very low and walks away.[149]

The captain and Gunsbourg were all for a wedding on board ship, but Nijinsky wanted a 'proper service in a church'.[150] Both bride and groom, of course, were Catholic. When Vaslav conducted Romola to her cabin that night she expected him to come in with her. In Hungary an engagement-ring gave the right to pre-marital intercourse. But Vaslav kissed her hand, smiling, and said goodnight. Having come thus far, he wanted to do everything properly. She was not sure whether to be flattered or offended, and even wondered whether Bolm might not be right.[151]

Next day Romola enjoyed the company's congratulations and noticed with a certain satisfaction that Grigoriev, who had become rather autocratic in the absence of Diaghilev, was obsequiously polite.[152] She had not the inkling of an idea that she was going to split up the Russian Ballet. Nor did she foresee how much she would come to love Nijinsky,[153] or the long years of suffering, which were to bring out in her heroic qualities she did not know she possessed.

A cable to Emilia Markus asking for Romola's hand was put into the best literary French by Gunsbourg and sent off by radio.[154]

Gunsbourg gave a gala dinner on board in honour of the engagement on the night of the 2nd, but the *Avon* was sailing through St Catherine's Bay, famous for its storms, and as the ship pitched and tossed, one member of the company after another hurriedly left the dining-room.[155]

Mimi Ramberg stood on the prow looking down into the wild waves; and as the wind roared around her, beating her hair and skirt, she howled aloud to herself, 'I want to drown! I want to drown!' In her unhappiness, it was touch-and-go whether she might indeed have taken her life, but she felt a hand on her shoulder. It was her admirer, Vladimir Romanov.[156] Either from pity or hoping to catch her on the rebound from Nijinsky he had come out of the night to save her – for the future.

The *Avon* sailed past Santos and Montevideo and up the Rio la Plata. On Saturday the 6th,[157] at Buenos Aires, she disgorged her passengers, some of whose lives the voyage had irreparably changed, for better or for worse. Nijinsky and Romola both stayed at the Majestic Hotel, he in a suite on the first floor, she in a room on the third. On Sunday Nijinsky went to inspect the stage of the Teatro Colón, which he found large and splendid. Romola went sight-seeing in the Palermo Park with the Batons. They rejoined each other that evening at dinner with Karsavina, who had arrived ahead of them. As one might expect, Romola found Karsavina charming.[158] Presented with a *fait accompli*, the ballerina was spared the horrors of a decision whether to interfere – something which would have been profoundly distasteful to her. Now, she had only to be as nice as possible and hope for the best. She wondered whether, had she been on board the *Avon*, she would have tried to persuade Nijinsky that his marriage must prove disastrous to the Russian Ballet; and she could not decide what she would have done.[159]

On Monday, 8 September took place the company's first rehearsal. Romola was allotted by Grigoriev *corps de ballet* roles in 'Prince Igor', 'Cléopâtre' and 'Schéhérazade'. Then she was given a glimpse of a new side of her fiancé's character.

Nijinsky was practising, and sent over a message that he wished me to keep on my dancing costume as he intended to give me a lesson. I was petrified. I tried to escape, but could not. Trembling, I went up, almost crying, and began my exercises *à la barre*. I looked at him. A strange person stood before me. There was no recognition in his face: the impersonal look of a master towards his pupil. I ceased to be his *fiancée*. I was just a dancer. I expected shouts and cursing *à la Maestro*, but instead found infinite patience . . . he always stopped me when I wanted to force any movement.[160]

While Oblokova went shopping for a *trousseau* and wedding presents, Gunsbourg busied himself with sorting out formalities over the wedding, which was to be on the Wednesday. Nijinsky being Russian and Romola Austrian, there were complications. On Tuesday Gunsbourg drove them to church for Confession. Nijinsky confessed to a priest who spoke no Russian or Polish; and Romola was made to promise to try to stop her future husband from dancing in the 'immoral' 'Schéhérazade'.

The civil ceremony was performed, on Wednesday, 10 September, at one o'clock at the City Hall in the presence of only a few of the friends. Romola wore a dark blue pleated taffeta dress with pink moss-roses at the waist and a black 'Secession' hat with a curved brim and a blue ribbon.[161] The Mayor addressed the happy couple in Spanish. They signed an elaborate scroll and became man and wife.[162]

The whole company attended the wedding breakfast at the Majestic Hotel. Muningsova recalled it in later years: 'It was an extremely awkward occasion, for there was not a single person present – except possibly Gunsbourg . . . – who could honestly congratulate bride or groom.'[163] Had Muningsova known how the engagement had come about, she would have had to make exceptions of Oblokova and Kovalevska too. Karsavina, who never did anything without giving thought to it, made a beautiful speech. Bolm spoke too, and said, 'Nijinsky has made many remarkable jumps in his life, but none so remarkable as the one he made today.' Not only was there to be a church wedding in the evening, but this was to be followed by a dress-rehearsal. Some day! Romola was tired, and, leaving the table, asked Mimi Ramberg to go upstairs with her. Mimi was by now calmer and resigned to her loss. Nijinsky soon followed them, bringing a piece of wedding-cake for Romola, which she ate sitting up in bed. Vaslav pecked the crumbs off her fingers, kissing them as he did so, one by one.[164]

And so to the Church of San Miguel, where Romola, in an ivory-coloured silk dress, an improvised tulle turban and white shoes, bought that afternoon, arrived late and noticed a look of disappointment on Nijinsky's face. In this Argentinian church, full of ornate clergy and strange fat fashionable ladies, the Austro-Hungarian bride was led up the aisle to the music of Wagner's 'Lohengrin' on the arm of her Russian-Jewish friend and united to the Russian-Pole, whose language she did not speak, in a ceremony performed in Latin and Spanish, which neither of them could understand. Thence by carriage to their hotel, where photographers were waiting, to be given a yellow-pink pearl. And on to the dress-rehearsal, at which the bride had to dance an Almée in 'Schéhérazade' before the critical eyes of her husband crouching in his role of Negro Slave at the Sultana's feet, and fell flat on her face. Finally, greatest ordeal of all, supper in the hotel bedroom and the awkwardness of silence and the doubt over what was to come later.[165] Journeys end in lovers' meeting. Yes, Nijinsky had got a girl at last (if that was what he wanted) and Romola had achieved her ambition. Could his sexual impulse survive all these ceremonies? For her, would the pursuit have been worthwhile, after all? 'We ate in silence. . . . He only smiled and served me attentively. We were both so embarrassed that we could not even express ourselves in pantomime. And when, after supper, Nijinsky kissed my hand and left me, I was so relieved that I almost cried from thankfulness.'[166]

Let us look ahead and see what happened to some of the characters who took part in the voyage of the *Avon*, because we shall not run into all of them again. Gunsbourg was sent, during the 1914–18 war, on a mission to the Caucasus, where it was supposed he was killed by revolting Cossacks, since he never returned. Rhené-Baton became Director of the Orchestra Pasdeloup, enjoyed a career as a minor composer and lived until 1940. Bolm stayed with Diaghilev until the second wartime tour of the USA, then remained in America as choreographer and teacher, dying in Hollywood in 1951. Grigoriev and Tchernicheva were with Diaghilev until his death, she having become one of his leading dancers. Muningsova became the celebrated Lydia Sokolova. Feodorov, the lover of Maicherska, remained with Diaghilev till the end and mimed the Father in Balanchine's 'Fils Prodigue' in Diaghilev's last season in 1929, but later in Paris had all his savings stolen and hanged himself. Hilda Bewicke married a distinguished Persian soldier and diplomat, General Arfa. Olga Khokhlova married Picasso.

Everyone knows what happened to Miriam Ramberg, who became Marie Rambert: not everyone knows the part that Nijinsky played in the fulfilment of her destiny. In place of the usual reasoning powers, Nature had endowed him with a certain mysterious and magical instinct. On board the *Avon*, going as he was to matrimony, breakdown and madness, he gave Ramberg the advice: 'Don't stay in the Diaghilev Company. This is not the place for you. Your work will lie elsewhere.' She never spoke to him again after the South American tour, but she took his advice. She left Diaghilev; and founded British ballet.

CHAPTER SEVEN

1913-1917

September 1913 – November 1917

Buenos Aires seemed to the dancers a town of narrow streets and undistinguished houses. 'The streets were crowded,' wrote Grigoriev, 'but only with men; there were few if any women to be seen at all. We were to discover later that women in Buenos Aires went about not on foot but in carriages.'[1] In spite of warnings that walking abroad might result in girls being abducted and sold into slavery, the dancers were allowed to wander about, to the astonishment of the natives, and to find their own rooms. Ramberg, choosing her lodgings, chanced on some sort of brothel, where she was propositioned by a man who had been on the *Avon*.[2]

The company's first performance – in 'Le Pavillon', 'Schéhérazade', 'Le Spectre' and 'Prince Igor' – was on 11 September. Eighteen performances in all were given, of which two were for the benefit of the subscribers to the Colón Theatre's opera seasons. It was the city's first sight of ballet, and the initial polite interest of the fashionable audience soon turned to enthusiasm.[3]

Romola was coached privately by the Maestro and by Kovalevska for her roles in 'Prince Igor', 'Schéhérazade' and 'Cléopâtre'; but her first official appearance with the company was in the mimed part of the Prince's Fiancée in 'Le Lac des Cygnes'. On this occasion her fears were soothed by Bolm, who was dancing the Prince, and who talked to her on stage. But when Nijinsky danced this role, he was 'no longer my husband, but the Prince himself'. There was no communication between them except in the manner of the role. Vaslav's absolute separation between art and life was brought home to her even more forcibly when she found herself gently turned away from his dressing-room before a performance. At such moments, when Nijinsky was 'becoming' a part, Romola was already conscious of 'an indescribable distance' between her husband and herself.[4]

Yet at the hotel Nijinsky was gay and mischievous; and he sent her roses every morning by the frowning Vassili. Progress in communication was slow, but with the aid of painstaking tuition from Gunsbourg Nijinsky laid before his wife confessions and revelations: the nature of his former relationship with Diaghilev, and the story of his brother Stanislav – 'He is insane. You have to know it.' He sent off to Diaghilev a letter announcing his marriage and stressing his unchanged friendship as well as devotion to the Ballet. Diaghilev was so understanding, Nijinsky naïvely believed, that he would give them his blessing.[5] Romola was not so sure:[6] but she could not imagine the Ballet could do without him.

Diaghilev was in Venice when he received the news. Misia Sert had been summoned to his hotel room that morning to play for him a score that had just arrived. She found him in nightshirt and slippers. 'Performing elephantine capers across the room, in his enthusiasm he seized my parasol and opened it. I stopped playing with a start and told him to shut it, as it brought bad luck to open it indoors and he was madly superstitious. Barely had I time to utter my warning when somebody knocked at the door. A telegram . . . Diaghilev turned livid. . . .'

Hysterically he summoned Sert, Bakst and the others. 'When the council of war was complete, the terrible event was discussed with greater calm. What had been Nijinsky's state of mind when he left? Did he seem preoccupied? Not at all. Sad? Certainly not.' Diaghilev ultimately decided to telegraph and forbid the banns. 'Alas! numerous confirmations continued to arrive: the marriage had taken place, it was irremediable. We immediately took Diaghilev, drunk with grief and rage, to Naples, where he launched himself on a frantic bacchanalia. But he was beyond consolation.'[7]* Apart from his disappointment as a lover and the crashing of his hopes for the company and for the future of Nijinsky as a choreographer, it was a felling blow for the great Diaghilev to have been tricked by a girl of twenty-three.

Reports of Nijinsky's marriage began to appear in the press. '*Un mariage bien . . . parisien*' was a sardonic headline in one French newspaper. '*Le danseur marié*' exclaimed another, jumping to the conclusion that Romola de Pulszky who had been Nijinsky's pupil was now to be his star. Benois wrote from Petersburg to Stravinsky in Switzerland.

Benois in Petersburg to Stravinsky in Switzerland, (?).9.13

. . . Serge is the Devil knows where. After discussing the Bach ballet with me in Baden, he was to have come to see me in Lugano and to have brought Ravel with

---

* By his own account (*Memories*, p. 135, footnote 2) Stravinsky was present when Diaghilev received the news of Nijinsky's marriage (but he places the event in the Montreux Palace Hotel). '. . . I had watched him turn into a madman who begged me and my wife not to leave him alone.'

him. But I have heard nothing from him, and since he has disappeared without a note, I am inclined to believe those charming gossipers (their news has probably reached you too) who say that Vaslav married a Hungarian millionairess and Serge, in his grief, has sold the company to an impresario. Have you any news of our dissolute genius Serge? Valetchka, who went to Paris (cursing his fate, poor fellow), also does not know anything.

Stravinsky confirmed the rumour.

Benois in Petersburg to Stravinsky in Switzerland, 28.9.13

Dear Igor Feodorovitch,

I was in Moscow and found your letter only on my return. The news about Nijinsky's marriage struck me like a thunderbolt. When did it happen? None of our friends is here in town at the moment, and I know of no one who can give me any information about it, since I do not want to talk to a stranger like Svetlov. I saw Serge and Vaslav almost on the eve of Vaslav's departure for Argentina, and there was no hint then about the coming event. Nijinsky was very attentively studying Bach with us, preparing the Bach ballet. Is it possible that he had no idea of it then? Be kind and tell me one thing: was it a complete surprise for Serge, or was he prepared for it? How deep was his shock? Their romance was coming to an end, and I doubt that he was really heartbroken, but if he did suffer I hope it was not too terrible for him. However, I imagine he must be completely bewildered in his position as head of the company. But why can't Nijinsky be both a ballet master and a Hungarian millionaire. The whole story is such a phantasmagoria I sometimes think I have read it in a dream and am an idiot to believe it.[8]

Diaghilev's despair did not prevent him attending to business. Hugo von Hofmannsthal was in Venice and negotiations over the Strauss ballet had to be pushed forward, even though Nijinsky could no longer be considered as its choreographer.

Hofmannsthal in Munich to Strauss at Garmisch, 30.9.13

In Venice I saw a lot of Diaghilev, Bakst and the very charming Lady Ripon and the conversation came round to 'Joseph' over and over again. . . . I entirely approve of Diaghilev's intention to employ Fokine and not Nijinsky as *metteur-en-scène* of this ballet.[9]

In Paris Astruc's great venture at the Théâtre des Champs-Elysées was foundering. The artists he had presented recognized the nobility of his endeavours on behalf of music, opera and ballet. It was arranged that there should be a final performance of 'Boris Godounov' on 6 November, and everyone would perform without payment. Diaghilev, presumably cutting short his Neapolitan orgies, attended this.[10] He then went to Petersburg. On 17 November Astruc's company went into liquidation.[11]

Romola was conscious of an improvement in her dancing under Nijinsky's watchful tutelage. He gave her traditional lessons and others of his own invention. 'The most difficult steps became easy if I carefully imitated his movements. The sense of harmony in the movement was the chief factor.' She overcame much of her nervousness, and her rendering of one of the Nymphs in 'L'Après-midi' pleased Nijinsky. But when she danced in 'Prince Igor', in which he had no part, she tried to dissuade him from watching. He insisted that he must see the performance, to judge it as a whole. Romola's fear of Nijinsky the artist returned, and 'as I saw him in the wings, I ran off the stage panic-stricken!' To her chagrin she was suspended for a week: and when she discussed the subject of her dancing with him, he told her that she had started too late to develop a perfect technique: 'But you could dance very beautifully certain dances which I will compose for you.'

Romola made the sensible decision to continue lessons with her husband, but never again to dance in public: she would serve him better by not distracting him with her problems as a dancer.[12] The result of this was to isolate her still further from the life of the company, and as she grew more distant from them so did Vaslav.

Through Gunsbourg Romola now discussed with her husband the question of a baby, and Gunsbourg relayed Vaslav's decision: 'For five years we shall live for art and our love, but the supreme happiness and the fulfilment of life and marriage is to have a child, and, after that time, when we will be in our permanent home, we shall have one.'[13]

After a month in Buenos Aires the company moved to Montevideo, where, although the public was even more receptive, only two performances were given. Another sea-voyage followed to Rio de Janeiro, where the first performance took place on 17 October. The tour was to end early in November. Romola had not been well in Montevideo, but in Rio she and Nijinsky went for drives in the forest, delighting in the flowers, the birds, butterflies and especially the ubiquitous little monkeys. They were less fond of the snakes which occasionally penetrated into their hilltop hotel.[14]

One day, according to Grigoriev, Gunsbourg was told that Nijinsky would not be dancing that evening. The Baron pointed out to Grigoriev that the dancer was breaking his contract: and there was the added problem of there being no understudy for the role of Harlequin in 'Carnaval', to be given in this performance.[15] Did neither of them know that Nijinsky had no contract?[16] The *régisseur* immediately got Gavrilov to rehearse Nijinsky's role, and then visited Vaslav and Romola, who were both adamant that Nijinsky should not dance that evening, in spite of Grigoriev's warnings. Nijinsky gave no explanation of his conduct and the next day was dancing as usual. Diaghilev was informed of what had happened by Gunsbourg. Such is Grigoriev's story. Romola Nijinsky denies that Nijinsky missed a

Nijinsky in 'Carnaval'.
Drawing by Jean Cocteau.

performance, and yet in the telegram which Diaghilev made Grigoriev send from Petersburg, according to the latter, the breach of contract was given as the reason for Nijinsky's dismissal. But Nijinsky had not had a contract since 1909. Grigoriev says he gave this incident, and the question of Nijinsky's marriage, much thought on the boat back to Europe.

It seemed to me that Nijinsky and the Ballet were all but inseparable. It was round Nijinsky that our now considerable repertoire had been largely built up; and the fact that Diaghilev had always concentrated publicity on him had resulted in his being identified with our Ballet in the public mind. Moreover, there was the new movement in choreography inaugurated by Diaghilev's collaboration with Nijinsky, about which so much had been said and written. I could not, in short, conceive how Nijinsky could be replaced; and yet, in the course of my five years' association with Diaghilev I had begun to understand the complexity of his character. He was not a man to depend on other people, however necessary to him they might appear to be; and now that Nijinsky was married I could not see how their collaboration could continue. Yet such was my faith in Diaghilev's immense resource that I felt sure he would find a solution to this problem. . . .[17]

Nijinsky and Romola sailed for Europe with the company.* Romola, who

* According to Grigoriev (p. 99) they sailed on a separate boat.

had found in Brazil that she was pregnant in spite of everything, felt sea-sick and the thought of childbirth frightened her. Vaslav cheered her by saying that the child, which he named 'Le Petit Nègre' in memory of South America, would be a marvellous dancer. They were beginning to be able to carry on a conversation in broken Russian and French; but to the end of his life even when Romola addressed him in Russian Vaslav answered in French.[18] Romola would speak enthusiastically of the beautiful dresses, hats and jewels and of a brilliant social life which she naturally felt was her due now that she had married the great dancer. But she soon found out that Nijinsky did not share her enthusiasm for worldly pleasures: he told her 'I am only an artist, not a prince, but anything I can have is yours. If these things make you happy, I will give them to you.'[19] The ship docked at Cadiz and the Nijinskys decided to travel from there to Paris by train, leaving the rest of the company to continue their voyage to Cherbourg.

Their plans were to call at Budapest for a few days, since Vaslav wished to meet Romola's mother, and then to go on a visit to Eleonora in Petersburg, where Bronia's baby Irina had been born in October. But first of all they expected to meet Diaghilev in Paris.

While we passed the frontier, at Hendaye, we were sitting in the dining saloon having dinner when Vaslav suddenly became livid, jumped up, and left. I went after him, and found him in our compartment – having fainted. I tried to summon a doctor immediately, but there was not one on the train. The *chef du train* brought some ice and smelling-salts; and as Vaslav came to himself he complained of intense headache, which he had often when on a long train journey. From that time I gave up smoking, as he could not stand even the smell of cigarettes.[20]

Diaghilev was not in Paris. The Nijinskys' short stay there, however, was a round of gaiety. The next stop was Vienna, where Romola's sister met them; and so to Budapest, where Emilia Markus had organized parties and press photographers. This lionization Nijinsky found distressing.

Emilia Markus and her doctor begged Romola not to have the baby. At the last moment, however, Romola decided that even death was preferable to an abortion. Vaslav was happy. 'An immense relief and pleasure was expressed in his face. He kissed me gently, and whispered: "Thank God. What He has given, nobody has the right to destroy." '[21] Romola, who had been infatuated with Nijinsky rather than in love with him before their marriage, now began to love him more and more because of his goodness.[22]

Nijinsky was becoming increasingly anxious about the completion of the two ballets on which he had been working, 'Joseph' and the ballet to Bach. All the preparatory work had been finished (some of it on the *Avon*), but rehearsals had been impossible in South America because of the intense heat, and Nijinsky had not been really fit since he left Rio.[23] On arrival in

Budapest he had cabled to Diaghilev to ask when rehearsals were to start and when he could begin work on a new ballet, and to press for the dancers being relieved of other commitments during the period of rehearsal.[24] While awaiting a reply, Vaslav made preparations to spend Christmas with his family.[25]

Grigoriev and the rest of the company had been greeted on arrival at Cherbourg by a welcoming telegram from Diaghilev. As soon as the *régisseur* arrived in Petersburg he was summoned to Diaghilev who showed him Nijinsky's telegram, then covered it with his hand – which 'he always did with any communication that annoyed him' – and wrote a reply, which he asked Grigoriev to sign. Grigoriev now found his initial fears about Diaghilev's resentment justified. 'By causing the answer to Nijinsky's telegram to go from me, he wished to show that their former friendship now counted for nothing and that their relationship had become purely formal.'[26]

The telegram arrived in Budapest two days before Nijinsky had planned to leave for Russia.[27]

Grigoriev in Petersburg to Nijinsky in Budapest (alleged text), 3.12.13

In reply to your telegram to Monsieur Diaghilev I wish to inform you of the following. Monsieur Diaghilev considers that by missing a performance at Rio and refusing to dance in the ballet Carnaval you broke your contract. He will not therefore require your further services. Serge Grigoriev, *Régisseur* of the Diaghilev Company.[28]

In view of the fact that Diaghilev knew perfectly well that Nijinsky had no contract (and therefore could not break one) even if Grigoriev did not, it seems possible that the latter's story of the missed performance and its being the pretext for Nijinsky's dismissal was a complete invention. Yet a message of dismissal was certainly sent. Nijinsky's first reaction to the communication, whatever its wording, was incredulity; his wife's was to burst into tears. 'Now, for the first time, it dawned on me that perhaps I had made a mistake; I had destroyed, where I had wanted to be helpful.' But Vaslav consoled her: 'Do not be sad. It is a mistake – and if it *is* true, I am an artist and I can work for myself.'[29] He sent a defiant telegram to Astruc:

Nijinsky in Budapest to Astruc in Paris, 5.12.13

Please inform the newspapers that I shall not be working any longer with Diaghilev.[30]

For some time, still refusing to believe in the reality of his dismissal, Nijinsky tried to find out from his former collaborators what was in

Diaghilev's mind. A few days later he wrote to Stravinsky (whom he had not seen since 'Le Sacre'):

Nijinsky in Budapest to Stravinsky, 9.12.13

Dear Igor,

I went with my wife to her parents' home in Budapest and there I immediately sent a telegram to Serge asking him when we could see each other. The answer . . . was a letter from Grigoriev informing me that I shall not be asked to stage any ballets this season, and that I am not needed as an artist. Please write to me whether this is true. I do not believe that Serge can act so meanly to me. Serge owes me a lot of money. I have received nothing for two years, neither for my dancing nor for my staging 'Faune', 'Jeux', and 'Sacre du printemps'. I worked for the Ballet without a contract. If it is true that Serge does not want to work with me – then I have lost everything. You understand the situation I am in. I cannot imagine what has happened, what is the reason for his behaviour. Please ask Serge what is the matter, and write to me about it. In all the newspapers of Germany, Paris and London, etc., it is reported that I am not working any more with Diaghilev. But the whole press is against him (including the *feuilletons*). They also say that I am gathering a company of my own. In truth, I am receiving propositions from every side, and the biggest of these comes from a very rich businessman, who offers one million francs to organize a new Diaghilev Russian Ballet [*sic*] – they wish me to have sole artistic direction and large sums of money to commission décors, music, etc. But I won't give them a definite answer before I have news from you.

My numerous friends send me letters of revolt and rage against Diaghilev – and propositions to help me and join me in my new enterprise. I hope you will not forget me and will answer my letter immediately.

Your loving

VASLAV.[31]

The letter was sent to Russia, but Stravinsky was in Switzerland and received it some time later. He felt that it was 'a document of such astounding innocence – if Nijinsky hadn't written it, I think only a character in Dostoevsky might have. It seems incredible to me . . . that he was so unaware of the politics and sexual jealousies and motives within the Ballet.'[32] Clearly Nijinsky's faith in Diaghilev's acceptance of his marriage was unshaken, since he had failed to perceive the connection between it and his dismissal. In spite of his 'confessions' to Romola, the result of his wish that she should know all about him, and despite what he was to write later in his *Diary*, at this stage he did not see his marriage as an impediment to continued friendship with Diaghilev.

In Petersburg Grigoriev was speculating that 'the violence of Diaghilev's reaction was due in part to the failure of Nijinsky's last two ballets. Diaghilev, I thought, must already have decided that Nijinsky did not have it in him to become a great choreographer.'[33] Grigoriev's inability to appreciate the originality of Nijinsky's art, together with his loyalty to Diaghilev, prevented his seeing the issue in its true light: but he was nevertheless astonished when Diaghilev told him that he intended to persuade Fokine to rejoin the company. 'Fokine's an excellent dancer and a no less excellent choreographer. Why not try?' He went to the telephone, and the conversation, wrote Grigoriev, 'lasted no less than five hours'. (Karsavina had several telephone calls of four hours or so from Diaghilev at moments of crisis.) Fokine

began by flatly refusing to have anything more to do with the Ballet. But Diaghilev was not deterred. He let him say all he wished, biding his time, and then protested at Fokine's accusations, defended his own standpoint, and embarked on persuasion as only he knew how. The result was that despite all Fokine's stubbornness (and he was of a far from tractable nature), after five hours of uninterrupted talk Diaghilev wore him down and obtained his promise to call the next day. As he replaced the receiver Diaghilev heaved a sigh of relief. 'Well, that's settled, I think,' he said. 'He was a tough nut to crack, though, all the same!'[34]

In *his* account of the incident Fokine makes no mention of this telephone conversation. He records that Svetlov persuaded him to receive Diaghilev at his own flat, and Diaghilev arrived and 'made a most eloquent speech, trying to convince me that he was now wholeheartedly on my side, that his infatuation with his favourite was now long forgotten, and that it was only I who could now save the art of the Russian ballet which I myself had created, and which now faced danger'. Fokine was persuaded, and agreed not only to re-stage his old ballets but to create seven new ones, of which the Richard Strauss work would be the first. He insisted in his contract that none of Nijinsky's ballets should be given under his regime. Fokine was also to be *premier danseur*, and a further clause in his contract specifically de-barred Nijinsky's re-engagement.[35]

Despite the fact that Grigoriev and others in the company had been hostile to Fokine when he left in the previous year, and in spite of the choreographer's wish that Grigoriev should be dismissed, which Diaghilev could not agree to, Fokine's return, according to Grigoriev, met with 'everyone's delight'. 'No one had really approved of the Nijinsky period in choreography. It had seemed to be leading us nowhere, whereas Fokine's return gave us fresh hope of success.'[36] Grigoriev's views on artistic matters had their limitations. Much work remained to be done on the repertory for the coming London season of both opera and ballet, but, wrote Grigoriev, 'strangely enough, Diaghilev seemed like someone who has shed a load and can at last breathe freely'.[37]

Diaghilev went off to Moscow in connection with work on the operas, and Grigoriev followed. On a visit to the Bolshoi Theatre Diaghilev was

Monsieur et Madame Nijinsky

prient *Mlle Mouirigs*

de bien vouloir leur faire le plaisir d'assister au

déjeûner qu'ils offrent Vendredi 19 à une heure[s]

dans le Salon Slave du Majestic Hôtel.

R. S. V. P.

74 Invitation to the Nijinskys' wedding breakfast.
75 Ekaterina Oblokova, Dmitri de Gunsbourg, Josefina Kovalevska, Romola Nijinsky, Nijinsky, Mme Rhené-Baton and Rhené-Baton at the Majestic Hotel, Buenos Aires, after Nijinsky's wedding.

76 Bronislava Nijinska, Nijinsky and members of his company in the new version of 'Les Sylphides' at the Palace Theatre, London.

77 Nijinsky and members of the Russian Ballet with Charlie Chaplin on a film set in Hollywood. Lydia Lopokhova in right foreground, Pierre Monteux in centre.

78 Nijinsky in 'Till Eulenspiegel'.

79 Nijinsky in practice clothes, New York.

80 Romola and Vaslav Nijinsky with Kyra.

81 Leonide Massine, 1920.
Drawing by Henri Matisse.

82 Diaghilev working in bed,
Grand Hotel, Paris, 1929.
Drawing by Michel Larionov.

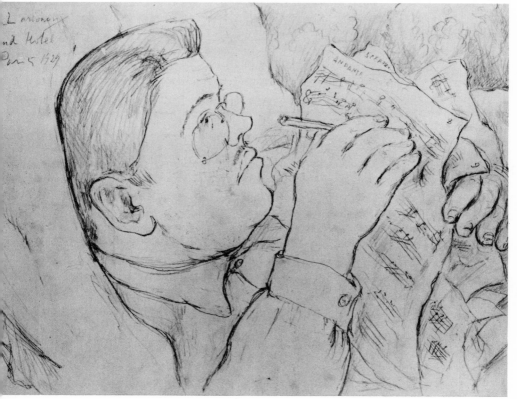

83 Romola and Vaslav
Nijinsky at Schloss
Mittersill, Austria, 1946.

84 At Virginia Water,
Surrey, 1949.

85 Una Troubridge's head of Nijinsky as the Faun and Wilfred de Glehn's portrait of Karsavina as Columbine in the Diaghilev Exhibition, Forbes House. Lydia Sokolova bought this plaster cast in a junk shop for ten shillings at the time of the Diaghilev Exhibition. Photograph by Leonard Taylor (Manor Studio, Southall).

86 Nijinsky in 'Le Spectre de la rose'. Photograph by Bert.
This was the photograph on the jacket of Mme Romola
Nijinsky's life of her husband which first interested
me in ballet.

taken by the appearance of a young dancer, Leonide Miassine, who was dancing the tarantella in 'Le Lac des Cygnes' and the Knight of the Moon in 'Don Quichotte',[38] and sent Mikhail Savitsky – a member of the Bolshoi *corps* who had danced in his company the year before – to tell Miassine that he wished to meet him. Miassine was flattered, and called on Diaghilev at the Metropole Hotel the next afternoon. Diaghilev told him that subject to Fokine's approval he would like him to dance the title role in 'La Légende de Joseph' – the role which was to have been Nijinsky's. Miassine was to make up his mind by the following day. The dancer was 'dazed and bewildered'. He had been on the point of giving up dancing to start on an acting career, and his friends advised him against changing his plans lest this tempting offer should ruin his chances in Moscow. Accordingly, when he returned to Diaghilev's hotel the next day, he had made up his mind to refuse. But Diaghilev's magic worked on this as on other occasions. 'I was just about to tell him that I could not accept his offer when, almost without realizing it, I heard myself say, "Yes, I shall be delighted to join your company." '[39] Miassine asked for two months' leave from the Bolshoi Theatre – and left for ever.[40] He travelled immediately with Diaghilev to Petersburg, where he had an audition with Fokine: this was a completely formal occasion, during which Miassine demonstrated his (then not very exceptional) technique, and the next day he was finally engaged.[41] He was eighteen: Grigoriev thought him 'strikingly handsome'. Diaghilev acknowledged that he was not much of a dancer as yet, and added, 'Of course, he's rather provincial. . . . But we'll soon put an end to that.'[42] From this moment Miassine became Diaghilev's constant companion. He was taken straight to the Hermitage to look at the pictures: his 'education' was begun without delay.[43]

Nijinsky only wanted to be back with the Diaghilev Ballet, but there was to be no olive-branch from Petersburg. He was determined that any other offer he took up must have serious artistic intentions: his art, and his opportunity to create, were all-important, and he would not consider appearing in music-hall. In vain impresarios sought his services and offered high salaries: in vain agents wrote to him and visited him in Budapest. Even Rouché, the new Director of the Paris Opéra, who offered him the post of *maître de ballet* and *premier danseur* for 100,000 gold francs a year, was turned down because of the limitations of the Opéra repertory. Romola knew that more than anything Vaslav wanted to create new ballets of abstract dancing – like 'Le Sacre' – as he had been encouraged to by Diaghilev.[44] But he must resign himself to the fact that if he formed a company he must administer it, train it, rehearse it and get engagements for it, besides dancing with it and making ballets.

In order to escape the insistent interference of Romola's mother and stepfather, the Nijinskys left for Vienna: and there the importunings of one impresario succeeded. Alfred Butt, owner of the Palace Theatre in London, offered Vaslav a contract for eight weeks in the spring of 1914, under which he could assemble his own company and plan his own repertory. According to Romola, 'Vaslav believed that this place was not a variety theatre, but one of the most distinguished houses in London, equal to Covent Garden or Drury Lane', and so he signed the agreement.[45] She overstates the case: Nijinsky could not fail to know that the Palace was a Theatre of Varieties – it was printed on the cover of the programmes – and Pavlova had appeared there for years. Nijinsky may have believed that the Palace was the *best* of the variety theatres, and overcome his reservations on being offered for his company £1,000 a week.

Bronia and her husband Kotchetovsky, who had resigned from Diaghilev's company in sympathy, came from Russia to Paris to meet Vaslav and discuss their plans. Nijinsky intended to employ thirty-two dancers, and to create new ballets, in addition to presenting, as requested, 'Le Spectre', 'La Princesse enchantée' (the Blue-bird *pas de deux*) and 'Les Sylphides'.

To carry out his plans Nijinsky needed new scenery and costumes. Bakst was the first to be approached, but he was unable or perhaps unwilling, through fear of Diaghilev, to co-operate.* But Boris Anisfeld, the scene-painter and designer of 'Sadko', accepted Nijinsky's commission, as did Mme Muelle who made the costumes for the Ballets Russes. Ravel also took Nijinsky's part and assisted him to choose music as well as providing a new orchestration for a slightly different selection of Chopin pieces which would constitute a new 'Les Sylphides'. The task of recruiting dancers for the company was taken on by Bronia and her husband, who went back to Russia for that purpose. None of the dancers whom Nijinsky auditioned in Vienna or Paris were at all suitable: but Bronia brought back a carefully selected group of Imperial School graduates who were sympathetic to Nijinsky, and these were engaged for one year.[46] The company was peculiar in that it contained only two men, Nijinsky and his brother-in-law Alexander Kotchetovsky. Nijinska was principal ballerina, and the other soloists were Mlles Boni (who had been with Diaghilev), Jvanova, Darinska, Jakovleva, Krasnitska, Larionova, Poeltzich, Ptitsenko and Tarassova.[47]

In February the Diaghilev company gathered in Prague, and many of the dancers heard for the first time of Nijinsky's dismissal and Fokine's reinstatement. During the German tour, which took the company to Stuttgart, Cologne, Hamburg, Leipzig, Hanover, Breslau and Berlin and

---

* The Nijinskys ran into him shortly after this outside the Savoy Hotel in London and he tried to cut them, exclaiming, 'I'm not allowed to talk to you!' (Romola Nijinsky conversations.)

ended in Switzerland at Zürich, Miassine was rehearsed by Fokine in 'La Légende' and took classes with Cecchetti. Fokine simplified the role of Joseph for Miassine.[48] The future leading dancer and choreographer made his début with the company as a watchman in 'Petrushka'. Fokine was dancing some of Nijinsky's roles, but the company was still deficient in principal male dancers. Diaghilev paid what was to be his last visit to Russia, and while there he re-engaged two notable dancers: Pierre Vladimirov, *premier danseur* of the Mariinsky, who had been with him in London in 1912 to dance two performances of 'Les Sylphides' in place of Nijinsky, and Alexis Bulgakov, the mime whose association with the Diaghilev company went back to the first night in 1909. He was to play Tsar Dodon in 'Le Coq d'or'. Maria Kuznetsova, an opera singer, was engaged to dance the Rubinstein-type role of Potiphar's wife in 'La Légende de Joseph'.[49]

In Paris Nijinsky and his sister began rehearsals for the London season. Romola felt that her sister-in-law disliked her: 'she seemed to resent everything that happened and blame it on me. I was the intruder in the Russian Ballet, in the family.'[50] The Nijinskys' arrival in London in February was much publicized. Lady Ottoline Morrell greeted them at the Savoy with armfuls of flowers, while Lady Ripon congratulated them on their marriage, telling Romola that 'it was always her wish that Vaslav should marry, and that she had tried in the past to introduce him to suitable young ladies.'[51] Gwladys Ripon wrote to Misia Sert that 'Nijinsky's marriage has predisposed everyone here in his favour'[52] – and Misia commented that the event had produced in a society whose memories of the Wilde *débâcle* were still fresh 'a wave of fine Puritan approval'.[53]

There remained two weeks for the completion of preparations, and the season was already fully booked. But things began to go wrong. Some of the trouble was caused by Diaghilev. Though he resented both Bronia's sympathy for Vaslav and her physical resemblance to him,[54] Diaghilev was well aware that she was a valuable artist. He had talked Fokine out of demanding her exclusion from the company, and now he brought a court action to prevent her appearing with Nijinsky on the grounds that her resignation from the Diaghilev Ballet had not been accepted. After much trouble Diaghilev lost the case.[55] Bronia, too, came in for criticism from Vaslav on an occasion when she felt unwell at a rehearsal, and Kotchetovsky insulted him in return. There was trouble with the management. Nijinsky was asked to call on Alfred Butt in his office: but he thought – or Romola told him – that Butt should come to him.[56] This misunderstanding with Butt was the first of several. During one scene Vaslav smashed a table.[57]

To Nijinsky, whose nerves were already on edge, working in the atmosphere of a music-hall was a humiliation. The first night was 2 March, and Romola was 'blinded with tears to see Vaslav dance, in his exquisite programme, after a clown's number and before a popular singer's act'.[58] The programme consisted of 'Les Sylphides', with re-arranged choreography to Ravel's orchestration of some new and some old Chopin numbers and a highly inappropriate décor of exotic vegetation by Anisfeld; Sinding's 'Danse Orientale' – the solo originally danced by Nijinsky in 'Les Orientales' and now performed by Kotchetovsky; and 'Le Spectre de la rose'. Cyril Beaumont was in the audience, and recorded the structure of the new 'Sylphides'. 'There was an overture provided by an Étude, then a Nocturne (Nijinska, Nijinsky and *corps de ballet*), a Mazurka (Nijinsky), an Étude (Mlle Boni), a Mazurka (Nijinska), an Étude (Mlle Jvanova), a Mazurka (Nijinska, Nijinsky), and a Nocturne (Nijinska, Nijinsky and *corps de ballet*).'

Beaumont 'anxiously awaited the rise of the curtain, but when the stage was revealed and the ballet proceeded I could not reconcile myself either to the new scenery, the different music, or the changed choreography. And when Nijinsky himself danced I have to confess that I was conscious of a pang of disappointment. He still danced with that rare elevation and feeling for line and style . . . but he no longer danced like a god. Something of that mystic fragrance which previously had surrounded his dancing in "Les Sylphides" had vanished.'

Kotchetovsky's *pas seul*, which 'was executed entirely *sur place* and consisted of admirably harmonized, if restricted, movements of the head, body, and limbs, clearly inspired by the Javanese classical dance', was greeted with enthusiasm. Then came 'Le Spectre', danced in front of a black velvet curtain. 'Both Nijinsky and his sister danced superbly, yet something of the old magic had departed.'[59]

The critic of *The Times* praised the dancing of Nijinsky and Nijinska in both ballets, and felt that 'Le Spectre' was quite the equal of the original production: but for him the new 'Sylphides' – though revealing Nijinsky's 'fine taste in figuration and his subtle skill in musical interpretation' – was 'just less than successful' by comparison with the original combination of music, choreography and décor which was an 'acknowledged masterpiece'.[60]

The audience's response, Beaumont felt, was polite and grew cooler as the evening progressed. This was partly due to the fact that during the two scene changes Nijinsky wished the auditorium to remain in darkness, and refused to allow the theatre manager, Maurice Volny, to have music played. Despite the number of people in the audience who had been regular followers of the Ballet at Covent Garden and Drury Lane, there were still sufficient music-hall patrons to resent this deprivation and grow restive. Nijinsky changed in the wings to make sure his wishes were adhered to. On the second night he went to his dressing-room, and on Volny's instructions the orchestra played a Tchaikovsky number from Pavlova's repertory chosen by the conductor, Herman Finck. When Vaslav heard of this, he became hysterical. Eventually 'Le Spectre' went on normally, but Nijinsky continued to protest vehemently in the morning.[61]

For the second week of the engagement 'Danse Polovtsienne' was announced, and for the third a new programme comprising 'Carnaval', 'L'Oiseau et le Prince' and 'Danse Grecque'. But on the evening of the 16th, after rehearsing all day, Nijinsky suddenly developed influenza,[62] and Butt had to announce that he was too ill to dance. A series of vaudeville turns was quickly put on in place of the ballet.[63] Romola had treated Vaslav with aspirin, which according to the doctors called in by Lady Ripon 'almost killed him, as he had an athlete's heart and was in an extremely dangerous condition'. The management of the theatre enforced the clause in the contract which put him in breach of the agreement if he failed to appear for three consecutive nights. He was not well enough to return, and the season ended abruptly, the total cost for properties, music and salaries devolving on Vaslav personally. Negotiations for a new arrangement failed, each side being dissatisfied with the other. Nijinsky had danced for the last time in London. His loyal company declared themselves content with the pay they had received and wanted only their fares to Russia, but Nijinsky would not hear of it and paid all thirty-two dancers a full year's salary from his savings.[64] It may be asked what money he had, since Diaghilev had never given him a salary. The answer is that for dancing at private parties such as the Aga Khan's he had been paid enormous sums. As Diaghilev had always settled his hotel bills, fed and clothed him and taken care of his mother's expenses, these were almost untouched.[65]

The comedian Fred Emney replaced the Russians at the Palace.

While these events were taking place, a reminder of happier times was provided by an exhibition at the Fine Art Society in Bond Street of portraits of Nijinsky in the roles for which he was famous: drawings of him as Harlequin, Petrushka, the Faun and the Spectre by Valentine Gross; in 'Le Pavillon' by Sargent; taking a call after 'Faune' by Glyn Philpot. There were three studies, including that in the costume for 'Danse Orientale', by Blanche; a statuette and etchings by Una Troubridge; and two drawings of him in 'Jeux' by the Beardsleyesque Montenegro, which the critic of the *Daily Telegraph* found 'repulsive' and 'a blot on the exhibition'. The same critic lamented the absence of any study of Nijinsky by either Bakst or Rodin.[66]

Lady Ripon wrote to Misia Sert about Nijinsky: 'There were some who believed that he did not wish to return to the ballet, but ever since he has been here he has been telling everybody how unhappy he is to be dismissed, and that all he wants is to go back.' Lady Ripon was being pressed by her friends to persuade Diaghilev to re-engage Nijinsky: and although she had divided loyalties, and felt that artistically Fokine augured better for the company than Nijinsky – since she thought that in Nijinsky's ballets 'the *corps de ballet* had become so disorganized that it was unrecognizable'[67] – her personal devotion to Vaslav was great. Clearly she was one to prefer such ballets as 'Le Spectre de la rose' to Nijinsky's audacious experiments. With regard to Diaghilev and his contracts, she wrote, 'he tells you anything that suits him at the moment!' and she was anxious to know from Misia how much he had 'tied himself up with Vladimirov'. She was also conscious of the 'gossip about his new friend' (Miassine). She seemed to believe – or pretend to believe – that Nijinsky hadn't 'the slightest desire to be the choreographer' and was 'ready to dance turn by turn with Fokine'. Unless something could be done to bring Diaghilev and Nijinsky together, Lady Ripon could only 'envisage the coming season with growing anxiety and a desire to go somewhere far away, where there will be no theatre, for when one begins to sacrifice Art to personal matters, it takes away every wish to have anything more to do with it'.[68]

Nijinsky's illness lasted two months, and he was advised that when he was well enough to work again, he should dance but abandon administrative work. During his convalescence he went for long walks with Romola in Richmond Park. As the time approached for the birth of the baby, the Nijinskys travelled to the Semmering in Austria for the privacy which Nijinsky thought essential, and then to Vienna.[69]

The repertory of the Diaghilev company for its seasons in Paris and London – their first without Nijinsky – was approaching completion. In addition to the Russian operas with Chaliapine which would be given in London, Stravinsky's opera 'Le Rossignol' – based on a Hans Andersen fairy-story – was to be produced with *chinoiserie* designs by Benois. The choreography for this work had been given to Boris Romanov, to spare Fokine, and also because the latter was not keen to compose any more choreography to Stravinsky's music.[70] Rimsky-Korsakov's opera 'Une Nuit de mai' had also been prepared. Fokine had arranged four works: the Strauss 'La Légende de Joseph', with flamboyant Veronese décor by J-M.Sert and costumes by Bakst, in which Miassine was to have his first major role; 'Les Papillons' to piano pieces of Schumann orchestrated by Tcherepnine, with a décor by Doboujinsky and costumes by Bakst; 'Midas' with music by Maximilian Steinberg, also designed by Doboujinsky; and Le Coq d'or'. Since Tcherepnine had not completed his score for 'The Red

Masks', which it had been intended that Gorsky should arrange, another ballet had been needed for the 1914 seasons. Fokine had wanted to produce Rimsky's 'Coq d'or' as a ballet suite for Pavlova two years before, but the ballerina had not thought it suitable. Fokine writes that he suggested to Diaghilev that 'Coq d'or' should replace Tcherepnine's ballet, and Diaghilev decided to produce the work as an opera-ballet.[71] At Benois' suggestion Diaghilev commissioned the décor and costumes from the Moscow painter Natalie Gontcharova. Benois' part in 'Coq d'or', however, was considerable. He had always longed to produce it since he had heard the work in 1909; moreover, since singers could so rarely act convincingly, he had the idea of removing them from the stage and having dancers mime the action. His idea was adopted by Diaghilev, and by Fokine (who was to claim it as his own). However, there would not be room for the soloists and chorus of the Bolshoi opera in the orchestra pit, so Benois decided to range them, identically costumed, in tiers at each side of the stage.[72]

The Ballet arrived in Monte Carlo in April, and on the 16th gave the first performance of 'Papillons', with Karsavina and Schollar as the two girls and Fokine as Pierrot. Fokine lost no time in reviving his neglected 'Daphnis et Chloë', which he now danced himself with Karsavina. 'La Tragédie de Salomé' was also revived – unsuccessfully. Diaghilev rejoined the company from Russia before the end of the Monte Carlo season.[73]

Nijinsky was invited to dance, at a fee of three thousand dollars, for the King and Queen of Spain at the wedding reception of Kermit Roosevelt in the American Embassy in Madrid. He travelled there with Romola's step-father and was given a warm welcome. Romola received a letter from him every day, 'of which I was proud, as I knew Vaslav never wrote to anybody, except his mother. He addressed me as "Femmka" or "Roma".'[74] On the way back to Vienna, Vaslav stopped off in Paris to attend the première of the Russian Ballet's season at the Opéra. This was on Thursday, 14 May, and included the first performance of 'La Légende de Joseph'. The newspapers were quick to spot him as 'many lorgnettes turned simultaneously' towards his seat. Though he no longer danced with the Russian Ballet, 'he seemed to me to be perfectly at ease', commented one observer. 'The society of the foyer can be equally attractive.'[75] According to Romola Vaslav went in the interval to Misia Sert's box, where her guests, including Cocteau, gave him a cool reception.[76] Before leaving Paris, Nijinsky had a lesson from Cecchetti. Miassine was sent by Diaghilev to take a class with him and to watch him at work. The *maestro*, using the gold-topped cane which Vaslav had given him years before, corrected Nijinsky's arm positions: 'Not curled up there – down there.' Miassine noticed that Vaslav accepted these corrections without ever answering back.[77]

Richard Strauss conducted the première of his ballet, which was given between 'Les Papillons', which the critics found disappointing (and again they thought the orchestration of Schumann a travesty), and a new version of 'Schéhérazade' with the third movement restored, danced by Karsavina, Fokine, Max Frohman and Cecchetti. 'La Légende' did not have the success which was expected of it: the various collaborators had failed to agree on a number of points and Fokine's choreography was uninspired. Miassine was overcome with nerves, but struggled through the performance.[78] What he lacked in dancing technique he made up for in stage presence and beauty. The first performance of 'Le Coq d'or' had been intended for 21 May, but the arrival of the costumes from Russia was delayed and the première took place four days later on a Sunday.* Karsavina danced the Queen of Shemakhan (sung by Dobrovolska), Jejerska was Amelfa (Petrenko), Bulgakov was King Dodon (Petrov), Cecchetti the Astrologer (Altchevsky), Kovalski General Polkan (Belianine). Nicolaeva sang the Cockerel, and Max Frohman and Grigoriev mimed the two princes Afrone and Guidone. 'Le Coq d'or', with its blazing red and yellow décor, was the real hit of the Paris season, though critical opinion was divided as to its success as a new way of presenting opera. Lalo thought the dances of Dodon and the Queen were not sufficient justification for imposing on the singers an immobility which detracted from their performances.[79] 'Le Rossignol' was given on 26 May, and the last première, that of 'Midas', which was rather an absurd work, took place on 2 June, Vladimirov dancing Amoun in 'Cléopâtre' in the same programme.

In reviewing 'La Légende', one critic, Alfred Bruncan, wrote: 'With his good taste M.Michel Fokine brings back to the Russian Ballet all the graceful attitudes and harmonious gestures which M.Nijinsky, with his grotesque ideas, sought to abolish.'[80] But this Paris season had proved a disappointment, and Jacques Rivière, staunchly loyal, put the blame firmly on Nijinsky's departure which 'has left a great void. One must say it boldly: the Russian Ballet was Nijinsky. He alone gave life to the whole company.'[81]

When the Paris engagement ended early in June, the company left immediately for London, where the German–Russian opera season had already opened at Drury Lane on 20 May. Performances had been given of 'Der Rosenkavalier' and 'Die Zauberflöte', and of both 'Boris Godounov' and 'Ivan le Terrible' with Chaliapine, as in the previous year. Chaliapine also sang in 'Prince Igor', the first complete performance of which opera in England took place on 8 June. The Ballet made its first appearance of the

---

* Fokine gives the advertised date as that of the première, forgetting the postponement (p. 233). Grigoriev gives the date as the 24th (p. 271).

season with the opera company that night, and Tchernicheva, Fokina and Bolm led the Polovtsian Dances, with Leon Steinberg conducting. The first full ballet programme was given the next day, and comprised 'Thamar' with Karsavina and Bolm, 'Daphnis et Chloë' with Karsavina and Fokine, and 'Schéhérazade' with Fokina and Fokine, Bulgakov, Fedorov and Cecchetti. This season was to be the only one during which Fokine ever danced in London.

The Times, on the morning of the première of 'Daphnis', published a letter from Ravel in Paris claiming that the version to be performed at Drury Lane without the chorus was 'a makeshift arrangement which I had agreed to write at M.Diaghilev's special request in order to facilitate production in certain minor centres'. Diaghilev was putting this version on in London 'in spite of his positive word', and Ravel considered this action 'disrespectful towards the London public as well as towards the composer'.[82] Ravel was always extremely precise in his demands, but music aside, he may, out of friendship for Nijinsky, have been trying to make things as difficult for Diaghilev as possible. Diaghilev replied the next day that the 1912 production in Paris with singing was an 'experiment' and 'it was clearly proved that the participation of the chorus was not only useless but actually detrimental'. He had then asked Ravel to produce the revised version which had been given in April at Monte Carlo with 'unanimous approval': and he felt that he had made 'every effort to present it in the most perfect manner to the London public, to whom I owe a very great debt of admiration and gratitude'.*[83]

Karsavina danced the role of Chloë at this performance: Fokina was to share the part with her, as she did that of Zobeïda in 'Schéhérazade'. Fokine was Daphnis and Bolm Darkon. The London public was enthusiastic. 'Papillons', given with 'Petrushka', on the 11th evoked memories of 'Carnaval', the firm favourite of previous seasons, but for Cyril Beaumont 'it remained nothing more than a dainty trifle. It had a definite charm of mood and was invested with poetry and lyricism; but it was too slight, too fragile, too intimate for a big theatre, and consequently failed to make a deep impression.' Karsavina, however, Beaumont found memorable. He had made her acquaintance – and that of Bolm – the previous year, and now decided to write a book about her. He visited her at the Savoy where she had already, with typical thoroughness, prepared a chronology of her career for him and the interview went well. But the war was to intervene, and the book which Beaumont eventually published was Svetlov's essay on the ballerina.[84]

On 15 June, in 'Coq d'or', Karsavina danced the Queen of Shemakhan,

* Grigoriev states that the Moscow chorus *did* take part in 'Daphnis', 'which made the last scene especially impressive' (p. 110). This is clearly not true.

with Bolm as King Dodon. Not surprisingly, London found the opera-ballet sensational. Charles Ricketts wrote in his Journal that the novel production delighted him 'beyond all reason' and went on: 'It is a most picturesque interpretation of the principle which obtained at the birth of Greek tragedy, and which still obtains in the Japanese No Dances. The interpretation was magnificent. Karsavina looked like a bewitching Hindu idol, her dancing and miming were incomparable.'[85] Osbert Sitwell felt that this was

a production such as none had dreamed of in the world of opera. . . . Besides giving us some of the most dramatic and haunting music of the past century, *Le Coq d'or* constituted a great satire. In its stilted, dream-like rhythms, displayed against a background of huge flowers and brightly-hued buildings, was to be felt a mockery of the great, a kind of joy in the doom of lordship. Fortunately for its success, the fashionable audience could revel in the beauty and strangeness of it without concentrating too much on its meaning or implications.[86]

Three days later, after the shared première of 'Le Rossignol' and 'Midas', neither of which aroused much interest, Sitwell noted with a sense of incongruity Stravinsky, 'with an air both worldly and abstracted, and a little angry', bowing to that same audience of 'clustered, nodding tiaras and the white kid gloves, that applauded him sufficiently to be polite'.[87]

In Vienna Vaslav and Romola were thinking of names for their baby, whose birth was overdue. Nijinsky was convinced they would have a son, and wanted to call him Vladislav, which Romola agreed to. Prince Montenuovo, the Minister of the Court, invited them to the première of Strauss's 'Elektra' at the Hofoper on 18 June, saying 'If this modern music won't hasten the baby's arrival, then nothing will!' They went, and the next day the baby was born. Romola's sister Tessa told her that 'as the nurse announced to him, "It is only a girl, but a nice one", for one second [Vaslav] lost his self-control, and threw his gloves on the floor.' But he then consoled Romola for the disappointment, and immediately became devoted to the daughter who was so like him. She was called Kyra.[88]

At the dress rehearsal of 'La Légende de Joseph', Charles Ricketts recorded, 'all little London was present and . . . Lady Diana Manners clambered over the balcony from one box to another before an enraptured house.'[89] London had been well primed for this new work as well as for the début of Miassine, and at its première on the 23rd the ballet was better received than in Paris. Miassine's dancing was a disappointment to an audience 'who had been led to expect a successor to Nijinsky', but as an actor – in what was largely a mimed role – he made some impression.[90] Miassine later recalled: 'I was now feeling much happier in Joseph, and was

344

encouraged by the warm reception I was given on the first night.'[91] Karsavina thought that Miassine's performance was 'quite remarkable. His very lack of virtuosity in those days lent pathos to the image he created, an image of youth and innocence.'[92] Karsavina now danced the role of Potiphar's wife for the first time, having 'accepted the part without my usual doubts as to whether I was fit for it'. Strauss, who was in London to conduct his ballet, and whose fiftieth birthday had been celebrated on the 21st by a music club reception which Stravinsky and Karsavina attended, advised the ballerina on her role at rehearsals and was sufficiently delighted with her performance to try to get her to dance whenever the ballet was given in Vienna in later years.[93]

Lady Ripon, wrote Romola, 'proved to be the most loyal friend Nijinsky ever had'. She had used her influence as prime mover of the Production Committee of the Russian Ballet Performances in London to oblige Diaghilev to engage Nijinsky to dance with the company, failing which the season would be cancelled. This done, she asked Vaslav to come to London at once, which he was delighted to do, and he set off towards the end of June. It was intended that he should dance three times in 'Le Spectre' and other works. But he found on arrival that only Lady Ripon, Gunsbourg and Trubecki took his part, while most of the company gave him a cool reception. After one rehearsal he could not bear this and wrote his thanks and apologies to Lady Ripon, leaving immediately for Vienna 'as he was afraid that if he saw the Marchioness again he would have to give in to her entreaties'.*[94]

The event which was to precipitate the war – the assassination at Sarajevo of the Archduke Franz Ferdinand on 28 June – had occurred as Vaslav was *en route* for London, and after his return to Vienna at the beginning of July he was pressed with letters and telegrams from Lady Ripon begging him to move to London with his family. The Nijinskys believed that she was still working to reconcile Vaslav and Diaghilev: they were to learn later that her fear of war was the true reason for her communications. But on the advice of Romola's doctor Nijinsky decided to stay in Vienna until the end of July; and then go via Budapest to Russia.[95]

The last night of the London season was 25 July, the ballets being 'Papillons', 'La Légende de Joseph' and 'Petrushka'. The ovations were loud and long, and the dancers brought Sir Joseph Beecham before the curtain and gave him a gilt laurel wreath.[96] After the safety curtain had been

---

* According to Grigoriev in a letter to Nouvel (quoted in Haskell's *Diaghileff*, pp. 259, 260) Lady Ripon fetched over Nijinsky merely on the chance of a reconciliation: Fokine's contract would have prevented Nijinsky appearing with the company. It seems likely that the real reason for Nijinsky's swift departure was that he realized this.

lowered, the applause continued, and Diaghilev enticed Karsavina back from her dressing-room, where she had begun to change, to take more calls – or rather to come round the curtain into the auditorium. 'I stood there for a brief moment, oddly confused; feeling as if I had violated the ethics of the theatre. The excited audience rushed forward: I turned and fled.'[97] 'Overwhelming demonstration of farewell to Karsavina,'[98] wrote Ricketts in his Journal that night: and to Gordon Bottomley he summed up, 'The new ballets have been admirable and have made up for the loss of Nijinsky. . . .'[99]

On the first night of 'Joseph' Count Harry Kessler, co-librettist of the ballet, had intimated that the projected German tour might not take place, but Diaghilev had dismissed the veiled warning.[100] It is surprising that so many people failed to hear the threat of war in 1914 – and that even when it did break out, they imagined it would be over in a few months. Karsavina had felt uneasy as the season drew to its close, and an 'acute longing to be home'.[101] But Diaghilev asked her to stay on another day, as he had something to discuss with her. He had not paid her anything for two years. This fact he had carefully mentioned to Joseph Beecham, with the result that the latter had turned up one night in Karsavina's dressing-room and given her £2,000 in notes. Having, no doubt, craftily calculated the result of his conversation with Beecham, Diaghilev wanted to borrow £400. This meant that Karsavina had to postpone her departure by one day in order to go to the bank for him.[102] The company dispersed for their holidays, and were due to gather in Berlin for the German tour on 1 October. When war was declared on 4 August Grigoriev had just arrived in Petersburg, the Fokines were in Paris, and Miassine was in Milan on the way to join Diaghilev and the Cecchettis in Viareggio. Karsavina's delay in London resulted in her being turned back by the Germans at the Russian border. She travelled back via Holland to England; and then finally, after a few weeks, she managed to reach Petersburg 'by means of varied locomotion'.[103] Her description of this journey was euphemistic. Her trials reached the newspapers, and on 27 August Charles Ricketts was to note in his Journal: 'Read in the paper of poor little Karsavina, the exquisite, the incomparable little mime, having to get through Germany with other Russian refugees in goods trucks and being herded in slaughter-houses.'[104]

The Nijinskys were preparing to leave Budapest, after spending a week with Emilia Markus, when they found the Russian frontier closed. The city was filled with marching troops, and Vaslav sighed, 'All these young men marching to their deaths, and for what?' Romola, who could only think of their own predicament, wondered at his concern for others. They had missed the diplomatic train, and now their hopes lay in being smuggled into

Italy by an uncle of Romola's. Before this could be arranged they were arrested and told that all three of them (Vaslav, Romola and Kyra) were enemy subjects and would be detained for the duration as prisoners-of-war. They were confined to Emilia Markus's house with orders to report to the police weekly.[105]

Diaghilev had signed a contract with Otto Kahn of the Metropolitan Opera House, New York, for an American season: and two of Kahn's conditions were that Diaghilev should accompany the troupe, and that Karsavina, Nijinsky and the other specified dancers should lead it. Necessity made a reconciliation seem possible. But Diaghilev did not understand at first that the Nijinskys were prisoners-of-war. Vaslav wrote that he had 'no right to leave Budapest because of the war'.[106]

Diaghilev in Florence to Stravinsky in Switzerland, 25.11.14

Nijinsky behaves so stupidly. He didn't even answer my detailed and, in my opinion, fair letter, and to my modest telegram requesting, 'reply paid', whether he had received it, he answered only: 'Letter received. Cannot come.' I am sure that his wife is busy making him into the first ballet master of the Budapest Opera. . . . I will write him a second, less modest and less reasonable letter and this miserable person will understand that now is not the moment for joking.[107]

Grigoriev was wrong in thinking that Diaghilev had lost faith in Nijinsky's choreography: for in this same letter to Stravinsky Diaghilev refers to another composition on which the composer was working. 'The invention of movement in "Noces" is definitely for Nijinsky, but I will not discuss the thing with him for several months yet.'[108]

After the initial shock, and the failure of various schemes to get out of the country with the aid of Romola's highly-placed relations, the family settled down to what they were convinced would be only a brief restriction of liberty. Hostilities were sure to cease by the end of the year. Romola was told by an official that her wisest move would be to divorce Nijinsky since he was an alien. Emilia Markus, according to Romola, held a similar view: the presence of a Russian in her family and her house was an embarrassment both to her and her husband. She had both affection and respect for her son-in-law – he was a great artist and a genius: but he was not working, and had no immediate prospects of work; so Emilia was supporting both her family and Romola's. Pardany tactlessly recounted victories over the Russians, which disturbed Vaslav and irritated Romola. Emilia's concern for Kyra was taken as interference by her daughter, and the Nijinskys gradually withdrew into their own part of the house to escape.

'We were completely isolated from the outside world,' wrote Romola. 'Vaslav and myself had to suffice for each other. I knew that he was happy in his marriage, and that he never blamed me for anything that had happened to him since.' During the winter they read Tolstoy, Chekhov and Pushkin, and Nijinsky explained these works to his wife. As they were reading Dostoevsky's *The House of the Dead* Romola 'could not help feeling . . . that I had brought a similar fate on Nijinsky. . . . When I spoke about it, he bravely replied, "Others are dying, suffering far more. I have my art in my soul; nothing and nobody can take it away. Happiness is in us; we take it with us wherever we go." ' As spring arrived they were able to go for longer walks, and Nijinsky found solace in nature. He had had little opportunity of exercising his art since internment began: he had been denied facilities to practise and in the summer had to content himself with the hard terrace of Emilia's house. But now Romola's cousin Lily de Markus, a pianist, began to play every day for him. He started to compose a new ballet on a medieval theme – which he had wanted to do for some time – and when Lily played him Strauss's tone-poem 'Till Eulenspiegel's Lustige Streiche' (Merry Pranks) he began to get ideas. Vaslav read all he could find about the thirteenth-century Flemish hero – a cross between Robin Hood and Robin Goodfellow – around whom an extensive mythology had grown. In his conception, based largely on the accepted 'programme' of the work, a number of these 'pranks' in which Till poked fun at the rich and exhorted the poor to rebel were to form the choreographic episodes. He planned group movement – 'making twenty people do the same movement as if they were one' – which was a development of his work on 'Le Sacre'. As a relief from his work on this ballet he would dance for Romola and her cousin the gypsy dances of Russia. He would suddenly be transformed into a wild, fierce, savage girl, trembling all over from the tips of his fingers to his toes, shaking his shoulders as if they were independent of the rest of his body. And then he would imitate the different ballerinas of the Mariinsky. 'We often begged him to show us how Kchessinskaya danced. But we loved it most when he showed us how the peasant women flirt whilst dancing. He had an inimitable way of throwing inviting glances, and undulating in such a lascivious manner as to stir up the senses of the spectator almost to frenzy.'

At the same time Nijinsky had begun to devise a system of notation for the recording of dances which was to occupy him for a number of years. He taught it to Romola as it progressed.

Life with her mother became more and more unbearable and Romola eventually travelled to Vienna to beseech her uncle in the War Council to send Vaslav and herself to a concentration camp. This he could not do, but he advised his niece to be patient, telling her of a plan to exchange Vaslav, through International Red Cross, for five Austrian officers in Russian hands. She returned to Budapest with renewed hope.

Kyra was now walking, jumping, and even dancing to the music of a street organ, and Vaslav was sure she would be a dancer. His devotion to her was his greatest solace. News came from Lady Ripon, and from one of Romola's aunts, that they were working to obtain Vaslav's freedom. Discussing his life with Diaghilev, Vaslav said, 'I will never regret anything I have done, for I believe that all experience in life, if made with the aim to find the truth, is uplifting. No, I do not regret my relations with Sergei Pavlovitch, even if ethics condemn it.' He had begun to doubt his love for Diaghilev, he told her, on the *Avon*, and considered becoming a preaching monk in Siberia. He recounted how he had first seen her in Budapest as she watched his rehearsals so intently, and he had thought 'A spoilt girl of society, and she possesses a soul.' Nijinsky ended by saying that if Romola ever met anyone she loved more, she was to tell him: her happiness mattered most to him.

Emilia Markus's machinations to rid herself of Romola and Vaslav culminated in a police interrogation: the officials had been informed that Nijinsky was working on a military plan which he was recording in a mathematical code. After days of investigation the police accepted that the 'plan' was Nijinsky's system of notation, and they congratulated him on it. The chief of police was most sympathetic to their predicament. Then, in the autumn of 1915, Vaslav was visited by a Hungarian impresario with the message that Diaghilev was taking the Ballet to North America, and that Nijinsky was needed there. Before long, word came that the police were transferring the three prisoners to Carlsbad in Bohemia: and the police chief suggested that they should break their journey in Vienna for Romola to see her doctor. 'We understood he showed us the way to liberty.'[109]

Meanwhile, in Viareggio, Diaghilev was trying to reassemble his company and make plans for future seasons. Trubecki was despatched to Poland to find dancers. Diaghilev had in mind new ballets to music of Stravinsky and eighteenth-century composers, with décors by Gontcharova and Larionov. In August 1915 Diaghilev and Miassine went to Florence, where they looked at paintings together.

Sometimes [wrote Miassine], Diaghilev would encourage me to try and reproduce the position and movements of the figures in certain paintings, particularly those of Tintoretto, Titian and Michelangelo. One afternoon in the Uffizi, while I was look-ing up at Fra Filippo Lippi's Madonna and Child, Diaghilev said to me: 'Do you think you could compose a ballet?' 'No,' I answered without thinking, 'I'm sure I never could.' Then, as we passed on into another room, I was suddenly aware of the luminous colours of Simone Martini's Annunciation. As I looked at the delicate postures of Gabriel and the Virgin Mary, I felt as if everything I had seen in Florence had finally culminated in this painting. It seemed to be offering me the key to an unknown world, beckoning me along a path which I knew I must follow to the end. 'Yes,' I said to Diaghilev, 'I think I can create a ballet. Not only one, but a hundred, I promise you.'[110]

Diaghilev was soon to give him the opportunity.

From Florence Diaghilev took Miassine to Rome, then, together with

Diaghilev, Massine and the gardener's boy. Caricature by Michel Larionov.

Sert and Misia, they drove to Switzerland and settled in the Villa Bellerive at Ouchy near Lausanne. This was to be Diaghilev's headquarters. Grigoriev was summoned from Russia, and after a journey through Finland, Sweden, Norway, England and France, arrived at the Villa to find Diaghilev surrounded by his new 'committee' – Stravinsky, Bakst, Larionov, Gontcharova, Miassine and the Swiss conductor Ernest Ansermet who was to go to America with the company. Grigoriev was immediately despatched back to Russia by the same circuitous route to gather a company.[111] Diaghilev was convinced that under careful guidance Miassine could become a great choreographer. Larionov was appointed to help him with 'Liturgie', a version of the Mass (in Diaghilev's original conception) with no music, but with stamping as in 'Le Sacre'. Several of the episodes were rehearsed, and Gontcharova and Larionov had begun the designs, but Diaghilev soon abandoned the work.[112] He next suggested to Miassine a ballet to music from Rimsky-Korsakov's 'Snow Maiden', and again with Larionov – who was to design the ballet – advising him, Miassine began to compose. The ballet would be called 'Le Soleil de nuit'.

Rehearsals progressed as the dancers arrived in Lausanne: Muningsova and Kremnev, who had been dancing in music-halls in London; a brilliant young Pole, Stanislas Idzikovsky, whom they had met in London and whose audition Kremnev had arranged with Grigoriev as he passed through; Gavrilov; Zverev; Woizikovsky and Slavinsky from Warsaw – Trubecki had got them out of Poland for a 'tuberculosis cure' in Switzerland; Tchernicheva; Bolm; and three pairs of sisters – Vera and Lida Nemchinova, Maria and Gala Chabelska, Luba and Nura Soumarokova.[113] Grigoriev had been sending his recruits from Russia in batches. He had failed to persuade Fokine or Karsavina to leave Russia in wartime. Since Diaghilev was hoping to have Nijinsky released by the time the American engagement began Fokine's absence did not worry him overmuch; but the company could not do without a leading ballerina. Olga Spessivtseva would not come from Petersburg, and instead Grigoriev engaged Xenia Makletsova from Moscow.[114]

Soon after Muningsova arrived Diaghilev told her that she was to be given solo roles, including Papillon in 'Carnaval', and that he was renaming her Lydia Sokolova, 'and I hope you will live up to the name of Sokolova, as it is that of a great dancer in Russia. Please forget from now on that you have ever been anything but Russian.'[115] By the time Grigoriev got back to Lausanne again most of the company had been assembled. Lydia Lopokhova, who had been in America since she left the company, would be joining them in New York, and she and Makletsova would take over Karsavina's roles. To fill the roles of Zobeïda, Cleopatra and Thamar, Diaghilev looked again for a successor to the exotic Ida Rubinstein: there had been Roshanara, Astafieva, Karsavina, and there had almost been Mata Hari. Although he thought it a makeshift Diaghilev agreed to Bakst's suggestion of engaging Flore Revalles, a tall and imposing French opera singer[116] whom the painter had seen as Tosca in Geneva.[117] She was to become popular in America. Diaghilev now had a company, but, with the exception of Bolm, he had been unable to provide for New York any of the stars Otto Kahn demanded. His only hope was Nijinsky, who he had by now realized was a prisoner of war.

Sokolova believed that the six months which the company spent in Switzerland were the happiest in their history, though the luxurious conditions of pre-war days had ended for good. Diaghilev was happy too, she felt, despite having to make frequent visits to Paris to get subsidies. 'We always knew when Diaghilev had been successful after one of his Paris trips, because Massine would be wearing another sapphire ring on his little finger. Massine, like Nijinsky, collected several of these, but whereas Nijinsky's had been set in gold, Massine's were set in platinum.'[118] Diaghilev's conviction that his new discovery had the makings of an excellent choreographer was his greatest encouragement, and to try out 'Le Soleil de nuit' and his new company he arranged two Red Cross charity matinées for December. On the 20th in Geneva Miassine's ballet had its first performance with Zverev as Bobyl and Miassine as the Midnight Sun. Despite the restrictions of Larionov's colourful but cumbersome costumes, the dancers performed with zest and the ballet was a success. Idzikovsky, Makletsova and Sokolova danced 'Carnaval' and Makletsova and Bolm 'L'Oiseau bleu'. With 'Schéhérazade' in place of 'Carnaval' – and Revalles making her début – the programme was given again at the Paris Opéra on the 29th, conducted by Ansermet. Diaghilev was delighted with the reception of his protégé's first ballet, and remarked to Svetlov: 'You see: given the talent, one can make a choreographer in no time!'[119]

On New Year's Day, 1916, the company sailed from Bordeaux for New York. Vaslav and Romola arrived in Vienna early in January, and they had no idea of how long they would remain prisoners. However, they were treated with exemplary courtesy and accommodated at the Hôtel Bristol, their departure for Carlsbad being postponed indefinitely. The Austrian conditions for Nijinsky's exchange had been prohibitive. Lady Ripon and Comtesse Greffuhle now enlisted the support of Queen Alexandra and the Dowager Empress Marie Feodorovna; the Emperor Franz-Josef of Austria interceded; and through the King of Spain the Pope himself[120] asked for Nijinsky's release – 'The best thing he has done in the war,' wrote the English writer and Churchill's secretary, Edward Marsh.[121] Diaghilev was given to understand that he could expect Nijinsky to be freed, though not before the spring.[122] While they awaited news, Vaslav and Romola were able to live an almost normal life. Nijinsky was given a pass to the Opera, and facilities to practise on the stage of the Theater an der Wien. Here he worked on his choreographic poem 'Mephisto Valse', classical dances – again in medieval spirit – to music of Liszt. In all there were to be forty-five dancers, and all the roles Nijinsky danced himself with perfect characterization. At the same time, working with Romola's brother-in-law Erik Schmedes, he conceived the idea of composing dances for Wagner's operas, which he hoped to realize in Bayreuth after the war. He met Kokoschka, who made a drawing of him; and he visited Arnold Schönberg – whose 'Pierrot Lunaire' he knew – at his villa in Heitzing and discussed music and dancing with him. Nijinsky also met Richard Strauss in Vienna, who was so delighted that Vaslav had choreographed 'Till Eulenspiegel' that he even offered to make alterations to his score, but Nijinsky had followed the programme minutely. After finishing 'Mephisto Valse', he began work on a Japanese ballet, but this was never completed.[123]

The Diaghilev Ballet had arrived in New York on 12 January 1916, and immediately began a week of intensive rehearsals. The first two weeks' performances in the city were to be at the small Century Theatre on Central Park West. Makletsova was to take the ballerina roles in 'L'Oiseau de feu' and 'La Princesse enchantée'. Lopokhova now joined the company, returning to ballet from her acting career, and Massine, whose name Diaghilev had simplified, created a new dance for her in his ballet. Revalles was Zobeïda, and Tchernicheva the Tsarevna in 'L'Oiseau de feu'. Nijinsky's roles were re-assigned: Bolm was to dance the Negro in 'Schéhérazade' (which he had done before), and the Prince in 'La Princesse enchantée' (which cannot have suited him); Massine would perform the Faun, Petrushka, and – later, when he had learnt the roles – Amoun and the Negro. At the last moment it seemed that disaster might strike. Bolm was ill for several days, could barely dance at all in the private performance on the Sunday evening, and had still not recovered his form by the first night.[124]

The opening programme on Monday the 17th was 'L'Oiseau de feu', 'Schéhérazade', 'La Princesse enchantée' and 'Soleil de nuit'. Massine thought the audience's response disappointing, and Diaghilev doubted whether the New Yorkers were going to appreciate his ballet. 'He told me,' wrote Massine, 'that Americans still seemed to think of ballet as light entertainment, to be enjoyed after a hard day at the office!'[125] The reviews next morning were aware of this problem, but highly enthusiastic. The *Journal of Commerce* pointed out that New York's familiarity with Pavlova and her dancers was no preparation for Diaghilev's repertory. 'The present ballet makes its appeal in a different way, to different senses. It is more of a command than an appeal. Those accustomed to the old ballet need education in the new to appreciate it. Abroad, it is said, they have learned to delight in it. Whether American audiences are sufficiently advanced to take to it at once is a question.'[126] For a public accustomed to classical dancing, as performed by Pavlova and Mordkine, a great adjustment needed to be made to respond to the totally new experience of the Fokine ballets. In London Diaghilev had

had the opposite problem: having brought up his audiences on a diet of Fokine, he found them unable to appreciate his 'Giselle' and 'Lac des Cygnes'. The new music of Stravinsky and the colours of Bakst astonished the Americans, who responded with admiration and respect. But much as Makletsova, Bolm and Massine were admired it was felt that a distinction was lacking through the absence of Karsavina and Nijinsky – and particularly Nijinsky. 'For thousands knew of the genius of Nijinsky,' wrote one columnist, 'where hundreds knew of the genius of the Russian *ensemble*. In a country where "personality" counts most in politics, business and art, the loss of the two chief "names" of a sudden was the most serious mischance that had happened to the Ballet in all its wanderings.' The same writer noted the absence of Nijinsky's wonderful leap in Bolm's Golden Slave, but added that this lack 'would never be noticed this time if it had never been seen before . . .'. In all the ballets the company were magnificent in their groupings. This, the American public had been told, was part of Diaghilev's conception of the ballet. 'Try as we may,' said this same critic, 'we can never come away from the Russian Ballet to think of it merely as an achievement of art. It is also a gospel, a philosophy.'[127]

Against the eulogies of the American press might be set the opinion of Carl van Vechten, the music critic who – as Paris representative of the *New York Times* – had seen the Ballet often in Europe and had been present at the first night of 'Le Sacre'. The fact that none of the 'stars' were dancing, he discovered, made a lot of difference. 'Often had we urged that the individual played but a small part in this new and gorgeous entertainment, but now we were forced to admit that the ultimate glamour was lacking in the *ensemble*, which was obviously no longer the glad, gay entity it once had been.' Massine, he felt, was neither a great dancer nor a great mime: he was no Nijinsky. Bolm had 'vitality and abundant energy' but not the skill in characterization attributed to him – and the same deficiency limited the otherwise polished dancing of Gavrilov. Makletsova was accomplished in technical tricks, but she lacked poetry or interpretative power. 'In such a work as "The Firebird" she really offended the eye. Far from interpreting the ballet, she gave you an idea of how it should not be done.' Lopokhova had charm and a 'roguish demeanour', but in her purely 'ballerina' roles taken over from Makletsova, 'she floundered hopelessly out of her element.' Tchernicheva made the most of the opportunities – mainly mimic – which she was given. Revalles did less than that: 'Her Cléopâtre suggested to me a Parisian *cocotte* much more than an Egyptian queen.' But in spite of these objections, van Vechten felt, Diaghilev had given New York 'finer exhibitions of stage art than had previously been even the exception here'.[128] This was exactly Diaghilev's view of the situation, and it was also the tenor of almost every press notice.

Besides 'L'Oiseau de feu' (with Massine as the Prince and Cecchetti as Kastchei), 'Schéhérazade', 'La Princesse enchantée' and 'Soleil de nuit', four other ballets were given in the first week: 'Les Sylphides' with Lopokhova, Tchernicheva and Bolm, 'L'Après-midi d'un faune' with Massine, 'Carnaval' with Lopokhova and Bolm, and 'Prince Igor' with Bolm. 'Schéhérazade' was given again at the Saturday matinée together with 'L'Après-midi', and as a result of complaints received after the first performances police witnesses were in the audience. John Brown, the Metropolitan General Manager, was obliged to order certain modifications before the ballets could be put on again.[129] A controversy over censorship sprang up in the papers. With 'L'Après-midi' the publicity about the Parisian scandal had prepared the ground for the rising of American gorges; but in 'Schéhérazade' the rub came nearer home. It was the idea of 'white' (albeit eastern) women taking negro lovers which was so abhorrent, and, wrote Carl van Vechten, there had even been 'talk of a "Jim Crow" performance in which the blacks were to be separated from the whites in the harem'.[130] While the police were taking *their* action, the Catholic Theatre Movement was busy circulating a private bulletin against the Russian Ballet.[131]*

The production during the second week of 'Le Pavillon d'Armide' with Makletsova, Bolm and Cecchetti, 'Petrushka' with Massine, Lopokhova, Bolm and Cecchetti, and 'Thamar' with Bolm and Revalles, completed the New York repertory and the engagement ended on the 29th. The company then set out on a tour. They spent ten days at Boston – the longest stay of the tour. Here Makletsova left them.[132] 'Cléopâtre' with Revalles and Bolm and 'Le Spectre' had their first performances in Chicago, after the company had danced in Albany and Detroit.

The American newspapers printed occasional reports of Nijinsky's vicissitudes in expectation of his arrival in time for the Ballet's second New York season. On 1 February Vaslav and Romola were summoned to the American Embassy in Vienna and told that the Ambassador had been successful in obtaining permission for Nijinsky to go 'on parole' to the United States to join Diaghilev. But there were conditions: Nijinsky should not return to Russia, and Romola and Kyra should remain as hostages. Nijinsky refused the latter, and eventually the condition was dropped in favour of assurances from the Ambassador. The next evening they left for Berne. There was a week's delay on the Swiss frontier, during which they were searched, and then they arrived at the Hotel Bernerhof. A dinner was given in their honour at the Legation, and they received a diplomatic passport.

* All the obstructions to smooth running during the American tours were attributed by Romola to the disapproval of Gatti-Casazza, the Metropolitan Director, and his 'Italian clique' of the engagement of the Ballet by Otto Kahn.

Two days later, in Lausanne, Nijinsky learned of his part in Diaghilev's contract with the Metropolitan Opera House, and although uneasy about the state of his relationship with Diaghilev he expressed himself willing to dance in the country which had worked for his freedom. He also heard that a case had been won for him in London for the money which Diaghilev owed him.*

While Vaslav and Romola were at Lausanne they were visited by Stravinsky who lived nearby at Morges. They got involved in heated arguments. Stravinsky had a grievance, too, against Diaghilev who had forgotten his promise to secure for him an official invitation to conduct his ballets at the Metropolitan Opera House.[133]

February drew to a close in Berne, and then news came in the form of a telegram from Astruc:

Astruc in Paris to Nijinsky in Berne, 1.3.16

Contact immediately Comte Daniel de Pradère, Councillor of the Spanish Embassy, who will facilitate your departure for America.[134]

The final arrangements were made, and on 24 March the Nijinskys arrived in Paris, where they had a day's grace before the boat sailed. Comtesse Greffuhle had done all that was needed, and Romola was able to prepare herself for the New World. With Vaslav she made

a tour of the leading dressmakers and millinery establishments. Nobody would have recognized us twenty-four hours later as we went to the Quai d'Orsay to catch the train. We were elegantly dressed, and followed by sixteen trunks, loaded with flowers, and accompanied by our maid and nurse and escort, Mr Russell [of the Metropolitan]. Many old friends and admirers of Vaslav turned out to say goodbye to us.[135]

At Bordeaux Nijinsky sent Astruc a visiting-card, 'avec tous mes plus vifs remerciments', which was probably accompanied by flowers,[136] then the party boarded the French liner *Espagne*. They took with them Bolm's fiancée whom they had promised to look after. During the voyage Nijinsky found in the ship's doctor, Louis Moret – a famous etcher – a companion who took great interest in his system of notation.[137]

From Boston the Russian Ballet tour had taken in sixteen towns, going as far west as Kansas City. They travelled in a special train of Pullman cars with their orchestra and technicians. On the 'one-night stands', a new and uncomfortable experience for the Russian dancers, they slept on the train: but in those cities where they performed for a few nights – such as Detroit, Chicago, Indianapolis, Cincinatti, Cleveland, Pittsburgh and Washington – they stayed in hotels.[138] The first night at Washington on 23 March was a

---

* According to Romola, the large sum of half a million gold francs. The money would be paid in America.

smart affair in the presence of the President and Mrs Wilson.[139] The news here reached the company that Nijinsky was on his way and would join them for their season at the Metropolitan.[140]

Nijinsky did not, however, arrive in time for the first night at the Metropolitan on 3 April: his ship was due to dock the next day. The programme for the opening performance comprised 'Le Spectre', 'Les Sylphides', 'Petrushka' and 'Prince Igor'. Only 'Le Spectre' was new to New York, danced by Lopokhova and – in Nijinsky's absence – Gavrilov. The sour critic of *Musical American* felt that 'Nijinsky's skill as a teacher does not equal his dancing abilities, for his pupil disported himself very heavily and without perceptible distinction or grace.' The same writer also noted that the two weeks at the Century Theatre 'apparently rubbed a good deal of gilt from the ginger-bread. There were no thronging cohorts at the Metropolitan Monday night and only modified raptures. . . .'[141] This second New York season had already occasioned some complaints in the press, since it took place during a regular subscription opera season. The continual repetition of ballets seemed like cheating to a part of the public – and in fact the repertory was to change scarcely at all with the advent of Nijinsky. Gatti-Casazza, the Director of the Metropolitan, whose Italian operas with Caruso were the staple diet, was unsympathetic to the Ballet, and it now reached the papers that even before the contracts were signed 'a liberal figure on the wrong side of the ledger was expected'. The season was privately subsidized, and even increased prices of admission offered 'no prospect of security against loss'.[142]

The *Espagne* docked in New York on 4 April, and the ship was immediately invaded by newspaper and camera men. Nijinsky was swamped, his muscles were felt, he was asked questions about the war, about his partners, about art, about Rasputin. When he was finally free from reporters and immigration officials he was met by Metropolitan representatives, members of the Ballet, Diaghilev and Massine. Diaghilev greeted Romola with a bouquet and kissed Vaslav on both cheeks, whereupon Nijinsky put his daughter into Diaghilev's arms. They then walked off together.[143]

But now it was Massine who was staying with Diaghilev at the Ritz, while Vaslav and Romola were at the Claridge. There was no real resumption of amicable relations between Diaghilev and Nijinsky: indeed, the first matter to crop up was Diaghilev's debt which Nijinsky insisted on having settled before he would dance with the company. Within a few days a private contract had been drawn up by the Metropolitan by which Nijinsky would dance eleven performances, and each week Diaghilev would pay a part of the debt through the Opera House from receipts.[144] The Press announced the settlement of the dispute, and mentioned that Diaghilev had 'protested that

$3,000 a week was enough for even a Nijinsky'.[145] Lydia Sokolova, writing home on 9 April, gave a picture of the disruptions and politics surrounding Nijinsky as they affected the company: 'Nijinsky is here and is making a lot of fuss – won't appear without tons of money, saying in the papers horrid things about the Ballet. You know just how they always turn around on those who make their names for them.'[146] Of course she was not in a position to know that Nijinsky had worked for years for nothing. Edward Ziegler, Otto Kahn's assistant, penned a verse which expressed everyone's frustration:

> O Mr Nijinsky,
> Where have you binsky?
> And if you are here
> Why don't you appear
> And save the ballet from ruinsky?[147]

It had been settled that Nijinsky should make his American début on Wednesday, 12 April. Diaghilev had arranged for him to have as many rehearsals as possible, including one with the orchestra.[148] To his interviewers Vaslav had declared himself 'in the pink of condition, and he looked it'.[149] But Sokolova thought that 'he had grown heavier and looked very sad. . . . He never spoke a word to anyone and picked his fingers more than ever.'[150] Grigoriev, too, commented on his 'vagueness and unfriendliness'.[151] The company, wrote Romola, treated her husband and herself with great courtesy, but not many were really friendly. Bolm was 'one of the few who kept aloof from petty intrigue' and was always loyal to Nijinsky.[152] During the first week at the Metropolitan, however, Bolm sprained a tendon, and as a result the programmes had to be changed. Sokolova's letter home continued: 'Yesterday Bolm was unable to dance "Petrushka" and so Kremnev rehearsed half an hour before performance and did the principal part.* . . . We have heard Diaghilev wants to give Bolm the slip now that Nijinsky's here, and so any part of his that Nijinsky won't do, Kremnev will get. . . .'[153] But Bolm was a considerable attraction too and was soon dancing again.

Sokolova felt that it must have been difficult – on top of everything else – for Nijinsky to return as *premier danseur* with the young Massine being schooled as his successor both in the company and in Diaghilev's affections.[154] But Massine did not feel this, nor was he disappointed in Nijinsky's dancing. He, too, saw in Nijinsky's reserve the evidence of his past tribulations. 'But when I saw him dance, I was astounded at the way his whole personality became transformed on stage. He had an instinctive effortless control of his

---

* Actually the Moor. (*Musical Courier*, April 1916.)

body; every gesture expressed the most tender and complex emotions. . . . After seeing Nijinsky dance, I realized I had seen a genius.'[155]

The programme for the matinée on 12 April was announced as 'Schéhérazade', 'Le Spectre', 'Prince Igor' and 'Petrushka' – but a slight mishap to Flore Revalles resulted in the first and third ballets being reversed. Mlle Revalles, who attracted much publicity on account of her pet snake which she kept in a cage or twined round her fingers when it was not on stage with her in 'Cléopâtre', received before the performance a letter signed by a cousin of the Kaiser, which, when opened, shot a cloud of talcum powder into her eyes.[156] The rearrangement of ballets allowed her to regain her composure before going on as Zobeïda. Her performance was impressive: but, remarked one critic, had it not been for her accident she would have been 'in direst peril of not having so much as one word in any newspaper on the occasion of the début of Nijinsky'.[157]

Nijinsky danced with Lopokhova in 'Le Spectre' and in 'Petrushka'. 'The Diamond Horseshoe was present in full force,' wrote Romola, 'and the audience was as brilliant as in the great Paris galas.'[158]* Nijinsky's entrance was greeted with a standing ovation and a shower of rose petals (probably organized by the management). The critic of the *Musical Courier* had no doubt that Nijinsky was the greatest of all male dancers: 'Where Mr Nijinsky excels all his fellow artists is in the absolute finish of line in his work. There is never a pause or an angle. Mr Nijinsky's dancing is an absolute and complete realization in movement of the melodic and rhythmical movement of the accompanying music.'[159] Another reviewer, Pitts Sanborn, music editor of the *Globe*, concluded that Nijinsky was 'not of this earth', and added that 'Le Spectre' would have been 'something for the tongue of angels, not of men, had Nijinsky had as partner Pavlova or Karsavina'.[160] In 'Le Spectre' Nijinsky had had little advance competition, but in 'Petrushka', the *Musical Courier* noted, 'he had to stand a very severe comparison because of the superb work of Mr Massine in the same role. Mr Nijinsky paid more attention to the puppet's soul and less to his mechanism than Mr Massine. Those who like this conception will prefer Nijinsky; those who prefer to have the fact that Petrushka is a puppet emphasized, Massine. Both are as fine as can be in their respective characterizations.'[161] Massine was to write many years later: 'Although I had identified myself with Petrushka, I soon realized that the role came more naturally to Nijinsky.'[162] The music critics noticed that Nijinsky's return to this ballet was accompanied by changes in the action, the *tempi*, and the 'shading in the orchestral accompaniment'.[163]

At the evening performance 'Thamar' was given on the same bill as the New York première of 'Cléopâtre', Revalles and Bolm dancing both.

---

* Though presumably not wearing their diamonds for the matinée.

Nijinsky's next roles two days later were in 'Carnaval' – in which Cecchetti (now sixty-six) replaced the sick Bolm as Pierrot – and in 'Les Sylphides', in which, according to the *Musical Courier*, 'his persistence in stroking his curls gave a touch of feminism to his performance . . . which was not relished by many of the audience.'[164] Lydia Sokolova danced Bronislava Nijinska's roles in 'Carnaval' and in 'Narcisse', which was given the following week. (The two performances of 'Narcisse' in New York were the only ones in America.) On the Saturday evening, 15 April, Nijinsky danced in 'La Princesse enchantée' and 'Schéhérazade'. Massine was to write of Nijinsky's 'incomparable' dancing in the former ballet: 'To convey the quivering motion of the bird's wings he fluttered his hands at such a dazzling speed that they seemed to have exactly the pulsating action of humming-birds. I learned later that he had done this by doubling the rate of his wrist movements.'[165] Reviewing Nijinsky in 'Schéhérazade' one critic revealed his racial feelings: 'The part of the negro who makes love to the princess is a repulsive one, but he tones down some of its unpleasantness. The impulse to jump on the stage and thrash him must be suppressed.'[166]

Lydia Sokolova thought that Nijinsky's dancing had deteriorated.[167] Grigoriev wrote that he improved gradually.[168] But Carl van Vechten, who was apprehensive before Nijinsky's first appearance, affirmed that 'it was evident that he was in possession of all his powers; nay, more, that he had added to the refinement and polish of his style. I had called Nijinsky's dancing perfection in years gone by, because it so far surpassed that of his nearest rival; now he had surpassed himself.' Writing of 'Le Spectre', which he thought best displayed the facets of Nijinsky's genius, he said:

His dancing is accomplished in that flowing line, without a break between poses and gestures, which is the despair of all novices and almost all other virtuosi. After a particularly difficult leap or toss of the legs or arms, it is a marvel to observe how, without an instant's pause to regain his poise, he rhythmically glides into the succeeding gesture. His dancing has the unbroken quality of music, the balance of great painting, the meaning of fine literature, and the emotion inherent in all these arts. . . . It is not alone the final informing and magnetized imaginative quality that most other dancers lack; it is also just this muscular co-ordination. Observe Gavrilov in the piece under discussion, in which he gives a good imitation of Nijinsky's general style, and you will see that he is unable to maintain this rhythmic continuity.[169]

Nijinsky's performance in 'Schéhérazade' suggested to van Vechten 'exotic eroticism expressed in so high a key that its very existence seems incredible on our puritanic stage': but somehow previous objections were forgotten as

This strange, curious, head-wagging, simian creature, scarce human, wriggled through the play, leaving a long streak of lust and terror in his wake. Never did

Nijinsky as the Negro Slave touch the Sultana, but his subtle and sensuous fingers fluttered close to her flesh, clinging once or twice questioningly to a depending tassel. Pierced by the javelins of the Sultan's men, the Slave's death struggle might have been revolting and gruesome. Instead Nijinsky carried the eye rapidly upward with his tapering feet as they balanced for the briefest part of a second straight high in the air, only to fall inert with so brilliantly swift a movement that the aesthetic effect grappled successfully with the feeling of disgust which might have been aroused. This was acting, this was characterization, so completely merged in rhythm that the result became a perfect whole and not a combination of several intentions, as so often results from the work of an actor-dancer.[170]

During the Metropolitan season Vaslav and Romola lived rather a busy social life, and Nijinsky also danced – in a black and gold 'Carpaccio Gondolier costume' – at a special benefit performance of *tableaux vivants* after Italian Masters, in aid of Venice flood relief. Society women stole most of his underwear for souvenirs.[171] This occasion was organized by Mrs Vanderbilt. All the great American families entertained Vaslav. Relations with Diaghilev were now purely formal, and disagreements frequent. Romola remained convinced that Diaghilev was intent on ruining her husband by telling everyone that Nijinsky was getting fat and petulant. Also, he showed no interest in Nijinsky's plans for 'Till Eulenspiegel' and 'Mephisto Valse'[172] – partly, no doubt, because they had been composed independently of him, and partly because all his hopes now lay with Massine. A further disagreement arose over 'L'Après-midi' which Massine had been dancing as he had been taught by Grigoriev and others. This was not exactly as Nijinsky had choreographed it, and he offered to rehearse the ballet. He also wished that Revalles should replace Tchernicheva as the chief Nymph. Diaghilev would not consider either of these proposals, and Nijinsky obliged him to cancel the performances advertised for the final week of the engagement, in which New York would have had its first sight of Nijinsky in a ballet of his own devising.[173] On the last day of the season, 29 April, a Saturday, Nijinsky danced in 'Le Spectre' at the matinée, and 'La Princesse enchantée' and 'Schéhérazade' in the evening. Diaghilev recognized the work of the specially selected orchestra of eighty by presenting them with an eight-foot-high floral wreath; and the orchestra was then dispersed.

Diaghilev was anxious to arrange a second American tour, since so many countries in Europe were closed to him in wartime. He took care to be reported in the newspapers as having liked America and wondered why he had never been before, and he praised the appreciation of the American audiences.[174] Otto Kahn wanted a coast-to-coast tour, and, according to Romola, 'even if a deficit were involved he did not mind, as he wished to educate the American public'.[175] In fact, he was trying to get into society.[176]

He was determined that Nijinsky should lead the company, but also thought it desirable that the next engagement should not be hampered by continual friction between Diaghilev and Nijinsky. Accordingly he persuaded Nijinsky that Diaghilev's presence was not required, and that Vaslav should be artistic director.[177] The company was thus to be rented from Diaghilev for the period of the tour, on condition that he was to remain outside the United States.[178] 'Everyone except Kahn, Nijinsky and Romola,' wrote Sokolova, 'realized this was madness . . .';[179] but Diaghilev had to agree. He had, however, accepted an invitation from the King of Spain for the company to dance at the Teatro Real in Madrid, and while in Spain he would be able to work with Massine on a new repertory. On 6 May, leaving Vaslav and Romola and Flore Revalles in New York, Diaghilev and the rest of the company sailed for Cadiz on the *Dante Alighieri*. The ship was full of screaming horses, many of which died on the way over.[180]

The Nijinskys moved to the Majestic Hotel, and their leisure time was spent with Caruso and other new friends. But Vaslav's chief pleasures were to walk on Broadway or to go to the 'movies'. On one occasion a luncheon party was given for Nijinsky and Isadora Duncan, and Isadora, just back from a very peculiar tour in South America[181] and temporarily reunited with Paris Singer, who proposed buying Madison Square Garden for her,[182] reminded Vaslav of the time when she had suggested that they have a child. She said, 'The idea did not seem to appeal to you then; I see you are changed now; you are less intolerant towards us women.' Vaslav replied, 'I did not change. I love everybody, as Christ did',[183] which, if truly reported, was rather an irritating remark.

Nijinsky's presence in New York was a constant source of news and gossip for the papers – some of it fanciful. The *New York Review*, for instance, reported on 13 May that Nijinsky had 'under consideration' an offer made to him by Annette Kellerman, the 'Diving Venus', for them to join forces in a new aquatic production.[184] But Nijinsky was now completely immersed in plans for his two new works and for the next season of the Russian Ballet, of which he was to be sole artistic director. One problem was to find a *prima ballerina* for the company, and the Metropolitan sent to Russia to investigate the possibilities. The next question was the designing of 'Till' and 'Mephisto Valse', since neither Benois nor Sudeikine, whom Nijinsky approached, would leave Russia during the war. Ultimately Rawlings Cottenet, one of the Metropolitan directors,[185] arranged for Vaslav and Romola to go to Greenwich Village and talk to a promising young painter, Robert Edmond Jones, who had worked with Max Reinhardt in Berlin. 'He was a tall, shy man,' wrote Romola, 'but he inspired confidence in Vaslav. . . .'[186] Jones gave a memorable description of Nijinsky at this meeting.

He is very nervous. His eyes are troubled. He looks eager, anxious, excessively intelligent. He seems tired, bored, excited, all at once. I observe that he has a disturbing habit of picking at the flesh on the side of his thumbs until they bleed. Through all my memories of this great artist runs the recurring image of those raw red thumbs. He broods and dreams, goes far away into reverie, returns again. At intervals his face lights up with a brief, dazzling smile. His manner is simple, ingratiating, so direct as to be almost humble.

The conversation took place in halting French, but Nijinsky seemed to be interested in the designs. As they talked Jones sensed

a quality in him which I can only define . . . as a continual preoccupation with standards of excellence so high that they are really not of this world. . . . There is in him an astonishing drive, a mental engine, too high-powered, racing – perhaps even now – to its final breakdown.* Otherwise there is nothing of the abnormal about him. Only an impression of something too eager, too brilliant, a quivering of the nerves, a nature racked to dislocation by a merciless creative urge.

Nijinsky's reaction to the drawings was simply 'Très heureux.'[187]

Vaslav bought a Peerless car which he learned to drive after a fashion, and in which he took Romola and the growing Kyra for rides. The family now moved – by car – to Bar Harbor in Maine to escape an epidemic of infantile paralysis, and there, with one or two friends nearby, they had the advantages of a swimming pool – where Nijinsky's prowess was noted by spectators – a marble theatre on a hill, and a Greek amphitheatre on the lawn. Vaslav played with his daughter on the grass and practised with his accompanist in the Greek temple. Here also he tried his hand – for the first time and with great success – at the game of tennis which he had misrepresented in 'Jeux'.† Once a week there was a concert in the theatre, where distinguished musicians performed. Nijinsky also composed some dances, one of which – 'Le Nègre Blanc' – he arranged to Debussy's Cake-walk.[188]

Robert Edmond Jones was summoned to Bar Harbor with his designs. The painter was overwhelmed with this commission and thought Nijinsky's conception of 'Till' a masterpiece and the choreographer 'at the very height of his creative power'.[189] Vaslav had asked him to work from books of the period, and was pleased with the costume sketches, which were full of life and colour. Jones's original idea for the décor was not entirely to Vaslav's liking, and Vaslav explained what he wanted.[190] He was to write in his *Diary* that the artist 'worried and worried. . . . I used to say to him, "Why should you be afraid? One must not be afraid." But he still worried. Evidently he

---

* Jones here seems to be wise after the event.

† I remember another outstanding dancer, Erik Bruhn, being introduced to the game of tennis one Sunday afternoon at the house of Mr William Low at Musselburgh, outside Edinburgh, and taking to it as a duck to water.

worried about the success of the ballet. He did not believe in me. I was certain of success.'[191] But as the two artists – each in his own way introverted – worked together, they evolved the final designs, described by Jones as follows: the front curtain – 'a huge sheet of parchment emblazoned with Til's device of the owl and the looking-glass, all blurred and worn, like a page torn from a long-forgotten manuscript of the Middle Ages'; the set – the market-place of Brunswick before the city hall and the 'brooding black mass of the cathedral', the buildings leaning towards each other in distorted fashion; the costume designs – 'the rosy-cheeked apple-woman with her big basket of apples, all red and green and russet; the cloth merchant in his shop; the fat blond baker with his long loaves of bread; the scrawny sweet-meat-seller, decked out in peppermint stripes of red and white, like one of his own candies; the cobbler carrying his rack of oddly-shaped shoes; the burghers, the priests, the professors in their long robes and their ridiculous shovel hats; the street urchins and the beggars; the three *châtelaines*, taking the air beneath peaked hennins that tower a full six feet above their heads, their trains streaming away ten feet, twenty feet, thirty feet behind them . . . and Til himself in his varied disguises – Til the imp, Til the lover, Til the scholar, Til flouting, taunting, imploring, writhing in his death agonies . . .'.[192]

Romola, in the meantime, was checking Nijinsky's contract which provided for a tour of the country lasting forty weeks, and three weeks in New York. The Metropolitan wished Nijinsky to dance five times a week: Romola managed to arrange this strenuous schedule so that he danced two ballets three times a week and one on the other evenings.[193] But on top of directing the company and travelling this threatened a great strain on Vaslav.

In June Diaghilev cabled to Otto Kahn from Madrid:

Diaghilev in Madrid to Kahn in New York, (?).6.16

Season ended yesterday admirably. Their Majesties attended every performance. Lopokhova, Tchernicheva, Bolm and Massine were introduced by me to the King, who spoke enthusiastically to them. He wishes us to return next spring. Has twice received Stravinsky, asked him to compose Spanish ballet. His Majesty wants us to give a few gala performances at San Sebastian in August. Diaghilev.[194]

These galas in San Sebastian provided the occasion for the premières of two new works which Massine had created in Spain in collaboration with Larionov. 'Las Meninas' to Fauré's 'Pavane' was inspired by the Velasquez paintings in the Prado: the costumes were by J-M. Sert after Velasquez, and the décor by the French painter Carlo Socrate. The ballet was intended by Diaghilev as a tribute to their Spanish audiences. The first performance was on 21 August at the Victoria-Eugenia Theatre: Sokolova, Khokhlova, Massine and Woizikovsky danced the leading roles, with Elena Antonova as the dwarf. Four days later Massine's other new ballet 'Kikimora' was given, with Chabelska and Idzikovsky. With music by Liadov and décor and costumes by Gontcharova and Larionov, this short Russian fairy-tale would become a year later the first part of 'Les Contes russes'. The third work which the company produced in Spain was a new version of the dances from 'Sadko' which Diaghilev entrusted to Bolm since Fokine's choreography of 1911 was almost forgotten. This was presented in Bilbao, with décor by Anisfeld and costumes by Gontcharova.

Nijinsky was now anxious to rehearse *his* two ballets, but Diaghilev could not dispatch the company to America until five weeks before the New York opening. Diaghilev had decided to retain a nucleus of dancers with him to plan new work, and so he, Grigoriev, Larionov and Gontcharova, the Cecchettis, Massine and some sixteen dancers – including Tchernicheva, Antonova, Evina, Maria Chabelska, Khokhlova, Woizikovsky, Idzikovsky and Novak – went to Rome, while the main body of the company set sail from Bordeaux on 8 September in the *Lafayette*. Nijinsky's biggest mistake, it was generally felt, had been his insistence that Grigoriev – the one person acquainted with every practical question in the management of the company – should not come back to America. In his place as *régisseur* Diaghilev had promoted Nicolas Kremnev, who was impetuous and tactless, and too much 'one of the boys' to have any authority. The business side of management was in the hands of Trubecki, Diaghilev's secretary and Pflanz's husband, and Randolfo Barocchi, who, although the husband of Lopokhova, had little knowledge of the Ballet.[195]

The season was to open at the Manhattan Opera House on 16 October, and when the company arrived in New York only three weeks remained in which Nijinsky could rehearse his new ballets, and the old repertory had to be polished up as well. Nijinsky did not show up to greet his dancers on their arrival,[196] and first met them at a morning rehearsal in the Grand Central Palace.[197] The two most important recruits from Russia were Marguerite Frohman, who, together with her brother Max, had danced for Diaghilev before the war, and the beautiful Olga Spessivtseva, whom Grigoriev had failed to entice to America for the previous season.

'Till' had a difficult birth. In rehearsals Nijinsky left it to Robert Jones to outline the scenario to the company[198] and they were slow to learn the new work. At one point the dancers became so exasperated by what they thought were Vaslav's shortcomings and by the failure of the management to intervene that they organized a two-day strike.[199] This Romola attributed to their refusal to dance to German music, and she remained convinced that the company as a whole – perhaps on Diaghilev's instructions – was intent on sabotaging Nijinsky's work.[200] In Rome Diaghilev and Grigoriev heard of the dissensions in the troupe, and Barocchi confirmed this in a telegram. More cables followed, until even Nijinsky had to wire asking Grigoriev to come to New York. With Diaghilev's approval the *régisseur* replied: 'Grigoriev declines the honour of rejoining the company while under your management.'[201] If Grigoriev's story is true this was rude and unhelpful, but by insisting that Grigoriev should be left in Europe Nijinsky had asked for it.

Despite the collaboration between choreographer and artist on the designs, there was further disagreement in this direction too. The scale model of the set was finished, and the scene-painters had begun their work painting the drops and flats on the vertical 'easel' frames in the scenic studios – the standard method in America, as in England. Nijinsky had wanted the work done the traditional Russian way, with the canvas laid on the floor, the painters walking over it in soft shoes with buckets of paint and long-handled brushes. This conflict was resolved after distress on both sides.[202] Pierre Monteux, who was conducting for this tour in place of Ansermet, now refused to conduct 'Till' because Strauss was a signatory to the Austrian manifesto against France, in whose army Monteux was serving when the Metropolitan got him six months' leave of absence. Dr Anselm Goetzl was engaged to conduct this ballet only throughout the tour.[203] Romola took Monteux's action as a personal attack on Vaslav.[204]

The costumes – which Sokolova thought were 'so striking' that 'they alone might have made a success of the ballet'[205] – delighted Vaslav; not so the sets· They were not high enough to give the effect of exaggeration in the buildings which he had wanted. Jones was summoned to Nijinsky's dressing-room· 'The walls . . . are papered in stripes of two tones of violent red. There is a pier-glass and a chaise-longue. On the dressing-table a number of stiletto-like knives, sharpened to a razor-edge, are ranged in an orderly row. The *maestro* is waiting for me in a flame of rage.'[206]* After his anger had exhausted itself, Nijinsky returned to the stage, and, jumping up to correct a dancer, fell and sprained his ankle. He was taken to a clinic and X-rayed: he was to rest for several weeks.

Confusion reigned. Rehearsals for 'Till' were to go on, but its première was postponed. Nijinsky was told that he could dance on tour, but possibly not in New York; and any idea of putting on 'Mephisto Valse' – for which Jones had made the designs – had to be abandoned.[207]

---

* At this point the luridness of Jones's account seems to reflect his own hysterical state of mind at the time: 'Torrents of Russian imprecations pour from his lips. The open door fills with frowning alien faces. Nijinsky switches to broken French. He lashes out at me with an insensate blind hate.'

Mme Romola Nijinsky's comment is 'Not true.' The 'stiletto-like knives' could only have been sticks of Leichner grease-paint.

Anna Pavlova sent Vaslav flowers.[208] She was appearing with her company at the Hippodrome in Charles Dillingham's 'The Big Show': it was an engagement which was to last five months – undertaken largely to pay her debts – in which she danced a condensed version of 'The Sleeping Beauty' sandwiched between vaudeville acts of spectacular proportions – with West Point cadets and four hundred minstrels – and an Ice Ballet: 'a jewel in a garish setting', commented one reviewer. As time went on her ballet became more and more vestigial – reduced finally to eighteen minutes – and her costumes by Bakst (the designs for some of which were to be used by Diaghilev five years later) were sewn with spangles to compete with the glitter of the other turns.[209] For Pavlova the presence of both Isadora and Nijinsky in New York at this time made matters worse, and it is perhaps understable that when Romola told the ballerina that Vaslav's ankle was only twisted, not broken, 'her voice dropped, as though she were disappointed'.[210]

The season opened on 16 October without Nijinsky, whose absence was felt at the box office. The repertory was the same as before, except that 'Narcisse', 'L'Oiseau de feu', 'Le Pavillon d'Armide' and 'Le Soleil de nuit' had been replaced by 'Les Papillons', Bolm's 'Sadko' and 'Till Eulenspiegel'. Lopokhova, Sokolova, Vassilievska and Gavrilov danced 'Sylphides'; Sophie Pflanz and Bolm led the Polovtsian Dances; Revalles resumed her roles of Zobeïda and Cleopatra (which Tchernicheva had been dancing in Spain) with Bolm as Amoun and the Negro, and Sokolova dancing Ta-hor; and 'Le Spectre' was given again with Lopokhova and Gavrilov. In 'Carnaval' Gavrilov was Harlequin, Lopokhova was Columbine, Pflanz Chiarina, Sokolova Papillon, Bolm Pierrot, Zverev Eusebius, Kremnev Pantalon, and Florestan was taken by a newcomer, Mieczyslaw Pianowski. Lopokhova, Sokolova and Bolm were to dance the leading roles in 'Papillons', whose première was scheduled for the end of the first week, but owing to Lopokhova's illness the ballet was postponed until the night of the première of 'Till Eulenspiegel', which was now to be Monday, 23 October. The only new ballet shown during the first week of the engagement was 'Sadko' with the choreographer in the title role.

Nijinsky's doctors decided that he was fit to dance 'Till'. Jones had solved the problem of the set by adding ten-foot-high canvases to the bases of the two flats, and painting them with 'an impression of foliage in broad washes of ultramarine'. Only the top of the scenery was fully lit. (The critics assumed that the effect was intentional, and approved.)[211] The dress-rehearsal was held on the day of the first performance. At this point the dancers knew the first act, which went smoothly: 'Nijinsky danced gaily,' wrote Sokolova, 'and without concern for the future.'[212] As Jones admired his finished set on stage, it was suddenly lit by a shaft of sunlight coming through a *lunette* in the ceiling; he was overcome by the beauty of it, fainted and was carried out.[213]* When the second part was reached, according to Sokolova, 'there was really no more ballet – just a few scrappy bits, under-rehearsed.' There were arguments, and Nijinsky left. And for the rest of the afternoon the company built up the ballet, relying on Nijinsky to know his own role.[214] He was to admit, three years later, writing about 'Till' in his *Diary*: 'It was "taken out of the oven" too soon, and therefore was raw. The American public liked my "raw" ballet. It tasted good, as I cooked it very well. I did not like this ballet but said, "It is good." '[215]

When the audience gathered on the 23rd, Pavlova was among them.[216] The performance opened with 'Papillons', which had as its setting discarded décor from 'Sylphides'.[217] This work made little impression on the critics who found the music in its orchestrated version poor, the choreography weak, and the costumes unimaginative (the 'restored' wings of the butterflies – on which what there was of drama depended – refused to stay in place, putting a jinx on the performance). It was seen as a pale shadow of 'Carnaval'.[218]

Then came 'Till Eulenspiegel'. Monteux had retired to a box, and Goetzl took up the baton.

The music of 'Till', like that of 'Die Meistersinger', surprises us with its un–German humour. Strauss orginally intended the work to be operatic: but the spiky themes, the absurd *charivaria* of orchestral effects, the flexible construction and the clarity of the story line, coupled with the universal appeal of the hero, provide ideal material for the ballet. The curtain, bearing the owl-and-glass device, rises to reveal the bustling market place of Brunswick on a late autumn afternoon.[219] Peasants and merchants throng the square, at the back of which tower the cathedral and the town hall. 'A species of whimsicality run riot sets before the astonished vision a medieval town that never was in any age and laves it in nocturnal blue touched with a few shafts of crepuscular light which illuminates the inverted cornucopia roofs of tiny houses tiled at crazy angles. . . .'[220] The characters – twenty of them – are costumed in exaggerated fashion as a comment on their lives and manners. Here are the notary, the priest, the merchant, the beggar, the lady of the castle, the ragged poor and the children stealing from the stalls. Here is the baker, carrying his bread in a basket as tall as himself, and there the apple-woman (Sokolova) with apple-cheeks and peasant costume, her fruit piled in a bundle on her head. Two policemen prowl suspiciously.

Suddenly a lithe youth in ragged Nile-green costume – tights, shirt and bodice, scarf and sash – and with a mop of unruly hair rushes into the square. This is Till (Nijinsky): he knocks down both the baker's bread and the apple-

---

* Romola Nijinsky wrote: 'When Jones . . . realized his miscalculations, he fainted and had to be taken home.' (p. 274.)

woman's apples for the poor to grovel for, and quick as lightning has tied up a group of citizens in a bundle with a flame-coloured bale of cloth. He then cuts them free and they fall to the ground. He disappears as quickly as he came, and the angry victims of his pranks march into the town hall to complain.

A little procession enters the market-place: a cowled priest is being followed by the noble ladies, by the learned men, by the poor, all listening to his preaching. To the beggars who ask him for money he counsels patience; then suddenly he pulls out his empty pockets, shrugs back his hood and – revealed as Till – darts off. The priests go off to the town hall for justice.

The congregation is leaving the cathedral – among them the Châtelaine (Revalles) and her two companions. They wear the most exaggerated costumes of all: elaborate silk brocade gowns with trains as long as the square is deep, and fantastically high headdresses, from the tips of which trail endless veils. The Châtelaine is being courted by a rich young cavalier in a cloak, who makes taunting obeisances to her with a hat which is all feathers. She spurns him, but Till's green tights are revealed beneath the cloak and the onlookers are convulsed with laughter. The ladies leave, their retainers entering the town hall to denounce the pretender.

The five robed men who now appear – with long beards, huge square spectacles and weird Don Basilio hats fashioned from rolls of parchment tied under the chin with ribbon – are professors of the university, arguing their abstruse problems. They are thrown into confusion by the arrival of a sixth, similarly dressed: a foreign scholar. As they struggle to understand him, he mocks them and shows them the poor people huddled in the square. Protesting, the professors in turn enter the town hall.

As dusk falls Till is heard singing, and he runs through the streets calling the poor to dance with him. It is a dance of revolution: all are equal. The crowd hoist the hero shoulder-high and carry him to the town hall; but drums roll and soldiers surround them. Till is brought before the Inquisitors who are clad in black with white crosses on their backs, and wear peaked caps. Till is still mocking, but all – priests, merchants, lords and ladies, professors – accuse him and he is condemned. His laugh is stopped only by the noose, and his figure hangs 'high in ruby light among the red lanterns'.

The poor people gather to reproach themselves for allowing Till to go to his death. But suddenly, out of a group of moaning women, springs Till – 'in a flight of toy balloons'. He has cheated even death: his spirit lives on.

Nijinsky had followed the programme of Strauss's music closely: the correspondence between Till's puckish theme on the clarinet and his antics on stage contained the spirit of the piece: but he emphasized the revolutionary aspect of Till's behaviour – in Strauss's programme Till annoys *everyone*, rather than inciting the underprivileged to riot – and whereas the Strauss synopsis ends with the rabble recollecting his tricks with nostalgia, Nijinsky chose to introduce an incarnation of Till's spirit in a climax recalling 'Petrushka'.

The ballet lasted only eighteen minutes. As the curtain fell, a storm of applause greeted what was to be the last new ballet by Nijinsky to be performed on any stage, and amid the flowers the choreographer and the designer held hands and took the curtain-calls together. There were fifteen in all.[221] 'C'est vraiment très, très heureux,' murmured Nijinsky.[222] Even Monteux was applauding from his box. Romola thought 'Till' was Vaslav's best work.[223] The programme continued with 'Le Spectre', danced by Lopokhova and Gavrilov, and ended with 'Schéhérazade' in which Nijinsky, unannounced, danced the Golden Negro.[224] After the performance the reporters clamoured for quotes. Flore Revalles said with great loyalty: 'I like to dance in "Till" better than in anything else, and I adore my costume.' Nijinsky, his magnanimity restored, pronounced Robert Edmond Jones to be 'a greater colour artist than Bakst'.

The patriotic and anti-Ballet Russe critic of *Musical American* attributed 'nine-tenths of the effectiveness and quick appeal' of 'Till' to Jones, whose designs Nijinsky 'with marvellously good judgement' had commissioned. But the choreographic and dramatic conception he found 'inconceivably paltry contrasted with the Rabelaisian comedy which in the concert hall enacts itself on the illimitable stage of the imagination. The spirit of the original has vanished for all the showy medieval accoutrements.'[225] But other critics were more enthusiastic. H. T. Parker of the *Boston Evening Transcript* felt that Nijinsky had 'retained, in matter and in manner, the flavour of the original folk-tale'.[226] Another voice stated that the ballet 'stood in a class by itself as a combination of musical, pictorial and terpsichorean art. The vividness, the depth of colour, was hardly less astounding than the deftness of it all.'[227] Another called this 'a brilliant performance, probably the most brilliant that the Ballet Russe has done in America . . . a triumph of stagecraft and choreography'; another 'a complete success'. Nijinsky's performance was seen as a 'fine . . . piece of mimic impersonation', a role to which he was 'exactly fitted'.[228] 'The keynote of Nijinsky's interpretation,' wrote Carl van Vechten, 'was gaiety. He was as utterly picaresque as the work itself; he reincarnated the spirit of Gil Blas.'[229] Perhaps the superlatives were partly due to the fact that not only was this a ballet created by Nijinsky and danced by himself but it was also the first Diaghilev ballet to have its première in the United States. 'Till Eulenspiegel' was also the only ballet performed by his company which Diaghilev never saw.

The occasion was notable too from the point of view of Richard Strauss.

It was twelve years ago, wrote one columnist, that the city had had a 'Strauss week'. Now it was having another. The following Thursday and Friday the first performance of the composer's 'Alpine Symphony' and selections from his opera 'Guntram' were given by the Philharmonic Orchestra in Carnegie Hall: and a week later 'Till Eulenspiegel' was given at a concert, again at the Carnegie, by the Boston Symphony Orchestra.

The night after 'Till' the performance opened with 'Les Sylphides', in which Marguerite Frohman and Spessivtseva made their American débuts; and then Nijinsky danced 'L'Après-midi' for the first time in America. The newspapers had wondered which version New York was to see, that of Paris or that of London. In this ballet, wrote the *New York Sun*, Nijinsky 'was said to have justified his fame as the most daring dancer on the stage', and much was expected. But 'Mr Nijinsky apparently believed in letting bygones be bygones. . . . At any rate there was nothing in his acting to bring the blush of shame to the cheek of modesty. But it was full of significance and rich in that special art of Mr Nijinsky, which is subtle in its inflections and intangible in its grace. Miss Revalles was the nymph, a part to which her slender and exquisitely drawn figure and her skill in statuesque posing well fit her.'[230] The ballet was performed with the same Bakst décor, less brightly lit than before.[231] The programme was completed by 'Prince Igor', and 'Petrushka' with Nijinsky. Both 'Till' and 'L'Après-midi' were given again before the Manhattan Opera House season closed on 28 October.*

Two days later the company set off on their second American tour, which was coast-to-coast and scheduled to last five months. There were sixty-five dancers and an orchestra of sixty, together with a number of technicians. The scenery and props, mechanical equipment and costumes went ahead together with the press agents, so that stages could be adapted and set before the dancers arrived in their twelve-car train. The musicians refused to sleep in upper berths, so the train was twice as long as it need have been. But Otto Kahn was sparing no expense.[232] The Metropolitan management took measures to stir up interest in the Ballet; art and fashion exhibitions reflecting the influence of the Ballet preceded the dancers, and, to Diaghilev's distaste when he heard about it, gramophone records were produced of 'Carnaval', 'Schéhérazade' and 'Sylphides' by the Ballet orchestra. There was talk of a film of the Ballet, but this did not materialize.[233] Kremnev became desperate, and tried to get a Metropolitan representative to take over the organization of the tour, but this only happened some months later. He wrote almost daily to Diaghilev and Grigoriev about the deteriorating morale of the company.[234]

* According to Mme Sokolova (*Dancing for Diaghilev*, p. 91) 'Till Eulenspiegel' was not repeated. But press reports prove that the ballet was given twice in New York, and Grigoriev's papers record twenty more performances during the tour.

The Ballet gave performances in Providence, New Haven and Brooklyn, and then in Springfield, where the troupe watched a football match, Nijinsky remarking to reporters that football and the Diaghilev Ballet had in common the fact that teamwork counted more than the excellence of any individual performer.[235] The next stop was Boston, where the season opened on 6 November. Barely had Nijinsky settled in than he was told of a rumour that he was a deserter from the Russian Army. This reached the newspapers, who reported him as saying that he was ready to fight, and did not believe that artists had any right to exemption.[236] Among friends in Boston was the painter Sargent who had drawn Nijinsky in London in 1911.[237] H.T.Parker of the *Transcript*, who had produced a thoughtful review of 'Till' on its première, now turned his attention to the Ballet on his home ground. The most notable performance was that of 9 November.

In 'Cléopâtre', wrote Parker

Mr Bolm mimed the high-hearted, fascinated, fated slave [*sic*] with large means, with as potent illusion, with a white-hot intensity of suggestion that lifted Amoun almost from melodrama into tragedy. Acting of the spoken word might hardly be more humanly eloquent, of joyous affection, sudden alarm, shrill entreaty and black woe than was the miming, half of the dance as well, of Miss Sokolova. With Cleopatra as with Thamar, there is that in Miss Revalles's personality and poses which suggests the viperous and voluptuous queen but her lack of technical resource and variety sorely limits her impersonation. Yet the acclaimed Rubinstein did hardly more with the part.

Sections of the audience were so inflamed by the passion of Sokolova's performance that they loudly demanded for her the curtain-calls which protocol decreed were for Revalles and Bolm.

In 'Le Spectre' Parker noted

the exquisite *pirouettes* that seem less feats of agility and exactitude than the eddies of an inner elation; the *entrechats* that cleave the air for the flash of an instant as foot meets and parts from foot in gossamer contact; the lovely and adroit play of arm and hand, head and body in flawless and flowing harmony and rhythm; the aroma of fancy distilling from the whole – a dance of the vapours and the gleams of the misty night, a dance of as sublimated a sentiment in girlish fancies. The white sparks kindled Miss Lopokhova too.

And finally Boston saw the other side of Nijinsky's genius, 'the acute and sensitive mind and feeling', in his performance in 'L'Après-midi':

this strange vision – as motionless, almost, as it has been mute – of pagan and primitive, yet of ultra-modern and a little perverse, fancy. Such feats of imagination, execution, illusion may the brooding Nijinsky, far-ranging and subtly tempered, achieve. The Italians have a word for the quality that shapes and savours them, even though they flower in a strange beauty. It is *morbidezza*.[238]

From Boston the Ballet moved on: Worcester – Hartford – Bridgeport – Atlantic City – Baltimore. Then, at the end of November, the company once again danced before the President in Washington, and Nijinsky was able for the first time formally and in person to express his gratitude for the part America had played in his release from internment.[239] In Philadelphia Nijinsky's first appearance was in 'Till Eulenspiegel'. The sets and costumes made a great impression, while Nijinsky's performance revealed 'a mimetic power which is remarkable and emphasizes the truth of the assertion that "speech was given man to conceal his thoughts." ' But this same Philadelphian critic noticed, in Vaslav's dancing in 'La Princesse enchantée', no distinct superiority to either Mordkine or Volinine. 'He has strangely heavy legs for a torso so light and well moulded.'[240]

The tour was proving disappointing: there was no shortage of warm applause for Nijinsky, but to his mind this was simply appreciation of his acrobatic skill, not understanding of the ballet. In November an interesting item had appeared in the *Washington Star*: this pointed out that

The Diaghilev Ballet, which came as a splendid surprise when first brought to this country as the play-toy of a group of wealthy art-connoisseurs, has drifted slightly toward the conventionality of the usual touring theatrical attraction, though still too large a proposition to play out a week stand as a matter of perfunctory custom. It has taken the star system which has of late been reflected so conspicuously in the drama and transferred it to the dance. The name, Nijinsky, is made so prominent that it overwhelms attention. It may be doubted whether American taste is sufficiently discerning in matters of dancing to understand the fine points of expression which would elevate a single interpreter beyond the merits of the picturesque and poetic atmosphere with which he is surrounded in such graceful and proficient co-ordination. The male dancer is still an exception in American attention, save when he appears as the dancing partner of a feminine star.

The author of this verdict concluded: 'So long as the auditor regards the dance as a superficial display, an appeal to the eye, more than an expression of an idea, the male dancing star, however graceful his poses and delicate his shadings in pantomime, is likely to be regarded more as a curiosity than as the artistic marvel which Nijinsky is conceded to be.'[241]

In desperation the Metropolitan management produced in December a publicity sheet disguised as a newspaper, entitled *Ballet Russe Courier*. In this were reprinted past notices of performances, together with advance information on the tour, gossip about the dancers – their exotic pets, their prowess in beauty competitions, the difficulty in pronouncing their names – a series of puns under the heading 'Baksterical Laughter', and an article on Bakst himself. Some of this would have disgusted Diaghilev; but the sponsors of the tour were determined to leave no stone unturned in order to fill houses and ensure a good reception for the troupe. One item in this paper was doubtless indicative of the situation in a number of towns: Richmond, Virginia, 'may have an evening with this superb organization if ten of our music-loving, artistically-inclined citizens will combine to form a guarantee fund in case the receipts should fall short of the sum pledged to the visiting company. In all probability the guarantors will not be called upon to make up any deficit.'[242]

The citizens rallied and the Ballet danced at Richmond for one night after leaving Philadelphia. Single performances were next given in Columbia and Atlanta – and in the latter town Nijinsky received a summons to appear within ten days before the military authorities in Petersburg. This seemed absurd and impossible, but – after rehearsing Gavrilov in one or two roles – he returned to Washington, where he was able to sort things out with the Russian Embassy. His exemption was re-confirmed, and he rejoined the company in New Orleans early in December.[243] In his absence Gavrilov danced 'Le Spectre' under his name.[244]

In New Orleans, out of curiosity, Romola wished to visit the celebrated brothels. Though Vaslav was reluctant, from his 'respect for womanhood', she insisted; and Nijinsky was most considerate to the inmates. 'He talked with them and offered them drinks. They were all amazed to see that otherwise he had no interest.'[245] (Nijinsky was to write, later, in his *Diary*: 'I will go to a bordello [in Zürich] because I want to understand cocottes. I want to understand the psychology of a cocotte. . . . I will give money to the cocottes, but will do nothing with them.')[246]

The repertory of the Ballet was often determined by what a particular town requested – and that in turn was conditioned by what it had heard. It was hardly surprising that 'Schéhérazade' was not to be performed in the South for fear of offending susceptibilities.[247] The dancers moved on: Houston – Austin – Fort Worth – Dallas – Tulsa – Wichita – Kansas City – Des Moines – Omaha. At Des Moines the limitations of the Coliseum prevented the use of the complete Bakst settings – for instance, 'Schéhérazade' was given without its heavy draperies – but the Ballet did not fail to produce 'an impression which will not soon fade, of grace, lightness, litheness, power and a fierce splendour'. The critic of the *Des Moines Register* felt that Nijinsky's Harlequin was necessary 'in order to assure the audience that he is really human', for in 'Schéhérazade' he was 'a lithe and powerful animal . . . a panther . . . the incarnation of something terrible in human nature'. In between these two ballets came 'Sylphides' with Lopokhova and Sokolova: 'These two Lydias are as light as thistledown in a breeze.' Though the house was not filled, the second balcony *was*. The price of $3.50 for the better seats had proved too much.[248]

The demands made on the principal dancers were great, and the whole company were exhausted by the conditions of the tour. It had been Diaghilev's practice to 'rest' only Karsavina and Nijinsky – and that but rarely – and understudies were the exception rather than the rule. Gavrilov was now established as Nijinsky's 'second', and Vaslav began to rehearse other dancers in principal roles. Zverev and Kremnev, Sokolova and Nemchinova were given new opportunities in this way.[249] Sokolova, for instance, was cast as the Girl in 'Le Spectre' – and this she regarded as a great honour. Her regret was that her début in this role followed her performance as Ta-hor, so that she had hurriedly to remove her brown make-up – and take another curtain call in the middle of doing so. The audience was enthusiastic, but she was unnerved. 'Dancing "Spectre" with Nijinsky was very frightening. He was always doing something unexpected. He would throw me in the air and catch me as I came down, or take his hand away at the moment of support in an *arabesque*. If I had come off my point then, the picture and atmosphere would have been ruined. He also puffed and blew.'[250]

The re-allocation of parts may have been partly due to Nijinsky's increasingly democratic ideas. Ever since the rehearsals of 'Till' in New York – and that ballet had had as its theme the rebellion of the under-privileged – two members of the company, Dmitri Kostrovsky, a newcomer, and Nicolas Zverev, both followers of Tolstoy, had attracted Nijinsky's attention. The Pole Kostrovsky, particularly, attached himself to Nijinsky and also lectured on his beliefs to the company. Much to Romola's displeasure the two dancers would come into Vaslav's compartment in the train during the company's journeys and preach Tolstoyan philosophy. Nijinsky began wearing the round-collared Russian peasant's shirt in place of a shirt and tie.[251] Romola 'would rather have seen him with Bolm, or others of the Imperial School graduates than with those *moujiks* – not on account of their origin, but because of an instinctive distrust I had of them'.[252] Whatever the cause, the re-arrangement of roles could be disconcerting. Nijinsky gave Zverev his role in 'Schéhérazade', and then, on account of the illness of the usual Chief Eunuch, took that part unannounced.[253] Romola was surprised by the 'outstanding miming of the old Eunuch [Cecchetti was in Italy]. I was so intrigued that I went back stage and found that the unknown artist . . . was Vaslav.'[254] There was some dissension, and a partial strike by the time the company reached Denver, the next stop after Omaha. Zverev occasionally danced 'Le Spectre' under Nijinsky's name,[255] as Gavrilov had done when he was away in Washington.

From Denver the route lay through the snow to Salt Lake City; and then early on the morning of Christmas Eve the dancers set off for Los Angeles, with two extra coaches on the train – a private car for Nijinsky, provided by the railroad company, and a baggage-car decorated for a Christmas party, in which a dance was given with music by the Metropolitan orchestra.[256] The company all received presents from the tree in Nijinsky's compartment. The snow was left behind, orange-trees appeared, and in Los Angeles the Nijinskys took a flat with Fred Fradkin, the concert manager, and his wife.[257] The Los Angeles engagement lasted from 27 December to New Year's Eve, 1917. Nijinsky visited the film studios in Hollywood, where Charlie Chaplin was making *The Cure*.* Chaplin described Nijinsky as 'a serious man, beautiful-looking, with high cheekbones and sad eyes, who gave the impression of a monk dressed in civilian clothes'. For several days Nijinsky watched the filming, and never smiled, although he told Chaplin that he admired him and wanted to come again. Chaplin was so unnerved by Vaslav's lack of response to his antics that he instructed the camera-man not to use any film. When Chaplin went to the ballet, he was captivated by Nijinsky's dancing. 'I have seen few geniuses in the world, and Nijinsky was one of them. He was hypnotic, godlike, his sombreness suggesting moods of other worlds; every movement was poetry, every leap a flight into strange fancy.' He visited Vaslav in his dressing-room as he was making up for 'L'Après-midi',† and the conversation was halting and seemed not to be getting anywhere.[258]

The Ballet arrived in San Francisco on New Year's Eve, and during a party at the hotel, Barocchi, who was reputedly clairvoyant, read everyone's palms. He foresaw for Romola a long and healthy life, but in five years' time some kind of separation from Vaslav. On looking at Nijinsky's hand Barocchi was visibly shocked. Vaslav asked if he was going to die, and Barocchi answered: 'No, no, certainly not, but . . . this is worse . . . worse.'[259]

The San Francisco season lasted two weeks, and for the second week Vaslav and Romola lived in a hotel in nearby Oakland. Nijinsky visited Berkeley University, and also had his first experience of flying.

The Tolstoyans were now rarely out of Nijinsky's presence: they held long conversations with him in Russian which Romola could not follow, and they resisted all attempts to get them to leave. In the company of Kostrovsky and Zverev, wrote Romola, Nijinsky 'reacted like a sensitive plant and folded himself up. He became silent, meditative, almost gloomy. . . .'[260] Kostrovsky induced Vaslav to become a vegetarian like himself – which Romola was sure would diminish his strength for dancing.

---

* Romola Nijinsky says *Easy Street*. (p. 286.)

† According to Chaplin Diaghilev had this ballet put on specially for him this evening. The management may have done, but of course Diaghilev was far away.

January saw the company through the Western States: Portland –
Vancouver – Seattle – Tacoma – Spokane – St Paul – Minneapolis –
Milwaukee. Now Romola hardly saw Nijinsky who was becoming weak and
irritable and whom the Tolstoyans were persuading to give up dancing and
work on the land. Romola told him that despite her devotion to him she
would not countenance the thought of his leaving dancing for peasant
farming. The matter came to a head when they arrived in Chicago towards
the end of January and she decided to return to Kyra in New York. As the
tour continued (Indianapolis – St Louis – Memphis – Birmingham – Knoxville
– Nashville – Louisville – Cincinatti – Dayton – Detroit – Toledo – Grand
Rapids – Chicago (again)) they communicated by telegram and telephone.
From Cleveland in February Nijinsky telephoned Romola with the news that
Diaghilev had cabled inviting him to join the company in Spain, and to go
on a second South American tour. She advised him to defer a decision until
he had consulted his New York lawyer.[261]

The next engagements were in Pittsburgh and Syracuse and the last
performance of the Diaghilev Ballet in the United States was in the
Harmanus Bleeker Hall, Albany, New York, on 24 February 1917, the
programme comprising 'Cléopâtre', 'La Princesse enchantée' and
'Schéhérazade'.*

Vaslav now rejoined Romola: to her relief he was wearing his rings and
his silk shirts again, and had abandoned his vegetarianism.[262] The rest of
the company – with some exceptions, such as Bolm who remained in
America for good – sailed back to Europe in various ships. By the terms of
his release Nijinsky could only dance in a neutral country, and the United
States were about to enter the war. The Ballet were due to give a series of
performances in Italy, in which, since it was an Allied country, he could not
dance; but their following engagement was in neutral Spain, and it was here
that he planned to rejoin them.

He made Romola presents of more jewellery and furs. From fear of being
torpedoed they both made their wills.[263] Dining with Cottenet one night,
Vaslav placed his American earnings in the form of a cheque under
Romola's napkin as a present for her.[264] Shortly after this they set sail for
Cadiz.

The main body of the company disembarked at Cadiz early in April, and
were met by Grigoriev, who escorted them to Rome, where Diaghilev and
the rest of his troupe were waiting to begin rehearsals for a season, opening
at the Teatro Costanzi on 9 April. Diaghilev, Massine and their friends

---

* Sokolova (p. 93) says the tour was 'cut short', but the *Ballet Russe Courier* had announced in
December a tour of seventeen weeks and it lasted in fact sixteen. There were tentative bookings
for Stamford, Connecticut on 14 March and the Princess Theatre, New York, on 15 March.

had been working hard throughout the winter, and a new era of the Ballet had begun. Though there were still works by Fokine and Nijinsky in the repertory, Diaghilev now placed all his hopes in Massine as a choreographer: one whom, wrote Grigoriev, 'he thought capable of becoming the very incarnation of all that was modern in art'.[265] In Rome Massine had been working on three ballets. The first, 'Les Femmes de bonne humeur', was based, at Diaghilev's suggestion, on Goldoni's play *Le Donne di buon' umore*. Diaghilev had also proposed using the music of Scarlatti, and the twenty-three sonatas eventually selected from the hundreds they listened to were orchestrated by Vincenzo Tommasini. Bakst produced elaborate eighteenth-century Venetian costumes and a Guardi set. It was also Diaghilev's idea that the recent one-act ballet 'Kikimora' by Massine and Larionov should be made into a long folk-tale ballet using more music by Liadov. From a wealth of folk- and fairy-tales the stories of the Swan Princess and Baba-Yaga were added to 'Kikimora', and the ballet was renamed 'Les Contes Russes'.

The studio in the Piazza Venezia in which Massine and the dancers worked on these ballets had become a *salon* in which not only Bakst, Stravinsky, Larionov and Gontcharova, but a new generation of artists gathered. These including Picasso, who was working with Massine on the ballet 'Parade', and who here met his future wife Olga Khokhlova.

The company gave four performances at the Costanzi, where the première of 'Les Femmes de bonne humeur' took place on 12 April: the ballet was danced by Lopokhova, Massine, Idzikovsky, the Cecchettis, Tchernicheva, Woizikovsky, Chabelska, Antonova and Khokhlova, and it delighted the Italian audience. At the same performance Stravinsky's early symphonic poem 'Fireworks' was played while the stage was occupied by a construction designed by the futurist Giacomo Balla, with lighting effects devised by Diaghilev which flashed on and off.

From Rome the Ballet travelled to Naples to give four performances at the Teatro San Carlo, then to Florence for a single night, and on to Paris for a season at the Châtelet. Here 'Les Contes russes', with Tchernicheva, Sokolova, Woizikowsky, Jasvinsky, Idikovsky and Kremnev, had its first performance on 11 May. 'L'Oiseau de feu' was also given that night, and as a tribute to the recent 'liberal' revolution in Russia Diaghilev arranged that Prince Ivan should receive at the end of the ballet not the crown and sceptre and ermine-bordered cape, but a red robe, the cap of liberty and the red flag. The public showed its disapproval and the former ending was subsequently restored.[266] On the 18th 'Parade' had its première.

'Parade' sprang from an idea of Cocteau's, and he had chosen Erik Satie to compose it because his spare and tuneful music, while being essentially

French, was still an antidote to Debussyism. Valentine Gross had introduced the poet and the composer. Then Cocteau had called in Picasso, the founder of cubism. The scene was the outside of a circus booth. The performers appeared in turn to lure spectators inside. First a Chinese Conjuror (Massine) did tricks with an egg; then a Little American Girl (Maria Chabelska) mimed the riding of a bronco, bicycled, danced ragtime, and imitated the flickering of moving pictures; lastly, two beautiful acrobats in blue and white tights (Lopokhova and Zverev) performed a lyrical *adagio*. The numbers of these dancers were punctuated by the antics of two Managers wearing immense cubist constructions and by a comic horse. There had been some disagreements over the creation of the work, Satie objecting to the sounds of typewriters, pistol shots and ships' sirens which Cocteau wanted to impose on the score, and Cocteau resenting the cubist Managers: but Picasso's ideas transformed what might have been a triviality into something marvellous. 'Parade' was a gay work which both dancers and audience enjoyed,[267] and it was unlike anything the Russians had done before.

Vaslav and Romola had endured a cold, rough voyage of thirteen days, and the Spanish ship was infested with rats which so frightened Romola that, braving the weather, she took to sleeping on deck. The Nijinskys decided to spend their holiday and await Diaghilev in Madrid. This city was new to Romola, but Vaslav had stayed a few days there when he had danced at the Roosevelt wedding in 1914: in March they found it cold and windy. They put up at the Ritz Hotel and immediately set out to explore the sights, visiting churches and the Prado, where Vaslav fell in love with Goya. The Los Caprichos etchings particularly delighted him.[268]

When spring came Vaslav and Romola used to sit in the gardens of the Prado and she translated for him from English the poems of Oscar Wilde and Rabindranath Tagore. Vaslav had met Tagore and had ideas of doing a ballet to one of his poems.[269] Meanwhile Kyra played among the irises. They were happy; and Romola thought Tagore was a good antidote to Tolstoy. But Tolstoy's influence was not effaced, as Romola found when some of her new clothes hanging in a cupboard were attacked by mice and she began to cry. Vaslav rebuked her gently. 'I give you furs, jewellery and anything you wish, but can't you see how silly it is to attach importance to them? And have you ever thought how dangerous for the pearl-divers and for the miners who provide your jewellery – they also have children, and yet they must endanger themselves daily for the adornment of women.'

They went to see gypsy dancers and Vaslav was very struck by the austere movements of the men. He imitated them and was soon on the way to becoming proficient at Flamenco.

379

Vaslav was working on his system of notation and practising at the Royal Theatre. Life was regular and peaceful, and the fine weather engendered a mood of optimism. He began to think that his troubles with Diaghilev were over.

One day Romola picked up a newspaper and read of the abdication of the Tsar and the formation of Kerensky's government. This had taken place on 15 March. Nijinsky thought the revolution would be a peaceful one and he welcomed it. He believed that it would make no difference to the artistic life of Russia and felt sure that Diaghilev would be appointed Director of the Mariinsky. He could envisage returning home to found his own theatre and school.

At the beginning of June the Ballet arrived.

Sergei Pavlovitch burst into the lobby of the Ritz and embraced Vaslav passionately. '*Vatza, daragoi moi, kak tui pajivayesh.*'

The greeting was as affectionate as if they had only parted a few hours ago, and no misunderstanding had ever occurred. It was the Sergei Pavlovitch of the old days. They sat down in a corner and began to talk. Hours and hours passed, and it seemed that the old friendship was restored. From that day on we were practically all the time with Diaghilev. The contract for South America was just brushed aside, and Sergei Pavlovitch simply said: 'We open in Madrid at the Theatre Royal, and then we will give some performances in Barcelona. Massine has composed new ballets. I want you, Vatza, to look at them and give me your opinion. Have you composed anything new? I want you to do so.'

Recent events in Russia were also discussed at great length, and Vaslav explained to Diaghilev his plans for the school and festival theatre. But Diaghilev objected: 'Why think of the future of ballet? That is not our task. Dance and compose for our company, and leave the future generation to look after itself. I do not wish to return to Russia; I have worked too long abroad – the artists at home would ask what I wanted there. They would say that I wanted to take advantage of the newly acquired possibilities of the liberty for which they had had to fight. They would say, "*Je suis vieux jeu, vieux régime.*" I could not survive in the new Russia. I prefer to stay in Europe.'

But Vaslav did not yet give up the idea of gaining Diaghilev for his plan. 'We can't go travelling about the world forever like a caravan of gypsies; we shall never be able to create real artistic work that way. We belong to Russia; we must go home and work there and make a trip to the West once in a while.'

Diaghilev's little circle, here as elsewhere, was formed of the elite of the advanced guard. He brought Picasso, who was very little known at that time, to us one day. He was reticent and very Spanish looking, and when he began to explain anything, he became full of excitement, and used to draw on the table-cloth, the menu cards, and on top of Sergei Pavlovitch's ivory walking-stick. Diaghilev was to me as a fatherly friend, protective and kind, at this time. Vaslav triumphantly said, '*Tu vois, femmka; je t'ai toujours dit qu'il sera notre ami.*'

Vaslav had told Romola how Diaghilev had forgiven Alexis Mavrine and Olga Feodorova. Romola observed: 'Vaslav was so happy that he would have done anything to please Diaghilev'; and there was no talk of contracts. Stravinsky too had arrived.

One evening [wrote Romola] we went to a theatre where Pastora Imperio was giving a recital. To us the name did not mean anything. We were told that she was a gypsy singer from Cadiz, that her fame extended to the Latin-American countries. She was the idol of Spain. As she appeared on the stage, behind the simple curtain, she did not make a great impression. We only saw a rather faded, stout southern woman, but the moment she began to sing, accompanying herself with movement and castanets, we forgot that she had no voice, that she was middle-aged and fat. With a few gestures she offered the history and the soul of Spain. Vaslav and Stravinsky, as well as Diaghilev, could not keep quiet on their seats, and, like three school-children, applauded, laughed, and cried, according to the mood this ageless marvel dictated.[270]

The Madrid season began and the King and Queen came to the ballet almost every night. Nijinsky danced in 'Schéhérazade', 'Carnaval', 'Le Spectre' and twice in 'L'Après-midi d'un faune'. King Alfonso was such an enthusiast that he attended rehearsals too – but then, he was in love with Grigoriev's wife, Liubov Tchernicheva.[271] Romola heard from the Duchess

*Lydia Lopokhova
in 'Les Sylphides'.
Drawing by
Pablo Picasso.*

of Durcal, a cousin of the King's, that he sometimes tried to imitate Nijinsky's leaps in private. This lady had fallen in love with Vaslav, and Romola, in her desire to bring out his worldly rather than his other-worldly side, positively encouraged her.

Now that the performances had begun, we had less time to go out with our friends, but I insisted that we should not give them up entirely, for I did not want Vaslav to isolate himself from the rest of the world and only live with Diaghilev and the Russian Ballet. I could not trust them after all that had happened in the past. As soon as they returned from their holiday, Kostrovsky and H.* practically installed themselves in our apartment, day and night. They hung around Vaslav after rehearsals. [Zverev] seemed to forget his courting [of Vera Nemchinova] and Kostrovsky his wife. The latter stood, with his shining, fanatical eyes, in the middle of the dressing-room, talking, talking, while [Zverev] pretended to listen with awe. Every second sentence was a quotation from Tolstoy, and Vaslav listened attentively. Either purposely or because he was unfortunately not only fanatical but also unintelligent, Kostrovsky mixed up the teachings of Tolstoy. He preached that art is not justifiable for its own sake, but must have as its end the spiritual development of the individual. He wanted to convince Vaslav that he should work for the Russian Ballet as long as it needed him, and then retire to the land, like Tolstoy.

One evening Romola saw Diaghilev in excited conversation with Zverev in a dark corner near the stage, talking 'not as an officer with his subordinate, but like two accomplices'. She was immediately convinced that the whole object of the Tolstoyan preaching had been to separate Vaslav from herself and that it had been organized by Diaghilev.[272]

This stay in Madrid was a crucial period in Nijinsky's life. Loving his wife and child, being friends with Diaghilev, even admiring the work of Diaghilev's new protégé Massine, he must have embraced the possibility of everybody working blissfully together without contracts for years to come, to the greater glory of art. Perhaps even the principles of Tolstoy could be reconciled with the Russian Ballet and married life. If Romola had not been an exceptionally strong character, this might indeed have happened. But she was a fighter by nature. She would not share Vaslav with the two Tolstoyans, whom she regarded as peasants; and at the thought that they were set on by Diaghilev to separate her from her husband she was up in arms. She has always maintained that Nijinsky was master in his own house and took every important decision himself. Yet she must at this time have decided at least to *try* to stop him going with the Ballet on the next tour in South America. It was Nijinsky's unwillingness to go to South America which led, as we shall see, to the final breach with Diaghilev.

In her distress Romola was uncertain whether Diaghilev wanted Nijinsky

---

* Zverev: Mme Nijinsky does not name him in her book.

back for the Russian Ballet on the old terms, i.e. without a wife to make trouble over contracts – 'It was all a carefully laid plan to estrange Vaslav from me and restore him to Sergei Pavlovitch's clutches' – or whether he wanted to put an end to Nijinsky's dancing career.

Sergei Pavlovitch knew Vaslav's character; he realized that only through altruism could he estrange him from marriage, normal life and art, and make Vaslav give up dancing for ever in order to cultivate the earth like a peasant.

I tried to provide as many distractions as possible for Vaslav, and we often passed the day with the Duchess [of Durcal], who was so obviously madly in love with Vaslav that he objected to going out alone with her, as I suggested. One day, we motored out to the Escorial, a dreary trip through barren desert, but at the last turn of the road we could not restrain an exclamation, for suddenly the grand austere building arose out of nothing, like a mirage, and dominated the whole horizon. The strict, imposing lines of the structure were overwhelming. Vaslav, rooted in admiration, said, 'Spain. Religious fanaticism expressed in granite.'

As he stood there, so small, so confident in the dazzling sunlight, before entering the gloomy pitiless home of the Inquisition, I wondered how it was that he did not see how the 'teachers' were trying, through religious fanaticism, to seize his soul and destroy him. . . .

At lunch, on the terrace, Vaslav seemed to have regained his mischievous ways. He said to me, 'Please, *femmka*, do not leave me so much alone with her [the Duchess]!' He was too discreet to give her away, but too honest not to put me on my guard.[273]

In spite of Diaghilev, the Tolstoyans and the Duchess, who was beautiful and had red hair,[274] Romola felt her marriage was a success and she loved Vaslav more all the time.

Our intimate life was ideally happy. Sometimes the strangest feeling would come over me, and I felt that the women of mythology may have felt as I did when a God came to love them. There was the exhilarating and inexpressible feeling that Vaslav was more than a human being. The ecstasy that he could create in love as in art had a purifying quality, and yet there was something intangible in his being that one could never reach.[275]

Then came Kostrovsky and Zverev, the common brutes, to spoil it all!

Vaslav began to wonder if cohabitation were only justified in case a child is born as the result. Before he had considered the state of my delicate health and the responsibilities of parentage, but now he suggested that either an ascetic life or a child every year was the right way. I immediately understood that this must be Kostrovsky's idea, in order to get me out of the way. One night, when they were discussing this subject, I declared open war.

It was three in the morning. I had listened for hours, seeing how cunningly they were trying to destroy our happiness, and at last, on the verge of tears, I exclaimed, 'Why don't you leave my husband alone? You don't dare to talk about his art, because you know that on that subject you cannot influence him. You are not his friends, but his enemies. If you want to create happiness, do so first in your own homes. Your wife, Kostrovsky, is miserable, your children without shoes, because you give your money away to strangers; and you [Zverev], if you want advancement, why not ask for it frankly? Vaslav Fomitch would help you. I forbid you both to interfere in our married life. Leave us, this place belongs to Vaslav and me.'

Vaslav had never seen me like this before, and for a moment he was taken aback, but then said, 'Please, *femmka*, they are my friends; do not try to withhold our hospitality.'

Kostrovsky and [Zverev] sat waiting, with impertinent provoking faces, to see how things would develop, but I turned round; 'Vaslav, you have to choose between the diabolical influence of these people and me. If within half an hour these people are still here, I shall leave you.'

I waited in the other room, and Vaslav came in to try and persuade me that they were both of good faith, but my determination was unshaken, and, as they were still there when the time was up, I went out into the night.

Next morning, Vaslav found me in the Prado and begged me to return, saying, 'It shall be as you wish.' From that day on, Kostrovsky and [Zverev] never entered our home any more; but in the theatre they still seized opportunities to get at Vaslav.[276]

Massine, as reserved a character as Nijinsky, though in a different way, watched Vaslav rehearsing 'L'Après-midi d'un faune'. 'I was thrilled by the way he demonstrated the most minute details of gesture and movement, correcting each dancer with calm assurance and complete understanding. He was an extraordinarily gifted choreographer.'[277] Vaslav thought 'Parade' showed a straining after modernism for its own sake, but he was fascinated by 'Les Femmes de bonne humeur'. Massine too had invented a quite new kind of movement – a flickering, jerky choreography inspired partly by the harpsichord sonatas of Scarlatti, partly by puppets, by Charlie Chaplin and the early cinema. Vaslav longed to help and encourage Leonide, and he went to the young man's dressing-room to offer to dance Battista, Idzikovsky's part, in the Italian ballet.[278] He also coached Idzikovsky privately for 'Le Spectre de la rose'.[279]

After their eleven performances in Madrid, the company went to give six more in Barcelona, another city where the Russian Ballet would be performing for the first time. The Duchess of Durcal followed them and Romola was 'rather glad'.

The evenings we spent with the Duchess of X., who was by this time desperately in love, and wanted to become Vaslav's mistress. Jealousy never entered into my head, and I was even rather pleased when Vaslav returned later than usual one night, but this escapade had quite a different effect upon him than I had expected. He was mournful, and told me frankly:

'*Femmka*, I am sorry for what I did. It was unfair to her, as I am not in love, and the added experience, that perhaps you wanted me to have, is unworthy of us.'[280]

Vaslav had resolved to tell Diaghilev he would not go to South America. The reason he decided to give – that he wanted a holiday – does not ring very true: he was only giving sixteen performances in Spain and dancing only in one or two ballets a night – not in four as in the old days – and this after a two months' holiday.

Lunching one day with Diaghilev [wrote Romola] the latter began to talk about our South American trip, but Vaslav said, 'I am not sure I will go, Sergei Pavlovitch, I need a rest, and do not like the idea of being separated from my child in war-time. South America will not be a creative trip artistically.'

Diaghilev, with a freezing smile, returned, 'But you have to go, you are under contract.'

'Have to?' said Vaslav. 'I have no contract.'

'You cabled me from America agreeing in principle. That is a contract.'

'But I also cabled that we would discuss the matter in Spain.'

'That is beside the point. In this country, a cable is a binding contract' – and S.P. laughed – 'I will force you to go.'[281]

Conversation must have been rather sticky during the latter part of this luncheon, which was to be the last meal Diaghilev and Nijinsky ever had together.

There was a rapid *dénouement*.

In the afternoon, Vaslav notified Sergei Pavlovitch that, as no contract existed, he would take no further part in the Russian Ballet, and we left for the station. But as we boarded the Madrid express, two men touched Vaslav's arm: 'M. and Mme Nijinsky, will you please follow us, you are under arrest.' We were aghast.

'On whose authority?' I ventured.

'On that of His Excellency the Marquess of Z., Governor of Catalonia, in the name of the King.'

We were escorted to the police station, where, with the aid of several interpreters, they explained that we had been arrested at the behest of Diaghilev – as Vaslav was breaking his contract. If he did not dance that night, he would be put in gaol. Vaslav was pale, but determined: 'Very well, put me there! I have no contract. In any case, I can't dance now; I'm too upset.' He sat down.

'M. Nijinsky, please promise to dance, then I will not have to imprison you.'

'No, I won't; I can't.'

'Show us the contract which Diaghilev pretends to have, and then Nijinsky will dance,' I said. 'Anyhow, you have no right to arrest me; I am a Russian citizen, and not a member of the Russian Ballet. I will complain at the Embassy at once if you do not let me go immediately.'

The prefect became rather uneasy, but, very much against his wish, released me. Followed by a detective, I dashed to the telephone, called up the Duc de Durcal in Madrid, who informed the authorities there of what was going on. Within an hour an order arrived from Madrid for our immediate release, and Señor Cambo, the eminent Spanish lawyer, arrived to take up our case with Diaghilev.

The Barcelona authorities now realized that they had made a dreadful blunder, and were full of excuses. It was too late to catch the train, so we returned to the hotel, where [Trubecki] and the Spanish director were awaiting us. The director cried out at once: 'The public are disappointed, they are returning their tickets by hundreds. It's you they want to see dance. I am ruined, because I have to pay Diaghilev whatever happens, and now I have not made a peso. My last season was a failure, too.'

Vaslav was sorry for him. 'For your sake, I will dance tonight. Tell the public, please, why I am late.'

Next day, Cambo discussed the situation with us. Spain was the only country in which a cable was a binding contract. So Vaslav was bound to go to South America. He regretted now that he had not listened more carefully to Laurence Steinhardt's [Nijinsky's American lawyer] shrewd advice, and that he had not shown him the cable drafted, word for word, by Kostrovsky and [Zverev]. But Cambo assured us that Diaghilev would have to grant Vaslav the terms he asked. So he drew up a contract, that Vaslav was willing to go to South America, and that his salary was to be the same as in the USA, payable, in gold dollars, one hour before the curtain rose at every performance. I insisted on such a clause. I did not want any lawsuits later on. If this clause was not fulfilled, the contract became void. It was originated by Fanny Elssler after she had been cheated many times by dishonest impresarios. Vaslav agreed to appear in all parts first danced by himself. The penalty for breaking the contract was twenty thousand dollars. Cambo and I went to Diaghilev with the contract. He received us in his drawing-room, with his usual tactics, sitting with his back to the window, and letting others talk while he listened. The contract was so cleverly drawn up that, while it fulfilled all his stipulations, there was no possibility of any trick being played on Vaslav. While Diaghilev's signature was being affixed, my mind went back to that meeting at the Bristol Hotel, years ago – how very different, and yet how very alike, the situation was.[282]

In this affair, even though Diaghilev used the cable as a trap for the unsuspecting Nijinsky, our sympathies are all with the older man, who had the struggle of keeping his company alive in war-time. Thus the famous friendship ended and it was at the Teatro Liceo in Barcelona, on 30 June, that Diaghilev saw Nijinsky dance for the last time.

Vaslav and Romola returned for a few days to Madrid and from there they dispatched Kyra to a sanatorium in Lausanne which specialized in the care of children.[283]

Diaghilev, Massine and their sixteen dancers remained behind once again when Romola, Vaslav and the company sailed for South America on 4 July in the *Reina Victoria Eugenia*.

Romola observed that Vaslav seemed worn out by the emotional upsets of the last few days. He now seemed to be resigned to the impossibility of working with Diaghilev again. He did not allow himself to be idle, however. He discussed his system of notation with Cecchetti and taught it to Kostrovsky and Zverev. One day Kostrovsky's wife called on Vaslav to help her: it turned out that her husband had epileptic fits. Vaslav determined to take him to see a specialist when they arrived in South America.

There was a young Chilean on board called Georges de Cuevas, whom Romola described as 'a typical gigolo, extremely well bred and dressed'. He flirted with her, adored Nijinsky, and begged to be allowed to serve them in any capacity. He was 'completely broke' and they thought he was on the look-out for an heiress, but 'he was amusing, played bridge excellently and danced the tango divinely.' Vaslav, who disapproved of ballroom dances such as the foxtrot and grizzly-bear, which he called '*frotter le plancher*', was delighted with the tango and learned from Cuevas to dance it 'with incredible elegance and smoothness'.[284] This new friend later inherited a Spanish title, married a Rockefeller heiress and as Marquis de Cuevas for a number of years ran a celebrated ballet company.

Maria Chabelska, one of the Polish sisters who had joined Diaghilev in Switzerland, was seldom seen without a book. One day Nijinsky, patrolling the deck with Ansermet, stopped to speak to her. '*Toujours lire, toujours lire!*' He looked at her book and exclaimed 'Newton! He was the man who saw an apple fall and invented – electricity.' Ansermet thought that it was part of Nijinsky's genius that he could not be satisfied with the everyday, the accepted truth – his mind soared beyond it to more extraordinary explanations or conclusions.[285]

Owing to Diaghilev's having insisted that his dancers travel in a neutral ship, they arrived at Montevideo rather than Rio as planned: and to recompense the impresario Mocchi for the cost of transporting them to Rio, Grigoriev put on a few free performances in Montevideo. Nijinsky was not allowed to take part in these since he would have had to be paid large additional sums.[286]*

---

* There are discrepancies between Grigoriev's and Mme Romola Nijinsky's accounts of this voyage and tour – as in many other matters. He says the Nijinskys followed the company to South America a few days later on a Dutch ship (p. 135). She says they travelled on the *Victoria Eugenia*, and describes Nijinsky's conversation with Cecchetti, Kostrovsky etc. (pp. 304–6). She does not mention the visit to Montevideo preceding that to Rio; and the thousand-mile voyage from Montevideo north to Rio on a British ship, *Amazon* (Grigoriev, pp. 136–7), she makes into a trip from Rio to São Paulo (p. 308) a matter of less than two hundred miles – and São Paulo is anyway inland. (Grigoriev says he motored there and the company went by train. p. 137.) Mme Nijinsky

In Montevideo* Kostrovsky was taken to see a specialist. As she spoke a little Spanish, Romola interpreted the diagnosis, which was that the unfortunate man was incurably and dangerously insane. He was to be sent back to Russia.[287] It is curious to conjecture how differently things might have turned out if this diagnosis had been made in Madrid. Romola would have had no reason to fear the Tolstoyan menace and might have encouraged Nijinsky to go to South America. Nijinsky would therefore never have had the difference with Diaghilev which led to their final break. He might have continued with the Russian Ballet for many years and made a number of new ballets. He might have revived his 'Sacre du printemps', with the result that it might have survived intact to this day. Continued work within the Ballet might have averted his illness or postponed it.

After their stay in Montevideo the company travelled on the British ship *Amazon* a thousand miles north to Rio de Janeiro. Vaslav and Romola drove straight to the Hotel Sylvestre where they had lunched with Kovalevska on the day of their engagement.

The Ballet were to give twelve performances in Rio. Grigoriev was in charge of the company, and his loyalty to Diaghilev made him regard the Nijinskys as enemies and treat them coolly. Other members of the Ballet followed suit. Vaslav felt that the majority of the company were giving him the cold shoulder, and he who loved his work began to dread going to the theatre.[288] Grigoriev complained that he had to put Barocchi in charge of Nijinsky.[289] When an accident happened the Nijinskys assumed it was a deliberate attack on Vaslav, probably instigated by Diaghilev.[290] This was interpreted by the company as persecution mania.[291] Things went from bad to worse. Grigoriev and others, such as Ernest Ansermet, the new Swiss conductor, who disliked Romola, would in later years and in the light of

places the Montevideo visit after Rio (pp. 308–9). I have accepted her statement that she and her husband travelled with the company – which is anyway confirmed by Chabelska's story – while taking for granted the order of the tour given by Grigoriev. Whether Nijinsky danced in Montevideo or not, and if he did not, why not, remains obscure, for Grigoriev is confusing (p. 136) – apart from being wrong (as I think) about the Nijinskys travelling separately and arriving late. He writes: 'Nijinsky was late in arriving at Montevideo, doing so only after two of our regular performances (that is to say those we had originally contracted to give) had already taken place with outstanding success. Shortly afterwards Mocchi informed us that the ship on which we were to go to Rio had been delayed, and asked us to seize the opportunity of giving our three extra performances at once. On learning that they were to be given, Nijinsky expressed a wish to take part in them. We therefore had to explain that he could only do so unpaid, since they were additional to the number agreed in his contract. The Nijinskys, however, refused to believe this and suspected a plot.' If the company were not meant to be in Montevideo at all, what is the meaning of 'two of our regular performances'? From Grigoriev's papers I deduce that eight performances were given in Montevideo, since about thirty-four ballets were danced.

* It appears from Mme Nijinsky's narrative that this happened in Montevideo, although she places the visit to Uruguay after that to Brazil. In Rio she would have had to interpret in Portuguese.

subsequent events assert that Nijinsky showed on this tour the first signs of mental illness.[292] This Romola Nijinsky flatly denies.[293]

One night Vaslav told Romola that 'L'Après-midi d'un faune' had been announced for performance in two days' time. He had danced it twice in Madrid, but still felt the management should have asked his permission to give it on this tour, and with the help of a friend he devised a way for getting his own back on Grigoriev. The scheme was the idea of Quintana, the son of the President of the Argentine, who happened to be in Rio at the time.

That evening [wrote Romola] the performance seemed to go very smoothly The *entr'acte*, during which I admired the colourful audience, seemed to me unusually long. 'Faune' was the next ballet on the programme. The public became restless; I wondered what could have happened. Vaslav's friends were smiling like conspirators. I went backstage; everything was ready, the scene lit, Vaslav in position waiting for the curtain to rise. But at one side of the stage there was a gesticulating group. The impresario, Grigoriev, Kremnev pacing up and down in a frenzy, [Trubecki] trying to hide a smile. The impresario was talking to two police officials. What had happened? They told me: 'Nijinsky, the author of "Faune" has brought an injunction to prevent the presentation of "Faune", as it does not legally belong to the Russian Ballet.'

Nijinsky, the dancer, however, stood waiting to begin his part in the 'Faune' according to the terms of his contract. 'But, Nijinsky the author and Nijinsky the dancer are the same person,' said one of the ballet. 'Sorry; have you anything in writing to prove that you have the author's permission to perform it – yes or no?' And 'Faune' had to be cancelled.[294]*

To friends outside the company Nijinsky seemed a delightful companion. In Rio the Russian Ambassador Tscherbatchkoi entertained Vaslav and Romola and drove them to his country house. The American Ambassador Edwin Morgan was another friend. The French Ambassador was no less a person than the poet Paul Claudel.[295] After seeing Nijinsky in 'Schéhérazade' he was in raptures and demanded to be introduced to him. The following night, however, Vaslav was dancing in 'Les Sylphides'. The poet found the old-fashioned romanticism of this ballet repulsive and was delivered of an epigram: '*Il-y-a une chose qui est pire que le mauvais: c'est la perfection dans le mauvais.*' (One thing worse than bad is perfection in the midst of badness.) The young composer, Darius Milhaud, one of the group called 'Les Six', was on his staff, and they had planned together two ballets, 'La Création du monde' and 'L'homme et son désir', which they hoped Nijinsky might stage.[296] These were later realized by the Ballets Suédois, with choreography by Jean Borlin. Milhaud was to compose a ballet, 'Le Train bleu', for Diaghilev in 1924.

* From Grigoriev's papers (not his book) it would seem that 'L'Après-midi d'un faune' was given once in Rio, once in São Paulo and four times in Buenos Aires.

Claudel later wrote of Nijinsky:

He moved like a tiger. There was no change of inert weight from one pose to another. His spring came from a buoyant partnership of muscular and nervous energy, like a bird on the wing. His body was not like a tree trunk or a statue, but a complete organism of power and movement. There was not a gesture, be it ever so slight (as, for example, when he turned his chin towards us, and the small head revolved on its long neck) which he did not accomplish magnificently, with a vivacity at once fierce and gentle and with an astonishing authority. Even in repose he seemed imperceptibly to be dancing, like those luxuriously sprung carriages which used to be called 'huit-ressorts'.[297]

Milhaud noticed 'How beautiful he was when he turned to speak to someone behind his chair. He turned his head, but his head alone, so precisely and rapidly that he seemed not to have moved a muscle.'[298]

The Nijinskys made friends with a young couple in Rio, Estrade Guerra the composer and his pianist wife, Nininha, who used to pick them up in Vaslav's dressing-room after performances. Guerra noticed that Vaslav continued dancing after the curtain went down and Romola told him, 'Don't worry. Vaslav isn't mad. He can't stop suddenly after dancing like that; the heart must regain its normal rhythm by degrees.'[299] In later years Guerra recalled

Nijinsky spoke French fairly well, not with complete fluency, but well enough to carry on a conversation. He seemed on excellent terms with his wife. She was likeable and sympathetic; pretty, with delicate features and fine blue eyes. There were two dancers whom he admired above all others, Karsavina and his sister, Bronislava Nijinska. He did not compare them, however, since they were so different. Sometimes one felt there was something mystical about him, but that did not strike me as anything unusual. I assumed it was typical of the Slav character. He was certainly highly strung, but not abnormally so for an artist. Intelligent? Most decidedly so. One of his most endearing aspects was the rather childlike, natural side of his character, without the slightest pretension. He was certainly conscious of his worth and knew quite well what he was about, but he was totally without vanity. Neither in private life nor on the stage was there anything effeminate in his behaviour. He expressed a desire to leave the Russian Ballet to go his own way and said that in any case this South American tour was to be his last. . . . When I heard subsequently that Nijinsky had become insane, I was unable to believe it. Nothing in our meetings in Brazil could have led me to foresee that.[300]

The journey from Rio to São Paulo was by train, and the costumes and scenery were placed in a van immediately behind the engine. A flying spark ignited this carriage as the train was going through a tunnel and the décor for 'Le Spectre' and 'Cléopâtre' was completely destroyed.[301] Fortunately the former was sufficiently simple to reproduce, and for 'Cléopâtre'

Grigoriev was able to adapt the sets for 'La Péri' which they were still lugging around with them although the ballet had never been produced.[302]* In São Paulo Nijinsky made friends with the head of the Research Institute, Calmette, a brother of the arch-critic of 'Faune';[303] and Lydia Sokolova, who had been six months pregnant when she last appeared on stage in Madrid – and who was on this tour as one of the staff – gave birth painfully and prematurely to a daughter on 1 September.[304]

The Ballet now sailed back down the coast to Buenos Aires, where Vaslav and Romola stayed at the New Plaza. They had friends here; they met Pavlova, whose company were also on a South American tour; and on 10 September their fourth wedding anniversary was celebrated with a luncheon given by the priest who had married them.[305] The season at the Colón Theatre opened on the 11th and proved, wrote Grigoriev, 'one of the most trying I ever managed'. This was partly due to difficulties with the impresario, as a result of which Grigoriev refused to go on with one performance, and partly because there was little applause – the audience having become Europeanized and believing that clapping was vulgar.[306] There was also the constant friction between Nijinsky and the *régisseur*. It is clear that they disliked each other. Grigoriev would claim in his memoirs that Nijinsky was already mentally unbalanced, but this is denied by Romola, and from his happy association with Claudel, Milhaud, the Guerras and their many diplomatic friends it seems improbable. Romola accuses members of the company of causing a series of accidents (presumably with the knowledge of Grigoriev, though she does not accuse him directly), and believes they were instigated by Diaghilev.[307] This too sounds improbable.

One night Vaslav trod on a rusty nail on the stage; on another he had to leap out of the way of a heavy iron weight falling from the flies. 'Petrushka' was brought into the repertory in Buenos Aires, and at one of the four performances the puppets' booth was not securely fixed, so that when Nijinsky gestured from the top of it at the Magician it collapsed and he had to dive into Cecchetti's arms. Romola was convinced that all these incidents were attempts to get from Nijinsky the penalty of 20,000 dollars which he incurred if he failed to fulfil his contract. Vaslav pitied his enemies, if they existed, and never blamed them. But Romola discussed the matter with her lawyer friend Quintana, who sent detectives to the theatre to watch over Nijinsky.[308]

The audience remained unaware of these goings-on and the season was a

* According to Haskell (*Balletomania*, p. 177, footnote) the décor for 'Contes russes' and the doors of the 'Schéhérazade' set were burnt; and 'Zverev painted a new set that was used for many years.'

success. Nijinsky was dancing his usual roles in 'Faune', 'Schéhérazade', 'Narcisse', 'Sylphides', 'Spectre', 'Petrushka' and 'Cléopâtre'; he still captivated the public, and he was always inventing new 'business'. In 'Schéhérazade', which he now danced in silvery-grey make-up, 'the audience rose with a scream' – and Romola with it – at the Slave's death leap. 'In that final jump, Vaslav, with the briefest touch of his head on the floor, flung himself into the air by the action of his neck-muscles, quivered, and fell. I ran backstage, but there was Vaslav practising *entrechats*! So convincing had his execution been that we all thought he was hurt.'[309]

On 26 September, 1917 the last of the company's twenty-three* performances took place at Buenos Aires, and Nijinsky danced for what was to be the last time with the Diaghilev Ballet, appearing in 'Le Spectre' and 'Petrushka'. He had told the Guerras that he intended to leave the Russian Ballet – and according to Ansermet, Vaslav and Romola had an idea of staying on in South America to start a school;[310] but they were longing to see Kyra and made plans to return to Switzerland. Before doing so Vaslav helped to organize a Gala matinée in aid of the French and English Red Cross in Montevideo, and this was to keep him in the country a month longer than he intended. He went to the dock to see off the company on their voyage back to Europe.[311]

Determined on his gala for the Red Cross, Nijinsky arranged it with a new diplomat friend, André de Badet. Artur Rubinstein was on tour in South America, and he was called in to share the programme, while a local pianist, Domingo Dente, accompanied Nijinsky. Badet wrote:

Vaslav had arranged some new dances for the Gala. Since only part of his stage wardrobe was available, he had to improvise his costumes, wearing the black velvet tunic and the white shirt and tights from 'Les Sylphides' with the pink slippers from 'Le Spectre de la rose'. . . . How could we have imagined that evening when we saw him bound from the wings, soar diagonally across the vast stage in two prodigious leaps and vanish in full flight on a third, like a sylph whose natural element was the air, that Nijinsky was dancing for the last time in a theatre? . . . His small, rather Asiatic head was poised, proudly and languidly in turn, on the column of his neck, muscular as a sculpture by Donatello. Domingo Dente played for him pieces by Chopin, for some of which Vaslav had composed aerial choreography for that single evening.[312]

So in his last public performance Nijinsky used his God-given talent in the service of the wounded and sick.

---

* Françoise Reiss says eight (p. 171).

CHAPTER EIGHT

1917-1950

November 1917 – April 1950

At twenty-nine – though he did not know it – Nijinsky had danced in public for the last time. His intention had always been to dance until he was thirty-five, when he would still be in his prime, then appear only in character roles, devoting himself to choreography and to the foundation and running of a school where he would teach other artists to compose ballets. He dreamed of a specially designed theatre in which great festivals would be held and all performances would be given *free*.[1] In this, as in so many other ways, his ideas were ahead of his time. But it was not destined that Nijinsky should be remembered as a schoolmaster or a festival director.

Nobody would ever see him, with declining years, give a performance which was less than perfect. Although tragedy awaited him there was another kind of tragedy – that of diminishing powers and fading inspiration – which he would be spared. He was to be remembered as the unparalleled artist of the dance and a pioneer of new forms. Sound in body and mind, he ceased to dance.

There were some who claimed or would claim in the light of after events, when they wrote books many years later, that Nijinsky had already shown signs of abnormality.[2] But he had never been like other people, and it was easy for an enemy or a rival faction to start the rumours that his nervousness, his reserve and his Tolstoyan inclinations were symptoms of incipient mania. Grigoriev, writing in the 1950s, described how, watching Nijinsky's final performance with the company in Buenos Aires, he 'tried to impress on [his] memory for the future a picture of his incomparable dancing . . . being convinced that [he] was never to see him dance again'.[3] This shows almost psychic intuition; and we are justified in suspecting an insertion by an editor and translator anxious to make the fact-crammed Russian chronicle more colourful in English. (It was perhaps this editor, my old friend Vera Bowen, who was responsible for describing the purely imaginary appearances of Pavlova and Chaliapine at the opening of the Russian season in Paris in 1909, the dancing of Nijinsky in 'Carnaval' in 1910, a year before he learned the role of Harlequin, Diaghilev's distress at the burning of Narodny Dom a month before the event, and Nijinsky's breach of a non-existent contract.)

We accept (not having ourselves been on the last South American tour) Mme Romola Nijinsky's account of the various accidents – the rusty nail, the falling scenery[4] – but Nijinsky did not mention these supposed attacks to her,[5] and it was she who enlisted legal and police help.[6] If the accidents were really accidents and not deliberate attacks on Nijinsky, it was his wife who was developing persecution mania and not he – and anyway, persecution mania is a symptom of paranoia and not of schizophrenia, the disease to which Nijinsky was to fall victim a year and a half later.

Rightly or wrongly, Vaslav and Romola felt that it was impossible for him to go on dancing with the Diaghilev Ballet. She thought that all the 'attacks', including that of Tolstoyan philosophy, were planned by Diaghilev. (She is entitled to her opinion, but one finds it hard to see why Diaghilev, however jealous, should set out to kill the goose that laid the golden eggs.) Still, it was Vaslav who took all decisions both regarding his career and his family.[7] He was undisputed master in his own house, and if he decided to leave Diaghilev it was probably mainly because of the latter's total absorption in Massine, not as a person but as a choreographer. When Diaghilev had begun to encourage Nijinsky as a choreographer, Fokine had felt that all the main opportunities would be given to the younger man: now Nijinsky felt the same about Massine. He was incapable of jealousy[8] and admired Massine's talent,[9] but he longed to create new ballets.

If Nijinsky *had* remained with Diaghilev during the last year of the war, spent by the company in Spain and Portugal, it is quite certain that Diaghilev would have been unable to pay him: for the Ballet was to have increasing difficulty in getting engagements and would be on the point of disbanding out of sheer poverty when they were rescued by an invitation to the Coliseum by Oswald Stoll in 1918. As it was, Vaslav's isolation from the world of ballet may have been the principal cause of his mental breakdown.[10]

While the Diaghilev Ballet remained in the neutral peninsula, the Nijinskys, after sailing back from South America, made for neutral Switzerland to set up house for the first time in a home of their own. But before they looked for a house they had to see their child. On arrival in Lausanne they went at once to the sanatorium where Kyra had been staying, and Romola observed, 'It was remarkable how the child changed the moment Vaslav entered the room. It seemed almost as though they had been one person split apart, and constantly wishing to be reunited. Sometimes I almost felt as if I were intruding on them.'[11]

In Russia the second revolution had taken place. Karsavina, now married to the British diplomat, Henry Bruce, was in Petersburg.

On the morning of the 8th of November I saw cadets marching down the Millionaya towards the Winter Palace; the eldest of them might be eighteen. Sporadic shooting started in the afternoon. Loyal troops had barricaded the Winter Palace Square and the access from side streets. The chief fighting was round the telephone exchange. For several hours I sat holding the receiver to my ear. . . . I could follow the exchange changing hands many times. . . . The other side of the river was cut off, all bridges up; a destroyer [the *Aurora*] faced the Palace from the Neva; the fortress was in the hands of the Bolsheviks. . . . The wine cellars all through the town were being looted. . . . It was a ballet night. I started from home soon after five. In about an hour's time I arrived at the theatre by many detours. By eight o'clock there was about one-fifth of the company at the theatre; after a short deliberation we decided to raise the curtain. The few performers on the vast stage were like the beginning of a jigsaw puzzle, a few clustered pieces here and there – the pattern had to be imagined. Still fewer people in the audience. A cannonade was faintly heard from the stage, quite plainly from the dressing-rooms. After the end some friends waited for me outside; we were going to supper with Edward Cunard, whose flat was opposite mine, near the Winter Palace. The square of the Mariinsky was free. . . . Pickets barred our street. . . . Cunard's flat was higher up the Millionaya than mine, only a hundred yards from the Palace Square. Machine-guns rattled with renewed zest; I had an uncomfortable feeling that I might get hit in the shin-bone. At supper we could hardly hear ourselves speak – field-guns, machine-guns, rifle-fire were deafening. Cunard brought out a pack of cards . . . the candles burned down. A grey winter light stole through the curtains. The fighting had died down – only an occasional boom of gun-fire. We broke up, the men escorting the ladies to their respective homes. From my window I could see the barracks. A solitary figure in soldier's uniform crept from the shadow of the gate and started running towards the Champs de Mars; a shot and the figure fell in the snow. I drew the curtain. In the morning we had a new regime – Lenin was Prime Minister.[12]

The Diaghilev Ballet also found themselves in the middle of a revolution in Lisbon that winter: this was soon over, but it had a dampening effect on their season.[13]

Vaslav had never heard of Lenin or Trotsky and wondered that power should be entrusted to men who had lived so long abroad.[14]

In December 1917 the Nijinskys took the Villa Guardamunt in the mountains above St Moritz. Vaslav then returned to Lausanne alone to fetch Kyra. Such a solitary journey was a novelty for him. 'To book a room in a hotel and to buy a railway ticket were experiences unknown to him', but 'Vaslav was very proud, and was full of adventurous feeling starting out on his first trip alone.'[15] While he was away his wife began to arrange the villa.

Our house looked like a real home, with all our personal belongings. The entrance was full of skis and toboggans, as I had decided to take part in all the winter sports. The house overlooked St Moritz, and the lake lay at our feet. Opposite was the beautiful Roseg Alp and the Piz Margna that sheltered us from the eastern winds, and snow glittering, snow everywhere, seven feet deep, that promised us a glorious winter. Vaslav and Kyra arrived, and in a few days we had fallen into our daily routine. I wanted to attend to everything for Vaslav, but he refused. 'A man should not be served by his wife, *femmka*.' The wardrobe of an old maid could not have been more perfectly in order and more spotlessly clean than Vaslav kept his things.

The balcony on the ground floor was cleared. There, every morning, for two hours, Vaslav did his exercises, with Kyra looking on and patiently watching Tatakaboy* dance, and when he leaped she used to cheer and clap her hands, then often Vaslav, forgetting his iron discipline, caught her in his arms and waltzed round singing, '*Votre amabilité, maia Kotyik, maia Funtyiki.*'†

This winter was a very happy one. We were constantly together undisturbed, and went for long walks all over the Engadine. I used to practise on the Dimson skeleton run; it was my favourite sport. Vaslav was simply worshipped by the servants. If he met the cook on the way up to the villa, he carried the parcels. If the coal was too heavy to put on the fire, he helped the maid, and he even flirted with the old laundress, brought her chianti, and chatted to her of her native Italy. He would play with all the children of the village. Sometimes we used to meet for an *apéritif* before lunch at Hanselmann's, where everybody goes during the season. Hanselmann, an Austrian by origin, the well-known *confiseur* of St Moritz, quite a personality, played a leading part in the life of the place. He became a staunch friend of 'Monsieur Nijinsky'. Vaslav appreciated his *Käsestängel*, gave him recipes for *Koulibjak*, and sometimes discussed the political situation with him at length.

We often went, too, to Dr Bernhard's. His house was the last word in Engadine style, and was the meeting-place of many interesting Swiss and foreigners. Our neighbour, President Gartmann, also entertained us.

Kyra was developing well, and looked lovely trotting beside Vaslav in her teddy-bear suit. They used to *luge* down the hill to Celerina at a breakneck speed. I was scared. 'Nothing will happen to my *amabilité* as long as we are together,' Vaslav used to say. The evenings we mostly spent quietly at home reading.

Vaslav accompanied me when I went skating, and, though he did not take part in any of the winter sports, he gave me remarkable advice on technique and balance. His instinctive knowledge was amazing.

* Kyra's name for her father.
† Nijinsky's name for Kyra.

Then Vaslav discovered sleighs that he could drive himself, and twice a week we would go off in the morning, the three of us, either picnicking or stopping at some roadside inn for lunch. We explored the glaciers, passes, and lakes of the Bernina. With the coming of the season many of our friends arrived from Paris and Vaslav seemed to be quite rested and soothed by the light-hearted gaiety of his *entourage*. As a surprise for me, he invited my sister and my brother-in-law Schmedes. Erik was a kind soul, and Vaslav had not forgotten his loyalty.

The spring came, and with it the foreigners departed; we were left alone again with the natives, whose life was quite patriarchal. It seemed remote and five centuries back to us. The celebrated sports centre had become a very quiet Alpine village again. In the evening, at the Hôtel Post, the notary, the Mayor, and the doctor, would meet to discuss the welfare of their little community. Vaslav loved to listen to their debate; it reminded him so much of Russia. We were so much in love with St Moritz that we did not wish to leave it even for a day.

The first timid crocuses pushed their way up and spring was officially here, but the torrents of melting snow kept us indoors more, and Vaslav resumed my lessons. He seemed lighter than ever; the number of his *pirouettes* and *entrechats* was infinite, and, watching him make his *battements* and *pliés*, it sometimes seemed to me that he was lighter than the snowflakes themselves. But his strength was of steel, and he bounded like india-rubber.

Practice or no practice, it was a strange thing for Nijinsky – no longer a prisoner of war – to spend a whole winter without appearing in a theatre. But his mind was active, and he was inventing.

He was full of ideas for new ballets. He composed a delightful version of Debussy's 'Chanson de Bilitis'. He said, 'I want you to dance Bilitis. I have created it for you. It obeys the same basic choreographic laws as the "Faune".' It was in perfect harmony with the movement of the music, with all its delicate feeling and sweet perversity. This ballet was in two scenes, the first Bilitis and her shepherd, their love, their youth on the green islands of Greece; the second, Bilitis and her girl lover, who shares her sorrows, and her pleasures.

Vaslav's other creation was his own life put into a choreographic poem: a youth seeking truth through life, first as a pupil, open to all artistic suggestions, to all the beauty that life and love can offer; then his love for the woman, his mate, who finally carries him off. He set it in the period of the High Renaissance. The youth was a painter; his master one of the greatest artists of the period, a universal genius, just as Diaghilev seemed to him to be. He designed the scenery and costumes for it himself, modern, and yet correct to the period. 'You know, *femmka*, the circle is the complete, the perfect movement. Everything is based on it – life, art, and most certainly our art. It is the perfect line.' The whole system of notation was based on the circle, and so was this ballet. It was in accordance with Vaslav's previous methods, but, unlike 'Faune' and 'Sacre', it was circular. The scenery was a design in curve, and even the proscenium opening was round. Vaslav worked out the whole design himself to the smallest detail, in blues, red and gold, Raphaelistic in style.

397

So the spring of 1918 found them isolated in their mountain retreat, while war and revolution raged around them.

Almost overnight our surroundings had changed. The frozen lake began to quiver, the slopes of the Alps, covered with fragrant flowers, had become a riot of colour, the pink alpen-roses, the sweet-smelling purple violets, and the cornflower-blue gentians. The snow retreated to the summits of the peaks, which were now so familiar to us and had each its own meaning for Vaslav. We used to run up to the Alp Giop and throw ourselves down among the flowers. And, while lying there in the scented pasture, we spoke of many things. I told Vaslav about my parents' unhappy marriage, and blamed my mother, but he stopped me. 'Don't be hard. You do not know the circumstances that made her act the way she did. We should never condemn anybody, nor have we the right to judge.' I often complained about the difficult times we were having to go through during the war, but Vaslav said, 'Do not look up to the more fortunate, look down to those worse off than yourself, and be thankful for your destiny.'

Romola had not been entirely well since Kyra's birth and she went into a Berne sanatorium for a minor operation. Vaslav arrived to visit her with his arms full of roses and spent a fortnight by her bedside. While in Berne he saw a dance recital by Clothilde and Alexander Sakharoff and told Romola 'You have missed nothing. It is merely attitudinizing, not dancing at all. *C'est du Munich.*' Romola saw that his artist's hunger to witness some new development was disappointed. But then Nijinsky had never really liked dance recitalists. In 1914 he and Romola had seen a performance by Argentina in London at the Savoy Theatre and commented, 'A dancer by himself is nothing, he has to have a frame. If the Almighty came down and danced from seven till eleven it would be boring.'[16]

In the autumn of 1918 Vaslav's patriarchal interest in household affairs showed itself in concern for laying in a good stock of fuel for the winter, and he helped chop the wood in the garden. He was always in and out of the kitchen, to the delight of the cook, lifting the lids of saucepans, and, if a cake was being baked, cleaning out the bowl with his finger as he had done as a child.

Kyra's Swiss nursery governess was married to a man who worked at the Palace Hotel. One day she was summoned to see him and on her return described with horror how he had been declared insane and taken off in a straitjacket. He had always been quite normal except for walking round the room for hours at night. When Romola told Nijinsky what had happened 'he became strangely silent and his face darkened'. The new governess, though Swiss, had been brought up in England and passed years in India, where she had studied *yoga*. In this, with his exploring mind, Vaslav became extremely interested.

This year [wrote Romola] the winter came early. When the snowing began, it went on for days and nights continuously. It was peaceful and warm; we seemed to be far away from the world, forgotten. The strange fascination of this isolated alpine village grew on us. In this sleepy whiteness, one morning the first news arrived from Bronia and '*Babouchka*'. They were well and did not need anything. They had received the money sent by Vaslav, but when the November Revolution took place they had fled to Kiev.

There was a letter enclosed for Romola, asking her to break the news to Vaslav that his brother Stanislav was dead. He had contracted pneumonia and Bronislava and her daughter Irina had visited him in the asylum a few days before his death.* Romola shirked her unpleasant duty for several days, knowing that Vaslav had loved his brother.

Finally I plucked up courage and went to him. He was drawing at the time. '*Regarde, femmka, ça c'est notre Kouharka* and this is Marie.' He showed me two lovely pastel portraits of the cook and the maid, transformed into Russian peasants, and a striking picture of Kyra. 'This is Funtyiki; you think it looks like her?'
I hated to spoil his happiness. 'Vaslav, I want to talk.' He sat down in the armchair, and I on the edge. Petting and caressing him, I buried my face on his shoulder, and said quickly, 'Stanislav is dead.' A long silence, then Vaslav lifted my face and asked how it happened. I told him, and burst into tears. He looked at me smiling, but with a strange and deep quietness. 'Do not cry; he was insane; it is better like this'; and he bowed his head. The same smile that he had had at his father's death came back again, and now I knew that Bolm had made a mistake, and that Vaslav was not heartless; on the contrary. But I felt it was strange – very strange.

Impresarios arrived at St Moritz with offers for Nijinsky, but they were all sent packing. Nijinsky would not dance until the war was over and he was free to plan his life in the way he wanted. Yet as winter came on, he was always busy composing choreography and designing. 'His drawings were all based on the circle, and he developed an amazing technique of producing portraits out of a few circles.' During the long winter evenings, at the suggestion of the new governess, they tried *séances* of table-turning and got some curious answers to their questions. This amused Vaslav.

Romola and Vaslav had worked out a system of arm signals whereby, as she returned from shopping in the town below, she could relay him the latest war news. At last in November she was able to signal that an armistice had been suddenly and unexpectedly declared. Romola ran up the steps of the villa with a newspaper. But when Vaslav read the peace terms he shook his

* Either Mme Romola Nijinsky did not understand the details of the letter exactly or she had forgotten them by the time she wrote her book. In this she states that the Soviet authorities had opened the doors of prisons and asylums, and that Stanislav, left to himself, had been burnt to death. Mme Bronislava Nijinska assures me that her elder brother died in bed from a liver complaint.

head. 'There can be no peace under those terms. War will go on, but in a hidden, different way.' So, with the instinctive and prophetic gift he had in common with certain other great artists, he saw in a flash something like the rise and fall of the Nazis and a second war – through which he and Romola were destined to live and suffer.

Diaghilev had finally succeeded – through the intercession of King Alfonso – in getting his company out of Spain and conveying them to London, where they had opened at the Coliseum on 5 September a season which was to last over six months. It was the first time Diaghilev had ever countenanced allowing his ballet to perform in a music-hall: they gave one ballet at each performance, sandwiched between Grock, the clown, and other turns.[17] Lady Ripon had died in 1917, but Juliet Duff and Lady Ottoline were in London to entertain Diaghilev, and he spent much time in the company of the Sitwell brothers, who were still in the Grenadier Guards. On 11 November Diaghilev and Massine dined with Osbert Sitwell in Swan Walk, Chelsea, and afterwards, before going on to a party in the Adelphi attended by the Bloomsbury group – including Maynard Keynes and Lydia Lopokhova whom he would later marry – they walked in Trafalgar Square and watched the Londoners celebrating the peace. 'The crowd danced,' wrote Sitwell, 'under lights turned up for the first time for four years – danced so thickly that the heads, the faces, were like a field of golden corn moving in a dark wind . . . there were many soldiers, sailors and airmen in the crowd which, sometimes joining up, linking hands, dashed like the waves of the sea against the sides of the Square, against the railings of the National Gallery, sweeping up so far even as beyond the shallow stone steps of St Martin-in-the-Fields.' Diaghilev, 'bear-like in his fur-coat', gazed on these revels 'with an air of melancholy exhaustion'.[18] Massine reacted differently: 'Pushed and shoved in all directions by the ecstatic crowd, I remained curiously unmoved. A sense of calm came over me, and I felt that life could now resume its normal course.'[19]

A week later, on 18 November, the Diaghilev Ballet gave its thousandth performance.

That winter Nijinsky read and liked Nietzsche's *Ecce Homo*, which had been written at Sils Maria nearby, and Maeterlinck's *La Mort*. He planned yet another new and original ballet.

It was to be a picture of sex life with the scene laid in a *maison tolérée*. The chief character was to be the owner, once a beautiful *cocotte*, now aged and paralysed as a result of her debauchery; but, though her body was a wreck, her spirit was indomitable in the traffic of love. She deals with all the wares of love, selling girls boys, youth to age, woman to woman, man to man.

'But, Vaslav, how will you be able to express it?' He danced, and succeeded in transmitting the whole scale of sex life. 'I want to show the beauty and the destructive quality of love.'

The part of the old *procureuse* was intended for Réjane.

Nijinsky set about sketching the choreography for this unusual ballet in an even more unusual way. He instructed Romola to stand before him motionless for a few moments, to empty her mind of all thoughts and then begin to dance. She was surprised as he had always regarded improvisation as inartistic. He assured her that this would be different. Vaslav hypnotized her. Romola, who had always been interested in psychic experiments, was a good subject for hypnotism. 'After a certain time,' she wrote, 'I began to dance, strangely fascinated by Vaslav's oblique eyes, which he almost closed as if he wanted to shut out of himself everything else but my dancing. When I had finished, he said that I danced with a wonderful technique all the different parts of his newly composed ballet. . . .' Romola was unaware of what she had been dancing, and every time she finished working with Nijinsky in this way she felt as if she were coming out of a trance and was irritable with the people around her. When she asked how he would develop the ballet he would not answer but fell into one of the long silences which were becoming more frequent with him. So the first draft of Nijinsky's last ballet – 'Les Papillons de nuit' he called it[20] – was danced out by his unconscious wife for the eyes of the choreographer alone.

Nijinsky decided that if it was impossible for him to return to Russia he would form his own company based on Paris, and would invite Massine to join it.[21] He asked Romola, who had once aspired to be the Vasari and chronicler of the art of her day, to put on record his artistic views.

They decided to celebrate the first Christmas of peace in style.

The 24th of December was passed in feverish preparations. The big pine-tree, which went right up to the ceiling, was brought into the drawing-room and placed near the open fireplace. We adorned it ourselves: it was a beautiful heavily laden tree, full of candies, toys, silver nuts, and garlands, and on the top Vaslav himself placed a shining silver star – 'The tree for Kyroschka'. He looked it over with a critical glance. He wanted it to be very lovely, and so it was. We enjoyed preparing it. Vaslav had helped me to wrap up the presents neatly in silver paper; one for each of the household. Vaslav also remembered many children and sick people in the village, and we went round to take them their parcels.

Our Christmas Eve was a peaceful and happy one. Kyra's eyes opened wide when she saw the beautiful illuminated tree which Tatakaboy, as she called her father, lighted for her. Next morning I slept late, and was awakened by the maid, who came in trembling and as white as a sheet. 'Oh, madame, as I went into the drawing-room I found the Christmas-tree fallen on the floor. It means bad luck.' I shivered. '*Femmka, c'est bêtise;* it only means that it lost balance, was overladen on one side. I can't understand it; I made it so carefully.' We went down to see it. There it lay on the floor, the silver nuts all round and the silver star broken in two. We pulled it up, tied it, and I tried to forget the incident.

In spite of his apparently serene life with wife and child in a comfortable home among the mountains Nijinsky's mind was in a turmoil: it had suddenly become a whirlpool of unanswerable questions. What was the purpose of life? Why had he been born? Why did God allow war? He had no regular routine of physical, professional work in class-room or rehearsal-room or on stage to keep the dark thoughts at bay. Did he miss his mother, his sister, Russia? Did he long for the protective love of Diaghilev? Did he miss the ballet, the public, the applause? The pleasant trivialities of everyday life seemed meaningless and idiotic. On his long solitary walks and as he sat up late at night by himself gulfs yawned.[22]

His mind was frantically busy. He invented a windscreen-wiper and an eversharp pencil. He pondered on mechanical problems and tried to simplify his system of dance notation. He bought quantities of paints and pastels. All this mental activity did not banish the black thoughts. Sometimes his wife would see him running, which she considered bad for the heart at such an altitude. Was he running to escape the horror in his mind?

Violent activity offered temporary relief. One Sunday it was decided that the family should sleigh over to Maloja. 'Kyra was glad,' wrote Romola, 'and Vaslav was very gay that morning.' But the excursion was disastrous and gave Romola her first indication that something was seriously wrong.

As it took us about three hours to get there, Kyra and I got very hungry during the long drive. The road was extremely narrow during the winter, as it needed clearing from the heavy snows and in certain parts there was always a space to await the sleighs coming from the opposite direction. Vaslav was as a rule a careful and excellent driver, but on this particular Sunday he did not wait, but simply drove on into the oncoming sleighs. We were in danger of turning over as the horses got frightened. The coachmen cursed, but this did not make any difference. Kyra screamed, and I begged Vaslav to be more careful, but the further we went the more fiercely he drove against the other sleighs. I had to clutch on to Kyra and to the sleigh to keep ourselves on. I was furious, and said so to Vaslav. He fixed me suddenly with a hard and metallic look which I had never seen before. As we arrived at the Maloja inn I ordered a meal. We had to wait. Vaslav asked for some bread and butter and macaroni. 'Ah, Tolstoy again,' I thought, but did not say a word, and bit my lips. Kyra was anxiously awaiting her steak, and, as it was laid before her and she began to eat, Vaslav, with a quick gesture, snatched the plate away. She began to cry from disappointment. I exclaimed, 'Now, Vaslav, please don't begin that Tolstoy-Kostrovsky nonsense again; you remember how weak you got by starving yourself on that vegetarian diet. I can't stop you doing it, but I won't allow you to interfere with Kyra. The child must eat properly.' I went with

Kyra to the other room to have our solitary lunch. We drove home very quietly without a word.

Vaslav decided to take part in the winter sports.

We attended the ski-jumps [wrote Romola], the bobsleigh and the skeleton races. We went riding and ski-ing. At the first lesson Vaslav asked our teacher to show him how to brake to stop, and the same morning he made telemarks. 'Well, well, the gentleman only needs a few corrections,' said the teacher, as Vaslav sailed down the slopes. 'He is of course a practised skier.' 'What do you mean? It is the first time he has had skis on.' 'Remarkable, such perfect balance; he bends his knees just perfectly, with the elasticity of a practised skier. You are fooling me.' But I was not surprised that Vaslav was so good; his wonderful training helped him in all sports.

. . . Vaslav took a liking to skeleton running, though I thought it was too dangerous a sport and told him so, but he was so proficient after a few hours' practice that I could not object. Skeleton running is done in a narrow ice-run built on the slopes of the Alps, with dangerous curves. The speed is terrific, as the skeleton is made out of steel and the person lies head downwards on the skeleton, which is guided by the displacing of the balance. Vaslav became brilliant in its execution. Very soon he asked me if I wanted to go down with him, lying as a dead weight on top of him. I loved it, and I had faith in Vaslav, but, even so, I had to shut my eyes when we went flying through the run. Sometimes he took Kyra down, and I could only stand and pray until they arrived safely in the valley.

But Nijinsky could not for long escape from his inner gloom, because he was in a state of nervous breakdown. Out walking with Romola he sometimes stopped and stood brooding for what seemed a long time, disregarding any questions she put to him.

One Thursday, when the governess and maid had their day off, Romola had an even more alarming experience than the expedition to Maloja.

I was making ready to take Kyra out for a walk when suddenly Vaslav came out of his room and looked at me very angrily. 'How dare you make such a noise? I can't work.' I looked up, surprised. His face, his manner were strange; he had never spoken to me like this. 'I am sorry. I did not realize we were so loud.' Vaslav got hold of me then by my shoulders and shook me violently. I clasped Kyra in my arms very close, then with one powerful movement Vaslav pushed me down the stairs. I lost my balance, and fell with the child, who began to scream. I stood up, more astounded than terrified. What was the matter with him? I was unaware of having done anything wrong. He was still standing there menacingly. I turned round, exclaiming, 'You ought to be ashamed! You are behaving like a *moujik*.' A very changed Vaslav we found when we came home, docile and kind as ever. I did not speak about the incident, either to him or to anybody else.

Nijinsky was turning out drawings at lightning speed until the floors of his study and other rooms were littered. It was no longer portraits or scenic designs that he produced, but strange eyes in red and black. 'What are these masks?' asked Romola. 'Soldiers' faces. War!'

Then he began to put down his thoughts in a diary. This he would not show Romola.

One day Romola went into the kitchen and noticed that the three servants seated round the table broke off their conversation and looked at her oddly. 'What has happened?' she asked. The young man who stoked the boiler said, 'Madame, forgive me; I may be wrong. We all love you both. You remember I told you that at home in my village at Sils Maria as a child I used to do errands for Mr Nietzsche? I carried his rucksack when he went to the Alps to work. Madame, he acted and looked, before he was taken away, just like Mr Nijinsky does now. Please forgive me.' 'What do you mean?' Romola cried; and Kati, the laundress, broke in excitedly: 'Mr Nijinsky is walking in the village wearing a big golden cross over his necktie, and is stopping everybody in the streets asking them if they have been to mass and sending them to church. He just spoke to me.' Romola ran down to the village and saw Vaslav stopping the passers-by.

I got hold of his hands [she wrote]. He seemed embarrassed at seeing me. 'What are you doing? What is this new nonsense? Vaslav, won't you stop imitating that old lunatic Tolstoy? You are making yourself into a laughing-stock.' He looked like a punished child, very sad. 'But, *femmka*, I did not do anything wrong. I just asked if they had been to church.' I pointed to Kyra's big golden Florentine cross. 'And what is this?' 'Well, if you don't like it – ' and he took it off. 'The world imitates me; all the foolish women copy my ballet costumes. They make their eyes seem oblique, and it becomes the mode, only because nature gave me high cheekbones. Why can't I teach them something useful, lead them to remember God. Why can't I set the fashion, since I do set fashions, that they should seek the truth?'

Romola could see the logic of this, but felt that he was putting his ideas into practice in an eccentric way.

Returning from another excursion, wearing his cross, Vaslav drove the sleigh so fast that he overturned it and threw Romola and Kyra into the snow. Romola remonstrated angrily with him and went home on foot with the child.

Of course he was home ahead of us. When I entered the house, the servant, who worshipped Vaslav, opened the door and said, 'Madame, I think Monsieur Nijinsky is ill, or perhaps very drunk, for he acts so queerly. His voice is hoarse and his eyes all hazy. I am frightened.' 'Don't be silly, Marie. He never drinks, you know. Artists have moods, but ring up the doctor and say I need him for Kyra, and put her to bed at once.' I went to our bedroom. Vaslav lay fully dressed on the bed, with the cross on, his eyes closed. He seemed to be asleep. I turned cautiously towards the door, and then noticed that heavy tears were streaming down his face. '*Vatza, qu'est-ce que tu as? Vatza, ne sois pas fâché.*' 'It is nothing; let me sleep; I have a dreadful headache.' He had had many of those lately.

On the pretext of Kyra having a chill Romola consulted the doctor, who stayed to tea and had a talk with Vaslav. He diagnosed 'a slight case of hysteria' and sent them a male nurse, who was to pretend to be a *masseur*, to keep Vaslav under observation. Romola noticed that Vaslav gave her 'a long, understanding look' when she introduced this man, but he made friends with him and they went for walks and drives together. For a time he seemed much more cheerful, played hide-and-seek with Kyra, and built snowmen in the garden.

At lunch one day, however, he announced that he had decided to give up dancing for ever and intended to farm in Russia.

I lost my temper [wrote Romola]. 'If you go you go alone. I have had enough; I can't become a peasant. I was not born one. Even if I love you I will divorce you and marry some manufacturer.' And in my bad temper I took off my marriage-ring, the heavy golden Brazilian circle, and ungraciously hurled it at Vaslav. He seemed very surprised. In the afternoon I received a huge bouquet of about five hundred carnations, with the ring in it.

At Nijinsky's suggestion Romola had asked her sister Tessa to stay, and her visit was marked by an increase of social activity. Vaslav spent thousands of francs on scent, shoes and sweaters, and accompanied the ladies to dances, dinners and ski-races. The Durcals arrived from Spain and invited them to tea. Asked what he had been doing lately, Vaslav put on a worldly air, leaned back nonchalantly on the sofa and said, 'Well, I composed two ballets, I prepared a new programme for the next Paris season, and lately I have played a part. You see, I am an artist; I have no troupe now, so I miss the stage. I thought it would be rather an interesting experiment to see how well I could act, and so for six weeks I played the part of a lunatic, and the whole village, my family, and even the physicians apparently believed it. I have a male nurse to watch me, in the disguise of a *masseur*.' Romola was overcome, torn between anger and relief. She was confirmed in her supposition that her fears had been groundless when the male nurse came, after ten days, to assure her from his long experience that Nijinsky was completely sane.

Nijinsky was watching the champion skaters practising, with Kyra seated in the sleigh beside him, when he spoke to a young stranger, Maurice Sandoz (who later became an author), who has recorded the occasion. Nijinsky was wearing a dark suit and a sealskin cap with a large copper crucifix hanging from his neck. He asked Sandoz, 'Can you tell me the name of this skater?' 'He's called Vadas. He comes from Budapest.' 'His skating comes from the heart, which is good.' 'Yes, there are greater virtuosi than him on the skating-rink, but no one so graceful.' 'Grace comes from God; the rest can be acquired by work.' 'But cannot grace also be acquired by work?' 'Grace which is learnt goes so far and no further. Inborn grace has no limits.'[23]

In Nijinsky's mind it seems that *die Gnade* and *die Anmut*, for which in French and English the same word serves, were one: that to him the Grace of God was the same as – or related to – that quality of which Leonardo wrote 'It is the extremities which lend grace to the limbs.' Perhaps he was right.[24]

The arrival of some Viennese friends, and particularly of the pianist Bertha Gelbar, Mme Asseo, decided Nijinsky to give a recital. This would be for an invited audience and there would be a collection for the Red Cross. All the hotel ballroom floors were of course polished parquet and therefore unsuitable, but in the Suvretta House Hotel, which Romola thought looked like an enchanted castle rising from the pine forests, Vaslav found a room which would do. He refused to say what he intended to dance, stating merely 'New creations', and set about making his costumes with the aid of an Italian dressmaker.

Shortly before five o'clock on the day of the recital, 19 January 1919, Vaslav, Romola and Negri, the dressmaker, drove to Suvretta House.

Vaslav was silent, just as before going to the theatre. I knew this mood and respected it. Before arriving at the Suvretta, I ventured to ask, 'Please tell me what Bertha Asseo must play for you.' 'I will tell her at the time. Do not speak. *Silence!*' he thundered at me. 'This is my marriage with God.' A slight uneasiness crept over me. Vaslav looked so menacing, so dark, in his fur-collared coat, with his Russian fur cap.

In this last recital, which began so embarrassingly that everybody remembered it differently, and went on to become so alarming, Nijinsky gave proof both of his genius and his madness. Never, perhaps, in history had an artist demonstrated so clearly how close the two are to each other.

About two hundred people, some uninvited, were seated on rows of chairs facing the empty space where Vaslav was to dance. Bertha Asseo was at the piano.

According to one account, Nijinsky first told his accompanist '*Jouez du Chopin*', then stopped her and said '*Non, jouez du Schumann*'.[25] Maurice Sandoz describes it differently. He remembered Nijinsky beginning with an interpretation of Chopin's Prelude No. 20 in C minor.

To each chord struck by the pianist he made a corresponding gesture. First he stretched out both arms in an attitude of defence, the palms of his hands raised vertically; then he opened his arms in a gesture of welcome, raised them in a movement of supplication then, to the fourth and fifth chords, let them fall noisily as if the joints were broken. . . . He repeated the movements for every sequence up to the final chord.

Then Nijinsky danced a number in the aerial style expected of him, and at the end of it placed his hands on his heart and said, 'The little horse is tired.'[26]

According to Romola

Vaslav entered in his practice kit, and, taking no notice of the public, went up to Bertha, and said, 'I will tell you what to play.' I was standing near the piano. There was an air of great expectation. 'I will show you how we live, how we suffer, how we artists create.' And he picked up a chair, sat down on it facing the audience, and stared at them, as if he wanted to read the thoughts of each. Everybody waited silently as if in church. They waited. The time passed. We must have been like this for about half an hour. The public behaved as if they were hypnotized by Vaslav. They sat completely motionless. I got rather nervous as I caught a glance of Dr Bernhard, who was standing in the background, and his expression confirmed me in the belief that my suspicion was justified. Vaslav was again in one of his strange dark moods. Bertha began as a prelude the first few bars of 'Sylphides', then 'Spectre'. She hoped to call Vaslav's attention to one of his dances. Perhaps then he would begin. I felt quite upset, and wanted to relieve the tension. I went over to Vaslav. 'Please won't you begin? Dance "Sylphides".' 'How dare you disturb me! I am not a machine. I will dance when I feel like it.' I fought desperately not to burst out crying. Never had Vaslav spoken to me this way, and before all these people! I could not bear it, and left the room. Mr Asseo and my sister joined me. 'What is happening? What is the matter with Nijinsky?' 'I do not know. I want to take him home. What shall we do?' We went in again, but by this time Vaslav was dancing – gloriously but frighteningly. He took a few rolls of black and white velvet and made a big cross the length of the room. He stood at the head of it with open arms, a living cross himself. 'Now I will dance you the war, with its suffering, with its destruction, with its death. The war which you did not prevent and so you are also responsible for.' It was terrifying.

Vaslav's dancing was as brilliant, as wonderful as ever, but it was different. Sometimes it vaguely reminded me of that scene in 'Petrushka' when the puppet tries to escape his fate. He seemed to fill the room with horror-stricken suffering humanity. It was tragic; his gestures were all monumental, and he entranced us so that we almost saw him floating over corpses. The public sat breathlessly horrified and so strangely fascinated. They seemed to be petrified. But we felt that Vaslav was like one of those overpowering creatures full of dominating strength, a tiger let out from the jungle who in any moment could destroy us. And he was dancing, dancing on. Whirling through space, taking his audience away with him to war, to destruction, facing suffering and horror, struggling with all his steel-like muscles, his agility, his lightning quickness, his ethereal being, to escape the inevitable end. It was the dance for life against death.

Romola's description recalls Marie Rambert's account of the tragic power

Nijinsky 1917–1950

Nijinsky showed when he demonstrated the dance of the Chosen Virgin to Piltz at Monte Carlo.

After Nijinsky's last dance tea was served.

That night he wrote in his *Diary*:

I want to live a long time, my wife loves me very much. She is afraid for me today – I acted very nervously. I behaved this way on purpose because the public understands me better when I am vibrating. They do not understand artists who are placid. One has to be nervous. I offended the pianist Gelbar. I wish her well, but I was nervous. God wanted the public to be in a state of excitement. The public came to be amused and thought I danced for their amusement. My dances were frightening. They were afraid of me, thinking I wanted to kill them. I did not. I loved everybody but nobody loved me and I became nervous and excited: the audience caught my mood. They did not like me, they wanted to go away. Then I started to do a joyful, merry dance, and they began to enjoy themselves. First they thought I was a dull actor but I showed them that I could do merry things. The audience began to laugh when I did. I was laughing in my dance. The audience laughed – they had understood my dance and felt like dancing too.

I danced badly; I fell when I should not have. The audience did not care because my dancing was beautiful. They felt my mood and enjoyed themselves. I wanted to go on dancing but God said to me: 'Enough.' I stopped.[27]

From now on Romola foresaw the end. There had been talk of whether she was fit to have another child: they both wanted a son. 'Cannot you find a man like Lombroso to examine us both?' Vaslav had asked. He wanted to be sure their child would be born fit both physically and mentally. And he felt the need of talking over with some wise man the trouble inside his head. Now Romola told him she had found a man as great as Lombroso – Professor Bleuler, the famous psychiatrist in Zürich. She made an appointment. Her mother and stepfather came from Budapest.

I am going away to Zürich. I do not want to do anything before my departure. Everybody is nervous. The maids have become stupid because they do not feel God. I feel Him, but I have not become stupid. I do not want to crack, but to say the truth. Oscar is telephoning to Zürich. He is afraid that people will not understand his name. He feels that nobody knows his name there and so he wants to make them understand it. His name is Pardany, and he pronounces it with an accent on every syllable. I do not care whether people know my name or not, and I am not afraid that people will not love me if they find out that I am poor.

When I was at school I used to shut myself in, pretending I was ill, so that I could read. I used to lie down and read, quietly. I want to write about the departure for Zürich, everybody is nervous because I did not care. I thought this journey was absurd, but I will go because God wants it. But if He did not wish it, I would remain. I am beginning to understand God. I know that he creates movement, and so I ask Him to help me. . . .

My wife came to me and told me to tell Kyra that I would not come back any more. My wife's eyes were full of tears and she said, trembling, that she would not leave me. I cried. God did not wish us to separate. I told her that.

I would not remain in Zürich if my wife is not frightened of me; but if she is afraid I would rather be in an asylum, as I fear nothing. Her soul was weeping. I felt my heart ache and said again that if she is not afraid of me I will come home again. She started crying and kissed me, saying that she and Kyra would never leave me whatever happens to me. I said, 'Very well.' She understood me and went away. . . .

I will go to Zürich and will see the town, which is a commercial town, and God will be with me.[28]

They travelled to Zürich by train. Romola wrote

I went alone to see Professor Bleuler. Vaslav did not want to accompany me. Bleuler was an old man with an infinite understanding in his eyes. I spoke to him about Vaslav, myself, our marriage, and life for almost two hours. 'Very, very interesting, all you tell me. I can assure you there is nothing the matter with you, my dear. Anyhow, we do not become insane; we are born it. I mean, the disposition is there. Genius, insanity, they are so near; normality and abnormality, there is almost no border between the two states. I should like to meet your husband; extremely interesting. If you spoke of any other man I might be worried, but the symptoms you describe in the case of an artist and a Russian do not in themselves prove any mental disturbance.' I was relieved, and came home happily. I told Vaslav how nice Bleuler was and that he thought I was healthy and that we could now have a son, and that he would like to make his acquaintance. Vaslav agreed, 'Of course, so would I; he seems interesting. I was quite sure everything was all right. After all, *femmka*, I was brought up in the Imperial School, and we were there under constant medical supervision. Since I left there, except for my typhoid, I have never been seriously ill.' In a happy mood, we went out shopping, and I noticed that Vaslav stopped before the window of a great departmental store where babies' layettes were exposed; he smiled, and I knew he was thinking of the son he so ardently desired.

Next day, about three in the afternoon, we drove across the bridge on the Lake of Zürich to the hilly side, where in a wood at a little distance the State asylum is built, a big old-fashioned building with iron-barred windows. But the smiling porter and the flowers which surrounded the directorial building, where Professor Bleuler received, took away the disagreeable impression. We sat for a few moments and then the professor came out. I introduced him to Vaslav, and they both disappeared in his study. Calmly I looked over the illustrated papers lying round: the *Illustration*, the latest numbers of the *Sketch* and *Graphic*. I was relieved that all this unnecessary anxiety was over; at last everything would be all right. We had had such a hard time these first six years of our marriage – the fight with Diaghilev, war prisoners, all the disillusion; but now at last the happy time would commence. The door opened within ten minutes, and the professor showed out Vaslav smilingly.

'All right. Splendid. Won't you step in for a second? I forgot to give you the promised prescription yesterday.' I smiled at Vaslav as I passed him, following the professor; what prescription I could not remember. As he closed the door of his study behind him, he said very firmly, 'Now, my dear, be very brave. You have to take your child away; you have to get a divorce. Unfortunately, I am helpless. Your husband is incurably insane.' I thought the sunray which passed through the window above the head of the professor was curiously full of dust. Why did he have that huge green table in the middle of the room? And those inkstands were irritatingly round – a circle; oh, yes, the Circle. That awful, that merciless circle of misfortune. I was vaguely hearing him ask me to forgive him for being so hard. 'I must seem to be brutal, but I have to be to be able to save you and your child – two lives. We physicians must try to save those whom we can; the others, unfortunately, we have to abandon to their cruel fate. I am an old man. I have sacrificed fifty years of my life to save them. I have searched and studied; I know the symptoms; I can diagnose it; but I don't know, I wish I could help, but do not forget, my child, that sometimes miracles happen.'

I did not listen; I had to get out of there quickly. I felt the place was going round with me faster and faster in a circle. I dashed through the door to the room where Vaslav was waiting. He stood near the table looking absentmindedly at the illustrated papers, pale, strangely sad, in his Russian fur coat with his Cossack cap. I stopped and looked; it seemed as though his face was growing longer under my gaze, and he slowly said, '*Femmka*, you are bringing me my death-warrant.'

Emilia Markus and Oscar Pardany arrived in Zürich on the following day. Romola was trying to work out some way in which she could care for Vaslav without having him confined in an asylum. Her parents thought otherwise. Nijinsky's condition was diagnosed as schizophrenia.

The idea that Vaslav was pronounced insane made them lose their heads completely. As they were unsuccessful in persuading me to seek a divorce, they decided to take our lives in their hands. My mother took me out for a walk, and, while we were away – Vaslav being still in bed, waiting for his breakfast – the police ambulance, called in by my panic-stricken parents, came, and the Hôtel Baur en Ville was surrounded by the fire brigade to prevent Vaslav's jumping out of the window, should he attempt it. They knocked at his door. Vaslav, thinking it was the waiter, opened, and was immediately seized. They tried to carry him out in his pyjamas. Vaslav, as I learned from the manager, asked, 'What have I done? What do you want of me? Where is my wife?' They insisted that he should come, and the doctor, seeing his quietness, asked the nurses to release him. Vaslav thanked him, and said, 'Please let me dress, and I will follow you.' When I came back at noon, I found his room deserted.

Desperately I ran to Professor Bleuler, who helped me to find him. He was in the State asylum among thirty other patients, but, by that time, Vaslav, owing to the shock, had had his first catatonic attack. Professor Bleuler deeply regretted this unfortunate incident, which brought on the acute development of the illness, which, under different circumstances, might have remained stationary. On his advice, Vaslav was taken to the Sanatorium Bellevue Kreuzlingen, where he not only found admirable care but kind-hearted friends in the Dr Binswangers.

Professor Bleuler had invented the word 'schizophrenia' in 1911 to describe a certain kind of mental disorder 'characterized by autistic thinking' – that is to say, a condition in which the patient is absorbed in wish-fulfilling fantasy as a means of escape from reality. This term was adopted as being more appropriate than *dementia praecox*. Typical symptoms are 'loss of emotional rapport with the environment; negativism or automatic obedience; individual logic in thought processes; and hallucinations'. Freud (1911) thought the illness was due to unconscious homosexual trends; Boisen (1936) considered that it came from an intolerable loss of self-respect. Many doctors have maintained that it is organic rather than psychogenic.[29] The schizophrenic suffers from 'a distortion of the usual logical relations between ideas, a separation between the intellect and the emotions . . . and a reduced tolerance for the strain of personal relations so that the patient retreats from social intercourse into his own fantasy life and commonly into delusions and hallucinations . . .'.[30] A recent theory of the Soviet Russian, Professor Pavlov, is that the disease is due to the nucleus of the nerve cells being fed insufficient carbon-dioxide.[31]

Diaghilev received the news of Nijinsky's illness in London. From the time years before when he had consulted Dr Botkine about his friend's health, he had believed that the threat of insanity was hanging over Vaslav: but in his usual manful way, he had kept this worry to himself. Now he admitted to Massine that he was not surprised that the blow had fallen, only that it had fallen so soon.[32] Marie Rambert, who had made her home in London since before the war and was married to the playwright Ashley Dukes, heard the news over tea with Diaghilev and Massine at the Ritz, and was surprised at Diaghilev's lack of distress when he told her Nijinsky was 'walking on all fours'.[33] But Rambert had always been emotionally demonstrative, and we can imagine that Diaghilev, having absorbed the shock in private, would be averse to joining in with anyone else's tears.

Leonide Massine, still no more than twenty-four, had developed into a most original and versatile choreographer; and his ballets, the fruit of wartime research and work, were being shown for the first time to London, along with works from the pre-war Fokine repertory, as part of the afternoon and evening mixed programmes at the Coliseum music-hall. Diaghilev had been reluctant to present his company under these conditions, but he had no choice if they were to survive, and the Russians proved popular, filled the house and captured a new audience. Lopokhova was now the star, and as Mariuccia in Massine's Italian ballet, called in England 'The Good-Humoured Ladies', and in 'The Midnight Sun', she proved irresistible to the English. 'Children's Tales' ('Contes russes'), which had evolved from 'Kikimora', now comprised three separate episodes to the music of Liadov, with Sokolova as the witch Kikimora and Idzikovsky as her cat, with Kremnev as the demon Baba Yaga and with Massine as the Knight Bova Koralevitch and Tchernicheva as the beautiful Swan Princess. Sokolova, herself a principal dancer now, noticed how whenever Diaghilev watched Idzikovsky as the cat he laughed till the tears streamed down his face.[34] This ballet was so popular that Stoll asked Diaghilev to give it as often as possible.[35]

Although the 'Italian' ballet and the two Russian folk ballets just mentioned were designed by Bakst and the more *avant-garde* Larionov, Diaghilev was beginning to turn to painters of the School of Paris for his décors. Picasso, with his 'Parade' in 1917, had been the first. Now he showed London 'Cléopâtre' in the new set of Robert Delaunay; and Charles Ricketts disapproved. 'The hideous setting was by the post-Impressionist round the corner, pink and purple columns, a pea-green Hathor cow, and yellow pyramids with a green shadow with a red spot. . . . Massine dances well. . . . He is stark naked save for rather nice bathing-drawers, with a huge black spot on his belly. Two or three idiot girls in the gallery shrieked with laughter when he came on.'[36]

In the spring the Diaghilev Ballet, after a fortnight in Manchester, moved to the Alhambra in Leicester Square for a proper season; and it was here that Massine scored his greatest success to date with 'La Boutique fantasque', danced to the sunny tunes of Rossini in André Derain's *faux-naïf* set, with himself and Lopokhova in the can-can.

Karsavina, having made her last appearance at the Mariinsky – in 'La Bayadère' on 15 May – braved exceptional perils to escape with her husband to England. Thence they had gone *en poste* to Tangier. Re-united with Diaghilev, she told him how the extra day he had asked her to stay in London after the 1914 season had cost her months of wandering.[37] Under the tuition of a Flamenco dancer, Felix Fernandez Garcia, engaged in Spain, Massine had become an expert on Spanish dancing, and he was working on his masterpiece 'Le Tricorne', which it was intended that Karsavina should dance. 'Our first collaboration in "The Three-cornered Hat",' wrote Karsavina, 'showed him to be a very exacting master. . . . On the Russian stage we had been used to a balletic stylization of Spanish dancing, sugary at its best: but this was the very essence of Spanish folk dancing.'[38] It is curious that, so soon after Nijinsky had lost his reason, the simple Andalusian Felix, who had hoped to dance his *farucca* in the

Spanish ballet himself, but who could neither stick to the strict *tempi* of a musical score nor adapt himself to the regulated life of a ballet company,[39] went out of his mind that summer and was discovered one night dancing on the altar steps of St Martin's-in-the-Fields. Karsavina and Massine danced the principal roles in 'The Three-Cornered Hat' in Picasso's wonderful set at the Alhambra on 22 July.

Now began for Romola Nijinsky thirty years of hope, despair, struggle, poverty and heroism. During the six months Vaslav was in Kreuzlingen she and the doctors entertained hopes of his recovery, but this was not to be; at the end of that time he grew worse, had hallucinations, was violent and refused food. The courageous Romola decided to try the experiment of taking him home, thinking it possible that familiar surroundings might have a beneficial effect. This necessitated day- and night-nurses under the constant supervision of doctors, and was expensive. Vaslav had his good days and his bad, but there was no real improvement in his condition.

In Switzerland Romola took her husband to be examined by Professor Jung and Professor Forel. Then, moving to Vienna, she consulted Professor Wagner-Jauregg, who told her that 'as long as a schizophrenic has periods of agitation there is a hope for an improvement towards normalcy.' Sigmund Freud said that psycho-analysis was useless in cases of schizophrenia. Romola kept Vaslav with her at home in Vienna most of the time. Only when he became very difficult to manage did she take him to the Steinhof Sanatorium. Once when she was briefly out of the country her parents committed him to the State Asylum outside Budapest, where he was badly treated. Romola hurried home and took him back to Austria.

On 14 June 1920 Romola gave birth – in the same room in the same clinic in Vienna where Kyra was born, and with the same doctor attending – to a second daughter, whom she called Tamara.[40]

In 1920 Diaghilev decided to revive 'Le Sacre du printemps', of which he still had the sets and costumes, only used seven times before the war. As nobody could remember Nijinsky's choreography Massine worked out a new version. Of this Grigoriev thought it 'lacked pathos, in which it differed notably from Nijinsky's'.[41] Sokolova gave a powerful rendering of the Chosen Virgin, Ansermet conducted; and it was clear the music had become acceptable, respectable and even a classic. Shortly after this Massine fell in love with a pretty, talented English dancer in the company, who had been given the name of Vera Savina. The pattern repeated itself and Diaghilev dismissed him as he had dismissed Vaslav seven years before.[42] This was cutting off his nose to spite his face, for with Russia isolated, with Fokine in New York and Nijinsky insane, Diaghilev was without a choreographer. He determined on an experiment at variance with all his other experiments, namely a return to tradition: he would mount one of the old classical ballets, against which his whole movement had been a revolt. He decided to revive the Petipa-Tchaikovsky 'La Belle au bois dormant', to be called 'The Sleeping Princess', at the London Alhambra in the winter of 1921, and to put it on for a run in the hopes of emulating the success of the musical comedy, 'Chu-chin-chow'. Bakst was summoned, and began designing several sets and hundreds of costumes.

At this time, Diaghilev met a young Russian, Boris Kochno, who became his secretary and was to write the libretti of later ballets.[43]

Bronislava had been running a school in Kiev since the Revolution and in 1921 she escaped with her mother and children to Vienna. Here Eleonora and Bronia saw Vaslav again, but he showed no sign of recognition.

Bronislava then joined Diaghilev in London and set about arranging some new dances for 'The Sleeping Princess', notably the 'Three Ivans' to the music of the coda of the *Grand pas de deux*. For three years she was to be choreographer to the company. In spite of the splendour of the production of the big Tchaikovsky ballet, and in spite of the presence of three wonderful expatriate ballerinas, Spessivtseva, Trefilova and Egorova, as well as Lopokhova, who took turns to dance the role of Aurora, supported by Pierre Vladimirov, the regular ballet audience was disappointed and the general public stayed away. 'The Sleeping Princess' was not a success and was withdrawn after 105 performances. Furthermore, Diaghilev had spent so much more of Oswald Stoll's money on it than he should have done that Stoll seized all the scenery and costumes, which made it impossible for Diaghilev to present the ballet in Paris or elsewhere.

It was at this low ebb in the Russian Ballet's affairs that the resilient Diaghilev came to an arrangement with the Monte Carlo Casino which would give his company a measure of security for the remaining years of its existence. Every winter the Russians would provide dancers for the Monte Carlo opera season, and would hold their own spring ballet season there before going on to Paris. These settled periods several months long would give them leisure to rehearse new works.

In 1923 Romola rented a flat in Paris at 50, Avenue de la Bourdonnais, near the Eiffel Tower. The experiment was made of taking Vaslav to the theatre, to the ballet and to watch Cossack dancers in a night-club, but the signs of interest he showed were soon over and he relapsed into his silent lethargic state again. When Romola was away, her sister Tessa kept house for Vaslav. Eleonora and Bronislava took a flat together in Paris.

Diaghilev came to see Nijinsky. This was the first time he had set eyes on him since they had parted in wrath in Barcelona six years before. He was met by a vacant stare. 'Vatza, you are being lazy. Come, I need you. You must dance again for the Russian Ballet and for me.' Vaslav shook his head. 'I cannot because I am mad.'

On 13 July 1923, Stravinsky's 'Les Noces', begun when the ink of 'Le Sacre' was hardly dry on his pen, was presented at last on the stage – at the Gaieté-Lyrique in Paris; and the choreography, instead of being by Nijinsky, as Diaghilev had intended in the old days, was by his sister.

The music which had been an extraordinary conception in 1916 when Stravinsky began to compose it, became even more extraordinary as he scored it between 1918 and 1923, and there has been nothing quite like it since. The preparations for a peasant wedding and its consummation were conveyed in snatches of song, now commonplace, now poetic, with invocations to the saints, drunken interjections and certain conventional remarks by parents and guests so traditional in Russian village life as to constitute a kind of indispensable liturgy. How strange – yet how typical of our century – that Stravinsky felt the need of this banal gibberish as the basis for his solemn music, in the way that Schwitters made grand compositions from a collage of bus-tickets! By this means all the nineteenth-century sentiment and sweetness about the idea of marriage were abolished with one blow. This marriage was like a death. The spoken and sung words had originally been intended to have heavy scoring like 'Le Sacre', but after a long process of brooding and elimination Stravinsky made the work a cantata with percussion, four pianos and a great bell to toll at the end. Gontcharova's sets were blank walls, the last with a door through which a bed was seen, piled with pillows. Her monochrome peasant uniforms in brown and white emphasized the universality of the two families and their friends, whom Nijinska piled up into epic groups and set going in a kind of swaying, stamping and twisting motion which had the inevitability of a cornfield swept by the wind. The result was one of the masterpieces of Russian art like 'Petrushka' and 'Le Sacre du printemps'.

That summer Romola, hoping for a miracle, took Vaslav on a pilgrimage to Lourdes. 'We spent several days there,' she wrote. 'I went with Vaslav to the Grotto. I washed his forehead in the spring and prayed. I hoped and hoped, but he was not cured. Maybe my faith was not deep enough.'

Diaghilev had a new friend, a young English dancer who had been given the name of Anton Dolin. In February 1924, arriving in Paris from Monte Carlo, they went together to visit Nijinsky. The flat was three or four flights up in a block built of grey granite. They were admitted by a Russian man-servant and shown into the drawing-room where Nijinsky was sitting, with Romola and their two daughters. 'Hardly a word was spoken,' wrote Dolin, 'but somehow in this man's face there was something more expressive than a volume of words. There were the same eyes I had seen in pictures, the same

415

beautiful mouth, the upper lip clean-shaven, and dark, hardly any hair on the head at all, white hands that were never still.' Dolin, both happy and sad, contrasted Vaslav's appearance with the Sargent drawing of him in 'Le Pavillon d'Armide', which Juliet Duff had given Romola[44] and which hung among other portraits on the wall. 'Diaghilev tried to make him speak. He wouldn't say a word. He just sat and laughed. I asked him something and he answered, "*Je ne sais pas.*" . . . I often wonder what Diaghilev's feelings were; whatever he felt, he succeeded in hiding. During tea Nijinsky would neither eat nor drink. He seemed powerless to do anything. He looked as healthy as any of us, yet somehow his brain refused to work. He sat in his chair, trying to understand. I think he did understand a great deal, but I believe his brain was tired.' The visitors left after an hour. 'He came to the door with us, said goodbye in Russian, and then, when Diaghilev asked if we should come again, nodded his head in a wistful way as much as to say: "I am very, very tired." '[45]

Bronislava Nijinska made several new ballets that year: 'Les Tentations de la bergère', a Versailles type of ballet to music of Montéclair in a set by Juan Gris; 'Les Biches' to a commissioned score of Francis Poulenc with designs by Marie Laurencin, which was a masterpiece of frivolity, the very epitome of the 1920s; 'Les Fâcheux', a Molière ballet to music by Georges Auric and with designs by Georges Braque; 'La Nuit sur le Mont Chauve' to Mussorgsky; and 'Le Train bleu', a ballet about sport and flirtation on a beach, with music by Darius Milhaud, Vaslav's old acquaintance from the French Embassy in Rio, a set by the sculptor Henri Laurens and a superb front curtain of running giantesses by Picasso. During rehearsals for the last work, in which Dolin did spectacular acrobatics in a Chanel swimming costume, Romola brought Vaslav to the Théâtre du Mogador. They entered unannounced just as Bronislava was coaching Dolin in his *pas de deux*. Dolin performed his back falls, leaps and a cartwheel: but there was no response from Nijinsky, and eventually his wife led him away.[46]

Benois, who had been curator of the Hermitage throughout the war and revolution, had recently arrived from Russia; and Diaghilev had given him the Gounod opera 'Le Médecin malgré lui' to design at Monte Carlo: but Benois could not bring himself to approve some of the new departures and Diaghilev for his part found Benois' work old-fashioned.[47] Bakst died in December 1924, leaving a son. Nouvel and Koribut-Kubitovitch still survived to help Diaghilev; and Svetlov was living in Paris, married to Trefilova.

Diaghilev could 'create' ballets through the agency of other people: but he also felt the need, in a sense, to 'create' the people. If he gave his friendship and affection to a young dancer, his highly developed pedagogic instinct made him want not only to educate him artistically, but to turn him into a choreographer. Because he failed to interest Dolin in choreography – and also because the independent Englishman was always running off to amuse himself with friends of his own age – Diaghilev lost interest in him.[48] His eye was attracted to a handsome, slightly-built young Russian with fine dark eyes called Serge Lifar. This boy had recently come out of Russia with a group of dancers from Nijinska's school in Kiev, and although he was comparatively inexperienced, he worked hard and his efforts aroused the interest of Diaghilev – as they were intended to do.[49] When Bronislava Nijinska heard that Diaghilev and Lifar were secretly experimenting with the choreography of a new ballet she was annoyed, having no faith in the creative ability of her former pupil; and just as Fokine had done when he heard of Nijinsky's secret rehearsals in 1912, she resolved to leave the company.[50]

It was not Lifar, however, who was destined to be Diaghilev's next great choreographer. I do not use the word 'great' carelessly: it is an extraordinary fact that all Diaghilev's principal choreographers from 1909 to 1929 had elements of greatness and originality and none was in the least like another. It was Fokine's invention of a more natural and expressive style of dancing, his revolt against the classicism of Petipa, that had made possible the conquest of the West. Nijinsky's mind soared ahead, and his works were forerunners of all the limitless experiments of modern dance in the age of space. Massine the eclectic, much influenced by the other arts, again found new styles of movement and, among other things, developed the comedy of manners in ballet. Nijinska, the versatile, could produce witty and exquisite trifles like 'Les Biches', but she also had her brother's epic vision and in 'Les Noces' she matched the splendour of Stravinsky's score. The last of the series was a young Georgian, also a refugee from Russia, who joined the company when they were at the London Coliseum in the winter of 1924–5. His name was Yuri Balanchivadze, later simplified to George Balanchine.

Of the varied ballets Balanchine produced for Diaghilev between 1925 and 1929 – comedies, *divertissements*, an English pantomime, experiments in constructivism and surrealism or with cinematic projection – two very different ones were masterpieces and have survived in the repertory of today: the neo-classical 'Apollon Musagète' to Stravinsky's score (1928), and the passionate, eccentric 'Le Fils prodigue' (1929) to Prokofiev's.

In 1926 Bronislava Nijinska went as ballet-mistress to the Colón Theatre in Buenos Aires (to which she was to return in 1932 and 1946) and in 1928 and 1929 she produced ballets for Ida Rubinstein's company, including Stravinsky's 'Le Baiser de la fée' and Ravel's 'La Valse'.

The dauntless Romola did not give up her hope of a cure for Vaslav. She tried Christian Science; she tried faith healers; and she visited Dr Coué at Nancy. In 1927 she heard that experiments in curing schizophrenia were being made by Professor Poetzl of the Vienna State Hospital, and she wrote to him. He replied that it was too soon to say whether the treatment he was trying might prove successful and that she should inquire again in a few years time.

Soon after her appearance in 'The Three-cornered Hat' Karsavina had gone with her diplomat husband to Bulgaria. Back in London, they had made their home in Albert Road, Regent's Park, near the Zoo. In 1926 Karsavina had returned to Diaghilev to dance in 'Roméo et Juliette' (music by Constant Lambert; décor by Max Ernst and Joan Miro) with Lifar, and now she was to resume her old role in 'Petrushka'.

Diaghilev thought that to see Karsavina in 'Petrushka' might give Vaslav the shock which would restore him to his right mind. The company were performing at the Paris Opéra. Romola was in America, so Diaghilev made the arrangements with Tessa. At the end of December 1928 he went with Lifar to the flat in Passy. Nijinsky was lying on a low mattress wearing a dressing-gown, 'either biting his nails till the blood came,' wrote Lifar, 'or somewhat affectedly playing with his wrists'. Lifar approached and kissed his hand. 'For a moment his eyes glowered at me from under the knitted brows, with the wild, suspicious glance of a hunted animal, then quite suddenly a wonderful smile lit up his face: a smile so kindly, so childishly pure, so luminous and undimmed, that I fell utterly under its charm.' At first he paid no attention to Diaghilev, but gradually became conscious of his presence, and 'from time to time, like a normal person, he appeared to be listening intently to what Diaghilev was saying'. Diaghilev pretended to Lifar that his only object in taking Nijinsky to the theatre was to have him photographed with the company, but Lifar saw through this affection of heartlessness and realized the intention behind the outing. 'By the way his eyes had lit up, I could see how much he was expecting from it, a very miracle in fact.' Diaghilev measured Lifar against Nijinsky and found the latter was shorter by half a head. Vaslav walked with a stoop. 'His legs were those of a great dancer, with immense globular muscles, though so flabby now that one wondered how they could possibly support his body.' Lifar shaved him.[51]

That evening at the Opéra Diaghilev sat with Nijinsky in a box. Various old colleagues came in the first interval to pay their respects but Vaslav was unresponsive. In the second interval he and Diaghilev went on the stage, which was set for 'Petrushka'. Karsavina described the scene.

Diaghilev spoke with a forced cheerfulness as he led Nijinsky on. The crowd of artists fell back. I saw vacant eyes and a passive shuffling gait, and stepped forward to kiss Nijinsky. A shy smile lit up his face, and his eyes looked straight into mine. I thought he knew me, and I was afraid to speak lest it might interrupt a slow-forming thought. He kept silent. I then called him by his pet name, 'Vatza!' He dropped his head and slowly turned it away. Nijinsky meekly let himself be led to where the photographers had set their cameras. I put my arm through his, and, requested to look straight into the camera, I could not see his movements. I noticed that the photographers were hesitating, and, looking round, I saw that Nijinsky was leaning forward and looking into my face, but on meeting my eyes he again turned his head like a child that wants to hide tears. And that pathetic, shy, helpless movement went through my heart.[52]

The photograph which was taken shows Benois and Grigoriev in dinner-jackets, Karsavina in her costume as the Ballerina with her left arm in Nijinsky's right, Nijinsky in a dark suit with a white shirt and a white handkerchief in his breast-pocket, Diaghilev in tails with his left hand on Nijinsky's shoulder and Lifar, dressed as the Moor. Nijinsky is looking down and sideways and smiling for the camera, and Diaghilev is smiling down at him in a would-be proud, fatherly way. When escorted back to the box, Vaslav grew flushed and hot. At the end he did not want to leave, and exclaiming, '*Je ne veux pas*', was led out.[53] The miracle had not taken place.

Marie Rambert was in the house. After the ballet she hurried backstage and at the top of the steps leading from the long corridor of artists' dressing-rooms she looked down to see Diaghilev helping Nijinsky into a car. She held back and did not approach him.[54] The man supporting Nijinsky by his other arm was Count Harry Kessler. In his Diary for Thursday, 27 December, 1928, Kessler wrote:

In the evening to a performance of Diaghilev's Ballet at the Opera. Stravinsky's 'Rossignol' and 'Petrushka'. After the performance I was waiting for Diaghilev in the corridor behind the stage when he approached in the company of a short, haggard youngster wearing a tattered coat. 'Don't you know who he is?' he asked. 'No,' I replied, 'I really can't call him to mind.' 'But it's Nijinsky!' *Nijinsky!* I was thunderstruck. His face, so often radiant as a young god's, for thousands an imperishable memory, was now grey, hung slackly, and void of expression, only fleetingly lit by a vacuous smile, a momentary gleam as of a flickering flame. Not a word crossed his lips. Diaghilev had hold of him under one arm and, to go down the three flights of stairs, asked me to support him under the other because Nijinsky who formerly seemed able to leap over roof-tops, now feels his way, uncertainly, anxiously, from step to step. I held him fast, pressed his thin fingers, and tried to encourage him with gentle words. The look he gave me from his great eyes was mindless but infinitely touching, like that of a sick animal.

Slowly, laboriously, we descended the three, endless-seeming flights until we came to his car. He had not spoken a word. Numbly he took his place between two women, apparently in charge of him, and Diaghilev kissed him on the brow. He was driven away. No one knew whether 'Petrushka', once his finest part, had meant anything to him, but Diaghilev said that he was like a child who does not want to leave a theatre. We went to eat in the Restaurant de la Paix and sat until late with Karsavina, Misia Sert, Craig, and Alfred Savoir. But I did not take much part in the talk; I was haunted by this meeting with Nijinsky. A human being who is burned out. Inconceivable, though it is perhaps even less conceivable when a passionate relationship between individuals burns out and only a faint flicker briefly lights the despairing, inert remains.[55]

Such was the last meeting of Diaghilev and Nijinsky, whose friendship had changed the world. Diaghilev died that summer. He had been suffering from diabetes and he neglected it. After a highly successful London season, his Ballet went to give what were to be their last performances at Vichy, and Diaghilev travelled with his latest protégé, the sixteen-year-old composer Igor Markevitch, to Munich. Here on 1 August Diaghilev went to a performance of his adored 'Tristan und Isolde', which was sung by Otto Wolf and Elizabeth Ohms.[56] Seated beside one he loved with the same love as he had given to Vaslav – a driving force in his procreative life – he listened to the divine Liebestod for the last time. So 'Tristan' was the last opera he heard; and it was Markevitch's first.[57]* Going on alone to Venice, he had become ill and telegraphed to Lifar and Kochno, who were with him at the Grand Hôtel des Bains de Mer on the Lido on 19 August, when he died. Misia Sert and Chanel had arrived, and Pavel Koribut-Kubitovitch reached Venice just too late.[58] The company, dispersed for their holidays, were horrified to read the news in the papers. They were out of work. The funeral, organized by Catherine d'Erlanger,[59] began with a service at the Greek church; then, wrote Lifar, 'the procession, wonderful in its solemn, silent beauty, re-formed, led by the magnificent black and gold gondola, bearing the coffin smothered in flowers, followed by that containing Pavel Georgievitch, Misia Sert, Coco Chanel, Kochno and myself, and a whole string of others, full of friends and mourners. Then, over the smooth ultramarine surface of the Adriatic, sparkling with golden sunshine, the body was wafted to the island of San Michele, and there borne on our arms to the grave.'[60] Lifar ordered a somewhat Mallarmean inscription to be carved on the tombstone:

Venise, Inspiratrice Eternelle de nos Appaisements
SERGE DE DIAGHILEV
1872–1929

* And the present author, aged fourteen, on his way with his mother and a cousin to see the Passion Play at Oberammergau, heard *his* first opera, 'Die Walküre'. in the same theatre, a year later.

420

There was no one able or willing to take over the direction of the Diaghilev Ballet. Neither Nouvel, nor Grigoriev, nor Kochno, nor Lifar, nor Balanchine had the inclination or the will or the prestige or the social contacts or the authority. After an extraordinary twenty years' Odyssey, steered by its valiant helmsman through an ocean of vicissitudes, the ship broke up, and it was every man for himself. Yet the members of the Diaghilev crew, dispersed or regrouped in different formations, would in the ensuing decades spread the love and knowledge of ballet throughout the world and promote the founding of national or municipal companies in six continents. Pavlova's company continued two years longer than Diaghilev's: she died in 1931.

In 1929 Romola Nijinsky was given work in the United States and as she could not take her husband with her, since the USA does not allow mentally unsound immigrants, she decided regretfully to install him once more in Kreuzlingen, where she knew he would be well treated. Nijinsky had been ill for ten years: for another ten he would be in the Swiss sanatorium. While Romola was on a lecture-tour in the USA, their latest flat in rue Conseiller Collignon was broken into and among objects stolen was the Sargent portrait of Nijinsky in 'Le Pavillon d'Armide' which had been given Nijinsky by Juliet Duff.[61]* In 1932 Romola heard that Eleonora Nijinsky had died in Paris: she never told Vaslav this, but would occasionally say to him that his mother was well though too old to come and see him.[62]

One of the tasks Romola undertook in order to earn money to keep Vaslav and herself was to write her husband's life. The idea had been suggested to her by Arnold Haskell, then working for the publisher Heinemann, in 1928. She began the book in America in 1930, assisted by Lincoln Kirstein, and finished it in England in 1932. Haskell was by now a literary agent, and he gave the book to Gollancz.[63] Shortly after this, Balanchine had a small company, Les Ballets 1933, appearing at the Savoy Theatre, with Tilly Losch and the young Toumanova. In a dressing-room at the Savoy, the theatre where Vaslav had enjoyed Gilbert and Sullivan with Diaghilev and Stravinsky in 1913, and where he and Romola had seen Argentina in 1914, next-door to the familiar hotel, Romola introduced the young Kirstein to Balanchine.[64] Kirstein was eager to advance ballet in the United States, and he invited Balanchine to America. From this encounter was born the School of American Ballet, and a series of ballet companies, the last of which, Balanchine's New York City Ballet, is now one of the foremost in the world.

* For three decades the famous charcoal drawing was lost to the world; then in 1958 it turned up in an exhibition of Sargent portraits at the Bohemian Club in San Francisco. It had been bequeathed to the club by the late Senator Phelan, an old balletomane, who had lived in Paris and who died in 1954. Romola Nijinsky brought an action to recover her property, but was unsuccessful, the club offering her a copy, which she refused.

Nijinsky by Romola Nijinsky, his wife, was published in England by Gollancz in 1933, and in the United States by Simon and Schuster in the following year. It went through several impressions. It was a vividly written and colourful story, in which Diaghilev necessarily played the part of villain. Romola hoped that it might be made into a film. In fact Alexander Korda had the idea of producing a film with John Gielgud as Nijinsky, but this was never realized.[65]

Early in 1936, Kyra Nijinsky married Igor Markevitch, Diaghilev's last protégé, at the Coronation church in Budapest. There would be one son of the marriage to continue the line of Vaslav and Romola.

In 1936 Romola published an English translation of Nijinsky's diary, which she had recently discovered in a trunk. *The Diary of Vaslav Nijinsky*, written at St Moritz in the winter of 1918–19, when the dancer was on the borderline between sanity and mental illness, immediately struck the world as a most extraordinary document.

That year Romola heard that the experiments in curing schizophrenia which had been made at the Poetzl Clinic had produced good results. She got in touch with the young Austrian Dr Sakel, who had invented this shock treatment, and arranged to meet him together with three distinguished Swiss doctors at Kreuzlingen Sanatorium, where Vaslav was still confined. Romola had trouble persuading Nijinsky's official guardians, appointed by the Swiss government, as well as the medical staff of the sanatorium, to give their consent to so novel and drastic a treatment; but the doctors found Nijinsky's physical condition to be good and thought the risk should be taken. Dr Sakel told Romola that if the treatment was not tried the patient's chances of recovery were non-existent: it might produce a cure or at least a partial improvement. 'Many of Diaghilev's and Vaslav's old friends,' wrote Romola, 'thought that it was better to leave him as he was. They were afraid that if he recovered he might be an unhappy man.' Nevertheless, she decided to take the risk, and it was arranged that Sakel himself should administer the treatment as soon as he was free.

In May 1937 Anton Dolin organized a charity matinée at His Majesty's Theatre in London to raise funds for Nijinsky. Lady Juliet Duff and Lady Diana Cooper were on the committee. John Gielgud recited a Prologue, and Martinelli sang in honour of Nijinsky. Lifar danced the 'Blue Bird' *pas de deux* with Prudence Hyman, and 'L'Après-midi d'un faune'; Margot Fonteyn and Dolin danced the Aurora *pas de deux* from 'The Sleeping Beauty'; Maude Lloyd appeared in 'Le Bar aux Folies Bergère' and Mary Honer and Harold Turner in the *adagio* from 'Casse-noisette'; Molly Lake, Diana Gould, Prudence Hyman and Kathleen Crofton danced Keith Lester's 'Pas de Quatre'; and Lydia Sokolova and Dolin's young pupil

Belita Jepson-Turner also took part. Constant Lambert conducted. At the end of the programme Karsavina, who had flown from Budapest, spoke about Nijinsky: for Dolin this was 'the most beautiful moment of all'.[66] When expenses were paid, there was £2,500 for Nijinsky.[67] A trust fund was now set up, known as the Nijinsky Foundation, to which friends were invited to contribute for Nijinsky's treatment.

Shortly after the Gala Dolin was motoring through Europe and called on Vaslav and Romola at the Kreuzlingen Sanatorium. Nijinsky was on the lawn with some of the other residents. Dolin was expecting to find 'a gross, fat man', but he saw 'only a slim, middle-aged man resting in a chair, looking ahead with wandering but far from vacant eyes'. Although at first apprehensive, Nijinsky soon seemed at ease, appeared to understand all that was said and made occasional remarks. Dolin asked him: 'Why do you not dance? You are lazy. Dance for me.' His answer came slowly and not with great conviction. '*Non, non, je ne veux pas maintenant.*' Vaslav showed Dolin his room: there were no pictures because, Romola said, he would break them when he lost his temper.[68]

In November 1937 an exhibition of Vaslav's drawings, water colours and pastels was put on by the Group Theatre at the Storran Gallery off Piccadilly, in aid of the Nijinsky Foundation. Herbert Read wrote in the Catalogue that the drawings – the product of an 'alienated' mind – were, in common with the art of young children or primitive peoples, 'direct or automatic expressions of the unconscious. . . . But these drawings have a general characteristic which immediately suggests the fully conscious art of Nijinsky – his ballets. Their rhythm is a dancing rhythm.'[69]

The treatment began at Kreuzlingen in August 1938.[70]

Every morning [wrote Romola] Vaslav was given an insulin shock to provoke an epileptic fit. The treatment was a great strain on the heart and the whole constitution. Every day it was like a major operation. During the hours in which Vaslav was lying in deep coma provoked by the insulin shock, I suffered indescribable anguish. . . . But seemingly he stood the treatment well, and when he recovered consciousness he would answer quite clearly and logically questions put to him. This was already an improvement, as for years he had been mute. Dr Sakel explained to me that this treatment was, as it were, opening the way into a pit, but that the real work was to build the bridge with reality by which his inner self, so long buried, might be drawn back into the outer world. The breaking down of his passive resistance and the unifying of his split personality must be done by someone who was near and dear to him. Therefore, I undertook the task myself.

Every afternoon I tried to interest Vaslav in small and simple matters, things which were related to his art, his youth or his hobbies. At first, it was an extremely thankless task. His tendency was to withdraw into himself. But I insisted and forced him to try to be active. One had to draw his attention to something and then sustain it. It might be a rose in the garden, which I would show him and make him gather. Or I would encourage him to listen to the piano or to watch a game of tennis. Later on, I took him out for walks in the town. I would draw his attention to the children. Dogs and cats made him afraid.

Professor Bleuler, who had first diagnosed Vaslav's illness in 1919, and who had long since retired, now came to observe the treatment. The medical staff at Kreuzlingen were impressed that this famous old man who had invented the term 'schizophrenia' should pay them a visit. Romola had not seen him for twenty years.

He arrived early one morning and was present when the insulin shock was administered to Vaslav. Later in the day we were all invited to Dr Binswanger's private house for a luncheon party. Dr Binswanger, the head of the Sanatorium Bellevue, was once Bleuler's pupil, and was naturally pleased to see his former master. Dr Sakel also joined us.

It was then that Professor Bleuler said to me: 'My dear Madame Nijinsky, many years ago I had the cruel task of informing you that, according to medical knowledge as it then was, your husband was incurably insane. I am happy today to be able to give you hope. This young colleague of mine,' and he took Sakel's hand, 'has discovered a treatment for which I searched in vain for over forty years. I am proud of him. And of you, because you did not follow the advice I gave you so many years ago to divorce your husband. You stood by him during those years of mental dimness, you helped him through this terrible illness, and now I believe you will be rewarded. He will once more become himself.'

I turned away to hide my tears.

The treatment was interrupted for a period of two months to give Vaslav a rest; then, as Dr Sakel was moving to America, it was continued daily for three months in the State Asylum of the Canton Berne at Münsingen.

In the mornings, Vaslav was under the care of the doctors. The rest of the day I looked after him, following the instructions of Dr Sakel. Here Vaslav had far more freedom. Dr Müller, following Professor Bleuler, who believed in re-education, encouraged every attempt to lead him back to normal life and to make him dependent on himself. Upon Dr Müller's advice we made longer and longer visits to Berne. The improvement was slow but steady and distinct. We now even ventured to take Vaslav to public places, to restaurants, concerts and the theatre, where we saw a performance by Trudi Schoop, the Swiss character dancer.

So marked was the improvement in Vaslav's condition that Dr Müller allowed Romola to take him away to an hotel in the mountains in the hope that he would gradually adjust himself to normal. Romola's devotion was to some extent rewarded and her courage in deciding on the new treatment was justified.

For nearly a year we lived in a small hotel in the Bernese Oberland, once more in the high mountains. Again Vaslav saw the seasons passing in the Alps as he had done in St Moritz. The two places were very similar. Everything went even better than we had hoped, and we seriously began to consider making a home for ourselves in Switzerland.

In June 1939 Serge Lifar, who had arranged an exhibition at the Musée des Arts Décoratifs in the Louvre to commemorate the tenth anniversary of Diaghilev's death, and who was planning a gala performance to raise money for Vaslav's treatment, came to see them.

The last meeting of Lifar and Nijinsky had been when the photograph was taken on the stage of the Paris Opéra. Lifar found Vaslav fitter, more supple and more sociable.

His face had lost its hopelessly timid and downtrodden expression, and he would readily respond to a question or a command. He no longer tore his nails to the quick. The nervous movements of his hands had found quite a different mode of expression. They had something of the dance, of the genuine dance – very beautiful at times. He never ceased playing with his hands, and his movements – especially round his head – were reminiscent, every now and then, of the plastic of Siamese dancers. But gone was his sly and childlike smile, a smile of confidence and good-natured benevolence. Its place had been taken by a hoarse laugh, deep and convulsive, which shook his whole body and threw it into sharp and angular plastic poses. In these, too, something of the dance was subconsciously expressed.

When we entered his room Nijinsky was talking to himself. He is always talking to himself, in a language of his own, quite unintelligible to others – a mixture of the most unexpected combinations of Russian, French and Italian words.

I asked him, 'Do you remember Diaghilev, Vatza?' and Nijinsky instantly answered – his reflexes are exceedingly quick, much quicker than those of normal people – 'Remember . . . yes, yes, he . . . remarkable . . . how he . . .' and suddenly the hoarse, terrifying laugh convulsed his whole body, jerked it hysterically into sharp, angular contortions.

A *barre* had been installed in the room and Lifar exercised at it in front of Vaslav, who responded by nodding, tapping his foot and counting. When Lifar danced part of 'L'Après-midi d'un faune', Vaslav pushed him aside and corrected him. Other dances he applauded.[71] But when Lifar tried a bit of 'Le Spectre de la rose', as if in reaction to the *entrechats*, Nijinsky, without *préparation* or *plié*, rose from the floor in a high jump, laughing.[72] A photographer was present and recorded this unexpected though hoped-for feat.

Among those who took part in the Gala were the ex-Diaghilev dancers Nemchinova, Dolin, Lifar and Tcherkas, the Spaniard Escudero, the Indian Ram Gopal, and the Opéra artists Lorcia, Darsonval, Schwarz and Peretti. The Nijinsky Foundation benefited by 35,000 francs.[73]

Vaslav began to act and behave quite normally. The insulin shock had decidedly freed him from hallucinations. The only signs of his illness now were his great timidity and a tendency to silence. He very much disliked any attempt to engage him in conversation and got rather excited if anybody persevered. But as even in his youth he was inclined to be silent, the doctor thought it best not to worry about this.

It was only natural that while we were trying to reconstruct a new life among the ruins of our shattered past, we paid very little attention to the outside world and its happenings. When we were sitting on our terrace one day, basking in the sunshine and admiring the mighty peaks of the Alps, our attendant came in with a newspaper. He seemed rather excited. The Germans had concluded a treaty with Russia, he said. It was in August 1939, if I remember right. The Swiss in the village seemed to be disturbed about it. As the days passed, some of the visitors packed up hurriedly and left for their native countries, and there was a certain panic which seemed ridiculous in these calm majestic surroundings.

Vaslav rather enjoyed observing people. As a youth, he used to sit with Leon Bakst at the Café de la Paix watching the passers-by. Now we went every morning to the little bar in our hotel. There we sipped our orange juice, looking at the crowds drift in from their walks or the swimming pool before lunch. Beromünster, the Swiss wireless station, broadcast the latest news at noon. One day the chatter ceased and there was silence when it was announced that Germany had refused the plea that it should not occupy Danzig. . . .

Then suddenly, as out of the blue, Vaslav spoke.

'So once more they claim "Deutschland, Deutschland, über alles". This is the beginning of the second act!'

The Swiss hotels soon emptied, but Romola arranged with the proprietor of their own that they should stay on indefinitely. Vaslav's male attendant was called up, but Dr Müller undertook to send a qualified woman. This was not a success.

Vaslav did not need any physical care; he needed a companion when I was not present, a person who could also act as a valet, to help him dress and undress, to shave him, and to serve his meals. But most of all he needed somebody with authority whom he respected and who would be able to impose his will and restrain him if necessary. I believed that an able nurse could easily do this, but I was mistaken. Vaslav immediately became antagonistic and did everything in his power to scare the life out of one nurse after another. Being a superb actor and mime, he looked at them so frighteningly and with such powerfully gloomy expressions that they became convinced that their last moment had come. They did not dare to stay with him alone or touch him. So my hopes of help and assistance vanished, and my mischievous Vaslav attained his aim. He simply wanted me to look after him day and night; he wanted to be alone with me and to be once more the boss in his own home.

This was a natural and healthy reaction which delighted his physicians and me,

426

as it was a sign of great improvement. But it put a tremendous load on me, as the responsibility was overwhelming. I had to assure Vaslav's bodily safety; but I was also answerable for his conduct towards society. What this means even when you are the guardian of a normal being most people can imagine, but what it is when you have to look after a schizophrenic patient is quite another matter.

Dr Müller, whom I consulted over the telephone, advised me to discharge the nurses, who were only annoying Vaslav by their presence. He very reluctantly said that in the circumstances we would have to abandon for the present our plan of leaving Vaslav at liberty, as he doubted whether I could stand the physical strain of being with him constantly without rest. He felt we could not do anything but bring him back to the asylum until the war was over.

But I was determined not to give up and to try the impossible. So I gave notice to the nurse, who anyway was spending her days strolling in the mountains or reading novels in her room, and took up my duties alone.

At first Vaslav was sweet and docile. He sat quietly when I shaved him, he helped me to tidy the room before we left for our morning walks, he accompanied me when I went shopping, he held the wool when I was knitting; it seemed to be plain sailing. Dr Müller was delighted and congratulated me.

There were, however, more trials in store for the indomitable Romola.

Perhaps Vatza felt that life was too dull here at six thousand feet above sea level and that it was high time to have a little excitement. During one of our walks, when we were climbing, he pushed me unexpectedly and with great strength so that I lost the ground under my feet and landed on the slope. What would have happened to me if Vaslav had pushed me a few moments earlier when we were walking along the precipice God alone knows. Was his action premeditated, or just a sudden impulse, I wondered. I knew that Vaslav's character was gentleness itself; he was never deliberately unkind to anybody. But I knew also that the schizophrenic patient acted on sudden uncontrollable impulses. That was its danger and what I had to watch out for. Was it possible to control Vaslav or to influence him? To use force was out of the question. Even when in the beginning of his illness those brutal doctors and nurses had put him in straitjackets and iron beds, it needed four male nurses and injections to overpower him. And with what results? He became a human wreck. I was determined that as long as I lived, no matter what he did, this would never happen to him again. I decided not to mention to anybody what had occurred but to watch even more carefully.

At the time of the incident, I stood up and laughed, and patted my skirt clean. Vaslav joined me in giggling as I said, 'Oh how funny, Vatzinko,' and energetically linked my arm into his. He seemed taken aback. I felt that he was wondering how I had the impertinence not to be frightened of him. I understood now he was trying to scare me. I knew that I had to keep the upper hand or my game would be lost.

Many years ago Professor Bleuler had advised me that 'one should never lose one's nerve when a mental patient becomes agitated or violent; on the contrary, then one must show utter fearlessness.' Even in an asylum, in surroundings designed to cope with such cases, with few and light pieces of furniture, unbreakable windows and automatically closing doors, it is difficult to counter the patient's attack. How far more difficult it is with strangers around, in a hotel where every object might mean bodily harm to one, and not least to the patient himself.

Next day, when as usual I took the breakfast tray into Vatza's room, with one powerful drive he landed the tray on the floor. I was dripping with tea; the scrambled eggs and stewed fruit were all over the furniture, the carpet, everywhere. Vaslav sat up in bed looking at me triumphantly. I bent down to pick up the unbreakable plates and cups, which I was wise enough to use, and to clean up. But Vatza was determined to make a real show. He threw at me first a chair and then the marble cover of the little table next to his bed. When even this did not have the desired effect of making me panic-stricken and of leaving the battlefield to him, with a foreboding expression he made one of his famous *grands jetés* and landed beside me, towering over me with threatening gestures.

At this moment, Vaslav looked very much as Ivan the Terrible must have looked. I saw in his veiled misty eyes that he was beyond hearing or understanding me. He was wild with emotion. But I did not move. I stood steadfast, looking steadily into his eyes with an energetic commanding expression. Vaslav gazed back. A few moments passed; it seemed eternity. Then almost imperceptibly he backed away. It was only a fraction of an inch, but I noticed it. I had won. I knew it, and with great gentleness and firmness I said, 'Vatza, please sit down.' He did so.

After this Vaslav settled down, his hallucinations receded, he seemed at peace and he allowed Romola to guide him. She now came to the conclusion that it would be best for them to move to the United States, where she had many friends and could earn money, and where, in addition, Vaslav would be near Dr Sakel, who was practising there. She applied through her American lawyer and friend, Laurence Steinhardt, for a visitor's visa for Vaslav. Her own visa was valid for another year. While she was awaiting this, she heard from Philip Morrell, Lady Ottoline's husband, that currency regulations would prevent his sending any more payments from the Nijinsky Foundation from England. Romola realized that their hotel-keeper, who had already moved them into two small back rooms on the top floor, would turn them out the moment their bills were not paid, and the American visa became all the more essential.

At Easter 1940, to her delight, she received a cable saying that the visa was granted and instructing her to report to the American Consul in Zürich. Unfortunately the information that Nijinsky was to come to America was released to the Washington press, and it was published in the Swiss papers on the morning Romola visited the Consul. He was annoyed and refused to grant the visa, saying that after their year was up if the war was not over, Vaslav and Romola would apply for an extension, and then he would be blamed by his superiors. Romola cabled desperately to the United States.

But the phoney war was now at an end, and as Hitler's victorious armies spread through Europe Romola felt that before she could arrange for the American visa – *if* she could arrange for it – she and Vaslav would be trapped penniless in Switzerland. With their Nansen passports they could only live in or travel through neutral countries. Hungary seemed to be the only alternative. If Mussolini declared war on the Allies (which he was to do on 11 July 1940) the escape route through Italy and Yugoslavia to neutral Hungary would be closed. Romola was advised to make use of her American visa and to leave Vaslav in a Swiss State Asylum. But reluctant as she was to repeat the experiences of the last war and rely on the charity of her parents, she decided to go to Hungary. Rather than risk cancelling all the good Vaslav's treatment had done him, she renounced comfort and security for herself in America and resolved to stay beside him. This was perhaps her most unselfish and heroic decision.

So on a hot July day, after a long, exhausting journey, Nijinsky and his wife returned to the city where she had first seen him dance in spring 1912.

'Crossing the Danube we saw the outstanding landmarks basking in the blazing sunshine; the chain of mountains encircling the city, the Royal Palace raised upon the hill which dominates the town, the Parliament, old Buda, the Island of St-Marguerite; sights once so familiar to us.'

From the start Romola felt they were unwelcome to her parents. In her book she had, after all, shown her mother in an unsympathetic light. Nobody came to meet the Nijinskys at the station, and when Romola rang up her home from the Ritz Hotel she was told Emilia Markus and Pardany were out of town. Vaslav, noticing Romola's embarrassment, said kindly, 'Don't worry. They did not receive your message in time.' Eventually Romola's parents, caring less, she thought, about being hospitable than for public opinion, came to the hotel and invited them to stay. The Nijinskys were installed once more in the same second-floor suite in the big house in the hilly suburbs that they had occupied in the first war.

Romola still hoped that the American visa might come through and that she and Vaslav might be able to travel through Yugoslavia to Greece and get a cargo-boat to the United States, but, as the weeks passed and she heard of the difficulties her lawyer was encountering, she gradually gave up hope. The Nijinskys resigned themselves to remaining in Hungary.

My family [wrote Romola] did not make life easy for us. They looked on Vaslav with mistrust. Nobody could have been more docile, quiet and good-natured than he was. Nevertheless, he could not disarm them. I was deeply worried, realizing the great mistake I had made in bringing him to my family's home where he had suffered so deeply in the past. It was an error with far-reaching consequences to place him here in this antagonistic atmosphere, charged with discord and suspicion, especially after the insulin shock treatment. Vaslav needed now to be surrounded with sympathetic understanding and kindly people. He was timid, like a child making his first contacts with life and society; he had to readjust himself to reality and his fellow human beings.

In March 1941 Yugoslavia broke off relations with Hitler and German troops poured through Budapest: within a month they would have penetrated to Greece. With Hungary completely dominated by the Germans and virtually ruled by the German Ambassador, Romola had cause to fear for Vaslav's life: the Germans exterminated mental patients. Hungary was still not at war with Russia, and Romola visited the Russian Consul in the hopes of getting visas to travel through Russia to America. But in June, Germany invaded Russia. Romola and Vaslav were in the town when she heard the news.

I stood rooted to the spot [she wrote]. Once more we would be prisoners of war. 'Roma, why are you so silent, what is the matter? What is worrying you?' asked Vaslav. I remembered the advice Professor Bleuler had given me years ago, that one must tell the truth and tell it gently. So I said 'The German Army has attacked Russia. If Hungary sides with Germany, we must face the fact that perhaps we may be interned again. Don't be frightened, we are together.'

To earn some money Romola began to write articles on art, but she was obliged to prove she was 'a pure Aryan' to the Literary Council before she was allowed to publish them. She also prepared a Hungarian edition of Nijinsky's diary.

In December 1941, after Pearl Harbor, Hungary declared war on Great Britain and the United States. When the consulates of those two countries began to pack up Romola begged them to take Vaslav and herself with them, but this they were unable to do. Romola's parents now asked her to leave. Her stepfather, being a Jew, though converted, was in danger, and Emilia was hiding other Jews in the house. The ground the family house was built on had been bought in Romola's childhood with money left her by her father, and she refused to budge. However, Vaslav was very susceptible to the unpleasant atmosphere and Romola began to look for somewhere else to live. Through her cousin, Paul von Bohus, she took a cottage in the country near Lake Balaton and for some months she and Vaslav enjoyed a peaceful existence, bathing and making excursions. Then, one day they had a visit from the local police, who searched them and clearly suspected they were Russian agents. They decided to return to Budapest.

Romola rented a small house on Svabhegy, a hill near the capital, and they moved in together with Brindus, a good-natured peasant who had been engaged to look after Vaslav, and who became devoted to him. The

Literary Council now withdrew Romola's permit to publish articles. In order to keep Vaslav clothed and fed and to provide fuel for his room, Romola would stop at nothing. She made a list of rich and distinguished people and went from door to door begging them to buy copies of the Hungarian edition of Vaslav's diary. One happy result of this humiliating and selfless task was that she met and made friends with Mr Quand, the General Manager of the National Bank of Hungary, who was able to help her financially in the following years.

All the time she was caring for and providing for her husband, Romola kept to herself her fears that he might be arrested as a Russian or exterminated as mentally sick. What burdens she had to bear! Wilhelm Furtwängler arrived from Germany to give a concert; and he terrified Romola by his description of trains filled with inmates of mental homes on their way to be put to death. She made frantic but vain efforts to have Vaslav sent to Switzerland.

In February 1943 the Nijinskys gave shelter to a young Hungarian officer who had walked two thousand miles from Stalingrad. From his description of Russian endurance and the plight of the German Army, they were more convinced than ever that an Allied victory was only a question of time. But as the German Army retreated, the German grip on Hungary tightened. All the able-bodied were called up, Brindus included; transport and fuel grew scarce and Jews had to wear large yellow stars. In April Romola went in the middle of a Russian air-raid to the Palace to see a relation of hers who was a Marshal of the Court, begging for a safe conduct to Switzerland. She was told that the Regent was powerless to help her, being entirely in the hands of the Germans, but received the following advice: 'Get some papers of some deceased relative whose age is about the same as Vaslav's (your Abbé can do that for you), and go towards the Austrian border, towards the lion's den. There you will be safer, there the control of the Gestapo is less severe. Don't go towards the East or Yugoslavia, it would be too dangerous. We Hungarians will shut our eyes.' Romola secured the papers.

Cousin Paul had found an inn in a forest near Sopron, a town on the Austrian border on the shores of Lake Neusiedler, whose proprietor specialized in hiding people and made good money out of it. Here the Nijinskys enjoyed their walks in the pretty country, and Vaslav learned some dances from their gypsy maid. In August 1944 the Russians entered Roumania and it was clear they would soon be in Hungary. People began pouring eastward through the town. On 15 October Admiral Horthy broadcast that Hungary had lost the war and must capitulate; but he was arrested and replaced by Szalassy, the head of the Hungarian Nazi Party.

For fear of being recognized, Romola and Paul decided that another move was essential, and they found lodgings in a nearby villa with a retired opera singer who was afraid of having her house requisitioned. Housework, fetching coal, picking up wood in the forest, and cooking occupied Romola's days. She was once more running out of money, and she decided to go to Budapest and sell some gold objects. As she could not leave Vaslav unattended she reluctantly placed him in a hospital in Sopron which had a department dealing with nervous diseases. When she broke the news to him of the arrangement she had made, he wept.

In spite of constant air-raids Romola was successful in Budapest and returned in a train crowded with fugitives, passing on the way sealed trucks bound for Auschwitz. Back at the inn, she and Vaslav and a group of friends would listen to the 'Voice of America' programme on the radio.

One snowy morning Romola was in the town seeing about a permit for fuel when there was a heavy American air-raid. It was evening before she could leave the shelter, and on her return home she found Vaslav in a roofless room, covered in dust. 'He just gazed steadfastly and silently at me.' Poor Romola took him back to the hospital, so that he should at least have a roof over his head and be near a shelter. The Hungarian Government arrived in Sopron. Now not only Jews but gypsies were to be put in concentration camps. The Nijinskys' maid came to say goodbye. Between air-raids Romola would run out to see if the hospital had been hit.

On 12 March 1945 Romola was hanging out washing when the house was shaken by tremendous explosions. It was an air attack on Vienna, seventy-five kilometres away.

Towards evening [wrote Romola] it began to snow heavily, and there was an uncanny stillness. We were sitting at supper when suddenly we heard knocking at the front door. I went out to see who it was and as I opened the door there stood Vaslav in his old grey winter coat, wearing his little Tyrolean hat and carrying a bundle in which his clothes and belongings were wrapped. Next to him stood the Polish attendant, Stan. 'Vaslav, my dearest, I am very happy that you are here,' I said, and I kissed him and escorted him to the table.

Stan informed us later, 'I had to bring Mr Nijinsky home, even if the danger of bombing is greater here. We have received orders to exterminate our mental patients by tomorrow morning.'

One afternoon Russian bombers were overhead and a bomb fell in the front garden. At two in the morning distant firing was heard. Romola woke Vaslav and together they ran into the woods. There was a full moon. Planes flew over and bombs began to fall. Romola put a plaid rug over Vaslav's head and prayed that he should not be killed by his own countrymen. 'But Vaslav pushed the rug back; kneeling with outstretched arms, he looked up at the bright sky with its circling Russian planes.'

Now for several days Romola and Vaslav hid in some caves in a nearby hill. There were two thousand others with them, including Cousin Paul, who had measles. This was the most sordid of all their experiences, yet Vaslav endured it. The Russian word for God is 'Bog' but Vaslav had a nickname for Him. Romola could reassure him by saying 'Bundenka is here with us.' Then he would grow calm.

In the early hours of Easter Sunday they thought the Germans must be gone for good and that there would be no more bombing, so they made for the villa.

Once installed at home, Vaslav fell asleep. The others tried to clean themselves while Paul went to bed with his measles, useless and helpless.

In the valley we could see the Soviet troops streaming towards the west like the advance of Genghis Khan, a most gruesome and magnificent sight. Thousands and thousands of tanks, heavy guns and cavalry, covered by hundreds of planes, rolled along through the green smiling spring countryside.

Within a few hours the town was occupied, the forest and all the houses were invaded. The Russian soldiers came into the houses in small groups.

Our gates were broken down and three tall young Russians carrying automatic machine-guns entered our house.

'Nemetski, Nemetski!' [Germans, Germans] they shouted loudly.

In a moment everybody in the house fled, panic-stricken, behind curtains and beds. Only Vaslav remained quietly lying on his couch while I stood beside him. The Russians shouted at me. 'Nazi?'

Vaslav, unexpectedly shouting still louder, replied in Russian. 'Keep quiet!'

The soldiers stood dumbfounded and lowered their automatics. 'A Russian? How does he come here? Is he a prisoner?'

'Yes, he is my husband, an artist.' I did not know that I had pronounced a magic word.

Next morning Romola was summoned before the Russian Commanding Officer, who was no less astounded to hear that she was the wife of the great dancer than that she had had to look after her sick husband for so long without aid from any government. He gave her some official papers.

Every house filled up with Russians and a friendly officer was billeted on the Nijinskys. Romola began to notice a change in her husband.

Vaslav used to stroll around the garden and lie in his garden chair, watching and wondering what was going on. He never asked any questions, just listened and listened, but his eyes became more and more attentive. They were not so dreamy and distant as they had been during the last twenty-six years. It seemed almost as if he were awakening from a long and deep sleep. Shyly, more and more, he approached the soldiers and sat down among them. It seemed that some inward barrier broke down and he seemed to melt towards the outside world. In the

433

evenings, he stood and listened to the plaintive, nostalgic sound of the balalaika for a long time.

For the first time since 1919 people did not stare at him, did not shrink from him because he had suffered from a mental illness. They spoke to him in the same nonchalant manner as they did to us.

At first I warned them: 'Leave Vaslav Fomitch alone, don't talk to him. He might get annoyed and impatient, he is afraid.'

But they just laughed. 'He won't be afraid of us,' they said. 'Let him alone to do what he wants.'

Romola began to wonder if by treating Vaslav as different from other people she and the doctors had made a mistake. She thought it probable that if she had been able to take him to Russia when he had first become disturbed, he would never have been seriously ill. The simple Russian soldiers had a better way with him than any doctor or nurse. Vaslav grew easier in his manner and spoke more. One evening, when the soldiers were singing and dancing, he suddenly stood up, jumped into the middle of them and began to dance. From then on the soldiers took to bringing him presents of food and clothes.

On the night of 5 May Romola was woken by the Russian officer, who said 'Go to Vaslav Fomitch and explain to him why all our planes are in the air; he might get frightened. We are going to fire all our guns. We are celebrating. The war is over.'

Even though Vienna was in ruins Romola felt that it must be the first stage of their westward journey. She and Paul got a lift to the city to reconnoitre the position. All the bigger hotels were taken over by the Russian Army, but the resourceful Paul forced his way into Sacher's, which was barred and bolted. The manager, who was sheltering a few old and distinguished customers, was trying to give the impression that the place was uninhabitable, but at the magic name of Nijinsky he opened his doors. With immense difficulty Romola and Paul returned to Sopron and fetched Vaslav to Vienna. In June 1945 they were installed in a palatial suite of rooms, with fine china and linen: but food was scarce and only available on the black market. Shortly afterwards Sacher's was requisitioned by the Russians. The Nijinskys were, however, allowed to stay on and after that Romola only had to take her place in the line of soldiers to be served plentiful meals.

In August the Russians allowed the Americans, British and French into Vienna, and the city was divided into zones. Russian headquarters was at the Hofburg, the Royal Palace in the heart of the city, the British at Schönbrunn Palace in the suburbs. Sacher's now passed into British hands, but the Nijinskys were again given permission to stay until they could make other arrangements.

There now came into their lives an Englishwoman who would prove a precious friend to them. Margaret Power, a widow of thirty-seven, was a passionate lover of ballet, besides being the most generous and warm-hearted of women. She had worked in the Foreign Office and in 1945 was posted to the Allied Commission in Austria. Before she left London, Cyril Beaumont had told her that she should try to find the Nijinskys as there was some money in the Nijinsky fund which they probably needed. One day in August Mrs Power made up a little parcel and set off from Schönbrunn to seek them out. She did not know they were at Sacher's, but remembered from before the war that the hall-porter there was supposed to know everything that went on in Vienna. She was amazed when he said 'They are upstairs. Where else in Vienna would they be?' Romola received the uniformed stranger with some reserve, but soon after Margaret's return to Schönbrunn telephoned to say how touched she had been by the contents of the parcel – tea, biscuits, chocolate and toothpaste – which only an Englishwoman would have been so thoughtful as to put together.

After that, Margaret returned often and was thrilled to meet Nijinsky, whom she found very silent.

One September evening [she recalled] we were sitting in the salon, Vaslav was in an armchair and Romola and I were going through some correspondence, when the lights failed. This often happened at that time; the Russians controlled the only power station and were not very good at maintenance. It was pitch dark as the curtains were drawn. Romola told me to sit quite still while she went to get a candle. She said a couple of words to Vaslav in Russian and found her way to the door. Suddenly I heard a movement, and a hand reached out and touched me on the arm. Vaslav said something soothing and gentle which I did not understand. He passed in front of me and sat on the sofa, taking my hand and patting it. And so we sat in the dark for a few moments until Romola came back with the servant, both carrying lighted candles. I said, 'M.Nijinsky has been taking care of me', and she replied 'He likes you very much. He calls you the English lady soldier.' At this I looked directly at Vaslav, meeting his eyes, which I had never dared to do before, and he smiled at me, murmuring something and again patting my hand before letting it go. We remained on patting terms for a long time after that, but we never had any conversation at any time. I used to chatter to him in French or English, but he never answered. I fell in love with him in Vienna and have remained so ever since.[74]

One winter day Romola and Vaslav were overtaken by a snowstorm in the Imperial Gardens and took refuge in the Hofburg where the collection of the Vienna picture gallery was on exhibition. Vaslav ran up the steps as if he felt at home, and Romola thought it must have reminded him of his visits to the Hermitage with his mother when he was a boy. He had not been inside a museum or picture gallery for twenty-six years, but he identified many of the paintings, naming Velasquez, Raphael and other artists. On Sundays, in the Hofkapelle, when he heard Masses by Haydn, Mozart or Schubert, superbly sung by soloists from the Opera and by the Vienna Boys Choir, Vaslav's face wore 'an expression of ecstasy'. He and Romola also went to a performance of 'The Queen of Spades'.

The Russians began to woo the Nijinskys, hoping that Vaslav would return to his own country. One evening a performance was given in his honour. Romola had expected opera but it was the ballet – his own old company – from Leningrad, who had carried on the traditions in which Vaslav had been brought up so many years ago. They danced 'Casse-noisette', a *divertissement* and Fokine's 'Les Sylphides'. Nijinsky 'clutched his hands and followed each step with a perceptible movement of his body'. Chabukiani, Sergeyev and the soulful Ulanova were dancing. Vaslav applauded 'with the abandon of a young enthusiastic student'. Next day, visiting Ulanova at her hotel, he was received with armfuls of roses.

In March 1946, in answer to a letter from Margaret Power, Anton Dolin wrote from Seattle that he had set aside $400 for the Nijinskys and asked if Margaret could find a way of paying them the equivalent. During the year he persevered in collecting further sums of money for them in America, just as he had done in England before the war.

The British were anxious to have Sacher's Hotel to themselves and Romola thought she ought to get Vaslav to the country, as to be continually surrounded by soldiers depressed him. Colonel Yarborough, the American Provost Marshal, offered a pass to the American Zone and arranged for Romola to inspect certain castles which were in the custody of the military authorities. So it was that in July 1946, after an anxious moment at the check-point between the Russian and American Zones, Romola brought Vaslav first for a few days to Salzburg, then to the romantic castle of Mittersill, perched high on a mountainside between Kitzbühel and Zell-am-See. Only now, though the war in Europe had ended more than a year before, could they at last feel that their wartime wandering and privations were really over.

Vaslav's rooms were on the ground floor opening on to the inner courtyard and with windows overlooking the Alps and the Salzach valley. He wandered freely about the ramparts and garden. Women came from the village to work in exchange for food, not wages; and thanks to American, French and British visitors who began to arrive at the castle, food was never scarce. The village priest celebrated Mass in the castle chapel. Margaret Power came from Vienna and played table tennis with Vaslav. 'Sometimes,' she remembered, 'he would kiss my cheek, always quite unexpectedly – not in greeting or farewell, but just out of affection.'[75]

As one season followed another [wrote Romola], we became so used to this romantic life, and so fond of the place, that we had almost forgotten the past. Once more Vaslav was free to go wherever he liked. For hours he sat in the park or in the courtyard, and we were not obliged to follow or watch him. This was the best thing that could happen to him. For years in the nursing home, he had been watched day and night. Through this constant observation he became very dependent on his companions. Later, during the war, I had to be with him constantly, trying to avert all disagreeable incidents or dangers. Now I was anxious that he should become more and more independent and therefore I let him alone. After a few months my method brought its result. Vaslav, who during the last twenty-seven years had lost the habit of expressing his desires, now very definitely began to say what he wanted or did not want.

During the winter of 1946–7 and again during the summer Romola made trips to Paris and London, where to her great relief, as her father had been born in Highgate and his birth duly registered at Somerset House, the Foreign Office were able to grant her a British passport. With the aid of Duff Cooper, the British Ambassador in Paris, she was successful in obtaining permission for Vaslav to live in England, and procured transit visas for the journey across France. She also arranged for a check-up of Vaslav's physical condition with Dr Rohr, his old doctor in Zürich. This took place in November 1947, and a diet was prescribed for his high blood-pressure.

The Nijinskys and Paul travelled straight from Switzerland to Calais, had a rough crossing to Dover – with Vaslav, the only one who did not feel sea-sick, waiting on Romola and Paul for a change – and motored to London through a dense fog.

They spent a few days in London. Romola felt that Vaslav was not fully aware that thirty-five years had passed since he was there last. He only knew he had been happy and successful there and people had been good to him, so he was delighted to be back. In the few years that remained the English authorities behaved considerately and Romola thought that 'Vaslav at last found a real asylum and complete freedom. Nobody ever worried him. The people who came in contact with him treated him as they would have done if he had never been mentally ill, and he responded with normal behaviour. During his entire stay in England he never became excited or upset.'

Alexander Korda, an old friend of Romola's in Budapest days, had made arrangements for them to stay at Great Fosters, a luxurious hotel near Egham in Surrey, just over a mile east of where the London–Exeter road skirts Virginia Water. It was a pretty, late-Elizabethan brick house and they spent Christmas there, very quietly. The rest of the winter passed peacefully, with

437

card-games or chess, walking and going to the local cinema. One film which Vaslav adored was Korda's production of Wilde's *An Ideal Husband*. He admired the Technicolor, which he had never seen before, fell in love with Paulette Goddard, and had to see the film through twice. Romola wrote to Miss Goddard, who sent Vaslav signed photographs.

Tamara Karsavina and Nadia Nicolaevna Legat, second wife and widow of Vaslav's old teacher, who had a ballet school in Kent, came to visit them. He took pleasure in talking to Mme Legat about the Imperial School and the Mariinsky Theatre.

In the spring of 1948 Romola found a small house called Whinmead at Virginia Water on the edge of Windsor Great Park. Vaslav enjoyed driving and walking in the Park or sitting in the garden. Romola sometimes took him to London and to the theatre. He saw the Indian dances of Ram Gopal, with whom he felt a close affinity, and applauded the lithe young Mexican Luisillo, who appeared with Carmen Amaya's Flamenco troupe at the Prince's (now Shaftesbury) Theatre.*

The fall of a horseshoe which was nailed over the front door of Whinmead heralded a run of bad luck. Romola fell and tore a ligament. She was laid up for eight weeks, and her illness made Vaslav restless and nervous. 'He took my foot in his hands and was full of attention.' Then Vaslav's attendant, whom he liked, gave notice, and it was hard to replace him. Alexander Korda had been going to make a film based on a story of Romola's and he had promised to get the Nijinskys to America. Now he decided he could not produce the picture and Romola was struck off the pay-roll.

Vaslav sat to a young Polish sculptor who, besides making a bust of him, took a cast of his foot. With Romola he visited the Legat School at Tunbridge Wells and stood godfather to the daughter of a young dancer. Margaret Power came sometimes to sit with him when Romola had to go out. He took up his drawing again. It was a quiet life, and Romola felt when she came into the room and he looked up at her and smiled 'with such charm and tenderness' that she was married to a rare spirit and all her struggles and sufferings had been worthwhile. 'It gave me the most perfect happiness to sit quietly in the same room with him. One felt protected, content in his presence, he emanated so much tenderness and goodness.'

Romola noticed that on his walks Vaslav would often hold his hand over the small of his back. This the local doctor, Dr Wilson, thought must be due to a nerve pain. He never complained of his health except of an occasional headache. But in the autumn of 1949 he had alarming attacks of

---

* It was on his visit to the Prince's that I saw Nijinsky for the only time, seated in a box to the left of the stage. Leon Hepner, the impresario, asked me to meet him, but I was too shy.

hiccups. Romola took him to London to Professor Plesch, a celebrated German physician, then retired, who diagnosed kidney trouble and ordered a stricter diet.

On Christmas Day Romola received news of her mother's death at the age of eighty-nine. Then the lease of their Virginia Water house was due to expire at the end of January and the landlord refused to renew it. On the 30th Romola had still not found another house, and as she packed Vaslav said 'Kak Tsigane! [Like Gypsies]' They returned for a few days to Great Fosters. 'Then,' wrote Romola, 'out of the blue, a perfect stranger, a Major Wright, who had heard of our predicament through some estate agent, called me up, saying, "I have a house near the sea, not far from Arundel. It has central heating. It is small, but very pleasant in the spring. I would be glad to lend it to Mr Nijinsky." ' It was too good to be true, and the offer was gratefully accepted. They motored down to Rustington in Sussex in a howling gale. Moving always made Vaslav nervous, but after a few days he settled down, and when the weather improved went for walks in the Duke of Norfolk's park at Arundel Castle. They were only a few miles from where Romola had stayed and studied with Miss Johnson as a girl. However, Nijinsky seemed to enjoy his walks less than he used to; his face was sometimes flushed and he would take any opportunity to sit down.

Serge Lifar telephoned from Paris to discuss a gala he was planning for June at which he hoped the Nijinskys would be present. This suited them quite well as Romola planned to take Vaslav to see a specialist in Switzerland in the summer. Lifar also said he was coming over with some artists of the Paris Opéra to televise, and would arrive on 2 April. Romola arranged to go up to London with Vaslav to see them. She went ahead to greet Lifar at the airport and on the afternoon of Sunday, 2 April, met Vaslav at Waterloo Station. He waved to her gaily from the train. They stayed at the Welbeck Hotel, where Lifar and his friend Jean Beau visited them. The BBC invited them to watch a rehearsal of the French dancers on the Tuesday.

That morning Vaslav complained of a headache, but wanted to go out. Romola took him round the corner to the Wallace Collection. He looked at the pictures carefully and stood for a long time before Lancret's painting of Camargo. At lunch he was in a good humour and signed some photographs.

We spent the entire afternoon at the Alexandra Palace watching the rehearsal of the Paris Opera Ballet. It all interested Vaslav immensely; he always adored mechanical inventions. Near him the chief engineer had placed a television set on which he could watch the performance while at the same time watching the dancing on the stage.

He was very much taken with Nina Vyroubova, whom he had seen dancing in Roland Petit's version of the old Taglioni ballet 'La Sylphide', a few months before, and who had now joined the Opera Ballet.

Her dancing enchanted Vaslav, who smiled at her all the time.

The rehearsal was interrupted by the tea which Mr Norman Collins, then Director of Television for the BBC, offered us. Serge and a few officials of the company were present. Vaslav seemed cheerful and happy.

When we returned home that evening, Vatza retired at once and had a light supper. He closed his eyes and did not wish to talk to us. Suddenly I noticed that he clutched his hands, and then, with the fingers of one hand, he tapped some dance movements as he used to do many years ago when he was composing and concentrating on new choreography. How strange, I thought. Then with his left arm he began to make *port de bras* round his head as he used to do while dancing the 'Spectre de la rose'.

On the Wednesday morning Romola felt anxious about Vaslav's condition and decided to consult her doctor.

I called him around ten o'clock and asked him to come at once. He was unable to do so. Vaslav had no temperature, but he refused to eat and lay limply on his bed. His pulse was slightly faster than usual. I began to telephone around to acquaintances in an effort to find a reliable doctor. It was already around three in the afternoon. Finally a very good Hungarian doctor was recommended to me. He had been practising in Germany and London lately. I called him and asked him to come at once, and he soon arrived.

He was alarmed by Vaslav's high blood pressure and took a blood test. He told me that until he got the report from the tests, he would be unable to begin any treatment as he might give the wrong medicine. He was not sure what had caused Vaslav's condition, and said, 'If he is suffering from arteriosclerosis, then he will need just a few injections. But if this is not the case, and he is suffering from the kidneys, we will be facing a far more difficult task.'

I begged him to do something at once, but he said he could not. I began to lose faith in all these doctors and phoned to Zürich, but Professor Rohr did not answer. I wired him. The hours passed. Vaslav was lying listlessly while I frantically telephoned around for medical help.

. . . The Hungarian doctor returned* and said the report was worse than he had anticipated. We decided that Vaslav should be taken next day to a clinic where treatment would be given. The doctor instructed me to dress Vatza the next morning and take him by taxi. He wished to avoid an ambulance so as not to alarm Vatza. . . .

I still did not realize that Vaslav's life might be in danger. Tremblingly I went to his room. He was sitting up in bed . . . and looking at the illustrated papers, smiling and interested. The attendant and I were quite relieved. But he had a bad night and was restless in the morning. His face became small and flushed and he

* The order of events in Nijinsky's final illness is slightly confused in Romola Nijinsky's *The Last Days of Nijinsky*. With her help Mme Nijinsky's account has been re-arranged here.

440

did not react to any of our questioning. He seemed dazed. We were unspeakably worried and summoned an ambulance. Never shall I forget how we took him to the clinic, wrapped up in blankets looking like a new-born baby, listless and helpless.

Throughout Thursday Romola tried to get help from Zürich. She was told that Professor Rohr had left for his Easter vacation and no one knew where he was. 'As I had the utmost confidence in him, I tried to persuade a Swiss broadcasting station to broadcast an announcement that Professor Rohr was requested to fly to London. But my call was in vain.'

During the night a priest came, but Romola would not allow him near Vaslav, in case he should realize he was dying. The next morning – Good Friday – Nijinsky lapsed into a coma. The doctors began to treat him with streptomycin and told Romola that if they could bring him out of the coma within twenty-four hours his life would be saved. Romola called in another consultant who said that Vaslav was 'beyond human help. His kidneys were gone.'

Romola was in a state of shock.

I stood by Vatza's bed while the attendant held his left hand which was bandaged and through which food and medicines were constantly administered intravenously. But he was quite unconscious. His eyes were closed all the time. . . . Vaslav moaned constantly and with his free hand he was wiping his face. The night passed. I was trembling. The anguish I felt was inexpressible.

There was a gradual improvement and on the Saturday morning he was better. 'The streptomycin had begun to act. He was coming out of the coma and understood what was going on around him. We all should be careful what we said. . . . He opened his eyes. They were clear and lovely. He looked at me with a tender, loving gaze.' Vaslav was able to sit up, looking bright, and his attendant spoon-fed him his breakfast. Everyone felt optimistic, and the doctor now said there was hope of curing the disease. But as Romola was talking in another room to the head nurse, Nijinsky's Swiss attendant, Schneider, called her. Nijinsky had fallen back against the pillow: his expression had changed. Suddenly he sat bolt upright and said '*Mamasha*'.

I don't know if he called his mother or me. And then he stretched out his right hand to me. I bent down and kissed it. . . .

I ordered the nurses to give him an injection, some oxygen. Vatza sighed just once. The sun beamed through the window. The nurses stood helpless, while the attendant laid Vatza back. His eyes and mouth closed.

Thoughts and feelings were racing in my mind, but the enduring thought was: 'You were privileged among so many millions of women to share his life, to serve him. God gave him to you. He has taken him back.'

Nijinsky 1917–1950

Thus Vaslav Nijinsky died in the presence of the woman who had been for thirty-seven years his wife and for thirty his breadwinner, nurse and second mother.

It was Holy Saturday, 8 April 1950. I was at a matinée of ballet at Sadler's Wells, sitting next to Lincoln Kirstein, the Director of the New York City Ballet, who had helped Romola in 1932 with the book which had changed my life; for I had now for several years been editing the magazine *Ballet*, which I founded, and was the ballet critic of the *Observer*. In the first interval an attendant told me I was wanted on the telephone. An editor of my newspaper said Nijinsky was dead and that I must quickly produce an obituary for Sunday's paper. I went backstage and was allowed to write and telephone in Ninette de Valois' office. It occurred to me that neither I, nor Lincoln Kirstein, nor Ninette de Valois would be where we were or doing what we were if it had not been for Diaghilev and Nijinsky; nor would the Sadler's Wells Ballet (the second of the two companies) be performing in this theatre, nor would the New York City Ballet, under Balanchine, shortly be making their first appearance at Covent Garden.

On the evening of Wednesday, 12 April, I was at Covent Garden, when Margaret Power, whom I knew then very slightly, came during an interval to tell me that Romola Nijinsky was rather upset as no one connected with the English Ballet had offered to be pall-bearers at Nijinsky's funeral in two days' time. I told her to reassure Mme Nijinsky, because it would never enter an Englishman's head to *offer* to be a pall-bearer; and I promised to arrange matters.

The funeral Mass was held at St James's, Spanish Place, behind the Wallace Collection, on Friday, 14 April. Besides Romola Nijinsky, a number of old colleagues – Tamara Karsavina, Marie Rambert and Lydia Sokolova – were present. The pall-bearers, paired off according to size, with the shortest in front, were Serge Lifar and Anton Dolin; Frederick Ashton and myself; Michael Somes and Cyril Beaumont. Of these only Beaumont had seen Nijinsky in his glory. He confessed afterwards that he had found the weight of the coffin almost intolerable. We slid the coffin into the hearse. Ashton and I did not go to the cemetery.

Two cars followed the coffin: in the first Romola, Karsavina, Dolin, Lifar and Beaumont; in the second, Marie Rambert, Frances James (formerly one of her dancers), Margaret Power and Rupert Doone, a member of the Diaghilev Ballet in later years, and a pioneer of ballet in England. The burial took place at the St Marylebone Cemetery in the Finchley Road. Afterwards, as the mourners moved away, Beaumont looked back to see a new figure standing by the grave. It was the Hindu dancer, Ram Gopal.

But Nijinsky was not to be allowed to rest in peace. *Kak Tsigane.* In June 1953 Lifar arranged for his body to be moved to Paris so that he should lie in the Montmartre Cemetery near Auguste Vestris, where Lifar intended to be buried himself. After disinterment, the coffin was taken to a chapel in the Marylebone Road, where regulations obliged that it should be opened to make sure the body was inside. The inner lead coffin was then placed in a new wooden one and this was conveyed to Victoria Station, where Nadia Legat brought a party of her pupils to adorn it with flowers. Margaret Power accompanied it. The second funeral service was held at about ten in the morning at the Russian Church in the rue Daru. Bronislava Nijinska had insisted that Vaslav be buried with the Russian Orthodox rites. Romola was in America and could not afford to come: Preobrajenskaya and Egorova were present, as well as Lifar and many dancers and singers of the Opéra. The Administrator and the Minister of Fine Arts made speeches.[76] This took place on 16 June 1953, just two weeks after the Coronation of Queen Elizabeth II.

Nijinsky's life can be simply summarized: ten years growing; ten years learning; ten years dancing; thirty years in eclipse. Roughly sixty in all. How long his memory will live in the minds of men we can only guess. As Sir Thomas Browne wrote, 'What song the sirens sang or what name Achilles assumed when he hid himself among women, although puzzling questions are not beyond all conjecture.'

BIBLIOGRAPHY

Agate, James. *Ego*, Vol. III. Harrap, London, 1938.

Alexander Mikhailovitch, Grand Duke. *Once a Grand Duke*. Farrar and Rinehart, New York; Cassell, London, 1932.

Astruc, Gabriel. *Le Pavillon des fantômes*. Grasset, Paris, 1929.

— 'Le Premier Feu d'Artifice' in *Revue Musicale*, 1 December, 1930 (Paris).

Barbier, George and Miomandre, Francis de. *Nijinsky*. Bernouard, Paris, 1912.

Beaumont, Cyril. *The Ballet called Giselle*. Beaumont, London, 1944.

— *The Complete Book of Ballets*. Putnam, London, 1937. Revised 1949, 1951.

— *The Diaghilev Ballet in London*. Putnam, London, 1940. [Beaumont: *London*.]

— *Michel Fokine and his Ballets*. Beaumont, London, 1935.

— *The Romantic Ballet as seen by Théophile Gautier*. Beaumont, London, 1932.

— *Vaslav Nijinsky*. Beaumont, London, 1932.

Bedells, Phyllis. *My Dancing Days*. Phoenix House, London, 1954.

Benois, Alexandre. *Early Memories of Diaghilev*, introduction to the catalogue of the Diaghilev Exhibition, 1954.

— *Memoirs*, Vol. II. Translated by Moura Budberg. Chatto and Windus, London, 1964.

— *Reminiscences of the Russian Ballet*. Translated by Mary Britnieva. Putnam, London, 1941.

Blanche, Jacques-Emile. *Portraits of a Lifetime*. Dent, London, 1937.

Bourman, Anatole (with D. Lyman). *The Tragedy of Nijinsky*. Robert Hale, London, 1937.

Braun, Edward. *Meyerhold on Theatre*. Methuen, London, 1969.

Buckle, Richard. *In Search of Diaghilev*. Sidgwick and Jackson, London, 1955.

Calvocoressi, M.D. *Music and Ballet*. Faber and Faber, London, 1938.

Carter, Huntley. *The New Spirit in Drama and Art*. Frank Palmer, London, 1912.

Chaplin, Charles. *My Autobiography*. The Bodley Head, London, 1964.

Bibliography

Chujoy, Anatole, 'Russian Balletomania' in *Dance Index*, Vol. VII, no.3, March 1948 (New York).

Clarke, Mary. *Dancers of Mercury*. A.& C.Black, London, 1962.

Cocteau, Jean. *Cock and Harlequin*. Translated by Rollo H.Myers. The Egoist Press, London, 1921.

— *Opium*. Stock, Paris, 1930.

— *La Difficulté d'Etre*. Paul Morihien, Paris, 1947.

Craig, Edward. *Gordon Craig*. Gollancz, London, 1968.

Dandré, V. *Anna Pavlova*. Cassell, London, 1932.

Debussy, Claude. *Lettres de Claude Debussy à son editeur*. Durand, Paris, 1927.

Dolin, Anton. *Autobiography*. Oldbourne, London, 1960.

— *Ballet Go Round*. Michael Joseph, London, 1938.

Dumesnil, Maurice. *An Amazing Journey*. Ives Washburn, New York, 1932. Jarrolds, London, 1933.

Duncan, Irma and MacDougall, A.R. *Isadora Duncan's Russian Days*. Gollancz, London, 1929.

Duncan, Isadora. *My Life*. Gollancz, London, 1928. Sphere (paperback), London, 1968.

Ede, H.S. *Savage Messiah*. Heinemann, London, 1931.

Fokine, Michel. *Against the Tide*. Leningrad and Moscow, 1962.

— *Memoirs of a Ballet Master*. Translated by Vitale Fokine; edited by Anatole Chujoy. Little, Brown, Boston and Constable, London, 1961.

Grigoriev, S.L. *The Diaghilev Ballet 1909–1929*. Constable, London, 1953. Penguin (paperback), London, 1960.

Guest, Ivor. *Adeline Genée*. A.& C.Black, London, 1958.

— 'Carlotta Zambelli'. *La Revue d'Histoire du Théâtre, III*. 1969.

Hahn, Reynaldo. *Notes: Journal d'un musicien*. Plon, Paris, 1933.

Harriman, P. L. *The New Dictionary of Psychology*. Vision Press; Peter Owen, London, 1952.

Haskell, Arnold. *Balletomania*. Gollancz, London, 1934.

— *Diaghileff*. Gollancz, London, 1935.

Hofmannsthal, Hugo von and Strauss, Richard. *Correspondence betweeen Richard Strauss and Hugo von Hofmannsthal*. Collins, London, 1961. [Hofmannsthal-Strauss.]

Hugo, Victor. *A Life related by one who has witnessed it*, Vol. II. William H.Allen, London, 1863.

Hyden, Walford. *Pavlova*. Constable, London, 1931.

Jankélévitch, Vladimir. *Ravel*. Grove Press, New York, and Calder, London, 1959 (paperback).

Johnson, A.E. *The Russian Ballet*. Constable, London, 1913.

Jones, Robert Edmond. 'Nijinsky and Til Eulenspiegel' in *Dance Index*, Vol. IV, No. 4, April 1945 (New York).

Karsavina, Tamara. *Theatre Street*. Heinemann, London, 1930. Revised edition, Constable, London, 1948. Dutton (paperback), New York, 1961.

Kchessinskaya, M.F. *Dancing in St Petersburg*. Gollancz, London, 1960.

Kessler, Count Harry. *The Diaries of a Cosmopolitan*. Translated and edited by Charles Kessler. Weidenfeld and Nicolson, London, 1971.

Khan, Aga. *The Memoirs of Aga Khan*. Cassell and Constable, London, 1954.

Kirstein, Lincoln. *Fokine*. British-Continental Press, London, 1934.

Kochno, Boris. *Diaghilev and the Ballets Russes*. Translated by Adrienne Foulke. Harper & Row, New York, 1970; Allen Lane The Penguin Press, London, 1971.

— *Le Ballet*. Hachette, Paris, 1954.

Legat, Nicolas. *Ballets Russes*. Methuen, London, 1939.

Lieven, Prince Peter. *The Birth of Ballets Russes*. Translated by L.Zarine. George Allen & Unwin, London, 1936.

Lifar, Serge. *Serge Diaghilev*. Putnam, London, 1940.

Lockspeiser, Edward, *Debussy*. Dent, London, 1936. Revised 1951, 1963.

— *Debussy, his life and mind*. Vol. II. Cassell, London, 1965.

Manuel, Roland. *Maurice Ravel*. Translated by Cynthia Jolly. Dobson, London, 1947.

Marsh, Edward. *A Number of People*. Heinemann and Hamish Hamilton, London, 1939.

— *Rupert Brooke, A Memoir*. Sidgwick and Jackson, London, 1918.

Martin, Ralph G. *Lady Randolph Churchill*. Cassell, London, 1969.

Massie, Robert K. *Nicholas and Alexandra*. Gollancz, London, 1968.

Massine, Leonide. *My Life in Ballet*. Edited by Phyllis Hartnoll and Robert Rubens. Macmillan, London, 1968.

Morrell, Lady Ottoline. *Ottoline*. Edited by Robert Gathorne-Hardy. Faber and Faber, London, 1963.

Mossolov, A.A. *At the Court of the Last Tsar*. Translated by E.W.Dickes; edited by A.A.Pilenco. Methuen, London, 1935.

Nijinsky, Romola. *The Last Days of Nijinsky*. Gollancz, London, 1952.

— *Nijinsky*. Gollancz, London, 1933. Penguin (paperback), London, 1960. Sphere (paperback), London, 1970 (pagination as in the Penguin edition). [Romola Nijinsky].

Nijinsky, Vaslav. *The Diary of Vaslav Nijinsky*. Translated and edited by Romola Nijinsky. Gollancz, London, 1937. Panther (paperback), London, 1962. [*Diary*].

Painter, G.D. *Marcel Proust*, Vol. II. Chatto and Windus, London, 1965.

Pevsner, Nicholas. *The Buildings of England: London (1)*. Penguin, London, 1960; revised 1962.

Propert, W.A. *The Russian Ballet in Western Europe, 1909–1920*. The Bodley Head, London, 1921.

— *The Russian Ballet, 1921–1929*. The Bodley Head, London, 1931. [Propert II.]

Proust, Marcel. *Lettres à Reynaldo Hahn*. Edited by Philippe Kolb. Paris, 1956.

Reiss, Françoise. *Nijinsky*. A.&C.Black, London, 1960.

Ricketts, Charles. *Self-Portrait*. Peter Davies, London, 1939.

Rimsky-Korsakov,N.A. *My Musical Life*. Translated by J.A.Joffe; edited by Carl van Vechten. Secker, London, 1924.

Bibliography

Rivière, Jacques. 'Le Sacre du Printemps' in *Nouvelle Revue Française*, November 1913 (Paris).

Rosenthal, Harold. *Two Centuries of Opera at Covent Garden*, Putnam, London, 1958.

Sandoz, Maurice. *The Crystal Salt Cellar*. Guilford Press, London, 1954.

Schneider, Ilya Ilyitch. *Isadora Duncan, The Russian Years*. MacDonald, London, 1968.

Sert, Misia. *Two or Three Muses*. Museum Press, London, 1953.

Seton-Watson, Hugh. *The Decline of Imperial Russia, 1855–1914*. Methuen, London, 1952.

Sitwell, Osbert. *Great Morning*. Macmillan, London, 1948.

— *Laughter in the Next Room*. Macmillan, London, 1949.

Slonimsky, Yury. 'Marius Petipa', edited by Anatole Chujoy, in *Dance Index*, Vol. VI, nos. 5 and 6, May–June 1947 (New York). [Slonimsky-Chujoy.]

Sokolova, Lydia. *Dancing for Diaghilev*. Edited by Richard Buckle. John Murray, London, 1960.

Sotheby & Co. Catalogues of sales of material relating to the Diaghilev Ballet: 15 October, 1963; 26 May, 1964; 13 June, 1967; 16, 17 and 18 July, 1968; 9 and 10 July, 1969; 15, 16 and 19 December, 1969.

Stier, Theodor. *With Pavlova round the World*. Hurst and Blackett, London, [1927].

Stokes, Adrian. *To-night the Ballet*. Faber and Faber, London, 1934.

— *Russian Ballets*. Faber and Faber, London, 1935.

Stravinsky, Igor. *Chronicle of my Life*. Gollancz, London, 1936.

— *The Rite of Spring, Sketches 1911–1913*. Boosey and Hawkes, London, 1969.

— with Robert Craft. *Conversations*. Faber and Faber, London, 1959.

— with Robert Craft. *Expositions and Developments*. Faber and Faber, London, 1962.

— with Robert Craft. *Memories and Commentaries*. Faber and Faber, London, 1960.

Svetlov, Valerien. *Le Ballet contemporain*. Designed by Leon Bakst. Golicke and Willborg, St Petersburg; translated by M.D. Calvocoressi, Brunoff, Paris, 1912.

— *Thamar Karsavina*. Translated by H. de Vere Beauclerk and Nadia Evrenov. Edited by Cyril Beaumont. Beaumont, London, 1922.

Terry, Ellen. *The Russian Ballet*. Sidgwick and Jackson, London, 1913.

Van Vechten, Carl. 'Vaslav Nijinsky' in *Interpreters*. Alfred A. Knopf, New York, 1917. Reprinted in *Dance Index*, Vol. I, nos. 9–11, September-November 1942 (New York) and in Paul Magriel: *Nijinsky*. Henry Holt, New York, 1946.

Vaudoyer, Jean-Louis. 'Variations sur les Ballets Russes' in *La Revue de Paris*, July 1910 (Paris).

Vaughan, David. 'Pavlova's American "Beauty" ', in *Ballet Review*, Vol. 3, No. 2, 1969 (New York).

Whitworth, Geoffrey. *The Art of Nijinsky*. Chatto and Windus, London, 1913.

Wilde, Oscar. *The Letters of Oscar Wilde*. Edited by Rupert Hart-Davis. Hart-Davis, London, 1962.

SOURCE NOTES

My sources are (1) printed books and articles in learned journals, (2) newspapers, (3) theatre programmes, (4) the Astruc correspondence in the New York Public Library, (5) certain unpublished manuscripts such as Diaghilev's Memoirs, Diaghilev's note-book, Grigoriev's note-books, the Romola Nijinsky-Lincoln Kirstein draft of Mme Nijinsky's biography, Nijinsky's copy of the score of 'L'Après-midi d'un faune' with his dance notation, Valentine Gross's typescript and manuscripts and Lady Juliet Duff's essay, (6) questionnaires answered for me by the associates of Diaghilev and Nijinsky, (7) conversations with some of the latter, of which I made notes.

In the list of books and journals in the Bibliography, the date of their first publication in English is given, or if they have not been published in English, their first appearance in French or another language. But the page references in my Notes are, for the sake of the student's convenience, given not to the first edition of a book, but to the latest and most available edition – perhaps paperback – published in England or America. Thus, in the Bibliography will be found: 'Karsavina, Tamara. *Theatre Street*. Heinemann, London, 1930. Revised edition Constable, London, 1948. [Notes refer to] Dutton (paperback), New York, 1961.' (I have made an exception to this rule in the case of the series of Stravinsky-Craft books. Since only two of these have been reprinted as one paperback, I have referred in all cases to the original editions.) Some books referred to have not, of course, been reprinted.

Notes such as 'Rambert conversations' or 'Grigoriev questionnaires' are self-explanatory.

In the Notes, books are referred to by the author's surname, or, if more than one work by an author is used, by the surname and the title (or abbreviated title) of the book. Departures from this practice are indicated in square brackets in the Bibliography.

Chapter One   1898–1908

1 Bronislava Nijinska conversations.
2 *Ibid.* Mme Nijinska put the number at between 100 and 150. Bourman wrote 'hundreds' on p.23 and 'one hundred' on p.24.
3 Karsavina: *Theatre Street,* pp.41 and 102.
4 Legat, pp.51, 52.
5 Bourman, p.19, lists the class-mates and their fates, but states that Feodorov was killed in error during the revolution. Mme Bronislava Nijinska says that the cause of his death was tuberculosis.
6 B.Nijinska conversations. Mme Romola Nijinsky had been misinformed when she wrote that Eleonora Bereda's father was a dancer, that he was of gentle birth and that he shot himself.
7 *Ibid.*
8 *Ibid.* All previous biographers have mistakenly postdated Nijinsky's birth and entry into the school by two years, giving him the dates which should have been Bronislava's.
9 Romola Nijinsky, p.25.
10 B.Nijinska conversations.
11 *Ibid.*
12 *Ibid.*
13 *Diary,* pp.53, 54.
14 B.Nijinska conversations.
15 Bourman, p.26.
16 *Ibid.,* p.27.
17 B.Nijinska conversations.

18 Legat, p.52.
19 Bourman, p.34.
20 Slonimsky-Chujoy, p.126.
21 Benois: *Early Memories of Diaghilev,* introduction to the catalogue of the Diaghilev Exhibition.
22 Benois: *Memoirs* II, pp.61 and 63.
23 Benois: *Reminiscences,* pp.187–90.
24 *Ibid.,* pp.211, 212.
25 *Ibid.,* pp.213–18.
26 Kchessinskaya, pp.81, 82.
27 Karsavina: *Theatre Street,* p.133.
28 Karsavina: speech at the opening of the Diaghilev Exhibition, Forbes House, November 1954, quoted in Buckle: *In Search of Diaghilev.*
29 Guest: *Zambelli,* pp.220–27.
30 Bourman, p.35.
31 Benois: *Reminiscences,* p.222.
32 *Ibid.,* p.187.
33 Kchessinskaya, pp.86, 87.
34 Karsavina: *Theatre Street,* p.147.
35 Karsavina conversation.
36 Imperial Theatres: information supplied by Mme Natalia Dudinskaya. Also mentioned by Bourman, p.36.
37 Bourman, p.36.
38 *Ibid.,* p.37.
39 Vladimirov conversation.
40 Bourman, pp.56–9, 94–6. These are two of Bourman's true stories, confirmed by Mme Bronislava Nijinska, though no

Notes

doubt some of their colouring has been considerably heightened.

41 B.Nijinska conversations.
42 Doubrovska conversation.
43 Romola Nijinsky, p.36.
44 Romola Nijinsky conversations.
45 Karsavina: *Theatre Street*, pp.135, 136.
46 Slonimsky-Chujoy, pp.125, 126.
47 Teliakovsky Diary, quoted in Slonimsky-Chujoy, p.126.
48 Legat, p.31.
49 Benois: *Reminiscences*, pp.229, 230.
50 Kchessinskaya, p.98.
51 Bourman, pp.82–4. Also Romola Nijinsky, p.41.
52 Benois: *Memoirs* II, pp.221, 222.
53 Karsavina: *Theatre Street*, pp.153, 154.
54 Bourman, p.84.
55 Duncan, p.118.
56 Information supplied by Mme Vera Krasovskaya.
57 Duncan, pp.119, 120.
58 Told the author by Mme Braikeivitch, the donor of the fine collection of Russian stage designs and pictures to the Ashmolean, at the time of the Diaghilev Exhibition.
59 Benois: *Memoirs* II, pp.223, 234.
60 *Ibid.*, p.234.
61 Diaghilev's speech at the Tauride Palace, quoted by Haskell, pp.160, 161.
62 Bourman, pp.90–93.
63 Letter from Diaghilev to Propert, 17 February, 1926, quoted in Propert II, pp.87, 88.
64 Fokine, pp.87–90.
65 Karsavina conversations.
66 Karsavina: *Theatre Street*, pp.158–60.
67 Legat, p.45; Karsavina: *Theatre Street*, p.162: *et al.*
68 Benois: *Memoirs* II, pp.230, 231.
69 Lifar, pp.167, 168. Lifar had this account from Mme Greffuhle.
70 B.Nijinska conversations.
71 Vladimirov conversation.
72 *Ibid.*
73 Karsavina: *Theatre Street*, p.151.
74 Information obtained by Mme Vera Krasovskaya from the Mariinsky Theatre Archives.
75 Bourman, p.100.
76 Information obtained by Mme Vera Krasovskaya from the Mariinsky Theatre Archives.

77 Fokine, pp.90, 91.
78 Facsimile reproduced in Fokine: *Against the Tide*, p.166.
79 B.Nijinska conversations. Although Fokine tells the story of the painted tights it was Mme Nijinska who told me that it was she who painted toes first on her own, then on the other dancers' tights.
80 Fokine, pp.93–6.
81 *Ibid.*, pp.96, 97.
82 *Ibid.*, p.101.
83 *Ibid.*, pp.102, 103.
84 Benois: *Reminiscences*, pp.225–7.
85 *Ibid.*, pp.106, 107.
86 *Petersburgskaya Gazeta*, No. 105, 17 April 1907.
87 *Theatre and Music*, No. 11170, 17 April 1907.
88 Information supplied by Mme Krasovskaya.
89 Schollar conversation.
90 B.Nijinska conversations.
91 Bourman, p.104.
92 *Ibid.*, pp.106, 107.
93 Diaghilev.
94 Benois: *Reminiscences*, pp.240–66.
95 Kchessinskaya, pp.40–42.
96 B.Nijinska conversations.
97 *Ibid.*
98 Bourman, p.117.
99 B.Nijinska conversations.
100 *Diary*, p.74.
101 B.Nijinska conversations.
102 Bourman, p.131.
103 B.Nijinska conversations.
104 *Ibid.*
105 *Ibid.*
106 *Ibid.*
107 *Ibid.*
108 Bourman, pp.133, 134.
109 B.Nijinska conversations.
110 Imperial Theatres: information supplied by Mme Natalia Dudinskaya.
111 Karsavina: *Theatre Street*, p.152.
112 Karsavina conversations.
113 Schollar conversation.
114 Imperial Theatres: information supplied by Mme Natalia Dudinskaya.
115 Benois: *Reminiscences*, p.243.
116 *Ibid.*, pp.245, 246.
117 *Ibid.*, pp.249–65.
118 Imperial Theatres: information supplied by Mme Natalia Dudinskaya.
119 Fokine, pp.129–33.

120 Diaghilev.
121 *Ibid.*
122 Benois: *Memoirs* II, p.246.
123 Benois: *Reminiscences*, p.268. Also *Memoirs* II, p.247.
124 Diaghilev.
125 Benois: *Memoirs* II, p.247.
126 Grand Duke Alexander Mikhailovitch: *Once a Grand Duke*, p.137.
127 *Ibid.*, p.138.
128 Karsavina: *Theatre Street*, pp.81, 82.
129 Diaghilev.
130 *Ibid.*
131 Benois: *Memoirs* II, pp.250, 251.
132 Diaghilev.
133 Benois: *Memoirs* II, p.251.
134 Karsavina conversations.
135 Diaghilev.

136 Benois: *Memoirs* II, p. 252.
137 Diaghilev.
138 M.Sert, pp.111, 112.
139 Bourman, p.140.
140 Reiss, p.51. Mlle Reiss had this information from Matilda Kchessinskaya.
141 Bourman, pp.141–4.
142 B.Nijinska conversations.
143 Baroness Budberg conversation.
144 Romola Nijinsky conversations.
145 *Diary*, p.63.
146 B.Nijinska conversations.
147 *Diary*, p.59.
148 B.Nijinska conversations.
149 Bourman, pp.151–5.
150 *Diary*, p.59.
151 *Ibid.*, pp.80–3.

Chapter Two *1909*

1 Romola Nijinsky, p.64.
2 Dandré, p.206.
3 Fokine, p.138.
4 Astruc, *Revue Musicale*, December 1930.
5 *Ibid.*
6 Benois: *Reminiscences*, p.266; *Memoirs* II, p.240.
7 Astruc, *Revue Musicale*, December 1930.
8 Astruc papers.
9 Astruc, *Revue Musicale*, December 1930.
10 Astruc papers: the contract is summarized in Astruc's report to the Tsar, November 1909.
11 Grigoriev questionnaires.
12 Karsavina conversations.
13 *Ibid.*
14 *Ibid.*
15 *Ibid.*
16 *Ibid.*
17 Grigoriev, p.17.
18 *Ibid.*, pp.14, 15.
19 *Ibid.*, pp. 15, 16.
20 Grigoriev questionnaires.
21 Grigoriev, pp.18, 19.
22 *Ibid.*, p.20.
23 Stravinsky: *Expositions*, p.25.
24 Kchessinskaya, p.111.
25 Grigoriev, p.23.

26 Astruc papers. Astruc's report to the Tsar, November 1909.
27 *Ibid.* Pro-forma.
28 Massine conversations.
29 Grigoriev, p.24.
30 *Ibid.*, pp.23, 24.
31 Lifar, pp.181, 182.
32 Astruc papers. Telegram from Diaghilev to Astruc, 12 March 1909.
33 *Ibid.* Telegram from Diaghilev to Astruc, 14 March 1909.
34 Benois: *Reminiscences*, pp.280, 281.
35 Karsavina: *Theatre Street*, p.192.
36 Benois: *Reminiscences*, pp.281, 282.
37 Grigoriev, pp.25, 26.
38 Fokine, pp.149, 150.
39 Grigoriev, p.26.
40 Astruc papers. Telegrams from Diaghilev to Astruc, 29 March 1909 and 3 April 1909.
41 *Ibid.* Only Diaghilev's reply to Astruc's demand survives. Telegram, 10 March 1909.
42 *Ibid.* Telegram from Diaghilev to Astruc, 31 March 1909.
43 *Ibid.* Same telegram.
44 *Ibid.* Telegram from Diaghilev to Astruc, 6 April 1909.

Notes

45 *Ibid.* Telegram from Diaghilev to Astruc, 7 April 1909.
46 Grigoriev questionnaires.
47 Benois: *Reminiscences*, p. 283.
48 *Ibid.*, p.283.
49 Astruc papers. Telegrams from Diaghilev to Astruc, 20 April 1909, 21 April 1909, 23 April 1909, 26 April 1909, 27 April 1909, 28 April 1909, 29 April 1909.
50 Karsavina conversations.
51 B.Nijinska conversations.
52 Astruc papers. Report to the Tsar, November 1909.
53 Karsavina: *Theatre Street*, p.193.
54 Karsavina conversations.
55 Astruc papers. Report to the Tsar, November 1909.
56 Grigoriev, p.27.
57 B.Nijinska conversations.
58 Svetlov: *Le Ballet*, p.86.
59 Benois: *Reminiscences*, p.287, also footnote.
60 Grigoriev, pp.28, 29.
61 Karsavina: *Theatre Street*, p.194.
62 Karsavina conversations.
63 Karsavina: *Theatre Street*, pp.194, 195.
64 Grigoriev questionnaires.
65 Karsavina: *Theatre Street*, p.196.
66 Svetlov: *Le Ballet*, p.86.
67 Painter II, p.146.
68 *Ibid.*, pp.17, 18 *et al.*
69 *Ibid.*, p.10 *et al.*
70 *Ibid.*, p.3 *et al.*
71 French Press.
72 *Ibid.*
73 *Le Figaro*, 11 May 1909.
74 Karsavina conversations.
75 Grigoriev, p.29.
76 Svetlov: *Le Ballet*, p.87.
77 *Le Figaro*, 17 May 1909.
78 M.Jean Hugo told the author this, but it is no doubt a well-known fact. Proust wrote for these papers.
79 *Le Figaro*, 19 May 1909.
80 Astruc, *Revue Musicale*, December 1930.
81 Benois: *Reminiscences*, p.289.
82 Romola Nijinsky, p.72.
83 Benois: *Reminiscences*, pp.289, 290.
84 *Ibid.*, p.292.
85 Compare illustration in Benois *Reminiscences*, facing page 297, and Plates 16 and 17 in this book.
86 Benois: *Reminiscences*, p.291.
87 *Ibid.*, p.291.
88 *Ibid.*, p.292.

89 The description of 'Armide' is largely based on Karsavina conversations (and, indeed, demonstrations), embellished by quotations from Benois, Fokine and Geoffrey Whitworth. I fitted these accounts of the action to the piano score, played for me by Brian Blackwood.
90 Benois: *Reminiscences*, p.244. I have changed Benois' past tense to the present.
91 Whitworth, p.40.
92 Karsavina: *Theatre Street*, p.197.
93 Romola Nijinsky, p.73.
94 Whitworth, pp.41, 42.
95 Karsavina conversations.
96 Karsavina: *Theatre Street*, p.198.
97 Fokine, p.107.
98 Karsavina conversations. Her actual phrase.
99 M.Jean Hugo's description to the author of how people behaved in those days.
100 Astruc, *Revue Musicale*, December 1930.
101 Vaudoyer: Introduction to the catalogue of Lifar's Exposition des Ballets Russes de Serge Diaghilev, Musée des Arts Décoratifs, 1939.
102 Kochno: *Le Ballet*, p.142.
103 Beaumont: *Complete Book*, p.685.
104 Karsavina: *Theatre Street*, p.198.
105 *Ibid.*, p.198.
106 Told the author by M.Jean Hugo.
107 Karsavina: *Theatre Street*, p.198.
108 *Ibid.*, pp.198, 199.
109 *Le Figaro*, 19 May 1909.
110 Karsavina: *Theatre Street*, p.199.
111 *Le Figaro*, 20 May 1909.
112 *Le Figaro*, 15 May 1909.
113 *Commedia*, 20 May 1909.
114 *Ibid.*
115 Astruc, p.133; Lieven, p.104.
116 Karsavina conversations.
117 Lieven, pp.87, 88, 104.
118 Karsavina conversations.
119 Karsavina: *Theatre Street*, p.200.
120 *Ibid.*, pp.282, 283.
121 Karsavina conversations. Mme Karsavina did not remember at whose house Nijinsky saw the Gauguin paintings. It was the author's friend Mme Jean Hugo who made inquiries in Paris and found that it could only have been Emmanuel Bibesco's. This was confirmed by Princess Marthe Bibesco, who added that her cousin, hard-up as he was, used to make Gauguin a small allowance.

122 It was M. Jean Hugo who described to the author the attitude of his father and the Jockey Club to the ballet.
123 Gautier in *La Presse*, 7 May 1838.
124 Karsavina conversations.
125 *Ibid.*
126 See the French press. See also Benois: *Reminiscences*, p.291.
127 Benois: *Reminiscences*, p.291.
128 Karsavina: *Theatre Street*, p.201.
129 Benois: *Reminiscences*, p.294.
130 Svetlov: *Le Ballet*, pp.98, 99.
131 Fokine, p.131.
132 *Ibid.*, p.130.
133 Stokes: *Russian Ballets*, p.89.
134 Johnson, pp.81, 82.
135 Benois: *Reminiscences*, p.298.
136 Lieven, p.80.
137 Benois: *Reminiscences*, pp.295, 297.
138 Description of 'Cléopâtre' based on Beaumont: *Complete Book*, and Johnson.
139 Lieven, p.102. He is quoting Benois.
140 Karsavina conversations.
141 Fokine, p.145.
142 Karsavina conversations.
143 Benois: *Reminiscences*, p.296.
144 Fokine, p.146.
145 Announcements in French press.
146 Karsavina conversations.
147 Grigoriev, p.35.
148 *Commedia*, 22 June 1909.
149 Karsavina conversations.
150 *Diary*, pp.141, 142.
151 Svetlov: *Le Ballet*, p.103.
152 Astruc papers. Letter from Astruc to Diaghilev, 15 June 1909.
153 *Ibid.* Astruc's report to the Tsar, November 1909.

154 *Ibid.*
155 *Ibid.* The bill, which was not honoured, exists.
156 Kchessinskaya, p.113.
157 Karsavina conversations.
158 Karsavina: *Theatre Street*, p.202.
159 Svetlov: *Le Ballet*, p.104.
160 Benois: *Reminiscences*, p.300.
161 Romola Nijinsky, p.80.
162 *Ibid.*, pp.80, 81.
163 Calvocoressi, p.136.
164 *Revue de Musicologie*, July–December 1962, p.34.
165 Quoted in Lockspeiser, Vol. II, p.169.
166 Astruc papers. Letter from Diaghilev to Astruc's firm, 19(?) July 1909.
167 *Ibid.* Letter from Diaghilev to Astruc's firm, 6 August 1909.
168 Romola Nijinsky, pp.81, 82.
169 Astruc papers.
170 *Ibid.*
171 *Ibid.*
172 *Ibid.* Letter from Mossolov to Astruc, 17 November 1909.
173 *Ibid.* Letter from M. Molodovsky to Astruc on behalf of the Grand Duke Nicholas.
174 *Ibid.* Letter from F. de Coubé to Astruc on behalf of the Grand Duke André.
175 *Ibid.*
176 *Ibid.*
177 *Ibid.* Letter from Martin to Astruc, 8 December 1909.
178 *Ibid.*
179 *Ibid.* Telegrams from Brussel to Astruc, Astruc to Brussel, Astruc to Elter, Litvinne to Elter and Astruc to Chaliapine, between 8 and 15 January 1910.

Chapter Three *1910*

1 Grigoriev, p.43.
2 Benois: *Reminiscences*, p.303.
3 Fokine, p.158.
4 Benois: *Reminiscences*, pp.303, 304.
5 Lieven, pp.106, 107.
6 Fokine, pp.158, 159.
7 Stravinsky: *Expositions*, p.129.
8 Grigoriev, p.38.

9 Benois: *Reminiscences*, p.304.
10 Lieven, p.106. Benois, who inspired Lieven's book, presumably showed Lieven a copy of Diaghilev's letter to Liadov, for he gives the date, 4 September 1909. If Diaghilev was still in Venice on that date, he had either lingered on after Nijinsky's return to Petersburg, or, if Nijinsky was

still there, he had missed the opening of the Mariinsky season.

11 Fokine, p.160.
12 Stravinsky: *Expositions*, p. 127.
13 *Ibid.*, p.128.
14 *Ibid.*, pp.128, 129.
15 Stravinsky: *Memories*, p.32.
16 Fokine, p.159.
17 *Ibid.*, p.159.
18 Haskell, pp.225, 226.
19 Kirstein, p.39.
20 Fokine, p.161.
21 Stravinsky: *Expositions*, p.129.
22 Grigoriev, p.40.
23 Calvocoressi, p.220.
24 Sotheby catalogues.
25 Grigoriev, p.42.
26 Imperial Theatres.
27 B.Nijinska conversations.
28 Benois: *Reminiscences*, pp.309, 310.
29 *Ibid.*, p.310.
30 *Ibid.*
31 *Ibid.*, also footnote.
32 *Ibid.*, p.311.
33 Fokine, p.151.
34 *Ibid.*, p.152.
35 Grigoriev, p.42.
36 Karsavina: *Theatre Street*, pp.212, 213.
37 Astruc papers. My reason for suggesting this date is Diaghilev's cable to Astruc about replacing 'Giselle' by 'La Belle au bois dormant', mentioned below.
38 Stravinsky: *Memories*, p.32.
39 Astruc papers. Telegrams from Diaghilev to Astruc, dated 2 February 1910, 8 February 1910; from Astruc to Diaghilev, 9 February 1910; from Diaghilev to Astruc, 10 February 1910, 11 February 1910.
40 I have no documentation for Mme Rimsky-Korsakov's opposition, though it is beyond question that she did oppose the production. Evidence for her protest after the event is the letter published in *Rech*, 7 August 1910. Diaghilev's reply to this from Venice was published 17 September 1910. A second letter from Mme Rimsky-Korsakov appeared in *Rech*, 12 October 1910.
41 Karsavina conversations.
42 *Ibid.*
43 Benois: *Reminiscences*, p.312.
44 Astruc papers. Letter from Schidlovsky to Astruc, 11 February 1910.

45 *Ibid.* Telegram from Astruc to Diaghilev, 15 February 1910.
46 *Ibid.* Telegram from Diaghilev to Astruc, 16 February 1910.
47 Stravinsky: *Chronicle*, p.52.
48 Astruc papers. Receipt exists.
49 *Ibid.* Telegram from Diaghilev to Astruc, 10 April 1910.
50 *Ibid.* Telegram from Gunsbourg to Astruc, 23 April 1910.
51 Benois: *Reminiscences*, p.312; reference to Metropolitan Opera in Astruc papers: telegram from Diaghilev to Astruc, 18 March 1910.
52 Benois: *Reminiscences*, pp.312, 313.
53 Lieven, p.112.
54 Benois: *Reminiscences*, p.313.
55 Karsavina: *Theatre Street*, pp.213, 214.
56 Lieven, p.115.
57 Benois: *Reminiscences*, p.312.
58 Fokine, pp.134-6.
59 Karsavina conversations.
60 Fokine, p.136.
61 B.Nijinska conversations.
62 Grigoriev, p.40.
63 Diaghilev's Black Note-Book, p.15.
64 Astruc papers.
65 *Ibid.* Draft of contract exists.
66 Karsavina: *Theatre Street*, p.215.
67 *Ibid.*, pp.214, 215.
68 Lieven, p.116.
69 Benois: *Reminiscences*, pp.313, 314.
70 Grigoriev, pp.44, 47.
71 Stier, p.237.
72 Stier, p.236; Grigoriev, p.44.
73 Karsavina: *Theatre Street*, p.219.
74 Grigoriev, p.44.
75 *Ibid.*, pp.44, 45.
76 Karsavina conversations.
77 Rimsky-Korsakov, pp.446, 447.
78 *Ibid.*, pp.292, 293.
79 Grigoriev, p.46.
80 *Ibid.*, p.46.
81 Fokine, p.155.
82 Benois: *Reminiscences*, p.316.
83 Fokine, pp.155, 156.
84 Whitworth, p.57.
85 Benois: *Reminiscences*, p.316.
86 Vaudoyer: 'Variations'.
87 B.Nijinska conversations.
88 Estrade Guerra in an interview with F.Reiss. Reiss, p.78.
89 Barbier and Miomandre, on the third and

fourth unnumbered pages of Miomandre's introduction to Barbier's drawings.

90 Cocteau: *La Difficulté*, p.70.
91 Grigoriev, p.47.
92 Proust, p.188.
93 Karsavina conversations.
94 *Ibid.*
95 Author's conclusion: see note 96.
96 Fokine, pp.153, 154.
97 Karsavina conversations.
98 Kochno: *Diaghilev*, p.48.
99 Grigoriev, p.43. See above p.118.
100 Karsavina: *Theatre Street*, p.220.
101 Benois: *Reminiscences*, pp.289, 290, 337, 338.
102 Karsavina: *Theatre Street*, p.220.
103 Benois: *Reminiscences*, p.313.
104 Svetlov: *Karsavina*, p.97.
105 *Ibid.*, p.47.
106 Benois: *Reminiscences*, pp.310, 311.
107 Stravinsky, letter to Roerich, 19 June 1910, from a copy in the composer's possession.
108 Benois: *Reminiscences*, p.311.
109 Stravinsky, letter to Roerich, 19 June 1910.
110 Quoted in Benois: *Reminiscences*, pp.314–316.
111 Painter II, p.164.
112 *Ibid.*
113 Cocteau: *Opium*, pp.163, 164.
114 Painter II, p.160.
115 Karsavinska conversations.
116 Benois: *Reminiscences*, pp.304, 305.
117 Stravinsky: *Conversations*, p.96; Lieven, p.246.
118 Benois: *Reminiscences*, pp.306, 307.
119 *Ibid.*, p.307.
120 Stravinsky: *Expositions*, p.129.
121 *Ibid.*
122 *Ibid.*
123 *Ibid.*, pp.130, 131.
124 Karsavina conversations.
125 Blanche, p.257.
126 Karsavina conversations.
127 *Ibid.*
128 Benois conversations.
129 Karsavina conversations.
130 *Ibid.*
131 Stravinsky, letter to Roerich, 19 June 1910
132 Stravinsky: *Expositions*, p.140.

133 Stravinsky, letter to Roerich, 19 June 1910.
134 Lieven, p.117.
135 Grigoriev, p.51.
136 Benois: *Reminiscences*, p.308.
137 Karsavina: *Theatre Street*, p.221.
138 *Ibid.*, p.284.
139 *Ibid.*, p.286.
140 *Ibid.*, p.285.
141 Karsavina conversations.
142 Grigoriev, p.52.
143 *Ibid.*, p.51.
144 Stravinsky, letter to Roerich begun at Ustilug and finished at La Baule, 19 June 1910; and another letter, 27 July 1910.
145 Stravinsky: *Expositions*, p.67.
146 Benois: *Reminiscences*, p.323.
147 The book Bakst wrote about this journey has not a single date in it.
148 Stravinsky: *Expositions*, p.134.
149 Benois: *Reminiscences*, p.324.
150 *Ibid.*, pp.324, 325.
151 Stravinsky: *Expositions*, p.134.
152 Astruc papers. Telegrams from Diaghilev in Venice to Astruc in Paris, 1 September 1910, and on subsequent dates up to at least 10 September 1910.
153 *Ibid.* Telegram from Diaghilev in London to Astruc in Paris, 10 October 1910.
154 Letter-card formerly in possession of Mlle Lucienne Astruc, 27 October 1910.
155 B.Nijinska conversations.
156 Lieven, p.142.
157 Benois: *Reminiscences*, p.327.
158 *Ibid.*, pp.326, 327.
159 Stravinsky: *Expositions*, p.135.
160 Benois: *Reminiscences*, p.327.
161 Fokine, p.185.
162 Stravinsky: *Memories*, p.96.
163 Benois: *Reminiscences*, p.328, footnote.
164 Astruc papers. Telegram from Diaghilev to Astruc, 14 December 1910.
165 *Ibid.* Telegram from Diaghilev to Astruc, 15 December 1910.
166 *Ibid.* Telegram from Diaghilev to Astruc, 18 December 1910.
167 *Ibid.* Telegram from Diaghilev to Astruc, 22 December 1910.
168 *Ibid.* Telegram from Diaghilev to Astruc, 24 December 1910.

Notes

Chapter Four 1911

1 Karsavina: *Theatre Street*, p.286 ('Diaghilev ... regarded the choreography of Fokine as belonging to the past.'); Morrell, p.227 ('Such ballets as ["Le Spectre de la rose"] did not interest [Nijinsky]. He said it was *trop joli* and was rather annoyed when people admired it.').
2 Benois: *Reminiscences*, p.345. An example is Diaghilev's cutting and editing of 'Le Lac des Cygnes'.
3 Duncan, p.58.
4 Reiss, p.102. Her interview with Larionov.
5 Deduction from correspondence and B. Nijinska conversations.
6 B.Nijinska conversations.
7 Romola Nijinsky, p.125. The first mention of Debussy's music in Diaghilev's Note-book was in September, 1910 (p.123).
8 B.Nijinska conversations.
9 *Ibid.*
10 *Ibid.*
11 Astruc papers. Telegram from Diaghilev to Astruc, 10 February 1911.
12 Vaudoyer: 'Variations sur les Ballets Russes', article in *La Revue de Paris*, 15 July 1910.
13 Lifar, pp.252, 253. He is quoting what Vaudoyer told him.
14 Fokine, p.180.
15 Astruc papers. Letter from Diaghilev to Astruc, 22 May 1911.
16 Karsavina: *Theatre Street*, pp.221, 222.
17 Sotheby catalogues.
18 Grigoriev, p.54.
19 *Ibid.*, p.58.
20 *Ibid.*, p.58.
21 *Ibid.*, p.55.
22 Benois: *Reminiscences*, p.343.
23 Romola Nijinsky, p.102.
24 *Ibid.*
25 Karsavina: *Theatre Street*, p.226.
26 B.Nijinska conversations.
27 Articles in *Novoye Vremnie* and *Le Journal de St Petersbourg*, 13 February 1911.
28 Sotheby catalogues.
29 Astruc papers. Telegram from Diaghilev to Astruc, 12 February 1911.
30 *Ibid.* Telegram from Gunsbourg to Astruc, 12 February 1911.
31 Romola Nijinsky, p.102.

32 Astruc papers. Telegram from Diaghilev to Astruc, 13 February 1911.
33 *Ibid.* Telegram from Diaghilev to Astruc, 14 February 1911.
34 *Ibid.* Telegram from Diaghilev to Astruc, 14 February 1911.
35 *Ibid.* Letter from Astruc to Diaghilev, 14 February 1911.
36 Kchessinskaya, p.123.
37 Astruc papers. Telegram from Diaghilev to Astruc, 2 March 1911.
38 *Ibid.* Telegram from Diaghilev to Astruc, 18 February 1911.
39 *Ibid.*
40 *Ibid.* First mentioned to Astruc in a telegram of Diaghilev's from Rome, 26 May 1911.
41 *Ibid.* Telegrams from Diaghilev to Astruc, 3 March 1911, 15 March 1911.
42 *Ibid.* Telegram from Diaghilev to Astruc, 12 March 1911 ('*Bakst arrive demain*').
43 *Ibid.* Telegram from Diaghilev to Astruc, 15 March 1911.
44 *Ibid.* I assume that it was on this lightning visit to Paris that Diaghilev became interested in 'La Péri', as the first reference to it is in his correspondence with Astruc is in a telegram from Beaulieu on 23 March 1911, two days after he left.
45 *Ibid.* From 23–25 March 1911 the telegrams were sent from Beaulieu.
46 *Ibid.* On 30 March 1911 Diaghilev telegraphed to Astruc from Beausoleil, '*Suis définitivement Riviera Palace.*'
47 Grigoriev, p.59.
48 Fokine, p.201.
49 Grigoriev, pp.60, 61.
50 Fokine, p.188.
51 Grigoriev, p.59.
52 *Ibid.*, pp.59, 60.
53 Astruc papers. Telegrams from Diaghilev to Astruc, 23 March 1911, 25 March 1911, 3 April 1911.
54 B.Nijinska conversations.
55 Grigoriev, p.59.
56 *Ibid.*, p.58.
57 Evidence as note 58.
58 The evidence that Stravinsky came over to Monte Carlo is the photograph, plate 41.
59 The evidence for Benois is the same as the preceding note. Also see Lieven, p.154.

60 Astruc papers. At least Gunsbourg was there on 1 May 1911 when Diaghilev telegraphed Astruc that he would arrive at the Majestic Hotel, Paris, on the next day.

61 The Botkine girls are in the photograph mentioned above.

62 Karsavina: *Theatre Street*, p.233.

63 Aga Khan, p.109.

64 Karsavina conversations.

65 Buckle collection. Letter from Bakst to Astruc, 29 March 1911.

66 Astruc papers. Telegram from Diaghilev to Astruc, 31 March 1911.

67 Drawing in Lucienne Astruc collection. Reproduced, plate 35.

68 Design for poster reproduced, *Comoedia Illustré*, 15 June 1911.

69 Poster in Buckle collection and possibly elsewhere.

70 Astruc papers. Telegram from Diaghilev to Astruc, 5 April 1911.

71 *Ibid.* Telegram from Diaghilev to Astruc, 21 April 1911, quoting telegram received from Rubinstein: '*Regrette mais nécessité de mon travail m'empêche venir dimanche. Pouvez absolument compter sur moi le vingt-trois. Amitiés.*'

72 Karsavina conversations.

73 Lieven, p.163. Grigoriev calls Muoratori '*régisseur*' (p.60), and Lieven calls 'Muratore' 'the former singer . . . in charge of publicity' (p.163).

74 Karsavina: *Theatre Street*, p.223.

75 *Le Monte Carlo.*

76 Kchessinskaya, p.125.

77 *Le Monte Carlo.*

78 Stravinsky-Craft questionnaires.

79 Plate 41. Referred to above.

80 B.Nijinska conversations.

81 Romola Nijinsky, pp.114, 115.

82 Benois: *Reminiscences*, p.340.

83 Karsavina: *Theatre Street*, p.240.

84 Press; Grigoriev, p.60.

85 Diaghilev's Black Note-Book, p.141.

86 Astruc papers. Letter from Diaghilev to Astruc, 27 May 1911. '*Quand Rubinstein a voulu monter une série de danses sur la musique compliquée de St Sébastien elle est venue à Monte Carlo pour 5 jours. Et tout a été fait quoiqu'elle fût tombée en plein dans la période si difficile de la création de Narcisse.*'

87 Benois: *Reminiscences*, p.341.

88 *Ibid.*, pp.341, 342.

89 *Ibid.*, p.341.

90 *Ibid.*, p.342.

91 Karsavina: *Theatre Street*, p.212.

92 Astruc papers. Telegram from Diaghilev to Astruc, 5 May 1911.

93 *Ibid.* Same telegram as above.

94 Benois: *Reminiscences*, pp.330, 331; Stravinsky: *Conversations*, p.98.

95 Benois: *Reminiscences*, p.331.

96 *Ibid.*, p.331; Karsavina: *Theatre Street*, p.234.

97 Karsavina: *Theatre Street*, p.231.

98 Benois: *Reminiscences*, pp.330, 331.

99 Karsavina: *Theatre Street*, p.231.

100 Grigoriev, p.62.

101 *Ibid.*, p.62.

102 Benois: *Reminiscences*, p.332.

103 Astruc papers. Telegram from Diaghilev to Astruc, 15 May 1911. The Roman telegraphist relayed the French expression '*ovations infinies*' as '*ovadons infibes*'.

104 Grigoriev, p.62.

105 Karsavina conversations.

106 Karsavina: *Theatre Street*, p.231.

107 Astruc papers. Telegram from Diaghilev to Astruc, 26 May 1911.

108 *Ibid.* Letter from Diaghilev to Astruc, 22 May 1911.

109 *Ibid.* Telegram from Bakst to Diaghilev, 24 May 1911.

110 *Ibid.* Telegram from Diaghilev to Astruc, 26 May 1911.

111 *Ibid.* Letter from Diaghilev to Astruc, 27 May 1911.

112 Grigoriev, p.137.

113 Adolphe Jullien in *Feuilleton du Journal des Débats*, 25 June 1911.

114 Astruc papers. Telegram from Diaghilev to Astruc, 31 May 1911.

115 Whitworth, pp.46, 47.

116 Valentine Gross, broadcast on Radiodiffusion française, 1951.

117 Cocteau in *Comoedia Illustré*, 15 June 1911.

118 At least according to a programme in the author's possession, dated 8 June 1911.

119 George Pioch in *Commedia*, 7 June 1911.

120 Karsavina conversations.

121 Karsavina: *Theatre Street*, p.241.

122 Lieven, p.143.

123 Fokine, p.190.

124 Kochno: *Diaghilev*, p.68.

125 Benois: *Reminiscences*, pp.333–5.

126 Braun, pp.113, 114.

127 Benois: *Reminiscences*, p.336.

Notes

128 Fokine, p.187.
129 Benois: *Reminiscences*, p.335, footnote.
130 Fokine, p.193.
131 Unidentified Press cutting.
132 Benois: *Reminiscences*, p.335.
133 Stravinsky: *Memories*, pp.33, 34.
134 *Ibid.*
135 Fokine, p.184.
136 Benois: *Reminiscences*, p.335.
137 Fokine, p.191.
138 *Ibid.*, pp.194, 193.
139 Benois: *Reminiscences*, pp.337, 338.
140 *Le Figaro*, 17 June 1911.
141 Pevsner, pp.314, 315.
142 Juliet Duff conversations.
143 Karsavina conversations.
144 Astruc papers. Telegram from Gunsbourg to Astruc, 3 August 1911.
145 Grigoriev, p.66.
146 Juliet Duff conversations.
147 Sir Michael Duff conversations, confirmed in a letter by the late Antonio Gandarillas, the popular Chilean who knew more about English society than most Englishmen.
148 Juliet Duff conversations.
149 Martin, p.151.
150 Hahn, p.214.
151 Covent Garden programmes.
152 *Daily Mail*, 21 June 1911.
153 Diaghilev.
154 Astruc papers. Telegram from Diaghilev to Astruc, 23 June 1911.
155 *The Times*, 22 June 1911.
156 *Observer*, 25 June 1911.
157 *The Times*, 26 June 1911.
158 *Ibid.*, 24 June 1911.
159 *Ibid.*
160 *Sunday Times*, 25 June 1911.
161 Bedells, pp.51, 52.
162 Diana Cooper conversation and letter.
163 Diaghilev.
164 *Daily Mail*, 27 June 1911.
165 *Ibid.*
166 *Ibid.*
167 Diaghilev.
168 *Sunday Times*, 23 July 1911.
169 *Daily Mail*, 28 June 1911.
170 Juliet Duff conversations.
171 Craig, p.84.
172 Ricketts, *passim.*
173 Juliet Duff, essay.
174 Stravinsky: *Expositions*, pp.140, 141.
175 Astruc papers. Telegram from Diaghilev to Astruc, 1 September 1911.

176 Grigoriev, p.68.
177 Benois: *Reminiscences*, p.345. But Benois says the costumes were by Korovine. According to the programmes only the lake décor was by him; the palace scene and all the costumes were by Golovine.
178 Astruc papers. Telegram from Diaghilev to Astruc, 25 September 1911.
179 *Ibid.* Telegrams from Diaghilev to Astruc, 13 October 1911, 10 October 1911.
180 *Ibid.* Telegram from Diaghilev to Astruc, 10 October 1911.
181 *Ibid.* Telegram from Diaghilev to Astruc, 15 October 1911.
182 Karsavina conversations. Her phrase.
183 Carter, p.23.
184 *Observer*, 15 October 1911.
185 Rosenthal, p.359.
186 Beaumont: *The Ballet called Giselle*, p.127.
187 *The Times*, 17 October 1911.
188 *Daily Mail*, 17 October 1911.
189 *Sunday Times*, 22 October 1911.
190 *Observer*, 22 October 1911.
191 *Daily Mail*, 17 October 1911.
192 *Sunday Times*, 22 October 1911.
193 *The Times*, 30 October 1911.
194 *Daily Mail*, 30 October 1911.
195 *Ibid.*, 4 November 1911.
196 Gordon Craig's Day book II in the collection of Edward Craig.
197 Kchessinskaya, pp.132, 133.
198 *Ibid.*, p.133.
199 *Daily Mail*, 15 November 1911.
200 Juliet Duff conversations.
201 *Daily Mail*, 15 November 1911.
202 *The Times*, 20 November 1911.
203 Astruc papers. Telegram from Diaghilev to Astruc, 15 November 1911.
204 Johnson, p.226. I have followed his account as it is the only one.
205 Kchessinskaya, p.134.
206 *Ibid.*, p.134.
207 Diaghilev.
208 Johnson, pp.226–33.
209 Beaumont: *London*, p.231.
210 *Sunday Times*, 3 December 1911 (and 28 July 1912); *The Times*, 1 December 1911; *Daily Mail*, 1 December 1911.
211 Kchessinskaya, p.134.
212 *Ibid.*
213 *The Times*, 1 December 1911.
214 *Daily Mail*, 1 December 1911.
215 *The Times*, 1 December 1911.
216 *Daily Mail*, 1 December 1911.

217 *The Times*, 1 December 1911.
218 Kchessinskaya, p.135. But she says Benois was present when he was not in London.
219 Astruc papers. Telegram from Diaghilev to Astruc, 3 December 1911.
220 Lady Juliet Duff's 'Birthday Book'.
221 *Daily Mail*, 11 December 1911.
222 Ricketts, p.175.
223 *Daily Mail*, 11 December 1911.
224 *Ibid.*
225 Ricketts, p.175.
226 *Daily Mail*, 11 December 1911.
227 Astruc papers. Telegram from Diaghilev to Astruc, 9 December 1911.

228 *Ibid.* Copy of telegram from Diaghilev to Keynote (an agency?), 11 December 1911.
229 *Ibid.* Telegram from Diaghilev to Astruc, 12 December 1911.
230 *Ibid.* Telegram from Diaghilev to Astruc, 15 December 1911.
231 *Ibid.* Telegram from Diaghilev to Astruc, 17 December 1911.
232 *Ibid.* Telegram from Diaghilev to Astruc, 16 December 1911.
233 Karsavina: *Theatre Street*, pp.240, 241. See also Bourman, p.212.
234 Drawing in the collection of the late Lady Juliet Duff.

Chapter Five *1912*

1 Stravinsky: *Expositions*, p.142.
2 Romola Nijinsky conversations.
3 Karsavina conversations.
4 Astruc papers.
5 *Ibid.* In the telegram from Diaghilev to Astruc, 21 September 1911, the dates had been 29 December 1911 to 1 February 1912.
6 *Ibid.* Telegram from Diaghilev to Kchessinskaya, 4 January 1912.
7 *Ibid.* Telegram from Diaghilev to Astruc, 8 January 1912 and another on which the date is indecipherable.
8 *Ibid.* Draft of contract exists.
9 Grigoriev, p.87.
10 Astruc papers. Letter from Astruc's office to Astruc in Nice, 21 February 1912.
11 *Ibid.* Telegram from Diaghilev to Astruc, 9 February 1912.
12 *Ibid.* Telegram from Diaghilev to Astruc, 9 February 1912.
13 Karsavina: *Theatre Street*, pp.225.
14 B.Nijinska conversations.
15 Romola Nijinsky, p.195. Bolm told her the story.
16 B.Nijinska conversations.
17 Karsavina conversations.
18 See plate 49.
19 Grigoriev, p.72.
20 Illustrated in *Ballet and Opera*, November 1948, pp.25–27.
21 Grigoriev, p.72.

22 *Ibid.*, pp.72, 73.
23 Karsavina: *Theatre Street*, pp.225, 226.
24 Astruc papers. Telegram from Diaghilev to Astruc, 20 February 1912.
25 Grigoriev, p.73.
26 Benois: *Reminiscences*, pp.343–6.
27 Astruc papers. Telegram from Diaghilev to Astruc, 6 March 1912; Grigoriev, p.74.
28 Grigoriev, pp.73–4.
29 Kchessinskaya, p.137.
30 Romola Nijinsky, p.12.
31 *Ibid.*, pp.12, 13.
32 Romola Nijinsky conversations.
33 Romola Nijinsky, p.13.
34 Bourman, p.222.
35 Kchessinskaya, p.138.
36 Astruc papers. The telegrams from Beausoleil begin on 19 March 1912.
37 *Le Monte Carlo*, 31 March 1912.
38 *Ibid.*, 28 April 1912.
39 *Ibid.*, 7 April 1912.
40 *Ibid.*, 31 March 1912.
41 *Ibid.*, 7 April 1912.
42 *Ibid.*, 14 April 1912.
43 Grigoriev, p.74.
44 *Ibid.*, pp.75, 76.
45 B.Nijinska conversations.
46 Rambert conversations.
47 *Ibid.*
48 See Rambert's anecdote on p.277.
49 Grigoriev, p.75.

Notes

50 Kchessinskaya, p.138.
51 *Comoedia Illustré*, the official Paris souvenir programme, 1912.
52 In this assessment of Diaghilev's character the author is not quoting any one person, but summarizing the impressions he received from many.
53 Fokine, pp.71, 72.
54 *Ibid.*, p.201.
55 Grigoriev, p.75.
56 *Ibid.*, pp.76, 77.
57 Astruc papers. Telegram from Diaghilev to Astruc, 17 April 1912.
58 *Ibid.* Telegram from Gatti-Casazza to Astruc.
59 Author's supposition, based on telegram, see note 60.
60 Astruc papers. Telegram from Bakst to Diaghilev, 19 April 1912.
61 Monte Carlo programmes.
62 Astruc papers. Telegrams from Diaghilev to Astruc, 25 April 1912 and 27 April 1912.
63 *Comoedia Illustré*, 15 May 1912, pp.638, 639.
64 Romola Nijinsky, p.135.
65 Astruc papers. Telegram from Diaghilev to Astruc, 2 May 1912.
66 Grigoriev, p.77.
67 *Comoedia Illustré*, the official Paris souvenir programme.
68 Sokolova, p.37.
69 Cocteau, note on the musical score.
70 Indication on the musical score.
71 *Le Figaro*, 14 May 1912.
72 Karsavina: *Theatre Street*, p.212.
73 Fokine, p.205.
74 The score, inscribed by Nijinsky with his choreographic notation and with indications of staging, is in the British Museum.
75 B.Nijinska conversations.
76 Romola Nijinsky, p.141.
77 *Ibid.*, pp.141, 142.
78 *Ibid.*, p.142, footnote.
79 B.Nijinska conversations. When Mme Bronislava Nijinska gave the reason for this jump I was able to point out to her the relationship of this stream at the right of the stage to the painted waterfall.
80 *Ibid.*
81 Grigoriev, p.79.
82 See page 202.
83 Grigoriev, p.79.
84 *Ibid.*, p.79.
85 *Ibid.*, p.79.

86 *Ibid.*, pp.78, 79.
87 Lieven, p.176.
88 *Commedia*, 30 May 1912.
89 *Le Figaro*, 30 May 1912.
90 *Ibid.*, 31 May 1912.
91 *Ibid.*, 3 June 1912.
92 Romola Nijinsky, pp.144-8.
93 Fokine, pp.204-9.
94 *Ibid.*, p.204.
95 *Ibid.*, p.209.
96 *Ibid.*, pp.209, 210.
97 *Ibid.*, p.209.
98 *Ibid.*, p.210.
99 Karsavina: *Theatre Street*, pp.238, 239.
100 Grigoriev, p.80.
101 Fokine, p.211.
102 *Ibid.*, p.211.
103 *Ibid.*, pp.211, 212.
104 Grigoriev, p.76.
105 Fokine, p.212.
106 Lieven, p.181. Benois told him this.
107 Jankélévitch, p.50.
108 *Le Figaro*, 9 June 1912.
109 Fokine, p.214.
110 Pierre Lalo in *Feuilleton du temps*, 11 June 1912.
111 Fokine, p.201.
112 Dates on certain designs which have changed hands since being seen by the author.
113 Fokine, pp.214, 215.
114 Vladimirov conversation.
115 Romola Nijinsky conversations.
116 Ricketts, pp.176, 177.
117 *The Times*, 13 June 1912.
118 *Daily Mail*, 13 June 1912.
119 *Morning Post*, 19 June 1912.
120 *The Times*, 19 June 1912.
121 *Daily Express*, 10 June 1912.
122 *Ibid.*, 17 June 1912.
123 *Daily Mail*, 19 June 1912.
124 Beaumont: *London*, pp.9, 10.
125 *Ibid.*, pp.15-17.
126 *Ibid.*, p.20.
127 Morrell, pp.226, 227.
128 *Ibid.*, p.227.
129 Juliet Duff, essay.
130 Duncan Grant, letter to the author.
131 Morrell, p.228.
132 Illustrated in *Comoedia Illustré*, 5 June 1913.
133 Morrell, pp.227, 228.
134 Augustus John: *Chiaroscuro*. I have stolen a phrase used by John of Oscar Wilde.

135 Blanche, pp.257, 258.
136 *Ibid.*, p.258.
137 Juliet Duff, essay.
138 *Ibid.*
139 *The Sketch*, 10 July 1912.
140 *The Times*, 9 July 1912.
141 *Ibid.*, 18 July 1912.
142 Juliet Duff, essay.
143 Guest: *Adeline Genée*, pp.125, 129. He is quoting an account by Mme Karsavina.
144 *The Times*, 10 July 1912.
145 *Morning Post*, 10 July 1912.
146 *Daily Express*, 10 July 1912.
147 *Daily Mail*, 10 July 1912.
148 *Sunday Times*, 14 July 1912.
149 Beaumont: *London*, p.38.
150 Ricketts, pp.177, 178.
151 *Ibid.*, p.179.
152 B.Nijinska conversations.
153 *Rhythm*, No. VI, July 1912.
154 Ede: *Savage Messiah*, pp.138–50.
155 *Ibid.*, p.191 footnote.
156 Marsh: *Brooke*, p.75. Letter quoted.
157 Stravinsky: *Chronicle*, pp.66–8 (but Stravinsky does not mention Nijinsky).
158 Astruc papers. A telegram from Diaghilev in London to Astruc in Paris, 30 August 1912, proves that Diaghilev was not yet in Venice. And on 21 September 1912 Diaghilev telegraphs to Astruc from the Lido that he will be in Paris on 25 September.

Chapter Six   *1912–1913*

1 B.Nijinska conversations.
2 *Ibid.*
3 *Diary*, pp.146, 147.
4 Karsavina conversations.
5 B.Nijinska conversations.
6 Debussy, p.111.
7 Grigoriev, pp.84, 85.
8 Astruc papers. Telegram from Diaghilev to Astruc, 12 December 1912.
9 *Ibid.* Copy of letter from Gunsbourg to Bewicke, 15 December 1912.
10 Rambert conversations. The information in the following four paragraphs – and indeed throughout much of this chapter – has the same source. Some of Dame Marie's recollections of the *Avon* voyage were incorporated in Mary Clarke's book *Dancers of Mercury*, but since she is a friend and told me these and further details I have attributed them to 'conversations'.
11 Szakats conversation.
12 Romola Nijinsky conversations. Some of these facts do not appear in Romola Nijinsky's *Nijinsky*, and some are stated differently.
13 Romola Nijinsky, p.14.
14 *Ibid.*, pp.15, 16.
15 Grigoriev, p.88.
16 Karsavina conversations.
17 Grigoriev, p.88.
18 *Ibid.*, p.88.
19 Romola Nijinsky, pp.19, 20.
20 *Ibid.*, pp.20–22.
21 Telegram 31(?) January 1913.
22 Telegram from Nijinsky to Astruc, 27 January 1913.
23 Grigoriev, p.89.
24 Beaumont: *London*, pp.42–5.
25 *The Times*, 5 February 1913.
26 *Daily Mail*, 6 February 1913.
27 Sitwell: *Great Morning*, pp.242, 241.
28 Beaumont: *London*, p.51.
29 *The Times*, 18 February 1913.
30 *Daily Mail*, 18 February 1913.
31 *Ibid.*, 20 and 21 February 1913.
32 *Ibid.*, 21 February 1913.
33 Sokolova, p.31.
34 Rambert conversations.
35 Here the author interpolates his own observations in the middle of a body of factual evidence by Dame Marie Rambert.
36 Grigoriev papers.
37 Bewicke conversation.
38 Grigoriev, p.90.
39 Rambert conversations.
40 B.Nijinska conversations.
41 *Ibid.*
42 Rambert conversations.
43 B.Nijinska conversations. '*Avec justesse*' was Mme Nijinska's expression.
44 Rambert conversations.

Notes

45 *Ibid.*
46 Karsavina: *Theatre Street*, pp.293, 294. I have rearranged the conversation as dramatic dialogue.
47 Rambert conversations.
48 *Ibid.*
49 *Ibid.*
50 Sokolova, pp.33, 34, 38, 39.
51 *Ibid.*
52 Romola Nijinsky conversations.
53 Romola Nijinsky-Kirstein MS.
54 Rambert conversations.
55 Astruc, p.287.
56 Grigoriev, p.91.
57 *Ibid.*, p.91.
58 Manuel, p.74.
59 Stravinsky: *Conversations*, p.62.
60 Valentine Gross, typescript in collection of Museum of Theatre Arts, London.
61 Rambert Conversations.
62 Agate, p.171.
63 Debussy, letter in private collection.
64 Boulez. Sleeve of CBS record 72533. Trans. Felix Aprahamian.
65 *Le Figaro*, 17 May 1913.
66 *Gil Blas*, 20 May 1913.
67 *Ibid.*
68 Lockspeiser, Vol. II, p.172.
69 Duncan and MacDougall, p.260.
70 Jacques Rivière, in *Nouvelle Revue Française*, November 1913.
71 *Ibid.*
72 Victor Hugo, p.274.
73 Valentine Gross, broadcast.
74 Cocteau: *Cock*, pp.48, 49.
75 Rambert conversations.
76 Romola Nijinsky, p.166.
77 *Ibid.*, p.166.
78 Manuel, p.74.
79 Romola Nijinsky, pp.165, 166.
80 Rambert conversations.
81 Astruc, p.286.
82 Stravinsky: *Conversations*, p.46.
83 B.Nijinska conversations.
84 Romola Nijinsky, p.166.
85 Stravinsky: *Conversations*, pp.46, 47.
86 Stravinsky-Craft questionnaires.
87 *Le Figaro*, 31 May 1913.
88 Laloy, in unattributed Press cutting.
89 *La Revue française de la musique*, April 1913.
90 *Gil Blas*, April 1913.
91 In an undated, unattributed cutting in the Arsenal.

92 *Le Monde musical*, April 1913.
93 *Commedia*, 31 May 1913.
94 Valentine Gross, typescript.
95 Karsavina conversations.
96 Johnson, pp.216–21.
97 Svetlov: *Karsavina*, p.62.
98 Grigoriev, p.94.
99 Valentine Gross.
100 Romola Nijinsky, pp.169–72.
101 Sokolova, pp.45–7.
102 *The Times*, 25 June 1913.
103 *Daily Mail*, 26 June 1913.
104 *Morning Post*, 26 June 1913.
105 *The Times*, 12 July 1913.
106 *Ibid.*
107 *Morning Post*, 12 July 1913.
108 *The Times*, 24 July 1913.
109 Letter from Bakst to Astruc, Buckle collection.
110 Astruc, p.286.
111 Benois: *Reminiscences*, pp.349–51.
112 Records of the Royal Mail Steam Packet Company, now Royal Mail Lines, Ltd.
113 Grigoriev, pp.95, 96.
114 Rambert conversations.
115 Romola Nijinsky, p.179.
116 Sokolova, pp.14ff.
117 Rambert conversations.
118 Sokolova, p.48.
119 Romola Nijinsky, p.185.
120 Rambert conversations.
121 Grigoriev, p.96.
122 Romola Nijinsky, pp.178, 179.
123 *Ibid.*, p.180.
124 Records of the RMSP Co.
125 Romola Nijinsky, p.181.
126 *Ibid.*, pp.182–4.
127 Rambert conversations.
128 Romola Nijinsky, pp.181, 182.
129 *Ibid.*, p.182.
130 *Ibid.*, pp.184, 185.
131 Rambert conversations.
132 Romola Nijinsky, pp.188, 189.
133 *Ibid.*, pp.187, 188.
134 *Ibid.*, p.188.
135 *Ibid.*, pp.190, 191. I have slightly rearranged the order of events recorded by Romola Nijinsky to fit in with the dates provided by the steamship company.
136 *Ibid.*, p.186.
137 *Ibid.*, p.186.
138 Records of the RMSP Co. Romola Nijinsky does not mention docking at Pernambuco. I have had to follow my

sense of probability in placing the events of this voyage, and to reconcile Mme Nijinsky's account of how long it took her to make friends with Nijinsky with Grigoriev's statement that 'After we had been at sea about a fortnight . . . [Nijinsky] was often to be seen in animated conversation with Mlle de Pulszka . . .' (p.96).

139 Grigoriev, p.96.
140 Sokolova, p.48.
141 Romola Nijinsky, p.195.
142 Rambert conversations.
143 Records of the RMSP Co.
144 Romola Nijinsky, pp.191, 192.
145 Rambert conversations.
146 Romola Nijinsky, p.193.
147 Rambert conversations.
148 Records of the RMSP Co.

149 Romola Nijinsky, pp.193–5.
150 *Ibid.*, p.195.
151 *Ibid.*, p.196.
152 *Ibid.*, p.197.
153 Romola Nijinsky conversations.
154 Romola Nijinsky, pp.196, 197.
155 *Ibid.*, p.197.
156 Rambert conversations.
157 Records of the RMSP Co.
158 Romola Nijinsky, pp.197, 198.
159 Karsavina conversations.
160 Romola Nijinsky, p.198.
161 Romola Nijinsky conversations.
162 Romola Nijinsky, pp.199, 200.
163 Sokolova, p.49.
164 Rambert conversations.
165 Romola Nijinsky, pp.200–202.
166 *Ibid.*, p.202.

Chapter Seven 1913–1917

1 Grigoriev, p.97.
2 Rambert conversations.
3 Grigoriev, p.97.
4 Romola Nijinsky, p.202.
5 *Ibid.*, pp.203, 205.
6 *Ibid.*, p.205.
7 Misia Sert, pp.120, 121.
8 Stravinsky: *Memories*, pp.134, 135. Letters quoted.
9 Hofmannsthal-Strauss, p.176.
10 Letter from Debussy to Stravinsky, 9 November 1913.
11 Letter from Astruc to the official receiver.
12 Romola Nijinsky, pp.203, 206
13 *Ibid.*, pp.206, 207.
14 *Ibid.*, p.207.
15 Grigoriev, p.98.
16 B.Nijinska conversations and Romola Nijinsky conversations.
17 Grigoriev, pp.98, 99.
18 Romola Nijinsky conversations.
19 Romola Nijinsky, pp.207, 208.
20 *Ibid.*, p.208.
21 *Ibid.*, pp.208, 209.
22 Romola Nijinsky conversations.
23 Stravinsky: *Memories*, letter from Nijinsky quoted pp.38–40.
24 *Ibid.*; Grigoriev, p.100

25 Romola Nijinsky, p.209.
26 Grigoriev, pp.99, 100.
27 Romola Nijinsky, p.209.
28 Grigoriev, p.100. The date is a guess based on the date of Nijinsky's existing telegram to Astruc.
29 Romola Nijinsky, p.210.
30 Astruc papers. Telegram from Nijinsky to Astruc, 5 December 1913.
31 Quoted in Stravinsky: *Memories*, pp.38–40.
32 Stravinsky: *Memories*, p.38.
33 Grigoriev, p.101.
34 *Ibid.*, pp.102, 103.
35 Fokine, p.204.
36 Grigoriev, p.103.
37 *Ibid.*, p.105.
38 Massine conversations.
39 Massine, pp.41–3.
40 Massine conversations.
41 Massine, pp.45, 46.
42 Grigoriev, p.105.
43 Massine conversations.
44 Romola Nijinsky, pp.210, 212.
45 *Ibid.*, p.211.
46 *Ibid.*, pp.211, 212.
47 Beaumont. *London*, p.78.
48 Grigoriev, p.106.
49 *Ibid.*, p.107

Notes

50 Romola Nijinsky, p.212.
51 *Ibid.*, pp.212, 213.
52 Misia Sert, p.122.
53 *Ibid.*, p.122.
54 Stravinsky: *Memories*, p.41.
55 Romola Nijinsky, p.213.
56 *Ibid.*, pp.213, 214.
57 Beaumont: *London*, p.83.
58 Romola Nijinsky, p.214.
59 Beaumont: *London*, pp.79, 80.
60 *The Times*, 3 March 1914.
61 Beaumont: *London*, pp.80–82.
62 Romola Nijinsky conversations; and *Daily Telegraph*, 17 March 1914.
63 Beaumont: *London*, p.83.
64 Romola Nijinsky, pp.214, 215.
65 Romola Nijinsky conversations.
66 *Daily Telegraph*, March 1914.
67 Misia Sert, pp.122, 123.
68 *Ibid.*, pp.122–4.
69 Romola Nijinsky, p.215.
70 Grigoriev, p.107.
71 Fokine, p.226.
72 Benois: *Reminiscences*, p.356.
73 Grigoriev, p.108.
74 Romola Nijinsky, pp.215, 216.
75 G. de Champdos in an unattributed cutting dated 16 May 1914 in the Arsenal.
76 Romola Nijinsky, p.218.
77 Massine conversations.
78 Massine, p.60.
79 Pierre Lalo in *Le Temps*, May 1914.
80 Bruncan, in unattributed Press cutting.
81 *Nouvelle Revue Française*, 1 July 1914.
82 *The Times*, 9 June 1914.
83 *Ibid.*, 10 June 1914.
84 Beaumont: *London*, pp.90–93.
85 Ricketts, p.199.
86 Sitwell: *Great Morning*, pp.244, 245.
87 *Ibid.*, p.245.
88 Romola Nijinsky, p.219.
89 Ricketts, p.236.
90 Beaumont: *London*, p.100.
91 Massine, p.61.
92 Karsavina: *Theatre Street*, p.245.
93 *Ibid.*, p.245.
94 Romola Nijinsky, pp.220, 221.
95 *Ibid.*, pp.222, 223.
96 Beaumont: *London*, p.101.
97 Karsavina: *Theatre Street*, p.305 [1930 ed.].
98 Ricketts, p.207.
99 *Ibid.*, p.204.
100 Grigoriev, p.111.
101 Karsavina: *Theatre Street*, p.248.
102 Karsavina conversations.
103 Karsavina: *Theatre Street*, p.252.
104 Ricketts, p.214.
105 Romola Nijinsky, pp.222–6.
106 Stravinsky: *Memories*, p.48. Letter from Diaghilev quoted.
107 *Ibid.*, p.50. Another letter quoted.
108 *Ibid.*, p.50.
109 Romola Nijinsky, pp.226–39. (Source for the preceding six paragraphs.)
110 Massine, p.70.
111 Grigoriev, p.114.
112 Massine, pp.73–4; Grigoriev, p.114.
113 Sokolova, p.69.
114 Grigoriev, p.115.
115 Sokolova, pp.68, 69.
116 Grigoriev, p.116.
117 *Ballet Russe Courier*, Vol. I, No. 1, December 1916. (Publicity publication of the Metropolitan Opera House.)
118 Sokolova, pp.69, 71.
119 Grigoriev, pp.116–18.
120 Romola Nijinsky, pp.241, 242.
121 Marsh, p.261.
122 Grigoriev, p.120.
123 Romola Nijinsky, pp.242–6.
124 *Journal of Commerce*, 19 January 1916.
125 Massine, p.80.
126 *Journal of Commerce*, 19 January 1916.
127 *Boston Evening Transcript*, 18 January 1916.
128 Van Vechten, *Dance Index*.
129 *New York Times*, 25 January 1916.
130 Van Vechten, *Dance Index*.
131 *New York Times*, 25 January 1916.
132 Grigoriev, p.119.
133 Romola Nijinsky, pp.247–54.
134 Copy of telegram from Astruc to Nijinsky 1 March 1916. Buckle collection.
135 Romola Nijinsky, p.255.
136 Visiting-card signed by Nijinsky. Buckle collection.
137 Romola Nijinsky, pp.255, 256.
138 Sokolova, p.76.
139 *Toledo Times*, 7 April 1916.
140 *New York Sun*, 30 March 1916.
141 *Musical American*, 9 April 1916.
142 *Washington Star*, 26 March 1916.
143 Romola Nijinsky, pp.257, 258.
144 *Ibid.*, p.260.
145 *New York Telegraph*, 10 April 1916.
146 Sokolova, p.78. She is quoting a letter she wrote home to her family, which they kept.

147 Discovered and sent to the present author by Mr Francis Steegmuller, the biographer of Cocteau.
148 Grigoriev, p.120.
149 *New York Evening Sun*, 19 January 1916.
150 Sokolova, p.77.
151 Grigoriev, p.120.
152 Romola Nijinsky, p.261.
153 Sokolova, p.79.
154 *Ibid.*, p.77.
155 Massine, p.86.
156 *Globe*, 13 April 1916.
157 *Ibid.*
158 Romola Nijinsky, p.261.
159 *Musical Courier*, April 1916.
160 *Globe*, 13 April 1916.
161 *Musical Courier*, April 1916.
162 Massine, p.87.
163 *Globe*, 13 April 1916.
164 *Musical Courier,* April 1916.
165 Massine, p.87.
166 Unattributed cutting dated 17 April 1916, in the New York Public Library.
167 Sokolova, p.77.
168 Grigoriev, p.120.
169 Van Vechten, *Dance Index.*
170 *Ibid.*
171 Romola Nijinsky, p.263.
172 *Ibid.* pp.262, 263.
173 *Ibid.*, pp.263, 264; unattributed cutting of April 1916 in the New York Public Library.
174 *New York Telegraph*, 1 May 1916.
175 Romola Nijinsky, p.265.
176 Romola Nijinsky conversations.
177 Romola Nijinsky, p.265.
178 Grigoriev, p.121.
179 Sokolova, p.80.
180 *Ibid.*, p.80.
181 Maurice Dumesnil, *passim.*
182 Schneider, p.203; Duncan, p.235.
183 Romola Nijinsky, p.266.
184 *New York Review*, 13 May 1916.
185 Romola Nijinsky conversations.
186 Romola Nijinsky, p.266.
187 Jones, *Dance Index.*
188 Romola Nijinsky, pp.266–8.
189 Jones, *Dance Index.*
190 *Diary*, p.111; Romola Nijinsky, p.269.
191 *Diary*, p.111.
192 Jones, *Dance Index.*
193 Romola Nijinsky, p.269.
194 *New York Telegraph*, 19 June 1916. Telegram quoted.
195 Sokolova, pp.86, 87.
196 *Ibid.*, p.87.
197 Romola Nijinsky, p.270.
198 Sokolova, p.89.
199 *Ibid.*, p.90; Romola Nijinsky, p.270.
200 Romola Nijinsky, pp.270, 271.
201 Grigoriev, p.124.
202 Jones, *Dance Index.*
203 *Ballet Russe Courier*, December 1916.
204 Romola Nijinsky, p.274.
205 Sokolova, p.89.
206 Jones, *Dance Index.*
207 Romola Nijinsky, p.274.
208 *Ibid.*, p.273.
209 Vaughan, *Ballet Review.*
210 Romola Nijinsky, p.273.
211 *Ibid.*, p.274.
212 Sokolova, p.90.
213 Jones, *Dance Index.*
214 Sokolova, p.91.
215 *Diary*, p.112.
216 W.B.Chase in an unattributed cutting in the New York Public Library.
217 *Musical American*, 28 October 1916.
218 Unattributed cuttings in the New York Public Library.
219 This description is put together from the accounts of Romola Nijinsky, pp.275–7, Sokolova, p.90, a review signed HTP (Parker) in the *Boston Evening Transcript* of 24 October 1916, and an unattributed review by W.B.Chase.
220 *Musical American*, 28 October 1916.
221 Unattributed cutting in the New York Public Library.
222 Jones, *Dance Index.*
223 Romola Nijinsky conversations.
224 Unattributed cutting in the New York Public Library.
225 *Musical American*, 28 October 1916.
226 *Boston Evening Transcript*, 24 October 1916.
227 Unattributed cuttings in the New York Public Library.
228 *Theatre*, December 1916.
229 Van Vechten, *Dance Index.*
230 *New York Sun*, 27 October 1916.
231 *Boston Evening Transcript*, 10 November 1916.
232 Romola Nijinsky conversations.
233 *Ballet Russe Courier*, December 1916.
234 Sokolova, p.91.
235 *Ballet Russe Courier*, December 1916.
236 *Ibid.*

Notes

237 Romola Nijinsky, p.278.
238 *Boston Evening Transcript*, 10 November 1916.
239 Romola Nijinsky, pp.278, 279.
240 *Public Ledger*, 24 November 1916.
241 *Washington Star*, 16 November 1916.
242 *Ballet Russe Courier*, December 1916.
243 Romola Nijinsky, p.279.
244 *Ibid.*, p.279.
245 *Ibid.*, p.280.
246 *Diary*, p.140.
247 Romola Nijinsky, p.281.
248 *Des Moines Register*, December 1916.
249 Romola Nijinsky, pp.283, 284.
250 Sokolova, pp.92, 93.
251 Romola Nijinsky conversations.
252 Romola Nijinsky, p.282.
253 Sokolova, p.93.
254 Romola Nijinsky, p.283.
255 Told to the author by Anton Dolin, who had it from Zverev.
256 Romola Nijinsky, p.285; *Los Angeles Examiner*, 27 December 1916.
257 Romola Nijinsky, p.285.
258 Chaplin: *Autobiography*, pp.205–7.
259 Romola Nijinsky, p.288.
260 *Ibid.*, p.286.
261 *Ibid.*, pp.289, 290.
262 *Ibid.*, p.290.
263 *Ibid.*, p.291.
264 Romola Nijinsky conversations.
265 Grigoriev, p.127.
266 *Ibid.*, pp.130, 131; Massine, pp.110, 111.
267 Sokolova, p.104.
268 Romola Nijinsky, p.293.
269 Romola Nijinsky conversations.
270 Romola Nijinsky, pp.293–6.
271 Told the author by Mr Anthony Diamantidi.
272 Romola Nijinsky, p.298.
273 *Ibid.*, pp.298, 300.
274 Romola Nijinsky conversations.
275 Romola Nijinsky, p.300.

276 *Ibid.*, pp.300, 301.
277 Massine, p.113.
278 *Ibid.*, p.113.
279 Idzikovsky conversations.
280 Romola Nijinsky, p.302.
281 *Ibid.*, p.302.
282 *Ibid.*, pp.302–4.
283 Romola Nijinsky conversations.
284 Romola Nijinsky, pp.304, 305.
285 Ansermet conversation; also (independently) Chabelska letter.
286 Grigoriev, pp.135, 136.
287 Romola Nijinsky, p.309.
288 *Ibid.*, p.312.
289 Grigoriev, p.140.
290 Romola Nijinsky, pp.311, 313.
291 Grigoriev, p.139; Sokolova, p.110.
292 Ansermet conversation; Grigoriev, p.139; Sokolova, p.110.
293 Romola Nijinsky conversations.
294 Romola Nijinsky, pp.306, 307.
295 *Ibid.*, pp.306–8.
296 Ansermet conversation.
297 Claudel: preface to French edition of Romola Nijinsky's *Nijinsky*, quoted in Reiss, p.167.
298 Milhaud: *Notes sans musique*, quoted in Reiss, p.168.
299 Interview with Guerra in Reiss, p.168.
300 *Ibid.*, p.169.
301 Grigoriev, p.137; Sokolova, p.108.
302 Grigoriev, p.137.
303 Romola Nijinsky, p.308.
304 Sokolova, pp.108, 109.
305 Romola Nijinsky, p.311.
306 Grigoriev, p.138.
307 Romola Nijinsky conversations.
308 Romola Nijinsky, pp.311, 313.
309 *Ibid.*, p.313.
310 Ansermet conversation.
311 Romola Nijinsky, p.314; Grigoriev, p.141.
312 Quoted in Reiss, pp.172, 173.

Chapter Eight   *1917–1950*

1 Romola Nijinsky, pp.294, 295.
2 Grigoriev, pp.137, 139–41; Sokolova, p.110.
3 Grigoriev, p.140.
4 Romola Nijinsky, pp.311, 313.
5 *Ibid.*, p.313.

6 *Ibid.*, p.313.
7 Romola Nijinsky conversations.
8 B.Nijinska conversations; Romola Nijinsky conversations.
9 Romola Nijinsky, p.297; Massine, p.113.
10 B.Nijinska conversations. See also Romola Nijinsky: *Last Days*, p.107.
11 Romola Nijinsky, p.317.
12 Karsavina: *Theatre Street*, pp.263–5.
13 Grigoriev, p.143; Massine, p.121.
14 Romola Nijinsky, p.316.
15 *Ibid.* p.319. From now on until we reach the beginning of 1919 it can be assumed, except where otherwise stated, that the source for descriptions of the Nijinskys' life is Romola Nijinsky's *Nijinsky*.
16 Romola Nijinsky conversations.
17 Massine, p.129.
18 Sitwell: *Laughter in the Next Room*, pp.1, 3, 4.
19 Massine, p.131.
20 Romola Nijinsky conversations.
21 *Diary*, p.99.
22 Here the author speculates on Nijinsky's state of mind.
23 Sandoz, pp.66, 67.
24 Here the author speculates.
25 Ansermet conversations. But Ansermet had the report at second hand from a friend.
26 Sandoz, pp.71, 72.
27 *Diary*, pp.167, 168.
28 *Ibid.*, pp.151–54, 161.
29 P.L.Harriman: *The New Dictionary of Psychology*, p.297.
30 Webster: *3rd New International Dictionary*.
31 Romola Nijinsky conversations.
32 Massine conversations.
33 Rambert conversations.
34 Sokolova conversations.
35 Grigoriev, p.151.
36 Ricketts, p.301.
37 Karsavina: *Theatre Street*, pp.247, 248.
38 *Ibid.*, pp.245, 246.
39 Sokolova, p.134.
40 Romola Nijinsky conversations.
41 Grigoriev, p.167.
42 Sokolova, pp.170, 171.
43 Grigoriev, p.172.
44 Juliet Duff conversations
45 Dolin: *Autobiography*, pp.32, 34.
46 *Ibid.*, pp.36, 37.
47 Benois: *Reminiscences*, pp.376–82; Grigoriev, p.198.
48 Haskell, p.334.
49 Lifar, p.355.
50 Grigoriev, p.205.
51 Lifar, pp.485–8.
52 Karsavina: *Theatre Street*, p.243.
53 Lifar, p.489.
54 Rambert conversations.
55 Kessler, pp.355, 356.
56 Munich programme.
57 Markevitch conversation.
58 Lifar, pp.511–24.
59 Misia Sert, p.164.
60 Lifar, pp.525, 526.
61 Romola Nijinsky conversations.
62 *Ibid.*
63 *Ibid.*
64 Lincoln Kirstein conversation.
65 Dolin: *Autobiography*, p.61.
66 *Ibid.*, pp.72, 73.
67 Dolin conversations.
68 Dolin: *Ballet Go Round*, pp.243–5.
69 Herbert Read: Introduction to Catalogue of drawings by Nijinsky, 1937.
70 Romola Nijinsky: *Last Days*. From now on Mme Nijinsky's second book will be, unless otherwise stated, the source for all references to the life of Vaslav and Romola Nijinsky.
71 Romola Nijinsky conversations.
72 Lifar, pp.529–32.
73 The sum is stated in Lifar's writing on a sheet of Opéra writing-paper stuck in the back of a souvenir programme of the gala which he sent to Lady Juliet Duff, who gave it to the present author.
74 Margaret Power, letter to the author.
75 *Ibid.*
76 *Ibid.*

INDEX

471

Index

Index

Index

Index

Index